THE
EARLY SWING ERA,
1930 TO 1941

THE
EARLY SWING ERA,
1930 TO 1941

Dave Oliphant

GREENWOOD PRESS
Westport, Connecticut • London

Library of Congress Cataloging-in-Publication Data

Oliphant, Dave.
    The early swing era, 1930 to 1941 / Dave Oliphant.
        p. cm.
    Includes bibliographical references and index.
    ISBN 0–313–30535–8 (alk. paper)
        1. Jazz—1931–1940—History and criticism.   2. Swing (Music)—History and
    criticism.   3. Jazz musicians—United States.   I. Title.
    ML3506.045 2002
    781.65'4—dc21   2001050119

British Library Cataloguing in Publication Data is available.

Library of Congress Catalog Card Number: 2001050119
ISBN: 0–313–30535–8

First published in 2002

Greenwood Press, 88 Post Road West, Westport, CT 06881
An imprint of Greenwood Publishing Group, Inc.
www.greenwood.com

Printed in the United States of America

The paper used in this book complies with the
Permanent Paper Standard issued by the National
Information Standards Organization (Z39.48–1984).

10 9 8 7 6 5 4 3 2 1

Copyright Acknowledgments

The author and publisher gratefully acknowledge permission to reprint the following material:

Excerpts from Gunther Schuller's *The Swing Era: The Development of Jazz, 1930–1945*,
copyright 1986, reprinted by permission of Oxford University Press.

Excerpts from the poem "Ben Webster" in Peter McSloy's *For Jazz: 21 Sonnets*, copyright
1995, reprinted by permission of hit & run press and Peter Townsend.

Excerpts from Richard M. Sudhalter's *Lost Chords: White Musicians and Their Contributions
to Jazz, 1915–1945*, copyright 1999, reprinted by permission of Oxford University Press.

Contents

Introduction		vii
1	Precursors to and the Birth of Big-Band Swing	1
2	The Name Black Bands	39
	Fletcher Henderson	40
	Bennie Moten and Count Basie	53
	Duke Ellington	65
	Jimmie Lunceford	78
3	The Name White Bands	97
	Benny Goodman	97
	Tommy and Jimmy Dorsey	112
	Artie Shaw	123
	Glenn Miller	132
4	Other Black Bands	147
	Louis Armstrong	147
	Luis Russell	156
	Chick Webb	161
	Earl "Fatha" Hines	167
	Cab Calloway	177
	Andy Kirk	195
	Lionel Hampton	209

	Erskine Hawkins	217
	Boots Douglas	226
	Oran "Hot Lips" Page	232
	Benny Carter	237
	Jay McShann	247
5	Other White Bands	263
	Paul Whiteman	264
	Casa Loma Orchestra	274
	Bunny Berigan	280
	The Bob Crosby Orchestra	287
	Charlie Barnet	296
	Gene Krupa	303
	Harry James	309
6	The Small Swing Groups	325
	Coleman Hawkins	326
	Jack Teagarden	331
	Benny Goodman	337
	Billie Holiday	343
	Lester Young	349
	Fats Waller	356
	Milton Brown	361
	Summa Cum Laude, et al.	367
	Duke Ellington	381
	Roy Eldridge and Buster Smith	386
	A to Z	397
	Selected Bibliography	429
	Index	433

A photographic essay follows page 262.

♪

Introduction

"The vision developed, by degrees, and gathered swing, momentum, energy."

—Mark Twain (1907)[1]

"Swing isn't music. . . . It's just a way of playing music. It isn't new. . . . It'll die."

—Irving Berlin (1936?)[2]

"I'm tellin' you you're gonna be blue when they're ain't no swing."
—from "Whatcha Gonna Do When There Ain't No Swing?" (Neiburg-Levinson, 1936)[3]

"All God's children got swing."
—from "All God's Chillun Got Rhythm" (Kahn-Jurmann-Kaper, 1936)[4]

"Sing me a swing song and let me dance."
—from "Sing Me a Swing Song" (Hoagy Carmichael; recorded by the Benny Goodman orchestra, with vocalist Helen Ward, 1936)[5]

"Philosophically, swing sought to involve the black culture in a platonic social blandness that would erase it forever, replacing it with the socio-cultural compromise of the 'jazzed-up' popular song: a compromise whose most significant stance was finally catatonia and noncommunication."

—LeRoi Jones (1963)[6]

"The Era of Good Feeling of the 30s, when the big bands symbolized a kind of romance and glamour and exotic beauty long gone from the world of entertainment."

—Ralph J. Gleason (1975)[7]

"In all of jazz there is no element more elusive of definition than swing.
. . . In its simplest physical manifestation swing has occurred when . . .
a listener inadvertently starts tapping his foot, snapping his fingers,
moving his body or head to the beat of the music."
                                        —Gunther Schuller (1989)[8]

During the Swing Era—generally defined as the years following the Stock
Market Crash of late 1929, with its consequent Great Depression, and
continuing at least up to the end of World War II in 1945—more Americans of all racial, social, and economic levels listened to, danced to, and
identified with the music of this time than during any other period of jazz
history. For some, the swing music of this era remains the most popular
type of jazz ever produced, whereas for others much of the so-called jazz
of the swing period represents merely a sentimentalized, diluted version of
the music, a commercialization of the basic ingredients of America's only
native art form.[9] From its beginnings jazz was a controversial music. The
difference of opinion on the Swing Era stems from a conflict between those
who find in particular examples of the music the spirit of a romantic age
and those who consider jazz to be a folk music related to blues and suffering and/or a serious form of highly sophisticated, artistic expression. The
reality, of course, is that the Swing Era was more complex than any one
interpretation of its music has taken into account. Both the depression and
World War II are now looked upon nostalgically as times of great hardship
and sacrifice, which eventually led to a better life for the population at
large; these were also times of close family ties, of group entertainment in
the form of public dances or listening together to the family radio, and
even as the beginning of the end of segregation. What is undeniable is that
the music of this period lives on for those who remember or first discover
its invigorating rhythms, its romantic melodies, and its arrangements of
lush or biting, gentle or driving sounds.

Most histories of the Swing Era published during the last decade of the
twentieth century focus on the ways in which the popular dance music of
the period reflected social conditions and the changes society was under-
going at the time, with the latter attributed in part to swing music and its
musicians.[10] Such studies also emphasize the rise of white bands which
came to dominate the world of swing music in terms of popularity and
access to the new mass media (phonograph recordings, movies, and radio
broadcasts and advertising), as well as the financial rewards that accrued
from the greater exposure to a mass public. Little has been said in such
studies of the aesthetic dominance that the black bands maintained
throughout the period, including the early years of the 1930s when it has
been implied that very little of significance was happening in jazz. Such
studies suggest that the depression stifled production of the music and that
only with the rise of the white bands after Benny Goodman's historic reception at the Palomar Ballroom in Los Angeles in 1935 did jazz recover

and go on to establish itself as the most popular form of American music between that date and the end of the Second World War. The present history looks closely at the black bands of the decade and compares and contrasts them with the white bands, up to the year of 1941, just prior to developments that would begin to undermine the hegemony of swing—specifically the return of the New Orleans form of polyphonic, group improvisation and the rise of bebop with its emphasis on individual solos and musical ideas rather than arrangements for dancing or as background to pop singers. Here as well the reciprocal influence of black and white musicians and bands on one another will be a major consideration. In addition to investigating the phenomenon of the big band, the present study also considers the small groups of the 1930s which, through the combo format, had not lost sight of the origins of jazz and which forecasted the return of the New Orleans style, as well as the creativity of the bebop quintets of Charlie Parker and Dizzy Gillespie.

Evidence of the enduring appeal of certain aspects—or of specific big bands—of the Swing Era lies in the fact that in the 1990s orchestras still bore the names of bands and/or their leaders from the 1930s. A Public Broadcasting System program, of March 15, 1997, was devoted to the music of Glenn Miller and of Tommy Dorsey, with that of the latter performed by "The Tommy Dorsey Orchestra" led by a former Dorsey sideman, trombonist Buddy Morrow. On this occasion, the first part of the program was billed as "Glenn Miller's Greatest Hits II," and began with "In the Mood," which from the time of its recording by Miller in 1939 was listed on the Hit Parade for more than half a year. Even a demanding jazz critic and historian such as Gunther Schuller has admitted that "the exquisite sense of suspended animation created in the diminishing riff repetitions [of "In the Mood"] . . . is surprising even after the 1000th listening."[11] The Miller half of the program ended with what was referred to as the band's "most popular theme song," "Moonlight Serenade." Ed Herlihy, who had been the announcer for Miller's shows and served as the announcer for this PBS program, observed that Miller's music recalled the "happy years when we were in a dancing mood." One striking fact about this presentation was that the band members on the stage and the dancers on the floor who were shown enjoying the music were all white, which suggests that certain types of swing music tend to attract only one race. Yet this has not actually been the case, for both whites and blacks listened to and danced to bands of either race; in fact today white aficionados more often than not prefer the music of the black bands.

The second part of the PBS program featured a tune by the Tommy Dorsey Orchestra, "Opus No. 1," which was arranged in 1944 by black trumpeter Sy Oliver, who had been largely responsible for the success of the Jimmie Lunceford Orchestra during the period from 1934 to 1939. Gunther Schuller calls "Opus No. 1," "one of the last end-stations of the swing-riff tune that had come to jazz a decade earlier from the Midwest and Southwest."[12] Most of the dancers televised on the dance floor were probably unaware of the race of the arranger, or of the fact that many arrangements played by white bands during the thirties were created by black arrangers. This points up two important developments during the thirties: the interrelationship of black and white and the vital role of the arranger in shaping a band's identifiable style. Other tunes featured in this second half of the program included "Song of India," with a trademark Dorsey vibrato solo reproduced on trombone by Buddy Morrow; "Hawaiian War Chant," with its de rigueur drum solo played by Louis Bellson, who recalled that he played it thousands of times during his tenure with Dorsey; "I'll Never Smile Again," the first hit by Frank Sinatra, who joined Dorsey in February 1940 but who had already established the indispensable role of the big-band singer during his tenure with the Harry James orchestra; "Dream," a sentimental song of the period that offered the much-needed view that "things are never as bad as they seem, so Dream"; "Marie" of 1940, the Dorsey orchestra's first million-selling record; and "Boogie Woogie" of 1938, which on being reissued in 1943 became a second million-selling hit. These few tunes indicate several characteristics of swing: a wide net was cast by arrangements, as they incorporated musical elements from or alluded to non-American cultures (here Indian and Hawaiian); the music was an outgrowth and extension of jazz from the 1920s; the prominence accorded to the drum solo was almost unheard of in the twenties; the vocalist became a standard and expected part of any performance; and record sales were both a key to the success of a band and led in some ways, as a consequence of the recording ban at the onset of the war in 1941, to the end of the big-band period of jazz history.

Yet another nostalgic television program, one from New Year's Eve 1997, sheds further light on the nature of the Swing Era. In a tribute to big bands, Erich Kunzel and the Cincinnati Pops provided a sampling of some of the tunes by the biggest names of the period, and in the process demonstrated the superior qualities of the original performances by masters of the swing style. Obviously the Pops program was intended as a form of homage rather than an attempt to reproduce in any very authentic way the music as played by inimitable orchestras that had worked for years to perfect theme songs that are now considered classic works of swing. This was true, for instance, of Benny Goodman's theme for his 1935 radio show, *Let's Dance*, which clearly had people of the time up and dancing to its smooth but stimulating rhythms. The Pops failed to capture anything of the spirit of this piece, and this was generally the case with every tune offered in tribute, from Ellington's "Take the 'A' Train" and Basie's "One O'Clock Jump" to Miller's "Moonlight Serenade." What was most painfully clear was that the featured soloists for the program—trumpeter Doc Severinsen, clarinetist Eddie Walters, trombonist Paul Hughes, and singer

Patti Paige—were incapable of approaching to any real degree the famous musicians whose solos they were given to reproduce. Severinsen, who had been with the Tommy Dorsey orchestra from 1949 and led the popular *Tonight Show* band during the tenure of Johnny Carson, was nothing short of impressive in the remarkable control of his horn at age seventy, but his version of Harry James's "You Made Me Love You" could not live up to the title of the song. The performance was totally lacking in the spine-tingling effect of the original. Likewise, Walters's rendition of Artie Shaw's "Begin the Beguine" was by comparison with the original not even a pale shadow—it was no more than meaningless doodles. Hughes's take on Tommy Dorsey's "I'm Getting Sentimental over You" was but one more example—along with Buddy Morrow's earlier imitations—of the virtual impossibility of reproducing a sound and technique that marked the work of a "lyric player and romantic balladeer" who, according to Schuller, "had no equal."[13] And finally, although Patti Paige did her best with Ellington's "Solitude," she too was unable to revisit the original with anything of its hauntingly affective feeling.

The failure of a "name" white band and pops orchestra in the 1990s to re-create convincingly some of the most famous tunes of the Swing Era and of World War II was not merely a matter of their being formed almost entirely of white players. Even a celebration of the centenary year of Duke Ellington's birth by the Lincoln Center Jazz Orchestra (LCJO), directed by Wynton Marsalis, was, with few exceptions, a far cry from the original work of the most distinguished of all jazz composers as it was performed by Ellington's own orchestra during the 1920s,'30s, and early '40s. Aired on television on May 12, 1999, *Swingin' with Duke* presented various well-known Ellington tunes played by the LCJO, along with film clips of performances by the Ellington orchestra from the early years. One shot of Ellington's unit at the Cotton Club showed the Duke's sidemen standing and delivering their parts without any reference to written or printed scores. It is possible that at the time of the film the music was dubbed, but it did not appear that this was the case. I personally recall a live performance by Ellington and his orchestra around 1972, in DeKalb, Illinois, and the sidemen all played without music stands. When not soloing, both Cootie Williams on trumpet and Harry Carney on baritone played their ensemble parts from memory. By contrast, the LCJO musicians were seated and clearly reading their parts off the music stands in front of them. Another difference between the two groups was to be seen in the manner of execution of the drummers. Whereas the LCJO drummer sat unmoving at his kit with a self-satisfied air, Sonny Greer, Ellington's percussionist during the leader's greatest period from 1926 through the marvelous 1941 recordings, could be seen in the clips moving among his instruments, yet always keeping the beat going while adding his special, subtle tone colors to the whole proceeding.

For the most part, the LCJO's performances of such classic Ellington pieces as "Black and Tan Fantasy," "In a Sentimental Mood," and "Harlem Air Shaft" departed so drastically from the original pieces that the results were necessarily disappointing. Also, one had the feeling that the LCJO musicians were playing at the music rather than entering into its true spirit. Perhaps this is the best that any such repertoire orchestra can hope to offer. However, on "Daybreak Express," the LCJO definitely turned in a better performance simply because it stayed closer to Ellington's original recording from 1933.[14] Even so, the LCJO could in no way approach Sonny Greer's rhythmic drive, the ensemble playing of the superb Ellington reed section, and the brief solo breaks by Barney Bigard on clarinet, Johnny Hodges on alto saxophone, and Freddy Jenkins on trumpet. Wynton Marsalis's own trumpet solo work on the television program contained little of a true jazz feeling, was almost wholly imitative, and consisted largely of showy phrases that never linked up with or developed any musical ideas. This was made dramatically clear by contrast when Marsalis brought on seventy-seven-year-old Illinois Jacquet to perform with the LCJO the tenor solo originally played by Ben Webster on the 1940 recording of Ellington's "Cotton Tail."[15] Marsalis commented that Jacquet "is our teacher" who shows us "how to look, how to present ourselves, how to play jazz," but it was nowhere evident in the LCJO's attempts at re-creating the Ellington sound. Jacquet himself remarked that Ellington's "music is a gift from God," and Illinois played it as such. He first delivered a fine performance of Ellington's "Sophisticated Lady," also originally recorded in 1940 and considered by Jacquet to be Duke's greatest composition.[16] After a clip of Ben Webster performing "Cotton Tail" with the Ellington orchestra, Illinois showed that he could pay true homage to both Ellington and Webster by rendering the piece with an astonishing depth of understanding and feeling and a technical control that will perhaps never be heard again— that is, not in terms of a swing-era interpretation, for once Jacquet is gone, there will be no other saxophonist who was present in the 1940s as an active and influential jazz tenorist in his own right and who at the end of the century could recapture the spirit of Ellington's music and of Webster's outstanding solo treatment.[17]

Ultimately, the value of such tributes, aside from the fact that the achievements of the big bands deserve such continued recognition, resides in their illustration of the unique qualities that, with rare exceptions, only the original performances can ever convey. What went into the making of swing-era music remains a fascinating study, and how and why the musicians who made the music were able to imbue it with qualities that can be replicated but by a select few still defies explanation, even after the chords, structures, and styles have been described and analyzed in detail. As with all jazz, there is in swing-era music an element of the indescribable and the unnotatable, which is what makes the music both so appealing and so difficult to discuss. Yet writers and readers alike persist in exploring the-ories, anecdotes, and histories that will satisfy a need to know more about this unique period in the ongoing story of jazz.

NOTES

1. Mark Twain, *Chapters from My Autobiography* (New York: Oxford University Press, 1996), facsimile edition, ed. Shelley Fisher Fishkin; originally published in the *North American Review*, No. DCVI (January 4, 1907): 11.

2. Quoted in Michael Freedland, *A Salute to Irving Berlin* (London: W.H. Allen, 1986), p. 167. Ironically, Berlin wrote many songs that became the basis of recordings by some of the leading swing musicians, such as "Blue Skies" (a version by Benny Goodman), "He Ain't Got Rhythm" (a version by Jimmie Lunceford), "You're Laughing at Me" (a version by Fats Waller), and "Marie" (a huge hit for Tommy Dorsey).

3. Lyrics sung by Midge Williams on *Bunny Berigan and His Boys 1935–1936* (Classics 734, 1993).

4. Lyrics sung by Ivie Anderson on *Duke Ellington and His Orchestra 1937 Vol. 2* (Classics 687, 1993) and possibly by Chuck Richards on *Fletcher Henderson and His Orchestra 1937–1938* (Classics 519, 1990).

5. *The RCA Victor Encyclopedia of Recorded Jazz*, Album 5 (New York: Jazz Club of America, ca. 1955).

6. LeRoi Jones (Amiri Baraka), *Blues People* (New York: William Morrow, 1963; Quill edition, 1999), p. 181.

7. Ralph J. Gleason, "Jimmy Lunceford," from *Celebrating the Duke*, rpt. in *Reading Jazz: A Gathering of Autobiography, Reportage, and Criticism from 1919 to Now*, ed. Robert Gottlieb (New York: Pantheon Books, 1996), p. 494.

8. Gunther Schuller, *The Swing Era: The Development of Jazz 1930–1945* (New York: Oxford University Press, 1989), p. 223.

9. Charles Edward Smith characterized the work of the "large popular 'name' bands" as "spineless and unoriginal" ("Swing," *The New Republic*, February 16, 1938, pp. 39–41; quoted in Lewis A. Erenberg, *Swingin' the Dream: Big Band Jazz and the Rebirth of American Culture* [Chicago: University of Chicago Press, 1998], p. 142).

10. The primary examples of this American Studies type of approach to jazz history are Burton W. Peretti's *The Creation of Jazz: Music, Race, and Culture in Urban America* (Chicago: University of Illinois Press, 1992); David W. Stowe's *Swing Changes: Big-Band Jazz in New Deal America* (Cambridge: Harvard University Press, 1994); and Lewis A. Erenberg's *Swingin' the Dream*.

11. Schuller, *The Swing Era*, p. 675.

12. Ibid., p. 688.

13. Ibid., p. 680.

14. This marvelous performance, from December 4, 1933, is included on *Duke Ellington: Daybreak Express* (RCA Victor LPV-506, 1964).

15. This performance, from May 4, 1940, is included on *In a Mellotone* (RCA Victor LPM-1364, 1956).

16. This performance, from February 14, 1940, is included in *The Ellington Era 1927–1940*, Vol. One (Columbia C3L 27, 1963).

17. Illinois Jacquet's solo on the May 26, 1942, recording of "Flying Home," with the Lionel Hampton orchestra, was perhaps the most famous tenor improvisation of the war years. It is available on *Flying Home: Lionel Hampton 1942–1945* (Decca MCA D-42349, 1990).

THE
EARLY SWING ERA,
1930 TO 1941

Chapter 1

♪

Precursors to and the Birth of Big-Band Swing

Styles or movements in the arts—whether of literature, painting, or music—do not begin or end with any particular date. Sometimes a single work or the death of an individual figure is used to mark the opening or closing of an entire style or movement, but this is more for the sake of convenience in surveying historical developments than for pinpointing when any particular style or movement started or stopped. Nonetheless, in designating the early Swing Era as extending from 1930 to 1941, it is possible not only to trace developments during an entire decade (including the extra year that preceded the entrance of the United States into World War II with its resultant disruption of the music industry) but also to commence with a year that saw the end of two major "hot jazz" careers: those of Joe "King" Oliver and Jelly Roll Morton, whose work in the 1920s represented in many ways the culmination of the New Orleans tradition that predominated during the first decade of jazz history and whose music would continue to have an impact throughout the 1930s.[1]

Oliver and Morton have been looked upon as two of only a handful of early jazz musicians who were not afflicted with the stiffness of ragtime. More important, both were the products of an age given to a form of popular music that depended largely on a technique of "spontaneous collective music" rather than a "worked-out orchestral language."[2] Even a piece by Morton recorded with his Red Hot Peppers on June 11, 1928, although titled "Georgia Swing," does not represent the orchestral form associated with almost all big bands of the Swing Era. On the Morton recording, there is no saxophone included and no sectional work as such. In contrast, big bands worked with three to five reeds, three to five trumpets, and two or three trombones, which were either featured strictly as a unit playing themes or riffs, exchanging call-and-response figures with another section, or stating as an entire band a melodic line made lush by an arranger's harmonic writing.[3] Instead of such sections, Morton's Red Hot Peppers consisted of banjo, tuba, and drums carrying the beat for the trumpet, trombone, and clarinet either playing simultaneously their differing lines or soloing against Morton's piano, which was persistently active behind the soloists with constant improvisation and inventive countermelodies of its own. Since there is an emphatic beat throughout, "Georgia Swing" could just as well have been labeled "Georgia Stomp," for "swing" came to mean in the '30s a smoother rhythmic drive, created in part by the more mellow string bass rather than the brassy oompah of the tuba, and a clearer, more homophonic music played by sections one at a time or sectional combinations performing a single line. It should be noted that Morton did use a string bass on his earlier 1926 Red Peppers recordings, being the first major band leader to do so. Nonetheless, the result of the changes taken together was the creation by the big bands of the thirties of a less complex music, less demanding on the ear, and easier for the listener to identify with melodically.

Although both Oliver and Morton lived on into the 1930s (Morton in fact dying in 1941), neither contributed new works after 1930 and only had an impact on the development of jazz through some of their solos or tunes from the twenties—in particular Oliver's breaks on "Dippermouth Blues" and "Snag It" (first recorded in 1923 and 1926, respectively) and Morton's "King Porter Stomp" (which dates from either 1902 or 1905 according to differing accounts[4])—which big bands made use of for their own commercial and artistic purposes. After 1930, Oliver did not make any significant recordings and Morton only recorded in 1938 and '39 in his original 1920s style. Neither Oliver nor Morton made the transition to the new music of the 1930s, although there is some indication that Oliver was attempting to recast his ensemble conception to meet the demands of dancers and listeners attracted to the big bands with their fuller sound and greater emphasis on virtuosic solos. Oliver had added more saxophones—which would come into prominence as jazz instruments of the thirties—to his Dixie and/or Savannah Syncopators, with Hilton Jefferson on alto sax contributing some influential solos in 1930 before he joined McKinney's Cotton Pickers in 1931 and the Fletcher Henderson Orchestra in 1932. An Oliver original like "Edna," recorded in April 1930, has been called "very good *ur*-swing,"[5] but the piece's "corny" sound of oompahing tuba, strummed banjo, and dated cymbal work is still rooted in the twenties, whereas the thirties preferred a string-bass, guitar, and hi-hat combination. And even if Oliver himself did not suffer from teeth and gum problems during the late twenties, as some accounts suggest, it is clear that his style of embellished melody lines was going out of fashion and was being replaced by the bravura approach of his protege Louis Armstrong. As for Morton, even though he asserted in later years that he had invented not only jazz but swing, his blend of ragtime and blues was becoming a thing of the past, and with the end of his and Oliver's recording contracts in

1930, these two giants of the twenties were left behind by the next decade's onward rush to something new.

In part, what the 1930s would develop as a new conception had actually already appeared as early as 1924 in the "contemporary . . . even rhythms of Armstrong's exuberant trumpet" solos with the eleven-piece Fletcher Henderson orchestra.[6] By 1927, Henderson made his first recordings with an expanded 12-piece band that included three cornets, two trombones, and three reeds, as well as the typical rhythm section of the day consisting of tuba, banjo, and drums. Also characteristic of the swing-era approach was Henderson's use of arrangements that combined "harmonized adaptations of New Orleans ensemble and straight homophonic writing, typical of commercial arranging of the period."[7] Although prior to 1925 "no very daring use" was made of the "new resources of instrumentation,"[8] over the period from 1923 to 1928, Henderson's band gradually developed its style "from a rough drive to an increasingly smooth but no less powerful kind of jazz."[9] Eventually, the entire Swing Era would rely "on the experiments of these years" and would build on Henderson's "base the best fruits of big-band jazz."[10] The evolution of a smoother, more fluid rhythm section was also a gradual development. Even though Jelly Roll Morton employed string bass player John Lindsay for the immortal Red Hot Peppers recordings of September 1926, other groups were slow to follow suit, with Henderson's John Kirby still recording on tuba as late as 1931. And although Armstrong had already freed himself from the collective mode of early jazz in such recordings as his "Potato Head Blues" of 1927 and his duet with Earl Hines on their "Weather Bird" of 1928, it would be years before other instrumentalists caught up with the trumpeter's ability to create improvisational lines with such linear logic and penetrating drive.

The difference between the King Oliver and Fletcher Henderson approaches to a band style are evident in two recordings each made of Oliver's tune "Snag It." Oliver's original, recorded in March 1926, was performed by a band of eleven musicians, consisting of two cornets, a trombone (played by Kid Ory), three reeds, and a rhythm section of piano (played by Luis Russell, who would later lead one of the most advanced swing orchestras at the end of the decade), banjo, tuba, and drums.[11] Although the brass and reed sections function much in the manner of those of swing-era bands—punctuating or commenting behind or following the soloists' statements—the effect is still a type of New Orleans group improvisation, especially at the beginning of the piece where Oliver's lead cornet is accompanied by several sidemen playing simultaneously their own lines. This traditional New Orleans style also is heard in Kid Ory's muted trombone solo delivered in the blues vein. Later, a shrill clarinet trio, which plays a kind of call answered by the brass, exhibits the basic pattern of alternating sections which will become the standard for swing-era arrangements. Following a vocal by blues composer Richard M. Jones, the King takes one of his most famous breaks, whose first four bars would, according to Hugues Panassié, be "quoted hundreds of times" by later bands.[12] Despite the fact that Oliver's solo may have appealed to the next generation of musicians and that Henderson and his arranger, Don Redman, were sufficiently impressed to make their own version of "Snag It," the Oliver recording remains dated largely because of the sound of the plodding rhythm section and of the uncomplementary brass and reed sections, weaknesses which would be overcome in the next decade when fluid rhythm sections and balanced brass and reeds became prominent strengths of the big-band style.

The Henderson version of Oliver's "Snag It" was recorded in January 1927, and follows the original closely, with Tommy Ladnier on trumpet reproducing not only the spirit of the King's general style but also his four-bar break.[13] Although calls by reed trios also imitate the original version, they are not shrill, and the brass responses are not so abrasive. The rhythm section, which is reduced to three with the absence of a tuba, is even now much smoother, and when the band goes into a double-time section toward the end of the recording, the effect is quite uplifting and achieves a cohesive swing by the entire ensemble. As Wilfrid Mellers indicates in his *Music in a New Found Land*, Henderson "was the first band-leader to insist that members of the group he established in 1923 should be technically proficient, able to read music, and willing to submit to the discipline of concerted effort."[14] Even earlier, in May 1926, only two months after the Oliver recording of "Snag It," Henderson's band recorded his own composition, "The Stampede," and as Marshall Stearns points out in *The Story of Jazz*, Henderson already had solved "the problem of making [ten musicians] play together as a team," and on "The Stampede," he even "led a truly swinging band of eleven jazzmen."[15] Indeed, "The Stampede" swings from beginning to abrupt ending, with inventive, technically impressive solos by Coleman Hawkins on tenor sax and Joe Smith and Rex Stewart on trumpet. The fact that part if not all of Stewart's solo was written out by Henderson—a practice in many later swing-era arrangements—is suggested when the ensemble concludes the performance by repeating some of the same figures as played by Stewart. This would seem to illustrate the assertion by Stearns that "the trick of making a big band swing had been amazingly simple. With the help of arranger Don Redman, Fletcher Henderson had figured it out in the early 'twenties. First a hot solo line was harmonized and written out for the whole section, swinging together. Then arrangers returned to the West African pattern of call-and-response, keeping the two sections answering each other in an endless variety of ways."[16] The section and full ensemble playing in the closing moments of "The Stampede" is superbly coherent, as the sidemen maneuver their way through complex written passages with a spirited, swinging drive. While the clarinet trio of

Oliver's "Snag It" also is present here, it is more musical, more exotic in the style associated with Duke Ellington, and yet just as swinging as the rest of the piece. Even the tuba of Ralph Escudero adds to the light swing–feel of the performance. All of this looks forward to developments in the 1930s that would become standard practice and underscores Stearns' view that a Henderson sideman (and the musician in any big band) "had to be able to 'swing' separately as well as with his section. And then the sections had to swing together, too. It meant endless rehearsals, a comparative loss of identity (except for the solo stars), and high-level teamwork."[17]

Another career in some ways comparable to Oliver and Morton's also came to a close in the year of 1930—that of the legendary cornetist Bix Beiderbecke. Dead the following year at 28, Bix made his final recordings in 1930, although his lasting fame and influence would stem from his solos on "Singin' the Blues" and "I'm Comin' Virginia," both dating from 1927. It is notable that "I'm Comin' Virginia" was composed by Will Marion Cook, a black band leader and composer from the period ending with World War I, but that a white jazzman made the tune famous. Although considered a pop tune, "I'm Comin' Virginia" is certainly a more serious work than "Barnacle Bill the Sailor" from 1930, which is an example of the typical novelty tune that jazz artists like Bix were accustomed to perform. The Barnacle Bill sort of fare was offered up even by Morton, as well as many lesser jazz figures in a tradition going back to the earliest jazz recordings by the Original Dixieland Jazz Band with its "Livery Stable Blues" of 1917. Indeed, Bix's very career began in the area of his hometown of Davenport, Iowa, with an outfit called Buckley's Novelty Orchestra. Recorded by a group of jazzmen brought together by singer-composer Hoagy Carmichael, "Barnacle Bill" resembles much of the rather lifeless material that Bix animated with his inspiriting tone and expressive lines during his years with the Paul Whiteman Orchestra, from 1927 to 1929. And just as his solo work could transform a pseudo-jazz symphonic arrangement of "Sweet Sue" into a thrilling few moments of brilliant improvisation, on "Barnacle Bill" the cornetist bursts through the broad humor of the tune and its lyrics to transmute the base metal of this music into a ringing string of golden notes.

Even though "Barnacle Bill" is not in itself a great jazz recording, it is yet highly instructive. For one thing, the personnel on this performance represents a number of historical developments, both with regard to jazz of the twenties and to the practices, relationships, and leaders of the music to come. The group recording "Barnacle Bill" in 1930 is identified as Hoagy Carmichael and His Orchestra, which was clearly a studio band brought together simply for a record-making session. But what was unusual at this time was the inclusion of trumpeter Bubber Miley, a black musician, with an otherwise all-white ensemble. Notable instances of this practice had taken place earlier—Jelly Roll Morton with the New Orleans Rhythm Kings (NORK) in 1923, Louis Armstrong with Jack Teagarden in March

1929, and Coleman Hawkins with the Mound City Blue Blowers in November 1929—but these were the exception within the recording industry, and mixed company was completely taboo during public performance. Carmichael's respect for and close relationship with black musicians accounts for his inclusion of Miley, who had just been released by Duke Ellington—the only occasion of such a firing in the entire career of this leader whose band members would in some cases remain with him for his entire lifetime. Miley has been credited with much of the original exotic sound of the Ellington band, but the trumpeter's drinking habits created problems on the job and forced Ellington to dismiss his star improviser, whose growl and mute techniques had been crucial to the early success of the organization. Miley solos in his growl style to fine effect on the other tune from this session, Carmichael's own song, "Rockin' Chair," which would later become a feature for Louis Armstrong and Jack Teagarden, as well as for Roy Eldridge, who recorded the tune with the Gene Krupa orchestra on July 2, 1941. Even without Miley present from 1930 on, Ellington would continue with many of that trumpeter's musical devices but would employ other outstanding soloists to utilize them, at the same time that Ellington would develop a much wider range of techniques and styles beyond Miley's own Oliver-based mute work that imitated human and animal sounds. In addition to indicating the new directions that Ellington would have to take without Bubber Miley, the trumpeter's presence on the Carmichael recording forecasts the eventual integration of jazz, which David W. Stowe has seen as impacting the whole fabric of the American social order during the Swing Era, by expressing "reverence for such cherished American ideas as liberty, democracy, tolerance, and equality, while holding firmly to the conviction that the experience of swing was both sign and engine of a fundamentally rational and ever-improving American society."[18]

In addition to Beiderbecke's solo on "Barnacle Bill," the recording features two other solos, one of which is by the future clarinet star and big-band leader Benny Goodman and the other by Bud Freeman, a tenor saxophonist of the Chicago school who would serve as a sideman with several important swing-era units, including Goodman's. The clarinetist's solo already exemplifies some of the ease of execution and the fundamental drive and swing that would later make him, for some, one of the greatest jazz improvisers in the New Orleans tradition.[19] The control and professional facility of Goodman's playing exhibited here would carry over into his work as a band leader-soloist in the mid-thirties, when almost single-handedly he made swing jazz the most popular music of the day. Also present on this recording are the Dorsey brothers, Tommy and Jimmy, who, like Goodman, would later help popularize jazz and would reap the economic benefits of such popularity. Other members of the Carmichael orchestra include the outstanding string duo of violinist Joe Venuti and guitarist Eddie Lang, as well as tubist Harry Goodman, who would later serve as string bassist in his brother's famous big band. Finally, "Barnacle Bill" features the drumming of Gene Krupa, who would first make his name with the Goodman band but then go on to form his own outfit, which, like Goodman's, would play charts written by black arrangers. Krupa also would spotlight a black soloist in his big band—Roy Eldridge on trumpet—just as Goodman featured in his combos such black soloists as pianist Teddy Wilson, vibraharpist Lionel Hampton, and electric guitarist Charlie Christian. On "Barnacle Bill," Krupa is heard most prominently toward the end of the recording when he strikes up a typical march routine, harking back to the beginnings of New Orleans jazz in the funerals and parades of the Crescent City. Although here Krupa concludes the affair with a dated cymbal crash, he would later become a prominent swing-era showman drummer, developing the use of his drum kit far beyond a simple time-keeping role that had characterized it for the most part during the 1920s.

Hoagy Carmichael, the nominal leader of the "Barnacle Bill" session, already was an important figure in jazz annals, primarily as the composer of a ragtime piano piece entitled "Star Dust" (1927), which became "the most famous of all popular songs" after its tempo was slowed down and Mitchell Parish set words to it in 1929.[20] This one tune would prove a perennial favorite with jazz improvisers,[21] but other Carmichael songs also served as jazz vehicles, in particular "Lazy River," "Georgia on My Mind," and "Lazy Bones," the latter recorded by the Casa Loma Orchestra in 1933, the year of its composition. The contributions of Carmichael look forward to the increasing importance of popular songs in the making of jazz, as well as the coming emphasis on vocalists, from the commercial crooners to the true jazz singers like Mildred Bailey and Billie Holiday. Carmichael sang renditions of his own "Lazy River" and "Georgia on My Mind" for other 1930 sessions with his studio orchestra, which also included Beiderbecke, trombonists Tommy Dorsey or Jack Teagarden, Jimmy Dorsey and Pee Wee Russell on clarinet or sax, Bud Freeman on tenor, and the string team of Joe Venuti and Eddie Lang. Teagarden's solo on "Georgia" is vintage "Big T," and at first Bix sounds like his old assertive self, but then fades out with a very melancholy falling off. Beiderbecke would be gone in less than a year from the time of the "Georgia" recording, and Bubber Miley would follow him in 1932. But the legacies of both these musicians would live on during the Swing Era in the playing of trumpeters like Bunny Berigan and Cootie Williams and, in the case of Miley, through the mute and plunger work of trombonist Tricky Sam Nanton. The decade of the thirties would owe much to the seemingly effortless, relaxed style of Beiderbecke and the bluesy, conversational, highly expressive approach of Miley, but cornet and trumpet players of the Swing Era would make their own contributions to a new brand of jazz, developing a note range and technical skill inspired by but even exceeding Armstrong's example. And while the clarinet would remain an important jazz instrument in the hands of Goodman and others, the saxophone would emerge as the most expressive jazz instrument of all, both in section work like that heard on the Carmichael orchestra's rendition of "Georgia on My Mind" and in solo improvisations as hinted at by Freeman in his exuberant break on "Barnacle Bill."

With the evolution of any art form, there are losses that are regretted by some and gains that are warmly greeted by others. Even though the Swing Era brought with it more independence for soloists, it may be that few if any solos in the thirties can compare with those by Armstrong on his Hot Five and Hot Seven recordings or those by Bix Beiderbecke on "I'm Coming Virginia" and "Singin' the Blues." For one thing, the solos by Louis and Bix were not intended for a dance audience so much as they were for discerning listeners to the phonograph. Some purists have objected to the eclecticism and commercialism of the Swing Era which they feel diluted jazz as an art music, but so many factors entered into the making of jazz, including its function as an enticing form of entertainment for dancers, that its very existence was almost from the first owing to a ballroom crowd. The fact that musicians such as Armstrong and Beiderbecke emerged as the result of a commercial demand cannot be ignored, even if their art transcended the service it rendered to a profit-making motive. The products they created in the process of catering to the public were due not only to the music industry's needs but to their own personalities, which could never be reproduced or replicated, both because of the special circumstances of their times and as a result of their own peculiar talents and intellectual qualities. Despite what may be considered certain unique achievements in the twenties, which could not by their very nature be repeated or improved upon, the decade of the thirties would produce its own singular moments of great jazz.

As often noted by commentators on jazz history, the Swing Era saw the saxophone supersede in many ways the trumpet as the dominant jazz solo instrument. For this reason the types of solo improvisations would change dramatically during the thirties. In addition, the role of the reed sections in big bands would bring to jazz a totally different dimension that involved not only a wide variety of new sounds but also a changed relationship between the various parts of the jazz ensemble. While the saxophone was present in jazz ensembles from almost the earliest recordings, its rise to a position of prominence and the development of its virtuosic and expressive possibilities would require the entire period from 1930 to 1941 before individual artists had mastered this instrument that was originally thought unacceptable for jazz. Once again, it was the Bix Beiderbecke recordings of 1927, with Frankie Trumbauer on C melody sax, that pointed the way for many of the saxophonists of the Swing Era. But even during the previous year, while Trumbauer was with the Jean Goldkette orchestra, he had impressed the musicians in the Fletcher Henderson band when the two groups battled at the Roseland Ballroom on October 6, 1926, and Goldkette's men literally blew Henderson's away. As Ted Gioia has characterized Trumbauer's approach, it was "less vertical, less built on spelling chords and interpolating substitute progressions"; instead, Frankie's lines "moved more ethereally, fashioned from an assortment of melodic phrases."[22] In addition to Trumbauer's own solo work, the Goldkette orchestra featured arrangements by Bill Challis, who as early as 1926 helped make this group what trumpeter Rex Stewart called "the first original white swing band in history."[23] Challis also arranged for Paul Whiteman's orchestra in the late twenties, but his writing for reeds is best showcased on a 1931 recording of "Stardust" by the Henderson band, with an outstanding solo by tenorist Coleman Hawkins. According to critic Phil Schaap, this one item "represents the culmination of the Goldkette-Henderson, Bix, Tram-Hawk-Rex admiration society."[24]

In tracing the development of the big band style, Richard Sudhalter discusses the orchestra of Isham Jones and observes that the final "two-chorus *tutti*" of its Brunswick recording of "Farewell Blues," from January 1923 (based on the 1922 New Orleans Rhythm King's recording of the same tune), is taken "at a broad, walking tempo" that "actually *swings* in a handsome, even modern, fashion, over a solid pulse laid out by John Kuhn's tuba and Joe Frank's drum."[25] Even earlier, Sudhalter suggests that Art Hickman's California orchestra, whose arrangements in 1919 for two trumpets and three saxes were scored by Ferde Grofé, created the first modern dance-band instrumentation and many of the jazz-band textures and sonorities for larger groups of instruments.[26] Sudhalter also includes Elmer Schoebel with NORK, Roy Bargy and Don Bestor with the 1923 Benson Orchestra of Chicago, and the unidentified arranger for the Jean Goldkette Victor recording of "It's the Blues," from March 27, 1924, among white figures who established "a frame of reference" that Don Redman used in writing for the Fletcher Henderson Orchestra of 1923–1925.[27]

In the field of literature, so much of creative writing is based on the work of predecessors. Homer and Virgil are the principal sources for a number of subsequent writers, including Shakespeare with his scene in *Hamlet* where the old player reproduces the death of Priam, the Trojan king, at the hands of Greek Pyrrhus. Homer's story of the fall of Troy in Book 8 of *The Odyssey* led to Virgil's version in *The Aeneid*, and in turn Shakespeare rang his own changes on this same event. In jazz too, one figure or group has depended for evolutionary developments on previous composers and/or soloists, such as Jelly Roll Morton with his "King Porter Stomp." This was the case especially with Fletcher Henderson's versions of Morton's classic tune, recorded both by Henderson's own orchestras of 1928, 1932, and 1933 and by the Benny Goodman orchestra of 1935. Other groups to record Morton's classic piece include Claude Hopkins' orchestra in 1934, Glenn Miller's in 1938, and Jimmy Dorsey and Cab Calloway's in 1940. Each of these recordings represents a different aspect of the Swing Era big-band style.[28] Comparing the period's versions with Morton's own recordings of his composition reveals several important facts about the nature of his form of jazz and both its impact on and difference from the music developed during the 1930s.

One early solo-piano recording made by Morton of his "King Porter Stomp" dates from 1924, and is much faster than his 1938 performance recorded for the Library of Congress, yet both versions support the view that Morton "perfected rhythmic techniques that altered the character of eighth-note lines so that they swung." He also "alternated intensities of eighth notes so that they gave the impression of strong-weak, strong-weak. These tendencies, plus a tendency to reduce the number of notes typically used as adornment, helped lend Morton's playing a lighter and more swinging feeling than was borne by ragtime."[29] The word "stomp" in the title of Morton's piece indicates that it is related to the blues, the other vital ingredient in much of jazz, and to the idea of a music with a strongly marked beat.[30] Even in the 1938 recording of his composition, Morton maintains a very clear 2/4 beat, at the same time that he manages to accent four counts per bar by (apparently) patting his foot. At the same time, the pianist improvises on his very striking themes, more fully here, as the LC recording notes by Orin Keepnews point out, than on Morton's previous recordings of his classic tune. But despite the contributions to jazz contained in Morton's recordings, Gunther Schuller takes the position that his music represented "the end of a line" and that we cannot "speak of a direct influence back to Morton" from major performers of the music. Schuller goes on to suggest that Morton's interest in "varied form" set him apart from "the theme-solo-theme format of later jazz [which] bored [Jelly Roll]."[31]

The Fletcher Henderson orchestra's 1928 recording of Morton's "King Porter Stomp" illustrates the typical "head" arrangement approach to such a tune. There is little in the way here of a written-out arrangement of the themes of Morton's piece—background figures played by the ensemble behind the soloists are kept to a minimum. Morton's tune already has become the basis of Schuller's "theme-solo-theme format of later jazz." The recording opens with solo trumpet played by Bobby Stark, who announces Morton's theme in a style that harks back to King Oliver's driving declaratory statements. Next comes Coleman Hawkins with a trilled phrase to begin his rather stiff solo, especially compared with his later, more fluid style. Jimmy Harrison's trombone break is, as Richard Sudhalter asserts, already behind the times in comparison with Jack Teagarden's smooth swing introduced in his New York recordings the year before.[32] The tuba also marks this 1928 recording as stilted when compared with the later recordings supported by the more supple double-bass. Even before coming to Henderson's 1932 arrangement of Morton's tune, it is clear from the orchestra's 1930 recording of "Somebody Loves Me" that the swing revolution is essentially in place. John Kirby's double-bass anchors the ensemble with a flowing beat that helps it float and Hawkins' tenor is swaying horizontally rather than producing straight-up staccato notes. On Benny Carter's superb arrangement of "Keep a Song in Your Soul" with its "fluently conceived syncopation,"[33] also recorded in late 1930, Harrison's trombone now exhibits some of the patented ease and tossed off turns of Teagarden.[34] But only with the 1932 "New King Porter Stomp" is the Henderson brand of swing fully accomplished, for here is truly something *new* in every sense of the word, beginning with Bobby Stark's opening muted trumpet solo, which is now daring and inventive, though still based on Morton's themes. Hawkins is more exploratory, extending the possibilities of his reed instrument with runs and across-the-bar embellishments. Walter Johnson, who had replaced Kaiser Marshall on drums, adds to the greater forward momentum, punctuating with sticks and pulsating with his shimmering cymbals. Kirby's double-bass now seems free to feed the beat from above and below the ensemble. But it is J.C. Higginbotham's trombone solo that achieves the overwhelming drive that makes this performance, as Schuller has said, "possibly the greatest recording Fletcher's band ever made."[35]

John Chilton even goes so far as to assert that "if there was a specific point marking the beginning of the Swing Era it was the day [December 9, 1932] these recordings ['Honeysuckle Rose' and 'New King Porter Stomp'] were made." Chilton cites "Honeysuckle Rose" as "the key performance" because it "was used as a vehicle for improvising rather than as a commercial arrangement interspersed with hot solos. It was this tactic that set the pattern many big bands later copied."[36] But "Honeysuckle Rose" is full of sloppy execution and the solo by Higginbotham cannot compare with his chorus on "New King Porter Stomp." More important is the fact that Morton's composition lends itself to a more imaginative arrangement. The closing ensemble, with call-and-response phrases from Morton's original work shouted by the brass and saxes, would become the trademark conclusion to many a swing-era performance. Gunther Schuller even asserts that "the final classic call-and-response riff-chorus" in Fletcher's 1932 recording of "King Porter Stomp" and "its remake by Goodman in 1935 was to become the single most influential ensemble idea in the entire Swing Era."[37] And while it may have been far from Morton's original conception, it is clear that much of the inherent swing and inventiveness of the Henderson recording is due to the fact that, as Mark Gridler observes, Morton's piano style involved "two or three lines at a time, much in the manner of a band. It was as though trumpet parts, clarinet parts, and trombone parts were being heard coming from a piano! Morton's playing featured a variety of themes and much activity within a single piece using stop-time solo breaks in the same manner as horns in a combo."[38] Gunther Schuller also notes in this regard that "the famous last chorus of Morton's 'King Porter Stomp' " consists of "full-voiced brass-like chords."[39]

Finally, John S. Wilson has said of Henderson's 1932 arrangement of "King Porter Stomp" that it "set the tone for the Goodman band and outlined the idiom that was to be known as 'swing.' "[40]

With its 1933 recording of "King Porter's Stomp," the Henderson orchestra would feature even greater participation by the ensemble behind the soloists and in this sense move closer to the arrangement Fletcher would make for the Goodman organization. But as Schuller indicates, this third version fails to approach the superb quality of the second. For one thing, even Dickie Wells's trombone solo, while different from the work of Harrison and Higginbotham and forecasting Dickie's fine breaks later for the Count Basie band, cannot hold a candle to J.C.'s unmatchable outing. Bobby Stark's final version of the opening solo, although superior to his first attempt, also falls far short of his second effort of 1932. Only Hawkins seems to improve on his previous improvisations, and Henry "Red" Allen does add a bit of new fire in his trumpet solo. Also, Kirby's bass and Johnson's drums do stoke the flames and lend the performance much of its fiery drive, which, if it were not for the band's 1932 reading of Morton's tune, would certainly gain for this effort a higher rating among the Henderson band's recorded output.

By September 1934, when the Claude Hopkins orchestra recorded its version of Morton's "King Porter Stomp," as arranged by trombonist Fred Norman, certain stylistic characteristics of the Swing Era were almost set in stone.[41] The piece swings from the first few beats, owing to the smooth pulsation of Henry Turner's string bass and the trumpet section's driving, high-note annunciatory opening phrases, which are so typical of the period in their combining of syncopation with an accented upbeat. In response, the sax section adds its own driving introductory phrases before Bobby Sands' tenor solo hints at Morton's main theme in a wonderfully whirling burst that is far removed from the original's four-square twenties style. Following altoist Gene Johnson's brief break, the trumpets return to state the tune's theme more fully, before the reeds begin to develop it even further. This is followed by a stirring trumpet solo by Ovie Alston that begins by swinging a held high note, shaken after the manner of Armstrong, and later Alston drives a repeated note by bending it up and down. The full orchestra does its variations on the stomp theme, and just before brasses and reeds respond to one another with riffs drawn from Morton's tune, a typical descending figure in the trombones helps add to the piece's energetic drive. Additional solos by clarinetist Edmond Hall, tenorist Bobby Sands, and trumpeter Ovie Alston add to the momentum. Then screaming trumpets provide a killer-diller ending that would become a standard feature of so many swing-era finales. It must be said, however, that in the end this performance is not on the same level with those by the era's name bands.

The variety of tonal shades and rhythmic patterns produced by the sections and soloists in the Hopkins orchestra is perhaps no greater than found in performances on jazz recordings of the twenties, but the effect of a wider spectrum is achieved by the arranger utilizing so many different combinations of brass and reeds against sax, trumpet, trombone, clarinet, and tenor solos, all swirling Morton's phrases as if a changing kaleidoscope of colors and shapes. Throughout the Swing Era, bands would attempt to vary more and more the sounds of instrumental blends and contrasts, yet employing almost always the basic approach of riff and call-and-response. Some groups emphasized certain sound elements over others; to differing degrees, all the bands included solos interspersed between the ensemble passages. Soloists were at a premium and were often hired away from one band by another. Like Henderson, most leaders stressed technical proficiency and teamwork, but as the number of bands increased, more was required than skill and practice to compete in the job market. Each band had to come up with a gimmick or a peculiar sound that set it apart. To maintain a high performance level both within sections and from soloists became more difficult as the decade wore on, largely owing perhaps to the demands of having to perform the same most popular tunes night after night. Yet it is amazing how many good bands there were during the Swing Era, how many inventive soloists, and how many effective arrangers who developed unique styles for so many outstanding groups. Once again, simply to listen to a single tune like Morton's "King Porter Stomp" as performed by a number of different bands is to appreciate how varied was the period of swing-era jazz.

According to an account by Red Norvo, his first wife, singer Mildred Bailey, was responsible for having "goaded Benny [Goodman] into buying scores from Jimmy Mundy, Edgar Sampson, and, perhaps most important, Fletcher Henderson." Norvo recalled that Bailey, "after listening to Benny Goodman's newly formed band during one of its early broadcasts, . . . remarked to the clarinetist that he seek out more distinctive arrangements. 'Go get a Harlem book' was her recommendation on one occasion."[42] Of the many arrangements Henderson did for the Goodman book, Morton's "King Porter Stomp" was one of the most outstanding. Recorded in New York even before the band's trip to California where its appearance at the Palomar proved a dramatic turning point in the fortunes of the outfit, as well as in the history of jazz, the Henderson arrangement was one of the pieces Goodman decided to play at the Palomar, thinking his band was finished and that they might as well enjoy themselves. Benny called the Morton tune and when "half the crowd just stopped dancing and gathered round the bandstand[,] I knew things would be all right from then on."[43] Although Gunther Schuller finds that it would have been difficult for the Goodman orchestra not to have lost *some* of the spontaneity in "a head arrangement by artists of Henderson's caliber,"[44] he yet considers Bunny Berigan's two solos on the Goodman 1935 recording of "King Porter Stomp" to be among Berigan's "very finest creative achievements."[45] Sudhalter agrees that Berigan's solos exhibit his "natural, unerring swing, a way of placing notes on the beat that conveys a sense of momentum and urgency even without the fervid quality so fundamental to Roy Eldridge's brand of excitement."[46] Sudhalter goes on to assert that "it's both forceful jazz, simply and logically constructed, and superior trumpet playing. For a trumpet player to begin a solo on this kind of *fortissimo* high note [pealing out a single massive high concert Db to fill his first bar], then use it as a structural pivot, returning to it five times in sixteen bars *without strain, without a hint of effect for its own sake*, is notable by any standard."[47]

While both Schuller and Sudhalter offer important insights in their comments on the Goodman orchestra's recording of "King Porter Stomp," they also raise two somewhat questionable points. In the first place, Henderson's arrangement for the Goodman orchestra parallels his orchestra's recording of "New King Porter Stomp," which is not a head arrangement but rather the very clear work of Henderson as an arranger. Also, most of the swing of the Goodman recording is generated by the arrangement rather than through the breaks taken by Goodman and his sidemen. Even though Berigan and Goodman undeniably contribute some swinging solos, much of what we hear involves more technical display than truly inventive phrasing and note choices. The problem with so many white musicians like Berigan, Goodman, and Artie Shaw is that, as Sudhalter perhaps unconsciously suggests, what we are being presented with in aural terms is superior technical playing rather than quality intellectual and emotional expression of the sort offered by Bobby Stark, Coleman Hawkins, and J.C. Higginbotham. The Henderson recording of "New King Porter Stomp" remains fresh, vigorous, stimulating, and memorable in ways that the Goodman recording cannot quite match. And yet it was by way of the Henderson arrangement for the Goodman orchestra that so many other white big bands recorded this piece by Jelly Roll Morton, making of his work of early jazz a mainstay of the later Swing Era.[48]

In discussing the Goodman recording, Lewis Erenberg cites John Hammond as having credited this performance with being the first to capture "the attack and freedom of the best coloured bands."[49] In his book, *Swingin' the Dream*, Erenberg is particularly interested in the idea of freedom as one of the most attractive features of jazz for white musicians and audiences. He equates the white desire for personal freedom during the Swing Era with the jazz performed and recorded by black musicians, and produced in turn by the many white big bands and smaller units of the period, heard on radio, at dance halls, on juke boxes, and on records. This idea had been treated at length by Burton Peretti in *The Creation of Jazz*, especially in his discussion of the Austin High Gang, which discovered jazz on Chicago's South Side with the bands of King Oliver and other New Orleans musicians. Subsequently, Richard Sudhalter, in his *Lost Chords*, has documented the white jazz groups active in Chicago as early as 1915, prior to the coming of such black figures as King Oliver and Louis Armstrong. Sudhalter also discusses the fact that the Jean Goldkette Orchestra, in which Bix Beiderbecke and Frank Trumbauer played, contributed significantly to the development of swing and of the big-band style, not only through the solos of Bix and Tram but through the highly influential arrangements of Bill Challis. Indeed, J.R. Taylor considers the early arrangements by Benny Carter for the Henderson orchestra to indicate an "interest in Bill Challis' work—particularly Challis' arrangements for the small Frank Trumbauer-Bix Beiderbecke recording groups."[50] The reciprocal impact of white and black musicians and ensembles on one another is incontrovertible, with benefits for both. Even before Sudhalter's mammoth, over 800-page volume presented evidence for the full range of white contributions to jazz, James Lincoln Collier had traced the music's biracial origins, beginning with the Creoles from Haiti and the Dominican Republic who immigrated to Louisiana and continuing with the input in New Orleans of blacks and whites. As Collier points out, "All sorts of people contributed to the making of jazz."[51] But it is still true that once a big-band procedure had been established—as it was with Henderson's arrangement of "King Porter Stomp" for the Goodman orchestra—that in the hands of most white bands such a procedure became little more than a cliché. There was little in the way of Erenberg's idea of freedom. This can be seen clearly in the case of Glenn Miller's September 1938 recording of "King Porter Stomp."

Gunther Schuller indicates that Glenn Miller, in the first year and a half of running his own unit, "was clinging to standard Goodman swing repertory: Henderson-style pieces like 'King Porter Stomp.' "[52] Of course, as Schuller also notes, such a piece was "already being transformed to some degree, cut to Miller's own stylistic cloth."[53] For one thing, following something of a Paul Whiteman symphonic opening, the Miller version of the Morton tune features the leader's trombone instead of a trumpet as in the Henderson and Goodman recordings. Miller's Teagarden-influenced solo certainly shows that he was capable of a very respectable performance on his instrument and that, as has been suggested, if Teagarden had not relegated Miller to doing mostly arrangements for the Pollack band and other groups of the late '20s and early '30s, he might have developed into an even more impressive trombonist. Other soloists in the Miller orchestra also give quite a respectable account of themselves—tenor sax first, then trumpet and alto sax—but not really on the same level with the Goodman sidemen and certainly not on the thrilling plane of the Henderson stars. The orchestra plays with crispness, and the sax section, with brass doing a type of doo-wah response, creates an undeniably delicious sound. The out section ensemble is nicely balanced and swings smoothly, concluding with the Henderson ascending phrase that he first used in "New King Porter Stomp" and then for the Goodman arrangement, which became a typical ending for many a swing-era tune. Although the Miller performance is quite well done, it essentially repeats what had come before, with only minor adjustments that hint at his own peculiar style that would make his orchestra immediately identifiable but would move it further and further from the *freedom* of jazz.[54]

Looking at the period from the perspective of some 60 to 70 years, it is perhaps easier to accept as largely true the fact that, as many black intellectuals have charged, the white big bands stole the blacks' music. So many of the radio jobs were only open to white musicians, and few of the black bands could compete with the popularity among dancers of the smoother white bands. Certainly the white bands of the 1920s, such as Goldkette's, had created its own music simultaneously with the black bands of the period. But in almost every case where a black composition was taken up by a white band, it was a far cry from the original. One such composition from the 1920s that would serve as the basis of a number of big band arrangements was King Oliver's "Dippermouth Blues," which also bore the title of "Sugar Foot Strut" or "Stomp." Dating from 1923 when King Oliver's Creole Jazz Band first recorded it, "Dippermouth Blues" was arranged in 1925, as "Sugar Foot Stomp," for the Fletcher Henderson Orchestra. Louis Armstrong was on hand to perform Oliver's classic solo, and like so many trumpeters thereafter, Louis hewed close to the King's style and the details of his performance. Schuller remarks that he gathers from listening to the Okeh recording of Oliver's "Dippermouth Blues" that "its great swing must have had an overwhelming effect in person in 1923."[55] It is evident that the structure of the King's solo and its "great swing" made it naturally alluring to arrangers like Redman in the '20s and perhaps even more so to arrangers of the Swing Era. But it is equally clear that even a formidable trumpet player like Harry James could not reproduce the power, intensity, and integrity of King Oliver's solo. On the September 1937 recording by the Benny Goodman orchestra of "Sugarfoot Stomp," arranged by Henderson, James's solo is unfortunately more showmanship, even showboating, than an example of the art of jazz. Technically, like other swing-era soloists such as Artie Shaw and (to a lesser degree) Tommy Dorsey, James is all over his horn and produces a good deal of excitement, yet he cannot match the emotive power and richness of Oliver's simpler lines and sounds. Goodman's clarinet solos, on the other hand, appeal more fully from their very natural swing and the relaxed, free-flowing ideas that he creates and communicates through the mastery of his instrument. This performance, in Henderson's very tasteful arrangement, certainly updates Oliver's composition, but it neither condescends to nor depreciates that earlier work. Rather, Henderson's arrangement (most significantly) and the Goodman orchestra's performance make "Sugarfoot Stomp" accessible to swing-era audiences, and even today it still can transmit something of the spirit of the original even if it does so in a less personal, more generic big-band style.

The question then arises, Were black musicians any more capable of reproducing Oliver's classic composition? The answer is found first in the 1925 Don Redman arrangement of the King's "Dippermouth Blues," renamed "Sugar Foot Stomp," with Armstrong playing Oliver's famous solo. Looking back on this performance after twenty-five years, Fletcher Henderson considered it his favorite out of all his recordings.[56] The reason is not difficult to ascertain. First, the tempo of this version lends itself to a maximum of swing without either dragging or being frantic—it is not so slow as the recordings of April 6 or even June 23, 1923, by Oliver and His Creole Jazz Band. It may be impossible to say who determined the tempi of Henderson recordings, or of those of other great bands, but the likelihood is that the leader set them himself. The difference this can make is exemplified by the case of the important Western Swing band led in the mid thirties by Milton Brown, whose tempi were always so right for the songs recorded by his Musical Brownies. This is clear from the one and only recording session headed up by his brother Derwood in February 1937 following Milton's death from a car accident in April 1936. The music can drag terribly, which must account in part for the 1937 recording session being the last held for the Musical Brownies.[57] With Fletcher Henderson, 1925 was just the beginning of his climb to the top of the big-band heap, but from this date his bands would regularly record tunes at tempi with a natural and infectious swing. As John S. Wilson says of the 1925 recording of "Sugar Foot Stomp," "it became the prototype of the Henderson big-band style with its mixture of driving beat, swinging ensembles and brilliant solo work."[58] Despite the fact that both the Oliver versions of his "Dippermouth Blues" are classics of their kind with a timeless spirit and penetrating sound, they do not achieve the same easy swing that is generated by the Henderson version of 1925.

As for Armstrong's playing of the Oliver solo, there is no denying that he knew the King's approach firsthand and had the technique to reproduce his notes with the same sort of inspiriting drive. Yet even Armstrong does not capture the soulfulness of Oliver on the April 6th recording, nor the unadorned intensity of the King's faster version of June 23rd. This points up one of the characteristics of great jazz—the inimitable nature of individual talent. It is rare or perhaps virtually impossible for one jazz musician to match the finest qualities of another. What endure in jazz are the essentially unique performances like those of King Oliver, and of course of Louis Armstrong when he was playing himself rather than attempting to replicate a solo by his predecessor. But aside from the "brilliant solo work" on the Henderson recording of "Sugar Foot Stomp," what stand out most are the swing of the entire ensemble and the surprising tonal and rhythmic shifts in the sectional writing (such as the three trumpets on the upbeats in the first statement of the theme, the highly influential clarinet trio, and the unusual ensemble fills between passages in Armstrong's solo), as well as the very full, rich sound of the eleven-man orchestra as it swings toward the end as one instrument in the style of Louis's cutting-edge horn. Later, in 1936, Armstrong would record a rendition of "Dippermouth Blues" with the Jimmy Dorsey Orchestra, and the approach then was in the dixieland vein, with drummer Ray McKinley's woodblock setting the style.[59] Dorsey's clarinet break recalls Johnny Dodds but is a smoother version of that twenties master (with a bit of Benny Goodman thrown in), while Louis's statement of the theme swings fully in the thirties mode and is, according to Max Harrison, "the best of all the countless recorded interpretations of Oliver's 'Dippermouth blues' solo."[60] Even in the Armstrong version the passion and intensity of Oliver's recording are replaced by a lighter good-time feel, which of course is characteristic of the dixieland style but not really of the King's much deeper music.

In 1931 Henderson arranged his own version of Oliver's "Sugar Foot Stomp," which is closer in its ensemble style to the original Creole Jazz Band recording of June 23, 1923, than to the 1925 arrangement by Redman, notably in Henderson's still faster tempo. In the same year of 1931 there were several Henderson recordings of the King's "Sugar Foot Stomp," one on March 31st, another on April 10th, a third on April 25th, a fourth on April 29th, and a fifth sometime in the summer.[61] The first version features five outstanding solos, including Henderson's on piano. Claude Jones's trombone chorus is technically daring, while Stewart's muted trumpet solo after Oliver's famous break is in Rex's own pixieish style, and therefore naturally removed from Oliver's more emotive power. Benny Morton matches Jones on trombone, but Coleman Hawkins is by far the star soloist. Although he tends to use a rather hard tonguing for half of his solo, Hawkins manages to swing in the most impassioned manner of any saxophonist up to this date, which would inspire nearly every tenor player of the Swing Era. A number of times, beginning with his first note ("a rugged low C"), Hawkins even reaches down to what in the early '40s came to be known as a "honk," favored by the Texas tenors who followed Coleman's lead.[62] Given the fact that both this March 1931 Henderson recording and the later 1937 version recorded by the Goodman orchestra were arranged by Henderson, it is clear that much of the ensemble swing is generated by the arranger's affinity for Oliver's original. The main difference between the two versions lies with the level of performance between the soloists in the Henderson and Goodman bands, and here it is evident that Henderson's sidemen recapture more of Oliver's classic jazz and yet do so without sacrificing their own voices or reducing themselves to mere imitators. Goodman's clarinet solos once again remain appealing as instances of his natural sense of swing, while Harry James's bows to Oliver lack an authentic ring and his own personal style seems overly exhibitionistic for its own sake. Nonetheless, the flamboyance of a James performance was highly popular with swing-era audiences, and when he is not held up for measurement against the King, James can still satisfy with his exuberant and flashy technique that always maintains a certain contiguity with the jazz tradition, which of course owes so much to a seminal figure like Joe Oliver.

In his extraordinary biodiscography, *Hendersonia*, Walter Allen writes that the various recordings of "Sugar Foot Stomp" by the Henderson orchestra "provide an interesting study of the variations possible within such a written score."[63] One curious fact about the development of Oliver's "Dippermouth Blues" as a vehicle for swing-era big bands is that, while Henderson's arrangement remained essentially the same (only the solo personnel changing), the April 10th and 25th recordings contain no direct statement of Oliver's trumpet solo. However, on the April 29 and the summer 1931 versions the King's break becomes something of the focal point of the two performances, with Rex Stewart playing the break muted. On all five of the recordings, the solos are outstanding. Benny Morton on the April 29 and J.C. Higginbotham on the summer sessions are especially effective; on these dates Hawkins, again, is quite impassioned but not so fluid, except on the April 29th cut where he irons out his chorus considerably. Only on the March 31st version does the Hawk play the "honks" mentioned above. The April 10th and 25th recordings are in a markedly more dated style than those of March 31st, April 29th, and the summer, with John Kirby on tuba on the first two instead of string bass (also on tuba for the April 29th cut); with Walter Johnson's cymbal work on the April 25th particularly harking back to the twenties; with Coleman Hawkins tonguing almost entirely on his breaks; and with a more shrill clarinet trio playing the tune's main theme. It is perhaps ironic that by returning to Oliver's 1923 original for more of its basic ingredients in the April 29th and summer recordings Henderson actually achieved a more swinging, updated arrangement and performance. Listening to Oliver's original recording, one cannot help but hear that he and his group generated a good deal of swing even at that early date, especially Oliver, with his driving open horn. Henderson's April 29th and summer 1931 recordings incorporate the well-known phrase shouted on the 1923 original: "Oh play that thing!" Likewise, Henderson ends the summer version with the same out-passage that concludes the 1923 recording. While the Henderson orchestra does not engage in the kind of group improvisation found on the Oliver original, the April 29th and summer 1931 "Sugar Foot Stomp" do exhibit the hot swing of that earlier period. As the decade would wear on, big bands would begin to lose touch with much of the hot jazz tradition and to substitute arranged passages for saxophone and brass sections in place of hot solos and any form of group improvisation. Although white bands continued to pay homage to the hot tradition by leaving opportunities—though fewer and fewer—for solos, these tended to become quite imitative of the black soloists or more bent on exhibiting technical skill, which consequently makes them less compelling in terms of artistic and emotive expression.

At the same time, it must be admitted that the black bands were influenced by what they heard the white players doing, either as soloists or as arrangers. Undoubtedly the most remarkable white jazzman of the 1920s, and probably of all white jazz history, was Bix Beiderbecke. Certainly, as Richard Sudhalter makes plain throughout his *Lost Chords*, almost every subsequent white player of the 1930s was indebted to Bix and emulated him in one way or another.[64] As for the impact Bix had on black musicians of the 1930s, this can be heard through the same Henderson recording session of April 10, 1931, which produced one of the versions of King Oliver's "Sugar Foot Stomp." On that date the Henderson orchestra recorded "Singin' the Blues," which was originally recorded by Beiderbecke on February 4, 1927, and has been considered to contain one of the finest examples of Bix's lyrical, logically constructed jazz. The difficulty for both black and white players thereafter to recapture the sound and swing of Bix's 1927 solo on "Singin' the Blues" is evident with every recording made by such groups as those led by Fletcher Henderson, Benny Goodman, and Lionel Hampton. In fact, in the case of the 1939 Hampton recording of "Singin' the Blues," the arrangement (probably by Benny Carter) simply avoids any reference to Bix's solo, including Coleman Hawkins' own solo, which never alludes to the Beiderbecke. As for the Henderson version of "Singin' the Blues," it was apparently arranged by Bill Challis for the April 1931 session. Here the soloists, Rex Stewart on cornet and Russell Procope on clarinet, play Bix's cornet solo and Jimmy Dorsey's clarinet break note for note.[65] Both soloists do a fine job of reproducing something of the spirit of those 1927 solos but not the special quality of the originals, especially in the case of the Bix solo with its purity and perfection of note placement and ringing sound that simply remain inimitable.

The other great recording by Bix and Tram, "I'm Coming Virginia," from May 13, 1927, was recorded live by the Benny Goodman orchestra at the Carnegie Hall concert of January 16, 1938.[66] Over ten years after the original recording, Bobby Hackett would try to reproduce Bix's solo and in doing so he was faithful to its lyrical spirit. However, while Hackett certainly approaches Bix's sound, Bobby muffs two crucial high notes, which Bix had executed flawlessly and with penetrating and poignant intensity. Towards the end Hackett clearly tires and concludes the solo weakly. In his *Lost Chords*, Richard Sudhalter has explained that at this time in his career Hackett's endurance was limited and that his agreeing to appear as a soloist on this occasion and "recreate" Bix's solo was perhaps an unwise decision: "He was nervous and his performance showed it; worse yet, he never got a chance on that momentous night to show off his own, by then, distinctively personal style."[67] Nonetheless, this is the closest approximation to the original Bix solo that any subsequent jazzman ever managed. Sudhalter notes that Bunny Berigan's earlier 1935 recording with a mixed group was "perhaps the day's highlight," but that Berigan takes the Bix solo "faster, as if deliberately eschewing the bittersweet nostalgia of Bix's recording. Bunny here is thoughtful, affectionate, as if commenting with some detachment on Bix and the song."[68] It should be noted that prior to Bix's recording of "I'm Coming Virginia," Red Nichols recorded quite a fine version of the tune in the company of the Whiteman band, on April 27, 1927. One wonders if Beiderbecke was influenced by Nichols's break, which seems to anticipate Bix's in sound and style, although ultimately they are quite different in feeling.[69]

It may be that both Berigan with his 1935 rendition of "I'm Coming Virginia" and Lionel Hampton with his 1939 version of "Singin' the Blues" were wiser not to attempt a recreation of the original Bix solos.[70] Another version of "I'm Coming Virginia" that is quite good and again does not try to duplicate the original cornet part is played by Harry James with Teddy Wilson's orchestra, recorded on April 23, 1937.[71] Berigan, like Hackett, does manage to recall something of the Beiderbecke sound even if he does not attempt to reproduce Bix's solo as such. With regard to the Hackett recreation of 1937, it was Irving Kolodin who came up with the notion of retracing "Twenty Years of Jazz" by revisiting such "landmarks of the popular music field as the Original Dixieland [Jazz] Band, Bix Beiderbecke, Ted Lewis, Louis Armstrong and the perennial Duke Ellington." Later Kolodin apologized for his idea "because it probably caused more trouble in listening to old records and copying off arrangements than it was worth," but then he goes on to say that it did bring out "that family feeling that all good jazz musicians have for their celebrated predecessors."[72] What should be borne in mind throughout all these comparisons and contrasts is that white and black musicians of the Swing Era were, in recording their own renditions of classic jazz arrangements or solos, paying homage to the great music they so deeply admired and sought to emulate. As Shorty Rogers said of his 1954 album, *Shorty Rogers Courts the Count*, he was "not trying to carve [Count Basie], that would be silly. It's our tribute to Basie and that's the whole reason we did it. It expresses the way myself and all the guys feel about him. He's meant so much to all of us and given so much to music we thought it would be nice to pay him this tribute."[73]

One additional example of the impact of Bix Beiderbecke on the subsequent history of jazz is his solo on "When," recorded with the Paul Whiteman Orchestra on March 12, 1928. This piece also includes a fine break by Frankie Trumbauer in the same vein as his solo work on "Singin' the Blues" and "I'm Coming Virginia," but it is Bix's second short break that contains a phrase that was picked up and repeated by Lester Young, the self-acknowledged admirer of Trumbauer, at the end of his Basie composition "Tickle Toe," recorded on March 19, 1940. Or it may be that Young heard this phrase in Benny Goodman's recording of "Could You Pass in Love?," cut on July 11, 1938. Although I confess that I cannot quite hear Bix's phrase in this latter piece, Edgar Sampson, according to Loren Schoenberg, wrote into his arrangement of "Could You Pass in Love?"—for Goodman's closing melody line—a phrase that "resembles" the one used by Lester Young from Bix's break on "When."[74] If Schoenberg is correct, his observation would indicate once again that black arrangers like Sampson and composer-soloists like Young were well aware of their white predecessors. This goes not only for the improvisational playing of a figure like Beiderbecke but for the work of white arrangers like Bill Challis of the Jean Goldkette Orchestra and Gene Gifford of the Casa Loma Orchestra.

The attractiveness to black leaders like Fletcher Henderson of the work of white jazz arrangers like Bill Challis is also revealed by the fact that in 1931 Henderson invited Challis to do an arrangement of Hoagy Carmichael's "Stardust" for the Henderson orchestra. According to Phil Schaap, as noted earlier, the recordings made by the Henderson orchestra during 1931 represent "the culmination of the Goldkette-Henderson, Bix, Tram-Hawk-Rex admiration society that had grown in warmth and music since their legendary first encounter at Roseland Ballroom on October 6, 1926." Schaap goes on to quote the recollections of Challis respecting the "Bix-inspired" arrangement he made for Henderson of "Stardust": "Fletcher wanted a little bit more of that type of flavor in his charts . . . which you might say was copied from the Goldkette influence. He wanted a little bit more of that trumpet color [Bix's cornet style and sound] and what's his name provided it . . . Rex Stewart, sure."[75] Stewart's solo, as constructed by Challis and performed by the Henderson sideman, does in fact achieve something of the feel of a Bix improvisation. Challis's work for the Paul Whiteman organization is evident in his use of chimes and a type of symphonic sound for the Henderson arrangement. Frequently criticized for its sloppy playing, the Henderson orchestra renders the Challis chart with striking precision and punch, yet with a sweetness typical of the Whiteman recordings. The March 1931 Henderson version of "Stardust," as arranged by Challis, also forecasts, along with Louis Armstrong's recording of the tune in the same year,[76] the popularity of this tune among swing-era big-bands, including renditions by Jimmie Lunceford (1934), Benny Goodman (1935), Tommy Dorsey (1940), Artie Shaw (1940—the latter arranged for swing band with strings by Lennie Hayton, a protege of Challis in the Whiteman organization), and Glenn Miller (1940), and even within the hardbop period, as indicated by a recording made by John Coltrane in 1963.[77]

In *Swinging' the Dream*, Lewis Erenberg speaks of the supplanting of hot jazz by sweet jazz during the early '30s. This view posits the notion that almost no important jazz took place between the Depression and Goodman's success in August 1935, which is a gross overstatement. Much of what Erenberg has to say in his book may apply more fully to white bands than to black ones. For example, Bennie Moten's band enjoyed its greatest recording session in 1932, producing some of the finest jazz of the entire decade. Many white bands also were involved in performing first-class jazz that in no way represents the typical sweet orchestras of the early '30s, such as Guy Lombardo's. Black bands naturally preferred to play hot jazz, or as Buster Smith put it in an interview, "rough" jazz, but they too had to play "that sweet stuff once in a while. It was all according to the kind of audience you had. You couldn't play our kind of music in some of the big places, the 'high collar' dances."[78] The issue of sweet versus hot is alluded to as early as a recording from 1931 by the Ben Pollack Orchestra, entitled "Sweet and Hot." What is most instructive about this recording is that jazz did not have to wait until Goodman's 1935 Palomar appearance to exhibit the essential characteristics of swing. While "Sweet and Hot" contains the title's two contrasting approaches to jazz, it also epitomizes the elements of swing, including a smoothly running string-bass line, played apparently by Harry Goodman, even though personnel for the date is listed with Harry performing on tuba. Brother Benny on clarinet already solos in his swingingly fluid style, which is fully in place for this 1931 session. Jack Teagarden's trombone solo tends to offer the hot side of the equation, whereas the saxes punctuate with sweet fills that typify some of the reed voicings of the later Swing Era. Richard Sudhalter declares that the band business itself tended arbitrarily and mindlessly to divide 1930s music into the hot and sweet categories. He suggests that the " 'sweet' category was actually something of a misnomer: it might more accurately have been labeled the 'not strictly for the swing fans' category." Sudhalter is referring specifically to the choice made in the late '30s by the Casa Loma Orchestra to include both approaches, which "had been in place from [the orchestra's] inception."[79] Schuller makes the same point about the Jimmie Lunceford tune, "While Love Lasts," recorded in May 1933, stating that half of it "is played in a sugary sweet style, including the brass, whereas the second part alternates between a better jazz style and an early form of dance-band swing—thus covering all stylistic bases."[80]

Just as black band leaders like Fletcher Henderson were attracted to the arranging work of Bill Challis and the sound of a white soloist like Bix Beiderbecke, so too were many black leaders led to imitate the style of the all-white Casa Loma Orchestra. The arranger for the Casa Lomans was Gene Gifford, who, according to Sudhalter, had served a "tough musical apprenticeship in the South and Southwest," where he played and wrote for various "territory" bands and even led "his own groups in Texas during the '20s."[81] Schuller credits Gifford's "Casa Loma Stomp" with bringing to white audiences a sense of real jazz, since, as the critic says, the young white college crowd that was so drawn to the Casa Loma sound had "unfortunately seldom heard any black music and authentic jazz at all."[82] Schuller also credits "Casa Loma Stomp" with advancing "more than any other piece of the early thirties . . . the idea of jazz instrumentals, at least in the guise of frenetic 'killer-dillers,' meant to be listened to as music, rather than as background for dancing."[83] Recorded in June 1930, "Casa Loma Stomp" offers many of the characteristics of swing-era big-band jazz, even though Schuller asserts that the orchestra "created the *illusion* of swing ... by substituting rhythmic energy and precision" in place of "swing in its highest and most relaxed linear form."[84]

After an unusual, symphonic-like opening, the theme of "Casa Loma Stomp," identified by Sudhalter as a Charleston figure, is played by the full orchestra in a peppy, infectious style.[85] This is followed by an impressive, driving trombone solo by Pee Wee Hunt and a rather stilted yet energetic tenor solo by Pat Davis. Biting trumpet fills behind the soloists look forward to the Goodman band's exciting trumpet section of the late '30s led by Harry James. The sax section with its precision playing in a passage involving a repeated rhythmic pattern of triplets leads to a call and response between reeds and brass that is a precursor of the decade's ubiquitous riffing in bands from Fletcher Henderson, Chick Webb, Count Basie, and Jimmie Lunceford to almost every white band of the period. (By decade's end so widespread was the use of riffs as a basis for big-band music that Artie Shaw reportedly tried his best to avoid using what he considered this boring device.[86]) The ending of "Casa Loma Stomp," with first its punctuating trumpets and then the brass moving up and the saxes descending in contrary motion, also forecasts the "killer-diller" finish to many a swing-era performance. As Sudhalter observes, this one piece "defines both the Casa Loma *sound* and Gifford's immense, even incomparable, contribution to jazz arranging." The critic also notes that Gifford's riff writing was "a primer and role model" for big bands "down to the end of the decade." [87] Through the work of its sidemen and arranger, the Casa Loma Orchestra set the stage for bands like Goodman and Basie to appeal to white audiences as creators of jazz rather than merely of dance music, emphasizing both imaginative solos and inventive, well-rehearsed and executed sectional writing.

Of course, the fact that most swing-era units produced danceable music would remain their primary attraction. Novelty numbers also continued to play an important role, just as they had on recordings in the '20s, including the banter between musicians on true jazz performances by Armstrong's Hot Fives and Jelly Roll Morton's Red Hot Peppers. Although the blues still exerted its influence on jazz of the '30s, vocal numbers as such tended more toward pop songs delivered to jazz rhythms. Hoagy Carmichael's "Lazy Bones," with lyrics by Johnnie Mercer, recorded by the Casa Loma Orchestra in June 1933, would be considered politically incorrect today, but at the time even black vocalists offered songs that depicted the life of Southern blacks in stereotypical form. What should be striking about the recording of "Lazy Bones," however, is not the patronizing lyrics but the more relaxed syncopation of this performance, and perhaps above all the lilting trumpet that plays the theme with a remarkably effective sweetness, not saccharine but genuinely romantic, a delivery that must have been the envy of later swing-era soloists. Other Casa Loma sidemen, especially Pee Wee Hunt on trombone and Clarence Hutchenrider on clarinet, are featured in hot breaks on "White Jazz" from 1931, and this piece also is notable for the drumming of Tony Briglia. Also from 1931 is the orchestra's version of "Smoke Rings," which again illustrates the sweeter, more romantic side of the band's personality. Here Pat Davis takes a rhapsodic solo that owes nothing to Coleman Hawkins and is even more convincing than the work of many later romantic tenor players of the period, while trombonist Billy Rauch ends the piece with what Schuller calls "a lyric style that anticipated (and almost matched) the later work of Tommy Dorsey." Sudhalter remarks that Rauch's "high F-concert at the end of Gifford's arrangement of 'Smoke Rings' was one of the standards by which *all* trombonists of the '30s judged one another."[88]

Another white band which surprisingly appealed to black leaders was that of Guy Lombardo. None other than Louis Armstrong admired the Lombardo sound and even recorded brother Carmen Lombardo's "Sweethearts on Parade" in December 1930 while Louis was the featured soloist with the Les Hite Orchestra.[89] Although the sax arrangement and playing and even Louis's opening trumpet sequence and his singing represent the sweet style, his solo following his vocal is as hot as one could wish, with the coda including a clever pre-boplike interpolation of a reveille bugle call. The influence of Lombardo's "sweetest music this side of heaven" on Armstrong's own orchestra, led by Zilmer Randolph, can be heard in its two versions of "Stardust" from November 1931. Once again, while the orchestra cloys with its syrupy reeds, Louis solos with hotly inventive lines, full of sixteenth-note runs, glissandos, dips, and triplets that displace Carmichael's theme, and exhibit what Gunther Schuller calls an "extraordinary rhythmic freedom."[90] After Louis's sweet vocal, backed by simpering orchestral fills, he improvises in the same swaggering manner trumpeter Harry James would adopt, including an octave glissando up to a high B flat and back down to low E on the staff. Schuller even traces James's later swing style to an eight-bar segment in Armstrong's solo on "Love, You Funny Thing."[91] This critic also makes the point that both Armstrong and Charlie Parker could create at a high level despite their being supported by a weak ensemble, and this goes as well for Bix Beiderbecke. Whether playing with his Hot Five or a sweet-style orchestra, Armstrong could offer the hottest licks of any trumpeter of the '20s or '30s and accounted in doing so for much of the style of the Swing Era.

The reciprocal influence of black and white bands on one another is fully demonstrated by various versions of Edgar Sampson's "Stompin' at the Savoy." Along with the work of Gene Gifford, this piece, as Gunther Schuller has noted, was one that set the " 'riff-instrumental' formula for dozens of white swing bands from Dorsey to Miller to Shaw and Les Brown."[92] First recorded in May 1934 by Chick Webb and His Orchestra, "Stompin' at the Savoy" refers in its title to the Savoy Ballroom in Harlem, advertised as "The Home of Happy Feet." Dancers flocked to hear the Chick Webb Orchestra, and "Stompin' at the Savoy" became "one of the unofficial anthems of the Swing Era."[93] Two other compositions by Sampson also impacted the Swing Era: "Don't Be That Way" and "Blue Lou," both of which were recorded by Webb in November 1934.[94] Each of these three works as performed by the Webb orchestra represents special characteristics of the Swing Era. In turn, as scored for and recorded by the Benny Goodman orchestra and other white and black bands of the '30s, Sampson's three compositions reveal many of the later developments of the swing period.

It is noteworthy that "Stompin' at the Savoy," along with "Sugar Foot Stomp," "King Porter's Stomp," and "Casa Loma Stomp," is not only in the '20s tradition of jazz with a strong beat but becomes during the Swing Era representative of the decade's own peculiar tendencies within the development of jazz and the big-band movement. Also in the grand tradition of the best jazz of the '20s was Jelly Roll Morton's "Black Bottom Stomp," recorded at his historic RCA Victor session of September 21, 1926, with his Red Hot Peppers, and yet in many respects it was ahead of its time. Morton's "Black Bottom Stomp" is typical of New Orleans jazz through what sounds like almost constant group improvisation between solo breaks, but as a matter of fact employs pre-arranged lines for the ensemble, which makes it basically the work of an arranger in the same way that Sampson's "Stompin' at the Savoy" was written out for Webb's orchestra, and later scored for Benny Goodman's orchestra. Vital to what Gunther Schuller calls the "unique forward momentum" and swing of Morton's tune is John Lindsay's pizzicato playing on his stringed bass, which Frank Tirro concisely points out "became a standard during the swing era." Tirro goes on to observe that with Morton's "Black Bottom Stomp" "we have an early recorded example of the bass used properly to supply the rhythmic life and harmonic ground so essential in the developing idiom."[95] In this regard, it is notable that Chick Webb's bassist, John Kirby, was responsible, along with the drummer-leader, for much of the powerful swing of the Webb orchestra on a piece like "Stompin' at the Savoy." Kirby would later go on to establish his own swing-era small unit that influenced any number of combos at the end of the decade.

Just as both "Black Bottom Stomp" and "Stompin' at the Savoy" are grounded by the string bass, the two pieces also share other similarities, even though the kinds of sound the two ensembles produce are quite distinct. Both compositions involve multiple themes, both employ punctuation by one group of instruments within the lines of another or of a single instrument, and both feature solo breaks that show off a sideman's improvisational skills. On the other hand, "Savoy" is more repetitious, depending largely as it does on repeated riffs, and the style is sweeter, with its use of muted trumpet and rhapsodic tenor. Once the themes of "Savoy" are stated, much more time is given over to solos than in Morton's composition. Finally, "Savoy" is less complex and therefore more danceable, which will be the tendency of the Swing Era with its simplification of jazz into a pattern of riff plus extended solos or even an entirely arranged piece with few if any solo breaks, rather than more of a balance between solo and ensemble, as in the Morton stomp.

Another source for jazz arrangements, quite different from the stomp tradition, was the burgeoning field of Broadway musicals. Jazz musicians like Red Nichols, Glenn Miller, and Benny Goodman, among many others, played in pit bands for such Gershwin hits as *Strike Up the Band* (1927) and *Girl Crazy* (1930). A September 1929 recording by the Luis Russell orchestra (under the name Lou and His Ginger Snaps) of a tune entitled "Broadway Rhythm" is suggestive of the beginning of jazz's dependence on the world of the musical (both of the American popular theatre and the Hollywood varieties) for much of its own music, that is, for band arrangements, solo improvisations, and original tunes based on the chord structures of popular songs like Gershwin's "I Got Rhythm" from *Girl Crazy*. The title "Broadway Rhythm" may actually refer to the New York street rather than to the playhouse district and the productions mounted there. But in the twenties Broadway and Fifty-first Street were in fact the home of the Roseland Dance Hall where Fletcher Henderson led the first big jazz band and where the Jean Goldkette Orchestra with Bix Beiderbecke did battle with Fletcher's outfit. As performed by Russell's Ginger Snaps, "Broadway Rhythm" is certainly representative of New York jazz of the period. Indeed, it is a "snappy" number, full of vigorous, shifting rhythms, stylish and smart in its pre-swing movement. At times it looks forward to the groups led by the preeminent New York stride pianist, Fats Waller. Solos by Charlie Holmes on alto, Bill Coleman on trumpet, Albert Nicholas on clarinet, Teddy Hill on tenor, and J.C. Higginbotham, all are peppy and quite advanced stylistically for this date, especially Holmes's alto and Hill's tenor. Pops Foster on string bass and Paul Barbarin on drums provide a solidly rocking rhythmic foundation. On the other hand, with "I Got Rhythm," recorded by Russell and His Orchestra in October 1930, the listener is thrust from the first bars into a pure Broadway pit-band reading of this Gershwin hit. The group in no way sounds like a jazz unit, not until J.C. Higginbotham cuts loose with an extended break that concludes with a bow to Jack Teagarden as he reaches for a blue note in the midst of an otherwise straight New York treatment. The vocal by crooner Vic Dickenson is also pure Broadway, and aside from the Higginbotham solo, only Greely Walton's brief ride on tenor relieves the hearer from the musical theatre recipe. Eventually, of course, "I Got Rhythm" would serve as the basis for countless Bebop tunes—unrecognizable as the Gershwin popsong but beholden to it for the melodic and harmonic underpinnings of some of the most inventive improvisations in jazz.

Seven years later, in September 1937, Chick Webb and His Little Chicks also recorded their version of Gershwin's "I Got Rhythm."[96] This is an example of the small-group recordings that were popular as offshoots of a big band, giving its personnel a chance to perform in a more intimate setting. The instrumentation also is characteristic of many small groups of the period, featuring something of a classical chamber ensemble sound with its flute, clarinet, piano, bass, and drums. Only the percussion instruments provide any type of jazz feeling, and this indicates how, as the Swing Era approached the end of the decade, many small ensembles tended to grow more classically inclined, playing an almost purely arranged music, and venturing further and further from any real jazz sound or spontaneous improvisation. Again, a piece like Gershwin's "I Got Rhythm" would, perhaps surprisingly, given the essentially non-jazz rendering of the tune by Webb and His Little Chicks, help lead the music back to its roots through the Bop Revolution instituted by Dizzy Gillespie, Charlie Parker, and others of the early to late 1940s. However, as we shall see, there were small groups other than Chick Webb's, such as the Lester Young combos and the Goodman sextets with Charlie Christian, which would be crucial to the development of Bebop and many of the later movements in jazz history.

Another Gershwin tune recorded by two important big bands of the '30s is "Liza" from *Show Girl*. Recorded by the Henderson orchestra in September 1934, "Liza" begins as a fairly straight reading of a broadway tune but is quickly transformed into a true piece of big-band jazz. A smooth swing is fully developed by bassist Elmer James, John Kirby's replacement after he joined Chick Webb, and the reliable drumming of Walter Johnson. The sections perform their variations on Gershwin's lines with precision and zip, ripping off phrases or bending them with drive and zest. Fills consist of bits and pieces of Gershwin's theme, which keep the performance from stating so directly and cloyingly its overly sweet popsong melody. The first soloist is either Russell Procope or Hilton Jefferson on alto, and the fluid but swinging style shows how far this instrument has come from the very stilted approach of its early practitioners. The trombone breaks, probably by Keg Johnson, are marked by his shaken high-notes that create a new sound for this once rather unwieldy horn. Benny Carter, also on alto, contributes a flowing solo that matches the earlier one by Procope or Jefferson but adds a tighter punch. Fletcher and his brother Horace both take a turn at the piano, with the former's more academic style in evidence in the introduction and his ragtime-influenced manner displayed in his closing, rather rare appearance as a soloist. In some ways this performance may be a prelude to the excessively smooth section work of so many big bands, an emphasis on section work over solos, but at this point both the sections and soloists are still offering a great variety of rhythmic, phrasal, and inventive sounds.

Almost four years later, in May 1938, the Chick Webb Orchestra also recorded a version of "Liza," arranged by Benny Carter. This version opens with Webb's drumming showcased before the rest of the unit joins him and three soloists take their turns. By this date the big band has begun its decline as a vehicle for inspiring jazz. Apart from an instance of the "mastery" of his drum kit, Webb does not provide with this performance anything particularly stimulating. The soloists try too hard to impress and fail to create choruses with appealing contours and felt expression. The arrangement does not allow for the kind of contrasts and rhythmic variety found in the Henderson chart, and the sections, precise in their execution, play little that is in any way novel or attractive. Although it is not clear who made the Henderson arrangement, it would seem from its high quality that it was either the work of Fletcher or Horace. In any case, the Carter version of "Liza" does not come up to the Henderson standard. This may be unfair to the Webb Orchestra, for he and his men certainly recorded more original and fetching work, as we shall see with later discussion of such tunes as "Stompin' at the Savoy," "Don't Be That Way," and "Blue Lou."

One further example of a poptune and its relation to jazz in the Swing Era is Irving Berlin's "He Ain't Got Rhythm," which may be something of a response to Gershwin's more famous "I Got Rhythm." In fact, Michael Freedland suggests that Berlin wrote his song "as if to get revenge on Gershwin."[97] Whatever Berlin's motive for the tune, as recorded by the Jimmie Lunceford Orchestra on January 26, 1937, "He Ain't Got Rhythm" represents the inventive uses swing arrangers and orchestra soloists made of such a work for the purposes of jazz. The lyrics of Berlin's tune, sung on the Lunceford side by tenor saxophonist Joe Thomas, suggest that without rhythm the subject of the song is "the loneliest man in town" because, as the lyricist's witty rhyme with "rhythm" has it, "no one is with him."[98] In one sense, this may have been true during the late thirties, for the whole country seemed in the swing groove, and those who were not with this rhythm were out of step with the times. Lunceford certainly had his own distinctive two-beat rhythm, and his version of Berlin's song is a perfect example of the leader's ability to employ a popsong as the basis for his own brand of swing, which was largely created by Lunceford's arranger, Sy Oliver, who adapted Berlin's piece to a popular orchestral style that Oliver himself helped establish. Using various instrumental combinations, Oliver repeats the Berlin theme in different voicings and with different rhythmic emphases, but always in the service of an easy, two-beat swing. In the passage following the vocal, Oliver has the trumpets and baritone spell out a chord from high to low by each holding in turn a different note. The variety of effects achieved in a two-and-a-half minute side made the Lunceford offering "an entertainment delight."[99] In addition to the arrangement, soloists in the Lunceford orchestra also took advantage of Berlin's tune for their own ends. In particular, electric guitarist Eddie Durham exhibits the potential for what would become an important new instrument in jazz. Durham's solo shows off his guitar's ringing, amplified sound and its special flexibility that Charlie Christian would make the most of not much later in the decade. Rather than being limited by popsongs, which in many cases were quite deadening, Lunceford and other band leaders—as well as a true jazz singer like Billie Holiday—transformed popsongs into highly inventive, sometimes moving, and almost always swinging works of enduring appeal.

The imaginative reach of swing is certainly greater than listeners were probably even at the time and especially now are fully aware. While there are many recordings which deserve the oblivion that they would naturally have fallen into were it not for series such as the one undertaken by Classics to reissue the complete sides of any number of bands from the Swing Era, there are many recordings which will reward repeated hearings. The following chapters will attempt to consider each band's output year by year, identifying the recordings by date, supplying information as to their availability on CD, vinyl disk, or cassette, and discussing arrangements and solos in order to suggest which sides are of more or less importance with regard to their contributions as jazz. Not every recording by a band or small group will be considered, but at least representative sides from each year of a band's existence. The "name" bands will be discussed first, beginning with the black and continuing with the white units, and these will be followed by what are termed "other" bands. The final chapter will treat the small groups which were so crucial to the artistic advancement of jazz. Finally, an A to Z section will provide concise information on selected band leaders, sidemen, singers, venues, and agents. While concentrating on the period 1930–1941, this volume also will attempt to reveal the continuum that has been vital to the making of this premier American music.

NOTES

1. Although King Oliver's most important work had been done by 1930, Albert J. McCarthy reports that he did record twice as the leader of the Bingie Madison band, in January and April 1931. According to McCarthy, Oliver can be heard taking a solo on "Stop Crying" and playing behind the vocalist on "One More Time." See McCarthy's *Big Band Jazz* (London: Barrie & Jenkins, 1974), p. 50. Morton would record again at the end of the decade, and a number of his sides are available on *Jelly Roll Morton: Last Sessions, The Complete General Recordings* (Commodore CMD-403, 1997). In the insert booklet to the Commodore CD, Butch Thompson suggests that "Get the Bucket," cut with a small band on January 23, 1940, "is a very funny parody of such swing-era vehicles as 'Christopher Columbus' and 'Tuxedo Junction.' Although it was probably not intended as satire,

one can certainly imagine Morton's delight in expropriating this kind of material" (p. 12). While the band sides on this CD are removed in some ways from the Morton style of the 1920s, they do not represent any significant afiliation with the swing-era conception.

2. André Hodeir, *Jazz: Its Evolution and Essence*, trans. David Noakes (New York: Grove Press, 1956), p. 33.

3. In *The Making of Jazz: A Comprehensive History* (New York: Houghton Mifflin, 1978; rpt. Delta, 1979), James Lincoln Collier notes that "polyrhythms, polyphony, things that are at the heart of jazz" were seen by arrangers with formal educations, such as Fletcher Henderson, Claude Hopkins, Luis Russell, Don Redman, and Jimmie Lunceford, "only as embellishments." Instead of the New Orleans polyphonic style, swing-era arrangers "conceived of a band arrangement . . . first in terms of a melody harmonized for a number of voices" (178).

4. Whichever of the two dates is taken, this would have made Morton age 12 or 15 when he composed this complex work, if his year of birth was 1890 rather than 1885 as he had claimed. Of course, he may have been something of a Mozartian prodigy. Lawrence Gushee is credited with discovering Morton's date of birth as 1890. See his article in *Storyville 98* (December 1981–January 1982), cited in *A Lester Young Reader*, ed. Lewis Porter (Washington: Smithsonian Institution Press, 1991), p. 224.

5. Martin Williams, liner notes to *King Oliver in New York* (RCA Victor LPV-529, 1966).

6. J.R. Taylor, liner notes to *Fletcher Henderson: Developing an American Orchestra 1923–1937* (The Smithsonian Collection R006, CBS Records P2–13710).

7. Hsio Wen Shih, "The Spread of Jazz and the Big Bands," in *Jazz: New Perspectives on the History of Jazz by Twelve of the World's Foremost Jazz Critics and Scholars*, ed. Nat Hentoff and Albert J. McCarthy (New York: Holt, Rinehart & Winston, 1959; rpt. Da Capo Press, 1975), p. 179.

8. Ibid.

9. Orrin Keepnews, liner notes to *The Birth of Big Band Jazz* (Riverside RLP 12–129, n.d.).

10. Shih, p. 178.

11. This recording is included on *King Oliver "Papa Joe" (1926–1928): King Oliver and His Dixie Syncopators* (Decca, DL 79246, n.d.).

12. Hugues Panassié, liner notes to *King Oliver "Papa Joe" (1926–1928): King Oliver and His Dixie Syncopators*. Jones had used the phrase "snag it" in a recording of Luis Russell's "Sweet Mumtaz" made on March 10, 1926, the day before Oliver's recording of "Snag It." "Sweet Mumtaz" is included in *The Luis Russell Collection, 1926–1934* (Collector's Classics COCD-7, 1992). Duke Ellington also borrowed from an Oliver tune for his composition "The Creeper," which, as Gunther Schuller points out, incorporates in a brass section break a four-bar passage from Oliver's "Snake Rag." See Schuller, "The Ellington Style: Its Origins and Early Development," in *Jazz: New Perspectives on the History of Jazz*, p. 251. As for Panassié's claim that Oliver's break was "quoted hundreds of times," I have as yet to discover a single instance, even after checking with several jazz cognoscenti, among them Dan Morgenstern of the Institute of Jazz Studies. However, this does not mean that Panassié may not be entirely correct. Martin Williams does observe of a 1930 Bennie Moten recording that "if the bass figure that introduces 'That Too,

Do' gets under your skin, listen to King Oliver's 'Snag It.' " Apparently Williams is referring to the phrase that Jack Washington plays on baritone (or perhaps bass) saxophone, which is the same as the Moten reed section's response to the two cornets' opening phrase on Oliver's "Snag It." See Martin Williams, liner notes to *Count Basie in Kansas City: Bennie Moten's Great Band of 1930–1932* (RCA Victor, LPV-514, 1965).

13. This recording is included on *Fletcher Henderson: Developing an American Orchestra 1923–1937*.

14. Wilfrid Mellers, *Music in a New Found Land: Themes and Developments in the History of American Music* (New York: Alfred A. Knopf, 1965; rpt. Oxford University Press, 1987), p. 311.

15. Marshall W. Stearns, *The Story of Jazz* (New York: Oxford University Press, 1970), p. 201.

16. Ibid., 199.

17. Ibid.

18. Stowe, *Swing Changes: Big-Band Jazz in New Deal America*, p. 74.

19. In *The Making of Jazz*, Collier suggests that Goodman was in fact always under the influence of the New Orleans style of jazz, that "his entire manner of playing is filled with the sound of New Orleans." Collier goes on to say that "the essential elements of Goodman's playing come from the old tradition" (p. 271).

20. Philip Furia, *The Poets of Tin Pan Alley: A History of America's Great Lyricists* (New York: Oxford University Press, 1990), p. 4.

21. Throughout his *The Swing Era*, Gunther Schuller discusses performances of Carmichael's "Stardust" by the following soloists: Louis Armstrong, Benny Goodman, Benny Carter, Charlie Christian, Tommy Dorsey, Roy Eldridge, Lionel Hampton, Earl Hines, J.J. Johnson, Murray McEachern (with the Casa Loma Orchestra), John Nesbitt (with McKinney's Cotton Pickers), Artie Shaw, and Ben Webster. The recordings on which these soloists appear date from 1928 to 1973. See the index to Schuller's *The Swing Era*, p. 911. Schuller does not include a solo on "Stardust" by Coleman Hawkins from 1931, perhaps because this particular recording with the Henderson band was not reissued until 1994. See my subsequent discussion of this piece.

22. Ted Gioia, *The History of Jazz* (New York: Oxford University Press, 1997), p. 87.

23. Rex Stewart, *Jazz Masters of the 30s* (New York: Macmillan, 1972), p. 12; cited in Gioia, p. 88.

24. Phil Schaap, insert notes to *Fletcher Henderson: The Crown King of Swing* (Savoy Jazz SJL 1152).

25. Richard M. Sudhalter, *Lost Chords: White Musicians and Their Contribution to Jazz, 1915–1945* (New York: Oxford University Press, 1999), p. 92.

26. Ibid., pp. 88–89.

27. Ibid., p. 89. Sudhalter goes on to say that "recorded evidence indicates that, rather than black precedent and white imitation (or its reverse), this appears after a time to have been a matter of independent and spontaneous gravitation toward universally accepted principles of ensemble organization" (p. 90).

28. Morton's tune would later contribute to the development of what was called in the 1950s the Progressive Jazz style, as represented by a recording of "King Porter Stomp" by the Pete Rugolo studio orchestra. While the use of timpani drums may

seem "progressive" here, they had been used on a Red Nichols recording as early as August 15, 1927. In his liner notes to *The Red Nichols Story* (Brunswick BL 54008, n.d.), Bill Simon writes that drummer Vic Berton "threw in accents and effects on the drums that had never been tried in jazz, and also introduced the tympani." Berton's timpani licks can be heard to fine effect on "Feelin' No Pain."

29. Mark C. Gridley, *Jazz Styles: History and Analysis*, second edition (Englewood Cliffs, NJ: Prentice-Hall, Inc., 1985), pp. 61–62. Morton's recording of his "King Porter Stomp" from December 14, 1939, has been considered the "best and most energetic of his several versions" (Martin Williams, annotations to *The Smithsonian Collection of Classic Jazz* [Washington, D.C.: The Smithsonian Collection of Recordings, 1987], p. 40). This 1939 version is available on *Jelly Roll Morton: Last Sessions, The Complete General Recordings.*

30. See the glossary of musical terms in Schuller's *The Swing Era*, p. 867.

31. Gunther Schuller, *Early Jazz: Its Roots and Musical Development* (New York: Oxford University Press, 1968), pp. 150–151.

32. Sudhalter, *Lost Chords*, p. 715.

33. Taylor, liner notes to *Fletcher Henderson: Developing an American Orchestra 1923–1937.*

34. According to Gunther Schuller in *Early Jazz*, the soloist here is Claude Jones, and this may be the case, but credit is given to Harrison on the Smithsonian Institution's 1987 album (see footnote 29 above). In any event, whoever the trombonist is, it is clear that he has listened closely to Jack Teagarden and learned his lessons well.

35. Schuller, *The Swing Era*, p. 324n.

36. John Chilton, *The Song of the Hawk: The Life and Recordings of Coleman Hawkins* (Ann Arbor: The University of Michigan Press, 1990), p. 78.

37. Schuller, *Early Jazz*, p. 268.

38. Gridley, *Jazz Styles*, p. 62.

39. Schuller, *Early Jazz*, p. 219.

40. John S. Wilson, "Fletcher Henderson," in *The Jazz Makers: Essays on the Greats of Jazz*, ed. Nat Shapiro and Nat Hentoff (New York: Holt, Rinehart and Winston, 1957; rpt. Da Capo Press, 1988), p. 228.

41. This recording is included on *Claude Hopkins and His Orchestra 1934–1935* (Classics 716, 1993).

42. Sudhalter, *Lost Chords*, p. 673.

43. Ibid., p. 561.

44. Schuller, *The Swing Era*, p. 9.

45. Ibid., p. 468.

46. Sudhalter, *Lost Chords*, p. 499.

47. Ibid., p. 500.

48. The Jimmy Dorsey Orchestra recorded "King Porter Stomp" repeatedly from the late 1930s, during 1945 and 1946 after the lifting of the recording ban, and even in the early 1950s. None of these many recordings adds anything particularly innovative or unforgettable to the piece in terms of jazz. Some versions take the tempo faster, add high trumpet work, feature a trombone trio, or contain more fully orchestrated sax fills, but the effect is nothing new in the way of jazz expression or development.

49. Erenberg, *Swingin' the Dream*, p. 74.

50. Taylor, liner notes to *Fletcher Henderson: Developing an American Orchestra 1923–1937*.

51. James Lincoln Collier, *Jazz* (New York: Oxford University Press, 1993), p. 200.

52. Schuller, *The Swing Era*, p. 667.

53. Ibid.

54. On April 23, 1940, a radio broadcast by Miller included a version of "King Porter Stomp," and on it the leader takes almost the same solo note for note— obviously not improvised but either written down or played over and over from the time of the first Miller recording of "King Porter Stomp" on September 27, 1938. The 1940 version has a better trumpet solo, the weak alto solo of 1938 has been dropped, and the ending jumps more, but it still does not offer the real swing of the black bands. The 1940 version is available on *Glenn Miller and His Orchestra: The Chesterfield Shows Volume II 1940/1/2* (Magic Compact Discs, DAWE 91, 1999).

55. Schuller, *Early Jazz*, p. 85.

56. See John S. Wilson, "Fletcher Henderson," in *The Jazz Makers*, p. 224.

57. See *The Complete Recordings of the Father of Western Swing: Milton Brown and the Musical Brownies* (Texas Rose Records, TXRCD 1–5, 1995).

58. Wilson, "Fletcher Henderson," p. 224.

59. The Armstrong-Dorsey recording of "Dippermouth Blues" is on *Louis Armstrong and His Orchestra 1936–1937* (Classics 512, 1990).

60. Max Harrison, *The Essential Jazz Record, Vol. 1 Ragtime to Swing* (London: Mansell Publishing Ltd., 1984; rpt. Da Capo Press, 1988), p. 341.

61. The March 31st recording is included on *Fletcher Henderson: Developing an American Orchestra 1923–1937*; the April 10th on *Fletcher Henderson: Tidal Wave* (Decca GRD-643, 1994); the April 25th on *Fletcher Henderson & His Orchestra: The Father of the Big Band* (Jazz Archives, No. 137, 159352, 1998); and the Summer 1931 on *The Crown King of Swing: Fletcher Henderson*.

62. Chilton, *The Song of the Hawk*, p. 70. I disagree with Chilton that Hawkins "seems to have been defeated by the banality of 'Twelfth Street Rag' " (p. 74). Hawkins' solo on the Euday L. Bowman rag tune strikes me as quite good—certainly more advanced in conception than the solos of the other sidemen on the fall 1931 recording by the Henderson orchestra.

63. Walter C. Allen, *Hendersonia: The Music of Fletcher Henderson and His Musicians: A Bio-Discography* (Highland Park, N.J.: n.p., 1973), p. 256.

64. Only after my own *Texan Jazz* of 1996 was in print did I discover, thanks to British poet and jazz critic Pete Townsend, the influence of Beiderbecke on a little-known Texas cornetist named Tom Howell. Townsend sent me a CD entitled *Blue Rhythm Stomp: Texas Jazz* (Marshall Cavendish Limited, 073, 1999), part of a series of Jazz Greats compiled in England by Tony Russell. Only one side by Fred Gardner's Texas University Troubadours is included, a piece entitled "No Trumps," but it is clear from Howell's playing on this tune that he had not only listened to Bix recordings but rather amazingly had mastered his sound and style. Only a few months later I came across *Jazz in Texas, 1924–1930*, compiled by John R.T. Davies and with liner notes by Brian Rust, which includes all four of the sides recorded on June 9, 1930, by Gardner's Troubadours (Timeless Records, CBC 1–033, 1997). Howell's muted cornet theme-statement on "Loveless Love" contains some Bix qua-

vers. On "Papa's Gone" Howell is not quite up to his work on "No Trumps"; here Howell is first open, playing some Bix rips and with his mellow ringing sound, and later he is muted. "Daniel's Blues" is clear evidence that the Troubadours were listening to the leading jazz lights of the day, for it opens with the theme of Ellington's 1928 "The Mooche" (not mentioned by Rust), and then shifts to a blues with the words made famous by Jimmy Rushing: "honey hang your head and cry." Here when Howell solos it is once again obviously in imitation of Bix.

65. This recording is included on *Fletcher Henderson: Tidal Wave*. As John Chilton says in his *The Song of the Hawk*, a clinker mars the introduction to the piece, but I do not hear that Rex Stewart "muffs some of the notes in his attempted recreation of Bix's solo" (p. 72–73). Chilton does say that the band produced another take and got the notes right in the introduction, yet that Stewart "blows a clinker during the early stages of his tribute solo but seems more assured than on the earlier recording; nevertheless the overall results amount to nothing more than a curio." Chilton does not identify the two recordings by specific dates and I have only heard the version of April 10th.

66. The Henderson orchestra actually recorded its own very respectable version of "I'm Comin' Virginia" on May 11, 1927, two days before the Bix version. The Henderson is included on *Fletcher Henderson & His Orchestra: The Father of the Big Band*.

67. Sudhalter, *Lost Chords*, p. 625.

68. Ibid., p. 501.

69. The Whiteman version of "I'm Coming, Virginia," with Red Nichols, is included on *Paul Whiteman & His Orchestra* (Jazz Archives No. 37, 157642, 1991).

70. Bunny Berigan's version of "I'm Coming Virginia" is on *Bunny Berigan and His Boys 1935–1936* (Classics 734, 1993); the Hampton recording of "Singin' the Blues" is included on *Lionel Hampton: Tempo and Swing* (Bluebird 66039–2, 1992). On "Whatcha Gonna Do When There Ain't No Swing?," which is included on the Berigan CD, Bunny plays a phrase at the end that echoes almost exactly Bix's closing phrase on "I'm Coming Virginia."

71. *Teddy Wilson His Piano and Orchestra with Billie Holiday* (Living Era CD AJA 5053, 1994). I had not heard this version at the time of writing *Texan Jazz* or I would have noted it as an example of James's superior work when not into his swaggering or showboating mode.

72. Irving Kolodin, liner notes to *Benny Goodman Live at Carnegie Hall* (Columbia Jazz Masterpieces, J2C 40244, 1988). Harry James is featured on "Shine," made famous by Louis Armstrong's March 1931 recording (included on *An Introduction to Louis Armstrong: His Best Recordings 1924–1938* [Best of Jazz, 4004, 1993]), although it is not clear to me that James's rendition is even based on Armstrong's 1931 recording. James does manages to play his notes at an impressive up tempo, but his version in no way achieves the swing of Armstrong's performance, lacking as it does the felt timing of Louis's rhythmic drive.

73. Quoted in Ralph J. Gleason, insert notes to *Shorty Rogers Courts the Count* (BM 720, BMG France, 1995).

74. Loren Schoenberg, insert notes to *Benny Goodman and His Orchestra: Wrappin' It Up: The Harry James Years Part 2* (Bluebird, 66549–2, 1995). Richard

Sudhalter also refers to Young's use of the Beiderbecke phrase in "Tickle Toe" (see *Lost Chords*, p. 460).

75. Phil Schaap, liner notes, to *Fletcher Henderson: The Crown King of Swing*. Schaap theorizes that Challis's written solo for Rex Stewart was perhaps based on an unknown performance of "Stardust" by Bix Beiderbecke, and when Challis acknowledges that this was a possibility, Schaap concludes that "there is no doubt that with this issue a 'lost master' has been restored."

76. See *Louis Armstrong: Stardust* (CBS Portrait Masters RK 44093, 1988). Gunther Schuller discusses and analyzes the two existing takes of Armstrong soloing on "Stardust" from his November 4, 1931, recording session. The music critic observes that the Armstrong version recasts Carmichael's melody through the trumpeter's highly inventive rhythmic vocabulary, and stresses the idea that "if anyone ever thought that swing had something to do with metronomic accuracy and playing only on or with the beat, here is a graphic illustration of quite the contrary. It underscores the point I was making in the definition of swing, namely, that swing is less a matter of accurate vertical placing of notes than it is their linear projection and inflection" (*The Swing Era*, pp. 174 and 176).

77. Gunther Schuller notes that an October 1928 version of Carmichael's "then brand-new 'Star Dust,' " as arranged by John Nesbitt for McKinney's Cotton Pickers recording under the name of the Chocolate Dandies, "lets us hear how orchestras used to play this piece in the late twenties, before it acquired lyrics and became one of the most successful sentimental ballads of all time." Schuller also points out that trumpeter-arranger Nesbitt takes "a fine Bix-like . . . solo near the end . . ." (*The Swing Era*, pp. 312–313). See John Coltrane, *Stardust* (Prestige Records, 7268, 1963), with Freddie Hubbard on trumpet, Red Garland on piano, Paul Chambers on bass, and others.

78. Don Gazzaway, "Conversations with Buster Smith, Part II," *The Jazz Review* 3, no. 1 (January 1960): 12, cited in Schuller, *Early Jazz*, p. 70.

79. Sudhalter, *Lost Chords*, p. 357. As an indication of how successful the Casa Loma Orchestra was in presenting the two sides of its musical coin, Sudhalter notes that it "led the 'sweet band' category in *Metronome*'s 1939 readers' poll" and yet the orchestra's lead trumpeter, Sonny Dunham, "wound up beside Bunny Berigan and Harry James on the first *Metronome* All-Star swing band recording session."

80. Schuller, *The Swing Era*, p. 205. "While It Lasts" is included on *Lunceford Special* (Columbia CS 9515, n.d.).

81. Sudhalter, *Lost Chords*, p. 341. Even before I encountered Sudhalter's book in 1999, I had discovered that clarinetist Clarence Hutchenrider, an important member of the Casa Loma Orchestra, was a native Texan. I had overlooked Hutchenrider in writing my *Texan Jazz* and only came across his work and the fact that he was a Texan, born in Waco, on June 13, 1908, while preparing for the present study of the Swing Era. Sudhalter interviewed Hutchenrider in 1985 and 1988, shortly before his death in 1991.

82. Schuller, *The Swing Era*, p. 635.

83. Ibid., p. 634.

84. Ibid., p. 639.

85. Sudhalter, *Lost Chords*, p. 345. All the Casa Loma sides discussed here are included on *Casa Loma Orchestra 1930/1934* (Jazz Archives, No. 54, 1992).

86. Ibid., p. 578. Sudhalter quotes Shaw as saying that he "was so sick, bored

to death, with all those riff things people were playing. . . . Tommy and Jimmy [Dorsey] had done the same thing; and Benny, and the Casa Loma band before him. It was all so formulaic: apart from the soloists, I thought Fletcher Henderson's was one of the most boring bands in the world."

87. Ibid., pp. 345, 343.

88. Schuller, *The Swing Era*, p. 641; Sudhalter, *Lost Chords*, p. 348.

89. This recording from December 23, 1930, is included on *Louis Armstrong: Mahogany Hall Stomp* (Living Era, AJA 5049, 1987).

90. Schuller, *The Swing Era*, p. 173. The two versions of "Stardust" are included on *Louis Armstrong: Stardust*.

91. Love, You Funny Thing is also included on *Louis Armstrong: Stardust*.

92. Schuller, *The Swing Era*, p. 215.

93. Anatol Schenker, liner notes to *Chick Webb and His Orchestra 1929–1934* (Classics 502, 1992).

94. These tunes as recorded by Chick Webb and His Orchestra are on *Spinnin' the Webb* (Decca GRD-635, 1994). Benny Carter's orchestra had previously recorded Sampson's "Blue Lou" in 1933.

95. Schuller, *Early Jazz*, p. 156; Frank Tirro, *Jazz: A History* (New York: W.W. Norton, 1977), p. 195.

96. This recording of I Got Rhythm from September 21, 1937, is included on *Spinnin' the Webb* (Decca GRD-635, 1994).

97. Freedland, *A Salute to Irving Berlin*, p. 166.

98. This recording is included on *Jimmie Lunceford* (Swingsation, GRD-9923, 1998).

99. Schuller, *The Swing Era*, p. 213.

Chapter 2

The Name Black Bands

Of the important big-band leaders of the Swing Era, all were active musicians in 1930, and most were still performing and/or leading a group in 1941. However, only about half the leaders of big bands were such in 1930; the other half would form a band or take over one later in the decade. Two of the seminal leaders during this period—Fletcher Henderson and Duke Ellington—had directed their own bands as early as 1923 and 1924, respectively. Each of the swing-era leaders was a fascinating figure, and each made a contribution to the development of Swing in the 1930s, but few of the leaders would professionally survive the 1940s and go on to direct big bands in the succeeding decades. The outstanding exceptions were Duke Ellington, Count Basie, Lionel Hampton, and Harry James. Two leaders who died in the 1940s—Jimmie Lunceford and Glenn Miller— might have managed to continue their successes of the 1930s and '40s, but to suggest as much would be mere speculation. Chick Webb died in 1939, and with his health problems would probably not have been able to continue as a drummer or leader even had he lived into the '40s or '50s. Other leaders—Benny Goodman, Earl Hines, the Dorsey brothers, Artie Shaw, and Cab Calloway—remained active as musicians and even directors of various groups, but none of these men achieved the same level of popularity that he had attained during the 1930s as the leader of a big band.

One test of a band leader and his band was whether they could make it in New York City. Some of the so-called Territory Bands, such as Andy Kirk and His Twelve Clouds of Joy out of Kansas City, did not appear regularly at the New York venues associated with the heyday of Swing, and others, such as the bands of Don Albert and Boots Douglas in Texas, did not tour much, if at all, beyond the state borders. Chicago's Grand Terrace was home for the entire period to the Earl Hines band, and Andy Kirk also played there often between 1936 and 1939. Both the Henderson and Basie bands also played the Grand Terrace and did radio broadcasts from there. Although the Kirk band had a successful tour of the East Coast in 1930, and played at the Savoy Ballroom and the Roseland in New York, for the most part Kirk's group was on the road. Not being in the Big Apple made it difficult for a group to capture the same large audiences as those attracted by the name bands of the period, which were often heard in New York or nearby eastern cities; such a presence meant that the bands there were able to reap the benefits of recording contracts, radio broadcasts, and commercial sponsorship.

The name bands enjoyed extended appearances at such New York venues as the Roseland Ballroom, the Cotton Club, the Apollo Theatre, and the Waldorf-Astoria, the Woodside, and the Pennsylvania hotels, as well as the Glen Island Casino at New Rochelle. The Goodman orchestra, accompanied by members of the Basie and Ellington orchestras, would appear in concert at Carnegie Hall in New York City. Among the second rank of big bands, that of Chick Webb was the featured unit at the Savoy Ballroom, which also welcomed other second-rank bands such as those of Erskine Hawkins and Charlie Barnet, as well as such name bands as those of Henderson, Basie, Ellington, and Goodman. Exposure in such prestigious venues assured the bands of media attention, profitable receipts, bookings elsewhere in the country, and what became avid fans and followers. Ultimately, however, it was the music of each big band that determined its success, and the name bands were most successful because they offered the most original, the most inspiring, and the most identifiable styles of swing music among the numerous groups active during the prewar period from 1930 to 1941. The name bands of Fletcher Henderson, Count Basie, Duke Ellington, and Jimmie Lunceford were the most original in terms of jazz performance, and therefore exerted the greatest influence on other groups, both the white name bands and the bands of the second rank. Even though the black name bands may not have profited as monetarily as some of their white counterparts, their recorded music lives on more fully as creative jazz than that of any other big bands of the era.

FLETCHER HENDERSON

Born in Cuthbert, Georgia, in 1898, Fletcher Henderson traveled to New York in 1920, intending to work as a chemist or pharmacist in the field of his college chemistry degree, taken at Atlanta University. While recording with many of the early female blues singers, Henderson found jobs for some of the sidemen accompanying the singers and together with these players fell into a full-time spot at New York's Club Alabam in 1923. In 1924, Henderson hired Louis Armstrong to strengthen his brass section, and Louis responded with the most advanced solos of the time, as on "Go 'Long Mule," "Copenhagen," and "Naughty Man."[1] On the first of these three tunes, it is clear by comparison with the corny breaks from the other players that Armstrong is simply so far beyond his band mates that it will take them some two years to catch up, as is evident for instance from "The Stampede" of 1926. Armstrong left the band in 1925, and two years later Henderson lost Don Redman, who had been his arranger from the first and had, as John S. Wilson puts it so succinctly, "developed the use of an entire section—the reeds or the brass—in a way comparable to the use of the single instruments in the smaller, extemporizing jazz bands. And he left open spaces for hot soloists, backing them up with prodding riffs, sometimes in the form of call-and-response between sections. In essence, this was the basic outline of big-band arranging as it was to remain for twenty years."[2]

After losing many of his sidemen in 1929, Henderson reorganized, hired altoist and arranger Benny Carter, began to write more of his own arrangements, and in 1931 made a number of celebrated recordings. James Lincoln Collier declares that Henderson's arrangement of "Just Blues" from April 1931 shows that Henderson was in fact the best arranger his band ever had.[3] Of course, as Gunther Schuller points out, Henderson's band also played a "distressing quantity of trite pop material," adding that "the titles tell the story: 'Sweet Music,' 'My Sweet Tooth Says I Wanna but My Wisdom Tooth Says No,' '. . . I Wanna Count Sheep Till the Cows Come Home,' all from 1931 and 1932."[4] Fortunately, there were other tunes, such as "Just Blues," that showed off to the best advantage the formidable talents of Henderson and his major sidemen. In addition, Fletcher's brother Horace also contributed to the band's book—in particular the 1931 "Hot and Anxious," which Schuller says "had a far-reaching effect on big-band history" in that it "presented a sure-fire formula for other, less gifted arrangers."[5]

Of the Henderson orchestra's "precarious years from 1928 to 1934," Schuller notes that every time the group's spirits lagged there was an injection of "new arranging and stylistic concepts."[6] In many ways, this characterizes the nature of the Swing Era and its dependence on arrangers for the success of its big bands, for the infusion either of novel ideas or of variations on the basic formula originated in the twenties. In the case of Benny Carter's arrangement of "Keep a Song in Your Soul," recorded in December 1930, this was an instance of an entirely new approach to big-band arranging. Schuller finds that this Carter chart "hit the mark . . . foreshadowing the swing style of years later." The critic asserts that the arranger "obviously had found the long-sought-after solution for making a section swing: the answer lay in syncopation." Schuller analyzes three different rhythmic arrangements of the tune's theme, indicating how the dotted-eighth-sixteenth-note rhythm of 1923 begun on the first beat of the bar was loosened up by 1928 to an eighth rest followed by an eighth-quarter-note pattern and then, by Carter's arrangement in 1930, to an eighth rest followed by a quarter-eighth-note pattern.[7] It is clear from the recording that this piece is indeed something entirely new in big-band jazz, that it is "one of the great arrangements in the Henderson book," with three fine solos by Claude Jones on trombone (others have credited the chorus to Jimmy Harrison), Carter on alto saxophone, and on trumpet Bobby Stark, whose break Schuller says sounds "*exactly* like Dizzy Gillespie of ten to fifteen years later. It must be heard to be believed."[8] Despite the fact that the piece opens with a tuba note (and John Kirby is on tuba throughout) and the first phrase ends with a single note on the xylophone à la Paul Whiteman, the arrangement has the reeds and brasses complementing each other, not just in a call-and-response mode but also with one section taking the theme entirely by itself or carrying part of it and then the other completing it. This makes for a smoother, more unified, more melodic flow. Especially unusual are the passages where the trumpets take the lead, with the first chair really driving the section, which would seem to foreshadow the style of lead trumpet played by Harry James with the 1937–1938 Goodman orchestra.

With Horace Henderson's "Hot and Anxious," of March 1931, the theme of Glenn Miller's immensely popular 1939 "In the Mood" is first used by a big band, having been played originally by Wingy Manone in his 1930 "Tar Paper Stomp." Aside from its theme, Horace's arrangement contains what Schuller calls "three primary elements": "(1) a steady four-to-the-bar 'chomp-chomp' beat, unvaried and relentless in all four rhythm instruments; (2) simple riffs . . . ; (3) the gradually receding 'fade-out' ending, preferably with bent blue notes in the guitar. Out of this formula Glenn Miller made a career, and many other bands, Negro and white, failed in the same ambition, but not for lack of trying." Schuller concludes that there is nothing special about the solos in "Hot and Anxious" but that its interest for other bands "lay in the new kind of swing feeling it presented. It was more illusion than real, but musicians felt comfortable in its 'groove.' It made no extraordinary demands on either player or listener, an obvious formula for wide success."[9] In April 1931, the Henderson band recorded, as we have seen, "Sugar Foot Stomp" and "Singin' the Blues," as well as a version of Fats Waller's delightful "I'm Crazy 'Bout My Baby." On this last tune, there are stirring solos by several of the sidemen, including Rex Stewart and Claude Jones, along with an unknown vocalist who does a decent job. The most impressive soloist is Coleman Hawkins, who takes an advanced break. John Chilton points out that in his sixteen-bar solo, Hawkins "reveals early signs of his experimentation with 'broken time' phrasing, creating musical ideas that didn't fall rigidly into two-or four-bar segments."[10]

Reedman and arranger Edgar Sampson joined Henderson for a recording session of July 17, 1931, and on "Radio Rhythm" Sampson's alto solo is a superb piece of swing. Also, his violin solo on "House of David Blues" shows the way for Western Swing—which will be discussed in the chapter on small-group jazz—but without that offshoot's countrified sound or rhythm. By this time, Coleman Hawkins is coming into his own on "Just Blues" and "House of David Blues."[11] John Kirby is still on tuba on these 1931 recordings, but he manages to play the instrument without the oom-pah sound and in fact achieves the equivalent of a "walking bass" on "House of David Blues" and "Radio Rhythm." On the latter, he helps to generate an extraordinary swing, along with drummer Walter Johnson. The division of brass and reed sections is clear throughout both of these pieces, and although this approach was originated by Redman, Fletcher, according to James Lincoln Collier, proved to be the superior arranger by using the formula "better than anybody in jazz." (Although Henderson arranged "House of David Blues," "Radio Rhythm" was arranged by Nat Leslie.) Collier quotes Dickie Wells to the effect that with a Henderson chart "you just had to play the notes and the arrangement was swinging. He didn't write too high—there wasn't any screaming—but his music used to make you feel bright inside."[12]

As noted in chapter 1, 1932 marked the recording date of Henderson's pacesetting "New King Porter Stomp." The following year saw another advanced score recorded by the band, that is, Coleman Hawkins's "Queer Notions," arranged by Fletcher's brother Horace. Although Gunther Schul-ler locates this "modernistic" piece of August 1933 "somewhat to the left of the main jazz tradition," he still considers it "authentic jazz" and the trumpet solo by Henry "Red" Allen to be "his greatest—at least from this period."[13] As Schuller also notes, another of the few pieces in this swing-era leftish tradition was Jimmie Lunceford's "Stratosphere" of September 1934.[14] Both "Queer Notions" and "Stratosphere" were essentially quite different from anything else recorded by these two bands, yet both pieces are immediately identifiable with the period. Unlike the modernistic work of Stan Kenton, which Schuller refers to and which other critics have seen as influenced by Lunceford (even though Kenton denied it), "Queer No-tions" and "Stratosphere" attempt to maintain a swing beat. One wonders whether swing-era couples were drawn to the dance floor or stood listening and waiting for the next, more predictable dance selection. As Benny Good-man recalled about the scene at the Los Angeles Palomar Ballroom in 1935, the couples there stopped dancing when the band began to play such tunes as "King Porter Stomp" and instead drew up around the band just to listen and applaud. Certainly in the early period of jazz history there must have been aficionados who preferred to listen to rather than dance to the music, and in the Bop and subsequent periods very few if any jazz enthusiasts would have attempted to dance to a challenging music that emphasized quick-changing rhythms and darting improvisations in place of a regular beat pattern. But the Swing Era was basically a period for popular dance music, and therefore pieces such as "Queer Notions" and "Stratosphere" were the exceptions which fascinate today precisely because they are excep-tional. Nonetheless, such composed music *was* part of the Swing Era and, as with much that was created during the period, looked forward to developments in jazz that are more associated with later styles and concepts which in fact had their roots in the early 1930s.

A more typical song and arrangement is "Happy Feet," from October 3, 1933, arranged by Horace Henderson and recorded under his own name.[15] "Happy Feet" had been recorded in February 1930 by the Paul Whiteman Orchestra, and that recording has been considered by Gunther Schuller to be, with its "crisp energy," among the Whiteman unit's "finest jazz scores."[16] In 1930, Whiteman had just made the Universal film *King of Jazz*, whose title, deriving from a photo caption in Whiteman's 1926 autobiography *Jazz*, was "a brilliant promotional ploy" but also reflected the reality of Whiteman's position at the time, "regardless of what the jazz purists may argue."[17] As Lorenzo Thomas has pointed out, Whiteman's vision of the future of jazz was a piece of "noble patriotism" and expressed his ambition " 'for jazz to develop always in an American way,' " even if Whiteman was not really thinking in terms of black jazz.[18] The differences between the Whiteman approach to jazz and that of Henderson are illustrated by comparison of the two versions of "Happy Feet."

Obviously much had changed between 1930 and 1933, but in many ways the basic approach of each orchestra on "Happy Feet" is essentially the same as it had been and would be throughout the careers of the two leaders. Although Horace is the arranger and nominal leader on the Henderson recording of "Happy Feet," the sidemen are those recruited by Fletcher, and the arrangement, with few exceptions, is identifiably in the Redman-Henderson tradition. As for Whiteman's rendition, it, too, is representative of his organization's approach. The soloists on the 1930 Whiteman version are Frankie Trumbauer, who plays a more flowing break than on his earlier work with Beiderbecke; Andy Secrest, who does an acceptable imitation of Bix; and Joe Venuti, who performs on violin with a subdued but still "hot" swing. The arrangement, which includes the usual Whiteman string section, aims at a rather bouncy symphonic beat that does in fact achieve a group swing that Henderson's orchestras had learned from Armstrong. There is variety in the Whiteman version through fills by different sections of the orchestra but no real use of the call-and-response pattern. The overall feeling is one of lightheartedness that still has an irresistible appeal. However, there is nothing special about the solos, and the arrangement is perhaps too busy to create the kind of intense drive that a Henderson unit could achieve through a leaner orchestration.

Right from the start, the precise, punchy trumpets that open the Henderson version with an attention-getting, five-note phrase initiate the piece's driving swing. This is followed by Horace on piano in a rather Hines-influenced, two-part introduction, in between which the trumpets repeat their five-note phrase. The trumpets then state the tune's theme (unrecognizable as the same Yellen-Ager composition played by Whiteman's orchestra) with unadorned simplicity, with only Walter Johnson's wonderful shimmering cymbal punctuating at the end of each phrase and later on with swirling fills by the reeds. The first true solo is by trumpeter Bobby Stark, who generates the kind of intensity—not by rapid tonguing but through speedy legato lines that move around the horn almost imperceptibly—that became characteristic of many of the top-rate trumpeters of the Swing Era. Stark is followed by Dickie Wells, whose shakes and high-notes are only part of the excitement of his break, which is marked by what André Hodeir would call "mobility and vehemence" and "impetuous effervescence." Hodeir considers Wells a "great jazz musician" in the same category with Armstrong (both of whose tone is, for Hodeir, enough to communicate something personal and moving), "one of those who swing the most," "majesty personified," and "one of the most perfect constructors of choruses in the history of jazz." As for Hodeir's description of Wells's construction of his choruses and his "sense of balance," this applies beautifully to the trombonist's solo on "Happy Feet": "The art of Dickie Wells seems to be governed by two essential ideas, *symmetry* and *contrast*." Hodeir goes on to say that "his choruses frequently begin with a kind of *doublet*—that is, a short phrase that is repeated, either identically or transposed, after a brief pause." The doublet is an instance of Wells's symmetry, whereas his "violent opposition of upper and lower registers, of forte and piano, of motion and repose" is an example of his contrast. Both these characteristics are present in Wells's solo on "Happy Feet," including the phrase that opens his chorus and is repeated lower, as well as the later phrase that shoots up and then is "doubled" below with the charm and wit that make his solos seem like self-conversations or a combination of direct comment followed by a contrastive aside.[19]

The final solo on the Henderson version is a short break by Coleman Hawkins, who just gets going when the ensemble reenters. Horace does not leave much room for solos in this piece and features rather the brass and reeds in alternating passages, which lend great variety to the performance yet maintain its exhilarating forward momentum. It should be noted that despite the shortness of Dickie Wells's chorus, he manages to make every note count and to link his solo with what had come before, which Hodeir also suggests is characteristic of the trombonist. Although it is undeniable that the Whiteman version of "Happy Feet" swings in its way, it does not offer the kind of high-level improvisation that is found in Wells's chorus. This is an important difference, because in the realm of jazz there were many bands that could swing but only rarely did they offer great, inventive jazz solos. In this vital respect, Fletcher Henderson's units outpaced most of the other swing bands of the era. Of course, it must be said that when Beiderbecke participated in a Whiteman performance, it was inevitably raised to another level of invention, lifting momentarily some of Whiteman's selections from sappy to the sublime, as on "Changes," "Back in Your Own Backyard," and especially "Sweet Sue."[20]

Two other 1933 sides recorded by the Henderson orchestra led by brother Horace are "Yeah Man!" and "I've Got to Sing a Torch Song."[21] On the former, according to John Chilton, Hawkins creates "some bold new thoughts" and "phrases that seem to defy musical gravity."[22] On "I've Got to Sing a Torch Song," Hawkins is not only given more solo space but perhaps the most enjoyed by any soloist up to this point in recording history. And he takes full advantage of the opportunity, not simply going on and on as so many later tenor soloists would tend to do, but making each of his phrases meaningful in a truly expressive way. The tempo is dreamy slow—another feature that makes this piece a foreshadowing of things to come. Hawkins in this atmosphere is at his rhapsodic best, his tone breathy as never before, his high register airy with a touch of the terminal vibrato that other tenorists such as Ben Webster would pick up from the master. Hawkins is unabashedly sentimental, but his technique is "hot" in the same sense as it is on his celebrated "Body and Soul" of 1939. He explores the theme and chords with characteristic imagination, if not so fully as he would at the end of the decade. The bridges to his choruses are marked by triplets and sixteenth-note runs that are totally under control yet at the same time fluctuate rhythmically within the bar lines by speeding up or slowing down. Every phrase, rather than being in his earlier staccato mode, is legato, which of course is appropriate to the ballad style. His conclusion is a kind of coda that underscores the emotive force of the entire solo, which also became a hallmark of much of his later work.

Jacques Morgantini has written of Hawkins's extended solo on "I've Got to Sing a Torch Song" that it provided "the taking-off point for further sumptuous ballads, interpreted with that beautifully-rounded warm, velvety tone" and that his "variations on a slow tempo would prove a guiding-light for many future tenor players."[23] Likewise, Albert McCarthy writes that Hawkins's solo prefigures "the rhapsodic ballad interpretations for which he became famous in the years ahead."[24] John Chilton quotes Howard McGhee as having said that before Hawkins's 1939 "Body and Soul" he "had never heard a horn play two choruses in a row," but Hawkins had done so in 1933 on "I've Got to Sing a Torch Song" where he plays two magnificent choruses.[25] Some of these same qualities and tendencies were already apparent in Hawkins's 1929 recording with the Mound City Blue Blowers of "One Hour," although that was in the context of a small group, as the 1939 "Body and Soul" would be. Also, it should be noted that Hawkins was capable of many different styles, as illustrated by his performances on the 1927 "St. Louis Shuffle" with Henderson and the 1929 "Wherever There's a Will, Baby," with Don Redman's McKinney's

Cotton Pickers, where in both cases he produces a more straight-ahead driving swing, as he does on "Hello, Lola," also from 1929.[26]

In September 1934, the Henderson band recorded "Shanghai Shuffle," which definitely exhibits great swing, with its string bass and guitar in tandem, and marvelous sectional writing and precision execution by brass and reeds alike, as well as fine solos, especially Buster Bailey on clarinet. It is instructive to compare this recording with the Henderson version of "Shanghai Shuffle" from 1924, as well as the recordings of "Singapore Sorrows" by Ben Pollack and His Californians from 1928 and of "Chop, Chop Charlie Chan (From China)" by Cab Calloway and His Orchestra from 1940. As indicated by this sixteen-year span, the use of "Chinese" music as the basis for a jazz performance was popular both early and late in the twenties and thirties. But more to the point is the fact that each recording illustrates the development of the big-band form of jazz and the changing styles that went along with it.

On the October 1924 Henderson recording of "Shanghai Shuffle," not unexpectedly the only really stimulating jazz is provided by Louis Armstrong's trumpet solo. The piece opens with a cymbal crash and closes with another sounding like a gong, which are intended to frame the work within a Sinolike setting. After the opening cymbal and drum figures, which suggest a rather monotonous rhythm supposedly associated with the Far East, muted trumpets state a motif that is slightly Chinese in character, followed by the sappy saxes which at one point slur up not quite an octave to achieve a somewhat Oriental sound. After a rather dreadful trombone solo by Charlie Green (normally a more effective soloist but probably straitjacketed by a written part), the theme is played by a combination of instruments that includes Don Redman on oboe in another attempt at a Far East effect. At last, Armstrong takes over and blows a series of rhythmically varied phrases, including a repeated one with a sort of hiccoughlike interval that may relate to the saxes' upward slur. Only toward the end of his solo does Armstrong allude to the tune's remotely Chinese theme, making it more interesting than it is on its own. Even though Armstrong's improvisation is inventive in a timeless way, it is dated somewhat by the accompanying tuba that pumps along on beats one and three of the "Fox Trot" pattern and thereby ties the solo too closely to a typical twenties sound. Again, other than Armstrong's solo, there is nothing to recommend this novelty piece as jazz.

Four years later, on April 26, 1928, the Pollack orchestra would record its version of "Singapore Sorrows," which is more immediately identifiable as based on stereotypical Chinese sounds. The opening here also features a Chinese crash cymbal but adds as well a familiar "Oriental" rhythm on the Chinese woodblock. (In Western music, it would appear that both of these instruments—the crash cymbal and the woodblock—were "brought

into use" by jazz musicians and that their true "home is the dance band."[27])
The percussion opening is followed by a symphonic introduction by the
full orchestra, complete with Chinese chords and a trombone section that
reminds one of a 1940s newsreel buildup to the latest world events. The
theme is then stated by the baritone sax, which contributes a further pseudo-
Chinese dimension to the piece. But the main difference between the Pollack
performance and the Henderson is that even with its Whiteman-like symphonic feeling "Singapore Sorrows" swings, and this is especially true after
the vocal by Pollack. Benny Goodman's clarinet break, like Armstrong's
on trumpet, transforms the piece, but in this instance into a showcase for
driving improvisations by first Benny and then Glenn Miller on trombone
and Jimmy McPartland on trumpet. Miller's extended trombone solo demonstrates once again how effective a soloist he could be in the hot vein,
and McPartland's Bix-inspired trumpet is the climax of the performance,
after which the piece ends with the predictable Chinese cymbal crash.

As good as the Pollack recording remains, the Henderson remake of
"Shanghai Shuffle," on September 11, 1934, is truly in a class by itself.[28]
What is amazing is that this recording could be based on the same
Rodemich-Conley tune as the 1924 version. One telling difference is the
inclusion of a clarinet solo by Buster Bailey, which alone lifts the overall
performance to another level. One wonders if Bailey had soloed on the
1924 version if it would have helped—probably not, because the arrangement was so novelty-oriented.[29] Information on the recording indicates that
Bailey was possibly a member of the Henderson band at the time of the
"Go 'Long Mule" date of October 7 but was "definitely" not at the October 10–13 recording of "Shanghai Shuffle."[30] On the 1934 version, the
trumpet solo by Irving Randolph has its moments and the alto break by
Hilton Jefferson is particularly fine, but the outstanding feature of this recording is Fletcher Henderson's arrangement and his sidemen who perform
it as an inspired and well-rehearsed unit. From the opening attack of the
stabbing trumpets and the first driving notes of Elmer James's string bass,
this is a thrilling piece of music in the best tradition of the Swing Era.
Significantly, Henderson as the arranger of this remake has eschewed any
Chinese gimmickry. The flutter-tonguing trumpets are the nearest thing to
exoticism, and this was hardly imported from afar but rather has been a
feature of jazz almost from the beginning. The tricky rhythms executed
precisely and with punch by the saxes are sheer fun to hear and follow.
And if the ending is already formulaic, it is at least not a piece of imitation
Chinese.

By the time Cab Calloway recorded his "Chop, Chop Charlie Chan
(From China)" on March 8, 1940, most everything that is characteristic of
the Swing Era had been repeated almost ad nauseam.[31] Of course, in the
following year, as we shall see, Duke Ellington still had plenty of surprises
in store for his avid followers. But even in 1940, Calloway was paving the

way for something completely new in jazz by way of his trumpeter, Dizzy Gillespie, even though Cab himself is often quoted as having objected to Dizzy's "Chinese music." Calloway was obviously not alluding to anything specifically Oriental in Gillespie's style but was referring more to his use of unusual note combinations, dissonances, and offbeat rhythms. Not that this is evident in Dizzy's solo on the 1940 recording of "Chop, Chop Charlie Chan," which for him is quite tame. More striking is Calloway's own mock-Oriental singing, which may be considered today rather politically incorrect, yet it is an example of Cab's genius for creating sounds that are both entertaining as such and swinging within the context of a jazz performance. The piece opens with the same type of Chinese cymbal crash as heard on the 1924 and 1928 recordings by Henderson and Pollack, but after the trumpet-section phrases vaguely suggest an Oriental atmosphere, the band plays a distinctly dissonant chord that turns this into a "modern" version of "Chinese" music and definitely looks forward to the Bop Revolution. The tenor solo, perhaps either by Chu Berry or Ben Webster, is vintage swing. After an early example of dissonance, the band settles into a rather traditional big-band swing groove. But again, it is Calloway's singing that creates something unique with its incorporation of imitative Chinese syllables that are perfect for his vocal acrobatics, his solid sense of swing, and his soaring notes that create such a rich harmonic blend with his sidemen's instruments.

If Henderson, through Don Redman's 1924 arrangement of "Shanghai Shuffle," inadvertently started the Chinese strain in jazz, he did not continue it but veered away from such exoticism and concentrated in his own arrangements on perfecting the basic sectional devices of the riff and the call-and-response established by Redman and other arrangers, black and white. (Henderson's use of the call-and-response is particularly well developed on his 1934 arrangement of W.C. Handy's "Memphis Blues."[32]) Nor did Henderson play an important role in the rise of jazz vocalists such as Cab Calloway, even though Fletcher had begun his career in the music field as a piano accompanist for many of the early blues singers such as Ma Rainey and Maggie Jones. Although vocals were common on Henderson recordings, as they were on many sides issued by jazz bands even in the twenties, Henderson never really featured singers and did not promote any of the star vocalists of the Swing Era. When he did employ a vocalist such as Dick Vance on "You Can Depend on Me," the singer spoiled the effect of what was otherwise a very fine arrangement.[33] What Henderson did do from the first was to hire outstanding sidemen, to assemble leading ensembles, and to make arrangements himself or to record arrangements by other musicians which were often models of their kind and influenced the entire movement of swing music. This is evident from such September 1934 recordings as "Down South Camp Meetin' " and "Wrappin' It Up," both arranged by Henderson. These particular arrangements are precisely in the style that Henderson used for the Goodman band. Not only that but in "Down South," following one of Henry "Red" Allen's major trumpet solos, the call-and-response exchange between Allen's trumpet and Hilton Jefferson's alto sax contains almost the same phrases played by Bunny Berigan to open the July 1935 Benny Goodman recording of "King Porter Stomp," as arranged by Henderson. In "Down South," Henderson also voices the reed section just as he would for the Goodman band, with so many other big bands following suit. Gunther Schuller speculates on the all but certain frustration that Henderson must have felt once he had developed "a distinctly new orchestral style in jazz, soon to be called 'Swing,' " which Goodman would sell "to a mass public" just after Henderson had disbanded his own orchestra in the same year he recorded "Down South."[34]

The clarinet trio in "Down South Camp Meetin' " recalls the use of this device in the 1925 Redman arrangement and Fletcher's own 1931 rendition of Oliver's "Sugar Foot Stomp." But once again, Henderson's 1934 form of jazz is far removed from Oliver's 1923 classic, and it has even less to do with Oliver's 1923 "Camp Meeting Blues" with its reference to the religious source for much early black music. What is symptomatic here of the decline of real jazz in many swing-era recordings is the overemphasis on ensemble work. Although all the sections—brass, reeds, and rhythm—play cleanly and with engaging energy and snap, there are only two solos, one by Allen on trumpet and the other by Jefferson on alto sax. (Hawkins had departed by this date and been replaced by Ben Webster.) The ubiquitous clarinet trio shows up again in "Wrappin' It Up," but overall this recording is even further from the 1920s style. The soloists, beginning with Jefferson on alto, are all quite splendid. Allen's two-part solo is in advance of Harry James, who, on the Goodman recording of the Henderson arrangement of "Wrappin' It Up," from May 28, 1938, swaggers as usual but in the second half is quite fine.[35] Before James on the Goodman recording, the alto solo by Dave Mathews is also noteworthy. But as Gunther Schuller points out, the Goodman orchestra tended to be "top heavy" and lacked the necessary foundation, because "the depth of feeling and support that a properly functioning rhythm section generates is just not present."[36] In contrast, the Henderson recording swings from below with a driving but relaxed beat. Another reason that the Goodman rendition does not come up to the Henderson original is, once again, the tempo—in comparison with the Henderson the Goodman drags. Perhaps by 1938 the white dancers were dictating such a slowdown.

Relaxed swing is also one of the outstanding qualities of the September 1934 Henderson recording of "Wild Party," around whose riff a clarinet weaves in an almost New Orleans style. Orchestral modulations are striking, as are all the many solo breaks and the drive that builds relentlessly. From the same session of September 25, the orchestra produced two other superb recordings: "Rug Cutter's Swing" and "Hotter Than 'Ell," the first arranged by Horace and the second by Fletcher. Both these tunes offer exciting jazz, with the Henderson rhythm section powering the soloists and ensembles throughout. Here Ben Webster really fills Hawkins's shoes as well as any tenor could, and in his own unique style. Another riff tune from earlier in the year is Henderson's own "Hocus Pocus," with Hawkins featured on his last recording date with the orchestra, his tone described by George Hoefer as "sweeter and even fuller" and within the reed section his "big tone making a solid wall of sound."[37] James Lincoln Collier rates Allen's brief, controlled solo on "Hocus Pocus" as among his best work, and Hoefer characterizes the entire performance as an instance of the sophisticated swing that can be discerned by this date.[38] Collier's view that black bands were finding work in the early thirties seems to contradict Lewis Erenberg's notion that there was no work for jazz musicians, period; Erenberg also claims that there was "a prolonged decline of jazz in the early 1930s."[39] Collier, on the other hand, declares that whereas white bands were having trouble finding jobs, "Blacks were preferred for the nightclubs and show spots, which wanted hot music, but they were not acceptable at the big, expensive, white-only hotel dining and dancing rooms."[40] Collier also asserts that because white bands played in hotels and restaurants, "they could play little jazz." He goes on to say flatly that "most of the recording by whites during the early thirties was of little value as jazz. The jazz records were being made by blacks" who "had the jazz audience, and it was they in the main who developed the big jazz band."[41] Certainly Fletcher Henderson was developing a "big jazz band" from 1923 onward. Other examples of his development of the form followed after he had disbanded his outfit in 1934 and started up again in 1936.

Perhaps the most important recording Henderson made in 1936 was of brother Horace's arrangement of Chu Berry's "Christopher Columbus." This was in fact the Henderson orchestra's first big hit, and would become, as Gunther Schuller suggests, "the kind of riff swing piece which later other bands—like Goodman, Harry James, Larry Clinton, Les Brown—were to grind into a rigid formula."[42] Making the new orchestra's recording debut a success on March 27 was John Kirby, who was back with his boss; Big Sid Catlett, who replaced Johnson on drums; tenorist Berry, who replaced Ben Webster; and Buster Bailey, who was with Henderson off and on from 1924, joined by advanced swing trumpeter Roy Eldridge. Once again, Henderson not only has earned the allegiance of players like Kirby and Bailey but also has attracted two of the leading swing soloists of the period in Berry and Eldridge. The brasses on top and the saxes answering below create a rocking background for the soloists, with Eldridge especially intense and Berry digging right in as the ensemble builds on Kirby's solid bass. Another fine recording from this session is the Henderson version of Edgar Sampson's "Blue Lou," which features more fully both Eldridge and

Berry, with the latter coming on with his trademark tight vibrato that generates a sense of urgency and intense drive. As good as this version is, it must be said that Chick Webb's original recording of "Blue Lou," from November 19, 1934, is hard to beat, with Chick's drumming, John Kirby's bass, and John Trueheart's guitar all laying down a beat that rivals that of Count Basie's later "All-American Rhythm Section." Nonetheless, Webb's recording does not offer the solo power of Eldridge and Berry. Finally, one other side from the March 27 session worthy of note is "Stealin' Apples," which opens with Fletcher playing his version of New York stride piano, followed by Chu Berry's warm tenor in a subdued but what came to be known as a booting solo. Bailey's break is perhaps a bit stiff at this date but effective even so, especially his high notes above the rest of the ensemble in the ride-out. Personally I find it affecting that Bailey is still with Henderson, for it says much about loyalty among the leader's personnel, as well as about Henderson's generous treatment of his faithful players. As we shall see, this was true as well of the great Duke Ellington.

Other sides recorded during 1936 that are worthy of a hearing include "Jangled Nerves" from April 9, "Grand Terrace Rhythm," "Riffin'," and "Mary Had a Little Lamb" from May 23, and "Shoe Shine Boy" and "Sing, Sing, Sing" from August 4. The last of these would, of course, become better known from the Goodman Carnegie Hall Concert of 1938, but the Henderson version is highly recommended, as are the other sides from 1936. Henderson's entire oeuvre deserves a better fate than being relegated to the work of a might-have-been great, when in fact so many of his sides remain superior to what have been considered the best recordings by a number of better-known leaders. It should be noted, however, that even with the fine recordings of "Christopher Columbus" and "Blue Lou," there is, as J.R. Taylor points out, a certain "hollow conservatism" that begins to creep into the Henderson sides by 1936, despite the startling trumpet work of Roy Eldridge.[43] Judged against the Henderson recordings of ten years before, certainly the 1936 sides are not revolutionary, but it is instructive to consider a performance like that of "The Stampede" from 1926 and to compare it with the rendition of the same Henderson tune (titled simply "Stampede") from March 2, 1937. Although the 1937 version does not offer the ecstatic soloing of Rex Stewart and Coleman Hawkins, it does contain everything characteristic of the Swing Era: a smoothness of execution by the sax section, contrasted by the sharp punctuations of the brass section; Israel Crosby's driving, almost melodic bass line; Walter Johnson's subtle cymbal work; brief but unified breaks by Emmett Berry on trumpet and Chu Berry on tenor; and the updated clarinet trio. Perhaps much has been lost in terms of jazz improvisation, but insofar as group interaction and overall swing, the 1937 version is light years away from the banjo and tuba-driven original.[44]

In 1937, Henderson once again had with him some of his earlier stalwarts. As noted in the recording of "Stampede," Walter Johnson was back, taking Catlett's place. Russell Smith, as Schuller points out, "played the role of a stabilizing, anchoring element in the brass players' world for nearly four decades" and served as Henderson's lead trumpet for sixteen years; and J.C. Higginbotham returned to the fold, having contributed so many outstanding solos to Henderson recordings from the first year of the decade.[45] Even though Albert McCarthy finds "little individuality" in "Rhythm of the Tambourine" from the March 2, 1937, session or "Back in Your Own Backyard" from the March 22 date, the latter seems to me to represent the Swing Era as well as any recording to this point, and would be as good a place for a listener to begin as any in the period.[46] Certainly a listener would be starting with the Father of the Big Band and would be able to hear immediately the foundational drumming of Walter Johnson, aided now by Israel Crosby on bass and Lawrence Lucie on guitar. Buster Bailey has been replaced by Jerry Blake, who brings a more up-to-date approach to the clarinet part, clearly influenced by Benny Goodman. This is true as well of the recording of "Sing You Sinners," from October 25, 1937, where Blake solos forcefully on Fletcher's full-blown swing arrangement, with Emmett Berry doing the honors on trumpet, and Peter Suggs effectively replacing Johnson on drums.[47] Emmett on trumpet and Chu on tenor add immensely to the easy swing of both "Back in Your Own Backyard" and "Sing You Sinners." The varied and well-played sectional work in these recordings is distinguished, and on "Backyard," it is good once more to hear Fletcher at the piano, but this time in a more modern style. Only Johnson's final cymbal on the March 22 side reminds one of the 1920s, but even this seems appropriate as a way of recalling how far Henderson and his orchestras had come in, as Collier would say, "the making of jazz." If these two pieces sound like the work of most of the other swing units of the late 1930s, it is largely because they all owed to Fletcher Henderson the creation of big-band jazz.

BENNIE MOTEN AND COUNT BASIE

In 1923 in Kansas City, a musical world away from the New York scene of Fletcher Henderson's beginnings as a recorded band leader, Bennie Moten initiated his own recording career in the same year that both Henderson and King Oliver made their first records as leaders. Born in Kansas City, Missouri, in 1894, Moten also would contribute fundamentally to the development of the swing-era big band. Just as Don Redman had helped to establish "a formula for employing a larger ensemble in an essentially homophonic style that could incorporate a true jazz solo," so Bennie Moten, along with other leaders from the Southwest, would make way for important stylistic features of the big band. Starting as a pianist rooted in ragtime and blues, as did Henderson, Moten first recorded with a six-man group that emphasized these early forms of jazz. Especially from ragtime he would derive the riff, the "repeated musical phrase" which "became the foundation for many of the most famous Kansas City and Southwestern compositions, and ultimately the heart of all the big-band music of the swing era."[48]

Like Henderson's first recordings in 1923, Moten's were awkward beginnings that did not indicate the great swing that by the early 1930s his groups would be capable of generating. Just as Gunther Schuller characterizes Henderson's recordings as influenced by those of King Oliver's Creole Jazz Band, but without the latter's "subtle inner energy linked to fluidity of movement," so he finds Moten's first recordings "rhythmically stiff beyond belief." Schuller does credit the Henderson band's first recordings "with a rhythmic drive that was a great improvement over the rather watery, aimless rhythm that had characterized most of their previous blues accompaniments," but he describes the Moten band as exhibiting no more than a ragtime that was "not even good" and "a simple, often 'crude' blues."[49] Nonetheless, as Schuller points out, it was both the ragtime riff and the blues material of the Moten band that would be combined in the Southwest to develop "a way of playing jazz which was eventually to supercede the New Orleans, Chicago, and New York styles."[50] Yet only slowly, between 1923 and 1929, did the Moten bands evolve into a unit that could compete with its eastern counterparts. A 1928 remake of "South," a catchy tune composed by Moten trombonist Thamon Hayes, became "one of the best-selling records of the entire 78 rpm era" and looked forward to the 1932 Moten recordings that were "such a watershed for the swing era."[51] Influenced by his hearing of Henderson's recordings and those of leaders such as Duke Ellington, and through his hiring away of such important sidemen as Eddie Durham, Bill (later "Count") Basie, and Oran "Hot Lips" Page from another southwestern band, the Oklahoma Blue Devils, Moten was able by 1930 to produce pieces like "Oh! Eddie" and "When I'm Alone," the latter foreshadowing the magnificent four-beat swing and "crisp brass figures" of his great 1932 recordings.[52]

By the time Moten's Kansas City orchestra traveled to Camden, New Jersey, in December 1932, to record at the RCA Victor studios, the leader had replaced all his original sidemen and had doubled in size his band's number to twelve from its six members of 1923. He now had newcomers Ben Webster on tenor sax, Eddie Barefield on clarinet and alto, and Walter Page on string bass, along with Durham on guitar and trombone, Dan Minor on trombone, Basie on piano, Lips Page, Joe Keyes, and Dee Stewart on trumpets, Jack Washington on alto and baritone saxes, Leroy Berry on rhythm guitar, and Willie McWashington on drums. In addition, the Moten orchestra included blues shouter Jimmy Rushing as its featured vocalist. This unit would cut several sides during what has been considered "one of the dozen or so most thrilling single sessions in this history of jazz. Here is the epitome of the Kansas City big band sound before it became absorbed into the swing movement."[53]

The first tune recorded on December 13 was "Toby," by Eddie Barefield, and it opens with Basie's piano setting the up tempo beat at which the soloists reel off their swinging breaks, with Ben Webster's whirling sax especially outstanding. At the furious pace of the call-and-response exchanges between reeds and brasses, it is simply astounding how crisply the two sections articulate their phrases. Sectional riffs accompany the bluesy choruses by Lips Page and Webster and the shorter breaks by Barefield, Minor, Webster again, and Durham on muted trombone (his guitar break having come right after Basie's piano introduction). "Moten's Swing," a Basie-Durham composition that became a "Kansas City Anthem," followed at a slightly slower tempo that produces what can truly be called a groove, created in part by Walter Page's solid string bass.[54] Barefield with his fluid alto and Lips Page with his very flexible, almost slithery trumpet are the featured soloists, along with the entire orchestra playing what Martin Williams characterizes as "original melodies on a rather sophisticated chord structure borrowed from a standard popular song." Williams also comments that the achievement of the Moten band by this date was to "*swing cleanly and precisely*" as a large group "according to the manner of Louis Armstrong."[55]

Other tunes from the 1932 Moten session also indicate how well his orchestra had come together as a swing unit and how much it would influence the swing movement. The "thrilling brass and reed riffing" on "Blue Room" is considered by Martin Williams "one of the most beautifully played passages in all recorded jazz," which "takes us into the later world of Count Basie."[56] The piece opens with the reed section showcased in a precisely played statement of the theme—not the overly sweet approach of so many later big-band sax sections—and then the orchestra builds with the help of stirring solo breaks and aided by some especially and unusually active percussion work by Willie McWashington. Durham's "Lafayette" is another riff tune that serves as a vehicle for choruses by Webster and Lips Page and some stride piano from Basie, as well as for Basie and Walter Page to work in tandem as they propel the rest of the group on top of their rhythmic drive. Basie is the star of the "Prince of Wales," striding with joyous abandon while the shouting brass match their "surging, inventive ... figures" heard on the powerful "Toby."[57] Gunther Schuller ranks "Toby," "Lafayette," "Blue Room," and "Prince of Wales" as "among the very finest orchestral jazz of that entire era."[58] Of "Moten Swing," Schuller writes that Lips Page's trumpet lines represent "an extension of Armstrong's rhythmic ideas," that he "is no longer playing 'changes' but is harmonically freed to produce pure melodic essence," and that here and in his best solos his artistry lies in "a minimum of activity with a maximum of expression, a lesson Lester Young was to extend several years later." Also, Schuller "marvels" at how quickly the Moten rhythm section of Walter Page, Basie, Berry, and McWashington had achieved a unified, horizontal, flowing 4/4 beat when only a year or two before it had still been "stiffly vertical." All this already places these Moten recordings "in the world of the Basie band of later years," in the estimate of Schuller, whose words echo those of Martin Williams.[59]

Unfortunately, the 1932 session was to mark the final recordings issued under the leadership of Bennie Moten, who would die unexpectedly in 1935 from a tonsillectomy. Although most of the sidemen drifted off, Count Basie managed to keep a few of them together and to recruit a number of other musicians from Kansas City and the Southwest, among them two tenor saxophonists, Lester Young and Herschel Evans. For a while, Basie co-led the group with arranger and altoist Buster Smith, who had recorded as a member of the Blue Devils in 1929.[60] Smith's very advanced, fluid style was matched by few alto players of the time (on occasion by Edgar Sampson) and in some ways was never equaled until the arrival of Charlie Parker at the end of the 1930s. But Smith did not record again until 1939, having missed out on the 1932 Moten session because he was still with the Blue Devils as coleader with Lester Young; only at the end of 1933 did both men finally join forces with Moten. But again, Smith missed out on being recorded with the Basie band in 1937 because he did not believe an offer from Decca would come to anything and left the organization before the session was held. Hot Lips Page also left Basie before the first recording session in 1937, in his case in order to become a leader of his own band. But the Basie unit would prove that in Lester Young and Herschel Evans it could boast an incomparable duo that offered contrasting styles that represented the two basic approaches to the jazz tenor saxophone. Although Evans was an adherent of the Coleman Hawkins style, which has been characterized as alternately "stormy" and rhapsodic, Young brought to his instrument and to jazz a cool, wry, laconic, melodically conversational manner that immediately made him, and therefore the Basie band, identifiably unique.[61]

Young himself credited his discovery of the Beiderbecke-Trumbauer recordings of 1927 with opening him up to his cooler style. As we have seen, other black jazzmen attempted to reproduce especially the Beiderbecke sound and mode of expression, whereas others imitated Trumbauer's skillful handling of his C-melody sax. Loren Schoenberg points out that on the Bennie Moten recording of "Rite Tite," from July 17, 1929, cornetist Ed Lewis and altoist Harlan Leonard quote from or reproduce some of the most famous breaks by Beiderbecke and Trumbauer. Lewis does not really approach the Beiderbecke sound, but he does demonstrate that he knew Bix's work, which is apparent as well from his playing on the July 16 recording of Moten's "Terrific Stomp." Schoenberg writes that Leonard

"resurrects Trumbauer's break from 'Singin' the Blues,' " and indeed Leonard recaptures convincingly the special quality of Frankie's C-melody sax.[62]
James Lincoln Collier asserts that "if Lester Young reminds us of anybody
in jazz it is Bix Beiderbecke. There is the same delicate strength, the same
attention to detail, the same concern for structure, the same ability to startle
us with twists in the melody."[63] Although Young also was attracted to the
technical facility of Trumbauer's playing, for some listeners it has been
difficult to reconcile Trumbauer's rather unimaginative though supple improvisations with Young's highly inventive and even more fluid manner.
But Collier has explained that Young must have been like other musicians
who "will often admire good technicians in a way that the fan will not,
because they recognize how difficult it is to do what the player is doing,
and many saxophonists of the 1920s took Trumbauer for a model."[64]
Other commentators have tried to make a case for Bud Freeman as a precursor to the Lester Young manner, describing the former's style as exhibiting as early as 1933 an alternative to the Hawkins school of tenor
saxophone playing by way of Freeman's cultivation of understatement, wit,
and emotional detachment.[65] Budd Johnson, another tenor player of the
period, also offered from his earliest recording in 1929 what Frank Driggs
calls a "fluent technique and an unusually light tone for that time. His style
already seemed personal and original, and he seemed to owe little to Coleman Hawkins."[66] Throughout the 1930s Johnson would develop independently a sound and style very much like that of Lester Young, but even so,
it was, despite any similarities with Trumbauer, Freeman, or Johnson's
ways of playing, Pres (short for President, as Young was called) who put
the cool, understated, conversational manner on the jazz map, both
through his solos with the Basie band and, as we shall see, through his
seminal recordings with small swing-era combos.

In 1936, John Hammond, the New York impresario and record producer, caught on his car radio the Basie-Smith band performing in a broadcast from Kansas City. As a result, the Basie unit was invited for an
engagement at the Roseland Ballroom in New York, and subsequently recorded its first sides on January 21, 1937. Previously, Lester Young had
spent a brief time with the Henderson orchestra between the death of Bennie Moten and Hammond's discovery of the Basie-Smith unit. But the story
goes that Henderson's wife disliked Lester's un-Hawkins style so much that
she saw to it that he was discouraged enough to leave. He was back in
Kansas City with Basie when Hammond heard the band on the air. But for
Gunther Schuller, the real stars of the first four records made by the band
were Herschel Evans and trumpeter Buck Clayton rather than Young. Further, Schuller avers that "the only partially redeeming side" of the four was
"Swinging at the Daisy Chain," where Evans plays "a wildly sinuous
bridge."[67] The critic especially objects to what he finds on Fats Waller's
"Honeysuckle Rose" to be some "borrowings from Henderson's famous

arrangement of 'King Porter Stomp.' " Henderson had generously given Basie a group of his arrangements at a crucial period when the Count found himself in Chicago at the Grand Terrace with not enough music.[68] Schuller is entirely correct that this piece is a mishmash of Jelly Roll's classic and "an unwarranted banal overlay of 'Tea for Two.' " Nonetheless, much of the Basie sound is already evident in these first recordings, especially the pianist-leader's own light touch, the rhythm section's relaxed drive, and the ensemble's rocking riffs, which Schuller notes were "still somewhat new to New York." Certainly "Roseland Shuffle" is the one tune that indicates the important role that Young will play, even if Lester's licks are not up to his best work, which had already been exhibited in a 1936 small-group session. In fact, Young's very finest performances were almost always with small groups, usually drawn from the larger Basie aggregation. Indeed, this reveals a significant aspect of the Kansas City tradition and the type of unit that the Basie organization represented: a big band attempting to swing like a small group.

Like other Territory bands, the Blue Devils of Oklahoma, in which several key Basie sidemen, including the leader and Lester Young, had worked before joining Moten, competed in order to hold on to their turf or to expand their audience. Southwestern bands traveling in the region would challenge those residents in particular cities to "cutting" sessions, and the winners would draw larger crowds and more money as a result of their victories. The Blue Devils defeated the Moten band in the late twenties, and this inspired Bennie to begin hiring away the rival musicians, including, as we have seen, Basie, Durham, Lips Page, and Walter Page. When the Henderson band toured the Midwest and reached Kansas City, Coleman Hawkins sat in on one of the regular all-hours cutting sessions where sidemen from the local bands tried to outshine one another. Hawkins reportedly was cut by Lester Young and other Kansas City tenor players, and in part this may have been because Hawkins, as primarily an orchestral player, was not so accustomed to the rough practice of cutting sessions as were the small-group-oriented Kansas City tenorists. On the other hand, Hawkins, too, would tend to do some of his best work with groups smaller than ten men, as on his 1929 "One Hour" and 1939 "Body and Soul" recordings. In many ways the most innovative jazz was developed within the small unit, and this was true as well even of a highly successful big-band leader such as Benny Goodman and his various combos, especially those featuring electric guitarist Charlie Christian. As for Young, he was basically an introvert, and must have felt more comfortable in the context of a small group. His 1936 recordings, made with a quintet composed of the Basie rhythm section and trumpeter Carl Smith, were revolutionary in nature, and are discussed in the chapter on small groups. Likewise, Young's later work with a septet made up of members of the Basie orchestra also shows him to have been an especially avant-garde figure when working within a smaller unit, as on "Dickie's Dream" and "Lester Leaps In" from 1939. But to hear what Lester could do in the larger setting of the full band one can listen to his solo on the air check recording of "One O'Clock Jump," from November 3, 1937.[69]

"One O'Clock Jump," the first big hit registered by the Basie band and eventually its theme song, was a tune that "soon every swing band pounced on" and "by 1940 . . . had been recorded a dozen times."[70] But the first Basie recording of the piece, from July 7, 1937, is not nearly so effective as the air-check version of November. Most important, Lester Young's solo on the first recording is extremely truncated and more forceful compared with his break on the air check. On this later outing, Pres illustrates perfectly Schuller's definition of swing: the listener cannot help but tap his foot, snap his fingers, and move his body and head in rhythm to Young's laid-back lines that seem tossed off effortlessly and yet are so structurally inventive and coherent, so thrilling in their easygoing drive. The other soloists also contribute effective solos, beginning with Herschel Evans, who plays another uplifting break similar to the one he created on the July 7 recording of "One O'Clock Jump." Evans is followed by Benny Morton on trombone, who picks up from his fine work with the Henderson orchestra in the early '30s, and by Buck Clayton, whose chorus is excellent but perhaps not up to his earlier performance on the July session, which Schuller considers one of Clayton's "finest creations."[71] One feature on the November recording unheard on the July date is a walking bass solo by Walter Page, accompanied by Freddie Green on guitar, who had just joined the Basie band for the July recording but who is not heard so prominently as he is on the air check from November. Green would become an indispensable addition to the Basie rhythm section and would help make it probably the most admired in the history of big-band jazz. The full-ensemble ride-outs of both the July and November versions of "One O'Clock Jump" are pure Basie in their stirring riffs shouted back and forth by brass and reeds. But above all it is the solo by Lester Young that stands out as an entirely new approach to jazz, a type of swing that in many ways represents the highest achievement of the Swing Era. Young had already recorded in this style the year before and would again in the context of the Basie big band and of several smaller units, but the November air check is perhaps the first full-band recording that captures Pres in his most influential form, his relaxed yet irresistible swing that would change jazz forever.

On the same 1937 air check, the Basie band is joined by one of the few true jazz vocalists, Billie Holiday, who sings a rendition of "I Can't Get Started" immediately following "One O'Clock Jump."[72] "I Can't Get Started" already had been recorded in April 1936 and in August 1937 by Bunny Berigan, who virtually made the Vernon Duke song his own property through his virtuosic trumpet solos.[73] Berigan's vocal on the 1937 recording, however, is not jazz so much as it is a rather artificial pop in-terpretation closely akin to the crooner variety. But in Holiday's hands (or throat) not only do the Ira Gershwin lyrics come to life, but also from her first notes she places us in a world of longing and sensuality that only she of all the swing-era singers could so convincingly convey. Along with Hol-iday's vocal is heard the obbligato tenor sax of Lester Young in but one example of the complementary and equally convincing accompaniments that Pres played behind Billie's vocals, mostly recorded with small units, many led by pianist Teddy Wilson. The unusual feature of Young's obbli-gato is that it begins before Holiday's vocal line and remains slightly offset from the melody she is singing, which gives to the performance an added quality of poignant yearning. The way these two artists work together rep-resents another facet of Lester Young's unique contribution to jazz. In all fairness to Bunny Berigan, it should be noted that he was one of the first jazzmen to accompany Holiday on record and to help make her early work freshly appealing on each rehearing. Holiday's recording of "No Regrets" dates from July 10, 1936, and includes Berigan on trumpet and Artie Shaw on clarinet doing a type of relaxed Dixieland jam in between Billie's vocal choruses.[74] But this is certainly a different approach to accompaniment and does not produce the special complementary effect of the Young-Holiday combination.

Another example of a Basie vocal-instrumental team that exhibits a symbiotic relationship is the pairing of Jimmy Rushing and Dickie Wells. However, Rushing was a blues singer, unlike Holiday, who sang almost exclusively pop songs, but with jazz interpretations that lent the melodies and lyrics nuances of sound and feeling that were hers alone. As for Rush-ing, when Wells accompanies him on "How Long Blues," from June 24, 1939, this is a more traditional blues relationship that goes back to the 1920s. Like Bessie Smith in the company of such instrumentalists as Joe Smith, Charlie Green, and Louis Armstrong, Rushing has his vocal lines echoed or commented on by Wells, who almost always follows at the end of a phrase, rather than paralleling or even anticipating the melody as Young does with Holiday. Other examples of the Rushing-Wells combi-nation are "Baby, Don't Tell on Me" and "Nobody Knows," both from March 19, 1939. All three of these pieces find the Basie band at a slower tempo than perhaps any other band ever had recorded or ever would. [75] Adding to the melancholy tone on "Nobody Knows" is Basie's organ, which underscores the vocal lament on "How Long Blues." Basie's chiming piano behind Buck Clayton's beautifully sad introduction is equally effec-tive in emphasizing the blues atmosphere of the piece. Wells's few moaning notes following Rushing's lyrics are concise but telling responses to the sorrowful singer. Once the full ensemble enters to express, as it were, its group empathy through short, repeated phrases—punctuated by Jo Jones's somber drums—the final effect is far different from the music of any other big band of the period, for the Basie band was above all a blues-based unit, whether riffing at a joyous up-tempo or almost dragging with apparent hopelessness and despair.

Although working within a simple and seemingly artless style, the Basie unit managed a remarkably wide range of expression. How wide is illustrated by "Harvard Blues," from November 17, 1941, on which Wells is rather humorous in his obbligato asides following Rushing's vocal phrases, and rightly so considering the fact that this piece is an "academic" blues.[76] The lyrics are credited to a "Mr. Frazier," who evidently was a Harvard undergraduate familiar with such legendary nineteenth-century campus figures as Reinhardt, "a most indifferent guy."[77] Although this piece may strike listeners as an incongruous combination of southern blues and Harvard satire, it supports Wynton Marsalis's remarks on the televised presentation of the LCJO's tribute to Ellington, from May 12, 1999, cited in the Introduction, which observed that jazz has gone "from outhouse to whorehouse to penthouse." In this instance, Basie's jazz reached the apex of intellectual sophistication at *the* university, where he and his sidemen were received with anything but indifference. Indeed, for Charlie Miller, a graduate who commented on the lyrics for the original Columbia album with "Harvard Blues," "The best thing about re-hearing [the piece] was Jimmy Rushing's magnificent and monumental gargle, riding over what to me has always been the greatest *big* band that ever played."[78] This meeting of jazz and academia was nothing new in 1941, for in the '20s college students were already attracted to the music. But more than ever in the Swing Era jazz found a following in all walks of life, from the ivory tower to the New Deal blue-collar worker. David W. Stowe, in *Swing Changes*, discusses "Harvard Blues" as a "kind of inverted blackface, comparing the cryptic ennui of a jaded Harvard sophisticate to the sexual or socioeconomic sorrow usually depicted in blues lyrics, [which] could be interpreted as an expression of existential solidarity."[79] Regardless of the interpretation one places on this encounter between academia and swing music, the fact of the matter remains that jazz was held in high regard by such intellectuals as Yale's Marshall Stearns and by Otis Ferguson of *The New Republic*, as well as by the dancers and bobbysoxers who flocked to the nightspots and matinee programs to hear their favorite bands.

The Basie organization had begun to build its reputation among critics and fans alike with its first appearances and recordings in 1937, producing many of its most memorable tunes with the return of multi-instrumentalist and arranger Eddie Durham, who, after working for two years with the Jimmie Lunceford Orchestra, rejoined a number of his former Blue Devils and Moten colleagues.[80] Durham's arrangement of "Good Morning Blues," from August 9, 1937, features, after Buck Clayton's wondrous muted solo and a bit of Basie piano, Jimmy Rushing's "plea" for Santa Claus to send him nothing for Christmas but "my baby back to me." The straightforward simplicity of this piece is once again characteristic of the Basie style, and Durham's arrangement epitomizes the clarity and lightness for which Basie became noted from his first recordings, but especially those made of Durham's tunes. From the same date, Durham's "Topsy" (also from August 9), as arranged by Jimmy Mundy, actually involves more activity by the ensemble behind the soloists than is usual with most arrangements done by Durham or Mundy. Durham's "John's Idea," from July 7, 1937, also arranged by Mundy, is more typical, being pared down to the essential elements of blues, riff, and call-and-response, but without the thicker harmonic texture of a Fletcher Henderson arrangement. It begins with the Count on piano playing what in 1938 would become the first phrases of the perennial Basie favorite, "Jumpin' at the Woodside." Accompanied by Green's guitar and Page's bass, the Count's piano, which here is heavily influenced by his teacher Fats Waller's New York stride, leads, after a brief ensemble break, into an impassioned chorus by Herschel Evans. This is followed by the ensemble working its way up the scalar ladder by repeating riffs in a call-and-response pattern that builds dynamically to a simple but powerful climax, after which Basie's piano returns with its light Wallerish stride. The ensemble reenters for more riffs, interrupted by a touch of Lester Young's tenor in a stop-time break that would be imitated endlessly. Then the brass and reeds ride out the piece with the same driving riff, punctuated by the trombones playing a single unison note, by Basie's rippling piano runs, and by Jo Jones's stick work, as slowly the band lowers the volume to a medium fade-out. The simple design of Mundy's arrangement, with its basic, driving riffs, subtle contrasts of instrumental colors, and varying dynamics, presents the most appealing traits of the Basie style. These same distinctive features would be repeated from this recording in 1937 throughout the rest of the leader's long and productive career.

Durham's own arrangements of "Blue and Sentimental," "Every Tub," "Swingin' the Blues," "Time Out" (a tune by James V. Monaco entitled "Pigeon Walk"), "Out the Window," and "Sent for You Yesterday and Here You Come Today" are Basie classics that were reproduced by the band for decades following their first recordings in 1937 and 1938.[81] "Blue and Sentimental," from June 6, 1938, features Herschel Evans's robust but dreamy, Hawkins-influenced sound and emotive force in what was the most famous solo showcase in the Basie book. As with the arrangement of "John's Idea," affective contrast is furnished here by Lester Young's clarinet, which is at once "sentimental" and penetrating in its leaner, more direct statement. "Every Tub," from February 16, 1938, is highlighted by an attention-getting opening chorus by Young and two intense breaks by trumpeter Harry "Sweets" Edison, both backed by the ensemble's biting riffs. Edison was only twenty-two years old at this time but played with great authority and tended to ride "on sustained notes (often blue notes) with a wave-like bent-note effect, a trait which Durham immediately picked up and featured in his background ensembles."[82] This description by Gunther Schuller fits perfectly Edison's two breaks on "Every Tub," as well as his brief solo on "Swingin' the Blues," also from February 16. This last piece by Durham is, as Schuller writes, "perhaps the most appropriately named title in the entire Basie library. For that's exactly what that band did: swing the blues."[83] Jo Jones's drum and cymbal work on "Swingin' the Blues" is prominent in setting from the first and continuing to the end the irresistible swing of this number, whose up-tempo pace illustrates the fact that the blues were not just played slowly and mournfully. The three-trombone break is a Durham trademark, along with his doo-wah brass section and his alternating of driving ensemble passages with short but intense solos (here by five sidemen: Benny Morton on trombone, Young on tenor, Clayton and Edison on trumpet, and Evans on tenor). "Out the Window," from October 13, 1937, opens with declarative brass in preparation for the string of breaks, beginning with a fine one by altoist Earl Warren or Jack Washington (who rarely took a solo), followed by Basie's stride piano, which at one point seems to allude to "Hold Tight (Want Some Sea Food Mama)"—in fact, two of the brass riffs later seem to echo a phrase from this same tune. Edison's muted trumpet again offers his bent blue notes, while Young's two breaks contain his signature phrases that speak directly to the listener with telling effect. Finally, "Sent for You Yesterday," also from the February 16, 1938, session, is another blues, this one with Jimmy Rushing belting it out in his very best shouting style. The band backs him superbly with its inimitable drive, slowed down here but no less puissant, with Edison's "wave-like bent-note" technique picked up, as Schuller has said, by Durham and transferred to the brass riffs. Taken together, this group of Durham arrangements epitomizes the Basie recipe which served him well during five decades of leading his always swinging, blues-driven bands.

Herschel Evans, Durham's fellow Texan, also contributed two classic arrangements to the Basie book, "Doggin' Around" and "Texas Shuffle," from June 6 and August 22, 1938, respectively.[84] These two pieces are notable both for their outstanding solos and for what Gunther Schuller considers in "Texas Shuffle" to be "another fine example of the cohesive ensemble swing the [Basie] band had by now acquired."[85] André Hodeir has focused his attention on Dickie Wells's solo on "Texas Shuffle" and finds that it exhibits his ability to play "with more intense swing than any but a few trumpeters have attained. Sometimes, in the manner of Lester Young, he even sacrifices everything else to swing, concentrating all his rhythmic powers on one or two notes repeated at greater or lesser length." Hodeir contrasts Wells's playing on "King Porter Stomp" with Fletcher Henderson by describing the way the trombonist on "Texas Shuffle" "knows how to use a calm vibrato to create a feeling of relaxation at the end of a violent episode."[86] James Lincoln Collier rates Evans's tenor solo on "Doggin' Around" as one of his best, along with his break on "John's Idea."[87] Basie's solos on these two sides have been singled out by Martin Williams as, in the case of "Texas Shuffle," "a good example of spontaneous logic of phrase and sound," and in that of "Doggin' Around" as "a classic of linking and occasionally contrasting melodic ideas" and "probably [Basie's] masterpiece."[88] Basie's spare style is exemplified best on "Texas Shuffle" and contrasts so dramatically with the approach of almost all other pianists of the period, especially the elaborate Art Tatum.[89] Williams also cites Lester Young's clarinet solo on "Texas Shuffle" as summing up Pres's historical importance: his light, almost vibratoless sound, his quiet swing with "a minimum of notes" that yet conveys "the most compelling ideas," his understatement, his "original and flexible use of the even, four beats," and his occasionally falling "a shade ahead of the beat or behind it."[90] Following Wells's second break, the somewhat Dixieland ensemble (with Young's clarinet on top) is rather unusual for the Basie group, but is a subtle touch and nothing like the heavy-handed revival of this older style by other big bands of the era. (This same Dixie-type jam occurs on "Jumpin' at the Woodside," where instead of Young's it is Evans's clarinet that slices through the group.) On "Doggin' Around," Jack Washington takes one of his infrequent but always solid breaks on baritone, and Young's tenor solo is vintage Pres as he speaks to the listener in a manner which is, by virtue of the fast-paced tempo of Herschel's tune, only slightly less intimate than his ballad work with Billie Holiday. Both of Evans's arrangements obviously brought out the best in the Basie soloists, as well as from the ensemble, which, as Schuller has said, achieves a coherence and group swing that few other bands could equal.

One of Lester Young's showiest performances takes place on "Clap Hands, Here Comes Charlie" from August 5, 1938.[91] Certainly, Pres's chorus on "Clap Hands" impressed countless tenors who went to school on this one recording, but at the same time it may be true that this more extroverted outing does not represent the "historical importance" of Young's work that Martin Williams hears in "Texas Shuffle." Nor is it on the same level with his recordings with Holiday or his small-group sides, such as "Lester Leaps In" and "Dickie's Dream." On "Taxi War Dance" from March 19, 1939, Young manages to work into his own style a bit of the tune's Indian motif, but more typical of Lester's playing are his solos on "Tickle Toe" and "I Never Knew" from March 19, 1940, and in fact he had by this time begun to repeat himself.[92] Following Herschel Evans's untimely death in 1939, Buddy Tate replaced his fellow Texan and would be the only tenor to solo on "Love Jumped Out" and "Rock-a-Bye Basie" from the March 19 session (sounding on the first almost like a clone of Evans and on "Super Chief" from May 31, 1940, more his own assertive self). But none of these recordings can compare with the earlier work of the band, represented by the Mundy, Durham, and Evans arrangements and the outstanding solos those pieces inspired. Although the Basie band continued to swing and would with different personnel produce many marvelous recordings after 1941, it would never match its classic years of 1937 and 1938. But then only a handful of big bands in the history of jazz has ever attained the high level of the Basie band at that time. As an ensemble, the Basie band could generate an incomparably relaxed swing, and as a collection of fecund soloists, the Basie men became models for future generations of jazz musicians and the delight of listeners around the world.

Although Basie himself was born in Red Bank, New Jersey, he and the men he worked with from the Southwest left their indelible blues-riff mark on the Swing Era. As one of the four or five most significant big bands of the 1930s, the Count Basie band remains unique in itself, with a sound that owes much of its distinctiveness to the leader and his exceptional rhythm section. Basie's ability to gather around him some of the top talent of the day, as soloists, arrangers, and sectional players, resulted in his creation of much of the most memorable and unmistakable music of any period in jazz history. And as Marshall Stearns observed early on, "If Benny Goodman became the 'King of Swing' . . . the man behind the throne was Count Basie," whose band "gave depth and momentum to the whole swing era while planting the seeds that later gave birth to bop and the 'cool' school of jazz."[93]

DUKE ELLINGTON

It is probably not coincidental that many of the successful big-band leaders were pianists. Other than King Oliver, the jazzmen who led the most enduring and even the short-lived but most accomplished and popular units were by and large piano players. Jelly Roll Morton, who is generally considered the first great jazz composer, Fletcher Henderson, who is consistently referred to as the Father of the Big Band, and Bennie Moten and Count Basie, who introduced the blues-riff idea most fully to jazz, all were pianists who came to their mature piano and band styles through an apprenticeship in ragtime and blues. Other bandleaders of the Swing Era who were pianists include Claude Hopkins, Luis Russell, Earl "Fatha" Hines, Lionel Hampton (although known primarily as a vibraharpist), Jay McShann, and above all Edward "Duke" Ellington, who, like Morton, Henderson, Moten, and Basie, grew up with ragtime and blues and moved on from there to develop his own approach to his instrument and to his unique form of orchestral writing. Although a number of other big-band leaders were noted virtuosi on clarinet and/or saxophone (Benny Goodman, Artie Shaw, Jimmy Dorsey, Benny Carter), on trumpet (Bunny Berigan and Harry James), on trombone (Tommy Dorsey, Glenn Miller, and Jack Teagarden), or as percussionists (Chick Webb, Gene Krupa, and Boots Douglas), none of these leaders, with the possible exception of Glenn Miller, created a distinctively original band style that began and essentially ended with his career. Noticeably missing from this list is Jimmie Lunceford, whose special case will be discussed subsequently. Other bands may have imitated the styles of Henderson, Basie, Ellington, and Lunceford, but none can compare with the authentic sound and artistry of each of these four giants of big-band swing.

It is clear from the many recordings made of "King Porter Stomp" that the various bands of the Swing Era were listening to one another, and especially that most were listening to Fletcher Henderson's band as the standard-bearer. This seems apparent not only with regard to such jazz classics as "King Porter Stomp" and "Sugar Foot Stomp" (the latter's clarinet trio said to have influenced "all the other bands—even that of Duke Ellington") but also with respect to pop tunes like "Posin' " and "Let 'Er Go."[94] On the other hand, Henderson himself seems to have been listening to Duke Ellington, if the former's recording of "All God's Chillun Got Rhythm," from June 30, 1937, is any indication—Ellington having recorded this same tune almost three weeks before on June 8. Even if it is merely a case of this particular piece coming to the attention of both band leaders when it first appeared in 1937 as part of the Marx Brothers film, A Day at the Races, their two recordings are nonetheless illustrative of certain similarities but also of fundamental differences between the leaders and their ways of creating swing. Ellington's vocalist in 1937 was Ivie Anderson, who sang "All God's Chillun Got Rhythm" in A Day at the Races. Although only Anderson is seen in the Marx Brothers film, the fact that the Ellington orchestra enjoyed a number of cameo appearances in films during the 1930s, starting with its "movie debut" in 1930 in Check and Double Check, starring Amos 'n' Andy, shows that the Duke and his men were on the top of the heap, and that even though Henderson had been the trailblazer for most big bands, it was Ellington who consistently played in some of the best-paying venues (beginning with his 1927–1930 tenure at the Cotton Club), earned accolades from critics and fans alike (both in the United States and abroad), and over the decade developed arguably the greatest big band of all time.[95]

Although it might be said that the 1937 bands of both Henderson and Ellington were not among their best ensembles, the approach of each band is fairly representative of its leader's work during the 1930s. "All God's Chillun Got Rhythm," as played by the Henderson band (in an arrangement perhaps done by Jerry Blake), pits sax section against brasses in the typical call-and-response pattern, at times varied by having trumpets and saxes answered by the trombones. The leisurely swing of the ensemble behind brief solos by Chu Berry, Emmett Berry, and Jerry Blake is perhaps more characteristic of the later '30s than the work of Henderson's bands from the early part of the era. Here there is not the drive nor the imagination of Smack's most outstanding bands, and the vocal by an unidentified singer takes the accustomed place of more solos and greater interplay between the sections. The ensemble passages before and after Blake's clarinet solo offer slightly sweet, generic swing phrases that by this date were standard with almost every band of the period, every band that is except Ellington's. Indeed, the Duke's version of "All God's Chillun Got Rhythm" reveals dramatically the difference between his own jazz conception and that of his rivals. Although there is use of a similar statement and answer pattern for the sections, the effect is almost like a distinct device, because Ellington will employ an unusual, at times dissonant, chord or voicing for the brass response to the saxes, changing thereby the entire complexion of the form. Not only this but from the very beginning of the piece his sidemen express themselves in their uniquely Ducal style. In addition, the rhythm section with Sonny Greer on drums creates a sound that is like that of no other band of the swing or any other period of jazz.

It is almost enough for contrast just to notice how cornetist Rex Stewart, a former sideman with Henderson, has now, through the Duke's encouragement, brought a new approach to his instrument. His notes—bent, slowed down, repeated, then suddenly darting about (on other Ellington sides he will develop more of his half-valve effects)—fit perfectly into the amazingly varied textures and rhythms of an Ellington performance. But Stewart's is but one style and one voice among many. The piece opens with three different tonal colors: After bassist Billy Taylor lays down the first beat, muted trumpets play a repeated, syncopated phrase answered by the clarinet, which, once the trumpets end their passage, goes into an ascending glissando that immediately identifies this work as Ellingtonian. Trombonist Tricky Sam Nanton then takes over with his talking plunger voice complete with growl, which distinguished the Ellington sound as early as his 1926 recordings when Bubber Miley employed this technique on "Choo Choo" (also the earliest of many train allusions in the Ellington oeuvre).[96] This is followed by Harry Carney's warm, singing baritone in its upper register, alternated with phrases ripped off with a gruff, guttural attack. Rex Stewart's jaunty chorus leads to the second of the three diverse trombone voices in the Ellington palette, that of the romantically sliding or rapidly tonguing, always richly swinging Lawrence Brown. (Juan Tizol on valve trombone is not heard from here but is on so many other outstanding Ellington recordings, including Tizol's classic collaborations with the Duke, "Caravan," "Pyramid," and "A Gypsy without a Song," and Juan's own original compositions, "Conga Brava" and "Perdido.") After Brown, there is more of Barney Bigard's subtle clarinet, in both the chalumeaux and soaring ranges, and last but not least the alto of Johnny Hodges, who absolutely takes one's breath away and brings tears just to hear his lifting, sonorous horn, swooping, arpeggiating, gliding, all seemingly with effortless ease. The piece concludes with the ensemble answering probably Cootie Williams's high, at times falling-off trumpet, and the saxes driving with, ingeniously, Carney's baritone on top. Then all's quiet but for Ellington's final piano note that punctuates as if with a period this less than three-minute swing-defining declaration.

At the same session, the Ellington orchestra was joined by Ivie Anderson for another rendition of "All God's Chillun Got Rhythm." Her vocal here is one of her finest efforts, along with the 1941 "I Got It Bad (And That Ain't Good)." Johnny Hodges, this time the only soloist, is even more impressive and awe-inspiring than on the purely instrumental version. If the vocalist on the Henderson recording listened to Anderson, he could only have drooled and then done his best to deliver the lyrics without feeling depressed. Ivie in her way fully complements Hodges, or vice versa. Both are rhythmically driving, although Ivie goes from almost solemn in her opening lines to totally upbeat, underscoring the tune's contrast between the blues brought on by troubles and the swing furnished by having rhythm. Sonny Greer's drum introduction to Hodges's chorus is so uplifting that the altoist can hardly help but soar. Like the Henderson, however, this side is limited in its appeal because it does not offer the variety of tonal colors, sectional contrasts, and distinctive solo voices heard on the all-instrumental recording.

Backing up two years, another performance by the Ellington orchestra that never fails to send chills up my spine is "Merry-Go-Round," especially its solos by Lawrence Brown and Harry Carney. Perhaps as English band-leader and critic Spike Hughes asserted in 1933 on hearing "Merry-Go-Round" at that time (under the title "King of Spades"), Brown's "solo work is altogether too 'smart,' or 'sophisticated,' if you will, to be anything but out of place in Duke's essentially direct and simple music."[97] Be that as it may, I personally would not find the recording of "Merry-Go-Round," from April 30, 1935, the same impressive performance without Brown's magisterial, for me direct-to-the-soul, solo. In fact, I could not do without a single note in what has remained for me, since I first heard it on the Columbia album *I Like Jazz* some forty-five years ago, the greatest example of swing I have ever heard. All the same soloists except for Nanton are present here, and all are in top form—not that they had slipped a step in 1937. The biting brass, answered by low-register saxes, opens this immediately pulsing number, which is aided all the way through by Wellman Braud's booming bass and Greer's shimmering cymbals and wondrous stick work. As Henderson could be with his early recordings, Ellington was a master of the right tempo, and here the relaxed, gently rocking "Merry-Go-Round" depicts a slow-paced rising and falling on that amusement park ride. The first break is by Cootie Williams on trumpet, a stirring announcement that has much of the intensity of a King Oliver solo but more relaxed and swinging than anything the King would have played. Barney Bigard comes next with bright sixteenth-note arpeggios, runs, and turns, while the ensemble responds below with contrastingly dark, almost brusque chords.

The ensemble, along with the Duke's rippling piano, then offers up a rich tapestry of sound, including some shakes that prepare for Lawrence Brown's entrance. The trombonist picks up on the trill-like shake motif of the ensemble and heightens the device's emotive power with greater emphasis, before bending his notes upward and adding even more emotion. Hodges carries on with the trill motif, beginning low and then swooping upward, after which Rex Stewart contributes a solo closer to his work with Henderson yet quite in keeping with the groove of the Ellington tune. Then the ensemble, with the trombones leading the way, prepares for a brief return of Bigard's clarinet before Harry Carney makes his appearance, in some ways imitating Barney's break. Carney begins his solo, then stops, blows a single low note, and then proceeds, creating a sense of expectancy in the listener to fine effect. He then runs the scales as smoothly as if he were playing Hodges's alto, ripping off notes on his big burly horn, moving from one register to the next effortlessly, while all the time making his marvelous statement with solid swing.

Once the soloists have completed their part, Ellington's ensemble writing takes over. Here the group swing is unbeatable, in terms both of the contrasting figures and of their execution by the various sections. After the trumpets state their thematic material, the saxes begin a kind of revolving, whirling motif, with the trumpets punctuating with sharp jabs. The three trombones then play a series of phrases that ends with the trio falling off their final notes. The out section is marked by some of Ellington's dissonant chords in the trumpets, and, as in "All God's Chillun Got Rhythm," the piece concludes with Duke's piano left with the last say. Nothing of this description can either accurately convey or truly account for the swing achieved by this performance—one must not only hear but feel the sounds that come from this group of exceptional musicians, the notes they were given to play and the way they make them their own, even as they express the composer's metaphorical idea for the musical depiction of a swinging ride at the amusement park.

Despite what I consider the infectious, irresistible force of recordings like "All God's Chillun Got Rhythm" and "Merry-Go-Round," these are not the best-known works of Ellington, or the recordings for which he is most highly rated as an artist. These two sides undeniably demonstrate the solid swing the Ellington orchestra could generate, yet this was but one type of music that Duke produced during the period from 1930 to 1941. Critics have unanimously ranked as the most important of his career the 1940–1941 band with Ben Webster and Jimmy Blanton. Even so, the beginning of the period saw the creation of one of his signature pieces, the 1930 "Mood Indigo," which, as Gunther Schuller points out, employs the classic New Orleans instrumentation of trumpet, clarinet, and trombone "in a totally new concept of sound" and, along with his 1928 compositions "Misty Morning" and "Awful Sad," features "an important element in the developing Ellington style: a kind of winding chromaticism *not* to be found in the faster dance numbers or stomps."[98] This slow, somber work would lead to another of Ellington's "three-minute tone poems," "Dusk," recorded ten years later on May 28, 1940, which, according to Schuller, presents in its last eight measures "musical sounds that had never occurred before in Western music and have rarely been heard even since then. Again timbre and color combine with harmony and voicing to create this unique blend."[99] One notable difference between "Mood Indigo" and "Dusk" is heard in the bass part, which in the former was played by Wellman Braud with a thumping beat and in the latter is performed by Jimmy Blanton with a light touch and at times a decorative series of sixteenth notes. This contrast between the 1930 and the 1940 Ellington style can be found even more fully in two other recordings: of "Ring Dem Bells" (created for the film *Check and Double Check*) and "Harlem Air Shaft" (Duke's musical re-creation of the sounds and smells of Harlem life, including jitterbugs "jumping up and down always over you, never below you").[100]

Recorded on August 20, 1930, "Ring Dem Bells" almost showcases Braud's big-toned bass, which is persistently present behind the string of soloists as well as the sectional work, as Wellman plucks either two or four beats, repeats a single note, double-times, and descends the scale slapping with determined drive. Likewise, Blanton, too, is featured on "Harlem Air Shaft," recorded July 22, 1940, but the difference is dramatic. Although Blanton contributes to every beat, he powers the ensemble more as part of the orchestra, even as his notes are clearly audible at all times. His bass lines are almost melodic, yet never vary from a straight four-beat rhythm. He plays higher up on the strings and then descends lightly with note choices that add greatly to the harmonic whole. One wonders about the difference for dancers of the two dates—in 1930 would they have been moved to follow Braud's booming bass or just listen, and would this have been the case in 1940 with Blanton's driving yet so inventive lines? Would the silences in "Harlem Air Shaft," where the orchestra stops playing, have prompted dancers to do some type of stop-time footwork or would they have paused to wait for the music to resume? Even though Ellington's music swings—in the sense that one can hardly keep from moving to the orchestral sounds—his jazz, it would seem, is primarily meant to be listened to intently. Unlike most of the other big bands, Ellington's orchestra offered a combination of swing and intellectual stimulation, the one appealing to the body, the other to the mind. In many ways swing as heard through the Ellington orchestra during the 1930s is the story of two simultaneous developments: the creation of compositions that offered what Schuller, as noted earlier, calls "faster dance numbers and stomps" and "musical sounds that . . . have rarely been heard." In fact, Ellington was constantly creating a wide range of works, some of which must have kept the dancers on the floor and others that kept the aficionados of jazz coming back for more, paying the ballroom fee just to listen.

"Ring Dem Bells" and "Harlem Air Shaft" represent but a few of the many facets of Ellington's artistry. Written for a Hollywood production, "Ring Dem Bells" demonstrates the leader's ability to create music for any type of setting, not just to perform songs such as "All God's Chillun Got Rhythm" which were the creations of other composers. It should be said, however, that when the Ellington orchestra did perform the works of other composers, it almost invariably made them more appealing than they were on their own or as performed by other musical groups. As for "Harlem Air Shaft," this piece's description of Harlem life recalls the fact that Ellington was originally inclined toward drawing and painting, and even "won an art scholarship to Pratt Institute."[101] His musical portraits of various black figures include those of tap dancer Bill Robinson in "Bojangles" and comic Bert Williams in "A Portrait of Bert Williams," along with sketches of his own sidemen, such as "Little Posey" (a musical description of trumpeter Arthur Whetsol) and "Weely (A Portrait of Billy Strayhorn)." Also, Ellington's aural depictions of a train ("Daybreak Express," 1933), a merry-go-round, a riverboat ("Showboat Shuffle," 1935—with Rex Stewart's first solo with Ellington and "one of his happiest"), a landscape/female nude ("Warm Valley," 1940), "a composite picture of the lady schoolteachers of Washington, who traveled and learned and spent holidays in Europe" ("Sophisticated Lady," 1940), and a series of images ("Sepia Panorama," 1940), all reveal the visual artist in Ellington.[102] Relatedly, there are Ellington's concertos for his sidemen, such as "Echoes of Harlem" (for Cootie Williams), "Clarinet Lament" (for Barney Bigard), "Trumpet in Spades" (for Rex Stewart), "Yearning for Love" (for Lawrence Brown), and "Jack the Bear" (for Jimmy Blanton), which make clear his ability to write works that were reflective of or that allowed for the expression of his musicians' personalities. Gunther Schuller characterizes this side of Ellington's art as a penchant for "pure composition," a category he "developed into a substantial autonomous musical expression, yet indigenous to jazz." Schuller goes on to suggest that the concertos were successors to "the vanguard of this effort," which was Ellington's thirteen-minute tone poem, "Reminiscing in Tempo," from 1935.[103] Ellington's need to write compositions that exceeded the three-minute recording limit was apparent in his 1931 "Creole Rhapsody," which continued from one side to the other of a 78 rpm disk. Other band leaders such as Artie Shaw also felt an urge to record pieces beyond the three-minute limit, but it was Ellington who would continue to expand his portraiture into extended works such as "Black, Brown and Beige" and his many suites depicting Latin America, the Far East, and scenes from Shakespeare and ballet. All these facets of Ellington's artistry began in the 1930s and make his music more than simply swing jazz, even though the swing ingredient is present to some degree in every composition he ever wrote.

In addition to the wide variety of compositions representing the more visual tendencies of Ellington's musical thought, which go hand in hand with the sounds and rhythms of swing, others of his works offer a definition of swing itself—in their titles, their creative modes, and their performances by his sidemen. Apart from Jelly Roll Morton's use of the term in 1928 for his "Georgia Swing" and Ellington's in 1929 for his small-group recording of "Saratoga Swing," the word "swing" was not generally found in titles prior to 1930. Rather, as we have seen, the word "stomp" was the common designation for a heavy, rocking rhythm associated with the blues. Ellington's 1930 "Rockin' in Rhythm," cowritten with his baritone player Harry Carney, was described by Duke as a piece that "was as close as an arrangement could possibly come to sounding spontaneous" and has been called "a number that would open the way to the glorious Swing Era of a few years later."[104] James Lincoln Collier says of certain Ellington themes like that of "Rockin' in Rhythm" that they "are as fresh and bright today as they were when he wrote them."[105] What makes this a precursor of the swing movement is the easy, relaxed rock of the piece, quite unhurried or even frantic as so much earlier jazz had been. The sound of the sax section, although pure Ellington in its clear but rich harmony, foreshadows the prominent role that the reeds would play in so many subsequent big bands. And as Ellington said, despite the fact that the piece is composed, it has about it a natural, spontaneous feeling, which in many respects came to be the opposite of much big-band writing of the period and eventually spelled in part the doom of the swing movement.

Ellington works that would be entitled swing numbers proliferated during the 1930s, beginning in 1932 with "It Don't Mean a Thing (If It Ain't Got That Swing)," which has been taken as a manifesto not understood until three years later when "white America figured out what [Ellington] meant and reserved network radio hookups and magazine covers for white bandleaders."[106] Schuller finds the performance of this "prophetic piece" with its "prophetic title" "by no means perfect" but "a quaintly vernacular definition of swing and also (for the time) a pretty good musical demonstration of it."[107] Nanton states the fetching theme, followed by Ivie Anderson singing the lyrics, while Carney provides a rocking obbligato. Perhaps the most swinging parts of the piece are the full ensemble's passage after Hodges's alto flight and Anderson's scatted, falling-off notes at the end. Ellington was surprised at the time that it was such a hit and that eventually "the world would take it . . . as the theme of an era."[108] Later in the same year Ellington's "Swing Low," an obvious allusion to the classic spiritual (the other half of that work having been used for Duke's "Sweet Chariot" of 1930), presents what the composer says "could very well have been called 'A Portrait of Freddy Jenkins,' because there is so much of his character in it."[109] Schuller labels this piece "a typical show number in the genre of 'Old Man Blues' or 'Double Check Stomp,' " the latter written for the 1930 film and the former recorded at the time in Hollywood.[110] Jenkins's conversational muted trumpet is backed by the smooth reed section led by Johnny Hodges on soprano sax. The saxes' a cappella-type passage shows the way for all future reed sections with its wonderfully unified execution and swing, just as Hodges's chorus on soprano shows how much he had learned from but how far he had gone beyond Bechet in applying a lighter swing feeling to his playing of Sidney's principal instrument.

Also related to the swing period are words like "jive" and "truckin'." According to Ellington, "jive" was first used on his recording of the 1933 "Jive Stomp" and he defined the term in its original sense as something that "swung, had spice or tonal zest."[111] The piece opens with a solidly swinging chorus by Harry Carney on baritone, interrupted logically by sectional interspersions. Credit for the swing again goes largely to Wellman Braud's driving bass and the insistent but subtle push of Greer's drum and cymbal work, as well as the fine sectional unity of and execution by the saxes. Another tune using the word "rhythm" in its title is Ellington's 1934 "Sump'in 'bout Rhythm," which Schuller considers "a rather sophisticated swing number featuring Duke's piano."[112] Not so heavy in its beat as "Rockin' in Rhythm," this piece remains relaxed at a faster tempo and finds Braud's bass much lighter than in 1930 or even 1933. The constant alternation of different sections and soloists retains the listener's interest throughout, with Nanton's plunger trombone coming in for highly effective short breaks that set off his distinctive voice among so many colorful sounds, including Duke's appealing dissonances at the piano and the fluttering sax section answered by the muted brass's type of stuttering punctuation. The title of the 1935 "Truckin' " refers to a popular dance of the mid-1930s and the piece features "a very hot hard-swinging vocal by Ivie Anderson" and a fine early solo by Ben Webster.[113]

In 1935 Ellington also composed one of his perennial favorites, "In a Sentimental Mood," which Schuller says "had nothing to do with 'swing.' " On the other hand, this lovely tune certainly typifies much of the decade's musical inclination toward sentimentality, with even a possible allusion to bandleader Tommy Dorsey as "The Sentimental Gentleman of Swing," which derived from the title of his own 1935 recording, "I'm Gettin' Sentimental over You." But as Schuller also notes, part of the reason that Ellington's creation of a potentially popular success did not attain in 1935 the attention of a Goodman or Dorsey recording was that "it was arranged in such a sophisticated manner that the emphasis was not on the tune but on the individual soloists' treatment . . . the timbral/textural variety Ellington could cram into this three-minute seven-second side, and the harmonic invention with which Ellington enriched the basic changes of the song."[114]

From the first notes of Ellington's uniquely florid piano introduction and the sheer beauty of Hodges's yearning soprano sax, this is one of the greatest recordings ever of a jazz ballad, without the syrupy sentiment so common to most ballads recorded during the Swing Era. Ellington was throughout the period a being apart, and as Ted Gioia puts it, "at the crest of the public's craze for big band music, Ellington remained a reluctant participant in the mainstreaming of hot jazz." Although most bands based their success on a repeated riff ("the undisputed musical signature of the era"), Ellington was ahead of his time in using, as Martin Williams says, "a variety of riffs to form continuous melodies," with the result, as Gioia points out, that many of his masterpieces were "dauntingly hard to sing along with." Williams also notes in this regard that "the less imaginative arrangers of the 'thirties and 'forties borrowed from Ellington's themes, effects, and backgrounds, two and four bars at a time, sometimes to turn them into simple, repeated riffs."[115]

Closer to the simple riff formula is Ellington's 1936 "Exposition Swing," which shows that he could play the game as well as any. But once again, this typical swing number is set apart both by his sidemen's special solo qualities and by the "timbral/textural variety" of Duke's writing. As he had on the 1935 "Truckin'," here, too, Ellington employs two bassists, which add greatly to the unrelenting drive of this "simple" piece. Ellington's additional bassist, Hayes Alvis, was the co-composer of the 1936 Ellington tune, "Swing Baby Swing (Love in My Heart)," which was recorded by an eight-man ensemble designated as Rex Stewart and His Fifty-Second Street Stompers. Ellington's sidemen recorded often as leaders of small groups, and although this may be one of the lesser efforts of such outings, it yet represents the very relaxed swing that was like no other among big or smaller bands of the era.

More representative of the larger orchestra's output and of the complexity of Ellington's compositions are two pieces from 1938. As Schuller writes of "Battle of Swing," this "1938 swing exercise rises above the norm—and its title. Indeed, it points brightly to the future: 1) to bop—with its unusual zig-zag figures, perky brisk tempo, and translation of the 12-bar blues into a distant stylistic world; and 2) to Ellington's own 'Cotton Tail,' with its daring unison lines."[116] Certainly this is not a performance that would have appealed to most listeners or dancers, for it demands too much concentration on the intricacy of the writing and the interplay between soloists and ensemble. In terms of swing battles, Ellington may have lost most of those during the mid-1930s, so far as popular success is concerned, but over the long haul he definitely won the war of respect and recognition. By 1938, however, even Ellington reaped the benefits of the swing craze, and, as Schuller says, "Duke now found himself garnering a level of respect from audiences [who attended his 'swing concerts'] as well as colleagues that was new in jazz history."[117] This year also saw the beginning of a "new spirit" in the Ellington orchestra, which is exemplified by its recording of Duke's "Steppin' into Swing Society."[118] Schuller declares that this piece "sets the tone and level for the entire next period in Ellington's development, leading eventually to the masterpieces of the early forties."[119] Following Schuller's wording, Ted Gioia notes that "Steppin' into Swing Society" "set the tone for Ellington's growing focus on medium-tempo swing charts, another trademark sound of the era."[120] Distinguished for its quiet, easy swing so different from the killer-dillers of the period, this piece obviously was not intended to take the society fortress by brute force. But as if to prove that he could mount an all-out attack, Ellington composed at the same time "Braggin' in Brass," a "complex swing chart" that Gioia considers a masterpiece and Schuller says is "a tour de force of unsurpassed brass virtuosity, still making players today shake their heads in disbelief."[121]

Also in 1938 Ellington and Juan Tizol collaborated on a composition that carried forward the Arabic motif of "Caravan" from 1937. Although "Caravan" and its successor "Pyramid" bear titles referring to the Middle East, the musical basis of these works is a Latin or Caribbean strain related to Tizol's Cuban heritage. The slow, sensual nature of these pieces, underscored in both cases by Greer's marvelous percussion work (using for "Pyramid" a handheld drum constructed of a tambourine "without the tinkles"), made them popular, according to Schuller, with stripteasers.[122] Tizol states the theme of both works on his valve trombone, and as Schuller says of "Caravan," it is "one of those melodies which, once heard, cannot be gotten out of mind."[123] A third collaborative effort by Ellington and Tizol recorded in 1938 is "A Gypsy without a Song," which Schuller calls "a masterpiece of period nostalgia."[124] This, too, was a common tendency during the Swing Era, especially in the forties with the onset of World War II. Stanley Dance stresses the serenity of "Gypsy," and this is yet another side of Ellington's music that sets it apart. "Gypsy" also demonstrates the artistry of the Ellington soloists who are in such total control of their instruments on this very demanding work. As Dance says of Hodges's solo, it has "been seldom equaled for serene beauty on the alto saxophone."[125] And this is not just a matter of technical dexterity, which too often is all that soloists in the big bands offered; rather, the Ellington sidemen always combined instrumental skill with a breadth and depth of expressive quality rarely matched by other musicians either soloing or playing as a section. As Schuller suggests, what makes "Gypsy" "a masterpiece" is the combination of Ellington's "subtleties of color" and his "players' contribution," including "the subtle intensification of melancholia that Brown achieves by his refined use of the slide (over Tizol's 'straight' version) . . . a subtle variant in expression."[126]

Along with serenity goes subtlety as one of the special Ellington attributes, and this can be heard in the 1938 "I Let a Song Go Out of My Heart," with Hodges again contributing some of his sumptuous sound on alto and "the Ellington band in full but subtle cry."[127] Schuller writes that this tune "prophetically predated and presaged a number of other fine moments in subsequent jazz history: Ellington's own 1940 hit 'Don't Get Around Much Anymore'; Glenn Miller's 'In the Mood' fade-away ending; and, much later, the sound that Gil Evans made into the hallmark of the late 1940s' Claude Thornhill orchestra."[128] George Avakian points out that "Don't Get Around" is in fact "a clever variation on 'I Let a Song Go Out of My Heart,' so constructed that the earlier tune becomes a perfect counter-melody to . . . 'Don't Get Around Much Any More' . . . except in the release, where the newer melody becomes a counter-melody for the old one."[129] No other composer-bandleader of the era brought so many nor such varied musical gifts to the creation of big-band music as did Duke Ellington, and the creations resulting from such gifts would continue unabated, especially during the next few years.

The year 1939 saw the addition of Jimmy Blanton on bass, and Billy Strayhorn as Ellington's collaborator with whom he would produce an outpouring of orchestral compositions. Before either Blanton or Strayhorn made their vital contributions, however, Duke recorded in March his "Subtle Lament," which illustrates what Schuller calls the " 'Ellington effect' . . . in full flowering: every harmonic touch, every daub of color, every timbral nuance used to maximum expressiveness."[130] In the blues line of "Mood Indigo" of 1930 and "Dusk" of 1940, "Subtle Lament" is notable above all else for the sectional writing and execution, aside from the lovely solos by Stewart on muted trumpet and Bigard on clarinet. The scoring for the reeds especially—so trademark Ellington in the penetrating lead of Hodges—and for the three trombones is simply exquisite. In November, bassist Jimmy Blanton would begin to make his revolutionary contribution to jazz history, but this was only with a group of duets recorded with Ellington on piano. The first of the big-band recordings featuring Blanton would not come until March 1940, when the orchestra recorded "Jack the Bear" and "Ko-Ko," both of which are the epitome of swing. Although Blanton's free-ranging bass helps lend a fresh vitality to these recordings, the drumming of Sonny Greer, who had been with Ellington from the beginning of his career, propels the band with new verve, owing undoubtedly to Blanton's youthful and inventive drive. And once again, it is the phenomenal writing for and execution by the sections that make these two works models of swing. Among the soloists, Nanton with his plunger adds to both recordings but particularly to "Ko-Ko" where he is so authoritative and direct in his intent to tell his story in no uncertain terms.

Blanton's special sound is highlighted fully on two other 1940 recordings, of Ellington's "Sepia Panorama" and "In a Mellotone." On the former Blanton gives a workshop in bass playing, both as a soloist and as an accompanist. On "In a Mellotone," he supports two of Duke's all-time leading soloists, Cootie Williams on trumpet and Johnny Hodges on alto.

Williams is showcased in particular on "Concerto for Cootie," which André Hodeir rated a masterpiece for so many reasons, including "its unusual
structure," "the simplicity and subtlety of the harmony," "sobriety," "an
economy of means . . . more valuable than the overloaded backgrounds
that the big modern band does not always know how to do without," the
soloist's "greater circumspection than he usually shows in a simple chorus-
after-chorus performance," and "the trumpet part" as "a bouquet of sonorities . . . phrases given to it by Ellington," which Cootie makes "shine
forth in dazzling colors, then plunges them in the shade, plays around with
them, makes them glitter or delicately tones them down; and each time
what he shows us is something new."[131] Hodeir also remarks that

there are few records in which the rhythm section of the band plays in quite such
a relaxed way, and by the same token there are few in which the band phrases with
as much swing. Naturally, this is not a torrid record like Hampton's *Air Mail
Special*. That kind of exaltation, which has its own appeal, is only rarely Duke
Ellington's line. But "Concerto for Cootie" is a perfect example of a performance
that is full of swing in a gentle climate.[132]

The other vintage Ellington sideman, Harry Carney, joins Hodges as
featured soloist on the 1940 version of "Sophisticated Lady," an Ellington
tune originally recorded in 1933. The piece opens with Carney high up in
his horn's register and then Hodges soars from there yet higher to increase
even more the emotive effect. Afterward Hodges plays an alto obbligato to
Carney's baritone theme statement as the pair create a strikingly unusual
blend, and even at one point some almost extinct simultaneous improvisation. This is followed by Duke's rippling arpeggios and then Lawrence
Brown's most romantic trombone. The final bars find the sax section softly
descending as if from the clouds as only Ellington would hear them with
his sophisticated imagination.

Although Ben Webster had recorded with Ellington previously, his solo
work on the 1940 "Cotton Tail" established his as one of the most distinctive tenor voices of the entire Swing Era. Schuller declares that not only
is Webster's solo one of his two or three greatest on record but also that
"Cotton Tail" is "a composition that both in its conception and performance was an important precursor of the big-band style of modern jazz.
Typically it did so years before anyone had heard of 'modern jazz.' "[133]
Schuller also notes that Webster "brought to the Ellington band (along with
Blanton) that bluesy, earthy rhythmic feel that came from the Southwest
and . . . what might best be described as a 'linear pulse,' otherwise known
as Swing."[134] James Lincoln Collier includes "Cotton Tail" among the dozens of Ellington compositions that "are the heart of the matter; alive with
fire and color, they constitute one of the great works of music created in
this century."[135] Another spotlight for Webster is Ellington's 1940 "All Too

Soon," which has been labeled "perhaps the most poignantly soothing of all Ellington ballad performances" and Webster's solo as an example of "his particular mastery of jazz ballad improvisation."[136] "Just A-Settin' and A-Rockin,' " a 1941 Billy Strayhorn collaboration, also features Webster in a relaxed setting that has Blanton's feeding bass in another fine supporting role.

Billy Strayhorn's major contribution to the Ellington book, the 1941 "Take the 'A' Train," is perhaps as well known as anything Duke himself ever wrote; in fact, Strayhorn's original 1941 composition became for some time the Ellington orchestra's theme song. Yet when all is said and done, it is Ellington, the creator of some thirty-five timeless songs, including "Solitude," "Satin Doll," "Prelude to a Kiss," "I'm Beginning to See the Light," and "Do Nothin' Till You Hear from Me," among those not discussed earlier (although the last of these furnished the musical figure for "Concerto for Cootie"), who stands as one of the greatest of all American composers, not only of still popular songs but of orchestral works that remain unique to jazz as well as to Western music. This survey has left out as many worthy Ellington recordings as it has included from the period 1930 to 1941, but even to the limited number discussed here very few if any bands of the Swing Era can measure up, at least not on the level of the quantity of quality performances produced by Duke Ellington and his superb cast of sidemen, many of whom were with him through all eleven years and some of whom remained with him to the end of his long and illustrious career.

JIMMIE LUNCEFORD

Unlike almost every other big-band leader of the Swing Era, Jimmie Lunceford was neither a virtuoso on any one instrument nor a singular vocalist on the order of Cab Calloway, nor was he known for his own arrangements or compositions (although he did in fact create a number of outstanding works), nor was his band heralded for exceptional soloists. And yet Lunceford was responsible for one of the most popular and instantly recognizable band styles of the 1930s. Like Fletcher Henderson, Lunceford was college educated, having graduated from Fisk University in Nashville. In 1926 he took a job as a music teacher at Manassa High School in Memphis, where he formed the nucleus of his famous orchestra. Following his students to Fisk, Lunceford kept the group together until they finished their degrees. In Dallas in December 1927, the band made two undistinguished recordings of "Chickasaw Stomp" and "Memphis Rag," and after becoming a permanent unit in 1929 and enduring hard times for several years, the group moved to New York in 1933 and made two test recordings for Columbia, which were not released until the 1960s. From those early tests of "Flaming Reeds and Screaming Brass" and "While Love Lasts," it is clear that by 1933 the orchestra already was the well-rehearsed unit that it would remain under Lunceford's leadership, and that the saxes were expertly led by alto saxophonist Willie Smith, who, like Henderson, held a degree in chemistry. André Hodeir writes of the Ellington orchestra that it "rarely had Lunceford's kind of precision," and according to Albert McCarthy, when Smith spent a year with Ellington in 1951, he irritated Duke's veterans in the sax section because of his "insistence on regular rehearsals."[137]

In the 1930s Ralph J. Gleason heard the Lunceford orchestra play dances and stage shows at such New York spots as the Apollo, Savoy Ballroom, Renaissance, Strand and Paramount Theaters, the Cotton Club, and the Bandbox. A Columbia University student at the time, Gleason would later write that "usually we can't return again, but this music [of the Lunceford orchestra] . . . brings back an era and a feeling and an emotion like an instant replay. There was never anything like it."[138] What made the Lunceford orchestra stand out from the rest of the pack—in particular from Henderson, Basie, and Ellington—was that its form of jazz was based primarily on "the sentimental songs and the cute ones and the tricky ones," rather than on the classic tunes of King Oliver and Jelly Roll Morton, on versions of ragtime and blues, or on complex compositions of the kind that Ellington created.[139] Certainly the Lunceford orchestra played riffs and even recorded a number of Ellington numbers, but these were not really the group's bread-and-butter material. As Gleason suggests, Lunceford made interesting music out of the "dreadful syrupy ballads" and the "Mickey Mouse music" of the period.[140] Also, the Lunceford style emphasized vocals, especially as sung by its male trio on a piece like "My Blue Heaven," which, as Gleason notes, was imitated by hundreds of college vocal trios.[141] Another distinguishing source for the Lunceford success was the band's showmanship, which Gunther Schuller calls "an entertainment delight."[142] But in addition to these more popular aspects of its appeal, the Lunceford orchestra offered many of the same ingredients as the other great bands of the era: "the incredible dynamics . . . the way it could whisper, and the great roar it got from the brasses and the amazing cohesion of that sax section . . . a variety and volume and an ever-changing tapestry of sound," and perhaps above all its ability to make "the whole audience meld together into one homogeneous mass extension of the music."[143] In the meantime, as Gleason recalls, what always puzzled him and other listeners was how Lunceford, dressed characteristically in his elegant all-white tuxedo and holding only his long baton, "could *look* so placid standing there in front of all that magic."[144]

An often reproduced photograph of the Lunceford orchestra, from a scene in a Warner Brothers short film, pictures the brass and reed sections on either side of Ed Wilcox seated at a white piano underneath a raised platform whereon is perched drummer Jimmy Crawford, with, to the far right behind the sax stands, tuba and string bass player Moses Allen, who, along with Crawford, had been on the 1927 recordings made by Lunceford's student band. The leader stands out front of the orchestra, with his face shown beneath the bottom rim of Crawford's bass drum, which has depicted on it a drawing of Lunceford's well-groomed head. The painted backdrop is above the section members and behind and to the sides of Crawford's drum kit—the drummer seated in front of his set of chimes— and pictures swirling music staves with eighth notes and flat and natural signs. All the musicians wear white tuxedo jackets, black trousers, and black bow ties, their mutes hanging on stands, their instruments resting on their right thighs, except for the trombones, which are held in the players' left hands with their bells above their left thighs. Lunceford is smiling, as are almost all his sidemen, especially Crawford and Moses. From the photo image, this is indeed a show band, and, as Gleason remarks, it "would have been great on television," but before the advent of that medium, Lunceford died mysteriously in 1947 and "the strange, living but impersonal organism that is a band disappeared."[145] Yet the recorded music lives on, and from hearing it, there is no doubt that, as Albert McCarthy says, "in its peak years, Lunceford's must rank with the Basie and Ellington bands of the same period as the greatest big bands in jazz history."[146]

One wonders why Columbia chose not to release "Flaming Reeds and Screaming Brass" and "While Love Lasts" when they were test recorded in 1933. Few other bands of that year could generate the excitement and drive of the first piece, which features a high trumpet passage that forecasts the way that later in the decade "the Lunceford trumpet section opened up the sky for the screamers."[147] Issued by Columbia around 1967 on an album entitled *Lunceford Special*, these two sides furnish early evidence of the orchestra's fundamental strengths: solid swing, precision execution, soloists who are not spectacular but whose breaks add appropriately to the mood or thrust of the tunes, and sectional cohesion that was perhaps unequaled by any other unit. This last quality is best exemplified by "While Love Lasts," where first the muted brass lay down a warm bed of sound supported by Moses Allen's big-toned bass and then the saxes play a sentimental passage that is so lovely and ahead of its time, and also so together, that the sentiment is beside the point. Ed Wilcox's classically trained piano lends the piece a classy and yet very swinging touch. What sounds like a xylophone also contributes to the stylishness of the performance, while Jimmy Crawford's percussion adds both taste and a smooth beat to the proceedings. An alto break by Willie Smith shows off, as Stanley Dance says, the leadman's "advanced musicianship," as he works into his rhapsodic solo a wonderful sixteenth-note turn.[148] Meanwhile, the ensemble employs syncopation in a lightly swinging manner that would become a Lunceford hallmark. All in all, this is a remarkable recording, and "While

Love Lasts" must have wowed live audiences even if it was never heard on victrolas of the time.

Fortunately, with 1934, the Lunceford orchestra began to record regularly. But its performances in that year of Ellington's "Sophisticated Lady," "Mood Indigo," "Black and Tan Fantasy," "Solitude," "Bird of Paradise," and "Rhapsody Jr." are not of the same quality or kind as the group's own arrangements of pop tunes. However, these Ellington compositions, as played by the Lunceford unit, do exhibit the orchestra's fine musicianship, in particular Wilcox's piano imitation of Ellington and even more so the fabulous sax section's togetherness in a virtuoso reading of the theme of "Sophisticated Lady." "Mood Indigo" opens with an extraordinary introduction that again displays some exceptionally fine work by the sax section, but this song also reveals some of the weaknesses in the soloists when Russell Bowles on trombone is rather clumsy in his delivery. Ultimately, however, as Gunther Schuller points out, the Lunceford version of "Mood Indigo" "is great *precisely because* it dared to depart from any preconceptions . . . the well-known theme stated very discreetly in muted brass while, virtually as foreground, clarinet and saxophones . . . escort the theme in a totally original bouncy staccato passage."[149] Sy Oliver's trumpet on "Black and Tan Fantasy" does not approach the emotional level of Bubber Miley's original break, but it certainly pays homage to that classic solo. As for Oliver's singing on "Solitude," it does not have the right tone to it for an Ellington ballad—Oliver turns it into a mere pop song rather than probing the meaning of the title's emotional state—and even the saxes, although they play with precision, do not capture the ballad's deep feeling. The two pieces never recorded by Ellington's own orchestra, "Bird of Paradise" and "Rhapsody Jr.," do not seem worthy of the master (which may explain why he never committed them to wax), but then it may be that in the hands of the Lunceford orchestra they just do not work, do not seem to hold together. Both come across as mere showpieces, with the brief solos more showy than substantive, with the possible exception of a Smith alto break on "Rhapsody Jr." In general, the Lunceford type of showmanship is a bit out of a place for performances of Ellington's haunting compositions. Lunceford may have been led astray from his more natural style by an obvious and understandable admiration for his fellow bandleader.

Other influences continued to sidetrack Lunceford from finding and following his own musical direction. The orchestra's 1934 rendering of Cole Porter's "Miss Otis Regrets" definitely falls short of the ghostly version by Cab Calloway. Also, the performances of two Will Hudson arrangements were, as Schuller says, "a momentary stylistic detour."[150] Hudson, as one of the arrangers for the Casa Loma Orchestra, brought to the Lunceford book a frantic pace that was really foreign to the more relaxed nature of the band's performance style. Also, the trumpet break on Hudson's "White

Heat" is purely an Armstrong imitation and on "Jazznocracy" both the trombone and tenor soloists are too beholden to Henderson's Claude Jones or Benny Morton and Coleman Hawkins. Even the Parish-Lunceford tune, "Swingin' Uptown," although an energetic outing, is essentially too much in the Henderson mold. The arrangement of "Rose Room" remains still indebted to Ellington (starting with Wilcox's piano introduction), although there are moments when the Lunceford style emerges, as in the relaxed two-beat swing, the delicate work of muted brass, the sharp articulation of the saxes, and the warm, full-toned tenor of Joe Thomas. But only with recordings of its own material did the Lunceford orchestra show its best and more authentic side, beginning with the leader's "Stratosphere" and continuing with the Sy Oliver-Lunceford collaboration "Stomp It Off," Oliver's "Dream of You," and Lunceford's "Rhythm Is Our Business."

Lunceford's "Stratosphere" has been singled out by Gunther Schuller as "a startlingly innovative (and so far roundly ignored) composition."[151] Schuller places this piece from September 4, 1934, in the company of two other "musical oddit[ies]," Coleman Hawkins's "Queer Notions" and Red Norvo's "Dance of the Octopus," both from 1933.[152] But Lunceford's "Stratosphere," although it is not perhaps a typical dance number but more of "an advanced composition falling almost outside the realm of jazz," still offers an unpretentious, straight-ahead drive that is characteristic of the leader's finest recordings.[153] This is even more true of the Oliver-Lunceford "Stomp It Off," from October 29, 1934, which once again showcases the precision of the orchestra's section work, especially the saxes' clipped phrases and the lighthearted call-and-response interplay between reeds and brasses. All the breaks, by trumpeter Tommy Stevenson, Thomas on tenor, Oliver on trumpet (who picks up on the orchestra's allusions to Slim Gaillard's "Flat Foot Floogie"), and Smith on alto, fit beautifully into the spirit and texture of the arrangement. Oliver's lovely "Dream of You," from the same October 29 session, survived to find its way into a 1997 Academy Award–winning Dutch film, entitled *Character*, which employs the Lunceford performance of the piece as part of the movie's intriguing plot (based on a 1938 novel by Ferdinand Bordewijk). Also, the fascinating 1956 recording of Oliver's composition, as arranged by Pete Rugolo, "is in the Lunceford tradition, though the modern touches are added to give it an extra cachet."[154] The original 1934 recording of Oliver's "remarkably sophisticated arrangement and composition" reveals "the magical way" the arranger-composer "could blend harmony and instrumental color with his own unique brand of relaxed swing."[155] The vocal by Oliver is quite convincingly dreamy and the trombone solos by Russell Bowles maintain the mood perfectly.

The showmanship of the Lunceford orchestra is fully illustrated by the leader's "Rhythm Is Our Business," with words by Sammy Cahn, recorded on December 18, 1934. After the attention-getting opening theme-statement, with its slowing, speeding-up trainlike pulse (reminiscent of El- lington but distinctive) and its fine solos by Smith and Oliver, four of the sidemen are named by Smith in his talk-vocal (echoed by Oliver and Tomp- kins), and each in turn struts his stuff: Crawford doing tricks with sticks, which make the "boys in the band all play hot licks"; Joe Thomas running the scales on tenor as a way of explaining why business "sure is swell"; Allen bringing with his solid bass "happiness to you"; and Stevenson mak- ing one think with his high-note trumpet "he's in the sky." Where Ellington composed concertos to feature the talents and personalities of his sidemen, Lunceford spotlighted his musicians in relationship to the orchestra's show biz approach, using lyrics to introduce the instruments of their trade and their uplifting effects. More than showcasing artistry, Lunceford concen- trated, as Schuller has indicated, on delighting through entertainment. This is not to say that soloists such as Thomas, Oliver, and Smith were slouches, but that the emphasis was less on individual expression and more on crowd-pleasing novelty touches, such as identifying the sidemen to the au- dience by name and through catchy lyrics designed to underscore their musical selling points.

The piece that highlights most fully the orchestra's teamwork is pianist Eddie Wilcox's arrangement of "Sleepy Time Gal." On the recording of this tune from May 29, 1935, no soloists are featured as such—Wilcox's piano break serves more as a link between two sectional sequences. Instead, the entire ensemble is the focus here, and especially the superlative playing of the saxophones led by Willie Smith. Again, there was probably no other band whose sax section could have matched the virtuosity of the Lunceford reeds, due obviously to Smith's insistence on being well rehearsed. Accord- ing to Stanley Dance's identification of the personnel, Lunceford himself performs an alto part rather than the recently added Dan Grissom, who would become one of the orchestra's star vocalists.[156] Schuller declares that "no modern 'Super Sax' group can equal or top [the Lunceford section's] hair-raising roulades and careening twisting turns." He goes on to add that "it is a feast for the ears to hear the band bounce through those marvelously buoyant syncopations in eleven-part voicings, balanced so well that one can rarely distinguish trumpets from saxophones from trombones."[157] An unidentified historian has been quoted as saying that "the Lunceford- rhythm was so intriguing that the label 'swing,' which is too general, didn't sufficiently describe it. It was also called 'bounce'—Lunceford's music was bouncing."[158] Following the muted trumpet introduction and after the opening sequence, in which the reeds state the theme at a leisurely pace (with Smith's clarinet on top), the four saxes (Smith, Lunceford, and La- foret Dent on alto and Thomas on tenor—baritonist Jock Carruthers ap- parently not present here) go into a written-out improvisation on the melody with bits of humor, double-time phrases, and precisely executed group trills. It is truly one of the most thrilling performances on record by a sax section during a period in which the reed choir tended to be the pride and glory of every big band. Lunceford's reeds not only led the way but also established a high level that, as Schuller has said, not even a modern "Super Sax" group could manage to attain.

Other sides cut in 1935 include "Swanee River," "Four or Five Times," "Oh Boy!," "Avalon," "Hittin' the Bottle," "My Blue Heaven," "Charmaine," and "I'm Nuts about Screwy Music." As the titles tend to suggest, each of these tunes exhibits another facet of the orchestra's many-sided entertainment personality. Opening with the expected precision playing of muted trumpets and more of the group trills and the smooth togetherness of the saxes, "Swanee River," from September 23, also includes a page out of Tricky Sam Nanton's book when Elmer Crumbley does his fine wah-wah plunger-mute imitation. "Four or Five Times," from May 29, once again shows off the splendid sax section but also a fine trombone trio; yet at the time what must have caught the attention of listeners most was surely Sy Oliver's singing of the lyrics. Typical of the Lunceford vocalists is Oliver's clear enunciation of the words, which looks forward to the clarity of a Nat King Cole delivery. Also ahead of its time is Oliver's final iteration of the title phrase in a falsetto voice. With "Oh Boy!," also from September 23, the Lunceford fan was introduced to the arranging skills of newcomer Eddie Durham, who in addition to doing arrangements for the group also played trombone and guitar. Here we find the Lunceford orchestra returning more to the big-band tradition represented by the Redman-Henderson call-and-response formula, but whereas a piece such as the 1934 "Swingin' Uptown" was overly a case of copycat, the Durham arrangement and the performance of "Oh Boy!" are in the unhurried, bouncy style of Lunceford. Gunther Schuller incomparably describes Durham's writing for the reeds, revealing how the arranger utilizes for the opening

two baritones not only in unison but in harmony. In fact he builds up the section gradually, adding the tenor after a few bars, and finally the two altos. Later on there are some very fast switches from saxophones to clarinets that add immeasurably to the sonoric variety, the illusion still further heightened by using the reeds in all their different registers: high soft saxes, low clarinets, high wailing clarinets, low somber saxes. Along with plenty of varied textures and colors in the brass, this offers a wide range of contrasts of the kind that Oliver excelled in and Durham here used as well to best effect.[159]

Durham's other 1935 contributions are "Avalon" and "Hittin' the Bottle," which I have discussed elsewhere.[160] As noted earlier, "My Blue Heaven," from December 23, features Lunceford's influential vocal trio, backed by a tasteful violin. But aside from these special attractions, it is Sy Oliver's dramatic arrangement that made "My Blue Heaven" one of Lunceford's most popular recordings. Jock Carruthers anchors the piece with his solid baritone and some of his infrequent but very fine improvisational work. This is Lunceford-rhythm at its most infectious, relaxed but driving, even through the romantic yet hip vocal trio, which concludes with a touch of barbershop harmony—a little something for everyone! Mostly there is what Gary Giddins calls Oliver's "illusory two-beat rhythm (the music was actually written in four but executed so as to emphasize the backbeat) that became Lunceford's primary trademark."[161] "Charmaine," another charming Oliver arrangement from September 30, features both an effusive solo by Joe Thomas and an effective vocal by Dan Grissom in his crooning tenor. And finally, Wilcox's arrangement of "I'm Nuts about Screwy Music," from December 23, illustrates Ralph Gleason's idea that the Lunceford orchestra could turn even "Mickey Mouse music" into the genuine jazz article. Willie Smith's handling of the corny lyrics even passes muster, but the instrumental solos and the ensemble execution are what carry the day. The crisp playing of all the sectional parts is exemplary, and along with Thomas's bursting-at-the-seams tenor break and Eddie Tompkins's closing high-note trumpet, the performance offers the three qualities the best big bands had in abundance and the public loved: "[p]ower, flash, and precision."[162]

Among the Lunceford recordings of 1936, representative pieces would include "Organ Grinder's Swing," "Harlem Shout," and "Running a Temperature." Oliver's arrangement of Will Hudson's "Organ Grinder's Swing," from September 1, has been called by Gunther Schuller "a minor classic of its kind," owing primarily to the "basic simplicity" of the arranger's treatment and his "imaginative use of dynamic and timbral contrast." Schuller cites particularly "a moment of true magic as whisper-soft saxes and rhythm enter with the simplest of blues-like harmonies, accompanying quietly trembling blues-ish guitar tremolos." He also notes that the arrangement comes "full circle" with the same opening clip-clop of Crawford's temple blocks, a duo first of Smith's clarinet and Oliver's muted trumpet, and then of Oliver with Carruthers's baritone for "a perfect ending to a perfect piece."[163] Symmetry, balance, discipline—this is another triad of essential traits of the Lunceford style. But, there are still other distinguishing attributes, which are exemplified by "Harlem Shout" and "Running a Temperature." The easy swing, the great variety of rhythmic patterns and instrumental timbres, the unexpected entries by single instrument or section (as when dissonant trumpet or trumpets suddenly scream out), the soloists who add their special voices—all of this is evident in "Harlem Shout," from October 14. (It might be noted that Carruthers's baritone break is taken almost verbatim from Harry Carney's opening solo on "Cotton Club Stomp" recorded May 3, 1929. This in no way detracts from the overall performance but only shows once more how much Lunceford's sidemen remained, as soloists, in the shadow of Ellington's, or those of Henderson as well.)[164]

Durham's version of "Running a Temperature," from October 26, illustrates Schuller's view that Lunceford's arrangers were often stimulated and even inspired by the lyrics of their novelty tunes, which helped bring to their arrangements "a welcome element of humor and wit."[165] This is certainly the case with "Running a Temperature," where the dramatic pyramid-building introduction, Smith's bent-out-of-shape melody statement, the whiny ensemble, the saccharine clarinet trio, Carruthers's down-in-the-mouth baritone, and Oliver's tongue-in-cheek plunger mute, all humorously reflect the theme of the feverish, lovesick singer burning up like a volcano. Here the Lunceford orchestra develops with swing the same classic doctor-patient love analogy as the one found in Shakespeare's sonnet 147. Durham achieves this analogic trick even more successfully than in his "Hittin' the Bottle," from September 30, 1935, which Schuller says "shows how well catchy lyrics, improvised solos, and ensembles could be integrated into a musically satisfying and nevertheless thoroughly entertaining whole."[166] To symmetry, balance, and discipline, then, we can add variety, surprise, humor, and magic to the inimitable Lunceford entertainment package.

With 1937 the orchestra continued to produce attractive, distinctive, and varied performances, including "Coquette," "The Merry-Go-Round Broke Down," "For Dancers Only," "Posin,' " "Put on Your Old Grey Bonnet," "Pigeon Walk," and "Annie Laurie." As Schuller observes, "Coquette," from June 15, was "perfect for slow close dancing," and even at its very slow tempo it swings "mightily, much aided by Crawford's powerful Chinese cymbal back-beat."[167] Nothing like Ellington's "Merry Go Round," the Lunceford recording of the similarly entitled tune, "The Merry-Go-Round Broke Down," also from June 15, is a piece of hokum featuring the call of a popcorn vendor, steam released from a calliope (provided by the hissing band members), a humorous vocal, something of a Dixieland jam, and a good time had by all because boy gets girl after all. (David W. Stowe, in *Swing Changes*, refers to a 1940 article by a University of Kansas professor who suggested that "the lyrics of many swing tunes . . . were sophisticated from a psychoanalytic point of view, and psychologically beneficial.")[168] Lunceford's band appealed to every audience, it would seem, but primarily its road tours were aimed at dancers, and "For Dancers Only," again from June 15, catered to that category of listener in particular. This Sy Oliver arrangement is a riff-based piece that finally has little to do with the riffs of Basie or Henderson or most of the other big bands, simply because it keeps its focus on the dancers rather than on showing off either soloists or section work as such. A trombone trio is the only exception, along with a brief break by Thomas on tenor, and yet even the trio offers simply the same driving, repeated riff, nothing fancy or intricate. Crawford's back-beat drumming emphasizes the forward momentum that is relentless, because the point is to keep the dancers gyrating and doing their thing. On the other hand, "Posin,' " from July 8, calls for the dancers to stop and assume a pose ("position's everything in life")—another way of involving those on the floor and keeping them coming back for more. This piece is just sheer fun, and so too is "Put on Your Old Grey Bonnet," from the same date, though at more of an up-tempo, with a double-time bass break by Moses Allen and some fine guitar work by Eddie Durham. As I have discussed Durham's arrangement of "Pigeon Walk" elsewhere, this brings me to "Annie Laurie," from November 5, and the addition of Trummy Young as Lunceford's stellar trombonist.[169] At the conclusion of "Annie Laurie," Young follows the screaming trumpet of Paul Webster with a high note of his own. But even earlier with his solo that comes after Thomas's shaking, quaking tenor, Young dazzles with his whirling phrases, glissando rips, and sixteenth-note turns. Young's technical prowess and his trumpet-high trombone work got the ear of every practicing and aspiring trombonist of the period, and was of course a feather in Lunceford's cap.

The next impressive outing for Trummy Young came on January 6, 1938, when the orchestra recorded "Margie." Willie Smith's playing of the theme is one of his loveliest unadorned statements, restrained but emotive. This is followed by Young singing the lyrics with a knowing tone before he picks up his trombone for a solo that ends both his chorus and the recording on a lightly tongued, glissandoed ascent to a high F#. One year later, on January 3, 1939, Young was again the star attraction in a Lunceford manifesto of the sort that Ellington had written in 1932 with "It Don't Mean a Thing (If It Ain't Got That Swing)." Sy Oliver and Young's big hit, "Tain't What You Do (It's the Way Hotcha Do It)," features Trummy as vocalist, backed up by members of the band in a call-and-response exchange. This piece also shows off Jimmy Crawford's drumming to best advantage, his cymbals and tom-toms lending the performance a special lowdown quality from first to last.

This final year of the decade offered a bumper crop of recordings by the Lunceford orchestra, including other Young vocals on "The Lonesome Road" (at an unusually fast pace for Lunceford and as compared with the recording of the same piece by Fats Waller of 1938), "Cheatin' on Me" (with a fine theme statement by Joe Thomas), "Ain't She Sweet," and "I'm in an Awful Mood." (These sides were recorded January 31 and 3, April 7, and December 14, respectively.) "Time's A-Wastin'," from January 3, has Oliver as a very effective vocalist on his own arrangement, which swings as solidly as any Lunceford recording. "Baby Won't You Please Come Home," from January 31, opens with a Dixie-type jam, complete with Crawford's cowbell, but then quickly moves into a late-thirties swing that finds Crawford's brushes pushing for all they're worth but with a relaxed drive that is totally up-to-date. Most of these tunes feature vocals (by one singer or a trio) rather than instrumental solos, except for sensational theme statements by the saxophonists, as on "Ain't She Sweet" where the altoist is Ted Buckner, who also plays the theme on "Well All

Right Then," from May 17. On the latter, Elmer Crumbley also takes a fine muted trombone solo, Crawford a brief drum break, and Thomas eight-bars full of his emotive vibrato.

By this time, both Sy Oliver and Eddie Durham were no longer with Lunceford—twenty-two-year-old arranger Billy Moore having had the mantel passed to him by Oliver when he left to join the Tommy Dorsey Orchestra. Moore's "Belgium Stomp," from September 14, 1939, leaves more space for instrumental solos, as well as the by now de rigueur screaming trumpet finale, which also is the case with Moore's "I'm in an Awful Mood," from December 14. Another arranger, Bud Estes, accounted for "I'm Alone with You," from the same date, which is still identifiably by the Lunceford orchestra, with Willie Smith and the sax section being put through their paces with unparalleled technique and finesse. "Uptown Blues," also from December 14, is one of the few blues ever recorded by Lunceford, with Willie Smith showing that he can do it all as he plays a sterling improvisation, including a stirring, ringing high note. Trumpeter Snooky Young also comes up with a fine solo effort of his own. Perhaps the most captivating side from 1939 is Eddie Durham's arrangement of "Lunceford Special," again from December 14, on which both Snooky and Trummy Young take driving solos and Snooky concludes the piece with one of the most spectacular high-note endings of the era.

In 1940, Billy Moore arranged a number of pieces that reflect perfectly the age of swing, especially his and Oliver's "I Wanna Hear Swing Songs," from January 5. Moore's "Bugs Parade," from the same date, also is characteristic of the period, with its flashy brass and pumped up sax section, Trummy Young's blaring trombone, Thomas's impassioned tenor, high notes by Paul Webster, and a familiar fade-away ending. On "I Wanna Hear Swing Songs," Trummy sings the typical lyrics, which naturally speak of moonlight and love, with Ted Buckner's alto and Thomas's tenor breaks completing the romantic scene. Likewise, Moore's arrangement of "What's Your Story, Morning Glory," from February 28, another of the almost unheard-of blues recorded by Lunceford, is cited by Schuller and Stanley Dance for the solos of Gerald Wilson on muted trumpet and Thomas on tenor (and in Dance's case for Smith's opening solo on clarinet) as "particularly striking."[170] Schuller also notes that Moore's arrangement exhibits "the band's almost obsessive insistence on variety."[171] Although these performances are executed with the Lunceford attention to detail, they lack the imaginative excitement of earlier arrangements by Oliver and Durham.

In 1941, the orchestra would record two arrangements by trumpeter Gerald Wilson, which in their offbeat, somewhat dissonant way represent another aspect of the Lunceford sound. With soloists exploring rather strange harmonies for Lunceford's men, with saxes trilling and alternating hushed and full-blown phrases, and with rapidly tongued passages and unexpected punctuations by the trumpets, "Hi Spook," from August 26, keeps the listener off balance and intrigued, evoking an image of dancers not knowing quite what to do. Like "Bugs Parade," "Yard Dog Mazurka," also from August 26, is reminiscent at times of "Jersey Bounce," and as Gunther Schuller observes, the opening of "Yard Dog Mazurka" was appropriated years later by Stan Kenton for his "Intermission Riff."[172] Here, pedal notes from the trombones and nice contrasts between soft and loud passages, with a delicate guitar interpolation, all make for an unusually varied fare in the best Lunceford tradition.

Given the wide range of material, the demanding arrangements, the insistence on precision and variety of presentation, and the general high quality of the solos, it is no wonder that the Lunceford style won high acclaim at the time and has since elicited glowing accolades from a critic such as Gunther Schuller. If listeners today are not so well aware of Lunceford and his sidemen (five of the original nine remaining with him right up to his death), certainly, as Ralph Gleason recalled, in his day "a whole generation of America loved their music."[173]

NOTES

1. These recordings are included on *Fletcher Henderson: Developing an American Orchestra 1923–1937*.

2. John S. Wilson, "Fletcher Henderson," in *The Jazz Makers*, p. 222.

3. Collier, *The Making of Jazz*, p. 183.

4. Schuller, *The Swing Era*, p. 323.

5. Schuller, *Early Jazz*, p. 276.

6. Schuller, *The Swing Era*, p. 8.

7. Schuller, *Early Jazz*, pp. 273–274. The recording of "Keep a Song in Your Soul" is included on *Fletcher Henderson: Developing an American Orchestra 1923–1937*.

8. Schuller, *Early Jazz*, p. 274.

9. Ibid., p. 277.

10. Chilton, *The Song of the Hawk*, p. 72. *I'm Crazy 'Bout My Baby* is included on *Fletcher Henderson: Tidal Wave*.

11. These sides are included on *Fletcher Henderson: Tidal Wave*. The unlikely tune, "My Sweet Tooth Says I Wanna (But My Wisdom Tooth Says No)," from July 31, 1931, also contains a fine violin break by Sampson, which is included on *Fletcher Henderson and His Orchestra 1931–1932* (Classics Records, 546, 1990).

12. Collier, *The Making of Jazz*, p. 184.

13. Schuller, *The Swing Era*, pp. 437 and 624.

14. This side is included on *The Jimmie Lunceford Orchestra: Stomp It Off* (Decca GRD-608, 1992). In his liner notes, Stanley Dance writes that Lunceford's composition is "rather prententious . . . tends to be too busy and not that easy to swing" (p. 6).

15. "Happy Feet" is included on *Fletcher Henderson & His Orchestra: The Father of the Big Band*.

16. Schuller, *The Swing Era*, p. 637.

17. Peter Dempsey, liner notes to *"The King of Jazz" Paul Whiteman: His Greatest Recordings 1920–1936* (Living Era CD AJA 5170, 1996).

18. Lorenzo Thomas, "The Bop Aesthetic and Black Intellectual Tradition," in *The Bebop Revolution in Words and Music*, ed. Dave Oliphant (Austin, Texas: Harry Ransom Humanities Research Center, 1994), p. 112.

19. Even though a December 21, 1943, recording with Dickie Wells on trombone, Bill Coleman on trumpet, and Lester Young on tenor is beyond the purview of this volume, I cannot resist mentioning Wells's solos on "Linger Awhile" and "I Got Rhythm," included on *Classic Tenors* (Doctor Jazz, FW38446, 1983), as wonderful examples of his later work that still exhibits the basic characteristics identified by Hodeir.

20. Hodeir, *Jazz: Its Evolution and Essence*, pp. 66–67, 70, and 70n. "Changes" is on the CD entitled *"The King of Jazz"*; "Back in Your Own Backyard" is on *The Indispensable Bix Beiderbecke* (Jazz Tribune No. 48, RCA Victor 66540–2); and "Sweet Sue" is on *The Bix Beiderbecke Story Volume 3* (Columbia CL 846). Richard Sudhalter cites Bix's solo on the 1927 "Changes" as a model of "clarity, balance, melodic organization, delivered with lift and assurance," but his solo on the 1928 "Sweet Sue," as Sudhalter acknowledges, shows "a deepening of thought and content" (*Lost Chords*, pp. 425 and 427).

21. "Yeah Man" is included on *Fletcher Henderson: Developing an American Orchestra 1923–1937* and "I've Got to Sing a Torch Song" is on *Fletcher Henderson & His Orchestra: The Father of the Big Band*.

22. Chilton, *The Song of the Hawk*, p. 86.

23. Liner notes to *Fletcher Henderson & His Orchestra: The Father of the Big Band*. Gunther Schuller does not comment on "I've Got to Sing a Torch Song," but Albert McCarthy does—the English critic proving a consistently dependable resource (*Big Band Jazz*, p. 72). Schuller does refer to another solo by Hawkins, on the 1934 Henderson recording of "It's the Talk of the Town," as being, along with "One Hour," one of his "breakthrough performances" (*The Swing Era*, p. 579; see also pp. 436–437). McCarthy also mentions "Talk of the Town," but this piece does not strike me as nearly so interesting as "Torch Song." The latter relates more fully to what Gary Giddins says of "One Hour": "He has everything under control—rhythm, intonation, melody, harmony, even the suspenseful romanticism (note the tension-building arpeggios in measure nine and ten) that remains at the core of the modern ballad style. Flawlessly conceived and executed, it carries the listener along with the force of its logic and character. More than the first entirely successful tenor solo, it's the first distinguished ballad improvisation in jazz" (*Visions of Jazz: The First Century* [New York: Oxford University Press, 1998], p. 124). "It's the Talk of the Town" is included on *Coleman Hawkins: Giants of Jazz* (Time Life Records, STL-J06, 1979).

24. McCarthy, *Big Band Jazz*, p. 72.

25. Chilton, *The Song of the Hawk*, p. 165. Before finding that Chilton states on page 88 of his book that Hawkins plays two choruses, I had asked Professor Richard Lawn of the University of Texas to confirm my notion that Hawkins does in fact play two choruses on "I've Got to Sing a Torch Song." Professor Lawn noted that the arrangement skips the repeat of the A section in the second chorus and goes to the bridge before returning to the A, thus breaking the expected form of A A B A. This truncating of the second chorus was apparently due to the dread

three-minute limit for recordings of the period, with this piece extending to three minutes and thirty-two seconds, which must have been right at the very maximum length of time allowed by the technology.

26. These sides, except for "Hello, Lola," as well as the version of "Sugar Foot Stomp" of April 29, 1931, are included on *Body and Soul: A Jazz Autobiography—Coleman Hawkins* (RCA Victor LPV-501, 1964). "Hello, Lola" is included on *Giants of Jazz: Coleman Hawkins.*

27. Percy A. Scholes, *The Concise Oxford Dictionary of Music*, 2d ed. (London: Oxford University Press, 1973), p. 108.

28. This side is included on *Fletcher Henderson: Tidal Wave.*

29. According to *Hendersonia*, Bailey had just joined Fletcher Henderson and was on the 1924 version. Although Gunther Schuller does not consider Bailey "an imaginative jazz artist . . . at best a fluent, technically well-equipped functional player," Bailey seems more than that on the 1934 "Shanghai Shuffle." However, Schuller is correct that in general Bailey's work is "devoid of the spontaneity one associates with major jazz figures" (*The Swing Era*, p. 814).

30. See personnel listing for "Shanghai Shuffle" on *Fletcher Henderson: Developing an American Orchestra 1923–1937.*

31. This side is included on *Cab Calloway* (Epic LN3265, nd).

32. Two takes of this September 12, 1934, recording are included on *Fletcher Henderson: Tidal Wave.*

33. This side is included on *Fletcher Henderson & His Orchestra: The Father of the Big Band.*

34. Schuller, *The Swing Era*, p. 323.

35. Martin Williams, in his annotations to *The Smithsonian Collection of Classic Jazz*, points out that Harry James's solo is "indebted . . . to Allen's original" (p. 48).

36. Schuller, *The Swing Era*, p. 28.

37. George Hoefer, liner notes to *Body and Soul: A Jazz Autobiography—Coleman Hawkins.*

38. Collier, *The Making of Jazz*, p. 186.

39. Erenberg, *Swingin' the Dream*, p. 69.

40. Collier, *The Making of Jazz*, p. 187.

41. Ibid., p. 188.

42. Schuller, *The Swing Era*, p. 326.

43. Taylor, notes to *Fletcher Henderson & His Orchestra: The Father of the Big Band.*

44. "Stampede" is on *Fletcher Henderson and His Orchestra 1937–1938.*

45. Schuller, *The Swing Era*, p. 579, in the text and in note 47.

46. McCarthy, *Big Band Jazz*, p. 74.

47. "Back in Your Own Backyard" and "Rhythm of the Tambourine" are on *The Father of the Big Band* and "Sing You Sinners" is on *Fletcher Henderson and His Orchestra 1937–1938.*

48. Schuller, *Early Jazz*, p. 246; Franklin S. Driggs, "Kansas City and the Southwest," in *Jazz: New Perspectives on the History of Jazz*, p. 191.

49. Schuller, *Early Jazz*, pp. 256 and 283–284. Schuller is discussing the two 1923 sides, "Elephant Wobble" and "Crawdad Blues," which are included on *Ben-*

nie Moten's Kansas City Orchestra 1923–1929 (Historical Records, vol. 9, ASC-5829–9).

50. Schuller, *Early Jazz*, p. 284.

51. Loren Schoenberg, liner notes to *Bennie Moten's Kansas City Orchestra: South (1926–1929)* (RCA Victor, 3139-2-RB, 1991).

52. Williams, liner notes to *Count Basie in Kansas City: Bennie Moten's Great Band of 1930–1932*.

53. John McDonough, "A Century with Count Basie," *Down Beat* 57 (January 1990): 36.

54. Albert Murray, *Stomping the Blues* (New York: Da Capo Press, 1987; rpt. of a 1976 publication).

55. Williams, liner notes to *Count Basie in Kansas City: Bennie Moten's Great Band of 1930–1932*.

56. Ibid.

57. Ibid.

58. Schuller, *The Swing Era*, p. 229.

59. Schuller, *Early Jazz*, p. 316.

60. "Blue Devil Blues," one of the two sides from the November 10, 1929, Blue Devils session, is included on *The Real Kansas City of the '20s,'30s & '40s* (Columbia/Legacy, CK 64855, 1996). The other side, "Squabblin,' " is rated much higher and is included on *Territory Bands, vol. 2, 1927–1931* (Historical Records, HLP 26).

61. Walter Allen calls Hawkins's solos on the April 10, 1931, recording of "Sugar Foot Stomp" "stormy." See Allen's *Hendersonia*, p. 261.

62. Schoenberg, liner notes to *Bennie Moten's Kansas City Orchestra: South (1926–1929)*.

63. Collier, *The Making of Jazz*, p. 234.

64. Ibid., p. 220.

65. Sudhalter, *Lost Chords*, p. 246.

66. Frank Driggs, "Budd Johnson: Ageless Jazzman," part 2, *Jazz Review* 4, no. 1 (January 1961): 17.

67. Schuller, *The Swing Era*, p. 236. "Swinging at the Daisy Chain" and the other sides from January 21, 1937, are included on *One O'Clock Jump: An Album of Classic "Swing" by Count Basie and His Orchestra 1937* (Decca, MCA-49394, 1990).

68. Ibid., p. 235.

69. This side is included on *Basic Basie: Airchecks from The Golden Count Basie Years: 1937–38 Lester Young, Herschel Evans, Billie Holiday, Buck Clayton and others* (Phonastic, NOST 7640, 1982).

70. Schuller, *The Swing Era*, p. 237.

71. Ibid.

72. This air check is included on *Basic Basie*, but the transfer from the original acetate, done in Sweden, is rather poor compared with the one made by Columbia for *Billie Holiday: The Golden Years* (Columbia Records, C3L 21, n.d.).

73. The 1936 Berigan version of "I Can't Get Started" is included on *Best of Jazz: The Swing Era: An Introduction to Bunny Berigan* (Best of Jazz Records 4021, 1995), and the 1937 version is on *Bunny Berigan: The Pied Piper 1934–1940* (Bluebird, 66615–2, 1995).

74. "No Regrets" is included both on the *Best of Jazz* Berigan CD and on *Billie Holiday: The Golden Years*.

75. These three Rushing vocals are included on *The Essential Count Basie Volume 1* (CBS, CJ 40608, 1987).

76. This side is included on *Blues by Basie* (Columbia, CL 901, n.d.) and also on *Best of Jazz: The Swing Era: An Introduction to Count Basie* (Best of Jazz 4026, 1995).

77. Comments on "Harvard Blues" on the record sleeve of *Blues by Basie* were written by Charlie Miller, class of 1941, who recalls the significance of a number of allusions in the lyrics, such as the line by Reinhardt stating that he "[c]an't keep dogs or women in [his] room."

78. Ibid.

79. Stowe, *Swing Changes*, p. 84. This critic goes on to note that in 1942 Harvard students "awarded Count Basie a doctorate in 'swingology.' "

80. Gunther Schuller writes that Durham's contributions to the Basie book helped "to solidify the band's performance and gave it a cohesive style, within the basic swing concept set by Basie" (*The Swing Era*, p. 238).

81. These sides are included on the Basie *Best of Jazz* CD, except for "Time Out" and "Out the Window," which are on *The Best of Count Basie* (MCA Records, MCA2–4050, n.d.). For a discussion of "Time Out," see my *Texan Jazz* (Austin: University of Texas Press, 1996), pp. 166–167.

82. Schuller, *The Swing Era*, p. 239.

83. Ibid.

84. "Texas Shuffle" is included on *Count Basie and his Orchestra: Jumpin' at the Woodside 1937–1943* (Jazz Roots, CD56015, 1991) and "Doggin' Around" on the Basie *Best of Jazz*. I have discussed both of these tunes in *Texan Jazz*, pp. 111–112.

85. Schuller, *The Swing Era*, p. 242.

86. Hodeir, *Jazz: Its Evolution and Essence*, pp. 69 and 72.

87. Collier, *The Making of Jazz*, p. 235.

88. Martin Williams, *The Jazz Tradition* (New York: Oxford University Press, 1983), p. 128.

89. For characteristics of Tatum's piano style, see under his name in the A to Z section.

90. Ibid., p. 130.

91. "Clap Hands" and "Lester Leaps In" are both on *Count Basie and His Orchestra: Jumpin' at the Woodside*, and "Clap Hands" is also on the Basie *Best of Jazz*. Young's solo on "Twelfth Street Rag" has been included by some critics, along with his solo on "Clap Hands," as "the very zenith of Lester's greatness," but other commentators have disagreed. See my *Texan Jazz*, pp. 32–33.

92. These two tunes are included on *Count Basie and his Orchestra: Jumpin' at the Woodside*.

93. Stearns, *The Story of Jazz*, p. 211.

94. See Jacques Morgantini's liner notes to *Fletcher Henderson & His Orchestra: The Father of the Big Band*.

95. Liner notes to *Duke Ellington at the Cotton Club* (RCA Camden CAL-459, 1958). In point of fact, the Ellington band first appeared in "a New York-shot short," *Black and Tan Fantasy*, in early 1929, but *Check and Double Check* was

its first full-length feature film. See liner notes to *Duke Ellington Vol. 10—Rockin' in Rhythm* (EPM 152312, 1995). Stanley Dance, in his notes to *The Ellington Era 1927–1940, Volume Two*, writes that the Ellington recording of "All God's Chillun Got Rhythm" "has been included for the benefit of those who fondly remember the band's appearance in the Marx Brothers film 'A Day at the Races.' " Unless by chance a scene with the Ellington orchestra was cut out of the video version of the film, only Ivie Anderson is seen in this 1937 movie. The occasion for Anderson's song is supplied by a scene in back of the racetrack stables where having rhythm is supposed to make up for the miserable conditions in which the blacks are living. Young black couples are pictured as dancing jitterbugs, and at the end of the film, all the blacks join in the triumphant parade after the hero and heroine's horse has won the steeplechase. Anderson's singing in the film cannot compare with the recording she made with the Ellington orchestra, nor can the playing of the song by the studio orchestra hold a candle to the Ellington ensemble's two recorded performances. In *The Swing Era*, Schuller discusses Ellington's score for the nine-minute film, *Symphony in Black*, recorded in March 1935, which the critic says contains "some of Ellington's most affecting music" (p. 72). After outlining Ellington's musical score for the four episodes of the film (which won an Academy Award for the best musical short subject) and characterizing it as mournful, moaning, and gloomy, Schuller concludes with a summation of the remarkable achievement of black music: "As depressing as this scenario may sound in description, the music somehow expresses hope. It is what we can observe so often in black music, especially the blues: the pathos of grief and despair, expressed without self-pity and sentimentality, without whimpering. The music, though inexpressibly sad, nonetheless radiates inner beauty and nobility" (p. 73).

96. "Choo Choo" is included on *The Birth of Big Band Jazz: Duke Ellington—Fletcher Henderson*. Nanton's plunger trombone can be heard on "The Creeper" from December 29, 1926, and his growl on "New Orleans Low Down" from February 3, 1927, both included on *Duke Ellington: The Beginning* (Decca DL 9224, n.d.).

97. Spike Hughes, "Impressions of Ellington in New York," in *The Duke Ellington Reader*, ed. Mark Tucker (New York: Oxford University Press, 1993), pp. 70–71.

98. Schuller, *Early Jazz*, p. 341. "Misty Morning" and "Mood Indigo" are included on *The Original Edward "Duke" Ellington Hits*, Vol. 1 1927/1931 (King Jazz, KJ 144 FS, 1993); "Awful Sad" on *Duke Ellington: "Hot in Harlem" (1928–1929), Vol. 2* (MCA Records, MCA-2076).

99. Schuller, *The Swing Era*, pp. 122–123. "Dusk" is on *The Indispensable Duke Ellington Vol. 5/6 (1940)* (RCA 66674–2 B, 1992).

100. Duke Ellington, as quoted on "Harlem Air Shaft" in the liner notes to *At His Very Best: Duke Ellington and His Orchestra* (RCA Victor, LPM-1715, 1959). "Ring Dem Bells" is included on *The Original Edward "Duke" Ellington Hits* and "Harlem Air Shaft" on *The Indispensable Duke Ellington*.

101. Duke Ellington, "Washington," from *Music Is My Mistress* (1973), excerpted in *The Duke Ellington Reader*, p. 17.

102. Schuller, *The Swing Era*, p. 72. The description of "Sophisticated Lady" is in Dance's liner notes to *The Ellington Era 1927–1940, Vol. One*.

103. Schuller, *The Swing Era*, p. 83.

104. Liner notes to *Duke Ellington Vol. 10—Rockin' in Rhythm*.

105. Collier, *The Making of Jazz*, p. 248.

106. Giddins, *Visions of Jazz*, p. 116.

107. Schuller, *The Swing Era*, p. 50.

108. Dance, liner notes to *The Ellington Era 1927–1940 Volume One*.

109. Dance, liner notes to *The Ellington Era 1927–1940 Volume Two*, which includes both "Swing Low" and "Sweet Chariot."

110. Schuller, *The Swing Era*, p. 57.

111. Dance, liner notes to *The Ellington Era 1927–1940 Volume Two*.

112. Schuller, *The Swing Era*, p. 69.

113. Ibid., p. 72.

114. Ibid., p. 71.

115. Gioia, *The History of Jazz*, p. 183; Williams, *The Jazz Tradition*, p. 118.

116. Schuller, *The Swing Era*, p. 103.

117. Ibid., p. 93.

118. Ibid.

119. Ibid.

120. Gioia, *The History of Jazz*, p. 184.

121. Ibid., p. 183; Schuller, *The Swing Era*, p. 93.

122. Dance, liner notes to *The Ellington Era 1927–1940 Volume Two*; Schuller, *The Swing Era*, p. 87.

123. Schuller, *The Swing Era*, pp. 87–88.

124. Ibid., p. 97.

125. Dance, liner notes to *The Ellington Era 1927–1940 Volume Two*.

126. Schuller, *The Swing Era*, p. 97.

127. George Avakian, liner notes to *The Music of Duke Ellington Played by Duke Ellington* (Columbia CL 558, n.d.).

128. Schuller, *The Swing Era*, p. 94.

129. Avakian, liner notes to *The Music of Duke Ellington*.

130. Schuller, *The Swing Era*, p. 105.

131. Hodeir, *Jazz: Its Evolution and Essence*, pp. 80, 84, 86, 90, and 93.

132. Ibid., p. 89.

133. Schuller, *The Swing Era*, p. 126.

134. Ibid., p. 583.

135. Collier, *The Making of Jazz*, p. 257.

136. Nat Hentoff, liner notes to *In a Mellotone: Duke Ellington and His Orchestra* (RCA Victor LPM-1364, 1956).

137. Hodeir, *Jazz: Its Evolution and Essence*, p. 89; McCarthy, *Big Band Jazz*, p. 251.

138. Ralph J. Gleason, "Jimmie Lunceford," from *Celebrating the Duke* (1975), rpt. in *Reading Jazz*, p. 496.

139. Ibid., pp. 497–498.

140. Ibid., p. 499.

141. Ibid., p. 494.

142. Schuller, *The Swing Era*, p. 213.

143. Gleason, "Jimmie Lunceford," pp. 495–496, 498.

144. Ibid., p. 497.

145. Ibid., pp. 496 and 500.

146. McCarthy, p. 254. The Lunceford film photograph appears on page 251.

147. Gleason, "Jimmie Lunceford," p. 500. "Flaming Reeds and Screaming Brass" is available on *Jimmie Lunceford: The Classic Tracks* (Kaz Records KAZ CD 317, 1996), and both it and "While Love Lasts" are on *Lunceford Special* (Columbia CS 9515, n.d. but a 1967 *Down Beat* article is mentioned in the liner notes by Stanley Dance).

148. Dance, liner notes to *Lunceford Special*.

149. Schuller, *The Swing Era*, p. 208.

150. Ibid., p. 206.

151. Ibid., p. 207.

152. Ibid., p. 437. Hawkins's "Queer Notions" was recorded with the Henderson orchestra and Norvo's "Dance of the Octopus" with the Paul Whiteman Orchestra.

153. Ibid., p. 516.

154. Liner notes to *Music for Hi-Fi Bugs Conducted and Arranged by Pete Rugolo* (EmArcy MG 36082, 1956).

155. Schuller, *The Swing Era*, p. 210.

156. See page 11 of the CD insert for *The Jimmie Lunceford Orchestra: Stomp It Off* (Decca GRD 608, 1992).

157. Schuller, *The Swing Era*, pp. 210–211.

158. See Alain Gerber's liner notes to *Jimmie Lunceford 2: "Harlem Shout" (1935–1936)* (MCA Records, MCA-1305, 1980).

159. Schuller, *The Swing Era*, pp. 211–212.

160. Oliphant, *Texan Jazz*, pp. 161–162.

161. Giddins, *Visions of Jazz*, p. 164.

162. Tirro, *Jazz: A History*, p. 227.

163. Schuller, *The Swing Era*, pp. 214–215.

164. This version of "Cotton Club Stomp" is on *Duke Ellington at the Cotton Club* (RCA Camden, CAL-459). It should not be confused with the one made later on April 22, 1930, which is reproduced on *Duke Ellington: Rockin' in Rhythm Vol. 3 (1929–1931)* (MCA Records, MCA-2077, 1970).

165. Schuller, *The Swing Era*, p. 212.

166. Ibid., p. 213.

167. Ibid., p. 215.

168. Stowe, *Swing Changes*, pp. 32–33.

169. Oliphant, *Texan Jazz*, pp. 164–166.

170. Stanley Dance, liner notes to *Lunceford Special*.

171. Schuller, *The Swing Era*, pp. 218–219.

172. Ibid., p. 219.

173. Gleason, "Jimmie Lunceford," p. 499.

Chapter 3

The Name White Bands

Although the Paul Whiteman Orchestra and the Casa Loma Orchestra were the earliest successful white big bands of the 1930s, these two organizations would not in the long run exert the same level of influence, reap the same financial rewards, nor receive the same adoration of listeners as would the next generation of white big bands. Even though some of the future big-band leaders grew up hearing Bix Beiderbecke and Frankie Trumbauer and in some cases even performing with those Whiteman stars, the new generation of leaders would develop their bands during a different time and would leave behind the stiffer, more formal approaches of the Whiteman and Casa Loma orchestras, largely as a result of hearing and even associating with black musicians of the era. Although in the first half of the decade segregation still precluded mixed groups in public, the new generation would participate in recording sessions with black musicians, and most of the white big-band leaders would eventually hire black players for their small or large units. Hailing from Chicago, Shenandoah (Pennsylvania), New York City, and Clarinda (Iowa), these future big-band leaders would bring to jazz some of the same lyrical qualities inherent in the playing of Bix and Tram but would apply them to a big-band setting either through their own soloistic talents and/or through arrangements created by them or by their sidemen.

BENNY GOODMAN

Born on May 30, 1909, on the West Side of Chicago, Benny Goodman was active as a professional musician at age fourteen. In 1924, he took a job with the Ben Pollack band, which had relocated from the Chicago area to Venice, California, where Glenn Miller also soon arrived to join the Pollack outfit. All the major white big-band leaders of the 1930s would at one time or another play together in some group or other before eventually starting their own bands. And although all the name bandleaders of the era were hugely successful, Benny Goodman, who took the plunge as a leader in 1934, would definitely make the biggest splash. The crucial role played by Goodman in broadening the appeal of jazz to a vast commercial audience is undeniable, and this is indicated by the fact that Gunther Schuller in his seminal 1989 study, *The Swing Era*, and Lewis Erenberg in his 1998 study, *Swingin' the Dream*, both begin their books with Goodman as the "King" of Swing.

Retelling the oft-told tale of Goodman's August 1935 triumph at the Palomar Ballroom in Los Angeles, Erenberg recounts the disheartening trip West during which, at each stop along the way to California, the band was greeted with less and less enthusiasm. When it appeared that the crowd at the Palomar was equally indifferent, even when "the orchestra opened with its more conventionally melodic numbers,"[1] Goodman, thinking this meant the end of the line for his unit, called for their Fletcher Henderson arrangements and "a roar rose from the crowd," and with that "the swing era, one of the defining moments in American popular music, was born."[2] As Schuller says, it was John Hammond, the wealthy New York promoter of jazz, who convinced Goodman, despite his seeing "little value in the music of orchestras like Henderson's," to hire Fletcher as his arranger—"It took Hammond to effect this collaboration."[3] And as Schuller concludes, "it was Fletcher (and Horace) Henderson's arrangements that turned the tide for Goodman."[4]

Before Goodman's rise to the Swing Era throne, he had certainly done much on his own to merit the high position he assumed in the minds of the audience that crowned him "King." From 1928 to 1933, he had made hundreds of studio recordings, had directed pit bands for Gershwin Broadway shows, had worked with all the leading white musicians of the period, and had recorded with two of the greatest black female jazz singers of all time, Bessie Smith and Billie Holiday (sessions arranged by Hammond). Like Bix Beiderbecke, who often performed brilliantly in rather mediocre company, Benny Goodman was a hot player who, as Schuller notes, could perk up any music with his solos that "momentarily injected an element of jazz."[5] Just one example is a Red Nichols & His Five Pennies recording of "The Sheik of Araby" from July 3, 1930.[6] Although this side features a Jack Teagarden vocal and his brother Charlie on trumpet and includes future big-band stars Glenn Miller and Gene Krupa, it is Goodman alone who provides any true jazz spirit to an otherwise rather lackluster affair. Goodman's solo is marked by many of his characteristic qualities, among them his technical facility, his fine sense of swing, and his turns, ornaments, and blues-ish touches, which make his solos consistently satisfying. As a big-band leader, he would attract a number of outstanding soloists who complemented his own always driving and at times exciting breaks. Also, it is to Goodman's credit that, as Ted Gioia points out, "Many jazz enthusiasts rejoiced in Goodman's conscious decision to emulate the hotter music of the Henderson orchestra—a direction that few white bands of the day were then taking—and bring this swinging style to the attention of the mass market."[7]

The Goodman band that traveled cross-country to California included trumpeter Bunny Berigan, who performs on three Fletcher Henderson arrangements recorded in July 1935 prior to the trip West. It can only be imagined what the Henderson band would have done with Fletcher's arrangement of "Sometimes I'm Happy," but for the most part the Goodman orchestra's performance is polite in comparison with the playing of a Henderson unit. However, it certainly is not as tame as the Goodman recording of "Goodbye," from September 27, 1935, which was used by the leader "as a come-on theme" at the Palomar rather than "Let's Dance," the better-known theme of his radio show.[8] The leader's decision to go ahead and play the jazzier arrangements like Henderson's "Sometimes I'm Happy" and "King Porter Stomp" turned out to be a momentous piece of resolve. For had he stuck with charts like "Goodbye," the history of the swing era might have been sadly different. Even so, "Sometimes I'm Happy" can at first almost put one to sleep. The dragging theme statement at the beginning of the piece is deadly, and only Berigan's somewhat swaggering entry livens things up. But the second half of Berigan's solo is truly a marvelous piece of jazz and one of the finest breaks ever taken by a sideman with the "King." Yet once again a tenor solo by Adrian Rollini almost has the listener sawing logs. The sax section is precise but on the saccharine side. The brass section provides some contrasting fire, but it quickly goes out, and not even Goodman's brief appearances help rekindle the flame. All this may be a bit unfair, because the Goodman band's sound and style of sweet swing are obviously quite different from the usually hard-charging approach of the Henderson bands. In some ways the more sophisticated, not so "rough" treatment of the tune by the Goodman unit may account for his organization's ultimate success, whereas the Henderson recordings may have been too aggressive, at least for a larger, less jazz-oriented audience. It may also be owing to the slower tempi for tunes like "Sometimes I'm Happy" and the later "Christopher Columbus" that the Goodman form of jazz proved more accessible to swing-era listeners.[9]

With the Goodman recording of "King Porter Stomp," which apparently was the piece that brought a roar from the crowd at the Palomar, the band as a whole definitely shows that it really could dig into a classic such as Morton's masterpiece. Also, Gunther Schuller finds "the low unison trombones behind Goodman's solo an ingenious revision of Henderson's original."[10] Berigan's statement of Morton's theme, though played with a mute, makes for a powerful opening, and even the much-maligned Harry Goodman's bass adds greatly to Berigan's driving delivery. Berigan's open solo following Red Ballard's trombone break is, like the rest of the performance, "alive . . . because of its buoyant spirit and expressive energy."[11] The call-

and-response by brass and reeds is certainly lively if still quite subdued compared with a Henderson performance. An arrangement by Spud Murphy of "Jingle Bells," from September 27, 1935, actually finds Goodman playing a hotter solo than on "Sometimes I'm Happy" and "King Porter Stomp"; Berigan again is quite engaging; and even Rollini's chorus has to it more of a rollicking swing. Although rather old hat by now, the clarinet trio is yet effective in keeping things going and providing a contrasting section. Joe Harris's vocal on another Henderson arrangement, of Johnny Mercer's "Santa Claus Came in the Spring," also from September 27, is typical of the very popular singers that would become attached to most every big band.[12] Harris sings more in the Jack Teagarden style on "Basin Street Blues," from November 22, which would be expected on the tune the Texas trombonist made his own. Harris's trombone solo also imitates, quite impressively, the Teagarden manner. This tune, again, was arranged by Henderson. However, on the whole, there are no soloists on these 1935 sides—except for Berigan—who challenge the best of the black sidemen with Henderson. And although the arrangements are mostly by Henderson, the performances tend to represent a more toned-down form of jazz.

From the overall evidence of the 1935 recordings, the Goodman orchestra was not destined to overshadow the great black bands of the era on the level of creative jazz, even though it did in terms of popularity. So what was it that so thrilled the crowd at the Palomar? One can only think that it had never heard a live orchestra of the quality of a Henderson, Moten, Ellington, or Lunceford. Henderson's bands had recorded superior performances from 1930 to 1934, Ellington's band the same, Moten's in 1930 and 1932, and Lunceford's in 1933 and 1934. Ellington, as we saw, also had been to Hollywood, where he recorded "Ring Dem Bells" in 1930. Was it that California audiences did not hear those groups' recordings because of the segregation of "race records" from the white market? Or was it simply due to prejudice that the Palomar audience received with open arms a white band unknowingly playing mostly black arrangements? All these factors may be part of the explanation, or not. In fact, it may simply be a case of the audience at that moment being ready for such music and of the band having played a live set with much more gusto than on its studio recordings.

It is known that the late-night NBC *Let's Dance* radio program, which broadcast the Goodman band from New York, was received at an earlier hour on the West Coast and was therefore listened to by Californians at a time when any would-be audience on the East Coast was already fast asleep. Just to have heard the Goodman band playing its swinging, infectious "Let's Dance" theme song, based on Carl Maria von Weber's "Invitation to the Dance," one would think would have been enough to have attracted the Palomar crowd, even though elsewhere in the country the piece seems to have fallen on deaf ears. Other explanations for the reception of Goodman are offered by Erenberg in *Swingin' the Dream* and Stowe in *Swing Changes* when they argue that the new populist spirit in the United States helped foster greater awareness of black culture and greater appreciation for its achievements, although how this would account for the appeal of Goodman's brand of jazz is not entirely clear. These two historians also attribute the increased opportunities for such music to the repeal of Prohibition. Whatever the reason for Goodman's success, where the better black bands had failed to gain a broad popular following, he, through his sudden popularity, clearly paved the way for greater exposure for other bands, including that of Count Basie, who organized his orchestra in 1935 and first recorded the following year, thanks again to John Hammond.

If Goodman's orchestra in 1935 did not reach the same level as the black bands in terms of jazz production, it would as a group develop with time a more distinctive style and spirit, even though no soloist would ever quite match the best work of Bunny Berigan. With the addition at the beginning of 1937 of Harry James on trumpet, the Goodman orchestra would become even more popular and would elicit even greater enthusiasm from its audiences. But even before the arrival of James as lead trumpet, soloist, and arranger, the band made a number of recordings in 1936 that show its growing improvement. For example, the Goodman version of "Christopher Columbus," from March 20, actually predates the Henderson recording by one week and is a praiseworthy rendition, even if the tempo drags a bit compared with that of the Henderson side.[13] Berigan plays with power and his solo definitely swings, as does the very fine break on trombone by Joe Harris. Goodman squeezes out of his clarinet some of his affectively silken smoothness as well as his "dirty" bends and blue notes. The Goodman version does not offer any solos of the same forward-looking caliber as those of Roy Eldridge and Chu Berry on the Henderson recording, but the overall performance approaches the high standards for jazz set by the black bands. A piece such as "Tain't No Use," from November 5, 1936, shows the smooth swing the Goodman band could achieve, whereas "Bugle Call Rag," from the same session, generates commendable energy, with a tenor solo by Vido Musso that is in the true spirit of the period, as are the breaks by Ziggy Elman on trumpet and Murray McEachern on trombone.[14] Gene Krupa by now has come into his own as a show drummer who genuinely adds to the ferment of many a performance. Best of all from the same November recording date is "Jam Session," which, like the first two pieces, was arranged by Jimmy Mundy, a black arranger who had come to Goodman from the Earl Hines orchestra. Krupa drives Vido Musso's tenor solo with snare-drum, and Elman delivers a stirring solo complete with "a dazzingly executed 5-bar descending and ascending glissando." However, Harry James will outdo Elman when he takes the solo spot for another version of "Jam Session" done on a 1937 radio broadcast, where Goodman's own solo is also far more effective.[15] The relaxed swing of "Did You Mean It?," also from November 5, is definitely infectious and goes far toward explaining why audiences, black or white, were drawn irresistibly to the dance floor when the Goodman band performed. Ella Fitzgerald's vocal, and even more her singing on "Goodnight My Love," also from November 5, is not only a plus but indicates one of the important contributions Goodman made to jazz and to racial relations.[16] In 1935, he already had begun to play in public with black pianist Teddy Wilson and would continue to hire other black musicians, among them vibraharpist Lionel Hampton and electric guitarist Charlie Christian—and Goodman was the first white bandleader to do so.

Other pieces recorded by the Goodman orchestra that predate versions by major black artists of the period include "He Ain't Got Rhythm" and "These Foolish Things."[17] The Goodman treatment of "He Ain't Got Rhythm" is from December 30, 1936, whereas the Lunceford orchestra would record the Berlin tune on January 26, 1937. The Goodman recording may excel even Lunceford's fine version, if for no other reason than the presence of Jimmy Rushing as Goodman's vocalist. As usual, "Mr. Five-by-Five" belts out the lyrics of this song in his inimitably robust voice.[18] However, in the case of "These Foolish Things," which Goodman recorded on June 15, 1936, with Helen Ward doing the vocal, this performance—and especially Ward's vocal—points up the vast difference between jazz musicians such as Rushing and Billie Holiday and the crooners featured by almost every white big band of the era. Two weeks later, accompanied by a star-studded group led by Teddy Wilson, Holiday would deliver the lines of "These Foolish Things" with her slightly gruff voice and her falls at the ends of phrases that offset the sentiment of the lyrics and yet make the words so deeply moving. Wilson's piano introduction sets the mood wonderfully, Harry Carney blows one of his magisterial baritone breaks, and Johnny Hodges furnishes an obbligato that underscores Holiday's floating, emotive notes.[19] In comparison, Ward's rendition comes across as overly romantic and not nearly so intensely felt, even though Ward also employs at times a fall at the end of a phrase. Murray McEachern's trombone solo, backed by George Van Eps on guitar, is likewise typical of the sentimental style of so many white trombonists, in particular Tommy Dorsey. The background figures from the band especially sweeten this version, and the ending leaves a rather cloying taste in the ear. Ward's vocal on "Sing Me a Swing Song (And Let Me Dance)," from May 27, is more appealing, for here she really swings, and both the ensemble's introduction and Goodman's break effectively build up to her entrance. Goodman's solo following the vocal is one of his more driving and inventive efforts. An even earlier vocal by Ward on "Goody Goody," from January 24, is a novelty piece that was bound to find a receptive audience, and of course success breeds acceptance even by a singer such as Ward who reportedly "hated ['Goody Goody'] when we cut it. Absolutely hated it. But I sure love it now."[20]

Two other Fletcher Henderson arrangements from 1936 are of the Alex Hill-Claude Hopkins-Roberto Williams tune "(I Would Do) Anything for You," and Henderson's "Down South Camp Meeting."[21] Henderson's own recording of the latter has been discussed in chapter 2. By comparison, once again, the Goodman is less assertive, and the solo by the leader and the ensemble passages are smoothly swinging but generally mild versions beside the Henderson original. The trio section is well played by the Goodman band and captures the spirit of Henderson's composition, but throughout the piece, beginning with the opening passages with their sax trills, there is not the same intensely driving execution as on the Henderson recording from 1934. Comparing these two recordings shows that big-band jazz had not progressed in terms of arranging or sectional work, for the Henderson unit already had established the standard, and the Goodman does not go beyond it or contribute anything special to the performance of the same piece.

Harry James's first session with the Goodman band was on January 14, 1937, and his presence as the leader of the "Biting Brass" gave the band even greater punch, as on "I Want to Be Happy," although here Gene Krupa becomes a bit too overbearing. Ahead of Ellington in recording on this same date "Chloe," which Duke would not cut until 1940, Goodman renders this piece with finesse and excellent swing. Pianist Jess Stacy takes a brief but delightful break, and the entire ensemble executes its parts with admirable precision. Nonetheless, there is not the character and depth here that is to be found in the Ellington version, which features Nanton's talking plunger-muted trombone, Lawrence Brown's warm, evocative tone, a haunting solo by Blanton on bass, Ben Webster's rhapsodic tenor, and Cootie Williams's climactic trumpet. Above all, what makes the Ellington performance so rich is his arrangement, which, as Nat Hentoff writes, "sound[s] as if it were an Ellington original."[22] It is perhaps unfair to compare these two versions, because it is like speaking of apples and pears, and to praise one rendition at the expense of another that is valuable in its own right does not do justice to valid differences. Also, for Hentoff to say that prior to Ellington's version of "Chloe" the song "had rarely, if ever, before connoted jazz of any kind" is to slight Goodman's very respectable recording that is certainly jazz of a kind.[23] As for the January 14 Goodman recording of "Rosetta," this has in the reed section's phrasing and voicing a distinctive sound clearly identifiable as that of the Goodman band, and Allan Reuss's guitar break is especially fine. Goodman's "Rosetta" is certainly different from the version produced in 1934 by Earl Hines and His Orchestra, which the Goodman recording has left far behind in terms of a smooth and cohesive swing. By this time it is quite understandable why the Goodman band could enjoy such a broad appeal and why black musicians such as Teddy Wilson, Ella Fitzgerald, and Jimmy Rushing would be eager to appear with the "King" of Swing.

Having elsewhere traced the source of Harry James's "Peckin' " to a solo by Cootie Williams in a 1931 recording of Ellington's "Rockin' in Rhythm," it is only necessary to note here that "Peckin'," from July 6, 1937, also shows off James's solo style, with its swagger that even upstages that of Berigan on "Sometimes I'm Happy."[24] "Can't We Be Friends," from the same date, although a very appropriate tune for the Goodman approach to swing, opens with the rather fumbling trombone of Murray McEachern and points up one of the persistent weaknesses of the band: other than Goodman (who solos effectively here), Berigan (whose tenure was brief), Musso (on occasion), Elman, and James, there were few really outstanding soloists. Later, as we shall see, Bud Freeman contributed significantly, and as mentioned earlier, Jess Stacy could with his rare appearances make a favorable impression. Also from July 6, "Sing, Sing, Sing," a showcase for Krupa's percussion work, is basically a boring piece, a riff driven into the ground while Gene whales away pointlessly. Even Goodman and James offer little worth a second hearing. That such a trance-inducing performance was quite attractive at the time reminds one that something similar is always fascinating to the youth of any age, which again demonstrates the fact of Goodman's broad appeal, including as it did college students, workers, and adolescents. More interesting is Mary Lou Williams's arrangement of "Roll 'Em," from July 7, on which Stacy takes a tasty chorus, after which the ensemble leads into and backs up well-conceived solos by Goodman and James, followed by a punchy call-and-response exchange between saxes and brass. Fletcher Henderson's arrangement of "When It's Sleepy Time Down South," also recorded by Goodman on the seventh, brings back the identifiable Goodman sax sound and a relaxed swing that obviously stimulates soloists Vido Musso and James to some solid breaks. Likewise, Henderson's arrangement of "Changes," from the same date, shows off the saxes' precision playing and a stair-step trumpet-section passage that builds to an in-your-face break by James.

It is hard to listen to Martha Tilton's vocal on "I Can't Give You Anything but Love," of September 6, and take it seriously, after having heard Fats Waller's later witty rendition from 1939.[25] In fact, after a while, many such Goodman tunes begin to pall, especially Tilton's singing of pieces such as "Let That Be a Lesson to You" and "Pop-Corn Man," from October 22.[26] These lack the satirical force of the Lunceford vocals and the imaginative solos and ensemble work that accompany them, which recalls a statement by Ellington quoted by Gunther Schuller from a February 1939 *Down Beat*:

It's not very difficult to understand the evolution of Jazz into Swing. Ten years ago this type of music was flourishing, albeit amidst adverse conditions and surrounded by hearty indifference.

. . . It is the repetition and monotony of the present-day Swing arrangements which bode ill for the future. Once again it is proven that when the artistic point of view gains commercial standing, artistry itself bows out, leaving inspiration to die a slow death. The present dearth of creative and original music is not, I'm convinced, due to a lack of talent.[27]

Ellington's view is illustrated to a certain extent by the Goodman recording of Edgar Sampson's "Don't Be That Way," from February 16, 1938. This tune, as played by the Goodman band, was one of its biggest hits and still holds up today. But the fact that it was originally recorded in 1934 by the Chick Webb Orchestra, in a lively performance that includes superior solos and more interesting contrasts and variety in the arrangement, supports Ellington's idea that mere repetition of what was once "creative and original music" is an indication of the loss of artistry that began to afflict such swing-era big bands as Goodman's. On the other hand, by recording its version of Oliver's "Sugar Foot Stomp," on September 6, 1937, the Goodman band did pay homage to that classic work and in a sense helped keep it alive.[28]

It can be said for the Goodman interpretation of "Don't Be That Way" that it is so different from the Webb that it *is* in a way "creative and original music." As Loren Schoenberg asserts, "While Webb's band had its share of outstanding soloists and the peerless drumming of its leader to commend it, the Goodman interpretations of these pieces [two different takes] are the definitive ones."[29] First of all, the tempo is just right for dancing, and both the sax section's mellow sound, with the conspicuous baritone an attractive touch, and the muted trumpets' crisp punctuations lend to the performance a freshness that it still retains. Goodman's solo entry also is just right, and both James and McEachern's breaks (the latter in imitation of Jack Teagarden), if not up to those of Webb's sidemen, are certainly serviceable. Only the fade-away ending was so overused during the period that, as Ellington warned, its monotony did bode ill. As for Basie's "One O'Clock Jump," recorded by Goodman at the same session, Schoenberg is accurate in owning up to the fact that there is no way that the Goodman version is definitive or anything close to the original.[30] But it is obvious that the Goodman interpretation is intended, like that of "Sugar Foot Stomp," as a tribute to Basie and his sidemen. Ellington again is right: it is not a matter of talent, there is plenty here but little creative originality. Nevertheless, the fact that a white band acknowledged the existence of a black band's theme song, through reproducing it in its basic style, reflects the deep respect that jazz musicians did feel for one another's work and certainly contributed to the beginning of a breakdown of racial prejudice during the 1930s. This is fully evident with the Carnegie Hall concert arranged by John Hammond in January 1938, which brought together musicians in the orchestras of Basie and Ellington, for a joint performance with members of Goodman's unit.

The Carnegie Hall Concert of January 16 was more of a symbolic production than it was a begetter of great jazz. In general the music is uninspired and uninspiring. Conceived in part as a tribute to "Twenty Years of Jazz," the program began with the Goodman band's versions of "Don't Be That Way," "Sometimes I'm Happy," and "One O'Clock Jump." Afterward, homage was paid to the Original Dixieland Jazz Band (ODJB) with a rendering of Nick La Rocca's "Sensation Rag," to Beiderbecke's solo on "I'm Coming Virginia," to Ted Lewis, to Louis Armstrong, and to Duke Ellington. The Bix and Louie renditions by Bobby Hackett and Harry James have been discussed previously in chapter 1. As for the intended ODJB tribute, this turned out to be more of a pathetic pastiche. Vernon Brown's trombone is an embarrassing attempt to imitate the countermelody style of the ODJB's Eddie Edwards, who, along with other members of the pioneering New Orleans band, had just recorded in 1936 what Richard Sudhalter implies are six unjustly neglected sides.[31] (One might wonder why the organizers of the program did not invite the ODJB to perform for themselves. The obvious answer lies in the controversy created by La Rocca, who "expressed contempt for anyone who tried to credit black jazzmen with any part in the creative process," which naturally would have defeated the purpose of the Carnegie Hall Concert.[32]) Ellington's "Blue Reverie" fortunately was performed essentially by some of his own men, Johnny Hodges, Harry Carney, and Cootie Williams, but not the Duke himself or his rhythm section—Stacy is on piano and a heavy-handed Krupa on drums. Hodges's chorus on soprano sax is superb, as usual, and one of the most satisfying solos of the entire concert; Harry Carney's brief, very lyrical break is delightful; and Cootie Williams's muted wah-wah and growl are in the grand tradition of Miley and Nanton. James's arrangement of "Life Goes to a Party" is one big-band piece that definitely offers a bit of excitement to the enthusiastic audience, with all three solos—by tenor Babe Russin (especially fine), Goodman, and James—giving the crowd something worth cheering about. But the Goodman band's encore of Horace Henderson's "Big John's Special" is far below the original 1934 Henderson recording—it is primarily a feature for James and Krupa's pathetic playing to the gallery. "Sing, Sing, Sing," also pitched to the gallery, was greeted with great hoopla and immediately became a best-seller.

The racial symbolism of the occasion was brought home fully with the mixed Jam Session based on Fats Waller's "Honeysuckle Rose." Lester Young solos effectively; Count Basie at the piano elicits for his part a burst of spontaneous applause; and both Buck Clayton and Johnny Hodges solo respectably. James, Goodman, and Krupa do not hold up their end in terms of quality work, their emphasis being once again on showmanship and exhibitionism. It must be said that such a jam session was not really the forte of any of the participants, with the possible exception of Basie and Young, who turn in the most satisfying moments. The other mixed groups were those of Goodman, his trio with Krupa and pianist Teddy Wilson, and his quartet with the addition of Lionel Hampton on vibraphone. The brand of toned-down jazz presented by the trio and quartet on pieces such as "Body and Soul" and "The Man I Love" is in dramatic contrast to the more stirring pieces such as "Avalon" and "I Got Rhythm," on the latter of which all the parties show their stuff, especially Hampton, whose improvisations are rather more stimulating than those of his colleagues. The polish of the groups is impressive and must have made it clear to the audience how well black and white could work together to produce the swing it had come to hear. Wilson on "The Man I Love" displays his impressive purity of sound and technique, and Krupa must be credited with providing a solid beat without the assistance of bass or guitar. Krupa's equally impressive technique is also fully in evidence, if, as usual, a bit too much so.

Following intermission, the big band came back with a Fletcher Henderson arrangement of "Blue Skies," "a celebrated best-seller in the Goodman record catalog since it was produced in 1937."[33] Not much can be said for it today except that it contains most of the Goodman band's typical features, including the punch of the trumpet section and James's attractive solo. The less said about "Loch Lomond," with vocalist Martha Tilton ("in pink party dress and blonde hair"), the better, even though this was evidently a popular sort of number that began to take over the swing movement and undermine its original relationship to jazz as such.[34] "Blue Room," the other Henderson arrangement, was intended to acknowledge, along with Irving Berlin's "Blue Skies" and Gershwin's "The Man I Love" and "I Got Rhythm," the vital contribution made to jazz by American popular music. Jimmy Mundy's "killer-diller" arrangement of "Swingtime in the Rockies" features Ziggy Elman's trumpet solo, which is more spectacular than anything James offers during this prestigious affair. After this came a tribute to the Jewish side of jazz, represented by Elman's fine "Frahlich" trumpet on "Bei Mir Bist Du Schon," also arranged by Mundy. The number of important Jewish jazz figures during the Swing Era included Goodman, Elman, Artie Shaw, and Bud Freeman, to name but a few. Of course, as indicated earlier, the popular song field was dominated by Jewish composers. Although the Jewish role as such may not have been a prominent aspect of the Carnegie Hall symbolism (was perhaps even played down), it was in fact a tremendously significant part of the story of the Swing Era. In speaking of this role, Lewis Erenberg remarks that Goodman, as a product of the poor Jewish Chicago west side, was able to serve as a cultural bridge between the white and black worlds because he, like many other Jewish artists, was able to understand both. As a white man, he was more acceptable to the majority society than an African American man would be. As a member of a marginal group that throughout history had known persecution and enslavement, however, he could appreciate the tensions, anxieties, and oppression in African American music and culture.

Both musical cultures, moreover, feature the blue note and the wail, as well as a delight in ecstatic release from the burdens of living.[35]

The trio rendering of "China Boy" has one of Goodman's best solos of the concert, as well as Krupa's most impressive display of his drumming skills, both abetted beautifully by Wilson's piano accompaniment. However, "Stompin' at the Savoy" by the quartet is mostly high jinks, as is "Dizzy Spells," where on both the emphasis is almost purely technique, of which all four players certainly had more than enough for showing off. Goodman's big band had recorded "Stompin' at the Savoy" in 1936, and that remains a more appetizing version of Edgar Sampson's original than is the quartet rendition. But then, as Gunther Schuller has commented, to hear Sampson's tune as it "was *supposed* to sound, one only need listen to Chick Webb's 1934 recording."[36] Yet it was important for the symbolism that even a second-rate performance of "Stompin' at the Savoy" should have been included in order to pay tribute to another fine arranger such as Sampson and indirectly to Webb's place in the jazz pantheon. It is to Goodman and Hammond's credit that so much of jazz history was in fact recognized by this first appearance of the music in the hallowed Carnegie Hall. Bringing respect to jazz was one of Goodman and Hammond's most meaningful contributions, and this concert at Carnegie Hall made possible other such appearances, including in 1939 Hammond's "Spirituals to Swing" concert and in 1943 the first in a series of concerts by the Duke Ellington Orchestra.

During the rest of 1938, the Goodman band recorded a number of Fletcher Henderson arrangements, among them "Wrappin' It Up," from May 28, which has been taken as the title of a CD tracing Harry James's final period with Goodman. At the beginning of 1939, the trumpet star left to form his own big band, but even before James left, Krupa departed in March 1938 and was replaced on drums first by Lionel Hampton and then by Dave Tough. Hearing a subdued Hampton on "Ti-Pi-Tin" and "The Blue Room," from March 9, the first post-Krupa cuts by the band, I personally want to yell "good riddance." What also helps make these two pieces satisfying is the presence of Basie guitarist Freddie Green and bassist Walter Page, as well as Lester Young, who solos beautifully on "Ti-Pi-Tin." With Dave Tough's arrival the band really swings in a relaxed way that it never had before—Schuller says that basically with Krupa "far too often the bass and drums do not swing; they merely keep time—and this, ironically, in the very band that was perceived as having initiated the swing craze."[37] Tough's effect on both Goodman and James's playing is immeasurably to the good. Also, the difference between the performance at Carnegie Hall and the Tough-led recording of Horace Henderson's "Big John's Special," also from May 28, is simply amazing. James really digs into himself rather than just showboating, and as a result comes up with one of his finest efforts ever, while Jess Stacy sounds right at home with his former

Chicago drummer chum. And the performance of "Wrappin' It Up" is totally worthy of the Henderson chart, and features again one of James's finest moments, as well as a quirky solo by Dave Mathews, who assumed the lead alto part, and a brief appearance by Bud Freeman, who had joined the band at the same time as Tough. And miracle of miracles, Martha Tilton's vocal on "Could You Pass in Love?"—also from this date—is a keeper, swinging with just the right feel and intonation. "Margie," from September 14, finds Goodman in top form, swinging in an infectious way that only he could manage at his best. James, too, is marvelous. This performance is every bit as good as the fine Lunceford recording.

The impact of Dave Tough and Bud Freeman on the Goodman band is summarized concisely by Richard Sudhalter when he writes that "it had a salutary effect on the leader: often, on these records, Benny's solos seem closer to the hot music spirit of Chicago days, the intensity and focus that illuminated his work with Ben Pollack."[38] These performances with Tough and Freeman certainly lay to rest the idea that white musicians could not compare with their black counterparts. Nonetheless, it should be said that "Margie," "Wrappin' It Up," and "Topsy"—the last of these, from November 10, with a particularly fine solo by Freeman—had all been recorded first by the black bands, and in the case of Henderson's "Wrappin' It Up" and Durham's "Topsy" were written by black composer-arrangers.

Bud Freeman's first solos are heard on "Lullaby in Rhythm" and "Sweet Sue," from April 8, the former arranged by Edgar Sampson, as was "Could You Pass in Love?" Freeman is quite good on "Lullaby in Rhythm," even though he is stiffer than Young. All the soloists on this tune are effective, including Vernon Brown on trombone, who gives a fine accounting of himself—indeed, it is one of his best efforts. On "Sweet Sue," all the soloists—Goodman, James, and Freeman—turn in splendid breaks, even though the tempo tends to drag a bit, unlike the tempi on "Big John's Special" and "Wrappin' It Up." Other solid performances during this period include "Russian Lullaby," from September 14, on which both Goodman and James shine; "Bumble Bee Stomp," from October 13, an up piece with Tough's ride cymbal maintaining the tempo and swinging as well; and "Smoke House," from November 10, a nicely relaxed, vintage piece of swing arranged by Fred Norman, a trombonist who contributed greatly to the Claude Hopkins band of 1934–1935. Freeman, in his first break on "Bumble Bee Stomp," starts well but then falters a bit, and the same goes for his second break—he tends to lose track of where he is going and falls back on a sort of Dixieland stiffness that frequently plagued his playing. He is better on "Smoke House." (On "Topsy" and "Smoke House," Lionel Hampton had come back to take Tough's place.) The Goodman band's recording of "Farewell Blues," from November 23, which includes one of James's last and best solos, is an updating by Jimmy Mundy of the famous NORK tune first recorded in 1922.[39] Certainly most everything has changed in sixteen years (for example, no thumping rhythm section with banjo), but listening to that 1922 recording one cannot say that the 1938 Goodman performance is superior in terms of jazz artistry. Paul Mares's muted trumpet contains as much quality jazz in it as James's ostentatious display, which is yet deeply rooted in the original classic tune.

In December, Bud Freeman was replaced by Jerry Jerome, a close imitator of Lester Young and even of Freeman. After Tough's departure, the drumming did not really miss a beat with Hampton, who adequately filled the percussion chair. But Hampton was then replaced by Buddy Schutz, who was preferable to Krupa but nothing special, and during the final months of 1938, the band did not record very interesting material, even though most of the arrangements were by Fletcher Henderson. The fare now offered up tended to be sentimental songs, such as "It Had To Be You," "I'll Always Be in Love with You," "Louise," and "You and Your Love," the first three from December 12, 15, and 23, and the last from May 4, 1939.[40] Not much jazz figured in these performances, mostly just imitative work at best. However, as Loren Schoenberg indicates, "a new recording contract, with Columbia, was about to be signed and arranger Eddie Sauter was already at work on music that would whisk Benny and the band off to destinations both new and challenging."[41] One quite different direction is indicated by the recording of Jimmy Mundy's "Solo Flight," from March 4, 1941, a feature for electric guitarist Charlie Christian.[42] But this was to be a short-lived tangent, because Christian was dead by early 1942, and this appearance is the only recorded example of his work within the orchestral format. Christian's highly inventive, long-lined melodic passages, with their soulful explorations of the blues idiom and a type of western rhythmic drive, are essentially out of place in the context of the Goodman brand of arranged swing. However, if this arrangement for the Goodman orchestra plus Christian does not show the guitarist at his best, his recordings with the Goodman sextet, and even more during late-night jam sessions at Minton's in New York, display more fully Christian's revolutionary talents and are discussed in the chapter titled The Small Swing Groups.

Although Goodman and other swing-era leaders such as Artie Shaw felt the need to grow as musicians and looked for new ways to develop their music, the listeners by and large were wired to the best-sellers and wanted to hear them endlessly. Gunther Schuller cites as an example Goodman's August 1939 recording of his version of Count Basie's "Jumpin' at the Woodside," intended, as the critic suggests, to stay up with or get ahead of the competition.[43] This may be the reason as well for another recording, from October 24, 1939, of the Goodman band's own theme song, "Let's Dance," which, despite its having been heard countless times before, is, according to Schuller, "a perfect performance, with not a musical hair out of place: everything sparkles, including Goodman's quicksilver tone and flawless execution."[44] Goodman's opening and closing breaks are essentially the same ones that he had first played over five years before to introduce his radio show, and they still can please, especially when he rides in so smoothly over the ear-catching theme stated swingingly by saxes and brass. But obviously Goodman was ready for something new, and he certainly got it in Eddie Sauter's 1940 "Benny Rides Again," which may have been just what the doctor ordered as far as Goodman was concerned, but it is doubtful that his listeners were ready for the modern, at times dissonant sounds of Sauter's arrangement. Swing is no longer the thing here, for even though it is present at times, now the focus is on the arranger's manipulation of orchestral chords and colors. Goodman's clarinet still sounds technically flawless but the ideas are studied, not spontaneous-sounding, and certainly not swinging in the same sense as his playing on "Let's Dance." Another new feature for Goodman was Sauter's 1941 "Clarinet à la King," which actually manages more swing in between all the classical allusions (Schuller identifying Brahms and Wagner) and "disjointed bits of dissonant harmonies."[45] Goodman is indeed more impressive here than on "Benny Rides Again" by virtue of his showing an ability to improvise with virtuosic fervor in Sauter's unusual key changes and against the allusive material that makes up this "progressive" composition.[46]

During the final years of the thirties, Goodman introduced to his lineup new vocalists in Helen Forrest and Peggy Lee. Schuller considers the former, next to Jack Teagarden and Mildred Bailey, the finest white jazz singer of the entire Swing Era "before the coming of Frank Sinatra."[47] Schuller analyzes fully and appreciatively the Sauter arrangement for the Forrest vocal on "How High the Moon," from February 7, 1940, as an example of Sauter's being unequaled as a "master of harmonic modulation in jazz."[48] But more important than any of the Sauter arrangements or the female vocals was Goodman's activities from 1939 to 1941 as the leader of a sextet featuring electric guitarist Charlie Christian. As noted earlier, this aspect of Goodman's work is discussed in the chapter on The Small Swing Groups, but in this regard it should be added here that Goodman's contribution to the Swing Era was fundamental to its meaning as a period in which jazz became a byword for all that the United States represented around the world: freedom of expression, cultural diversity, imaginative and uplifting music, and racial equality. It is true that the last of these was still not a reality in this country, but thanks to Benny Goodman, swing music stood for such an idea and such an ideal toward which the citizenry was beginning to gravitate, to the rhythm of his own clarinet, his big band, his small groups that incorporated black musicians, and the many other swing units whose arrangers and arrangements Goodman respected, supported, and promoted.

TOMMY AND JIMMY DORSEY

Like Benny Goodman, Jimmy and Tommy Dorsey had fully paid their dues before they formed their own big bands, the two together in 1933 and then each with his own unit beginning in 1935. Even before this, the brothers, who were born in Shenandoah, Pennsylvania, on February 29, 1904, and November 19, 1905, respectively, had worked together in numerous bands and had recorded with their own Dorsey Brothers Orchestra beginning in 1928, although this did not become a regular unit until 1933, making its first recordings as such in early 1934.[49] Although the brothers split up and went their separate ways—Richard Sudhalter has detailed colorfully and sympathetically their fraternal love-fight relationship—both would create two of the most successful big bands of the Swing Era, and both came to this success through experience with the leading orchestras of the 1920s. Tommy recorded in 1924 with the Jean Goldkette Orchestra, which included at the time Bix Beiderbecke and Joe Venuti, and Jimmy made his debut on records with the Scranton Siren, also in 1924. Jimmy and Tommy were both sidemen in the Paul Whiteman Orchestra when it recorded in 1927 with Beiderbecke and Frankie Trumbauer, and in the same year, Jimmy played the clarinet solo on the classic Bix and Tram recording of "Singin' the Blues." Jimmy recorded as well with Jack Teagarden in such groups as Goody & His Good Timers (1928), The Whoopee Makers (Ben Pollack's Orchestra, 1929), and Jack's own orchestra of late 1933 and early 1934. Both Dorsey brothers were multi-instrumentalists, with Jimmy influencing many black saxophonists through his technique on the alto, whereas Tommy, who began on trumpet, recorded impressively on that instrument but even more so on the trombone for which he became best known. Although ultimately neither is recognized today as a major jazz musician, each brought to the Swing Era virtuosic instrumental skills and a talent for leadership that resulted in two of the most popular big bands of the period.

Although Jimmy was the elder Dorsey, the superior improviser, and his own band remained the original that the two brothers had started together, it was Tommy's orchestra of 1935 that enjoyed the greater success and was in fact one of the first big bands to attract a large audience for its smooth, romantic rhythms and expert execution. Tommy's repertoire was less in the jazz idiom than Jimmy's, but this probably accounted in large part for his greater success commercially. Tommy's hit records during the period were many, beginning with "I'm Gettin' Sentimental over You," from September 26, 1935, which the Dorsey Brothers Orchestra had first recorded in 1932 "to a resounding non-success." As Gunther Schuller goes on to say, "From such a performance it would have been hard to predict that in a few years this song would become Tommy Dorsey's all-time hit and, in its pleasant way, forever identified for millions with the entire Swing Era."[50]

Schuller claims that Tommy "was one of the greatest trombonists of all time—in any field" and that "as a lyric player and romantic balladeer . . . had no equal. Indeed he virtually invented the genre."[51] Tommy's control of his instrument at a very soft level and his seamless movement from lower notes to higher is immediately impressive. But if this is jazz, it is only distantly related. And yet, however Dorsey's music is defined, it has a lilt and loveliness that is undeniably attractive, and irresistibly so. Apart from Tommy's elegant playing of the theme of his hit tune, there is not much more to this piece, except for two passages by the saxes—also marked by fine control—that seem far advanced in terms of romantic expressiveness. Other big bands would obviously pick up on Tommy's approach and cash in on it as well. As we have seen, one band's successful recording generally translated into versions of the same piece by most every other competing group. However, no other trombonist attempted to duplicate Tommy's 1935 trombone showcase from which he acquired his label of "The Sentimental Gentleman of Swing."

During the same year of 1935, Tommy's orchestra recorded "Weary," with its "dreary" rhyme in a vocal which, as the lyrics sung so wretchedly by Buddy Gately put it, "I can't endure." There are other vocals by Gately that are even more dreadful, such as "Please Believe Me."[52] But as with Tommy's first try at "I'm Gettin' Sentimental Over You," it would be difficult to imagine from the Gately vocals that Tommy would at the end of the decade feature a singer such as Frank Sinatra who often said of his leader: "My greatest teacher was not a vocal coach, not the work of other singers, but the way Tommy Dorsey breathed and phrased on the trombone."[53] Fortunately, Tommy also had the services in 1935 of a female vocalist by the name of Edythe Wright, who, on "I'm Shooting High," belts out her lyrics with style and swing.[54] Tommy's trombone break, although quite short, also shows his ability to swing. It is clear, as Schuller points out, that because the Dorsey brothers had come up through the ranks of some of the lesser bands of the '20s and early '30s, they necessarily emulated such orchestras as Whiteman's and emphasized "a commercial pop/dance repertory" while "adhering to a modicum of jazz."[55] However, in 1935 Tommy also instituted a small group, taken from his larger orchestra (Schuller referring to this as a form of segregation, "a neatly separatist policy"), in order to play a type of sophisticated Dixieland, and on the sides issued under the name of his Clambake Seven the trombonist would, along with his sidemen, forge some excellent, extended hot jazz solos. These sides are discussed in the chapter on The Small Swing Groups.

Despite his evident ability to play real jazz, far too many of Tommy Dorsey's recordings are of the Gately variety—especially those featuring this mercifully soon forgotten vocalist. The overwhelming tendency of Tommy's recordings is toward a businessman bounce or such sentimental numbers as "You Started Me Dreaming."[56] On this last-named piece, from

March 25, 1936, we at least find Gately replaced by Jack Leonard, but Leonard is no Sinatra, and not even Tommy's trombone could have rescued such a saccharine piece from the oblivion it fully deserves had it not been for a CD series such as The Chronological Classics. One replacement who does make more of a difference is Dave Tough, who brings greater swing to the band—as he did to the Goodman unit—when the drummer took over for Sam Weiss, whose timekeeping even Sudhalter characterizes as "a clattering recital of 1920s 'dixieland' band gimmicks."[57] Sudhalter is speaking of Weiss's work with Artie Shaw in 1936, but it applies as well to his playing with Dorsey in 1935. In another context Sudhalter mentions that Bud Freeman found his time with Benny Goodman to be like "big band factory work."[58] One wonders how Dave Tough endured the miserable string of dull pop tunes recorded by Tommy Dorsey. Apparently the opportunity for Freeman and Tough to perform in the Clambake Seven somehow made up for what seems worse than factory work when it comes to the assembly line of sentimental drivel that Tommy's big band so frequently turned out. Only Edythe Wright's vocals could on occasion be something of a saving grace, as with "You" from March 25. Tough's presence has smoothed the beat wonderfully and makes Wright's job that much easier and her delivery much more satisfying for the listener. Of course, this is all relative, considering that we are still in the world of sentimental ballads with no relief furnished by even one hot solo. At least on "Robins and Roses" and "You Never Looked So Beautiful," from the same March 25 session, the ensemble is allowed to add a bit of punch, Tough throws in some wakeup punctuation now and again, and on the former Max Kaminsky contributes a few hot bars on trumpet and on the latter Joe Dixon does the same on clarinet. Wright also is fetching on "It's You I'm Talking About," from March 27, on which Tough's drums again contribute to the swing, but the ensemble's part is essentially corny and all too clichéd, at least in hindsight. Nonetheless, such numbers must have kept the couples dancing and listening, and eventually they did make way for more imaginative work.

Perhaps the word "imaginative" is too strong for the music of Tommy Dorsey's big band. It may apply to some of the solos and to some extent to the material chosen for arranging, but in general there is little that challenges the ear or stretches the mind. As Schuller views it, the Dorseys tried "to be all things to all people (including the sales-minded recording executives)."[59] Even so, it was indisputably the eclecticism of the Dorsey bands that led them into a repertoire that had been little explored by other groups, or at least not so successfully. Paul Whiteman, of course, had covered just about every base, from Charleston, stomp, and Dixieland to a symphonic swing arrangement such as "Sweet Sue" and almost out-and-out classical works such as Gershwin's "Rhapsody in Blue." Also, Whiteman had led the way in terms of the back to the classics movement of the '30s with a

1929 recording of "Song of India," based on the Rimsky-Korsakov ballet-opera *Sakdo* as arranged by Ferde Grofé. Nonetheless, it was Tommy who really initiated the development known as "swingin' the classics," beginning with his rendition of "Song of India," from January 29, 1937. Like Whiteman, Tommy also could go in the opposite direction, back to the Dixieland and even the boogie woogie roots of jazz. As noted before, Tommy formed his Clambake Seven as an outlet for a type of updated Dixieland, but he also would have the big band perform a classic Dixieland piece such as "Royal Garden Blues," first recorded by Beiderbecke in 1927. Arranged by Paul Weston for Tommy's big band, "Royal Garden Blues," recorded on April 3, 1936, opens with a spirited jamlike statement of the theme, and then moves into a big-band section before Tommy's respectable Dixie-flavored solo. The entire performance revisits the twenties tradition with taste and swing, spiced up by kicks from Tough's drums and a lively break by Bud Freeman on tenor.[60]

The other early jazz genre of boogie-woogie was brought back into fashion by the Dorsey band's version of Pinetop Smith's "Boogie Woogie," as arranged in 1937 by Deane Kincaide. This piece was not recorded by the big band until September 16, 1938, and before this Count Basie had recorded his own "Boogie Woogie (I May Be Wrong)" in March 1937, Goodman had recorded Mary Lou Williams's boogie-influenced arrangement of "Roll 'Em" in July 1937, and the Bob Crosby Orchestra recorded its "Yancey Special" in March 1938, but it was the Dorsey version of "Boogie Woogie" that caught the attention of so many other big-band leaders, after which most every big band had to have a boogie number. As Pat Hawes declares, "Tommy Dorsey had the biggest hit of all with Deane Kincaide's brilliant arrangement of Pinetop's tune with Howard Smith at the keyboard. Dorsey gave this number considerable exposure on broadcasts and live appearances and the record sold more than four million copies overall!"[61] Typically, this arrangement smoothes out the rough barrelhouse nature of the original and makes it appetizing for the swing-era audience. But again, there is no denying the appeal of this version, which varies the rifflike theme by moving the motif around from one section of the orchestra to another, with the saxes trilling, the clarinet on top, the trombones on the bottom pumping away, and the trumpets punctuating in between. Tommy concludes the piece with his smooth trombone as a final touch, as if to give the leader's "sentimental" seal of approval.

An even earlier black musical form that preceded ragtime, boogie, and Dixieland was what was originally referred to as the Negro spiritual, which was the basis of an arrangement entitled "Yes Indeed," recorded by the Dorsey orchestra on February 17, 1941—complete with hand clapping. This arrangement for Tommy's big band was done by Sy Oliver, who had come over from the Lunceford orchestra. The Dorsey version was based essentially on the same themes as the head arrangement of Lunceford's

"Well All Right Then," recorded in 1939 at the last session before Oliver left to join Dorsey. Oliver even says "Well all right then" at one point in the lyrics of the Dorsey version, on which Jo Stafford joins Oliver for the vocal. Stafford is unbelievably inept in the role of a "spiritual" singer, and not even the tune's subtitle, "A Jive Spiritual," can justify her totally wrong treatment. As for Oliver's vocal part, it converts what derives, at least distantly, from sacred music into a piece of kitsch. Many of the band's vocals tend to lower the musical level rather than to heighten it, as with "Once in a While," from July 21, 1937, which begins with a beautiful theme statement by Tommy on trombone but then goes downhill when Jack Leonard sings the lyrics.[62] In light of the poor quality of so much of Tommy Dorsey's music, it is curious to learn that for Leonard as a vocalist as well as jazz-oriented sidemen such as Bud Freeman, Tommy was looked upon as an ideal leader, one who respected his musicians and furnished them, according to Leonard, with "wonderful arrangements."[63] Although to some degree Tommy and his arrangers paid their respects to the history of black music, jazz as such was never the main concern. The exceptions are found primarily with solos by sidemen such as Bunny Berigan, Pee Wee Erwin, and Bud Freeman.

On "Song of India," the emphasis from the first is on the melody, only slightly jazzed-up by the trumpets' syncopated response to the saxes' theme statement. But the whole complexion of the performance changes with Berigan's solo, which, like a Beiderbecke entry in a Whiteman tune, turns the focus from the pseudo-classical to swinging, creative jazz improvisation. This is even more the case with "Marie," which was on the other side of "Song of India." "Marie" opens with Tommy's elegant trombone theme statement, is followed by a Leonard vocal responded to by the band's jive-like phrases (including another directly out of Lunceford), and leads to breaks by Berigan, Dorsey, and Freeman. Once more the entire atmosphere is altered by Berigan's solo, which Schuller cites as an example of "how a jazz improvisation may transform fairly innocuous song material into highly creative art." Schuller calls Berigan's "one of his finest, most sweepingly authoritative solos," a " 'composed' solo, a major statement in its own right."[64] After this, Dorsey contributes a bit of jazz in his own muted break, and then Bud Freeman continues the groove with a swinging improvisation to finish out the side. Another example of Freeman's work is on the cut of "Smoke Gets in Your Eyes," from July 20, 1937, which begins, as so often, with a muted Dorsey theme statement. Freeman's extended solo and, after a brief break by trumpeter Pee Wee Erwin, a second but shorter piece of improvisation are both quite engaging in their storylike lines, and illustrate why Freeman was possibly, according to Benny Goodman, an influence on Lester Young.[65] But these moments are by and large the exception among Tommy Dorsey recordings. On "Who?" from October 14, 1937, the same formula of Tommy's flawless theme statement and

Leonard's vocal with band responses is followed at least by a solo from Pee Wee Erwin, which, though it lacks Berigan's artistry, does swing and climbs into the upper register impressively. Tommy's muted break is again jazzlike and Bud Freeman's solo even includes a number of unexpected honklike low notes that effectively interrupt the flow and create a bit of welcome surprise. Erwin and Freeman likewise take extended solos on "Little White Lies," from December 6, 1937.[66] Yet for the most part the sequence of theme statement, vocal, and solos becomes quite predictable and certainly not very stimulating intellectually, although obviously this was not Dorsey's aim. Success called for a dependable, recognizable formula that would automatically appeal to a mass audience.

The sure-fire secret to success by the end of the first two years of the forties was to have a vocalist of the caliber of Frank Sinatra. Three among many vocals recorded with "Old Blue Eyes," as he would be referred to in later years, are the 1940 version of "Stardust" and the 1941 renditions of "I'll Never Smile Again" and "Dolores."[67] Sinatra came over from the Harry James orchestra in early 1940, replacing Jack Leonard, and accompanied by The Pied Pipers, with their ooh-ahh fills, Sinatra contributed to the band's growing popularity with yet another version of the ever-popular "Stardust." This recording, like the one of "I'll Never Smile Again," has absolutely nothing to do with jazz, but once again, Dorsey's object was success—not art. There is no swing to these mood pieces, which are at such slow tempos that they could only make listeners comatose or allow them to dance cheek to cheek in a dreamy state that was clearly more attractive to most dancers than having to listen closely to a jazzman's complex musical thought. (Schuller notes that the "romantic nostalgic balladry" of such pieces began with Ellington's 1930 "Mood Indigo," but of course Dorsey's approach is a world away from the evocative instrumental voices of Duke's recording.[68] In fact, "I'll Never Smile Again" shows how far by 1941 a white band such as Dorsey's had degenerated from the profoundly rich sound and expressive humanity of Ellington's 1930 classic.) "Dolores" is a bit more upbeat, but barely, and although Sinatra's voice and delivery are artistic in their way (control-wise, for example), this is still not jazz and lacks the kind of imaginative response to lyrics represented by the singing of a Billie Holiday. Under Sy Oliver's influence, the Dorsey band would, as Schuller says, belatedly and reluctantly perhaps enter the Swing Era, but this comes primarily after 1941 with hits like the 1944 "Opus No. 1."[69]

To hear more real jazz, it is necessary to listen to Tommy's brother Jimmy and his big band, which, for one thing, recorded compositions more in the jazz tradition, such as Jelly Roll Morton's "King Porter Stomp," Duke Ellington's "In a Sentimental Mood," Eddie Durham's "Moten Swing," Edgar Sampson's "Stompin' at the Savoy," and Count Basie's "One O'Clock Jump." As Schuller points out, Tommy Dorsey "never performed or recorded" these particular jazz standards, works that are fully identified with the Swing Era and represent some of its finest jazz offerings, but his older brother certainly did—to what effect we shall see.[70]

In Louis Armstrong's biography, *Swing That Music*, published in 1936, he mentions Jimmy Dorsey several times, calling him one of the "great swing players" along with other white jazzmen such as Jack Teagarden and Frank Trumbauer.[71] It may seem strange that Armstrong would only cite white musicians as examples of great swing players, but in all likelihood these choices were not Armstrong's but those of his ghostwriter, for the book is filled with literary allusions that make it suspect that Armstrong was the principal author, as in the references to Mark Twain, Walt Whitman, Edgar Allen [sic] Poe, and "great writers" who "didn't think only about what people wanted to have them write—they went on swinging their stuff."[72] Even so, it would have been natural for Armstrong to think of Jimmy Dorsey in 1936, for in the summer of that year he recorded with the Dorsey orchestra and, as Gunther Schuller sees it, the "encounter . . . came off rather well, in fact. The band was disciplined—more so than any Louis had ever recorded with—and played with a fine laid-back beat and a balanced homogenized sound. Louis . . . thrives on the Dorsey sides."[73] (This 1936 session is discussed fully in chapter 4.)

Although Jimmy Dorsey, like his brother, would record a great deal of material played in a nonjazz approach, the elder Dorsey did create works that are more rooted in the jazz tradition, including, as noted before, such jazz standards as "King Porter Stomp," "Moten Swing," and "One O'Clock Jump." Although the last two were not recorded by Jimmy until after 1941, he did record versions of "Stompin' at the Savoy," "Don't Be That Way," and "In a Sentimental Mood" in 1936 and 1938. Equally jazz-associated pieces such as "I Got Rhythm," "The Darktown Strutter's Ball," and "All of Me" also received treatments by the Dorsey orchestra that place them within the more standard jazz repertoire. But above all, pieces such as "Contrasts," "Dolemite," and "Turn Right" make it possible to rank Jimmy's "with the best of the white swing bands" and to hear why as an altoist he impressed the likes of Charlie Parker.[74]

Novelty numbers abound in the Jimmy Dorsey discography, and one of these is "Parade of the Milk Bottle Caps," yet at least this piece does offer some jazz-oriented moments. In the orchestra's book from the time that the two brothers were still together, "Parade," as recorded on July 7, 1936, has been aptly described as "a jaunty, strutting piece" on which "the band seems to enjoy itself."[75] Jimmy's alto break is too brief to give much of an idea of his virtuosity or his best improvisatory form, which unfortunately is true of many of his solo appearances. Later work would, however, indicate more clearly his impressive qualities on the alto. Even on the recording of "When Ruben Swings the Cuban," from August 7, 1936, which features a vocal, vintage trumpet breaks, and the expected high note all by Louis Armstrong, Dorsey turns in a brief but fine alto solo that shows his capacity for producing substantial work. This suggests that had Dorsey not felt it necessary to perform within the confines of a popularity contest among the competing big bands he might have developed more fully as a jazz artist.[76] Armstrong seemed to recognize Dorsey's potential, as he yells out on the recording, "Ah, swing it brother Jimmy."

After Tommy's departure, Bobby Byrne, who was sixteen years old when he joined the Dorsey brothers band in 1934, took over the trombone seat in Jimmy's orchestra. On July 27, 1936, at age eighteen, Byrne was the featured soloist on the orchestra's rendition of Duke Ellington's "In a Sentimental Mood," and Gunther Schuller notes that Byrne "at times seems to have been an even more astounding player than Tommy" and that "no classical trombone player of the time could have come even close to matching, for example, Byrne's clean, effortless, elegant work on 'In a Sentimental Mood.' "[77] Indeed, the entire performance of Ellington's classic piece is so fine that Ellington's original excels only by way of interpretation rather than anything to do with the quality of the music produced or of Dorsey's faithfulness to the spirit of Ellington's composition. Byrne solos on three separate occasions, and although on each the trombonist hews closely to the theme, he manages to vary his statements with unusual note choices that are not heard on the Ellington recording of 1935. Throughout the side, the orchestra presents a very convincing version of the piece, full of respect for Ellington's haunting melody. As for Dorsey's alto solo, it is tastefully done but nothing special. With Sampson's "Stompin' at the Savoy," from the same session, the Dorsey rendition recalls the original Webb recording perhaps more than does the Goodman version. The sax figures are nicely played by the reed section and the brass with ooh-wah hats adds what would become a typical swing-era touch. Trumpeter Shorty Sherock delivers a fine trumpet solo, and Skeets Herfurt's tenor break is quite good as well.[78] Dorsey's two alto solos are a bit stiff, and even corny when in the first he goes into a pattern of rickety triplets. Drummer Ray McKinley kicks the band along well enough, but behind the piano by Bobby Van Eps, the drums are too Dixielandish for the tune's basic swing style.

On "I Got Rhythm," from March 3, 1937, the Dorsey orchestra creates a very original, driving version of this tune that had already in the earlier part of the decade received a number of notable readings by other groups and would become the basis of many a bebop chart in the 1940s. The frenetic pace of trumpeter Toots Camarata's arrangement is handled wonderfully both by the orchestra and by Dorsey, who is featured on clarinet first and later on alto, with in between a solid solo by tenorist Charlie Frazier. Dorsey really gets after it on his clarinet and achieves a fully satisfying solo that is played against an all-out full ensemble. Although his alto break is quite brief, Dorsey does give evidence that he was capable of some daring phrases, even though rarely did he allow himself to indulge in such. His slower, more romantic clarinet is heard in a snippet on "I Can't

Face the Music," from March 3, 1938, and is so good that it makes one long for more. This particular piece also includes a vocal by June Richmond, a black singer hired by Dorsey, who apparently took her on at about the same time that Artie Shaw contracted with Billie Holiday. Richmond does not offer any competition to Ellington's Ivie Anderson on this treatment of blues-based lyrics, and certainly she was not in the same class with Holiday. As for Dorsey's version of "Don't Be That Way," from March 16, it seems closer to Goodman than to the original recording by Chick Webb. In fact, this performance is not very interesting from any angle, with even the trombone break by Byrne a poor imitation of Jack Teagarden. Jimmy's alto is probably the only novel touch, whereas his three appearances on clarinet, although good, are essentially too close to Goodman. On "I Cried for You," from March 29, Dorsey shows another side to his clarinet work, with a very low-keyed, expressive theme statement that is quite appealing.[79] Behind him the band plays a figure that seems to have been lifted from Lunceford's 1934 version of "Rose Room." This piece contains one of the few decent piano solos by Freddy Slack, and it also features some high trumpet-section passages arranged by Camarata, something that would become overworked as the Swing Era continued into the forties.

The most famous swing instrumental by the Dorsey orchestra was "John Silver," arranged by Ray Krise and recorded on April 29, 1938. An allusion to "Popeye the Sailor Man" thrown into this arrangement would be more at home in a witty bebop improvisation but perhaps was inevitable given the title of the tune. Dorsey's doodlings on alto are an indication that this really is not a serious piece, and the same goes for the trombones' humorous comments. The call-and-response pattern is not an integral part of this mixed bag, which ultimately does not amount to much, despite one of Byrne's better hot breaks. The orchestra's treatment of "The Darktown Strutters' Ball," from the same date, is also pure novelty, including Richmond's nowhere vocal. About the only thing to be said for this piece is that it forms part of the boogie-woogie revival of the late thirties. As Gunther Schuller observes, Jimmy's discography "is much too filled with . . . pop ephemera of the time to be able to make a case for [his] orchestra as a jazz ensemble of first rank or of major importance."[80] This is even true of "Dusk in Upper Sandusky," again from the same date, which derived from an earlier Dorsey Brothers piece entitled "Dorsey Stomp." Although Richard Sudhalter implies that both pieces are in "the line of descent" of Jimmy's better work, "Dusk in Upper Sandusky" does not offer anything of real substance—it is primarily a showcase for drummer Ray McKinley, who despite using everything in his drum kit arsenal does not have much to say percussion wise.[81] Dorsey's alto rides are sheer technical displays, and the piece itself in no way lives up to its "Tiger Rag" pedigree. Schuller is correct that nothing mentioned thus far places the Dorsey orchestra in the front rank of jazz units. But the group's best work was still to come, and in particular the recording of "Dolemite," which Schuller for some reason never mentions.

One rather amazing piece by the Dorsey orchestra is "All of Me," from March 3, 1939, with eighteen-year-old Helen O'Connell as the vocalist. Schuller does not refer to this recording either, and this is quite surprising, for there are at least three aspects of this side that make it exceptional. First, the vocal by O'Connell predates by two years the marvelous version of this song recorded by Billie Holiday in 1941. O'Connell even sounds like Holiday in several places, although ultimately Helen renders the lyrics with her own cool yet tender feeling. Dorsey's alto solo is surely one of his most rhapsodic on record and shows that on occasion he could play on a level with Johnny Hodges and in fact went beyond the Ellington sideman in terms of a more modern sound and execution, which obviously would have caught Parker's ear. The third truly remarkable feature of this recording is Bobby Byrne's obbligato behind O'Connell. So high is the trombone at times that it sounds like a trumpet, and Byrne's commentary recalls in its way the combination of Jimmy Rushing and Dickie Wells, if not quite Holiday and Lester Young. This, of all the recordings cited thus far, aside from the Dorsey version of Ellington's "In a Sentimental Mood," deserves repeated hearings, for it is a subtle, very rewarding performance by the orchestra as a whole but especially by O'Connell, Dorsey, and Byrne. Another excellent side is "Contrasts," from April 30, 1940, which served as the orchestra's theme song (first recorded in 1932) and originated in Jimmy's youth when he wrote it to show off his technique. Later it was his feature with the Paul Whiteman orchestra, titled then "Oodles of Noodles." Dorsey again demonstrates his very modern alto style on the 1940 version of "Contrasts," which Schuller cites as an example of Jimmy being able "in the ballad department" to "easily vie with his competitors."[82] The title is illustrated by Dorsey's alto in slow, rhapsodic passages on either side of the piece's bridge where the orchestra shifts to double-time. This is an approach worth hearing as well, and is even more dramatic in the orchestra's version of "Tangerine." Dorsey seemed drawn to differing poles in his work, as indicated by the titles of two other pieces from 1940, "Turn Left" and "Turn Right," from December 9, 1940, and February 3, 1941, respectively.[83] In his own playing, he was fully capable of performing at fast and slow speeds, matching his ideas to the set tempo and delivering meaningful lines and figures. Of course, he also was guilty of the inane break, but there is enough evidence of his artistry to prove that he was at given moments an important link in the development of jazz alto.

The best proof of Dorsey's advanced alto conception is found on the recording of "Dolemite," from July 17, 1940. As John Lissner indicates, this arrangement by Camarata "marks a new and more powerhouse Dorsey sound—heavier, blacker, very different from his previous orchestras."[84] Adapted from a big-band recording by Erskine Hawkins, "Dolemite" is a riff-based piece that opens with the saxes down low and then higher up in a rich upper-register sound that makes for an extremely effective contrast. Against the riffs, Dorsey's two alto breaks are notably free wheeling and yet quite cohesive in their musical expression, in particular the first. Although neither break sounds like Parker, the first is at times as daring as the Bird would be and certainly as flowing and even as angular in its way. Dorsey ends the piece with a clarinet break that is more in the typical swing vein, not so imaginative or forward-looking as his alto solos. Also on this piece are fine trumpet and tenor solos that are much more driving and forceful than anything heard on earlier Dorsey recordings. Buddy Schutz on drums is an improvement over Ray McKinley in that the former is more of a true big-band percussionist rather than a basically Dixieland drummer.

At this point there is the beginning of some really solid swing to the Dorsey band. Schutz's presence on "Contrasts" also seemed to make a difference by encouraging a more flowing style for the band and the soloists in place of McKinley's cowbell punctuations. "Turn Left," like "Dolemite," is also marked by contrasts, such as the low baritone sax against the high brass and the soft passages followed by louder ones. Some of the writing is heavily influenced by Lunceford, and even Dorsey's alto solo seems to have Willie Smith in mind. The trombonist has definitely been listening to Trummy Young and comes up with a break worthy of Lunceford's star. Also like "Dolemite," "Turn Left" swings mightily, and even more so its alter ego, "Turn Right." Both these companion pieces were arranged by pianist Joe Lippman, and the latter opens with string bassist Jack Ryan setting the pace alone for eight bars, followed by the reeds calling with a coy female softness and a bass clarinet responding with a certain declarative urgency. Then the reeds reply to the muted brass, after which Dorsey on clarinet embellishes the haunting theme. At this point a fine up-to-date extended tenor solo relates to the theme but features some free improvisation on a very imaginative level, including great registral variety and unrelenting drive. Then Schutz kicks the ensemble into high gear, before Dorsey enters on alto with a solo that is not so impressive as on "Dolemite" but quite venturesome in its leaps and swoops, as was the tenor's. The conclusion is one of the most satisfying of any Dorsey recording, as it brings the piece full circle with the return of the bass clarinet, some clarinet-trio arpeggios, and the high brass driving home the final theme-related notes.

On alto Dorsey also is in fine form for the opening of the beautiful Harold Arlen ballad "When the Sun Comes Out," from February 3, 1941. If Helen O'Connell's vocal is not so effective here as on "All of Me"—her control is not quite up to what it was on the latter—it may be more passionate and is, in this sense, as John Lissner says, "remarkably mature" for a singer of nineteen.[85] From the August 1, 1941, "Charleston Alley," a tune written by Horace Henderson for the Charlie Barnet band, it is clear that trumpeter Shorty Solomson had been listening closely to Harry James, but Shorty's solo is less showy and for that reason rather more appealing. Dorsey's alto solo is less satisfying than his work on "Dolemite" and "Turn Right," but those were apparently high-water marks in his career. Ironically, Dorsey's success after this was greater than ever and yet the basis of that success—vocal numbers featuring Bob Eberly and Helen O'Connell—had almost nothing to do with jazz. This is indicated by "Tangerine," from December 10, 1941, which was performed by the Dorsey band in the 1941 film *The Fleet's In*.[86] In contrastive sections, the first sung slowly by Eberly and the second up-tempo by O'Connell, "Tangerine" presents the two vocalists in what would prove one of a number of Latin-flavored works that were big hits for the Dorsey orchestra. Other such hits included "Green Eyes," "Bésame Mucho," "María Elena," and "Amapola." As Gunther Schuller rightly assesses these pieces, "none of them related to jazz in the slightest."[87] But by this time—the beginning of the war years—Jimmy Dorsey already had established himself as a highly successful big bandleader and an influential alto saxophonist, which, given the competition during this period, was a considerable achievement, and perhaps even more so when one considers that his brother also had made his mark independently with one of the handful of name white bands of the era.

ARTIE SHAW

Although the black name bandleaders were by and large pianists, with the exception, as we have seen, of Jimmie Lunceford, the white name bandleaders were either clarinetists or trombonists. Benny Goodman was foremost a clarinetist, even though he did record on the alto saxophone—for example, in 1931, with the Ben Pollack orchestra.[88] Jimmy Dorsey perhaps made more of an impact on the development of jazz as an altoist, but he began principally as a clarinetist and continued to play his first instrument throughout his career. Artie Shaw, who was born in New York City on May 23, 1910, began on saxophone and played it on occasion with his various bands, but his primary instrument was the clarinet, through which he made his most important musical statements. One difference between the black pianist-leaders and the white clarinetist-leaders may lie in the fact that the former were both instrumentalists and arranger-composers of great distinction. Basie may have served more as an editor of his sidemen's compositions and arrangements than as an original creator of written scores, but the Count's spare, blues-based piano set the style for most of his band's performances. Henderson and Ellington each guided his respective orchestra by furnishing it with the material to be played and by allowing for ample solo space for a wide variety of sidemen. In the case of Artie Shaw, he as the leader was himself the star soloist—and to a lesser extent this was true as well of Goodman and the Dorsey brothers. In certain respects, these differences between the black and white orchestra leaders determined the degree to which the former involved more of the jazz tradition in their work than did the latter. However, it is true that Artie Shaw, more than the other big-name white leaders, did write a considerable amount of material for his groups and made a few excellent arrangements, even though none of his pieces became a standard in the jazz repertoire.

Like Goodman and the Dorsey brothers, Artie Shaw was active in jazz circles in the twenties. He was invited in 1924 at age fourteen to join the Ben Pollack orchestra in California, and when he turned down the offer because he was happy with his job with the Austin Wylie orchestra in Cleveland, Goodman at age fifteen was hired instead. In the late twenties and early thirties in New York, Shaw, again like Goodman and the Dorsey brothers, was contracted for a great deal of radio work. According to Richard Sudhalter, Shaw's first "strictly 'hot' record date appears to be an August 15, 1934, session." This was with "a racially mixed band" and Shaw came on "vigorous and surprisingly hot" but still under the influence of such clarinetists as Matty Matlock, Sidney Arodin, and Goodman.[89] On November 20, 1934, Shaw recorded with Frankie Trumbauer and His Orchestra, and on "Troubled," Artie's solo sounds at times indistinguishable from the work of Goodman.[90] On April 13, 1936, Shaw appeared on the first recording by Bunny Berigan in his classic rendition of "I Can't Get Started." On this side Shaw does not solo, but he does briefly on another piece recorded at the same date, "A Melody from the Sky," on which he displays his fine control and purity of sound.[91] Shaw's first big ear-catching appearance came on May 24, 1936, at the Imperial Theater in New York City, on the occasion of "a milestone event in jazz history: the first real jazz concert," organized by Joe Helblock, owner of the Onyx Club.[92] Although the Casa Loma and Bob Crosby orchestras were the headliners and the bands of Louis Armstrong, Tommy Dorsey, and Paul Whiteman also were featured, it was Shaw and his string quartet plus rhythm section that "caught the attention of some of the music industry's movers and shakers."[93] Although the other outfits emphasized "the hot, brassy side" of jazz, Shaw presented "a softer alternative" and as a result Shaw's one piece, "Interlude in B-Flat," which he himself had written for the concert, "proved to be the evening's high point" and led soon afterward to Shaw forming his own orchestra.[94]

As the leader of yet another swing band, which like Whiteman's included strings, Shaw was by no means an immediate hit. His first group toured around and made a number of recordings with Brunswick, but it did not have an impact on the listening public. Always an outspoken critic of his own audience as "by and large musically illiterate," Shaw disbanded and reorganized, eliminating the string quartet and naming his fourteen-piece group Art Shaw and His New Music.[95] (Gunther Schuller considers Shaw's estimate of his original orchestra and its "superiority" an indication of the leader's "lack of artistic objectivity and lack of self-criticism," because he misjudged "the quality and nature of his own art." Schuller even views Shaw's work as evincing "little sense of jazz as a *creative music*." ⁹⁶) One piece recorded with his new orchestra on September 17, 1937, and entitled "Shoot the Likker to Me, John Boy," was written by Shaw and features black vocalist Leo Watson.⁹⁷ There is nothing special about the piece itself nor its performance—it sounds like a typical swing tune played by most any other group. As for Shaw's clarinet work, it is technically flawless and swings, but still there is nothing distinctive about it. However, the following year, on July 24, Shaw's group would make a hit recording of "Begin the Beguine," a tune from Cole Porter's 1935 Broadway show, *Jubilee*. Inspired by the composer having watched "native dancers perform the beguine on the island of Martinique," "Begin the Beguine" would, through Jerry Gray's arrangement, catapult Shaw and his orchestra into instant fame and would mark a turning point in the leader's life.⁹⁸ After a surprisingly crisp single-note opening by the brass, the leader's warm clarinet states the beguine theme in the low register against sharp punctuations by the trumpets and then sax figures followed by muted brass. The arrangement and performance offer an easy swing that is immediately captivating, with the romantic sax section and Tony Pastor's lyrical tenor solo adding to the piece's inviting mood. Later a clarinet trio and some call-and-response passages between Shaw and the ensemble lead to his concluding glissando that climbs into the upper register and then reaches a climax with his series of ascending notes played perfectly in staccato style. Whether Schuller intended to apply to "Begin the Beguine" his idea that Shaw's band achieved for each Broadway show tune "the kind of treatment its mood and lyrics seemed to indicate," it certainly seems true of this piece, which is "a far cry from the formula-like arranging styles of most late-thirties' swing bands."⁹⁹

Although the popularity of "Begin the Beguine" made it the number one record in the country in 1938 and placed the handsome clarinetist and bandleader in the limelight, which led to Shaw's successive marriages to movie stars Lana Turner and Ava Gardner, Gunther Schuller can lament that in terms of jazz Shaw's repertoire abandoned a recent and belated "waking up to the pre-eminence of black composers, arrangers, and bandleaders" and began to "favor forgettable pop tunes."¹⁰⁰ But in fact what even Schuller himself cites as an example of "a straightahead Henderson-style" arrangement of "What Is This Thing Called Love?" was recorded by the Shaw orchestra on September 27, two months after "Begin the Beguine." Even so, despite the fact that "What Is This Thing Called Love?" demonstrates Shaw's ability to improvise effectively, and with some intricate phrases quite different from anything Benny Goodman ever tried, the arrangement and performance do not offer anything particularly new or imaginative. Aside from Shaw, the soloists on trumpet, tenor, and trombone all make their driving contributions, and yet there is nothing remarkable about any of their breaks. Certainly the soloists and the arrangement cannot compare with those of the Henderson recordings—Shaw's lack the same level of invention, even if they approach at times the same intensity. More convincing examples of Shaw's jazz-oriented recordings are "Comin' On" and "Back Bay Shuffle" from the same July 24 session that produced "Begin the Beguine." On those two pieces, the former written by Shaw, we find both the leader and his sidemen in swinging grooves that make one think, at least in the case of "Back Bay Shuffle," of Lunceford and Basie. Also on this session Billie Holiday recorded for the single time during her brief tenure with the Shaw orchestra, singing as only she could on "Any Old Time," another Shaw original. Tony Pastor's tenor solo on this last piece is by no means up to a Lester Young, but it is quite good in its own right. Shaw is perhaps best on "Back Bay Shuffle," differing here from Goodman through his more biting attack and rather metallic tone, but he also is quite himself on "Any Old Time" when he plays in his warm, lyrical vein.

One of Shaw's most lyrical recordings is "I Surrender, Dear," from August 19, 1939, which Gunther Schuller praises for its "marvel of a side-ending cadenza."[101] This piece also shows off Shaw's abilities as a leader with a clear notion of what he wanted from his sax section. Shaw explained that "for the sax-soli section, where the saxes are practically breathing together," he had written "a clarinet solo and we scored it for the sax section."[102] The section's phrasing is truly exceptionable and even vies with the Lunceford reeds, although the sound is more tinged with sentiment and less swinging. Overall, there is much worthy of being heard in this performance, not the least Shaw's opening theme statement with its very lovely and not overdone vibrato. Shaw's technical virtuosity is evident on any number of recordings, but especially on "I Surrender, Dear," or a piece such as "Pastel Blue," from March 12, 1939, where the clarinetist reveals his simultaneous technical and expressive qualities. His classical-like cadenza with its high-note ending on "Pastel Blue" soars into the stratosphere where the sound becomes almost inaudible it is so "beyond the instrument's usual range."[103] Shaw's technical virtuosity and expressiveness also are evident on two W.C. Handy tunes, the world-renowned "St. Louis Blues," from November 28, 1939, and the less well-known "Chantez-les bas," from September 7, 1940.[104] On both Handy pieces, Shaw makes apparent his obvious appreciation for the roots of jazz and his understanding of the classic blues form. His opening clarinet on the latter is wonderfully authentic, as is the muted trumpet that follows him, but unfortunately the performance is marred by the entry of a sappy string section, which happens all too often on Shaw recordings in the last years of the decade. (Schuller refers to the strings on works such as "Chantez-les bas" as forming "an oppressive glutinous blanket of musical taffy."[105]) Mercifully this is not the case with "St. Louis Blues," which is a straight big-band performance without the intrusion of saccharine violins. This second Handy piece was the occasion for one of Shaw's freest and most satisfying improvisations, as well as the basis for a fine, swinging treatment by the entire ensemble; it also includes a booting tenor solo by Georgie Auld. The "St. Louis Blues" rendition was taped from a radio broadcast done at the Cafe Rouge of the Hotel Pennsylvania in New York City, which would seem to account for its greater swing and more free-wheeling spirit.

Shaw recalled that in broadcasting from the Cafe Rouge there were no limitations placed on the band, "no one to tell us we were running out of record space."[106] As a result, Shaw and his band cut loose on "St. Louis Blues," as well as two other tunes, his original "Everything Is Jumpin' " and an arrangement of "At Sundown." Dating from a broadcast of October 20, 1939, "Everything Is Jumpin' " is an apt description of this swinging five-minute performance. The live audience can be heard in the background urging on Shaw and his sidemen—not that Buddy Rich, who had taken over the drum seat, was not enough by himself to drive them to an intensity rarely achieved by any other white big-name band. (Shaw himself said of Rich that the drummer "provided the fire we never had before."[107]) "At Sundown," from October 25, is even more relentlessly driving at four minutes in length, and features fine breaks by Les Burness on piano and Auld on tenor, while Shaw delivers some of his most thrilling musical moments—he himself, on hearing the air check discs (which he managed to save from being thrown out by NBC), was "astonished at the absolute freedom" of the Cafe Rouge broadcasts.[108] Other on-the-air Cafe Rouge performances, from November 11, include "My Blue Heaven," which compares favorably with the 1935 Lunceford recording, and "Diga, Diga Doo," which has little in common with a 1928 version by an Irving Mills studio orchestra with Jack Teagarden as the star soloist (and including as well breaks by Jimmy Dorsey on alto sax and clarinet). The differences between the fluidity of Shaw in 1939 and Dorsey's basically stiff approach in 1928 illustrate the great technical change that had come over clarinet playing during the intervening eleven years. The trombonist on "Diga, Diga Doo," however, has not really advanced beyond Teagarden, but then in 1928 Big T was years ahead of his time technically, as well as in the essentially "black" feeling of his low-down, earthy style. Although Shaw's version of "My Blue Heaven" is quite good, it cannot be said to update the Lunceford—in fact it seems to owe its interpretation almost entirely to his 1935 recording, including Georgie Auld's tenor, which harks back to Joe Thomas's solo. Nonetheless, the Shaw rendition swings all the way and is a valid remake of the Lunceford side.

Unlike Tommy Dorsey, Artie Shaw often paid his respects to the great black bandleaders. This is evident in an outstanding piece such as "One Foot in the Groove," another Shaw arrangement, dating from March 17, 1939. Here the biggest influence is Basie, especially by virtue of the fact that this is a riff tune. Even though the riff was a form that Shaw could denigrate on occasion, his band's performance is quite respectable.[109] Auld is exceptionally good here and clearly combines, as Richard Sudhalter observes, the qualities of Basie's two great tenors, Lester Young and Herschel Evans.[110] Of course, all of this had been done before, but there is no denying that Shaw could imitate the black bands at a high level. Another Basie-derived performance is Shaw's version of "Oh! Lady Be Good," from June 22, 1939, which also seems to owe something to the Goodman-James recording of "Life Goes to a Party." Gunther Schuller cites "Traffic Jam," another side from the June 22 recording session, held in Hollywood, as evidence that the Shaw band had "finally arrived at the level of virtuoso excitement and collective drive that Bennie Moten had already attained in 1932 on 'Toby,' from which piece, by the way, the Shaw-McRae effort seems to have borrowed copiously."[111] "Lover, Come Back to Me," a recording made the previous January 17, also elicits high praise from Schuller, who says that with this and "other performances from that period, the Shaw orchestra suddenly reached a new plateau, from which it was then able to begin the final assault upon the throne of the Kingdom of Swing, in order to topple the King himself, Benny Goodman."[112] The section work in this piece is truly superb, especially where, as Shaw noted of his arrangement, "the four saxes play as one instrument."[113] This performance owes little to the black bands, at least directly, because more than anything it is an arrangement rather than a piece containing spontaneous solos. Another swinging piece from the June 22 session, "Serenade to a Savage," does offer fine trumpet solos and a break by Georgie Auld on tenor, but once again these are indebted to Basie sidemen, especially Auld's solo, which owes much to Herschel Evans. This piece also exhibits the influence of Lunceford in the brass figures supported by Buddy Rich's tom-tom rhythm.[114]

Shaw's biggest hit other than "Begin the Beguine" was another Latin American number, "Frenesi," from March 3, 1940, arranged by black composer William Grant Still, who did six arrangements for a studio session. Gunther Schuller considers "Frenesi" "quite jazz-less," and even though that perhaps overstates the case (with brief tenor and trumpet solos obvious exceptions to any such categorical judgment), the arrangement (which opens with strings) is definitely more in the line of Gershwin and a Broadway musical than it is within the jazz idiom.[115] (An air check of "The Carioca," from August 19, 1939, does offer evidence that the Shaw band could transform a Latin-based piece into a true work of jazz. Here the solos are quite good and Buddy Rich's drumming generates a solid drive.[116]) One Shaw recording to receive special accolades both from Gunther Schuller and Richard Sudhalter is his version of "Stardust," from October 7, 1940.[117] Schuller remarks that Shaw plays "magnificently, not only topping his effort with a stunning high A but 'singing' the whole solo with a loving, warm lyric feeling that no other clarinetist of the time could have matched."

Despite this ringing endorsement, Schuller actually finds trombonist Jack Jenney's solo "the most memorable moment . . . for all its romantic cast, a major breakthrough statement, both in technical and expressive terms."[118] Sudhalter praises trumpeter Billy Butterfield's "glowing opening solo (and section lead)" and compares Jenney's trombone solo with Coleman Hawkins's classic interpretation of "Body and Soul," recorded a week earlier. Sudhalter points out that Jenney "never states the melody directly but refers to it obliquely from time to time." As for Shaw's solo, Sudhalter declares that it "became one of the set-pieces of the jazz canon, alongside Beiderbecke's and Trumbauer's 'Singin' the Blues' choruses, Armstrong's 'West End Blues,' and Coleman Hawkins's epic transformation of 'Body and Soul.' "[119] This indeed is elevated company, and perhaps Shaw's solo deserves its place among those illustrious "set-pieces"—certainly Schuller is correct that the clarinetist's lyric feeling was at the time unmatched. But what detracts from the performance is, once again, the strings, which make an already sweet-sounding piece absolutely cloying. Sudhalter can find an "organic richness" in Lennie Hayton's writing for the strings that for me remains merely a surfeit of artificial sweetener.

As Schuller indicates, Shaw began his rise to stardom by employing a string quartet as part of his fusion or "Third Stream"–type of approach, so there is nothing unusual about his continued attraction to a blending of classical and jazz elements. Nonetheless, it always seems a failed attempt, even in such pieces as Ray Conniff's "To a Broadway Rose" and Paul Jordan's "Suite No. 8," both of which are lauded by Schuller, in the former case for being "far ahead of its time" and in the latter for being "far removed from the world of 'arrangements' and dance numbers and pop tunes."[120] All this is undeniable, as is the fact that in "Suite No. 8" Hot Lips Page "brought a native vitality to the piece, that without [his and Georgie Auld's] solo contributions it would not have had."[121] But as Schuller also suggests, such solos may be considered "stylistically extraneous to the work," which begins as a straight classical string piece and then moves into a swinging, jazz-oriented work heavily influenced by Duke Ellington's "more 'formal' extended compositions."[122] Like many of Shaw's recordings in this vein, "Suite No. 8" ends up a mishmash, and although interesting as an experiment, it satisfies neither as classical nor as jazz, nor as a fusion of the two musical worlds. Although well rehearsed and at times inspiriting, such works lack a unified effect and leave the listener torn between traditions that create different, even opposing expectations. Although one may find Jordan's introductory section of "Suite No. 8" appealing as an evocative modern classical work for strings, the mood it creates is disrupted and in a sense ruined by the equally appealing jazz that follows, with the result that the latter has an unsettling effect and seems out of place even though it exists in its own right. Ultimately, such experimentalism must be seen as but one more facet of the Swing Era, which in no way limited itself to a single style or a predictable formulaic pattern. As will be particularly evident in the chapter on small groups, the impact of the epoch's experimental tendencies would have far-reaching effects on the future of jazz, and this was true as well of the kind of fusion compositions encouraged by Shaw. According to the leader's own account, he worked with such arrangers as Jerry Gray in the same way that Ellington and Billy Strayhorn collaborated, and it might be added, as would such figures as Miles Davis and Gil Evans during the late 1940s.

Clearly Artie Shaw was a highly eclectic musician and bandleader. He organized a great variety of units, employed arrangers of every imaginable persuasion (Bill Challis, Lennie Hayton, Jerry Gray, Fred Norman, William Grant Still, Paul Jordan, Ray Conniff, Margie Gibson), hired sidemen with widely divergent styles (for example, Hot Lips Page, who was essentially a blues man in a basically non-blues band—Still's respectable "Blues," of December 4, 1940, notwithstanding), and featured vocalists as different in approach as the true jazz singer Billie Holiday and the sappy crooner Tony Pastor.[123] In 1939, Shaw hired eighteen-year-old Helen Forrest as his featured vocalist, and as Schuller has noted, she, "as much as Shaw himself, contributed substantially to the band's popular success, mainly by the sincerity and unmannered communicative directness with which she could deliver a song, even a mediocre one."[124] Certainly "Deep Purple," recorded on March 12, 1939, is not a mediocre song, and Forrest renders it with all the feeling it deserves, whereas Shaw maintains the romantic mood better than any other clarinetist of the period could have.[125] An air check, from November 11, 1939, also pairs Forrest and Shaw on "Moon Ray," which may not be as fine a song as "Deep Purple," but Forrest also delivers it with telling directness, and a rather amazing maturity for the singer's age.[126]

Part of Shaw's success with the listening audiences may have derived from the extraordinary range of materials and styles that he attempted. He noted that "in those days, nobody thought of having a dance band do concerts, but that's really what we were doing, because half the time there'd be let's say 9,000 people in the Palomar, and probably 75 of them out there dancing. The rest were watching."[127] Shaw himself seemed primarily interested in musical experimentation. He constantly sought to grow as a musician, was never satisfied with himself or the bands he put together, even when the public responded favorably. In fact, Shaw was inclined to dismiss his listeners as uninformed and intrusive, and he frequently abandoned them despite the fact that he was, in the opinion of the public that idolized him, the most talented clarinetist of his generation. As Gary Giddins has observed, Shaw's rejection of stardom remains a mystery for "those of us who haven't the holy gift."[128] Equally mystifying is, as Gunther Schuller points out, the great discrepancy between Shaw's high standards and some of the low-quality, tasteless work he produced.

A piece like "Temptation," from September 7, 1940, is another Latin-related work that is a sheer hodge-podge of big band, strings, and Holly-wood ending. The alto saxophone solos are almost gratuitous bows to jazz, and not very good ones at that, whereas Shaw's glissando is pure exhibitionism with no other musical purpose. Gunther Schuller reserves his harshest attack for a work such as "Concerto for Clarinet," from December 17, 1940, which the critic considers "anything but a true concerto . . . a pastiche thrown together out of some boogie-woogie blues, clarinet-over-tomtom interludes, a commonplace riff build-up towards the end, all encased in opening and closing virtuoso cadenzas for the leader's clarinet."[129] Richard Sudhalter agrees with Schuller, but he indicates that Shaw himself called the "Concerto" "a fraud, a pasteup, slung together for use in *Second Chorus* (a 1941 movie starring Paulette Goddard) and issued on two sides of a twelve-inch 78 rpm record."[130] Shaw also observed that the "Concerto" issue on flip sides "doomed it to instant oblivion in those days," whereas Schuller reveals that the piece "was published and seriously studied by clarinetists and classical musical teachers, and it is still played nowadays by high-school and college orchestras, trying to show their 'progressiveness.' "[131] Shaw certainly wished to be progressive in his music making, and in his own words, he definitely intended through the "Concerto" "to show [him and his] band spreading out a little and doing things that were not altogether standard dance-band fare." Somewhat contradicting Sudhalter's report, Shaw found the "Concerto" to be "a good show-piece for clarinet and for the rest of the band, and I thought everyone swung like crazy on it. My part was entirely improvised."[132] The opening of "Concerto" is typical of a sentimental film score, and the boogie-woogie bit comes as a rude contrast. As for the various solos by the sidemen, there are indeed a number of swinging breaks on the first side, especially what sounds like a Dickie Wells–inspired trombone break by Jack Jenney and an Armstrong imitation probably by Billy Butterfield. But the second side is given over almost entirely to Shaw's pointless solo and cadenza, which, although they amount to very little musically, showcase the clarinetist's incomparable technique, with a high note held as the stirring finale.

Artie Shaw undoubtedly was the master exponent of the romantic side of swing-era jazz, and could fashion hot solos as well, briefly doing so on the second side of his "Concerto for Clarinet." The romantic facet of his playing is fully apparent with his opening theme statement on 'I Cover the Waterfront,' from January 23, 1941, arranged by Lennie Hayton.[133] Shaw's more progressive side is found in a piece like "Nocturne," from November 12, 1941, arranged by Jerry Sears, which Gunther Schuller considers successful in blending strings with saxes.[134] At times reminiscent of certain phrases in *Porgy and Bess*, although in no way rooted in black music as Gershwin's opera is, "Nocturne" is almost a purely "classical" treatment—Shaw's clarinet part containing nothing in it of the jazz tradition. Ultimately, Shaw is, as so many commentators have noted, an enigma, a chameleon, changing his musical colors either to suit himself or the audience he despised or pretended to. What is clear in the end is that Artie Shaw was a major figure in the Swing Era, both as a soloist and as a bandleader whose groups played every type of music associated with the period. Although he may not represent one of the crucial creators of jazz as such, he was a formidable performer on his principal instrument and a bandleader who elicited from his sidemen some of the most memorable recordings of the late 1930s, with a piece like "Begin the Beguine" clearly representing one very popular side of the big-band era.

GLENN MILLER

If Artie Shaw stood for much of the glamour of the Swing Era—by virtue of his virtuosity as a performer, his marriages to movie stars, and his band's many hit recordings—Glenn Miller epitomized its romantic idealism, its need for an all-American type of innocence reflected in good, clean musical entertainment. It was in fact Miller and his orchestra that captured the hearts of an entire worldwide generation of listeners and dancers. A radio broadcast on an air check recording declares, "Midst spotlights and celebrities the Glen Island Casino opens its 1939 season" at the "mecca of music for moderns" with Glenn Miller, "one of the nation's foremost swing trombonists." On another air check recording, the announcer apprises Glenn that on the Make Believe Ballroom's poll his orchestra has been voted the Number One Band in the nation, garnering more than twice as many votes as its nearest competitor. On the second air check, the announcer goes on to say that Miller has given audiences "a host of swell arrangements, songs old and new, ranging all the way from 'Danny Boy' to 'Tuxedo Junction.' " On hearing this announcement with its presentation of a bronze plaque certifying that Miller's was the "Number One Danceband," the crowd in the background cheers and applauds ecstatically.[135] As Gunther Schuller says of "the extremely popular 'Danny Boy,' " this piece, with its "variety of mutes, producing a gorgeous velvety sound and texture, never heard before in or out of jazz . . . was the ultimate 'romantic' sound, and when set in a slow tempo, as it invariably was, it was seductive and irresistible."[136] Although "seductive," such music was fully acceptable, unlike so much of what was considered the untamed, uninhibited animalism of jazz. If Glenn Miller could include a few "dirty notes" in his solo on "Little Brown Jug," these were hardly objectionable, set as they were in the context of a very polite form of jazz. And if Miller's brand of swing was for the most part rather far removed from the jazz tradition, emphasizing arrangements over spontaneous improvisation, even so, by late 1939 the leader had "evolved out of [his] sonoric experiments . . . a sound world that was unprecedented in the history of music—and unique (except by imitation)."[137]

The romantic side of the Miller repertoire does not tell the whole story of his orchestra and its recordings and broadcasts. Given the opportunity to play more standard jazz material, he and his sidemen could turn in highly swinging ensemble performances and even quite inventive improvisations. Indeed, the Miller organization, like a number of basically non-jazz big bands of the swing period, could on occasion produce a very valid form of jazz, even though it knew—or at least its leader was fully aware—on which side the bread was buttered. This means that the success of Miller and his orchestra was assured by their romantic, seductive platters, not their renditions of such classic jazz numbers as "King Porter Stomp" and "Farewell Blues" or late thirties jazz compositions such as Eddie Durham's "Wham (Re Bop Boom Bam)," "Slip Horn Jive," or "Glen Island Special." Nonetheless, with these latter numbers the Miller orchestra created some of its truest jazz recordings, even though it was the group's sentimental, more immediately recognizable numbers such as "Moonlight Serenade," "In the Mood," and "A String of Pearls" that gained a popular following which in some quarters has not diminished even to the present day. Still and all, the Miller orchestra was fully capable of competing at times with the more jazz-oriented big bands of the era, and it is this side of the group's production that perhaps has been slighted simply because it made a name for itself with its less purely jazz-based recordings. Certainly the leader himself had paid his dues as a jazz musician and knew and frequently dipped into the jazz repertoire for some of his more impressive performances in the sense that they featured his sidemen in rousing and at times quite inventive improvisations.

Born in Clarinda, Iowa, on March 1, 1904, Glenn Miller studied music at the University of Colorado and in 1925 joined the Ben Pollack orchestra in Venice, California. The first, surviving recordings of the Pollack orchestra, with Miller as the possible arranger of "'Deed I Do," were cut in December 1926.[138] When the Pollack group arrived in New York in 1928, it included at the time, in addition to Miller, such future stars as Benny Goodman, Bud Freeman, and Jimmy McPartland, among other sidemen. During this period, Miller became active as a studio musician for numerous recording sessions and was in on many dance jobs along with Goodman and Tommy Dorsey. He worked with Red Nichols and his various groups, and was present on November 14, 1929, for the historic recording by Red McKenzie's Mound City Blue Blowers of "One Hour," which included Coleman Hawkins's seminal tenor solo. Miller's trombone break on this recording is respectable, if at times somewhat shaky. His broad vibrato has in it something of the mellow, romantic style that would mark most of his solo work with his own band in the late 1930s. Never considered an outstanding trombonist, Miller made a name for himself more as an arranger, even though his writing in 1934 for the Dorsey Brothers band has been considered "disappointing" by Gunther Schuller, who finds Miller's arrangements of "Milenberg Joys," "Basin Street Blues," "St. Louis Blues," "Weary Blues," and "Dippermouth Blues" "marred by stylistic incongruities—certainly in relation to the venerable 'classic' jazz repertory here involved—and a fussy clutteredness that did not serve these simple pieces well. The results were rather mechanical and artificial as the players were caught at cross-purposes with the material."[139] The mystery with Miller—different in kind from that of Artie Shaw with his type of split personality—is how he eventually developed his "famous reed section sound," which for Schuller has few parallels "in Western music," a sound so special that this critic can think of hardly any other "quite so unique, quite so mesmerizing—and, more astonishingly, so resistant to becoming tedious."[140] Schuller suggests that "invention and creativity in the arts" remain a matter of mysterious processes that cannot be rationally explained, but he goes on to say that "in some dim and groping way Miller had been looking for 'the sound' for a long, long time."[141]

After arranging for the bands of Smith Ballew, Ray Noble, Glen Gray, Ozzie Nelson, and Vincent Lopez, Miller organized his own band in January 1937 and made his first recordings the following March. Previous to forming his own unit, Miller had arranged in a wide variety of styles, primarily a combination of jazz and popular music. With his own band, he began to develop arrangements "more in a jazz or swing vein" and to showcase sidemen who represented "the major stylistic soloist conceptions," including those of Hawkins, Armstrong, and Goodman.[142] Experimenting with various reed section sounds—"a rich somewhat sombre four-part sax ensemble in the lower register"; "two clarinets and two tenors, each pair in thirds an octave apart (well known from 'Sunrise Serenade')"; with brass and reeds alternating as in Henderson's call-and-response pattern but doing so with "the choirs one beat apart" instead of with one or two bars separating their exchanges—Miller searched for a sound that would distinguish his orchestra from that of Goodman, which was based largely on the Redman-Henderson formula.[143] According to Leonard Feather, it was during Miller's period with Ray Noble that he first discovered his "reed section voicing (clarinet over four saxes) that later proved a key factor in the success of his own orchestra."[144] Schuller observes that in using this "distinctive clarinet and saxophone sound" for what the critic calls Miller's "lyric instrumentals"—"virtually a new genre created by Miller"—that the bandleader, in his arrangement of "Moonlight Serenade," from April 4, 1939, invented an opening "as irresistibly magical today as it was forty-five years ago [from the date of Schuller's statement written in the mid 1980s]."[145]

The slowed down tempo of "Moonlight Serenade"—strikingly so for a typical call-and-response arrangement—evokes through its ravishing reeds and muted brasses a dreamy mood that is indeed, as Schuller says, mesmerizing. The classical purity of the clarinet solo by Wilbur Schwartz, in the mode of Goodman and Shaw, is the closest the piece comes to jazz improvisation, for the focus of the entire performance is on achieving a romantic mood rather than stimulating the listener through creative musical thought. As Schuller points out, Miller reduced his musical "palette to a limited and precisely selected choice of colors" in an attempt to appeal to "wide public acclaim . . . his exclusive aim."[146] This same approach was repeated for all the "lyric instrumentals," such as "Sunrise Serenade," "Tuxedo Junction," "Danny Boy," "Star Dust," "At Last," and "Tchaikovsky's Piano Concerto." Largely a subdued form of jazz, a Miller performance in speed and volume is far slower and lower than that of most any other big band of the era. Even though "Tuxedo Junction" contains many of the traditional jazz elements—trumpet solos supported by riffs and sectional call-and-response exchanges—they are so diminished in intensity that the effect is to turn them into a type of opiate, a soothing, low-keyed sound that induces a relaxed, romantic frame of mind. This is far removed from most jazz as originally conceived and performed—its object originally having been to excite and uplift, to start a listener inadvertently "tapping his foot, snapping his fingers, moving his body or head to the beat of the music."[147] Miller's object was more to relax his listeners, primarily couples, and to place them in a romantic frame of mind that would make each feel sentimental about the other. His success in doing so is indicated by the mass audience he attracted through his radio programs and the unprecedented financial rewards he reaped from the sponsorship of such a commercial firm as Chesterfield cigarettes. Lewis Erenberg reports that Chesterfield paid Miller a quarter-of-a-million dollars a year, and this did not include proceeds from recordings, personal appearances, and movies such as *Orchestra Wives* and *Sun Valley Serenade*.[148]

It is difficult and perhaps even foolish to argue with success, but in considering the relationship between Glenn Miller's music and jazz, there is for some listeners an element of sacrilege in the commercialization of America's most important native art form. The reaction to this type of jazz would soon develop through the so-called Bebop Revolution, and yet contrary to Irving Berlin's claim that swing would die, it has enjoyed in the last decade of the twentieth century a revival that has once again made the Miller-Goodman-Dorsey-Shaw brand of jazz hugely popular among the nation's youthful dancers.[149] Nonetheless, most of Miller's music, as Gunther Schuller has said, "is connected to jazz by only the slimmest thread," even if it "was often a music of considerable beauty and, unlike so much popular commercial music, never offensive."[150] The flimsiest ties with jazz are found in what must have been quite appealing to a mass radio audience: the Chesterfield cigarette ads, which incorporated allusions to the jazz parlance for purposes of marketing their now lawsuit-prone product. One ad from a Miller Christmas Eve show offered a set of verses with such phrases as "a stocking full of tunes," "singing and ringing and rocking the stand," "trumpets are blaring and bursting with pride," "the Chesterfield smokers are satisfied," and "it's time to forget all your worries and cares." This is followed by the band's version of "Jingle Bells," which does not contain the same level of jazz found on the 1935 Goodman rendition with Bunny Berigan on trumpet but does end with a decent bit of trumpet improvisation of its own. After a performance by the Miller band of "Elmer's Tune," with the vocal by Ray Eberle and The Modernaires, the announcer calls this piece "a community thing," because the lyrics refer to candy maker, baker, farmer, "man in the street," and "the cop on the beat," among those who "all sing Elmer's tune." The lyrics also employ the phrase "swinging any old way," which is not quite true of the Miller approach, for his orchestra's performances were rehearsed to a fare-thee-well. There was nothing sloppy about his "final presentation," including the vocals as sung by The Modernaires, who, on a piece like "So You're the One," can render the tune through a bit of scat singing that to a degree jazzes up the group's type of barbershop harmonization. Of course, many of the vocals were corny novelty pieces with crowd-pleasing appeal. "Jack and Jill," or as the lyrics aptly put it, "silly Jack and Jilly," also alludes to the jazz tradition when it says of Jack that he "boogie-woogied with the farmer's daughter." But again, the jazz connection is thin (and perhaps the sexual meaning of boogie-woogie was lost on the lyricist), because the intent is to cater to a "mass appetite" by performing "with impeccable polish and skill" arrangements not complex in nature, thereby satisfying the "slow and lazy" musical mind of the listener.[151]

In discussing an early Miller recording titled "Community Swing," from June 9, 1937, Gunther Schuller identifies the "essential ingredients of Miller's later style," including the "six-man brass section with its biting, sharply etched, slightly piercing timbre."[152] (The title of this early work is certainly prophetic in light of a piece such as "Elmer's Tune," which, as we saw, could be referred to as "a community thing.") The sectional antiphony on this 1937 recording is notable, the trumpet solo is fiery and penetrating, and the swinging clarinet break shows the positive influence of Goodman. Bass and drums drive the group well, and as with so many later performances, Miller lowers the dynamics suddenly after a drum break, goes into some nice, soft syncopation, and then abruptly concludes the piece with a loud, dramatic ending. In 1937, Miller had not yet developed his characteristic clarinet-sax sound, which later he would apply to almost every selection. On "Stardust," from a 1939 Glen Island Casino broadcast, the sound of this combination of clarinet and saxophones is quite shrill in comparison with its more mellow use on "Moonlight Serenade" and most of the other arrangements where it appears. Probably the early application of what would become Miller's tried and true sound must have startled and possibly pleased the 1939 crowd. However, this version of "Stardust" is overall a very weak rendition of the classic song, with a clarinet trio at the end almost a pathetic use of that 1920s device. The tenor break is Hawkins-inspired, while the extended trumpet solo is rather awkward and more a series of triplets that go nowhere than a jazz construction with a purposeful sense of direction. (A later version of "Stardust," from January 29, 1940, is much improved and includes a fine trumpet solo by Clyde Hurley.)[153]

Even a memorable solo such as Bobby Hackett's famous twelve bars on "A String of Pearls," from November 3, 1941, lacks the musicality of true jazz—it too seems more an exercise in arpeggiated figures.[154] At times the Miller orchestra's instrumental breaks, as on the radio broadcast of the pop vocal "Everything I Love" (which again employs the predictable clarinet-sax sound), seem simply gratuitous, adding nothing much to the performance and coming across as little more than a pale imitation of jazz. In attempting to convert every type of music into the Miller sound, the leader even offered an arrangement of Tchaikovsky's first piano concerto. One can hear the live audience singing along with the orchestra as it plays the famous theme, a clear indication of how well Miller knew his listeners. Of course, the popularity of "swinging the classics" had been created by earlier white big bands, but Miller always knew a good "community thing" when he heard it. Perhaps surprisingly, here the tenor break actually does Tchaikovsky's classical theme justice as a basis for jazz, even though the rest of the performance tends to make the concerto a neither-nor work. Similarly, the Miller radio performance of "Song of the Volga Boatmen" is a blend of jazz and a Russian folksong, and once again the results are rather neither-nor. A plunger trumpet solo imitates black jazz but seems out of place in the context. An alto solo by Ernie Caceres is certainly a respectable piece of playing, but ultimately the entire piece seems pointless, especially its Hollywood ending. None of this is perhaps as objectionable as the Miller version of the Ellington-Strayhorn classic, "Take the 'A' Train." Here the arrangement actually extracts the jazz blood from this masterwork, leaving Miller's version an anemic rendition. The clarinet-saxophone sound at the end turns " 'A' Train" into a saccharine if well-intentioned tribute.

On the other hand, there are arrangements that reveal a more authentic jazz side to the Miller personality. "Little Brown Jug," for example, truly swings, and the tenor solo is a solid contribution, not a throwaway break. The execution by the reed section, especially in the trilled passages toward the end, is exceptional in its achievement of a unified sound. "Pennsylvania 6–5000" also exhibits some excellent solo work, with the tenor (most likely Tex Beneke) heavily influenced by Lunceford's Joe Thomas. As Schuller notes, Miller much admired the "medium dance tempo" perfected by Lunceford, and this is a fine illustration of the critic's point.[155] "A String of Pearls" also shows the Lunceford influence in the breaks by the two tenors, Beneke and Al Klink, and here, too, is the call-and-response pattern alternated one beat apart, as noted by Schuller. The best Miller swing tune of them all remains "In the Mood," from August 1, 1939, which reflects once more the influence of the classic Redman-Henderson call-and-response pattern.[156] The swaggering trumpet solo by Clyde Hurley is one of the most satisfying breaks by a Miller sideman, and Tex Beneke engages in a fine exchange with his fellow tenorist Al Klink. The fade-away ending followed by a loud trumpet section ascending the scale five notes at a time, until a single trumpet tops off the passage with a final five notes up to high C, is still an effective conclusion to this memorable performance.

On a National Public Radio program aired on July 29, 2000, Miller trombonist Paul Taylor traced the history of the "In the Mood" motif back to the Wingy Manone recording of "Tar Paper Stomp" in 1930 (called "Jumpy Nerves" in 1939), through Fletcher Henderson's "Hot and Anxious" of 1931, on to a recording by the Mills Blue Brothers of "There's Rhythm in Harlem" in 1935, and finally to an Artie Shaw broadcast in 1938.[157] According to Taylor, the "final ending" of the Miller version would "part everyone's hair," and did so from the first time the orchestra tried it out at the Glen Island Casino. Taylor reported that in order for the orchestra to know when it should play the ending loud, after having gradually diminuendoed a number of times, teasing the crowd, Maurice Purtill, the drummer, would hit his cowbell lightly as a signal. Contrary to what other commentators have suggested, Taylor claimed that Eddie Durham did not contribute to the writing of "In the Mood," that only Joe Garland arranged the piece. In the interview, Taylor never really discussed Miller's piece as a work of jazz, but rather he emphasized the effect of the "teasing" dynamics, of the group's playing to the crowd. In the Miller orchestra's studio recordings and live performances, any jazz element—such as a hot solo or an intense, driving swing—almost always takes a backseat to the effect to be achieved through arranged sounds intended to hold the listener spellbound, rather than draw him or her into a creative line of musical thought.

But again, it is not that Miller's sidemen were incapable of a hotter, more intense jazz; it is a case rather of their rarely being given the opportunity within the orchestra's more sedate settings. And then, why alienate the audience Miller had so carefully cultivated, by throwing a Shaw tantrum or going off on an experimental tangent or disturbing the listener by expecting of him or her too much in the way of intellectual effort? Through his more popular, commercial appeal Miller had by 1941 achieved what no other recording group had done in fifteen years—sell a million copies of one record. With sales of the orchestra's "Chattanooga Choo-Choo" exceeding one million by two hundred thousand copies, this one side earned Miller a gold plaque from Bluebird records. Arranged by Jerry Gray and recorded on May 7, 1941, "Chattanooga" features a vocal by Tex Beneke and The Modernaires and takes full advantage of one of the favorite sources for blues and jazz: the railroad association.[158] Apart from the imitation train motif in the opening section of "Chattanooga" and the swing rhythms of the Modernaires, however, riffs and drum breaks are the only jazz elements to be heard on this side—there are no horn solos. A novelty piece emphasizing an upbeat lightheartedness, "Chattanooga" is one consistent side of the popular Miller coin, with the other offering the dreaminess of "Moonlight Serenade" and "Moonlight Cocktail."[159] Bill Finegan's arrangement of "Slow Freight," from March 31, 1940, is a work related to "Chattanooga" and includes solos by trumpeters Dale McMickle and Clyde Hurley, the former muted and the latter open, which provides for an effective contrast. This piece also includes the motif of "Tuxedo Junction," played by McMickle, and a bit of the call-and-response pattern. Nevertheless, only occasionally did Miller and his arranging corps lean toward the styles of the major black bands.

Two tunes composed by Eddie Durham, "Slip Horn Jive" and "Glen Island Special," represent works that are more in the Henderson and Basie line, which is understandable because Durham had been a part of the Basie organization. Both charts date from 1939 and feature solos by Beneke, Klink, Miller, and Hurley. Beneke and Hurley turn in excellent breaks on "Glen Island Special," from July 26, and their work on "Slip Horn Jive," from June 2, is also decent, although Beneke is somewhat corny in spots. Even though the orchestra swings these pieces quite well, both would have been improved in performances by Henderson and Basie. One of Klink's better solos comes on "Boulder Buff," from May 7, 1941, the same session that produced "Chattanooga." "Rug Cutter's Swing," a Horace Henderson tune, was recorded by the Miller orchestra on January 29, 1940, and this interpretation swings in the Miller mode, which gives it a distinctive sound, and yet the orchestra definitely does justice to Henderson's original. Solos by Hurley, Beneke, and Miller are all quite fine, and Beneke even lays claim here to being a "Texas tenor," coming on bold and a bit eccentric. The fade-away and then the loud ending bear the recognizable Miller stamp.[160] A third Durham original, "Wham (Re Bop Boom Bam)," which was recorded by a number of other big bands at the end of the decade, was broadcast on September 10, 1940, from Boston, with Marion Hutton singing the lyrics.[161] The famous "salt peanuts" phrase later recorded by Dizzy Gillespie appears here, but other than this the only jazz links are found in the driving percussion work and an energetic brass section. Durham's arrangement does "jump," as the announcer says, but no soloist makes an appearance. On the other hand, solos abound on "I Dreamt I Dwelt in Harlem," from February 25, 1941, and all are quite legitimate improvisations.[162] Ultimately, however, these more jazz-oriented sides or broadcast numbers were the exception and do not today represent the immediately identifiable Miller approach.

That Miller not only knew the jazz tradition but throughout this period returned to it on occasion is clear from three sides based on the early jazz repertoire: "Farewell Blues," "Johnson Rag," and "The Booglie Wooglie Piggy." In the case of the first, recorded on August 1, 1939, this version completely transforms the original work (recorded by the New Orleans Rhythm Kings in 1922) into a big-band swing piece, with the fiery solos by Beneke and Hurley fitting well into the style, and Miller's trombone break is especially good—even showing him capable of a Teagarden-like technique. The trumpet section passages are especially forceful, with sax responses quite unusual for the Miller unit, as is the killer-diller ending. "Johnson Rag," from November 5, 1939, swings well, and Beneke and Klink both contribute driving solos, while Hurley's trumpet break is uncharacteristically weak. The orchestra's sudden diminuendo and then slow buildup to a dynamic ending once again bears the Miller stamp. Probably the most dramatic example of this approach comes on Bill Finegan's arrangement of Morton Gould's "Pavanne," recorded on April 18, 1939. Meanwhile, Jerry Gray's arrangement of "The Booglie Wooglie Piggy," from May 7, 1941, is quite advanced, opening with a very sophisticated orchestral sound. This again is from the same session that produced Gray's arrangement of "Chattanooga," and both tunes are novelty numbers with a typical Beneke vocal backed by The Modernaires. Chummy McGregor on piano does the boogie bit, whereas Beneke turns in one of his most impressive, up-to-date tenor solos, showing that he must have been listening to the leading black tenors. Like all the name orchestras of the era, the Miller could swing most any type of piece, which is illustrated by "Pagan Love Song," recorded on June 27, 1939.[163] Beginning with Miller's "hot" trombone break, all the solos are full of verve and imagination: Klink on tenor, Hurley on trumpet, and Beneke on tenor. The ending offers quite a bit of razzle-dazzle, with Maurice Purtill kicking the group along with his drum break and his accompanying percussion work.

For many listeners, as Gunther Schuller has indicated, Miller's music, regardless of its tenuous ties to jazz, "epitomized the era for vast numbers of Americans," and still does.[164] There is no denying that Glenn Miller was a dominant force among the major white bands and that, as Schuller also notes, his music represented "a high order of craftsmanship."[165] But for the thrill of deeply stimulating jazz and its imaginative improvisatory flights, the recordings and broadcasts of Glenn Miller are not the recommended source. Although they have their moments, in comparison with the name black bands, the Miller performances do not in the end satisfy on the same high level as truly authentic jazz. Today Miller's music offers more than anything a nostalgic trip to a prewar era of jukebox Saturday nights, honey lambs, reverie, and make believe. For those "in the mood" for the idyllic, uncomplicated sound of romance, the best place to hear this is in the opening, still entrancing strains of "Moonlight Serenade."

NOTES

1. Erenberg, *Swingin' the Dream*, p. 4.
2. Ibid.
3. Schuller, *The Swing Era*, p. 8.
4. Ibid.
5. Ibid., p. 13.
6. *Jack Teagarden, Vol. 1* (Jazz Archives No. 51, 157022, 1992).
7. Gioia, *The History of Jazz*, p. 142.
8. Hymie Schertzer, quoted by Mort Goode in the insert notes to *Benny Goodman and His Orchestra: Sing, Sing, Sing* (Bluebird 5630–2-RB, 1987).
9. All the sides discussed in this paragraph are included on *Sing, Sing, Sing*.
10. Schuller, *The Swing Era*, p. 21.
11. Ibid., p. 22.
12. "Jingle Bells" and "Santa Claus Came in the Spring" are on *Bunny Berigan: The Pied Piper 1934–40.*
13. This side is included on *Sing, Sing, Sing.*
14. "Tain't No Use" is included on *The Indispensable Benny Goodman Volume 3/4 (1936–1937)* (RCA Victor, NL89756[2], 1963); "Bugle Call Rag" is on *Sing, Sing, Sing.*
15. This version of "Jam Session" is included on *I Like Jazz* (Columbia, JZ1, n.d.).
16. These two sides are included on *The Indispensable Benny Goodman.*
17. These two sides are included on *Benny Goodman and His Orchestra: Sing, Sing, Sing.*
18. These sides are included on *Sing, Sing, Sing.*
19. This recording, from June 30, 1936, is included on *Billie Holiday: The Golden Years.*
20. Quoted by Mort Goode in his insert notes to *Sing, Sing, Sing*. Both "Goody Goody" and "Sing Me a Swing Song" are included on this same CD.
21. These two sides are on *Sing, Sing, Sing.*
22. Nat Hentoff, liner notes to *At His Very Best: Duke Ellington and His Orchestra.*
23. Ibid. "I Want to Be Happy" and "Chloe" are included on *Sing, Sing, Sing.*
24. Oliphant, *Texan Jazz*, p. 212. I also discuss James's other well-known arrangement, "Life Goes to a Party," on p. 213.
25. This side and all the recordings discussed in the previous paragraph are included on *Benny Goodman and His Orchestra: The Harry James Years, Volume 1* (Bluebird, BMG 66155–2, 1993).
26. These two sides are included on *The Indispensable Benny Goodman.*
27. Schuller, *The Swing Era*, p. 23n.
28. Both of these sides are on *Benny Goodman and His Orchestra: The Harry James Years, Volume 1.*
29. Loren Schoenberg, insert notes to *Benny Goodman and His Orchestra: The Harry James Years, Volume 1.*

30. "One O'Clock Jump" is on *Benny Goodman and His Orchestra: The Harry James Years, Volume 1*.

31. Sudhalter, *Lost Chords*, p. 21.

32. Ibid., p. 16.

33. Kolodin, liner notes to *Benny Goodman Live at Carnegie Hall*. All the tunes from this concert mentioned here are included on this album.

34. Ibid.

35. Erenberg, *Swingin' the Dream*, p. 72.

36. Schuller, *The Swing Era*, p. 29.

37. Ibid., p. 28. "Ti-Pi-Tin" and "The Blue Room" are included on *Benny Goodman and His Orchestra: Wrappin' It Up, The Harry James Years, Part 2* (Bluebird, BMG 66549–2, 1995).

38. Sudhalter, *Lost Chords*, pp. 262–263.

39. All the sides discussed in this paragraph are included on *Benny Goodman and His Orchestra: Wrappin' It Up, The Harry James Years, Part 2*. I agree with the estimate of Loren Schoenberg in his insert notes to this CD when he writes that on "Farewell Blues" James delivers "one of his very best solos with the band."

40. Ibid.

41. Ibid.

42. "Solo Flight" is included on *Solo Flight: The Genius of Charlie Christian* (Columbia, CG 30779, 1972).

43. Schuller, *The Swing Era*, p. 36. The critic does not identify the specific day for this recording, but it must be August 10, and was issued on a Columbia album, 35210, according to Tom Lord's *The Jazz Discography* (Vancouver, B.C., Canada: Tom Lord Reference Inc., 1992), p. G372. Schuller says of this side that although the Basie "was a masterpiece of its kind, far outclassing Goodman's 1939 imitation," the Goodman recording represents "one of [the band's] best 1939 performances, generating a deeper fuller sound and avoiding some of the excessively bright clipped staccato style it normally favored."

44. Schuller, *The Swing Era*, p. 36. This version of "Let's Dance" is included on *Benny Goodman's Greatest Hits* (Columbia CK 65421, 1997).

45. Schuller, *The Swing Era*, p. 40.

46. These two Sauter pieces are included on *Benny Goodman's Greatest Hits*.

47. Schuller, *The Swing Era*, p. 34.

48. Ibid., p. 32.

49. Sudhalter, *Lost Chords*, p. 359.

50. Schuller, *The Swing Era*, p. 649. "I'm Gettin' Sentimental over You" is included on *The Best of Tommy Dorsey* (Bluebird, BMG 51087–2, 1992).

51. Schuller, *The Swing Era*, pp. 677 and 680.

52. Both these tunes are included on *Tommy Dorsey and His Orchestra 1935–1936* (Classics, 854, 1995).

53. Quoted in Mort Goode's insert notes to *The Best of Tommy Dorsey*.

54. In *Lost Chords*, Richard Sudhalter says of Wright that she "was at best an adequate singer" (p. 836, n. 38), but compared with Gately she's a marvel. Sudhalter reveals that Wright was Tommy's lover and so no one could convince him to keep her off the recordings. "I'm Shooting High" is included on Classics CD 854.

55. Schuller, *The Swing Area*, p. 646.

56. All the sides mentioned in this paragraph are included on *Tommy Dorsey and His Orchestra 1935–1936*.

57. Sudhalter, *Lost Chords*, p. 578.

58. Ibid., p. 263.

59. Schuller, *The Swing Era*, p. 646.

60. "Song of India" and "Royal Garden Blues" are included on *The Best of Tommy Dorsey*.

61. Pat Hawes, insert notes to "Boogie Woogie Stomp" (Living Era, CD AJA 5101, 1993). The Dorsey recording is included on this CD as well as on *The Best of Tommy Dorsey*.

62. Both these sides on are *The Best of Tommy Dorsey*.

63. Goode, insert notes to *The Best of Tommy Dorsey*.

64. Schuller, *The Swing Era*, p. 683.

65. Sudhalter, *Lost Chords*, p. 565.

66. All these sides with Berigan and Freeman are included on *The Best of Tommy Dorsey*.

67. All three sides are included on *The Best of Tommy Dorsey*.

68. Schuller, *The Swing Era*, p. 690.

69. Ibid., p. 685.

70. Ibid., p. 692. Tommy Dorsey did perform in 1937 such traditional jazz numbers as "Dippermouth Blues," "Weary Blues," and "Ja-Da," and as we have seen, he recorded "Royal Garden Blues" in 1936.

71. Louis Armstrong, *Swing That Music* (London: Longmans, Green, 1936; rpt. New York: Da Capo Press, 1993), p. 107. In his Foreword to the reprint, Dan Morgenstern points out that "one is left with the hunch that it was the ghostwriter or editor (who may have been one and the same) who had read *Tom Sawyer*, not Armstrong (though he certainly might have), and who thought that any account of life on the Mississippi should include Twain," especially as the classic American author was "never mentioned in [Armstrong's] later autobiographical writings or interviews" (p. x).

72. Ibid., pp. 44, 108, 29.

73. Schuller, *The Swing Era*, p. 191.

74. Ibid., p. 651. In *Visions of Jazz*, Gary Giddins quotes tenorist Dexter Gordon as having said that Parker "had a lot of Lester in his playing, and also Jimmy Dorsey." When questioned about the Dorsey influence, Gordon replied, "He was a master saxophonist, Bird knew that" (p. 332).

75. John Lissner, insert notes to *Contrasts: Jimmy Dorsey & His Orchestra* (Decca, GRD-626, 1993).

76. "When Ruben Swings the Cuban" is included on *Louis Armstrong and His Orchestra 1936–1937* (Classics 512, 1990).

77. Schuller, *The Swing Era*, pp. 650–651.

78. Both "In a Sentimental Mood" and "Stompin' at the Savoy" are included on *Contrasts: Jimmy Dorsey & His Orchestra*. John Lissner credits Herbie Haymer with the tenor solo, but from personnel listed for the 1936 recording Haymer was not in the orchestra, only joining the organization in 1938.

79. All four sides are included on *Contrasts: Jimmy Dorsey & His Orchestra*.

80. Schuller, *The Swing Era*, p. 651.

81. All three sides are included on *Contrasts: Jimmy Dorsey & His Orchestra*.

82. Schuller, *The Swing Era*, p. 651.

83. "All of Me," "Contrasts," "Turn Left," and "Turn Right" are included on *Contrasts: Jimmy Dorsey & His Orchestra*.

84. Lissner, insert notes to *Contrasts*.

85. Ibid.

86. "When the Sun Comes Out" and "Tangerine" are included on *Contrasts*.

87. Schuller, *The Swing Era*, p. 648, n. 16

88. *Jack Teagarden, Vol. 1 1928/1931* (Jazz Archives, No. 51, 157022, 1992).

89. Sudhalter, *Lost Chords*, pp. 575–576.

90. *Bunny Berigan: The Pied Piper 1934–40*.

91. *Bunny Berigan and His Boys 1935–1936* (Classics, 734, 1993).

92. Chris Albertson, insert notes to *Begin the Beguine: Artie Shaw and His Orchestra* (Bluebird, 6274-RB, 1987).

93. Ibid.

94. Ibid.

95. Ibid.

96. Schuller, *The Swing Era*, pp. 695 and 697.

97. This side is included on *Artie Shaw: His Best Recordings 1937–1942* (Best of Jazz, 4016, 1994). Unless indicated otherwise, all the Shaw sides discussed here are on this CD.

98. Albertson, insert notes to *Begin the Beguine*.

99. Schuller, *The Swing Era*, p. 700.

100. Ibid., pp. 697 and 698.

101. Schuller, *The Swing Era*, p. 702. This side is included on *Artie Shaw and His Orchestra: Personal Best* (Bluebird, 61099–2, 1992).

102. Interview with Shaw by Orin Keepnews, insert notes to *Personal Best*.

103. Graham Colombé, insert notes to *His Best Recordings*.

104. These two sides are on *Personal Best*.

105. Schuller, *The Swing Era*, p. 704.

106. *Personal Best*. All the Cafe Rouge sides are included on this CD.

107. Quoted by Graham Colombé in the insert notes to *His Best Recordings*.

108. *Personal Best*.

109. See Sudhalter, *Lost Chords*, p. 578.

110. Ibid., p. 587.

111. Schuller, *The Swing Era*, p. 702.

112. Ibid., p. 699. This side is included on *Personal Best*.

113. *Personal Best*.

114. This side is included on *Begin the Beguine*.

115. Schuller, *The Swing Era*, p. 703.

116. The "Carioca" air check is included on *Begin the Beguine*. A version of "Carioca," from January 23, 1939, is found on *His Best Recordings 1937–1942*.

117. This side is included on *Begin the Beguine*.

118. Schuller, *The Swing Era*, p. 704.

119. Sudhalter, *Lost Chords*, pp. 591–592.

120. Schuller, *The Swing Era*, pp. 710 and 706. These two sides are included on *Personal Best*.

121. Ibid., p. 709.

122. Ibid.

123. "Blues," in two parts, is included on *Begin the Beguine*.

124. Schuller, *The Swing Era*, p. 699.

125. "Deep Purple" is included on *Begin the Beguine*.

126. "Moon Ray" is included on *Begin the Beguine*.

127. *Personal Best*.

128. Giddins, *Visions of Jazz*, p. 205.

129. Schuller, *The Swing Era*, p. 705. This work is included on *Personal Best*.

130. Sudhalter, *Lost Chords*, p. 593.

131. Schuller, *The Swing Era*, p. 705 n. 37.

132. *Personal Best*.

133. On *Personal Best*.

134. On ibid.

135. *Glenn Miller: A Legendary Performer* (RCA Victor, CPK2–0693, 1974).

136. Schuller, *The Swing Era*, p. 671.

137. Ibid., p. 671.

138. Sudhalter, *Lost Chords*, p. 322.

139. Schuller, *The Swing Era*, p. 649. "Dippermouth Blues" as performed by the Miller orchestra faithfully reproduces the Oliver tune, complete with the shouted phrase, "Oh play that thing," but this is a popularized rendition that takes the soul out of Oliver's classic. Miller himself plays Oliver's solo on trombone and his maudlin, Dixielandish version devalues a golden moment in jazz history, as well as debasing a worthy tradition carried on by Armstrong, Henderson, and even Jimmy Dorsey.

140. Ibid., p. 661.

141. Ibid., p. 663.

142. Ibid., p. 664.

143. Ibid., pp. 665–666.

144. Leonard Feather, *The New Edition of The Encyclopedia of Jazz* (New York: Bonanza Books, 1962), p. 333.

145. Schuller, *The Swing Era*, pp. 667–668.

146. Ibid., pp. 672 and 666.

147. Ibid., p. 223.

148. Erenberg, *Swingin' the Dream*, p. 169.

149. Freedland, *A Salute to Irving Berlin*, p. 167.

150. Schuller, *The Swing Era*, p. 669.

151. Ibid.

152. Ibid., p. 664. "Community Swing" is included on *The Best of Benny Goodman & Glenn Miller* (Madacy Entertainment, Sony Music Special Products, STP2 3487, 2000).

153. This version of Stardust is included on *Glenn Miller: Swing Legends* (Nimbus Records, NI2001, 2000). In my *Texan Jazz*, I overlooked the fact that Hurley was a Texan, born in Fort Worth on September 3, 1916, and educated at Texas Christian University, where he played for four years (1932–1936) in the school jazz band before joining Ben Pollack in 1937, after which he was called up by Miller in 1939.

154. "A String of Pearls" is included on *Glenn Miller: Moonlight Serenade* (Bluebird, 61072–2, 1992).

155. Schuller, *The Swing Era*, p. 674.

156. "In the Mood" and "Pennsylvania 6–5000" are both included on the radio broadcast cassette, *A Legendary Performer*, but the studio recordings from August 1, 1939, and April 28, 1940, are included on *Glenn Miller: Moonlight Serenade*.

157. Gunther Schuller covers the same history of "In the Mood" in his *The Swing Era*, except for the mention of a 1938 Shaw radio broadcast. Schuller does refer to Shaw as having played but never recorded the piece. See *The Swing Era*, p. 674.

158. "Chattanooga Choo-Choo" is included on *Moonlight Serenade*.

159. "Moonlight Cocktail" is on *A Legendary Performer*.

160. "Rug Cutter's Swing," "Boulder Buff," "Slow Freight," "Slip Horn Jive," and "Glen Island Special" are all included on *Swing Legends*.

161. This version of Durham's "Wham" is included on *Glenn Miller and His Orchestra: The Chesterfield Shows Volume II 1940/1/2*.

162. Ibid.

163. "Farewell Blues," "Johnson Rag," "Pavanne," "Pagan Love Song," and "The Booglie Wooglie Piggy" are all included on *Swing Legends*.

164. Schuller, *The Swing Era*, p. 674.

165. Ibid.

Chapter 4

Other Black Bands

Along with the four great name bands discussed in chapter 2, there were at least a dozen additional black units active during the period from 1930 to 1941. These organizations also made singular contributions to the history of jazz and at times competed successfully with the name bands, even outdueling them on occasion, as when Chick Webb's band faced off against that of Count Basie at the Savoy in one of the many "Battles of the Bands" held at that famous dancehall. Some of these bands were designed primarily to feature instrumental stars such as Louis Armstrong, Earl "Fatha" Hines, and Hot Lips Page, or a singer such as Cab Calloway. In such cases the band itself was not the major attraction but rather the soloist or singer, and with respect to Armstrong and Page, the star instrumental soloist was also the band's notable vocalist. Other bands—like those of drummer Chick Webb, vibraharpist-pianist-drummer Lionel Hampton, and altoist-trumpeter Benny Carter—frequently spotlighted their leaders as instrumental soloists, but were at times outstanding in themselves. Although black units other than the name black bands could showcase a soloist of the stature of Armstrong, a singer as entertaining and unique as Calloway, or a multi-instrumentalist as talented as Hampton, most of these organizations also presented the work of such influential arrangers as Edgar Sampson, Jimmy Mundy, and Mary Lou Williams, performances by pace-setting ensembles, and solos by sidemen who were illustrious in their own right. As a group, these "lesser" black bands made a mark on the Swing Era that was almost equal to that of the name bands and certainly vital in its way to the development of jazz in this second major decade of the music.

LOUIS ARMSTRONG

As the musician who is credited with single-handedly changing the emphasis in jazz from an art of collective group improvisation to one of soloistic virtuosity, Louis Armstrong had perhaps made his most remarkable contributions to the music by 1928 when he recorded such masterpieces as "West End Blues" and "Weather Bird." But this does not mean that Armstrong no longer produced important or even pathbreaking solos, for he did. However, the company he often kept during the 1930s did not always serve him quite so well artistically. The small groups led by Armstrong in the late 1920s involved more give and take between Armstrong and his sidemen, which, especially in the case of pianist Earl "Fatha" Hines and his part on "West End Blues" and "Weather Bird," resulted in seminal recordings.

Many commentators have lamented the big-band settings during the thirties in which Armstrong found himself, at times surrounded by essentially nonjazz musicians. Some critics have laid the blame for the poor aggregations at the feet of the trumpet star's manager, Joe Glaser, who was responsible, as James Lincoln Collier has pointed out, for choosing the musicians in the bands, making the bookings, selecting the tunes, and in general running the business of Armstrong's career. Collier indicates that Glaser was little interested in Armstrong's development as an artist but more concerned to direct him "toward popular material, movies in which he played the grinning darky, radio shows where he jived with Bing Crosby, and whatever else was necessary to build Armstrong as a celebrated public figure who could make them both rich."[1] Yet it was not always the case that the big bands with which Armstrong was the featured soloist were mediocre or filled with nonjazz sidemen. Dan Morgenstern disagrees with Collier and contends that "it makes no sense to judge an Armstrong big band by the same standards as are used for Ellington, Basie or Goodman. It is not intended to be a self-sufficient creative unit; it is essentially there to back a virtuoso instrumentalist and singer who in a very real sense is the whole show."[2] But regardless of the band context in which Armstrong appeared, the trumpeter could still elevate most every performance to a level rarely reached by other jazz musicians. This was achieved through the extraordinary solos he fashioned, frequently based on popular songs with often little to recommend them until Armstrong transformed their sentimental melodies and trite harmonies into the stuff of swinging jazz.

Just as Louis Armstrong was ahead of all other jazz musicians in the architectonic structure and swing of his 1924 solos with the Fletcher Henderson orchestra, so in the 1930s the trumpeter led the way in extending his instrument's range, both in terms of note production and of emotive expression. In 1930, on his recording of "You're Lucky to Me," Armstrong would for the first time hit a high F, which Gunther Schuller calls a "new Olympian height."[3] Like so many of the trumpeter's performances during the '30s, this one is not especially interesting except for his wondrous singing tone in the piece's opening section and his concluding solo's dazzling glissando up to that Olympian note. His vocal is lackluster, owing in part perhaps to the uninspiring lyrics by Andy Razaf, who did much better work on "What Did I Do to Be So Black and Blue" and Fats Waller's "Ain't Misbehavin' " and "Keepin' Out of Mischief," which were sung more effectively by Armstrong in 1929 (the first two) and 1932. The orchestra seems adequate, and a baritone sax solo is effective enough, but clearly the purpose of the group behind Armstrong is to support him as the star attraction. Another piece that characterizes much of Armstrong's recording output in the thirties is "Chinatown, My Chinatown," from November 3, 1931.[4] As Louis tells the listener in his introductory sing talk, while the orchestra in the background plays the theme at breakneck speed, this is a novelty number in which the trumpet and saxes will have an argument, which means, as it turns out, a traditional call-and-response exchange. When the saxes can be heard—the volume level on their part being lowered when Armstrong sing talks to the listener—the section performs admirably what the trumpeter refers to as its "getting away." But just when one is tuning into the reeds, Louis comes back with some of his banter, full of phrases that became predictable on his later recordings, such as "You rascal you" (also the title of a tune recorded by him in 1931) and "Look out there." As for Armstrong's trumpet work, it is composed of what would also become quite predictable: short, repeated phrases answered by the orchestra, half-valve glissandos into the upper register, and high notes held and often shaken for bars at a time. Once the listener has heard the corny jokes and the displays of pure showboating, they grow somewhat tiresome as the years go by.

Fortunately, Armstrong also produced a number of exceptional solos during this period. Two of these are the "Stardust" recordings of 1931, discussed previously in chapter 1. In 1932 Armstrong also recorded two versions of "Between the Devil and the Deep Blue Sea," accompanied by the Les Hite orchestra. Both Collier and Gunther Schuller rate all four of these performances as some of Armstrong's finest, with the latter saying that "his playing on these particular recordings is beyond anything he had previously achieved."[5] Although once again the ensemble is far from noteworthy, it seems to work well enough in highlighting the soloist, and is much better on the second of the two versions of "Between the Devil," more forceful and more clearly audible than on the first where it is relegated to the background. The intensity of the trumpeter's two performances is striking, even though he uses a mute on both versions, only taking it out for his concluding strains. Although Schuller may be correct that Armstrong surpassed his previous playing, it is difficult to find the solos on "Between the Devil" as infectious and technically fascinating as his work in the twenties. Certainly there is not the same type of inventive playing involved in his performances of the thirties, nor the driving swing that he had exhibited on those earlier recordings that showed the way for so many other jazz soloists. Another recording from 1932, of "Home (When Shadows Fall)," contains one of Armstrong's frequent cadenzas, which, once again, does not compare favorably with his stop-time choruses recorded on the 1926 "Cornet Chop Suey."[6]

More impressive, and rather typical of Armstrong's work during the Swing Era, are his recordings from 1932 of "All of Me" (January 27) and "Love, You Funny Thing" (March 2), the former of which he would frequently return to in the forties and fifties. On both pieces Armstrong again performs at first with a straight mute that does not lessen—may in fact increase—the impassioned power of his playing.[7] His vocals are very fine, with his knowing inflections for "oh baby" or just "oh," and his wordless interpolations that add to the sentimental impact of the lyrics. "Love, You Funny Thing" has a touching melody line, which, after Armstrong's vocal, he and the ensemble play together evocatively, with the trumpeter straying off at times to release intensely felt phrases. As Gunther Schuller has observed, "Armstrong was at heart a lyric player . . . with a highly developed sense of embellishment."[8] This is quite evident on these two pieces, as is Schuller's observation that Armstrong "preferred moderate or slower tempos."[9] In contrast, a piece such as "Swing That Music," from May 18, 1936, is taken at a much faster clip than was customary with the trumpeter during the thirties.[10] Here the Luis Russell–led ensemble generates tremendous swing for an Armstrong-supported orchestra, and although the tempo is furious, the trumpeter manages his signature glissandos and repeated notes, the latter varied by shifting rhythms and changing intensity of dynamics and drive. He definitely shows on this one piece that he was still one of the greatest, if not the very greatest, jazz musician alive. Two other tunes from 1936, which also exhibit more swing in an Armstrong performance than is customary for him during this period, are "I Come from a Musical Family," from April 28, and "Mahogany Hall Stomp," from May 18.[11] Both these sides were cut with the Luis Russell ensemble, which is not only a swinging unit but its sidemen contribute brief but punchy solos: Snub Mosely and Jimmy Archey on trombone, Greely Walton on tenor, Leonard Davis on trumpet, and Charlie Holmes on alto. In a moderate tempo, these pieces rock along nicely, with Pops Foster's bass leading the way, until in the case of "I Come from a Musical Family," the tune slows to a curious coda in which Armstrong reverts to a more lyrical mode. Proof that Armstrong could swing anything at any tempo is found in "Mexican Swing," from May 13, 1938. This Latin-flavored piece features a real rapport between soloist and ensemble, as well as a fine tenor solo by Bingie Madison.[12]

Another orchestra that backed Armstrong in 1932 was that of Chick Webb. James Lincoln Collier ranks "Hobo, You Can't Ride This Train," one of the sides recorded with the Webb orchestra on December 8, 1932, as among Armstrong's very finest recordings of the 1930s.[13] An original Armstrong tune, "Hobo, You Can't Ride This Train," as Dan Morgenstern observes, was "spawned of the Depression" and "is a blues that really romps."[14] Like Duke Ellington's "Wall Street Wail" of December 1929, Armstrong's original piece documents something of the historical period, which is characteristic of jazz and other forms of American music. In this sense jazz provides, along with the other arts, a perspective on social developments of the day, comparable in Armstrong's case to "The River" section of Hart Crane's poem *The Bridge* from early 1930, with its depiction of "Rail-squatters ranged in nomad raillery."[15] As the tough but jovial brakeman, Armstrong repeatedly tells the hobo that he cannot ride the train, but at the end of the tune he relents and says, "You're alright with me son . . . I think I'll let you ride." His reference in the lyrics to riding the rods again recalls the Crane poem; also, in both there is the feeling, as the poet suggests, that the hobos are in touch with their times and with the real America. Ultimately, of course, it is the music of the Armstrong-Webb recording of "Hobo" that makes this work endure rather than the words of Louis's gravel-voiced raillery. Opening with a bell (played by Mezz Mezzrow) and Chick Webb's brushes on snare drum in imitation of a train starting up, this performance is notable not only for Armstrong's soaring glissandos and spectacular tonal qualities—Dan Morgenstern writes that "never before or after did he sound like he does on these 1932–33 Victor recordings"—but also for the way the Webb orchestra swings probably better and is more complementary behind the trumpeter than any big band that ever backed him up.[16] The tenor solo by Elmer Williams is superb, but it is Charlie "Big" Green's shaking trombone that truly delivers, in Morgenstern's word, a "caloric" break, along with the one he takes on "You'll Wish You'd Never Been Born," from the same date, which was the last recorded by Armstrong's former mate from the Fletcher Henderson orchestra of 1925.[17] The trumpeter's own playing here is not marked by any striking ideas but is amazing rather with respect to its virtuosity, range, and glorious sound. For a depression song, this must have been joyously uplifting at the time, and almost seventy years later, it is still a stirring piece of music, timeless in its ability to thrill the ear and move one almost to tears.

In January 1933, Armstrong recorded with what reedman Budd Johnson, who was with him at the time, considered the trumpet star's worst band. Nonetheless, the group did produce a few sides that have garnered praise from Gunther Schuller and George Avakian, although mostly for brother Keg Johnson's trombone work on "Some Sweet Day," from January 27, "Mahogany Stomp," from January 28, and especially "Basin Street Blues," also from January 27. Budd's tenor breaks on "Sittin' in the Dark," from January 26, and "Some Sweet Day" also are quite noteworthy. Louis's expansive solo work on "I Gotta Right to Sing the Blues" and "He's a Son of the South," from January 26, is particularly fine (even with a few miscues in the latter), and his swinging vocal on "Honey, Do!" is a true delight. Pianist Teddy Wilson, who also participated in the January 1933 session, remarked that Louis "had a combination of all the factors that make a good musician. He had balance . . . this most of all. Tone. Harmonic sense. Excitement. Technical skill. Originality. Every musician, no matter how good, usually has something out of balance. But in Armstrong, everything was in balance, all the factors equally developed . . . Lyricism. Delicacy. Emotional outbursts. Rhythm. Complete mastery of the horn."[18]

Another session on April 24, 1933, produced in "Laughin' Louie" "one of Armstrong's greatest" solos, according to Avakian, and in the judgment of Dan Morgenstern and Stanley Crouch, it is "a magical performance."[19] "Mississippi Basin" and "Dusky Stevedore," from this same session, seem even more impressive, as is his playing on "Mighty River" from an April 26 date, which produced as well a fine trombone break by Keg Johnson on "I Wonder Who" and a lively rendition of "St. Louis Blues."[20]

Although physical problems during 1934 and 1935 limited Armstrong's output, he did record "Got a Bran' New Suit" with the Luis Russell band on October 3, 1935.[21] Here Armstrong's vocal is smoothly rhythmic, mellow, and infectious, and is followed by swinging breaks by Greely Walton on tenor and Charlie Holmes on alto. Armstrong's solo on a previously unissued take is delivered with a relaxed if somewhat restrained swing, marred by slight flubs but more swinging in places than the take that was issued by Decca in 1935, although admittedly the latter is superior in its construction.[22] Gunther Schuller observes that on a piece like this, where Armstrong has grown more subdued, the trumpeter has "brought a new maturity to his art."[23] The same singing tone is present, but there is a relaxation in his delivery that makes it more rhythmically satisfying. This carried over into what was one of Armstrong's most outstanding recording sessions of the decade, held on May 18, 1936.

Six sides from the May 18 session, in collaboration with the Luis Russell Orchestra, are among the most notable Armstrong made during this period: "Lyin' to Myself," "Ev'ntide," "Swing That Music," "Thankful," "Red Nose," and "Mahogany Hall Stomp." Two of these pieces—the more swinging, medium-tempo sides, "Swing That Music" and "Mahogany Hall Stomp"—have been discussed earlier. As for the other four, all represent some of Armstrong's most expressive vocals, with his clear enunciation and unfailing sense of rhythm an obvious influence on such singers as Billie Holiday and Nat King Cole. Louis's vocal on "If We Never Meet Again," from April 29, is equally fine.[24] With regard to Armstrong's vocal jazz, George Avakian has written that

Louis developed a whole school of jazz singing, based on a literal interpretation of the folk and blues singers' approach to the voice as an instrument. Louis showed that the emotional meaning of a lyric can be expressed through vocal inflections and improvisations of a purely instrumental quality just as effectively—more in fact—as through words. This line of development paralleled the growth of his instrumental influence. It still embraces every jazz and popular singer today.[25]

As for Armstrong's trumpet playing on "Lyin' to Myself," "Ev'ntide," "Thankful," and "Red Nose," it is tastefully dramatic, with on the first an amazing cadenza and a wondrous building up to the final high note, which is matched and perhaps even exceeded in the latter regard by "Ev'ntide." "Thankful" also exhibits some of Armstrong's passionate drama, and includes two impressive solos by Jimmy Archey on trombone and Charlie Holmes on alto. Speaking of Armstrong's performances on the two ballads, "Ev'ntide" and "Thankful," Gunther Schuller writes that "he invents grandiloquent and masterful improvisations, his tone purer and bigger than ever. A new authoritativeness exerts itself, as he takes even the relatively complex changes of 'Thankful' and invents magnificent new free-floating arching lines over them, great cathedrals of sound."[26] On "Red Nose," Armstrong's vocal is backed by a muted obbligato from lead trumpet Louis Bacon, whereas on "If We Never Meet Again," Armstrong plays an obbligato behind Bingie Madison's romantic tenor, recalling Louis's many obbligatos for Bessie Smith and other blues singers in the twenties. Certainly all of these recordings in 1936 with the Luis Russell band are far removed from the twenties style, but Armstrong remains the master of every aspect of jazz performance, from vocal, trumpet solo, and obbligato to his driving of the ensemble and inspiring his fellow sidemen in their own highly effective solos.

In 1936, Armstrong also recorded with the Jimmy Dorsey Orchestra, as noted in chapters 1 and 3. Although most of the numbers were novelty tunes, with the exception of "Dippermouth Blues" and "Pennies from Heaven," Armstrong's singing is even more markedly clear, void of his usual gravelly sound, more appealing in a popular manner.[27] In fact, by comparison with Bing Crosby and Frances Langford, who appear with Armstrong on "Pennies from Heaven," Louis's vocal rendition is, in its musicality, dramatically superior to the crooning of the two white singers, even given the corny lyrics of "Skeleton in the Closet." As for his trumpet work, this has been praised especially in the case of "Skeleton," which the Dorsey band plays with great gusto and in the process achieves a finer effect than similar "spooky" pieces such as "Hell's Bells" and "Hi Spook" recorded by the Lunceford orchestra in 1937 and 1941, respectively.[28] Gunther Schuller finds the performance of "Skeleton" has "a light airy Henderson-style swing" and notes again that Armstrong's tone is pure and rich, his ideas flowing from him "with devastating ease."[29] Schuller does not rate the Dorsey band's recording of "Swing That Music," from August 7, 1936, so highly as the earlier one with the Luis Russell orchestra, calling the later Dorsey version "frantic" and overly "driven."[30] Nonetheless, here Armstrong is simply spectacular in his own driving solo, building to an intensity that is his alone, even as he keeps pace with the frantic Dorsey band.

Prior to recording with the Dorsey Orchestra, Armstrong joined with another white group to cut a side titled "Yes! Yes! My! My!" Billed as Louis Armstrong and His Orchestra, as were Satchmo's recordings with the Luis Russell unit, this session was held on February 4, 1936, and included in its personnel Bunny Berigan on trumpet, Stan King on drums, and Al Philburn on trombone.[31] Berigan's lead trumpet is prominent both behind Armstrong's vocal and in driving the entire ensemble, but it is Al Philburn who takes the solo spotlight with a fine Teagarden-inspired break, which throughout features that Texan's typical triplet turns. Armstrong's own solo is full of swinging phrases, niftily maneuvered, with the concluding note not exceptionally high but wonderfully well placed and supported to great effect by the ensemble's final chord. In August 1936 and in March and April of 1937, Armstrong recorded with such groups as The Polynesians, Andy Iona and His Islanders, and The Mills Brothers, but these are not particularly worthy of comment.[32] The Hawaiian impact on jazz is most notable perhaps in its introduction at the time of a steel-guitar sound with its exaggerated vibrato, which showed up in recordings by Western Swing groups. Louis's singing demonstrates once again his ability to handle any style with taste, even if the material has little or no value as jazz. Probably the best of these sides is "Darling Nelly Gray," recorded on April 7, 1937, with The Mills Brothers, which contains a decent trumpet solo and a delightful jive vocal.[33]

According to Gunther Schuller, 1938 was a lean year for Armstrong in the recording studio, as he was somewhat forgotten in the midst of the tremendous popularity of the big bands, which relegated his status to something of an eclipsed star.[34] Nonetheless, Armstrong did record several sides that both Schuller and James Lincoln Collier consider among his best of the period, in particular, "Jubilee" and "Struttin' with Some Barbecue."[35] "Jubilee" is notable for the "climactic high F" with which Armstrong ends this marchlike piece, and Richard Sudhalter observes that

in bar 26 of the final chorus, Louis holds out the concert G, corresponding to the word "of" in the phrase "carnival of joy," for three and a half beats (instead of the eighth-note assigned to it in the song), before landing on the F for "joy." It amplifies the phrase and the concept of real, untrammeled joy behind it. Only the extraordinary artistic mind of Louis Armstrong could have conceived of that, and at so purely instinctive a level.[36]

As for "Struttin' with Some Barbecue," it is even more spectacular in offering in the final few bars "not merely a high note, but a series of wildly flapping glissando effects that defy both description and notation."[37] In attempting to distinguish between the jazz of the 1920s and that of the 1930s, it is useful to compare Louis's original version of "Struttin' with Some Barbecue," from December 9, 1927, with his rendition of January 12, 1938.[38] For the sessions that first produced "Struttin' with Some Barbecue," which are considered among "the most astonishing days in jazz history," Armstrong made five classic recordings in the company of Kid Ory, Lil Hardin, Johnny Dodds, and Johnny St. Cyr.[39] Backed by a thumping rhythm laid down by St. Cyr's banjo and Hardin's piano, throughout "Struttin' with Some Barbecue" Louis's ringing trumpet is so full of energy and vitality that there is nothing quite like it in jazz. When he departs from the melody line to embellish it with virtuoso licks, he is not always entirely in control because his notes are simply bursting with invention and exuberance. But it is this unconstrained energy that conveys an infectious quality to his playing which cannot be expressed by a more flawless execution. With the 1938 version, Armstrong is more assured, more in control, and more powerful in his delivery, and the Luis Russell band complements him with a background that showcases and thereby enhances his brilliant sound and technique. Both recordings are masterful performances, with each representing a different side of Armstrong's jazz artistry.

"I Double Dare You," from the same session of January 12, 1938, which produced "Jubilee" and "Struttin' with Some Barbecue," also has been singled out by Collier for its "long solo at the end . . . made up of a sequence of completely formed phrases, each four, five, or even six measures in length, and each cut and lapped to fall at unexpected places across the rigid four-bar segments of the song. Many phrases end on the fourth beat of a measure, a practice later to become widespread with the beboppers."[40] "True Confession," also from January 12, "So Little Time," from May 13, and "Naturally," from June 24, all find Louis at his lighthearted best. In 1939, he tended to be "drifting along," and then in 1940 he began to record with small groups, which would lead in 1941 to the establishment of his All-Stars, with Jack Teagarden and Earl "Fatha" Hines. But also in 1941, on November 16, Armstrong recorded again with Luis Russell and what Max Harrison has called "an altogether degenerate survival" of the latter's band. Despite the "neutral character" of the Russell group, Armstrong produces "one of his very best recordings" in "When It's Sleepy Time Down South," a tune he had previously recorded in 1931 and 1933 (Louis's solo on the latter called by Gunther Schuller "soulful").[41] Harrison declares that Armstrong's solo "contains not a superfluous note," that its "almost classical focusing on essentials distills all the qualities he brought to music."[42] It is true that this recording includes many, if not "all," of the trumpeter's contributions to jazz; but mostly it exhibits his broad, singing tone, his ability to embellish a tune with just the right rhythmic and harmonic note choices, and his dramatic flair. However, because it is a ballad taken at an even slower tempo than his 1931 version, this piece does not contain much in the way of his exemplary swing; but the latter is deliciously present on the cut of "Cain and Abel," from May 1, 1940.[43] Along with recordings cut in 1940 and 1941 with the Russell band, Armstrong also made a group of sides with a sextet that included Sidney Bechet, who takes some fine breaks on "2:19 Blues" and "Down in Honky Tonk Town."[44] Armstrong's subsequent All-Star recordings represent in many respects his return to a type of Dixieland style, coinciding with a New Orleans revival that began to compete with the big bands and with the emergent bebop movement. Although by the end of the thirties Armstrong was no longer the leading figure in jazz, he had certainly held his own during the period and even, as Harrison suggests, continued his "musical growth . . . right through the 1930s," proving beyond a doubt that he remained still a pillar in, if not the very foundation of, every era of jazz history.[45]

LUIS RUSSELL

As we have seen, Luis Russell's orchestra served in the capacity of backup for the virtuosity of Louis Armstrong. But the Russell unit was established some eight years before Armstrong began to front it in 1935, and by 1929 had changed from a New Orleans–style to a New York–style aggregation, from a collective ensemble playing interpolated solos to one playing " 'advanced' arrangements and 'originals,' heavily featuring its roster of soloists."[46] Albert J. McCarthy has asserted that "it is doubtful if any contemporary group could equal the ensemble swing that Russell was able to produce with the personnel he led. The numbers that he and other musicians, within the band, contributed to its book were ideal for displaying both its surging ensemble power and the individuality of its soloists." McCarthy refers to a statement made by Henry "Red" Allen that "there may have been bands who could better Russell's in several respects, but none who could outswing it."[47]

According to both McCarthy and Gunther Schuller, the finest recordings by the Russell orchestra date from 1929 and 1930. Of the May 1930 sides, "Louisiana Swing," from the 29th, is singled out for special commendation, with McCarthy finding it "the best performance from this date" and Schuller calling it an impressive composition "with its entirely original bridge."[48] Both critics also praise the solo work of Russell's sidemen, in particular J.C. Higginbotham on trombone and Henry "Red" Allen on trumpet. Two other sides also recorded in 1930, "Saratoga Drag" and "Ease on Down," are considered by McCarthy to "exhibit some of the spirit associated with the band."[49] Beginning with "Louisiana Swing," the Russell unit begins to exhibit some of the smoother swing that will become characteristic of so many other bands of the thirties. This is even more evident on "Saratoga Drag," from December 17, 1930, when the sax section is totally together, the writing and playing are no longer frantic as on the exciting but rather exaggerated "Panama" and "High Tension" of September 5, and Pop Foster's bass is flowing rather than slapped. Allen's two trumpet solos on "Saratoga Drag"—separated by a spirited break by Greely Walton on tenor—offer a newer, more daring reach for his instrument, extending beyond

Armstrong's strongly on-the-beat rhythm. Allen's lines are horizontal rather than vertical, his arpeggios achieving a forward momentum, his notes leaping at times from high to low but in an effortless flow that does not interrupt the overall development of his headlong improvisational thought. Schuller indicates that on "Louisiana Swing" the trumpeter plays "with a relaxed sustained poise that contrasts with his more fidgety, restless work of the time."[50] This is true as well for Allen's solo on "Saratoga Drag," which is, once again, amazingly advanced for the date of this performance. Finally, Charlie Holmes's alto saxophone also represents a more flowing, smoother sounding style, with less of the sweet tone of a Johnny Hodges and moving toward the less adorned, more direct approach of a Charlie Parker at the end of the decade.

The ensemble playing on "Saratoga Drag" is especially impressive. The reed and brass sections complement one another, but not so much in the style of a Fletcher Henderson call-and-response exchange. Here the brass tends to comment on or even complete what the saxes have to say, or vice versa, and when they play as a full group, the effect is an increase in energy and power, a more intense drive in terms of what McCarthy accurately describes as Russell's surging ensemble. What lends the entire performance such energetic swing is largely Pops Foster's bass, which is not surprising because, as McCarthy avers, "when basic jazz qualities are considered [Foster] rates as one of the greatest of all jazz bass players."[51] The tempo is faster on "Ease on Down," from December 17, 1930, and this, too, adds to the surging drive of the ensemble, yet the group maintains control despite the furious pace. The soloists, Walton on tenor, Higginbotham on trombone, and Allen on trumpet, are all spectacular in their ability to keep the momentum going even as they create their truly superb breaks. Walton is all over his horn, Higginbotham delivers some startling, intense shakes, and Allen drives for all he's worth. This is not exactly the type of dance music that would become the fashion later in the decade, for it is a bit too hot. Perhaps, as the title of one Russell side suggests, it was too "Primitive" for most listeners of the late 1930s, but it should still be appealing for those inclined to hear all-out hot jazz played by a rolling, sweeping eleven-piece ensemble.

In 1931, the Russell orchestra recorded four tunes that all find Henry Allen in great form, as is Dickie Wells, who has replaced Higginbotham. On two of these pieces, "You Rascal, You" and "Goin' to Town," from August 28, Pops Foster's bass and Paul Barbarin's drums provide solid swing for the ensemble and soloists. On both tunes, Dickie Wells is more extroverted and forceful on his breaks than would be the case with his later work with Basie. However, André Hodeir remarks that on "Goin' to Town" Wells's solo "is a kind of synthesis of all [his] principal characteristics: attack, glissando, vibrato, 'bite,' and freedom of rhythmic construction."[52] Vocalist Chris Bullock's contributions are not embarrassing but neither are they jazz, especially on "Say the Word," from the same date, which is almost entirely in the sweet category, with a type of Paul White- man symphonic syncopation. On this piece, Allen's trumpet solo furnishes just about the sole jazz touch. Albert J. McCarthy considers the fourth piece from this session, "Freakish Blues," an original by Russell and Barbarin, "an attractive tune that, now and then, calls to mind the popular song 'Red Sails in the Sunset.' "[53] What is particularly noteworthy about this per- formance is that it is essentially the same as that of "Freakish Light Blues," credited to Russell and Barbarin and recorded February 1, 1929, by King Oliver and his orchestra, which at the time included the cocomposers, as well as Charlie Holmes. The trombone solo, originally performed by J.C. Higginbotham, is on the 1931 version rendered by Dickie Wells, but is almost note for note the same as on the 1929 recording. Henry Allen, who was with Oliver in 1930, does not hew so closely to the trumpet part of the earlier version, using more of a Bubber Miley style of wah-wah mute. Only two years separate these two recordings, and the personnel is much the same; even the new members seem quite aware of the original version, as indicated by Wells's trombone part, which may have been completely written out or picked up from the 1929 recording. All this points up the fact that Russell continued to live off his earlier work—Gunther Schuller observing that another Russell-Barbarin piece, titled "The Call of the Freaks," was recorded by Oliver in 1929 and also by a Russell orchestra in the same year.[54] However, "The Call" and "Freakish Blues" are not at all the same tunes, yet both are "stompy, moody minor-key piece[s], which must have sounded captivatingly 'weird' to listeners in 1929."[55] Even though, according to McCarthy, the orchestra's Okeh recordings on Sep- tember 5, 1930 of "Panama" and "High Tension" were on a par with its January 24, 1930 recording of "Saratoga Shout," which by consensus is one of the orchestra's greatest recordings, the Okeh company, as Schuller notes, must not have been that captivated, because it did not renew a con- tract with Russell after 1930.[56]

In 1926, Russell units had recorded compositions by the leader titled "Sweet Mumtaz," "Plantation Joys," and "Dolly Mine" (the last of these, like "The Call of the Freaks," cocomposed with Barbarin), and in 1930, as we have seen, "Saratoga Drag" (cocomposed with Greely Walton) and "Ease on Down" (cocomposed with a Williams). After this, "Freakish Blues" (dating from 1929), "Ghost of the Freaks," and "Hokus Pokus" were Russell originals among the recorded work of his orchestra in 1931 and 1934, even though most of the other material came from the pop song repertory.[57] Russell may never have established a clear personal style, es- pecially, as Gunther Schuller indicates, during the period when Russell's orchestra served as a backup for Louis Armstrong.[58] Nonetheless, in some ways Russell improved on or anticipated certain developments among the big bands, in particular those of Fletcher Henderson and Jimmie Lunceford.

For example, the Russell group recorded "You Rascal, You" on August 28, 1931, almost a month and a half after Henderson had recorded it on July 17.[59] On three Henderson takes of "You Rascal, You," the only outstanding feature of the recordings is Coleman Hawkins's solos, which are each different and create what John Chilton calls "a series of interesting variations on what is a very simple harmonic sequence."[60] Russell may have picked up on this tune from Henderson, but Luis's version is in no way similar to Fletcher's. Even though both have rather lame vocals (the Henderson with sideman Rex Stewart on the first take and Claude Jones on takes two and three; a superior effort by Chris Bullock on the Russell), the instrumental arrangements are quite distinct, with much better swing on the Russell and fine solos by Greely Walton, Dickie Wells, and Henry Allen. Walton actually achieves a smoother chorus than Hawkins, and Wells is almost as exuberant as he is in his outstanding breaks on "Goin' to Town." The ensemble behind Allen is terrific in its swing, and the trumpeter thrills with his spirited, ringing ride-out.

On August 8, 1934, Russell would record "Hokus Pokus," the title of which recalls Henderson's version of Will Hudson's "Hocus Pocus" from March 6, 1934. But Russell's tune is entirely different from that of Hudson, and the performances of the two works show quite differing approaches to big-band jazz. The Henderson recording is, as noted earlier in chapter 2, an example of sophisticated swing taken at a rather slow tempo, with Coleman Hawkins's solo highly rated for its control and fuller, sweeter tone. Henry "Red" Allen's solo on the Henderson also exhibits these same qualities, which are a change from his earlier work with the Russell band. Gunther Schuller finds Allen's playing with Russell to have been "some of the best early solos by the fiery and at times quirky 'Red,' " whereas his work with Henderson, including "Hocus Pocus," is marked by sustained intensity, a harnessing of his "fertile imagination," and a "full control of his ideas."[61] Unlike Henderson's "Hocus Pocus," Russell's "Hokus Pokus" is a moderately fast number, featuring fine tenor solos by Greely Walton, as well as a brief but driving solo by Rex Stewart. (It is notable that Henderson and Russell's bands attracted some of the same outstanding sidemen.) Albert J. McCarthy has suggested that "Hokus Pokus" shows the influence of Jimmie Lunceford, which may be true, but in fact the Russell motif found in Irving Berlin's 1937 "He Ain't Got Rhythm" predates both that composition and the Lunceford recording by two-and-a-half years.[62] This may be a matter of hearing in retrospect what was actually original with Russell, which holds true as well for Russell's recording of "My Blue Heaven," also from August 8, 1934, made half-a-year earlier than the 1935 Lunceford version. Of course, Russell may have heard the Lunceford version before it was recorded, and McCarthy is correct in saying that the Russell is "unusual in lacking a solo," although Jimmy Archey on trombone does play the theme as something of a solo, whereas the trombone solo on the Lunceford is more of an improvised break, as is the playing of baritone saxophonist Jock Carruthers.[63] As for the ensemble writing in Russell's "My Blue Heaven," it is quite different from the Lunceford arrangement by Sy Oliver, with Russell looking forward to Miller's use of the clarinet on top of the reed section. The vocals on the two versions also differ, with Sonny Woods doing the honors on the Russell and a trio singing on the Lunceford. This is not to say that one version is superior to the other but that the notion of influence seems rather questionable on the basis of the recorded evidence. It may be that Russell has not been credited with a rather eclectic originality simply because he recorded some of the same tunes or, in the case of "Hokus Pokus," entitled his composition too much like one already in existence and performed by a band with a bigger name.

Other tunes recorded by Russell on August 8, 1934, include "At the Darktown Strutters' Ball" (on which vocalist Sonny Woods alludes to Morton's "Jelly Roll Blues" and altoist Henry Jones, according to Gunther Schuller, tries to imitate Don Redman), "Ghost of the Freaks," "Primitive," and "Ol' Man River." Schuller considers the first two and the last of these to be "filled with aural delights, both in solo and ensemble terms," even though he also calls "Ol' Man River" a "virtual plagiarization of Duke Ellington's 'Old Man Blues' of 1930, reminding everyone that Duke's version was itself deeply indebted to Jerome Kern's classic."[64] Once again the issue of influence seems a bit muddled by the fact that the source of both the Russell and Ellington recordings is Kern's "Ol' Man River." Even so, there is no doubt that Charlie Holmes's alto solo on the Russell owes something in style to Ellington's Johnny Hodges. On the other hand, the Rex Stewart and Jimmy Archey solos owe little or nothing to the styles of the Ellington sidemen. As Schuller terms it, Stewart's cornet solo is mostly a "hair-raising virtuoso tribute to Herbert L. Clarke," the cornet virtuoso, pedagogue, and author of basic exercise books.[65] Regardless of the origins of this performance, it is still a swinging performance from first to last. On "Primitive," which owing to its rather subdued drive Schuller finds "anything but 'primitive,' " Stewart also contributes a "remarkable" and "quite unorthodox solo."[66] And once again, the Russell orchestra certainly generates some intense swing, which was characteristic of the group from its inception up to this final session before Armstrong apparently saved it from having to break up for lack of bookings.

Even though the Russell band's recordings have been seen by this date as unequal to its output in 1930, it still could manage some very stimulating efforts. In fact, "Ghost of the Freaks" seems to indicate that Russell might have been able to establish his group as a major contender had he not been forced by economic considerations to succumb to a supporting role behind Armstrong. This piece hints at the more relaxed, sophisticated style that would develop during the next few years of the Swing Era and features an especially fine alto solo by Charlie Holmes, who, like Russell's entire ensemble, deserves to be better known for his solid, forward-looking swing. In addition, the various versions of the "Freaks," as composed or cocomposed by Russell, trace something of the history of jazz as it developed over a five-or six-year period, which in even such a short span of time has often given rise in jazz to many significant changes. It has been said that in the arts there is no such thing as progress, because Homer and Shakespeare speak today as clearly and profoundly as ever, and perhaps even more so, with the same holding true for Bach, Mozart, and Beethoven, Leonardo Da Vinci, Michelangelo, and Delacroix. Nonetheless, it is possible to see "progress" in individual artists. A soloist such as Charlie Holmes developed from a rather stilted style to one with a smoother flow of ideas, which again illustrates the difference between jazz in the late 1920s when Holmes worked with King Oliver and the mid 1930s when he recorded with the Luis Russell Orchestra. Both Holmes and Russell emerged from the Oliver hegemony to help produce a new approach to jazz and their contributions remain a remarkable part of the Swing Era's larger story.

CHICK WEBB

Although Henderson, Basie, and Ellington guided their bands from the piano and Lunceford from up front with his baton, Chick Webb provided his orchestra's rhythmic drive from the stool of his drum set. Although afflicted physically from a childhood accident, Webb managed to become the first great swing-era percussionist, influencing through his "tremendous creativity and originality" the major stars among the period's drummers, from Sid Catlett and Jo Jones to Gene Krupa and Buddy Rich.[67] Webb has been credited with making the drummer, "that central source of pulsation and color, . . . increasingly important in jazz."[68] As for Webb's band, it was one of the most popular during the late 1930s, and the compositions by its principal arranger, Edgar Sampson, not only accounted for part of Webb's popularity but also proved the basis for hit recordings by Benny Goodman. At the time of a 1937 battle between the bands of Webb and Goodman—considered "one of the key jazz events of the 1930s"—Goodman was riding the crest of his greatest popularity, and yet Webb's band clearly bested the "King of Swing" in a showdown at the packed Savoy Ballroom, with Goodman's drummer Gene Krupa bowing to Webb in recognition of defeat and saying at the time that he had never been "cut by a better man."[69] Nonetheless, when Webb and his band had taken on the orchestra of Duke Ellington two months earlier and when it came up against that of Count Basie eight months later in January 1938, Webb could not compete on the same level. Dave Dexter of *Down Beat* magazine observed that Webb's "music lacked the black characteristics found in the bands of Ellington, Basie, Lunceford, Earl Hines. It was the charts mostly."[70] Although Dexter does not specify what he considered "black characteristics," it is clear that the Webb band did not establish a distinctive voice in the same way as Ellington, Basie, and Lunceford, and yet at times the drummer's group could swing as well as any of the period's name bands and he himself was undoubtedly one of the finest percussionists of the era.

Born in Baltimore in 1902, Chick Webb was active in jazz beginning in his early teens when he played the Chesapeake Bay area with his lifelong friend and band member, guitarist John Trueheart. In 1924, Webb and Trueheart moved to New York where Webb found his first full-time work with Edgar Dowell's band. His first engagement as a leader came in 1926 at Manhattan's Black Bottom Club, which was made possible by Duke Ellington, his "most vociferous champion."[71] Reportedly, Webb was a reluctant bandleader, but once he committed himself to the role, he became obsessed with putting together a top band and improving it by hiring the finest sidemen. As early as 1931, Webb's band included some of the outstanding soloists of the thirties, among them Jimmy Harrison on trombone, Benny Carter on alto sax, and Elmer Williams on tenor. The group's March 30 recording of Louis Armstrong's 1926 "Heebie Jeebies," as arranged by Benny Carter, features a fine solo by Harrison, who would die prematurely only four months after this recording date, as well as a break by Elmer Williams that Gunther Schuller calls a "searching beat-freed tenor solo, quite linearly fluent despite its rangy contours."[72] Webb's band at this point was capable of a swing that is a bit reminiscent of Bennie Moten's band at about the same time. Don Kirkpatrick's rocking piano is typical of the early thirties and adds effectively to the closing passage. But in some ways "Heebie Jeebies" and another tune more associated with the 1920s, "Darktown Strutters' Ball," cut on December 20, 1933, are rather the exception among the Webb recordings of 1931 and 1933.[73]

More often Webb's offerings were popular, sentimental pieces, as with three sides from March 30, 1931: "Blues in My Heart" (a Benny Carter composition which is not a blues as such), "Soft and Sweet" (composed by Edgar Sampson), and "On the Sunny Side of the Street" (with a vocal and trumpet solo by Taft Jordan that imitates a style that will, for this song, always be associated with Louis Armstrong, even though it must be said that Jordan certainly at this early date could render the Armstrong style with impressive finesse). Jimmy Harrison's last recorded breaks on "Soft and Sweet" are one of the saving graces of a piece that is marked by a shrill, dated clarinet trio and a somewhat sappy melody. As Albert J. McCarthy points out, this recording is good "more because of the solos than any great individuality of approach." Of Harrison's appearance, McCarthy states that his "beautifully conceived solos with a warm tone and fluent technique . . . underline his importance as one of the great trombonists of jazz."[74] Elmer Williams's occasional ecstatic bursts on tenor and a fine trumpet solo by Louis Bacon are the other appealing features of "Soft and Sweet." With "Darktown Strutters' Ball," the Webb band predates the Luis

Russell recording of this same tune by some nine months and compares favorably with the latter's excellent swing. Once again, the soloists generate the infectious drive of this recording, in particular Elmer Williams on tenor, Sandy Williams (who replaced Harrison) on trombone, and Pete Clark on clarinet. The ensemble swing is also quite remarkable, and Webb on drums is heard more prominently, though not so fully as he will be later in the decade. Also making his presence heard and felt is John Kirby on string bass; with his addition, Webb now had, with himself on drums and John Trueheart on rhythm guitar, one of the finest rhythm sections of the day.

For Webb, 1934 was a banner year, with his orchestra recording several Edgar Sampson originals that would become standards of the swing repertoire. Two sides from January 15 are not especially distinguished on the same level with later Sampson compositions, but both "When Dreams Come True" and "Let's Get Together" offer several fine solos, including the Hodges-influenced alto work of Sampson and some bright moments by Sandy Williams on trombone and Elmer Williams on tenor. "Let's Get Together," whose theme is credited to Webb, was arranged by Sampson and shows off the entire band to good advantage, even though this is not so swinging as "I Can't Dance (I Got Ants in My Pants)," recorded on May 9. Even though the novelty vocal by Taft Jordan on "I Can't Dance" is quite forgettable, the trumpeter's solo, the exceptionally crisp ensemble playing, and Sandy Williams's hot trombone all make this a satisfying performance. On the other hand, "Imagination" and "Why Should I Beg for Love" would seem, in Dave Dexter's view, to be almost wholly lacking in the kind of jazz normally identified with black bands. One suspects that an agent such as Irving Mills must have had a hand in the recording of these two pieces, especially as "Imagination" features a rather dreadful vocal by Chuck Richards and little to recommend it as jazz, other than two Armstrong-like breaks by Taft Jordan. "Why Should I Beg for Love" does contain some warm muted trombone statements by Sandy Williams and another convincing Armstrong imitation by Jordan, although the latter's vocal is pretty hard to take. This last piece was recorded at the same May 18 session that produced Sampson's classic "Stompin' at the Savoy," and with this performance the Webb band can be heard driving as never before, its relaxed swing generated by Webb's drums and Kirby's bass, which inspire the soloists to some high-level choruses. Albert McCarthy calls this "one of the best of Webb's earlier recordings" and cites its uncomplicated swing as the basis for such a judgment. McCarthy singles out Sandy Williams for his "great fluency and relaxed phrasing," but he also identifies trumpeters Mario Bauza and Reunald Jones as contributing fine breaks, as well as Elmer Williams on tenor and Peter Clark on clarinet.[75] Even though Clark's playing cannot compare with Benny Goodman's smooth execution, Webb's clarinetist is not embarrassing, and overall Gunther Schuller rates this first version of "Stompin' at the Savoy" as superior "in terms of swing and rhythmic energy" to the later Goodman hit recording of Sampson's classic.[76] The superiority of Webb's recording is especially notable because the Goodman version is in no way negligible. McCarthy for one recognizes the fine solos turned in by Joe Harris on trombone and by Adrian Rollini on tenor, as well as the "relaxed performance" of the entire Goodman orchestra.[77]

On July 7, the Webb band recorded another outstanding Sampson tune, "Blue Minor." This riff finds the band playing more in the style of the black name bands, with the soloists utilizing some growl effects, a rougher attack than usual, and a generally hotter approach than is found on such sentimental tunes as "True," "Lonesome Moments," and "If It Ain't Love," recorded at the same session. In September, the Webb orchestra recorded another version of "Blue Minor," which Gunther Schuller considers "a superior remake," yet the two versions are virtually identical with, for example, the alto solo by Sampson essentially note for note the same.[78] More interesting than another go at "Blue Minor" is "That Rhythm Man," which features striking trumpet work by Bobby Stark, an exuberant break by Sandy Williams, some pumping, big-toned bass notes from John Kirby, and superb section playing with drive and bite. But the most outstanding performance from this recording date is undoubtedly Sampson's "Blue Lou," which begins with an annunciatory statement by the ensemble that is quite ear-opening. Kirby's bass fully adds to the relaxed pulse of this piece, which features a fine trumpet break by Stark and some wonderful pre-Basie piano by Don Kirkpatrick, who had returned to the band after being absent for three years. Also furnishing a type of Freddie Green relaxed drive to Sampson's tune is John Trueheart's rhythm guitar. Overall, this is one of Webb's most completely satisfying sides. On Mario Bauza's "Lona," also dating from this September session, Sampson is featured on alto, as is Kirkpatrick in a Walleresque piano solo. This is a pleasant enough piece, but in its appeal is not up to "Blue Minor," certainly not to "Blue Lou," nor even to "That Rhythm Man."[79]

On November 19, 1934, the Webb orchestra recorded another Sampson classic, "Don't Be That Way," which once again Goodman would cash in on, first performing it at the 1938 Carnegie Hall concert. As Albert McCarthy notes, this is the first time that Webb really "comes to the fore" with his own drumming, and in combination with Kirby and Trueheart, he swings the unit in a more solid manner than Goodman's orchestra could ever match. Also cut at this November session was Don Kirkpatrick's "What a Shuffle," which, with its catchy riff figure and more daring breaks by the sidemen, is more stimulating than most of Webb's earlier recordings and suggests why the band was so popular at the Savoy Ballroom, where it is said that Chick could communicate with the dancers on the floor, translating "into percussive terms what [the lindy hoppers] were doing out there."[80] But it is with the 1936 "Go Harlem," the 1937 "Clap Hands!

Here Comes Charlie," which precedes the Basie version by over two years, and "That Naughty Waltz" that the Webb band really began to come into its own, and of course this was the band that outplayed the Goodman band in the 1937 battle at the Savoy. (One critic observes that although the Webb version of "Clap Hands" "may miss the magic of Basie's 1939 version . . . the controlled exaltation of its closing bars is still something to be wondered at."[81]) On these recordings Pete Clark shows how far he has advanced on clarinet, and on "Clap Hands" he even turns in a boisterous baritone break that outdoes anything he had recorded on the so-called licorice stick. Also outstanding on "Clap Hands" is Teddy McRae on tenor. Much of the excitement of these 1936 and 1937 sides is generated by Webb's drumming. For Burt Korall, the 1937 "Harlem Congo" is at "the heart of Webb's art" because it exhibits his "inner drive."[82] Speaking of "Go Harlem," "Clap Hands," and "Harlem Congo," Gunther Schuller asserts that "Webb is virtually the only swing era drummer on whose recordings one can aurally shut out the other instruments and still have a consistently rewarding musical experience," owing to Webb's combination of "exceptional soloistic talents with an impeccable sense of time and, above all, an uncanny ability to articulate with total clarity every sound he produced."[83]

Webb's success as a bandleader was enhanced beginning in June 1935 when seventeen-year-old Ella Fitzgerald made her first recording with Chick's band of a tune entitled "Love and Kisses."[84] One year later, on June 2, Ella and Chick combined for a recording of what has been "considered the theme of the ensuing years": Hoagy Carmichael's "Sing Me a Swing Song and Let Me Dance."[85] Benny Goodman and his twenty-year-old vocalist, Helen Ward, also teamed up to record this same Carmichael tune in 1936, and it is instructive to compare the two recordings. Ward's inflections are quite seductive, and she definitely swings the lyrics, which include such phrases as "brother give me high notes" and "give the rhythm man a chance / sing me a swing song and let me dance." Goodman basically carries the day with his rich, liquid clarinet breaks, while Gene Krupa kicks along the high-flying band. This is a fine performance, but it does not quite have the power of the Webb, which is marked by fuller sound, a razzmatazz drum break by Chick, and a more rhythmically engaging Fitzgerald vocal in which she refers to the drummer by name as "beating it out." Ella's opening lines are not heard in the Goodman recording—"When a body meets a body on the ballroom floor, / then a body asks a body: 'What's a swing band for?' "—but both bands answered that question emphatically by offering music that irresistibly drew dancers to the floor to perform their gyrations, splits, and paired acrobatics. A tune recorded by Ella and Chick on October 29, 1936, just in time for that year's presidential election, was entitled "Vote for Mr. Rhythm," which once again has the vocalist referring by name to the drummer, whose platform the band is "running on," which promises "to swing it from now on." The lyrics have Ella voting twice to "Let freedom ring" and soon "We'll all be singing / Of thee I swing."[86] This not only looks forward to Martin Luther King's famous phrase but also supports the view of David W. Stowe in his *Swing Changes* that the Swing Era played an important role in bringing the races closer together. Certainly Chick Webb's drumming, which on "Vote for Mr. Rhythm" features some of the battery of instruments he employed—from cowbell and snare and bass drums to temple blocks—not only made his fellow percussionists such as Gene Krupa and Jo Jones vote for him, but also gained for the big little man the admiration and respect of so many listeners, black and white.

Ella Fitzgerald's biggest hit with the Webb orchestra was "A-Tisket, A-Tasket," recorded on May 2, 1938, but this, like most of her songs, was a novelty piece that does not show her at her best. More impressive as a vocal and with better support from Webb's unit is "Oh Yes, Take Another Guess," from January 14, 1937. Here the vocalist swings the tune solidly, and the lyrics—about a woman's determined survival of the man who has walked out on her—call for an upbeat feeling that Ella conveys with convincing force. As for her version of "Organ Grinder's Swing," from November 18, 1936, this offers some jivy scatting that lends special pep to the final section, even though this performance does not compare favorably with the fine Lunceford version of August 1936. Ella is quite effective on "I Want to Be Happy," from December 17,1937, and Chick swings the band with his wonderfully relaxed drive. "I'm Just a Jitterbug," from the same May 2 session that produced "A-Tisket, A-Tasket," features Ella's more popular rather than jazz-related style, which would eventually predominate in her work. But this is definitely an infectious performance, and Chick contributes a terrific break. Fitzgerald worked best in a rocking, syncopated piece such as "Wacky Dust," from August 17, 1938, which has clean ensemble support and a nice muted trombone solo by Sandy Williams, which seems something of an answer to Tommy Dorsey. Ella's version of " 'Tain't What You Do," from February 17, 1939, is competent enough, but when one has heard Trummy Young's definitive rendition from January 1939, nothing else will do.

A number of critics regretted that Webb and his band essentially took a backseat to Ella Fitzgerald once she became the star attraction.[87] On the other hand, some of these same critics acknowledge that Ella opened doors that had been closed to Webb and might have remained shut without her part in the organization. The reasons for Webb not having received the support he deserved before Fitzgerald's appearance may be many and complex. Not only did Webb suffer physically as a result of his chronic illnesses, but apparently he was subjected to prejudicial treatment, as would appear to be the case from a promotional photograph taken of the drummer as he demonstrated a Zildjian cymbal in the alley behind the firm's factory in

Massachusetts.[88] Fitzgerald probably helped Webb overcome some of the prejudice simply because she brought offers that would otherwise not have come his way. Without Ella, Webb was "a moderately successful attraction," but with her as his featured vocalist, he rose to prominence as leader of one of the most popular big bands of the era.[89] Yet in terms of jazz, Chick himself remained the most important member of his organization.

For those who first heard Chick Webb on jukeboxes, it was his band's 1938 recording of the Benny Carter arrangement of Gershwin's "Liza" that most caught their attention.[90] Not only does this side from May 3 contain Webb's impressive, razzle-dazzle solos, which have been considered better recorded than most of his others, but it also features more of Bobby Stark's "fierce, attacking" trumpet, which combines "drive and logic," as well as a surging break by Sandy Williams.[91] Also from this same May 3 session is the marvelous "Spinnin' the Webb," with a swaggering solo by Stark, Sandy Williams recalling something of J.C. Higginbotham, and another clearly recorded master class by the leader on the art of relaxed swing drumming. On August 18, 1938, the orchestra recorded "Who Ya Hunchin'?" with Webb again at the top of his form and a virtuoso trumpet solo by Taft Jordan, who, as Gunther Schuller observes, has now "dropped his Armstrong act and . . . opt[ed] for the by now more popular Harry James and Ziggy Elman."[92] This piece also is notable for the punch of the brass section, abetted by Webb's driving percussion. The final recording made by Webb with his orchestra came on February 17, 1939, when the group cut Webb's own tune, "In the Groove at the Grove," which is a powerful performance and one that seems even more remarkable once one learns that Webb was only four months away from his death by spinal tuberculosis and obviously playing in pain, unable to walk, and having to be carried off the stand by his faithful valet. Webb's heroic efforts for his listeners, for his sidemen ("who were as thrilled by him as the audience"), and for posterity were fortunately recorded for any who would hear Chick's "bass drum shots" that Artie Shaw caught live at the Savoy and many years later still felt vibrating in his chest.[93]

EARL "FATHA" HINES

Like Ellington and Basie, Earl "Fatha" Hines was a pianist-leader of one of the finest of all swing-era bands, associated from 1928 to 1940 with Chicago's Grand Terrace Ballroom. Born on the outskirts of Pittsburgh on December 28, 1903 or 1905, Hines was a major jazz pianist by 1928 when he recorded with Louis Armstrong as a duet on King Oliver's "Weather Bird," with Armstrong's Hot Five on "West End Blues," and with Armstrong and his orchestra on "Muggles." One of the big three among swing pianists—the other two being Art Tatum and Fats Waller—Hines was considered by Teddy Wilson to have had "the most powerful rhythmic drive, more . . . than Art or even Fats." Wilson also observed that "swing is not an objective word, but my conditioning of the swing feeling was the way Armstrong and Hines played on the Hot Five records—not the others [Fred Robinson on trombone, Jimmy Strong and Don Redman on reeds, Mancy Cara or Dave Wilborn on banjo, and Zutty Singleton on drums], just Armstrong and Hines."[94] James Lincoln Collier finds that Hines mixed stride piano

with the primitive blues tradition, [which] gave him a style that was rhythmically powerful, with a preference for single lines of notes, or . . . simple rhythmic figures spelled out with a hard attack in octaves. Hines is a banger at the piano. . . . Not for him the flowing or rippling right-hand figures of the Harlem stride players. Figures break off in midflight. The melody jumps into the bass. . . . His playing, in sum, is charged, powerful, rocky and inventive.[95]

In terms of Hines's place in the development of jazz piano, John S. Wilson asserts that Fatha "changed the piano from a sort of solo-centered fellow traveler of jazz to a full-fledged member of the jazz ensemble with all the rights, privileges and responsibilities that this implies."[96]

At the end of 1928, on Hines's birthday, the Grand Terrace Ballroom opened and Hines was invited to front a band, which cut its first sides within six weeks of the ballroom opening. Commenting on the Hines band's 1929 recordings, Norman Field asserts that, although the tracks show "signs of a new ensemble settling in with fresh repertoire," they "have a charm that may fairly be called ingenuous, without any of the 'faint praise' sometimes implicit in that term."[97] This ingenuousness can be sampled with "Sweet Ella May," the first tune recorded on February 13, 1929. Included in the personnel are cornetists George Mitchell, who had recorded with Jelly Roll Morton's Hot Peppers in 1926, and Shirley Clay, who "with his powerful, broad-toned solos . . . most captures the attention of a later generation of record listeners"; banjoist and guitarist Claude Roberts, who also would figure in the performance of "Boogie Woogie on St. Louis Blues," from February 13, 1940, which includes what has been called "unquestionably the most famous of all Hines' recorded piano pieces"; bassist Hayes Alvis, later to star with Ellington; arranger and reedman Cecil Irwin; and clarinetist, altoist, and baritone saxophonist Lester Boone, who states the theme on baritone with a full-bodied sound and buoyancy that at the time only Harry Carney could have equaled or surpassed.[98] Hines's renowned right-hand "trumpet-style" piano can be heard to fine effect on "Sweet Ella May," and although his own prancing approach would change little over the next five decades, his band of the 1930s would mature into a unit that was the envy of other leaders such as Goodman and Lunceford, who hired away from Hines his arranger Jimmy Mundy and his trombonist Trummy Young, respectively.

Gunther Schuller makes the point that because Hines relied on arrangers to shape his band that it never developed "a single cohesive recognizable style" like the bands of Ellington and Basie. The critic goes on to say that "what was recognizable was [the Hines band's] rhythmic energy, its penchant for lively tempos, its spirit. These qualities emanated from the band's leader, for it was the particular Hinesian *interpretation* of these many diverse arranging styles that brought some degree of unity to the band." Schuller also suggests that the band's "hard, clean, urgent ensemble sound" was "surely a reflection of Hines's own sharply defined, flinty piano sonority."[99] It is Hines's shouting, dancing piano style, with its drive and clarity, that makes his band's performances almost immediately recognizable, so that in that regard at least a Hines band did achieve recognition as distinct from other big bands of the period. Although Albert McCarthy makes it clear that on the early 1929 sides by the Hines band that "the highspots of the recordings are, inevitably, Hines's own solos," this would not always be the case.[100] By 1932, when the band recorded again, the leader began to add a core of sidemen who, in Hines's words, came "together like a team trying to win the World Series," and who as soloists made their marks on a level approaching that of the pianist-leader, although in quite different styles that were largely more in keeping with the developing tendencies of the swing movement.[101]

On July 14, 1932, the Hines band recorded for the Brunswick label six tunes (with "I Love You Because I Love You" being cut in two versions—one as a vocal and the other as an instrumental).[102] The first piece was a Fats Waller original, titled "Oh! You Sweet Thing," which opens with Hines's ringing piano, followed by a muted trumpet that leads into some superb ensemble work, with the saxes leaning toward the sweet side while the slapped bass of Quinn Wilson drives the whole unit with a powerful, irresistible force. The first full-blown solo is by Darnell Howard on alto, and it is quite advanced compared with most of the solos of the 1929 band. A trombone break by William Franklin also is solid, and is followed by a fine Hines solo, and then more of the energetic drive of the ensemble, kicked along wonderfully by drummer Wallace Bishop. This one tune shows the "strides" Hines's unit had made toward developing into a highly competitive big band. The second tune, "Blue Drag," features an outstanding break by clarinetist Omer Simeon on baritone and an inventive, wide-ranging solo by Hines, as well as some startling ensemble work, once again driven by Wilson's bass and some deft drumming by Bishop. Gunther Schuller discusses a recording of this same tune on Columbia, which he says was rejected and when reissued on a Time-Life series "was not a particular service to Hines."[103] But the version on Brunswick to my ear in no way exhibits the problems of intonation and of Hines "being completely lost in the fifth through eighth bars of his solo," as Schuller suggests, nor are the saxes "whiney" or the brass "ragged" or "blary."[104] Indeed, the

"Blue Drag" on Brunswick is a wholly delightful performance, as is "Sensational Mood," which begins with the exact same opening as on the Bennie Moten recording of "Somebody Stole My Gal," from October 31, 1930, which so far as I can tell has not been noticed. Schuller simply says that "Sensational Mood" was "one of those 'flag-wavers' which every band from the early thirties on had to have in its 'book'—especially since the success of 'Casa Loma Stomp' " (the latter recorded on June 12, 1930).[105] The Hines performance of "Sensational Mood" is quite in keeping with its title, and after the opening bars that replicate the Moten recording, the rest of the Hines tune is an entirely different piece, with the Hines piano quite in contrast to Basie's on "Somebody Stole My Gal," although the Basie offers, as Martin Williams puts it, "a moment of light-hearted joy" and some amazingly and rather unusual quick finger-work by the Count.[106] The Hines pace is much faster than the Moten recording, the drumming of Bishop is in the same category as that of a Chick Webb, and all the soloists deliver some scorching breaks, especially Walter Fuller on trumpet. As for Hines himself, he is in top form—all over the piano and yet with his hallmark energy and drive fully intact. The ending is like a soundproof door suddenly being shut on a marvelous performance, a conclusion that couldn't be better.

On February 13, 1933, the Hines band recorded two classic Hines originals, "Rosetta" and "Cavernism." This version of "Rosetta" is quite slow compared with other recordings of the tune and in this way shows off the full sax section, anchored by Simeon's baritone. Mainly, as would be expected, the performance features Hines's ornamental approach to his own tune, with right-hand "trumpet" bursts, tremolos, and rippling embellishments. Simeon's solo on alto is especially engaging, and unusually long for a Hines sideman, covering two full choruses. This version of "Rosetta" differs from the one described by Albert McCarthy, because it does not include a vocal by Walter Fuller.[107] In comparison with a later rendition of September 12, 1934, the 1933 version is less in the swing mainstream and Hines's piano is not so rich as on the 1934 recording, where Fatha bangs, embellishes, and trumpets, but in a smoother, swing-style manner. The 1933 "Cavernism," arranged by Jimmy Mundy, is a driving side, with Fuller's trumpet leading the way to what Gunther Schuller suggests is a highly influential violin solo by Darnell Howard, which the critic feels certain that Bob Wills must have listened to, probably through "a nightly broadcast from the Grand Terrace over a nationwide NBC network hookup."[108] Stanley Dance reveals that "from 1934 onwards, two radio wires—WMAQ and WNER—gave [the Hines unit] more air time than any other band."[109] Although Howard's violin would certainly have impressed Wills, Darnell's jazz break has nothing in it of the characteristic southwestern hillbilly or honky-tonk sound characteristic of Wills and His Texas Playboys. Even more impressive is Howard's violin solo on "I Want a Lot of Love" from the recording session of October 27, which also contains the first outing by Hines's new trombonist, Trummy Young. This date also produced "Take It Easy," another swinging side in the "Cavernism" mode, with Hines's ringing piano heard through the ensemble in the same way as Jelly Roll Morton would improvise behind and through his Red Hot Peppers. (In this regard, John S. Wilson points out that of his two great predecessors, James P. Johnson and Morton, Hines descends more strongly from Morton.[110]) On "Take It Easy," the riffs played in a shout and response by reeds and brass are in their driving energy something of a contradiction of the tune's title, unless the phrase "take it easy" refers to the relaxed swing of this piece that must have caught the attention of Fletcher Henderson, whose band was invited to spell Hines's at the Grand Terrace when the latter went on the road. It was during one stay at the Grand Terrace that Henderson established his theme song, "Christopher Columbus," which elevated his unit from a "$400-a-night band to a $1000-a-night."[111] But as Hines himself asserted, "the Grand Terrace was no Grand Terrace without us, because we were there so long. When people came to Chicago and the club was mentioned, they naturally thought of us."[112] This seems a modest way of putting it, for Hines's piano and his very versatile bands were a tough act to follow.

Another pair of fine recordings by the Hines band in 1933 are "Harlem Lament" and "Bubbling Over," also from October 27. Arranged by bassist Quinn Wilson, "Harlem Lament" once again features Hines's rippling runs, at one point behind Charlie Allen's muted trumpet, when the pianist serves as a "superb accompanist, selecting the particular type of ornamentation most suited to a particular solo or ensemble."[113] On his own, Hines lets go with lightning-fast runs, tremolos, and a drive that always maintains a strong pulse. Stanley Dance describes this piece as a "piano concerto," and it does suggest such a comparison with the classical form, especially when one considers the range of Hines's technical facility.[114] Gunther Schuller lists six different aspects of the pianist's performance on "Harlem Lament": recomposition of the theme, building the solo climactically, right-hand octaves and tremolos, dialogue between hands, "vertiginous careening runs," and "at solo's end a simplification of continuity to ease things back into the band ensemble's next chorus."[115] "Bubbling Over," a Hines original arranged by guitarist Lawrence Dixon, has more of the leader's amazing piano—a high-stepping, driving chorus—but also another impressive appearance by Trummy Young on trombone, as well as some exuberant solos by Fuller on trumpet and Cecil Irwin on clarinet. Even though, as Schuller points out, the solos by Fuller and Irwin are flawed by wrong notes, this does not keep "Bubbling Over" from doing just that with drive and exuberance, which may account for the loss of complete control in a few spots by the trumpet and clarinet.[116] Certainly the playing of Trummy Young is a new plus for the Hines band. Although the 1933 recordings were impressive, those of 1934 marked the real arrival of the Hines band, as it "assumed, along with Fletcher Henderson and Lunceford, a front leadership position in jazz."[117]

One tune that achieves a swing comparable to that of Lunceford is "Julia," from March 27, 1934, arranged by multi-instrumentalist George Dixon. Walter Fuller's vocal rendition also recalls something of the Lunceford approach, as does the peppy two-beat treatment, but one that is in Hines's own driving, energetic style. There are fine efforts from Fuller on trumpet and Young on trombone, and percussion work by Bishop that is once again on a par with that of Chick Webb. Also from this same session is "Darkness," which evokes an Ellingtonian touch in Fuller's plunger growl trumpet, although some of the opening passages may remind a listener of a Lunceford piece such as "Stratosphere" recorded later in September of the same year.[118] Like the Lunceford, and any number of Ellington pieces, "Darkness" features a soaring clarinet passage by Darnell Howard, and Omer Simeon's alto at times is reminiscent of Johnny Hodges. All in all, this is a forward-looking piece, except for the conclusion that slows down to a rather clichéd, anticlimactic ending. "Madhouse," a side from the previous day, March 26, is praised by Gunther Schuller along with major pieces by Ellington, Lunceford, Basie, and Webb.[119] Although Schuller does not analyze "Madhouse" as he does "Blue" of the same session, both tunes find Quinn Wilson on tuba, which in "Blue" the critic calls a strange anachronism.[120] This is truer of "Blue" than of "Madhouse," where it is apparent that the tuba does not call attention to itself as so dated but at times quite effectively imitates the string bass in its time-keeping role. Nonetheless, the tuba had been so relegated by this time to a past tradition that it is difficult to understand why Wilson reintroduced this horn. As Milt Hinton points out, after Ellington's bass man, Wellman Braud, was heard on "Ring Dem Bells," from October 1930,

we were all strictly sold. The horn had value before amplification, but after hearing Duke's band—which we always went back to—the rhythm section seemed to have more flow to it, even with the two-beat. Bass horn and banjo together were a little rigid and stiff. When Freddy Guy played guitar and Braud the string bass, Duke's rhythm section sounded so wonderful and fluid. . . . I believe the bass sound carried more then than it does now, for the simple reason that we played two beats (to the bar), which gave the strings more time to vibrate, and you could hear the two different pitches. Boom, boom, boom . . . the sound still rings in my ears, this wonderful sound in the Savoy Ballroom in Chicago, where I'd go to hear the Ellington and Henderson bands.[121]

Surely the most impressive performance by the Hines band of 1934 is "Swingin' Down," from March 27. How to achieve the title's description is demonstrated by ensemble and soloists in a style that seems a carryover from the hot jazz period yet sounds right at home in the Swing Era. From the explosive opening, with Wilson plucking his string bass for all it's worth, and Bishop kicking the band with all his battery, including cowbell and Chinese cymbal, this riff number is unrelenting in its drive, with Hines plugging his piano in between the winds' breathing spaces to keep the intensity at "White Heat." To say this is in no way to suggest that the Hines band was imitating the likes of the Casa Loma or the Goodman orchestras, the former with its tune of that title and the latter with its breakthrough into the widest popularity of any jazz band the following year. For no white band of the 1930s could swing on the same level with this Hines performance, and not even the Casa Loma's "Stomp" was in the same category with this energetic jazz. Albert McCarthy especially points to the "closing ensemble chorus which has crisp work by the trumpet section."[122] But it is the drive, the sheer dynamism of this recording that elevates it to a position above every other "killer-diller" of this or most any other year in jazz history. On the basis of this recording alone, which Gunther Schuller does not discuss, that critic's assertion that his "ears narrow the peak period" of the Hines band "to 1934" is fully confirmed.

"Swingin' Down" was not the last of the great 1934 recordings by Hines and his men, for after the March 27 session, the band made a group of sides for Decca, which also shows the unit in top form. As Schuller indicates, many of the Decca recordings from September 1934 derive from the 1920s repertoire—above all, "That's a Plenty," "Maple Leaf Rag," "Copenhagen," "Angry," and "Wolverine Blues."[123] Yet, as would be expected, Hines updated these classic tunes, at the same time as he "juxtaposed" them "with [Jimmy] Mundy's newest creations, like 'Fat Babes,' and 'Rock and Rye.' "[124] On "That's a Plenty," Hines's piano is everywhere but never intrusive, always contributing some distinctive figures behind the soloists. Although this is a good, driving performance, it does not in the end come to much. As for "Fat Babes" and "Rock and Rye," these suggest "why Benny Goodman hired [Mundy] in the following year."[125] "Fat Babes" features an extended three-trombone break and section writing for the saxophones that finds the reeds leaping and swinging in a new way, while the riff ending would become a typical swing-era touch. "Rock and Rye" generates a more ferocious drive, with Quinn Wilson's furiously slapped bass and the three trombones in no way timid. The trumpets are becoming more exhibitionistic by this date and punch out their lines with power, the saxes meanwhile being put through some amazing paces. All the soloists add to the intensity of the performance, as does Hines's ringing piano punctuations. The ending slows down to an intriguing contrast with its rather solemn, almost classical coda. Hines's version of Scott Joplin's classic "Maple Leaf Rag" retains the basic notes but embellishes them more and plays them faster than the composer would have wished. But what stands out on this side is the work of the sax section, which gives the Lunceford reeds a run for their money.[126] "Angry" finds Hines in very daring form, with tremolos and great swing. His ambitious solo illustrates Leonard Feather's notion that Hines was "the Houdini of jazz piano," being able to extricate himself from most any musical straitjacket by finding the right notes that can release him from what seems a tangle of wrong tones.[127] Likewise, on "Wolverine Blues," Hines exhibits more of his daring piano, with leaps into the upper register and dives back into the bass, but always with masterful control. Darnell Howard on clarinet also manages some of the same acrobatics, as he does on "Copenhagen." On the latter Trummy Young on trombone makes his mark in advance of his better-known work with Lunceford some four years later, but this is even truer of the remake of "Cavernism," where Trummy's trills and falls are trademark features of his playing. As Howard did on the 1933 version, he contributes here a fine, very swinging violin break. For the ending of Hines's original tune, arranger Mundy adds some unusual vibraphone notes to close out this smoother rendition of what was the band's theme song before it was replaced by "Deep Forest."

On February 12, 1935, the Hines orchestra recorded a number of pieces that seem aimed more at a dance audience rather than at jazz listeners. This is the case especially with a tune such as "Rhythm Lullaby," with its sort of ricky-ticky trumpet theme statement and Fuller's derivative Armstrong vocal after the tra-la-la treatment by the Palmer Brothers. Only Hines's piano behind the saxes' sweetish passage saves it from turning saccharine. Although "Disappointed in Love" also features another vocal by the Brothers, Trummy Young offers some virtuosic licks that make this side worthwhile. Trummy also makes a brief but effective appearance in "Japanese Sandman," the tune that Paul Whiteman first recorded in 1920; Albert McCarthy calls the Hines version "splendid."[128] Even more impressive is the 1935 remake of "Bubbling Over," an arrangement by Mundy that features Bishop's drumming, Young's quick tonguing and a few of his high notes, Howard's virtuosic clarinet, some Armstrong trumpet by Fuller, Hines's darting, daring piano, and an intense overall swing that is more characteristic of the 1934 recordings. "Blue" once again has the trumpet playing a ricky-ticky theme statement, and even Bishop does some rather corny work on his snare rim. Next to "Bubbling Over," the best of the 1935 sides is the remake of "Julia," despite another derivative Armstrong vocal by Fuller. Hines, Wilson on bass, and Bishop on drums achieve a pulsating swing that drives the ensemble and inspires some fine short breaks by Fuller and Young. These six sides would be the last the Hines orchestra would record until 1937.

The first side cut in '37, on February 10, was "Flany Doodle Swing," which shows the possible influence of the Count Basie band. Budd Johnson, who has replaced Cecil Irwin after his accidental death in May 1935, solos in a Lester Young vein, even though Budd had developed his own manner independently of Pres's celebrated storytelling style. Johnson's own approach is clearer in his marvelous tenor solo on "Pianology," where Darnell Howard also contributes a fine clarinet break. Albert McCarthy considers this one of the best Hines recordings from the period, and this is an accurate assessment.[129] Almost as good, according to McCarthy, is "Rhythm Sundae," but this piece, which opens with some inimitable rippling and trumpeting piano by the leader, is taken up with "a curiously old-fashioned beat and rhythm" and contains only one solo by a sideman, a fine break by Trummy Young.[130] Gunther Schuller calls "Inspiration" "somewhat inspiration-less," and unfortunately this is true, except for Hines's piano, although Schuller feels that even the leader has "lost a lot of his drive and inventiveness."[131] On the other hand, Stanley Dance reports that with a tune like "Ridin' a Riff," from April 10, 1937, the Hines unit "overwhelmed Fletcher Henderson's in an Indianapolis battle of music."[132] This side features some strong, clean trumpet from Ray Nance, who would later join the Ellington band, good alto and tenor breaks by George Dixon and Leon Washington, respectively, and some flashy drumming by Oliver Coleman. The leader's piano toward the end is truly sparkling, despite Schuller's regret that "the repetitious chain of diminished chords . . . is not worthy of Hines."[133]

On March 7, 1938, the Hines group recorded "Solid Mama," arranged by Jimmy Mundy, and McCarthy finds the ensemble strong and solos by William Randall on clarinet, Hines on piano, and Dixon on trumpet "attractive."[134] The ensemble passage following Dixon's first brief appearance sounds very much like Lunceford, whereas the typical swing ending is Goodman-like, which is not surprising, because, as noted earlier, Mundy later arranged for Benny Goodman. Another side from the same 1938 recording session is "Goodnight, Sweet Dreams, Goodnight," which is a fairly innocuous big-band number, offering little more than a mild jazz treatment of a pop tune, except for a nicely constructed, melodic trumpet solo by Pee Wee Jackson.[135] Although for Schuller and McCarthy the superior Hines ensembles were those he led from 1934 to 1937, Stanley Dance has preferred the 1939–1942 orchestras. Personnel changes after 1937 certainly altered the character of the Hines orchestra, and this is perhaps most noticeable with respect to the drum chair, which was taken over by Alvin Burroughs, who had originally starred with the Oklahoma Blue Devils. In replacing Wallace Bishop, Burroughs brought to the Hines unit a different style, one more given to the use of cymbals for driving the group, which in some ways looks forward to the work of a modernist such as Kenny Clarke. This and other changes to the Hines orchestra beginning in 1939 probably account for the appeal to a listener like Dance.

On July 12, 1939, Hines and his men recorded Budd Johnson's "G.T. Stomp," where Burroughs makes his presence felt and heard with his cymbal and smooth brush work both behind the soloists and in something of a solo break. Even though the piece opens with some typical piano from the leader, the arrangement is a bit new for a Hines production, especially "a stirring climax devised by Earl to accompany the [Revue] chorus as it left the floor one by one."[136] Fuller and Edward Simms in their trumpet solos have essentially left behind the Armstrong influence and are emphasizing greater speed and angularity in the creation of their breaks, looking forward with Burroughs's drumming to the bebop period. In Budd Johnson's arrangement of "Grand Terrace Shuffle," Trummy Young's replacement, John Ewing, picks up where that trombone star left off after he joined Lunceford and even goes Trummy one better in his controlled smears, blares, and shakes. Here, too, Budd Johnson exhibits his Pres-like approach on tenor that includes some of the false fingering and honks that would be imitated by the likes of Illinois Jacquet and other Texas tenors. Another new trombonist, Edward Burke, is heard on " 'Gator Swing," from an October 6 recording session, with his buzz or "kazoo mute."[137] One of Budd Johnson's finest riff arrangements is "Father Steps In," which features Burroughs's drumming, along with excellent solos by Robert Crowder on tenor; Budd himself on alto, which reveals him to have been as advanced on this instrument as he was on tenor; and a driving ride-out by Fuller on trumpet. Other Johnson arrangements include "Piano Man" (a showcase for the leader's piano); "Riff Medley" (which offers some of Johnson's best Pres-like tenor, Hines's swinging piano, Fuller and Simms in something of a trumpet duel, some fine alto by Leroy Harris, and a top drawer drum break by Burroughs, whose snare shots and stick work expertly drive the ensemble from the piece's opening bars); and "XYZ" (with more of Johnson's Pres-style tenor, plus Harris with some swirling alto, Fuller's soaring trumpet, Johnson again, Ewing's brash trombone, Wilson's slapped bass, and drum rolls and stick work by Burroughs).[138] All these pieces have the mark of Johnson's arranging style, with its emphasis on the riff, either in the Basie or the Lunceford mode. "Number 19," yet another Johnson arrangement, recorded on February 13, 1940, is, like "Riff Medley," especially reminiscent of Lunceford. "Number 19" opens with some razzle-dazzle drumming by Burroughs, and after the ensemble states the theme, Hines solos before George Dixon on alto takes a break, followed by the tenor of Crowder, some inspiriting trumpet by Fuller, and more of Dixon's soaring alto. Based on the Hines orchestra's recordings of this period, Stanley Dance has declared that this was "undoubtedly the most exciting and homogeneous band of [Hines's] career."[139]

Although Budd Johnson had left Hines briefly and was not present on the recording of his "Number 19," he returned for several key sides on June 19 and December 2, 1940, and on April 3, August 20, and October 28, 1941. "Call Me Happy," from June 19, arranged by Buster Harding, is a swinger from first to last, with breaks by Fuller on trumpet, Burke on trombone, and Johnson on tenor that maintain the energy even as they offer some dazzling ideas. "Tantalizing a Cuban," also from June 19, is a Hines original arranged by Budd Johnson and opens with the leader's piano accompanied by guitarist Claude Roberts (along with shouts from George Dixon), followed by an aggressive bass solo by Wilson and some fine brush work by Burroughs, after which Hines returns and Budd Johnson takes a bursting at the seams tenor break. Johnson's finest moment comes not on tenor or alto but on clarinet, another member of the reed family that he had mastered over the years. This time he solos on a blues number titled "Jelly, Jelly," from December 2, which also features a vocal by Billy Eckstine and electric-guitar interpolations by Hurley Ramey. Of all the clarinet solos recorded during the swing era, there is nothing quite like Johnson's "magnificent New Orleans style clarinet wails" on "Jelly, Jelly."[140] Johnson's stratospheric clarinet even looks forward to the dazzling work of a later Texan, reedman John Carter, who was part of the free jazz movement of the 1960s through the early 1980s.

In 1941, Alvin Burroughs was replaced by Rudy Traylor, who brought even more of a razzle-dazzle style of drumming to the Hines orchestra, beginning with the April 3 "Up Jumped the Devil," a Jimmy Mundy original. In a way this piece is a feature for Traylor's drumming, for other than a chorus by Hines and a very brief tenor break by Franz Jackson, there are no major solos and more attention is given to Traylor than any other sideman. Buster Harding's "Windy City Jive" from August 20 finds Johnson soloing again on tenor, along with trumpeter Pee Wee Jackson, who makes a very strong showing, Tommy Enoch also on trumpet, and John Ewing on trombone. This piece, like Harding's "Call Me Happy," from June 19, 1940, is closer to the Basie vein than earlier Hines recordings, and even the leader's piano has a Basie feel to it. This is the case as well with Hines's own original, "The Father Jumps," recorded on October 28, 1941, which features more of Pee Wee Jackson's strong trumpet, as well as a fuller tenor outing by Johnson. One thing about the performances of 1941 has not changed from Hines's beginnings: they still exhibit the fierce energy and drive so characteristic of a Fatha-led ensemble, which made it at times the equal of the best bands of the entire era.

CAB CALLOWAY

Born in Rochester, New York, on Christmas Day 1907, but raised in Baltimore, Cab Calloway started in music "as a relief drummer, master of ceremonies and singer/entertainer," working in the mid 1920s in Chicago, where he attended Crane Law School, "intending to be a lawyer, as was his father," and then in New York City, first with a group known as Marion Hardy's Alabamians and later with one called The Missourians.[141] After appearing with the latter in New York in 1928, Calloway returned to Chicago and worked again with the Alabamians, fronting this band when he went back to New York for a debut at the Savoy Ballroom in October 1929. Afterward he began to work once more with The Missourians and eventually changed the name of the group to Cab Calloway and His Orchestra. Beginning in 1931, Calloway and his unit spent a year at New York's Cotton Club, and with a recording in that year of his own "moaner" tune, "Minnie the Moocher," Cab gained national acclaim as a "scat" singer, leading from that time up to 1948 one of the most successful big bands of the day.

From the first what distinguished Calloway's orchestra is that it was built around a singer rather than an instrumental player, and that Cab "surrounded himself with a real jazz orchestra, something no other bandleading vocalist cared (or managed) to do."[142] Although the primary focus on most recordings was the vocalist himself, Calloway did tend to give ample solo and ensemble opportunities to his sidemen, and his orchestra members were excellent all-around musicians, as well as, in many cases, outstanding soloists; the group's repertoire exhibits "great diversity and breadth" in its "stylistic range."[143] Similarly, Calloway's own singing style, which "clearly owes a great deal to the vaudeville tradition that shaped much early jazz," is marked by a "voice of remarkable range" with "excellent diction" and affective phrasing.[144] Gunther Schuller has considered Calloway "a magnificent singer, quite definitely the most unusually and broadly gifted male singer of the thirties."[145]

According to Frank Driggs, "there was nothing [Cab Calloway] could not do with his voice . . . going all the way from bass and baritone right up to tenor and even to high falsetto when needed."[146] All of Calloway's vocal acrobatics are evident on his recording of "St. Louis Blues," from July 24, 1930, including Cab's "high-pitched" notes, his "high-powered frenetic energy," and his type of triple-tongued articulation of a string of scatted syllables.[147] Opening with plunger trumpet by R.Q. Dickerson and growl trombone by De Priest Wheeler, this version of W.C. Handy's classic tune finds Cab entering with a long held note reminiscent of an Armstrong trumpet or a Johnny Dodds clarinet break from the 1920s, while behind the singer Earres Prince swings away with some Jelly Roll–like piano. Among the early Calloway recordings, there is nothing quite like Cab's vocal exhibition on this piece, which would become more characteristic of his later style, along with his pop or sweet approach found on such early recordings as "Dixie Vagabond" and "So Sweet" from March 3, 1931. As for the driving lead trumpet in the closing ensemble on "St. Louis Blues," Albert McCarthy indicates that this was "characteristic of The Missourians on their own recordings" even before Calloway took over the group.[148] The powerhouse drive of the early Missourians, who originally were from St. Louis, is best illustrated by "Some of These Days," from December 23, 1930, which both McCarthy and Gunther Schuller cite as outstanding, with Schuller stating that this "incredibly virtuosic," "spectacular" piece was "a staggering technical achievement for its time and, if memory doesn't fail me, the fastest tempo achieved by any orchestra up to that time."[149] The superfast staccato-style trombone break by Wheeler is most impressive. Also from this period are the first recordings of two of Calloway's perennial hits, "Minnie the Moocher" and "St. James Infirmary," which he first recorded on December 23, 1930, and March 3, 1931, respectively. On the latter, Calloway displays his remarkable vocal range, while Walter Thomas, the principal arranger for the orchestra at this time, takes an ear-catching sixteenth-note solo on baritone sax. One of the most curious pieces is "Sweet Jenny Lee," recorded on October 14, 1930, with a trumpet solo by Reuben Reeves that recalls Bix Beiderbecke and a tenor solo by Andrew Brown that is close to the work of Coleman Hawkins. This performance may have inspired a later recording, of the same tune, by Milton Brown and His Musical Brownies, cut on January 27, 1935, with the styles of early swing jazz and Western Swing clearly exemplified by these two equally valid renditions. Another Calloway side from the same October 14 date is "Happy Feet," recorded earlier in February 1930 by Paul Whiteman and in 1933 by Fletcher Henderson, as discussed in Chapter 2. Calloway's version is notable for the powerful trumpet solo, probably by Lammar Wright. With most all the Calloway sides from this period, his orchestra still utilizes a tuba rather than a string bass, which accounts largely for its rather plodding, pre-swing feel.

The Calloway orchestra's varied repertoire is illustrated by "Yaller," "The Viper's Drag," "Doin' the Rhumba," "Mood Indigo," "Farewell Blues," "I'm Crazy 'Bout My Baby," "Blues in My Heart," "Black Rhythm," "Six or Seven Times," and "My Honey's Lovin' Arms," among other sides from 1930 and '31. Despite the orchestra's respectable and at times engaging versions of these widely varying works composed in the '20s and early '30s, Calloway's group does not represent an emerging swing unit on a par with the name bands of the same years nor even a second-rank orchestra like that of Chick Webb. What interests Gunther Schuller most about "Yaller" is that it is "a remarkable theme . . . an amazingly outspoken protest song about prejudice against half-castes," but there is little here to recommend the piece as a work of jazz.[150] In fact, at times Cab's vocal is even reminiscent of Al Jolson, as Schuller himself has noted.[151] "The Viper's Drag," as Schuller also points out, is representative of the many jazz compositions allusive of marijuana and opium use.[152] Here Cab's wordless singing is quite atmospheric, and the instrumental mute and growl effects (à la Ellington's men), a fine baritone solo, and an open trumpet break all are well played. "Doin' the Rhumba" is a Latin-flavored number, with a fine trombone break by Wheeler and some of Cab's vocal falls, rapid strings of words, and smooth, facile movement from one register to another. "Mood Indigo," from March 9, 1931, like the orchestra's version of Ellington's "Creole Love Song," from May 6, 1931, is a close imitation of the Duke's October 1930 recording but fails to create the poignant quality of the original, partly it would seem from its being taken a bit too fast and from altering and thereby enervating some of the song's familiar rhythms. "Farewell Blues," a classic from 1922, also is taken faster than the original, and yet even with tuba and a chink-chink rhythm by the drummer, this piece manages to approach a smoother swing style. Also, here Cab's scat solo is a driving piece of jazz, as is Wheeler's captivating "freak" trombone break. "I'm Crazy 'Bout My Baby," like "The Viper's Drag," was composed by Fats Waller, and the former especially reveals the distinctive vocal styles of Cab and Fats. A Waller version of "I'm Crazy 'Bout My Baby," from August 1, 1936, is a comic treatment of Alexander Hill's lyrics, achieved by Fats's explosive overemphasis of the initial B in baby, along with his many humorous asides that comment on and urge on his sidemen. Cab, on the other hand, sings this much straighter for him than usual, with only an occasional leap into the upper register, with his characteristic lift of a note with a rising "hey." All the soloists on this tune are outstanding, and, once again, despite the fact that the tuba still anchors the rhythm section, a fairly fluid, driving swing is generated by the entire ensemble.

"Blues in My Heart," as noted earlier, is a Benny Carter composition, recorded by Chick Webb on March 30, 1931, with Calloway's version being made on May 6. Cab's reading of Carter's piece closely resembles the Webb recording, down to a closing muted trumpet and a few notes on vibraphone. Louis Bacon's vocal on the Webb in no way comes up to Cab's in terms of control, but the overall performance by Calloway's orchestra lacks the rhythmic pulse of Webb's, which is accounted for by the faster tempo of the latter; the swing of its string bass, guitar, and drums; and the generally superior execution by Chick's band. It is clear from this and almost every other piece by the Calloway orchestra recorded during the early part of the decade that it did not create a level of swing comparable to that of the Webb unit, and this was due in part to Cab's bass player sticking with the tuba instead of switching to the stringed instrument. When Jimmy Smith did change over on occasion, as with the September 23 recording of "You Rascal, You," the November 18 "Without Rhythm," and "The Scat Song" of February 29, 1932, the difference is dramatic. "You Rascal, You" even approaches to a degree the various Fletcher Henderson versions of this tune made in the summer of 1931, even despite the continued presence of Morris White's banjo on the Calloway recording. Certainly there is no soloist comparable to Coleman Hawkins in the Calloway orchestra at this time, but on the other hand, Claude Jones's vocal on the Henderson versions cannot compete with Cab's subtle handling of the lyrics. Indeed, no other big band with the possible exception of Moten's, which had Jimmy Rushing as its vocalist, could offer a jazz singer as effective as Calloway, and this is especially evident on "Without Rhythm" and "The Scat Song," with Cab at his improvisational best on the latter. On "The Scat Song," also, the orchestra is now into a full-blown swing style, and here, too, as Schuller asserts, all the solos are excellent.[153] Schuller also singles out "Black Rhythm," from November 6, 1931, as an example of the Calloway unit's "many excellent integrated solo breaks," as well as "its solid full-ensemble sound," but this piece seems more a symphonic exercise, a kind of mishmash of styles—arranged, Schuller assumes, by Thomas—rather than a work of true jazz.[154]

On "Six or Seven Times," from June 6, 1931, also by Fats Waller, the Calloway orchestra is still in the 1920s style with its pumping, almost plodding tuba. Cab's vocal and his novel whistled passage, although illustrative of his control, are more representative of his showmanship than his musicianship so far as jazz is concerned. Even though Calloway exhibits a gift for vocal versatility, we miss in him the emotive power of the great female blues singers or the poignancy of a Billie Holiday. Cab and his ensemble's call-and-response exchanges with altoist Walter Thomas, although well performed, do not have to them any real imaginative force, neither are they inspiriting nor inspiring. Compared with the Jimmie Lunceford recording of "Four or Five Times," from May 29, 1935, Calloway's "Six or Seven Times" had yet to attain the smooth swing and ingenious interplay of sections, the Lunceford reeds' masterful execution of fills and figures, and the charming, rhythmic style of Sy Oliver's singing, with at the end his own effective version of a falsetto leap. It may be unfair to compare these two tunes that share similar themes and lyrics, but they point up where the Calloway orchestra was compared with the kind of swing and instrumental precision that the name bands were already beginning to achieve. As for "My Honey's Lovin' Arms," from June 17, the Calloway orchestra's performance of this piece represents another instance of the sweet style, as well as a rather dated clarinet, especially when one recalls the fluidity and the rich tone of a Benny Goodman by 1931.

On September 23, the Calloway orchestra recorded "Bugle Call Rag," which elicits high praise from both Albert McCarthy and Gunther Schuller, with the former labeling it a "spirited version" that "highlights the drive of the band and its Midwestern heritage" and the latter commenting that it exhibits "a rich sampling of instrumental solos."[155] Cab's jiving on this piece in the form of encouragement to the soloists—"talk to me"; "gonna wake up"; "goin' to town"—is but one of his many approaches to the use of words in a performance. "You Can't Stop Me from Lovin' You," from October 12, exhibits another: his playfulness with the song's lyrics, which in this case were made for such with their reference to the loved one putting tacks in his shoes and rocks in his corn flakes. This tune also features a type of "lassus trombone" trio, with smears characteristic of the piece by that title written by Henry Fillmore, and demonstrates the many musical styles incorporated into jazz of this or any period. Yet another of Cab's vocal practices is found in "You Dog," from the same date, with Cab's rocking and soaring delivery supported wonderfully by Bennie Payne's piano. Lammar Wright on trumpet offers an especially outstanding break, something of a rhythmically updated version of King Oliver. The October 21 recording of "Ain't Got a Gal in This Town" presents Cab's "mournful wail," rhyming predictably with "frail," his word for a "chick" or "broad." This piece also shows off the singer's ability to swoop from one register to another with total control, to bend his notes but always to end his phrases right on the money. Meanwhile, the orchestra backs him with a complementary wailing sound, first through the tuba's somber sustained notes and toward the end with a muted growl and wa-wa trumpet. "Between the Devil and Deep Blue Sea" of the same date may be, as Schuller suggests, a put on, but whatever Cab's attitude toward the song, his performance reveals once more his great versatility in terms of styles, as he moves from what seems a straight crooning delivery to a jivy syllabic improvisation.[156] The range of Calloway's styles is certainly amazing, and his orchestra matches him appropriately in every case.

By 1932, the Calloway orchestra could on occasion play in the full-blown swing style (except for Morris White's banjo), as evinced by its February 29 recording of "The Scat Song." Jimmy Smith's string bass smoothes out the flow of the music and the reeds are swinging better as a section in this Harry White arrangement, which Gunther Schuller commends as a "gem, excellently performed," with again "a rich sampling of instrumental solos."[157] On March 14, the unit recorded "Strictly Cullud Affair," which exhibits a solid swing that can compare favorably with that of Ellington and Lunceford. "Aw You Dawg," from the same recording session, also swings well and features what sounds like a driving solo by trumpeter Lammar Wright, again inspired by King Oliver but updated in the smoother swing style. However, the tenor break is too rickety and straight up; at this point Calloway's band still did not include a really outstanding reedman. Yet by June 7, Calloway had added Eddie Barefield on clarinet, alto sax, and baritone, and it would seem that it is he who contributes a fine baritone break on "Dinah." This date also marks the replacement of bassist Jimmy Smith by Al Morgan, whom Schuller calls a "strong New Orleans bass player (and disciple of Pops Foster)."[158] Throughout, "Dinah" generates a solid swing, with Leroy Maxey's drums becoming more prominent and, in tandem with Morgan's booming bass, driving the group with greater forward thrust. In addition to representing part of the evolution toward a full-fledged swing movement of the mid and late '30s, several of these tunes evoke something of the era of Prohibition, with its mob activities, the common packing of "artillery" and mowing down of adversaries, and the attraction of drugs, with references to Chinatown and Calloway's frequent phrase, "kicking the gong around," another allusion to marijuana use. Indicative of an early awareness of the concept of swing is Cab's singing of the line "the King of Swing is gonna give the bride away" in "Minnie the Moocher's Wedding Day," recorded on April 20. In many respects Calloway and his orchestra epitomize this period both sociologically and musically. Through such features as song titles, lyrics, dance styles, popular venues, and references to the media (for example, Fletcher Henderson's recording of "Radio Rhythm"), jazz has always tended to reflect cultural and social changes in each decade, as David W. Stowe reveals about the 1930s in his *Swing Changes*.

Beginning in June 1932, Calloway recorded extensively, even in the middle of the Great Depression, thanks to "his first longer residency at the Cotton Club that had made him and the orchestra the talk of the nation."[159] Indeed, no other orchestra of the period exceeded Calloway's in the quantity of recordings, not even Duke Ellington's. And once again, the wide variety of styles represented by Calloway's 1932 sides is remarkable. Included are examples of the various themes that he returned to regularly, among them the marijuana or opium motif and the Gal, Lady, and Harlem series: "Reefer Man," "My Sunday Gal," "Eadie Was a Lady," "Harlem Holiday," and "The Man from Harlem." Likewise, in terms of orchestral arrangements or styles, there also is a wide range to be heard in the 1932 recordings. The sessions dating from June 7, 9, and 22, September 21, November, 9, 15, and 30, and December 7 offer a little of everything: the surprisingly smooth swing achieved in "Old Yazoo," with the ensemble powered by Al Morgan's string bass and Leroy Maxey's drum kicks; superb sectional work in "Angeline," with Cab doing something of an Armstrong-style vocal; a passage in "Swanee Lullaby" featuring bass clarinet and clarinets; the rather strange "Git Along," with fine muted trumpet behind Cab's vocal but a sappy contribution by Chris Bullock as vocalist and Roy Smeck with a nonjazz, almost hillbilly guitar; and something of a throwback to the late '20s in Benny Carter's instrumental, "Hot Toddy," which Gunther Schuller calls a "flagwaver" with "some of the feel of Moten's 'Toby' and 'Prince of Wails' (recorded four months later) but not the latter's clarity of execution or incomparable dynamic energy."[160] Both Schuller and Albert McCarthy single out for approval "I've Got the World on a String," the former praising Morris White's "terrific" rhythm guitar and the latter Doc Cheatham's "lyrical" trumpet, which he also plays on "I Gotta Right to Sing the Blues."[161] On the latter, Cab delivers the lyrics as convincingly as did Jack Teagarden, who used the tune as the theme song for his own big band. The fine trumpet solo on "Wah-Dee-Dah" is more in the hot rather than the sweet or lyric vein, just as Cab's vocal is more infectious in his swinging scat line. Calloway's vocal on this last piece illustrates, as does that on "The Man from Harlem," an important point that Schuller makes as to Cab's vocals being "fully integrated into a jazz *orchestral* concept."[162] "The Man from Harlem," a Will Hudson original, finds Cab utilizing a type of Fats Waller talk style of narrative. The ensemble behind him is exceptionally fine, with Maxey's drums providing great drive, as they do on "My Sunday Gal," where brief solos seem to float up from the driving ensemble and where Maxey's fine performance may remind listeners of Chick Webb. Hudson's "Gotta Go Places and Do Things" is heavily syncopated and far from the smoother swing style of "Old Yazoo," but it does contain a good trumpet break and more of Maxey's strong drum work. Although Calloway's varied mix of styles, both vocal and orchestral, may not have allowed him to establish a single identifiable sound, the fact remains that his was a highly entertaining program, and it always included outstanding jazz of some type in most every recording.

On December 7, 1932, the Calloway orchestra recorded Will Hudson's "Hot Water," which, despite a different introductory section, is essentially Hudson's "Casa Loma Stomp," recorded November 2, 1930, by the Casa Loma Orchestra.[163] What is most distinctive about the two recordings is that the Casa Loma version is frantic rather than swinging. As Gunther Schuller has said, the Casa Loma "kind of swing was somewhat mechanical and stiff," and this is particularly true of its drummer's punctuations in "Casa Loma Stomp," but also in its reed section's ensemble passages.[164] The Calloway orchestra's drummer, Leroy Maxey, adds much to the smoother flow of the music, even though, like Tony Briglia for the Lomans, Maxey can at times end phrases with rather tacked-on licks on the cymbal or snare. However, at other times Maxey's rim-shots definitely contribute to the drive rather than coming, as with Briglia, as afterthoughts. As for the Calloway reeds, they now articulate their passages with great precision and swing. There may not be a soloist on the Calloway recording to compare with the Lomans' PeeWee Hunt and his charging trombone, but overall Cab's performance is much more in the swing mode and ultimately more satisfying in that regard.

From September 18, 1933, the Calloway orchestra's recording of trombonist Harry White's "Evenin' " finds Cab singing in a style that would become another of his trademarks—a type of dreamy, languorous manner, with his patented shaking, falling notes, and even a kind of trill on certain syllables (especially those beginning with or containing an "r"). Again, a muted trumpet—by Doc Cheatham—complements Cab's delivery, as does Bennie Payne's celeste. Most familiar is the version of "Minnie the Moocher," from December 18, 1933, with Cab's inimitable soaring lines and long glissandi echoed by the orchestra's chorus (as they are on "Zaz Zuh Zaz" of November 2). This arrangement is considered by Schuller to be "much enriched by swirling guitar, piano, and vibraphone embellishments, especially in Cab's final out-of-tempo cadenza: a whole sound-world new to jazz."[165] As Schuller also asserts, "the Calloway recordings are full of wonderful surprises. There is hardly a side which does not offer several musical delights, sometimes tiny, sometimes major." Schuller makes another important observation about the Calloway orchestra when he says that the recordings strike "an excellent balance between [Cab's] vocal displays and the orchestra's involvement."[166]

On January 22 and 23, 1934, the Calloway orchestra recorded six sides that reveal how fully the unit and singer had entered the Swing Era, and in many ways anticipated a number of what would become the name bands, black and white. " 'Long about Midnight," as Albert McCarthy has indicated, shows off "the drive and expertise of the ensemble" and offers "excellent solos by Swayzee and White."[167] Most impressive of the six sides with respect to a solo outing is Will Hudson's "Moon Glow," one of four fine recordings of works by this white composer, the other three being the previously mentioned "Hot Water" and "Hotcha-Razz-Ma-Tazz" from January 23 and "Moonlight Rhapsody" from September 4. "Moon Glow" is not only a highly romantic rendition in a swing style that would not be developed by most big bands until the end of the decade, but it also contains in the almost unheard-of-before alto artistry of reedman Eddie Barefield what Gunther Schuller considers "a major breakthrough" in terms of a solo feature for one of Cab's sidemen and "a major musical statement of its time."[168] Earlier, McCarthy had commented that "Barefield took full advantage of this rare opportunity, playing a fine flowing chorus with overtones recalling Benny Carter—it is sad that at the time he had so few chances to be heard at this length."[169] The tune opens with a mellow setting consisting of a single accented note by muted trombone, answered by muted trumpets completing the theme (in 1955 made famous by the film version of William Inge's *Picnic*). Clarinet flourishes by Arville Harris contrast beautifully with the opening, followed by the reeds stating the theme once more before Eddie Barefield takes over for his extended, virtuosic alto solo, full of wondrous rushes of sixteenth notes against the leisurely pace of the ensemble. Barefield's final blaze of notes does, as Schuller suggests, look forward to the dazzling alto display of Eric Dolphy on "Stormy Weather" of 1960.[170]

As if to prove that his orchestra could swing at an up-tempo with the best of the big bands, Calloway recorded "Jitter Bug" at the session of January 22, 1934. Once more this piece is a marvelous blend of Cab's shouting, jiving vocalizing and snatches of superb instrumental breaks, especially again by Eddie Barefield, whose alto can be heard in the background. Just as "Moon Glow" demonstrates an advanced romantic conception, "Jitter Bug" places the Calloway orchestra at the forefront of the jitter bug craze that would take the country by storm some three years later when, by 1937, "the best jitterbugs were incorporating acrobatic 'air steps,' judolike variations in which partners would roll and flip each other over the back."[171] "Jitter Bug" is an original by Cab and his trumpeter Edwin Swayzee, on which Al Morgan's string bass drives powerfully and the four-man reed section (referred to by Cab in his jiving lyrics) plays as well as any in the decade. In the same vein is Hudson's "Hotcha Razz-Ma-

Tazz," with lyrics by Andy Razaf, although Cab also does his own type of "Chinese" jiving on wordless syllables. On the September 4 "Chinese Rhythm," an original by Calloway and his trombonist Harry White, Cab gives the fullest version of his imitation Chinese-language jazz. It is White who contributes the most forceful solo on "Hotcha"—a ripping break that illustrates Schuller's view that White was "a fine trombonist in the Higginbotham tradition."[172] Barefield also provides an abbreviated example of his exceptional alto work on "Hotcha" and then is given more space to work his magic on "Chinese Rhythm." On the latter, Cab opens with some of his sung, stereotypical Sino talk and then with his explanation in English of the need for one to have Chinese rhythm. Following a splendid extended clarinet break, probably by Arville Harris, Cab returns with an absolutely amazing tour de force performance, with leaps into the upper register and a type of double-time of Chinese syllables. Bennie Payne's Chinese touches on piano combine with Cab's vocal and breaks by the various sidemen to create yet another cross-cultural encounter, reflecting the fact that jazz has always been open to and profoundly enriched by every influence from the varied worlds of musical expression.

Two other recordings, "Margie" and "Avalon," also from September 4, 1934, recall the later versions made by the Lunceford orchestra. Although the Calloway renditions are quite good, they lack the cachet that Lunceford achieved with his distinctive sound and rhythm. Once again, Calloway's eclecticism may have worked against him in the sense that he did not establish a sound for his band that was readily identifiable, apart from his own unique vocals that are indeed immediately recognizable as his alone. But this does not mean that the performances by the Calloway orchestra are necessarily of a lower quality jazz-wise. Even so, the Calloway orchestra at this point could not boast the kind of unified sound represented by Lunceford's "Margie"—where the vocal and the band's playing are so much of a piece—nor a soloist of the star quality of Trummy Young. Not even Barefield's solo on "Moon Glow" satisfies so fully as Willie Smith's alto break on "Avalon," simply because the latter is so much a part of the larger performance rather than simply a virtuosic display. A final side from the September 4 session that produced "Margie" and "Avalon" is "Weakness," a tune by Cab's trumpeter, Edwin Swayzee.[173] Here the ensemble behind Cab's straight vocal is vintage swing, with the second trumpet solo, probably by Doc Cheatham, somewhat in imitation of Armstrong but in the smoother swing style—comparable in this regard to Lammar Wright's updating of Oliver on "You Dog" and "Aw You Dawg." The rhythm section, with Morris White on guitar, Al Morgan on bass, and Leroy Maxey on drums, is in superb form and truly competitive with the best rhythm sections of the era.

With the first recording session of 1935, new personnel in the Calloway orchestra paved the way for superior solo and ensemble work. Claude

Jones, who had been with the Fletcher Henderson orchestra in 1930 and '31, brought the trombone section up to the full complement of three and made possible some excellent trombone trios. With the return of William Thornton Blue on clarinet and alto, replacing Eddie Barefield, the reed section came into its own as a flexible, virtuosic unit. Blue had recorded with Calloway in 1930, soloing on "Nobody's Sweetheart" with what Gunther Schuller calls a "shrill, bright, and very eccentric clarinet . . . heard in all its raspy dirty overblown effectiveness."[174] But on "Good Sauce from the Gravy Bowl," the first side cut on January 21, 1935, Blue, it would seem, takes a straight alto solo, as well as an especially good alto release on "Keep That Hi-De-Hi in Your Soul," from the same date. Perhaps on "Good Sauce" the "shrill, bright" break on clarinet also is his. If this is Blue on these two sides, he demonstrates his skilled handling of both instruments, which in the case of the saxophone must have carried over to his sectional work as lead alto, because the reeds now play as a unit with greater precision and swing. (Although Frank Driggs identifies the soloist on "Keep That Hi-De-Hi in Your Soul" as Eddie Barefield, the discography for Classics CD 554 lists Blue as having replaced Barefield for the January 21 session that produced both "Good Sauce" and "Keep That Hi-De-Hi.")[175] Also on "Good Sauce," Claude Jones contributes a solid trombone break, while on this tune and "Keep That Hi-De-Hi," he obviously adds to the very striking trombone trios, which would become something of a regular feature of the Calloway recordings. Particularly fine examples of the trombone trio are to be heard on "Miss Otis Regrets" and "Nagasaki" (both from July 2, 1935, and with, on the latter, two fabulous solos by Jones) and on "You're the Cure for What Ails Me" (from January 27, 1936). Also notable is the trombone section's shaking break on "Peckin' " (from March 3, 1937). As for the reed section's more unified playing, this is most impressive, apparently under Blue's leadership, on "Miss Otis Regrets," "Nagasaki," and "Baby, Won't You Please Come Home?" (from July 2, 1935), on "I Love to Sing" (from January 27, 1936), and on "Are You in Love with Me Again?" (from May 21, 1936). Neither Schuller nor Albert McCarthy comments on any Calloway recordings from 1935, although the latter does say that between 1935 and 1937 "the band had been strengthened by the arrival of such musicians as trombonists Claude Jones and Keg Johnson, saxophonists Garvin Bushell and Ben Webster, bassist Milt Hinton and guitarist Danny Barker."[176]

Frank Driggs is certainly right to include "Nagasaki" among "the most important recordings by Cab Calloway," for this performance has everything: fine work by the reed section, an outstanding trombone trio, a smart ensemble call-and-response, Jones's excellent solo, and another by newcomer Irving "Mouse" Randolph on trumpet. "I Ain't Got Nobody," from the same July 2 session, is an equally good side, with the reed section quite together, a very nice alto solo by Blue, good piano by Benny Payne, and a swinging ensemble on the ride-out that matches the best of any other band at the time. In addition, "I Ain't Got Nobody" also contains one of Calloway's finest scat breaks, which shows him using his voice to achieve the same kind of imaginative improvisation as produced by top instrumentalists of the day. On "Baby, Won't You Please Come Home?" Cab does some of his amazing high note "yells," whereas on "You're the Cure for What Ails Me," from January 27, 1936, he sings the Harold Arlen lyrics with a very effective straight delivery, and then on "Jess's Natu'lly Lazy" and "Are You in Love with Me Again?" from May 21, he spreads it on thick, parodying first the black stereotypes of the former (reminiscent of Hoagy Carmichael's "Lazy Bones") and then the typical romantic ballad. "You're the Cure" predates by some nine months the recording by Lunceford of "Running a Temperature," from October 26, 1936, with the lyrics of both songs playing on the lovesickness motif. The Arlen lyrics are perhaps even more catchy—and timely—than those of Milton Pascal, with Cab capturing wonderfully the humor of the line about being a "weaky lamb" who with his sweetheart's love can suddenly "shoulder Boulder Dam." Not only do these various performances illustrate Calloway's versatility but also they reveal his ability to bring off any song style and whatever subject matter. Whether Cab or his managers chose the songs makes no difference, because, regardless, he delivers them after his own inimitable manner. All three tunes recorded at the January 21 session were by Harburg and Arlen, whereas for the session of September 15, 1936, all four tunes were by Davis and Coots. Two of the Davis-Coots songs, "Copper-Colored Gal" and "Frisco Flo," belong to Cab's Gal and Lady series (as does "My Gal Mezzanine" from March 3, 1937), while Davis-Coots's "The Hi-De-Ho Miracle Man" is another in the group of songs employing the Ho-De-Ho, Hi-De-Hi or Hi-De-Ho phrase. The fourth piece by the Davis-Coots team is "The Wedding of Mr. and Mrs. Swing," with its clever line, "Do you promise to swing with no one else but him?" Calloway's talent for realizing a cast of characters and his versatility in creating jive phrases and ballad moods made his performances immensely popular at the time and are still a satisfying form of jazz vocal artistry.

For those who prefer the instrumental side of big-band jazz, the Calloway orchestra also offers a gratifying listening experience in this regard as well. This is especially true beginning with the recordings of May 21, 1936, which include cameo appearances by tenorist Ben Webster and the bass work of Milt Hinton. "Love Is the Reason" contains an unusual trombone and trumpet sequence that builds up to Webster's marvelous break. In addition to what Gunther Schuller calls Webster's "velvet-glove approach," Ben's solo here harks back to his 1932 solos with the Moten band when the tenorist would shake and bake. But it is his patented warm, mellow sound that predominates, as it would on his major solos with the Ellington orchestra in 1940 and '41.[177] Gentle Ben's style has been aptly described in a poem by Peter McSloy: "the broad, warm breeze / He blew, recumbent, couchant on the sound, / Speaking his natural tongue, that priceless ease, / Coaxing a sigh from the hardest reed he found."[178] Unfortunately, most of Webster's breaks on the Calloway sides are too brief to allow him to stretch out and do not really feature him as the major soloist that he could be. Webster's solo on "Are You in Love With Me Again?—also from May 21—is sandwiched between two fine breaks by Randolph on trumpet, but more impressive is the reed section as a whole, which swings wonderfully. On "Copper-Colored Gal" and "The Wedding of Mr. and Mrs. Swing," from September 15, 1936, and "My Gal Mezzanine" and "That Man Is Here Again," from March 3, 1937, Webster's breaks are clearly recognizable as such, but he just gets started when Cab or the ensemble interrupts. Aside from his relatively more extended solo on "Love Is the Reason" from May 21, Webster's breaks on "Peckin' " and "Congo," from March 3, 1937, present his talents most fully. On "Peckin'," Webster is truly himself, with a high shake, emotive falls, and that marvelous warm, unsentimental sound that only he derived from the tenor. (It is worth noting that the Calloway recording of Harry James's "Peckin' " predates both the famous Goodman version of July 6 and the Ben Pollack of August 26, with Cab's lively rendition of the lyrics describing this as "the dance we all should do.") On "Congo," Webster takes three breaks, and these are all at an up-tempo which he negotiates with smooth, flawless drive, so different from the staccato style of early tenorists, including his mentor Coleman Hawkins before he grew rhapsodic.

As for Milt Hinton, his bass artistry is heard best on "When You're Smiling," also from May 21, 1936, where he is more active than Al Morgan was and is concerned not just to keep the beat but to contribute melodically, his lines almost singing. On "Don't Know If I'm Comin' or Goin'," from March 3, 1937, Hinton provides this piece—which is deeply into the swing-era's sweetish reed sound—with an even smoother swing than Morgan had ever managed, even once the latter had dropped his more slapping New Orleans style, as heard on "I Love to Sing," from January 27, 1936, Morgan's last recording session with Calloway. Hinton also is quite effective on "Congo," where he helps maintain the fast tempo almost imperceptibly, blending beautifully into the overall performance, which includes "voodoolike" fills from the brass, an "exotic" clarinet trio, some suitably "tribal" drumming by Maxey, and fine solos by Webster, Garvin Bushell on clarinet, and probably Randolph on trumpet. Despite the fact that, as Albert McCarthy has said, Hinton, Webster, and the other sidemen served in a "subservient role" to the leader's vocalizing, except on a purely instrumental piece like "Congo," Calloway did showcase his orchestra more than any other star singer.[179]

Following the arrival of Chu Berry to replace Ben Webster in the summer of 1937, Calloway's sidemen would slowly be featured more prominently than ever before. One side that indicates this trend even comes as early as the March 17 session, on which two tunes were recorded, "Wake Up and Live" and "Manhattan Jam."[180] Although unissued at the time, "Manhattan Jam" is a type of Dixieland original by Harry White, a feature for clarinetist Garvin Bushell, who on occasion plays long glissandi like those of Ellington's Barney Bigard. More engaging than either this piece or "Swing, Swing, Swing," from March 3, which Frank Driggs includes among "the most important recordings of Cab Calloway," is "Wake Up and Live," especially owing to Cab's vocal handling of some tricky rhythms in the theme, but also because Ben Webster takes a brief solo, as does Irving Randolph, while Leroy Maxey furnishes some very fine touches on drums. But with Chu Berry's appearance at the August 24 recording session, it is clear that Calloway looked upon this tenorist as worthy of greater exposure than the leader previously had granted to any of his other sidemen.

Chu Berry's first breaks are on "I'm Always in the Mood for You" and "She's Tall, She's Tan, She's Terrific," from the August 24 session, both tunes once again by the team of Davis and Coots. Although the tenorist does not enjoy space enough to stretch out in his two brief appearances on each of these sides, he does make it clear that he is not indebted that much to either Hawkins or Webster when it comes to his style of drive. Berry's distinctive approach is heard more fully on "Go South, Young Man," from the August 31 session, which is yet another Davis-Coots tune. Here the tenorist really charges in and shows that not only can he build intensity in the short span of his two brief breaks but that the structural shape of his ideas is peculiar to him alone. On the second break, Berry finishes off with just the right flourish to render a satisfying end to his brief performance. Two other sides that contain impressive outings by Berry are "Mama, I Wanna Make Rhythm" and "Queen Isabella" (a version of Berry's "Christopher Columbus"), also from August 31. On the first the tenorist is afforded more space than Webster had been, and on the latter he is featured more than any previous sideman, taking advantage of a full chorus to construct a driving, imaginative solo that has his special sweet sound, which is yet in no way cloying. Berry's final appearance from this date is on "Savage Rhythm," which, like "Queen Isabella," is another instrumental. Here Randolph solos first on trumpet and then Berry plays a stirring break that justifies Frank Driggs's inclusion of "Savage Rhythm" among the Calloway orchestra's "most important recordings." This tune, also by the team of Davis and Coots, puts the reed section through its paces, has a brief break by the trombone section, and finds the ensemble swinging hard on the out passage, driven by Maxey's "savage" drums. But Berry is clearly the star of this recording, and it seems that Calloway must have valued his new tenorist, because Berry definitely received most of the spotlight, especially on two purely instrumental sides.

The first side from the December 10 session is "Every Day's a Holiday," which offers a rather generic big-band sound, although the Calloway orchestra may have been ahead of the other units in its use of a silken reed sound for this gently swinging tune. Cab handles the lilting rhythms as skillfully and infectiously as he did on "Wake Up and Live," and Chauncey Haughton on clarinet takes a delightful break. Berry comes in only briefly at the tag end.[181] On Hoagy Carmichael's "Jubilee," Cab sings the lyrics in a more relaxed manner that is, although smooth and personally expressive, ultimately less invigorating than the version recorded just a month later by Louis Armstrong and the Luis Russell Orchestra. As Richard Sudhalter has written, "Jubilee" "has never been played or sung better" than by Armstrong, and the backing he received from the Russell unit, with Pops Foster's bass booming right along, is truly far more inspiriting than the Calloway recording, despite the fact that Berry plays a delicious break and none of the Russell sidemen solos.[182] Naturally Cab and Louis take center stage on both recordings, but there is no doubt that the latter creates a work of genuine jazz whereas the former manages only a convincing piece of popular entertainment. Most commentators on Calloway's career tend to see it as an extension of the vaudeville tradition, from which Armstrong also emerged to a certain extent but definitely outgrew by dent of his superior artistry both as a singer and a trumpeter. A curious item recorded by the Calloway orchestra is "In an Old English Village," from December 10, 1937, which features a sweet muted trombone (in no way equal to Tommy Dorsey's for control) and finds Cab putting on something of an English accent. Both the Dorsey-like trombone and the vocal are an apparent attempt to compete with the white bands. "(Just an) Error in the News," from the same date, is not really jazz, just popular dance-band music in the sweet style. "A Minor Breakdown (Rustle of Swing)," also from this date, is an instrumental rejected by the Vocalion label, which suggests that the band had lost something of the energy and drive of the earlier Calloway groups. Not even Berry's brief appearance saves this side from sounding rather like just another big-band chart. Although "Bugle Blues," from the same date, is offered by Albert McCarthy as evidence that "the band was a fine one," this is certainly not a thrilling performance, and the solos by Berry, Randolph, and Bushell are nothing special.[183]

With the session of January 26, 1938, the listener is treated to six sides, out of which essentially half are instrumentals. Although "I Like Music (with a Swing Like That)" is largely a feature for the sidemen, it does contain a vocal by Cab. The two strictly instrumental sides bear the by now de rigueur swing word in their titles: "Rustle of Swing" and "Three Swings and Out." Brief solos by Berry highlight three other vocal sides from this date: "One Big Union for Two" (with a rather subdued Chu playing the theme, doing a bit of obbligato work behind the vocalist, and then bursting out on his final freer break); "Doing the Reactionary" (with the ensemble supporting the vocalist effectively and Berry making the most of his few bars); and "Foolin' with You" (where Berry opens with the theme and demonstrates why, as Leonard Feather has written, with his "soft sound and lush, mellow tone" Chu belongs with Webster and Hawkins "among the earliest figures to bring full maturity to the tenor saxophone").[184] On the last of these three sides, Cab is into his yell-singing style, and the ensemble really swings, with nice figures behind the vocalist at the close. Except for Berry's solo on "Rustle of Swing," this is a rather corny piece. And in keeping with its title, "Three Swings and Out" certainly doesn't hit one out of the park, but Berry, who is allotted a full chorus, with interruptions by the ensemble, does make it past first base. On "I Like Music," Cab, after his introductory vocal, calls on "Chu" by name to swing out some jive, which he does beautifully, followed by breaks by Randolph on trumpet, a few bars by Milt Hinton on bass, probably Keg Johnson on trombone, and Leroy Maxey with some drum work before the ride-out. Berry also opens the Duke Ellington composition, "Azure," recorded on March 23, and here Chu shows most fully why he was rated by fellow musicians as one of the big three of the swing-era tenors, leaning (on his longer solo) in the narrative direction of Lester Young but with the more rhapsodic manner of Hawkins. As for Calloways's singing of the lyrics to Ellington's classic, it may not do the piece true justice, because Cab's vocal fails to evoke the haunting quality of the original. Nonetheless, Berry's opening and closing breaks are closer to the Ducal mood, and the reeds are featured in some intricate lines played with lovely precision.

One other side from March 23, 1938, "At the Clambake Carnival," is a Berry original, which Frank Driggs again includes among the Calloway orchestra's most important recordings. As might be expected, Berry opens his own tune with a rather booting solo, on which, according to Gunther Schuller, "the real Chu Berry can be heard,"[185] followed by one of trombonist Keg Johnson's more relaxed efforts, Bennie Payne on vibes, and Chauncey Haughton on clarinet, after which the whole ensemble plays a type of dixie jam. (The title of Berry's piece and its Dixieland flavor at the end recall Tommy Dorsey's band-within-a-band, his Clambake Seven, to be discussed in Chapter 6 on small groups.) Nothing about this performance seems especially notable, however, and does not really show the warmth or imagination Berry exhibits on "Foolin' with You," which, although a minor ballad by Harry White, obviously inspired a fine effort from Chu. A more impressive outing from Berry is found on the recording of "Jive (Page One of the Hepster's Dictionary)," as the subtitle has it, from August 30, 1938. Here, on this jive version of a Jericho-like spiritual, Berry works the chords beautifully, moving from eighth to sixteenth notes and with an overall warm and mellow sound. Schuller has charged that Berry "lacked the warm, fully-centered tone that a great ballad player must have," and this may be true, but certainly here and on "Foolin' with You" and "Azure," Chu's sound is warmly emotive.[186] Of Berry's major recordings, Schuller prefers "Lonesome Nights" from August 28, 1940, to the more frequently praised "A Ghost of a Chance," from June 27, 1940. Schuller finds that on the latter Berry's vibrato "was too regular, automated," and this may be a fair judgment in the case of "A Ghost of a Chance," although it might be said simply that Chu utilized a light instead of a heavy vibrato.[187] Over either "Lonesome Nights" or "A Ghost of a Chance," I prefer, as does Albert McCarthy, Berry's "enthusiastic, bustling style . . . at a medium to medium-fast tempo," as on "Bye Bye Blues" and "Come on with the 'Come On,' " both from June 27, 1940.[188]

It is instructive to compare "A Ghost," which is given over entirely to a virtuosic performance by Berry, with the Calloway recording of "Willow Weep for Me," a feature for altoist Hilton Jefferson, from January 16, 1941. For one thing, Berry and Jefferson's performances reveal how far Chu, Hilton, and the jazz saxophone had come since the days of King Oliver when Jefferson soloed on such a piece as "Shake It and Break It" from September 10, 1930. Jefferson's alto solo on the Oliver side, though influential at the time, due to its already greater flexibility, was still rather in a vertical, staccato style.[189] By 1941, Jefferson and Berry both had developed a smoother legato manner, or what McCarthy, in writing about Hilton's "Willow," describes as flowingly "elegiac." McCarthy goes on to say that "Jefferson was not perhaps an outstanding jazz improviser, but he was very good at this type of melodic variation."[190] For his part, Berry embellishes the melody of "A Ghost" with runs, arpeggiated phrases, and stirring leaps that transform the material into a new, personalized composition, which was crucial to the maturation of the saxophone's role in jazz. As for "Lonesome Nights," this Berry feature finds the tenorist playing with a sweeter sound, and McCarthy, like Schuller (or vice versa, since the latter follows McCarthy chronologically), considers the tenorist's performance "one of his greatest solos at slow tempo."[191]

With the session of August 30, 1938, Cozy Cole replaced Leroy Maxey as Calloway's drummer, and the new sideman's more subtle presence is evident on "Jive." On February 20, 1939, Cole was the featured soloist for "Ratamacue," which Gunther Schuller correctly judges, along with two other spotlights for the drummer, "Crescendo in Drums," from July 17, 1939, and "Paradiddle," from March 8, 1940 (arranged by Dizzy Gillespie), to be "disappointing, both as virtuoso display pieces and as compositional vehicles."[192] These three features for Cole essentially come to little as music—with "Ratamacue" and "Paradiddle," according to Burt Korall, being "based on two drum rudiments and their variations," or what Schuller describes as "endless snare drum triplet patterns," which reflect the studious nature of Cole as a highly respected percussionist but do not necessarily translate into enjoyable listening.[193] Another feature for a member of the rhythm section is "Pluckin' the Bass," from August 30, 1939, with Milt Hinton simultaneously slapping and plucking his strings; however, this piece is perhaps more noteworthy for marking the first solo outing by Dizzy Gillespie, Calloway's latest addition to his trumpet section.[194] But even the future Bebop star does not offer much here that is satisfying musically. More appetizing is Gillespie's break on "Boo-Wah-Boo-Wah," from August 5, 1940, on which he plays not in an advanced style but a distinctive one. His most advanced conception is found on "Bye Bye Blues" and "Cupid's Nightmare," the latter a broadcast transcription from January 1940, an experimental type of composition by Don Redman.[195]

Joining Gillespie on "Bye Bye Blues" was trombonist-vibraharpist Tyree Glenn, who solos on vibes with tremendous swing, doing on this instrument what few if any other vibraharpists have ever done: playing simultaneous lines of different character. On both "Pluckin' the Bass" and "Boo-Wah-Boo-Wah," Chu Berry also swings mightily. Just as Berry had acquitted himself well on Ellington's "Azure," Chu also comes off wonderfully on the fine Calloway version of the Ellington-Strayhorn classic, "Take the 'A' Train," from July 3, 1941, as does a muted Jonah Jones, another new trumpeter who is featured on "Jonah Joins the Cab," from March 5, 1941. Jones, as McCarthy says, "plays with power and an impressive broad tone" on the March 11 recording of the Benny Goodman tune, "A Smooth One," made famous by Goodman's sextet featuring electric guitarist Charlie Christian.[196] "Calling All Bars," a Benny Carter instrumental from May 15, 1940, shows the entire band in great form, supported by Cozy Cole's as it were behind-the-scenes percussion work. Fine solos are turned in by Gillespie, Berry, and Tyree Glenn on trombone, and although Schuller may be correct that Dizzy's two breaks are characterized by a repetitive circularity, they yet are pitched in a distinctive new voice.[197] Another feature for Milt Hinton is "Ebony Silhouette," from January 16, 1941, this time showcasing Milt's bowed bass. Still other purely instrumental recordings during 1940 and 1941 include "Limehouse Blues," from July 27, 1940, which showcases some of Cozy Cole's best extrovert drumming, which is true as well of Chu Berry's two in-your-face breaks, as well as Gillespie in full control of his fleet-fingered style; "King Porter Stomp," from the same date, features driving solos by Tyree Glenn on trombone, Jerry Blake with a rasping clarinet, Gillespie prefiguring the bop mode, and Berry bursting at the seams; and "Tappin' Off," from March 11, 1941, is highlighted by a surging Chu Berry.[198] Encouraged by Cab's yells and kicked by Cole's percussion, the band plays the Jelly Roll Morton classic with a powerhouse delivery, concluded by Cozy's lesson in big-band drumming. All these instrumental sides furnish evidence that the Calloway orchestra, when not backing up the leader's vocals, "outswung most of its competitors."[199] It is certainly clear that Calloway hired some of the strongest players available and that his orchestra was truly the training ground for a new generation of jazz stars.

Although Calloway's orchestra members indicated some of the trends to come, Cab himself continued with his same entertaining ways, recording a number of typical tunes: "The Jumpin' Jive," on July 17, 1939; "Boog It," on March 8, 1940; "Topsy Turvy (Hard Times)," on May 15, 1940; "Geechy Joe," on March 5, 1941; and "St. James Infirmary," on July 3, 1941. On July 24, 1941, through his inimitable swing and the lyrics' allusions to the many characters in his songs, Calloway summed up the past decade with "We Go Well Together," as if in reference not only to his own stylistic traits but also to the association of the leader with his sidemen. "Boog It" and "Topsy Turvy," from a January 1940 broadcast transcription, show off Cozy Cole and Milt Hinton's wonderful rhythm work and Chu Berry's marvelous tenor, including on "Boog It" what became known as the Texas honk.[200] In these final years of the early Swing Era, the Calloway Orchestra offered in some ways the best of both worlds: a superior vaudeville act and an advanced jazz band with exceptional soloists, a solid rhythm section, and outstanding charts by such arrangers as Benny Carter ("Lonesome Nights" and "The Lone Arranger"), Andy Gibson ("Special Delivery" and "Willow Weep for Me"), Buster Harding ("Bye Bye Blues"), Don Redman ("Cupid's Nightmare"), and Edgar Battle ("Topsy Turvy"). "The Lone Arranger," from May 15, 1940, and "Special Delivery," from March 5, 1941, are typical swing-era pieces, the former a smoothly driving number that features two fine breaks by Berry and Cozy Cole's expert drumming, and the latter a flag waver on which Berry really blows and goes.

Regardless of what aspect of the Calloway organization one prefers, there is no denying the enduring allure of a piece such as "The Jumpin' Jive," with the leader and his jivy, hep lingo sung in an infectious style, his sidemen joining in as a lively chorus, Cozy Cole's sticks punctuating with taste, Milt Hinton's firm pulse laying down a solid, unobtrusive beat, Chu Berry's big-toned tenor booting with the best in the business, Irving Randolph's muted trumpet fueling the drive, and Keg Johnson's smooth trombone grooving with flawless swing. This was a complete entertainment package that almost no other band could offer, and surely accounts for the long career of the leader and the staying power of so many of his sidemen, with trumpeter Lammar Wright and reedmen Walter Thomas and Andrew Brown still in the band from the original Missourians of 1930. In itself, the Cab Calloway Orchestra represents most every development of big-band jazz from 1930 to 1941, with the leader singing everything from ballads and jive and novelty numbers to original character studies and classic pieces by such contemporaries as Ellington and even Glenn Miller (Cab's "Chattanooga Choo Choo," of July 3, 1941, recorded two months after the Miller version of May 7), with some of Calloway's sidemen in the last two years previewing Bebop as the next major movement in jazz.

ANDY KIRK

The creation and spread of Swing was a national phenomenon, with every region of the country having an impact on this most popular of jazz movements. Denver, Colorado's mile-high city, was no exception, despite the fact that it was not one of the major centers of jazz and was largely isolated from the territories that most often spawned the leading figures of Swing and of the other developments in jazz history. Nonetheless, Denver was home to two crucial figures who influenced the growth and popularity of Swing: Wilberforce J. Whiteman, father of Paul Whiteman and teacher of both Jimmie Lunceford and Andy Kirk; and George Morrison, a violinist whose dance orchestra tutored a number of early jazz musicians, including multi-instrumentalist Sonny Clay, who, like Morrison-proteges Lunceford and Kirk, would go on to become a popular band leader himself, in Los Angeles. Eventually, both Lunceford and Kirk would eclipse at the national level not only Morrison, their former employer, but also Paul Whiteman, the "King of Jazz" in the 1920s.[201]

In his autobiographical account, *Twenty Years on Wheels*, Kirk, who was born in Newport, Kentucky, on May 28, 1898, but moved to Denver in 1904, reveals that his schooling in Colorado was exceptional for the times. (While Andy was at East Denver High, Willie Smith, Lunceford's lead alto, studied at South Denver High.)[202] Kirk recalls verses learned in German, his ability to wander the city without encountering prejudice of any kind (except from Texans who had moved to the Rockies), and the fact that his "first jazz 'instruction' was from white musicians, and certainly not in school. I don't recall we'd even heard the word jazz then." It was only in the little clubs in Kansas City, which he first visited in 1925, that Kirk "got 'educated' in jazz and blues." He does not "remember much about the weather" in Kansas City, but he says he will "never forget the heat from Bennie Moten's five-piece band at a little after-hours club on 18th street. It was the first time I'd ever heard a band like that. It was *swinging*."[203] In time, Andy Kirk also would lead a swinging Kansas City band, known from coast to coast as the Twelve Clouds of Joy, "the first regional band after Bennie Moten's to attain nationwide popularity."[204]

Originally led by Terrence Holder, the group that would become the Twelve Clouds of Joy worked out of Dallas at the time that Andy Kirk joined up, which was in the fall of 1926. Kirk comments that "Texans liked competition," and as he was the only "Northerner in Holder's band . . . did the Texans ever make fun of the way I talked!" He goes on to say that in joining up with Holder he heard for the first time "Southwest-style jazz," in particular the tenor playing of Budd Johnson, and later the band of Jack Teagarden, who "demolished the old stereotype of colored bands having a monopoly on jazz and Whites on sweet music."[205] Kirk himself had begun on tenor, studying in Denver with Franz Rath, who had played clarinet with the Boston Symphony, but he was hired by George Morrison to play tuba. Eventually Kirk taught himself the string bass and the bass sax, but more importantly he began to write and arrange, influenced, he reports, by Jelly Roll Morton, who, on his trips through Denver, "often played with a George Morrison unit" and whose "stompin' . . . showed up in patterns" Kirk "used later in arrangements" for his own band.[206] After Holder abandoned the Twelve Clouds in 1928, the band elected Kirk as its new leader and only then did the unit take on the name Andy Kirk and His Twelve Clouds of Joy. As a member of the Northeast Amusement Company, the Clouds settled in Tulsa, traveling between park pavilions there and in Oklahoma City. Soon, however, Kirk and his men would become a Kansas City band, when the Pla-Mor, seeking competition with its rival, the El Torreon Ballroom where Cab Calloway was featured at the time, was contracted in 1929 to replace Chick Scoggins. The success of the Twelve Clouds of Joy, according to Kirk, was that it was "first and last a dance orchestra" because "people were dance crazy in those days. And if you played the kind of music they liked to dance to, that's what mattered. As I've said, our band didn't stress jazz, though we played it. We emphasized dance music—romantic ballads and pop tunes and waltzes—Viennese as well as standard popular waltzes like 'Kiss me again' and 'Alice Blue Gown.' I loved to play waltzes."[207] In some ways, the biggest influence on the Clouds of Joy in terms of jazz came with the almost accidental addition of pianist-composer-arranger Mary Lou Williams, by consensus the "first woman jazz musician of real stature."[208]

The first recording session for the Clouds of Joy was held on four days, circa November 7, 8, 9, and 11, 1929, in Kansas City. The regular pianist, Marion Jackson, had failed to show up for the audition in October, and Mary Lou Williams was hurriedly recruited at the last minute, but she was so good that she turned out to be "a big factor" in the band "landing an excellent two-year recording contract."[209] The first tune recorded by the group was "Mess-A-Stomp," written by Mary Lou, on which she takes a fine Hines-inspired piano solo, while Kirk's brass bass is heard from the opening bars. Albert McCarthy writes, "[T]his first title recorded . . . proves beyond any doubt that the band could swing."[210] On "Cloudy," Kirk's own tune, the leader takes a brief tuba solo, although McCarthy considers Kirk never to have been "an outstanding instrumentalist."[211] "Casey Jones" is a novelty piece, also by Kirk, with imitation train effects, which will be improved on by the band's recording of "Casey Jones Blues," on March 2, 1931 (credited to Blanche Calloway and Her Joy Boys). Andy and Mary Lou's "Corky Stomp" is marked, as McCarthy says, by "tight ensemble work";[212] again, there will be a later "Corky," of March 7, 1936, featuring the band's then tenor star, Dick Wilson. Mary Lou's "Lotta Sax Appeal," a showcase for her husband John on baritone sax, also looks forward to one of the band's major recordings, a remake in 1936 of the same piece, but with the spotlight once again on tenorist Dick Wilson.

What is most striking when the 1929 sides are compared with "I Lost My Gal from Memphis," the first tune recorded only five months later at sessions held April 29 and 30 and May 1, 1930, is the smoother swing and greater precision of both ensemble and solo work. And this is true as well of Kirk and Williams' "Loose Ankles," the second tune pressed, which includes a violin break by Claude Williams and which in the ensemble passages definitely shows the influence of the Trumbauer-Beiderbecke recordings. Albert McCarthy even hears in tenorist Lawrence Freeman's solo something of Trumbauer's playing style.[213] Not so effective is the Clouds' version of King Oliver's "Snag It," although trumpeter Harry Lawson's rendition of the famous Oliver break is quite commendable. Kirk has explained in his autobiography that because "Moten had been *the* band on Okeh" that the Brunswick and Vocalion people wanted the Clouds to do the same sort of "thing like 'Snag It,' 'Mary's Idea,' and 'Dallas Blues.' That type of number was the smaller part of our library. The bigger part we could play only in person."[214] "Snag It," "Mary's Idea," and "Dallas Blues" all are backward looking compared with "I Lost My Gal from Memphis," even though "Dallas Blues" contains an excellent piano solo by Mary Lou, more good trumpet work by Lawson, and a solid break by trombonist Allen Durham. Closer to the relaxed swing of "I Lost My Gal" is "Honey, Just for You," with a decent tenor solo by Lawrence Freeman. The Clouds' version of the frequently recorded "You Rascal You" finds Durham contributing some of his most fluid trombone work, while Lawson supports vocalist Billy Massey with some nice trumpet responses. This recording compares favorably with those made by Fletcher Henderson, of whom Kirk has recalled that it was Smack's band "that really opened our ears" when the Clouds played opposite the Father of Swing at the Pla-Mor in Kansas City.[215] Of course, Kirk did not have a soloist of the caliber of Coleman Hawkins, but he did have an improving organization, with a fine drummer in Edward McNeil, who was beginning to come into his own on recordings like "Saturday" and "Sophomore," from the session of December 15, 1930. This last pair of tunes combines pop elements with moments of true jazz, which would in some ways characterize much of the Clouds' recording history.

From the time of the Clouds' recording in support of Blanche Calloway in 1931, it would be five years before the band returned to the studios. The first side cut, on March 2, 1936, "Walkin' and Swingin'," has been called "the best recording of the band" and Mary Lou Williams's arrangement "one of the finest in large-band orchestration."[216] As would be expected after half a decade, the difference in the band's sound is worlds apart from the 1930–1931 recordings, although Mary Lou's piano is still rooted in Hines, just more so on this particular side. The ensemble is now more evenly balanced, with both brasses and saxes of equal quality, whereas earlier the brasses had been the stronger section. The only solos are those by Mary Lou and Dick Wilson, whose tenor introduces a smoother Chu Berry–influenced sound. Naturally the presence of Booker Collins's string bass adds greatly to the relaxed swing, as does Ben Thigpen's smooth drumming. The other two sides from this March 2 session are a laid-back, un-aggressive version of "Moten Swing," which pays homage to the original 1932 recording by duplicating its final out passage, and "Lotta Sax Appeal," with Wilson given full rein to show his stuff, as is trombonist Ted Donnelly. In some ways as "appealing" as the fine solos by Wilson and Donnelly and short breaks by clarinetist John Harrington and trumpeter Harry Lawson on "Lotta Sax Appeal" is the ensemble playing, which is by turns mellow and crisp—the mild reeds complemented by the piquant punch of the brass, creating what Albert McCarthy calls a "subtle balance" and a "light ensemble sound."[217]

The following day, March 3, the Clouds recorded "Git" and "All the Jive Is Gone." Drummer Ben Thigpen does the novelty vocal on the former, another piece with "an easygoing relaxed beat" and with pleasant breaks by Paul King on trumpet and Wilson on tenor.[218] Wilson is more engaging on "All the Jive Is Gone," which is the first side to feature Pha Terrell as the vocalist who would help gain the band national recognition but would also direct it away from a jazz-oriented approach toward more popularized material. The next day, March 4, the Clouds cut three more sides: "Froggy Bottom," "Bearcat Shuffle," and "Steppin' Pretty." The first of these is a rather lazy riff with none of the drive of a Moten or Basie performance. Although Charles Fox considers "Bearcat Shuffle" to include one of Wilson's finest solos, I personally prefer his work on "Steppin' Pretty," which is an apt title for this tune with something of a Lunceford-like lift. Fox locates Wilson's style in relation to Coleman Hawkins's as "roughly the same . . . as Hershal Evans,' " with the difference that Wilson has a "light dry tone . . . suggestive of Lester Young's, while at faster tempos he could push as impetuously as Chu Berry."[219] Wilson's solo on "Bearcat Shuffle," predating Evans's recorded work with the Basie band, does suggest Hershal's sound but lacks tension, the sense of barely controlled emotion that is trying to erupt at all times, a feeling Evans created in even a very few notes. On "Steppin' Pretty," Wilson is more adventuresome, moving suddenly into the upper register and, as Gunther Schuller has described his style, delivering lines that are "sinuous and unpredictable, taking odd, unexpected turns that broke through the usual automated fingering patterns."[220] This also is true of Wilson's solos on "Corky" and "Christopher Columbus," from March 7, 1936, with the tenorist's solo on the former praised by Schuller for its "concise, compact statements" and "relaxed free-floating swing."[221] Although Wilson's tenor solo on "Christopher Columbus" has its own compelling personality and is interesting in and of itself, it does not achieve the drive and exuberance of Chu Berry's on the Henderson recording, which was made almost three weeks after the Clouds' version. Perhaps, as Schuller suggests, this was by design, and perhaps it is only fair to see Wilson's work as Schuller does: instead of "Berry's tendency to a kind of run-on breathlessness, Wilson balanced his solos by interposing quick flurries of notes with more sustained phrases."[222] Albert McCarthy finds Wilson's melodic invention another attractive side to his playing, as revealed on the March 11 recording of "I'se a Muggin'."[223] Unfortunately, Wilson and Berry, who were born a year apart, both died in 1941, at ages thirty and thirty-one, respectively, without, one would think, reaching their full potential. However, as Schuller suggests, in Wilson's case it would have necessitated his being with a better band, or at least one that offered him more opportunities to solo and more challenging material.[224]

The side that proved the biggest hit for the Clouds was "Until the Real Thing Comes Along," first recorded on March 11, 1936, for distribution by Columbia in England, but issued by Decca after a second recording made on April 2. Pha Terrell's singing of the lyrics probably sold the side, along with the rather sentimental style of the orchestra. After one has heard Fats Waller's rendition from November 3, 1939, it is difficult to take seriously the Clouds' essentially sappy recording. When Terrell sings "I'd be a beggar or a knave for you," one hears Fats's aside, "Whatever that is," and when Terrell asks "What more can I say," Fats's improvised lines immediately come to mind: "Do you want me to rob a bank? Well I won't do it." Even so, the Clouds' recording was requested repeatedly by audiences of the day everywhere the orchestra toured. Another tune, "Blue Illusion," recorded the next day, on April 3, was in the same romantic vein, with muted trumpets repeating the theme as first sung by Terrell and with Mary Lou playing some cocktail-style runs in the background, after which the vocalist concludes, as he does on "Until the Real Thing," in a falsetto voice. Yet another tune of this sort is "Cloudy," also from April 3, and here at least Wilson contributes one of his melodic inventions, but overall, like so many of the Clouds' offerings, this piece does not come to much, blending popular and jazz elements in a rather unsatisfying mix. A fairly dreadful novelty vocal such as "Give Her a Pint (and She'll Tell It All)," from April 7, can include some fine ensemble and solo moments, but the corny tune detracts from one's ability to enjoy even those rare moments, and even on an instrumental such as "Puddin' Head Serenade," of April 10, Wilson can play some quite pointless doodles. It becomes difficult to endure much of the Clouds' inane material for the sake of a few seconds of mildly interesting jazz. "Fifty-second Street," recorded on the final session of December 9, 1936, opens with a nice peppy swing, but even though this piece pays tribute to the New York street "where swinging got its start," as with so many of the Clouds' sides following the success of "Until the Real Thing," this number comes to little or nothing. Even the tribute to Mary Lou Williams, "the main attraction" of "The Lady Who Swings the Band," offers little more than a Waller-like stride piano. These two pieces, like "Until the Real Thing," are the work of the team of Cahn and Chaplin, and even though their tunes tend to make up some of the unit's better material, they still cannot compare with the compositions of the name bands.

Gunther Schuller characterizes the problem with the Clouds when he says of "Wednesday Night Hop," the first side recorded at the session of February 15, 1937, that this "could have been a more successful riff number but for the Leslie Johnakins arrangement."[225] One wonders how this essentially dull piece could have inspired dancers at the "hop." For one thing, it shifts styles so often that it must have frustrated most sock hoppers. And the worst part of it is that this was among the few instrumentals recorded by the Clouds, because the vast majority of its material now featured Pha Terrell's predictably sappy vocals, one of which, "Downstream," from the same February 15 session, epitomizes the nonjazz tendency of the orchestra. The only "soloist" is the baritone with a theme statement, no improvisation, and with the ensemble, as the lyrics say, just "drifting downstream." The best instrumental from the whole of 1937 and 1938 is "In the Groove," cut on this same date of February 15. On this piece, Dick Wilson takes one of his better solos, which Schuller has transcribed to illustrate the tenorist's "inventive urge to explore advanced harmonic and rhythmic realms" and the fact that Wilson solos in "the unusual, hard-to-play key of B major."[226] This side also offers a fine trumpet break by Paul King and some of Mary Lou's jaunty piano. "A Mellow Bit of Rhythm," a Mary Lou composition, recorded on July 26, finds Wilson contributing an okay break, John Harrington's clarinet better than usual, and Ben Thigpen more active on drums, but the piece does not really cohere. Another Cahn-Chaplin tune, "In My Wildest Dreams," also from July 26, has more of Pha Terrell's romantic crooning (which can have a certain charm, especially on the next couple of cuts, "Better Luck Next Time" and "With Love in My Heart," that is hard to reconcile with the fact that he was discovered by Kirk working as a nightclub bouncer). On the first of these tunes, Wilson plays with a broader sound that is less interesting than his normal balancing of light, fluid lines with sudden flourishes. On "With Love in My Heart," Wilson is quite good, achieving what Charles Fox calls "a lyrical stance . . . very much his own," and the whole band really swings momentarily before Pha returns, ending as so often on a bit of a falsetto note.[227] It must be said that on a piece such as "What's Mine Is Yours," from July 27, both Wilson and Mary Lou's solos help make this a highly successful romantic rendition, which must have been the type of performance, along with the success of "Until the Real Thing," which prompted Joe Glaser, "the prominent booking-agency," to sign the orchestra to "lucrative tours."[228]

On December 13, 1937, the Clouds recorded "Lover, Come Back to Me," which Wilson opens with more of his broadly romantic style. This is another of many smooth performances that the orchestra was regularly recording, with Pha Terrell clearly singing with great confidence. But there is by now almost no real jazz being produced by the unit, which should remind one of Andy Kirk's autobiographical comment that the group played what appealed most to its audience and did not concern itself with performing just jazz. At times, as on "Poor Butterfly," of the same date, the sax section could demonstrate its rather distinctive sound, abetted by the presence, as Albert McCarthy notes, of Wilson's very personal tone.[229] On the next session, of February 8, 1938, the orchestra recorded "Twinklin'," "nothing less than a mini-concerto for piano and orchestra composed and arranged by Mary Lou Williams."[230] As Gunther Schuller points out, here there is a definite Basie influence on Mary Lou's piano style, even though she does reel off some more daring runs than the Count generally attempted.[231] For his part, McCarthy hears in the pianist's solos an "occasional reversion to ragtime modes."[232] Good ensemble work shows what the band was capable of, but like so many of the Clouds' sides, this one ultimately amounts to very little. Mary Lou's penchant for boogie woogie piano is heard on her "Little Joe from Chicago," cocomposed with Henry Wells and also recorded on February 8. In Mary Lou's autobiographical account of her life, she recalls that it was due to her success with "Roll 'Em," her arrangement written for the Benny Goodman orchestra, that the Clouds "had to start featuring boogies."[233] Beginning under the influence of Hines and moving during this time more toward Basie, Mary Lou exhibits throughout her Clouds recordings an eclectic artistry, handling all the popular piano styles of the period, as indicated by some fine stride piano on her composition "Mess-a-Stomp" from September 9 and on "Jump Jack Jump" from October 24, her Teddy Wilson approach on "What Would People Say" from September 12 (in her autobiography calling Wilson "a genius"), her Walleresque touch on "Julius Caesar" from December 5 (in her autobiography listing among the major jazz piano inspirations Hines, Wilson, and Waller), and her dreamy, romantic side on "How Can We Be Wrong?" from September 9 and "But It Didn't Mean a Thing" from December 6.[234] A tune such as "Breeze (Blow My Baby Back to Me)," from October 24, with its allusive Lunceford lick, makes one wonder if the Clouds had any particularly identifiable sound of their own. It would seem that only soloists such as Mary Lou, despite her eclecticism, and Dick Wilson provide the orchestra with much in the way of distinctive voices—Terrell's vocals are perhaps recognizable as his but remain largely generic in nature. Aside from their pianist and star tenorist, the Clouds seem basically an anonymous orchestra.

At least in the period from 1936 to 1938, Kirk and His Twelve Clouds of Joy do not exhibit any special development as an organization. With the success of Terrell's vocals, the orchestra became primarily a purveyor of a form of romantic jazz, as exemplified by Kirk's own composition, "Sittin' Around and Dreamin'," from October 25, 1938. This is as good a romantic dance piece as was produced during the Swing Era, with nice work by the reed section, some unusual alto spots, an effective break by Wilson, and a capable vocal by Terrell. Orrin Keepnews cautions against making comparisons "between particular works or specific artists, leading to the assertion that one is 'better' than another." His position is that "none of this actually has anything at all to do with creativity."[235] On the other hand, Stanley Crouch defines swing as a "combination of grace and intensity," and this critic implies that without both these qualities being present, so that "sorrow rhythmically transforms itself into joy," there is no authentic jazz.[236] It is perhaps representative of the somewhat one-sidedness of the Clouds' output that the group was entitled just the Clouds of Joy, because there is little in their music of sorrow that "transforms itself into joy." This is illustrated by their October 25 recording of "What's Your Story, Morning Glory?"—especially when compared with the recording by the Lunceford orchestra of the same song, from February 28, 1940. Although Dick Wilson is clearly a finer tenor soloist than Lunceford's Joe Thomas, here the latter's effectiveness within the framework of Billy Moore's blues arrangement is greater than Wilson's contribution on this particular tune. Again, the Lunceford recording achieves what Crouch has defined as a transformation of the sorrow of the blues form into the joy of "grace and intensity." This combination is almost totally missing here and in all other Clouds recordings. Even though the Clouds' version is presented as essentially a pop song, with Terrell's vocal sung in a heavily syncopated manner, followed by Wilson's rather pointless break, there is one aspect of this recording that is unusual among most of the Clouds' sides of this period, namely, it builds to a climax rather than simply concluding without any sense of closure. (This is evident, for example, in the December 5 "Dunkin' a Doughnut," with its undramatic, abrupt ending.) So often with a Clouds performance there is neither a "combination of grace and intensity" nor any feeling that the piece had a meaningful point to make, other than to present the theme, the vocal's lyrics, and the compulsory yet almost incidental solo or two.

Despite the fine tenor playing of Dick Wilson and the occasional solo contributions of other sidemen, including in particular Mary Lou Williams, as well as the frequently excellent balance between the sections, the Kirk orchestra ultimately was a minor big band because it emphasized the sentimental over the meaningful musical statement. Limited to its type of dreamy drifting and floating (as in the lyrics to "Clouds" of December 5), the outfit never established any sense of direction, any feeling in the listener of a deepening of musical thought. "Mess-a-Stomp," of September 9, 1938, certainly updates the same piece recorded by the Clouds under that title in 1929, and "Toadie Toddle" of September 12 declares itself in the lyrics to be something "ultra new," as compared with the Clouds' "Froggy Bottom" of 1936, but these tunes do not represent any significant developments in themselves. In comparison with so many sentimental sides recorded by the orchestra, they do stand out as examples of greater swing and a more forceful style of ensemble playing, although, as Albert McCarthy notes, the Kirk orchestra never becomes "frenetic" in its style of swing.[237] Like "Mess-a-Stomp" and "Toadie Toddle," "Mary's Idea," of December 6, also re-visits an earlier piece by the same title (or a similar one in the case of the sequel to "Froggy Bottom"). Here the "idea" is not one that offers much to inspire either the pianist-composer herself, whose break is beholden to Basie for most of its inspiration, or the other sidemen in their solos. Both the first trombonist and the clarinetist turn in flawed performances, and the piece ends again without having made any particular statement. Two other pieces from this same session suggest in their titles the problem with the Clouds: "But It Didn't Mean a Thing" and "(I Don't Believe It but) Say It Again." Once more, both Wilson and Williams offer decent breaks on the first, and Wilson's distinctive tenor voice is clearly identifiable on the second. "Say It Again" also finds the Clouds producing a fine rocking swing, with Thigpen kicking the group along nicely, and Mary Lou taking one of her more swinging solos. The finale even includes a nice stop-time break by Wilson that ends the proceedings on a more upbeat note than usual. Still, the lyrics of the first of this paired set of songs tells it all: "You kissed me but it didn't mean a thing. / When you caressed I wanted you to cling. / You never gave me your heart."

The following year of 1939 did bring with it some new sounds from the Kirk orchestra, which was largely due to the arrival of two sidemen, Floyd Smith on electric guitar and Don Byas on tenor, and a female vocalist, June Richmond. The first sides recorded this year, "You Set Me on Fire" and "(I Guess) I'll Never Learn," on March 16, are again in the romantic, sentimental vein (with Wilson in good form on both and Terrell in his element). An instrumental by Mary Lou Williams, "Close to Five," finds her playing some of her finest relaxed piano on this piece and the ensemble swinging well (though once more with no buildup to any kind of climax). The big hit from this session was a feature for Floyd Smith, "Floyd's Guitar Blues," which was "no doubt a highly influential recording for many guitarists of the day."[238] Gunther Schuller calls the piece "rather shallow musically" and Charles Fox characterizes Smith's electric guitar on this "oddity" as "Hawaiian Gothic."[239] Along with the new use of the electric guitar (at least new for the Clouds, because Lunceford's Eddie Durham had recorded on this instrument previously), there was the orchestra's rather unusual return to a blues. Fox has indicated that the Clouds, like other Kansas City big bands, catered to "audiences that liked blues and riffs and expected to be able to dance to the music" and thus they "fulfilled all those demands."[240] This is true, but only to the extent that beginning in 1939 did the Clouds play more blues than in the previous three-year period, a development resulting as much from the addition of singer June Richmond as from the replacement of guitarist Ted Robinson by Floyd Smith. As for riffs, these, as Fox points out, were "deployed" by the Clouds "quietly, almost unobtrusively, creating a very controlled, almost dainty, species of excitement."[241] Most of the fare offered by the Clouds was of the sentimental variety and probably appealed greatly to audiences who preferred the danceable over the imaginative improvisations or driving riffs of an outfit such as Basie's.

During his less than one-year stay with the Clouds, Don Byas apparently soloed sparingly, what with Wilson still remaining the star tenor (although his outings seem limited almost entirely to ballads). On "I Wanna Go Where You Go—Do What You Do Then I'll Be Happy," from March 23, 1939, Byas first makes his presence felt on this classic swing treatment. For excitement, none of Wilson's breaks can compare with the two brief passages delivered by Byas, especially the first with its amazing swirl of notes, which is followed up with an almost equally stirring outburst full of rips and offbeat patterns. Before Byas's breaks, singer June Richmond and the ensemble swing more solidly than perhaps on any other Clouds recording. Although Richmond had been the featured vocalist with the Jimmy Dorsey orchestra, her stay with Dorsey, as Gunther Schuller says, cannot match "her later work with Andy Kirk."[242] This is definitely one of her best efforts with the Clouds, putting some real pep in the whole performance. On "Please Don't Talk about Me When I'm Gone," from November 15, Richmond also swings this piece effectively, singing toward the end a bit of jive. Here, too, Don Byas takes a break that adds to the more advanced feeling of this performance. When these two newcomers join forces, the Clouds create a distinctive sound, one that departs dramatically from the sentimental tendencies of most of their other material. Richmond also inserts more of the blues into the Clouds repertory, with such tunes as Billie Holiday's "Fine and Mellow" (on which the orchestra exhibits more punch than usual, with a rare Basie-like intensity) and a certain Jackson's "Take Those Blues Away," both recorded on June 25, 1940. Another blues is entitled "Big Jim Blues," the work of trumpeter Harry "Big Jim" Lawson and Mary Lou Williams. Of this last piece, recorded on November 15, 1939, Schuller writes that Lawson's "poignant blues theme . . . is turned into a hauntingly beautiful arrangement by Mary Lou Williams, in a manner not unlike some of Ellington's late 1930s mood pieces. Simple pastelish voicings predominate, then are combined in infinitely subtle variants."[243] Yet another piece that shows the Clouds moving away from their usual material is "Wham (Wham, Re, Bop, Boom, Bam)," credited to Eddie Durham, who composed it for the Glenn Miller Orchestra. Recorded by the Clouds on January 2, 1940, "Wham" uses the "bop" word and the phrase "killer-diller" in Richmond's singing of the lyrics, as well as the line "Some folks say swing won't stay, and that it's dying out, / but I can prove it's in the groove and they don't know what they're talking about." Here again, Byas takes a driving solo, one that foreshadows something of the bop movement in its speed and dexterity. This last piece also is notable for one of the rare drum solos taken by Ben Thigpen.

The rest of the January 2 session was devoted to Pha Terrell's ballad singing, which is quite appealing on "Love Is the Thing." The contrast between Richmond's blues work and Terrell's ballads must have made for a winning combination with audiences of the time. The Clouds' wider variety of material is represented as well by a fine piece concocted by Dick Wilson and Mary Lou Williams, entitled "Scratching in the Gravel," recorded on June 25 and featuring some fine muted and open trumpet by Harold Baker, another newcomer who contributed to the band's greater punch. On this number Wilson takes a solo that Schuller describes as a "tribute to uncluttered simplicity," which begins beautifully with a sudden descending figure quite unlike most anything he had previously recorded.[244] This is a particularly satisfying performance from beginning to end. Still another novel piece of work is found in June Richmond's singing of "Fifteen Minutes Intermission," which really rocks, as the ensemble swings out and Baker's trumpet adds some intensity to the proceedings, as do Fred Robinson's driving trombone and even Smith's more traditional guitar. Compared with the Cab Calloway version of this same tune, recorded two days later than the Clouds' rendition, on June 27, 1940, Kirk's unit definitely turns in a more engaging performance—the Calloway including only a brief break by Chu Berry.[245] Although the Calloway orchestra was more often superior to Kirk's, the latter could on occasion hold its own against the competition. "Take Those Blues Away" from the same session as "Scratchin'" and "Intermission" also builds to greater punch at the end than usual, and along the way the ensemble is lightly but solidly swinging and the orchestration features some new wrinkles with regard to sectional contrasts.

On July 8, 1940, the Clouds recorded four sides, and of these, only one, "Little Miss," is an instrumental, with Terrell making his final sides with the orchestra on "Now I Lay Me Down to a Dream" and "There Is No Greater Love," while Richmond vocalizes on "Midnight Stroll." "Little Miss" features, as Albert McCarthy indicates, "the light, floating sound" of the reeds "associated with the band," as well as strong solos from (according to McCarthy) Lawson on trumpet and Wilson, who really swings on this number.[246] "Midnight Stroll" finds the trumpets punctuating with the sharpness of Basie's brass section and with a typical swing buildup to Richmond's vocal. Terrell's two ballads are essentially uninteresting, but it is instructive to compare the Ellington treatment of "There Is No Greater Love," from January 27, 1936, to the Clouds' version. This tune by Isham Jones is lovely in and of itself, but only Ellington's orchestra does it justice, investing it, as Stanley Dance observes, "with an individuality that gives it lasting appeal."[247] The difference is not only that Ellington's version does not rely on a balladeer to deliver most of the feeling through love lyrics but also that the Clouds' recording lacks the very distinctive voices of Lawrence Brown on trombone, Johnny Hodges on alto, and Art Whetsol on trumpet. The three Ellington sidemen each in turn bring out a differing facet of the melody through instrumental range and interpretive expression. Dick Wilson, the only soloist on the Clouds side, does shape a lusciously romantic chorus, embellishing the theme with some perfectly executed turns and flourishes, and the Clouds ensemble does play with precision and warmth. But nothing can match the Ellington version in terms of the relationship between ensemble and soloists or the singing quality of each sideman's rendering of the theme. The tonal colors created by the Ellington arrangement, his tiered piling of one section on top of another, and his writing for the reed section all give the piece, as Dance says, a "lasting appeal." Wilson's solo is impressive on its own, but it does not contribute to an overall composition in the same way as do the soloists and ensemble in the Ellington performance. Again, it is perhaps unfair to compare, as they say, apples with oranges, and certainly the Clouds' version is effective as a swing-era ballad, but it does not reach the level of unified artistry that marks the work of an Ellington.

On November 7, 1940, the Clouds recorded a piece titled "The Count," which does not seem to refer to Basie but is in fact more a nod in the direction of Ellington, at least by way of the ducal sound of Fred Robinson's talking muted trombone. The clearest allusion to Basie comes with Wilson's solo, which is very like the work of Lester Young. Overall, however, this piece has its own sound which, except for Wilson's tenor break and Mary Lou Williams's piano, might not be recognized as the work of the Clouds. Indeed, this is an unusual piece in the sense that more is going on in the arrangement; more soloists are featured (trombone, piano, trumpet, and tenor); the bass, guitar, and drums generate a more pronounced beat; and the ensemble builds to a very pointed ending. One commentator has even heard in this number a "hint of the bop which was just around the corner."[248] Following this comes the Clouds' swing version of "Twelfth Street Rag," which is a rousing rendition arranged by Williams and features fine solos by Baker and Wilson.[249] Blues, boogie woogie, and rag have all entered the Clouds' repertory at this point, even as the orchestra is showing signs of moving toward the advanced conceptions of bop. Trombonist Henry Wells has taken over for Pha Terrell in the ballad-singing department, and in some ways this does not seem much of a loss, for even if Wells does not have the control of Terrell, he still gets the job done. At the session of January 3, 1941, another boogie woogie number was recorded, titled "Cuban Boogie Woogie," on which June Richmond does the vocal, the lyrics of which include the phrase "a Cuban band with something new to say," another prophetic indication of the coming Cuban influence on beboppers such as Dizzy Gillespie. Along with this forward-looking piece, the Clouds would record their jumping version of Ellington's 1930 "Ring

Dem Bells," with Mary Lou's piano chords replacing Sonny Greer's chimes. Ironically, as Gunther Schuller notes, Mary Lou's piano solo is in "Basie's aphoristic style"—which is something of a reversal of the Ellington-style trombone in the tune titled "The Count."[250] Other solos are by Wilson, Baker, and Smith on guitar, and all three are excellent, with Wilson really digging in more forcefully than usual and even producing a honk that would become popular in the '40s. Wilson's energetic break on this number would be one of his last solos, making it for that reason all the more remarkable and poignant.

The final Clouds recording session of the period under consideration here came on July 17, 1941, with four sides cut, although only the first two, "Big Time Crip" and "47th Street Jive," are worth discussing. The two ballads sung by Wells unfortunately marked a low point in the orchestra's output. Both "Big Time Crip" and "47th Street Jive" are boogie woogie numbers, the last to be recorded by Mary Lou Williams with the Kirk Orchestra, for afterward she would leave the Clouds for a career as a leader of small groups, which included various notable figures in the bop movement. Gunther Schuller has characterized Williams as an "advanced conservative" and as later taking "a more *pre*servative position," based in part on her incorporation of such styles as those of Hines, Waller, and Basie.[251] Nonetheless, as both a pianist and a composer-arranger, she was crucial to the jazz-oriented side of the Clouds' achievement, and "Big Time Crip," a composition credited to her and Henry Wells, served to inspire Dick Wilson to one of his better late efforts. Wilson's last recorded solo was taken on "47th Street Jive," with Mary Lou beating it out eight-to-the-bar and June Richmond belting out what has been called her "sophisticated urban blues."[252] Charles Fox hears Wilson sounding in his final break "unwontedly like Ben Webster," and Albert McCarthy finds the tenorist "consistent as ever, though the material is trite."[253]

In many respects, the problem with Andy Kirk's Clouds was that more often than not their material was beneath the organization's talented members and was designed mostly to appeal to dancers and sweethearts rather than to jazz fans. All the same, the Clouds reflect the many changes and adaptations that swing bands of the period went through in order to survive, and along the way they did produce many outstanding performances. The unit also represents such developments during the Swing Era as the move toward a greater dependence on ballad singers; a return to blues, ragtime, and boogie woogie; a revisiting and reworking of those styles and the unit's own early material into swing arrangements; tributes to such name bands as those of Ellington, Basie, and Lunceford; the popular introduction of the electric guitar; prophetic touches of bebop; and the loyalty of such sidemen as Dick Wilson, John Harrington, Harry Lawson, Ted Donnelly, Booker Collins, and Ben Thigpen, who made possible a consistently high level of performance if not a clearly identifiable sound on the order of that of an Ellington or Basie. Above all, perhaps, the Clouds exemplify the degree to which prominent dance orchestras of the period applied swing to every form of popular music.

LIONEL HAMPTON

After working with the Benny Goodman organization, several of that leader's proteges left to form their own big bands, among them Harry James, Gene Krupa, and Lionel Hampton. Although Hampton only began his own big band in September 1940 and did not record with it until the very end of 1941, he had led from 1937 a number of pickup groups for an RCA Victor contract. Long before this, Hampton had been a member of West Coast bands, including that of Les Hite, with whom Lionel recorded in October 1930 as part of a backing unit for Louis Armstrong. It was Armstrong who encouraged Hampton to concentrate on the vibraphone, the instrument on which he would make his greatest mark as a jazz soloist, taking his first solo and the first in jazz history on vibes on "Memories of You" during that same 1930 recording session.

Born in Louisville, Kentucky, on April 12, 1909, and raised in Chicago, Hampton originally played drums, first with the *Chicago Defender* Boys' Band, and continued to do so from the time he moved to California in 1928. Hampton also played piano (in a two-fingered percussive style) and sang—his first vocal recorded in 1929 with the Los Angeles–based Paul Howard orchestra on "Moonlight Blues."[254] But it was as a vibraphonist in the Benny Goodman Quartet that Hampton first gained fame from his ability to play with great energy for countless choruses. Goodman had discovered Hampton when the vibraphonist was leading his own group in Los Angeles, and after recording in August 1936 with Goodman, Teddy Wilson, and Gene Krupa, Hampton was invited to go on the road with the Goodman band. During his four-year stay with Goodman, Hampton was allowed and encouraged to record with his various pickup groups, which usually were drawn from the Goodman personnel and from the bands of Duke Ellington, Count Basie, and other orchestras of the late 1930s. Like Cab Calloway, Hampton would prove in the 1940s, as Gunther Schuller has said, that he "and big orchestras were made for each other." However, as Schuller also suggests, with the pickup groups of the '30s and even those of later years, Hampton seemed to have "little actual influence on the outcome of these sessions," for he was more interested in "the sheer joy of performing" rather than in exercising leadership in the way an Ellington or Lunceford did.[255]

Although Hampton was the central figure in his pickup groups, just as Cab Calloway was with his own orchestra, many of the performances by what were billed as Lionel Hampton and His Orchestra featured a number of the leading musicians of the era, and for this reason the recordings at times remain of more interest for the playing of his sidemen than for that of the leader himself. Nonetheless, Hampton's presence seems crucial to the swing and drive of so many of these recordings, and especially when he solos on vibraphone as he does on "Jivin' the Vibes," from February 8, 1937, with the orchestra composed of personnel from the Goodman band. As so often happened in smaller groups such as this ten-piece unit, a section player like Ziggy Elman (the only trumpeter on the side) had a greater chance to show off his stuff, and Hampton's opening break on vibes sets the stage for Elman to play more forcefully than usual. On "The Mood That I'm In," from the same session, Hampton is the only soloist, singing first in his rhythmically pleasing voice and then playing a lovely chorus on vibes. With "Hampton Stomp," also from this same date, most of the sidemen are featured, including Hymie Schertzer on alto, Arthur Rollini on tenor, and Krupa on drums, while the leader lays out as a soloist.

Returning as a soloist on "Buzzin' Around with the Bee," cut on April 14, Hampton opens on vibes and is followed by three of Ellington's men, Johnny Hodges, Cootie Williams (with his growl mute), and Lawrence Brown (imitating the bee buzz). Hampton also solos after the Ellington men and then drives the ensemble effectively in its out passage. Although Gunther Schuller considers a sideman such as Hodges "only half the artist when not embraced by Ellington's harmonies and enveloped in his orchestral colors," the critic does concede that the altoist is "still obviously a confident performer," and in any case it is always good to hear him in whatever context.[256] The same is true of Lawrence Brown, who, as Schuller points out, is especially fine on "Stompology," also from April 14, as is Hampton, whose vibes solo is more adventuresome than on the previous sides. Hodges is his usual lyrically brilliant self on the April 26 version of "On the Sunny Side of the Street," with Hampton backing him up on vibes to fine effect, after which the altoist plays a lovely obbligato behind Lionel's vocal and then an equally lovely theme statement over the leader's vibes. "Rhythm, Rhythm," also from April 26, opens with Hodges and then features in turn Jess Stacy's piano, Allen Reuss's guitar, and Buster Bailey's clarinet, before Hampton takes over on vibes, swinging with gusto, aided wonderfully by Cozy Cole on drums. Hampton's piano work is featured on "China Stomp," again from April 26, and although Schuller has found Lionel's two-fingered "mindless . . . pyrotechnics" inappropriate to the instrument's "great capacity for a variety of tonal nuances and touch," this performance is amazing nonetheless, ranging as it does over almost the entire keyboard while driving relentlessly and with enough different tonal combinations to maintain a listener's interest from first to last.[257] Certainly Schuller is correct in his assessment of Hampton's piano playing when it comes to the August 16 "Piano Stomp." As for "Drum Stomp," from the same session, Hampton features himself on drums along with Eddie Barefield's very attractive clarinet. The tempo of this piece, which was intended obviously to show off the leader's ability to keep the beat at a breakaway speed, is not handled by Jonah Jones as well as it is by Barefield, and Jones's insistent trumpet is also less satisfying.

One of the more cohesive sessions was held on September 5, 1937, with mostly personnel from the Goodman band. On a second take of "The Object of My Affection," the group works quite well together, and Hampton sings one of his more delightful vocals. Ziggy Elman is especially effective here, as well as on "Baby Won't You Please Come Home," "Everybody Loves My Baby," and "After You've Gone." Jess Stacy also is outstanding on the second take of "The Object of My Affection," whereas Hampton heats up "Everybody Loves My Baby" with a driving vibes solo and sings liltingly on "After You've Gone." On "I Just Couldn't Take It Baby," Elman again is quite effective, and Allen Reuss's guitar adds much to the ensemble sound. Taken together, the sides from 1937 reveal the various talents of the leader and incidentally spotlight sidemen who may have played better in other, more crafted formats but who in supporting Hampton as the star of the date made for the most part impressive music of their own.

On January 18, 1938, Hampton was joined once more by Cootie Williams, Johnny Hodges, Jess Stacy, and Allen Reuss, as well as Edgar Sampson on baritone sax, Billy Taylor on bass, and Sonny Greer on drums. Williams's growl trumpet and Hodges's obbligato alto behind Hampton's vocal and his soaring solo on "The Sun Will Shine Tonight" are examples of those Ellingtonians' special qualities. As would be expected, both Williams and Hodges are right at home on "Ring Dem Bells," where Stacy replaces Greer's chimes with piano tones, as would Mary Lou Williams on the Clouds' 1941 version. Sampson takes a nice baritone break on the Ellington tune, as he does on his own composition, "Don't Be That Way," while Hampton on vibes, Hodges on alto, and Williams on trumpet embellish the melody with evocative feeling. On July 21, Hampton was in the company of members of the Goodman and Basie bands plus Benny Carter and John Kirby, both of whom had been with Fletcher Henderson early in the decade. Harry James on trumpet and Carter on alto each play a solo on "Shoe Shiner's Drag," as does Herschel Evans, who really upstages his band mates before Carter returns on clarinet to play an even more impressive break. James is featured on "Any Time at All," along with the four saxes (Carter, Evans, Dave Mathews on alto, and Babe Russin on tenor), in a fine sectional passage, and Russin blows a marvelous obbligato behind Hampton's vocal. "Muskrat Ramble" again has excellent breaks by Evans and Carter on tenor and clarinet, respectively, as well as a swaggering solo by James, a lesser effort by Russin than his obbligato, and Hampton finishing things off nicely with what Gunther Schuller calls one of his "above-average . . . improvisations."[258] From a session on October 11, Budd Johnson from the Hines band takes a fine but uncharacteristic tenor break on "Down Home Jump," and Hampton again delivers another above-average improvisation as the ensemble riffs behind him on his own original tune. A driving Walter Fuller on trumpet opens "Rock Hill Special," a second Hampton original, before the leader does some of his two-finger piano, followed by Fuller, more of Hampton's amazing two-finger work, then what I take to be a terrific example of Budd Johnson's tenor, and a swinging conclusion with Hampton back on vibes. A third Hampton original in a row, "Fiddle Diddle," has Fuller muted, Hampton vocalizing, and then on vibes, with his playing over the ensemble producing a wonderfully ringing sound. Although Schuller may be correct that Hampton seems "content to unhesitatingly wend his way through vibraphone solo after solo" without bothering with "much artistic and stylistic control" over his groups, the results are by and large quite satisfying, and once again it is good to hear sidemen such as Benny Carter, Babe Russin, and Budd Johnson revealing facets of their talents that are not so evident in other settings.[259]

On April 3, 1939, Hampton was joined by Chu Berry, Irving Randolph, Milt Hinton, and Cozy Cole from the Calloway orchestra, among other sidemen, for a version of Ellington's seminal thirties tune, "It Don't Mean a Thing (If It Ain't Got That Swing)." Berry seems more relaxed here than on his sides with Cab, and Hampton's vocal and vibes solo are undistinguished but unusual in their rather low-keyed manner. Clyde Hart is tasteful on piano in his few bars, as he is in an extended appearance on "Shufflin' at Hollywood," recorded on April 5 with a sextet including Berry, who is more his old self in a sort of fidgety mode, as he is on "Denison Swing," where Schuller has "the distinct impression that the energetic shuffle rhythm and bright tempo were Berry's idea, not Hampton's," with the latter on piano definitely into some of his "mindless pyrotechnics."[260] Berry, Ziggy Elman, and Clyde Hart are all effective on "Ain'tcha Comin' Home," from June 9, as is Hampton on vibes, with Danny Barker accompanying him nicely on guitar. Schuller finds Hampton's version of the "Twelfth Street Rag" another of his mindless displays on piano, but this side from June 13 is salvaged in part at least by five Ellingtonians: Rex Stewart on cornet, Lawrence Brown on trombone, Harry Carney on baritone, Billy Taylor on bass, and Sonny Greer on drums.

The session that most impressed listeners at the time and continues to stand as one of the best of Hampton's pickup productions came on September 11, when he was supported by Dizzy Gillespie, Benny Carter, Coleman Hawkins, Chu Berry, Ben Webster, Clyde Hart, Charlie Christian on unamplified guitar, Milt Hinton, and Cozy Cole, with all the arrangements being done by Carter. The gathering together of four of the major saxophone stylists in one unit was in itself the basis for a rare recording session. In addition, this marked the first recording date for Charlie Christian, and although he served more as an accompanist than a soloist, his skills in the former capacity are clearly significant. The first of four tunes recorded at the September 11 session was "When Lights Are Low," of which John Chilton writes that "from the first moment it's apparent that the rhythm section . . . achieved a remarkable blend. Each man's contribution is clearly discernible yet the overall impression is of one emphatic pulse."[261] As for the soloists, Benny Carter is the first on his own original tune, and his eight bars have been described as an excellent example of the altoist's "rhythmic subtleties," with the suggestion of "a three-against-four pattern in the last two measures."[262] Chilton quotes André Hodeir on Hawkins's solo, which is "aggressive, and tense to the point of exasperation, showing off in the treble of the instrument with an amazingly powerful sound, utilizing an unusual 'growl.' He takes a solo with ferocious roughness, shaking everything around him, neglecting the melody for a sensual excitement which is not without beauty."[263] The second tune, "One Sweet Letter from You," again showcases a solo by Hawkins, on which Chilton finds that the tenorist "moves closer to top form in his concluding eight bars, but the ideas seem to be held in check. The stand-out feature of the track is Hampton's idiosyncratic vocal, which is inspiringly backed by Christian's crisply chorded guitar fill-ins."[264] Gunther Schuller also praises Christian's fills as compelling, but rather than remarking on Hampton's vocal, this critic rates his vibraphone solo as one of his three most "exceptionally sensitive" ballad treatments.[265] With regard to Chu Berry's part in the session, Chilton views this tenorist as showing on "Hot Mallets" how he "was increasingly intent on incorporating new harmonic twists into his bustling, skilful solos."[266] Gillespie's muted trumpet opens this Hampton original, on which the vibist really swings, powered by the rhythm section. The final number, "Early Session Hop," a Teddy Wilson tune, has been called "a truly innocuous theme" on which Webster shows his obvious allegiance to Hawkins, because "Ben hadn't developed his musical poise" at this point.[267] Indeed, so close is Webster's tenor sound to that of Hawkins that in 1964 George Hoefer and RCA Victor credited this solo to the latter, including the track on *Body and Soul: A Jazz Autobiography—Coleman Hawkins*. Certainly Webster's solo is not one of his best, but it is in his own voice and with foreshadowings of things to come in the tenorist's warmer yet still robust tone. Carter takes another brief break, and Hampton again drives with power, bringing the proceedings to an impressive close.[268]

On October 30, 1939, Hampton's orchestra included once again Ben Webster on tenor, Ziggy Elman on trumpet, and Clyde Hart on piano, as well as Toots Mondello and Jerry Jerome on reeds, Al Casey on guitar, Artie Bernstein on bass, and Slick Jones on drums. Of the five sides recorded at this session, Gunther Schuller commends especially "The Munson Street Breakdown," "I've Found a New Baby," and "I Can't Get Started" as "tasteful" and "exuberant" performances by Elman on the first two pieces and another instance of Hampton's sensitive ballad work on the third.[269] The last two of these tunes were arranged by Fletcher Henderson, whereas the other three on the session were charts by pianist Clyde Hart. "Gin for Christmas" features Hampton on drums, whereas "Munson Street" (with a boogie woogie rhythm laid down by Bernstein and Hart) and "I've Found a New Baby" showcase the leader's two index fingers on piano and, on "Munson Street," his smooth runs on vibes. Although Hampton's vibes on "I Can't Get Started" are emotive, the ensemble playing leaves something to be desired. "Four or Five Times" is the only tune of the five that finds Hampton vocalizing, including a jive exchange with a muted Elman, and includes a break by Webster, as does "Gin for Christmas." The latter has been aptly described as "a manic blues," on which Elman really cuts loose.[270]

On December 21, 1939, both Benny Carter—this time on trumpet—and Coleman Hawkins joined Hampton once again for three sides—four including a second take of "Dinah." In addition to Carter, Hawkins, and Hampton, the "orchestra" consisted of Edmond Hall on clarinet and a rhythm section of Joe Sullivan on piano, Freddie Green on guitar, Bernstein on bass, and Zutty Singleton on drums. As John Chilton observes, Hawkins's chorus on the first take of "Dinah" "can be counted among [his] greatest achievements," although on the second take "each of the main soloists (Carter, Hawkins and Hampton) explores creative alternatives based on ideas he had formulated on the first attempt, but both the phrasing and the note content of these new endeavours are different from the originals (giving a fine insight into the mental agility of these three superb jazz musicians)."[271] Quite different is Hawkins's approach to "My Buddy," but again his solo, though less cohesive, is still a worthy contribution, as is Hampton's rhythmically and motivically varied vibe work. When "Singin' the Blues" was recorded by the Fletcher Henderson orchestra on April 10, 1931, Hawkins formed part of the organization but did not figure in the solo work since the Henderson version, as noted in Chapter 1, was intended as a tribute to the Trumbauer-Beiderbecke recording of 1927, in particular, Bix's famed cornet break. On the Hampton recording of December 1939, there is no attempt to duplicate that 1920s performance, and Hawkins's solo is in a laid-back, sensuously smooth style that says much about the difference between the hot approach of the late twenties and the rather cool manner of the late thirties. Benny Carter's relaxed muted trumpet is about as far from Beiderbecke's at times intensely passionate open cornet as one can get, and Hawkins's playing has more in common with Lester Young's horizontal, unhurried phrasing than with Coleman's own earlier vertical urgency. Again, as suggested in Chapter 1, the Hampton group's swing treatment of the song that served as the basis for Beiderbecke's seminal recording represents a clear distinction between two types of jazz. In addition, Hawkins's solo here indicates the impact of Lester

Young's cooler style and its influence not only on Coleman (the other great tenorist of the Swing Era) but also on almost every tenor player to come.

The same sort of relaxed, sensuous style characterizes the first of five tracks recorded by a Hampton pickup unit on February 26, 1940. "Shades of Jade," a tune by reedman Toots Mondello, features Hampton's tender vibes and a yearning break by Ziggy Elman, as well as a lush opening sax section of two altos and two tenors, played by Mondello, Buff Estes, Jerry Jerome, and Budd Johnson, with responses from Elman. The Goodman-Hampton riff, "Till Tom Special," again features Elman's muted trumpet, this time in a more lusty, swaggering manner, but here the central soloist is tenorist Budd Johnson, who turns in a delicious chorus. This date's version of "Flying Home," which would become Hampton's trademark tune, is "surprisingly listless," according to Gunther Schuller, but as a slower, more gently rocking arrangement than Lionel's killer-diller tracks of later years, it serves as another showcase for Budd Johnson's fine tenor work.[272] Johnson's style at this point owes little either to Hawkins or Young and includes several "Texas honks" which would become typical of his fellow Texan Illinois Jacquet's later exhibitionism. Hampton's vibes are wonderfully relaxed, and yet both he and Elman end the piece in a solid groove. "Save It, Pretty Mama" has decent if unexceptional blueslike solos by Mondello on alto and Elman on trumpet and lovely lyrical outings by Johnson on tenor and Hampton on vibes. "Tempo and Swing" opens with Johnson and Mondello trading choruses and really driving on this piece by Hampton's wife Gladys. On vibes Hampton follows with a more relaxed swing, until Elman leads the ensemble in a hot outsection. This session may be "listless" for some, but for others it may be found to offer very relaxed yet swinging jazz that contrasts greatly with the hectic, overblown recordings made by many of the bigger bands of the day.

During May, July, and August 1940, Hampton recorded with even smaller groups. The first two sessions of May 10 and July 17 were with the Nat "King" Cole Trio: Cole on piano, Oscar Moore on guitar, and Wesley Prince on bass, plus drummer Al Spieldock and Hampton on piano, vibes, or drums. The session of August 21 was again billed as "Lionel Hampton and His Orchestra" but included only Marlowe Morris on piano, Teddy Bunn on guitar, Douglas Daniels on tiple (a small guitar), Hayes Alvis on bass, Kaiser Marshall on drums, and Hampton on vibes. The standout performances on these sides, other than those by Hampton himself, are by Cole, Moore, and Bunn, but these are small-group sessions with rhythm instruments rather than with horns. It has been thought that Lionel Hampton took his cue for organizing his various pickup groups from Teddy Wilson, who had recorded with such smaller units as early as July 1935 when he and a sextet backed vocalist Billie Holiday. Wilson recorded throughout the rest of the 1930s with various groups, and in 1939, after leaving the Goodman organization, he, like Hampton, formed his own big band, but as Gunther Schuller has noted, Wilson "was unable to establish a recognizable and memorable orchestral identity."[273] Teddy Wilson's small-group sessions are considered in Chapter 6.

At the end of 1940, Hampton recorded with sextets on December 19 and 20. This time the groups, billed as "Lionel Hampton and His Sextet," included Marshall Royal on clarinet and alto sax, along with various rhythm instruments and Sir Charles Thompson on piano and Ray Perry on violin. Gunther Schuller praises Perry for his "unusual contributions on amplified violin," singling out performances of "Altitude" and "Fiddle Dee Dee" from December 19 and "Bogo Jo" and "Smart Aleck" from December 20, which aside from "Open House" and "Bouncing at the Beacon" are the only real jazz pieces out of the eight sides recorded on these two dates, the others given over almost entirely to pathetic vocals by drummer Lee Young and Evelyn Myers.[274] Electric guitarist Irving Ashby is an integral part of this Hampton sextet, the group sound of which on "Fiddle-Dee-Dee" is very close to that of Django Reinhardt and the Hot Club of Paris, with Perry's sound on "Altitude" recalling Stéphane Grappelli. Marshall Royal, who would later star with Count Basie's big band, is effective on clarinet on "Bogo Jo," "Open House," and "Smart Aleck," with Ashby sounding close to Charlie Christian on the last of these sides, on which Perry, Hampton on vibes, and Thompson on piano all turn in fine performances. "Bouncing at the Beacon" is another boogie woogie piece, featuring Hampton on piano as well as Royal on alto, although neither offers anything of consequence.

On April 8, 1941, Hampton recorded four sides with the same group, but with Karl George added on trumpet (having recently been with Teddy Wilson's big band) and Shadow Wilson replacing Lee Young on drums. "Give Me Some Skin" is largely devoted to some topical jive talk of the period between Hampton and the group as chorus, but it also includes a tasty break by Perry. Aside from Hampton's drumming display, Royal's hot clarinet is showcased briefly on "Chasin' with Chase." George's trumpet leads "Three-Quarter Boogie," which contains another snatch of Perry's amplified violin, as well as brief breaks by George, Royal, Ashby, and Thompson, but mostly soloing by Hampton on vibes. This would be the last of the small-group sessions prior to Hampton forming his first big band and recording with it beginning on Christmas Eve 1941.

From the last small-group dates, Marshall Royal, Karl George, Ray Perry (on violin and alto sax), and Irving Ashby all would join the Hampton big band, along with a number of future stars, including Ernie Royal and Joe Newman on trumpet and Dexter Gordon and Illinois Jacquet on tenor. On trombone, Hampton's featured soloist would be Fred Beckett; his pianist and chief arranger, Milt Buckner, has been credited with inventing "the locked-hands (or block chord) style," made famous by George Shearing and later by Red Garland of the Miles Davis Quintet.[275] The first tune recorded by Hampton's band was "Just for You," a ballad featuring the leader's romantic vibes, with fine work by the five-man sax section (anchored by Jack McVea on baritone) and a solo by Beckett concluding with a gorgeous high note. "Southern Echoes" is a smoothly rocking performance with the brass section employing mutes to good effect. Hampton sings the vocal, and McVea takes a mildly rousing break. In general this is typical big-band swing of 1941, nothing exceptional. The second ballad, "My Wish," is even more generic. It is only with the final number, "Nola," that the band shows a bit of the high-powered energy Hampton units would be known for in years and decades to come. The leader's vibes state the theme before the ensemble begins to dig in, leading to Buckner's romping locked-hands break, after which the orchestra builds—only diminished from time to time by Hampton's rather lame vibes but aided by a driving break by Royal on clarinet—to a climax with the expected high-note trumpet ending. With a solid group of sidemen and with the leader's versatility as a multi-instrumentalist, vocalist, and magnetic showman, this unit was assured of a success that it achieved beginning in 1942 with its first hit, a Buckner arrangement of "Flying Home," which, unlike the earlier version of February 1940, would make for Lionel Hampton and His Orchestra a permanent place in the history of big-band jazz.

ERSKINE HAWKINS

Like Jimmie Lunceford's orchestra, which he first put together from his students at Fisk University, the 'Bama State Collegians was a group originally made up of students at the State Teachers' College in Montgomery, Alabama. A territory band like so many in the Kansas City and Southwest region, the Collegians were active in the early thirties in Alabama and the nearby area before trying their luck in New York in 1934 under the leadership of J.B. Sims. After appearing at such venues as the Harlem Opera House and the Fox Folly, and touring upstate New York, the band was not able to find further work in the northeast, but two years later, twenty-year-old trumpeter Erskine Hawkins, an ex-'Bama State Collegian, was appointed the orchestra's leader and the group returned to New York for a residency at the Savoy Ballroom alongside the Chick Webb band. From 1936 until the first part of 1938, the group retained the Collegians name, but afterward, when it began to record for RCA Victor in the autumn of 1938 (having recorded previously for the Vocalion label), the group was billed as Erskine Hawkins (The Twentieth Century Gabriel) and His Orchestra.[276] Gunther Schuller writes that Hawkins "is little remembered today, and yet his orchestra was one of the most popular for many years (especially at the Savoy Ballroom), and its accomplishments are well worth recalling." Schuller attributes the "admirable consistency of performance in its soloists, ensemble work, and its arrangers . . . in large part to the fact that the orchestra's personnel over a period of a dozen years rarely changed." This was the case with a number of the other important big bands, including especially those of Ellington and Lunceford, although Schuller finds Hawkins's band neither as "spectacular" nor "original" as the units of those two leaders.[277]

Although the Hawkins orchestra is not among the name bands of the Swing Era, "Tuxedo Junction," a tune written by the leader, his alto saxophonist William Johnson, and his tenorist Julian Dash, is familiar to every devotee of the Glenn Miller story. Recorded by the Hawkins orchestra on July 18, 1939, "Tuxedo Junction," which would become one of the most popular of all Miller recordings, predates the latter's rendition by some seven months, and according to Albert McCarthy, the Hawkins original "is far superior to the better known Glenn Miller version."[278] Reportedly, the tune's riff "was the standard sign-off for all bands appearing at the Savoy Ballroom," but only after the Hawkins band, while awaiting Chick Webb's to arrive, began improvising on the melody did the piece become a hit with the audience and on being recorded became "an instantaneous success."[279] The piece is immediately recognizable as the same as that recorded by Miller, but it is also clear from the very first that this is a different type of band. The ensemble sound is more mellow and not so sweet, the swing more relaxed yet more propulsive, and the trumpet solo is not merely an integrated break but a true feature for the soloist, allowing him to work into his notes a very personal inflection.[280] The first trumpet in the Miller version is stiff by comparison, and although the second trumpet's somewhat growly break is more engaging, the third is again more functional than creative. Also, the background figures behind Hawkins and clarinetist Haywood Henry are more supportive in a jazz sense—that is, in their rhythmic and emotive feel—just as Henry's solo is much more exploratory than most anything ever played by a Miller sideman. The muted solo by the major Hawkins trumpeter, Wilbur "Dud" Bascomb, also is more a work of jazz rather than merely an arranged element in the overall Miller format. Bascomb's wonderful phrasing and note choices are very much identifiable as his own and make his contribution a very individual part of the entire performance. Ultimately, the Miller recording does not come off as inventive jazz but rather as an arrangement with only a limited jazz feeling, with the emphasis more on evoking a mood instead of offering an opportunity for soloists to express themselves artistically. As for swing, the Hawkins really has it, whereas the Miller achieves what can only be called pseudoswing, if even that. The latter is basically a showpiece rather than a work of creative jazz.

Another tune recorded by the Hawkins orchestra prior to a version by the Miller orchestra—although by only two weeks—is Jelly Roll Morton's classic "King Porter Stomp." Cut by Miller on September 27, 1938, his arrangement of Morton's tune opens with a type of concert buildup à la

Paul Whiteman, and although four different soloists take their turns at the changes, the effect remains largely one of a formal, concertized reading of Morton's masterpiece. Miller's trombone theme statement and slight improvisation are agreeable enough but at times a bit too stiff in a rickety style. The best of the four soloists is the tenorist, but even he tends to go through the motions, especially when he plays a series of rather stilted arpeggios. The muted trumpet is too influenced by Harry James, his notes and emphases too consciously chosen to impress. Although the altoist is technically secure in his playing, his phrasing, like Miller's, is too rickety and conveys little or no real jazz feeling. The reed section's theme statement is blemished by the brass's hand in and then out of the bell wa-wa that sounds artificial and even forced. The ending is close to the Morton original but is played with almost no conviction.

The Hawkins recording of "King Porter Stomp"—made on September 12, 1938—also begins as something of a concert buildup to the leader's rather bravura trumpet. Both Albert McCarthy and Gunther Schuller find that too often Hawkins's trumpet is eccentric, erratic, and bombastic (both critics comparing Hawkins's style to that of Ziggy Elman).[281] This is the case here with the Morton tune, although in comparison with the Miller version, it must be said that Hawkins does instill more intensity into the performance than any of the Miller soloists. Although the other Hawkins soloists are only allotted very brief appearances, each gives a more convincing account of himself, with Julian Dash's tenor break swinging intensely, Haywood Henry's baritone driving with power, and Dud Bascomb's muted trumpet articulating his notes with just the right inflection. The call-and-response episode between Hawkins and the ensemble also generates more intensity than anything on the Miller side. Nonetheless, neither of these performances can compare favorably with those recorded by Fletcher Henderson and Benny Goodman, and in many ways the Miller and Hawkins versions reveal how Morton's tune has pretty much lost its vitality through a too formal treatment, a rather exaggerated, even staged approach that begins to plague swing-jazz in the last years of the 1930s.

More successful during 1938 and 1939 and even as early as 1936 are original pieces composed by Hawkins's sidemen, pianist Avery Parrish, altoist William Johnson, and trumpeter Sammy Lowe. Parrish's "Strictly Swing," from October 20, 1938, is an easy-rocking piece with a well-played alto break by Johnson, a very nicely swinging trumpet solo by Bascomb, what sounds like a two-baritone theme statement, a muted trombone (probably by Robert Range), a string bass release, and some of Hawkins's high-note trumpet. (Gunther Schuller notes that in the mid 1940s Hawkins added a second baritone, but here it sounds like he has already employed a pair, with Haywood Henry undoubtedly one of the two.[282]) Johnson's "A Study in Blue," from the same October 20 session, has been called by Albert McCarthy an "attractive" piece, particularly for its fine solos by

Dud Bascomb on trumpet and Julian Dash on tenor, but this composition is, like the "King Porter Stomp" arrangement, too much of a concert-type treatment of the blues and does not have the authenticity of an Ellington or a Basie performance.[283] Johnson's "Swingin' on Lenox Avenue," from May 14, 1939, is much more appealing and shows how the hand in and out of the bell wa-wa can be used more naturally and effectively. Mainly this piece offers another of Dud Bascomb's very personal trumpet solos, one of Johnson's smooth alto breaks, a swinging outing by tenorist Julian Dash, a few tasteful bars by Parrish on piano, and some relaxed but intensely driving ensemble work for the outchorus. On the same session of July 18, 1939, which produced the recording of "Tuxedo Junction," the Hawkins orchestra cut Sammy Lowe's equally swinging "Hot Platter," with its very fine section work by the reeds; a different approach from Dud Bascomb, which shows how varied his ideas could be; and Haywood Henry's impressive clarinet work over the ensemble's Dixie-like jam. Also from this same session is Lowe's "Gin Mill Special," with more of Bascomb's excellent trumpet and Dash's tenor, which can recall something of both Chu Berry and Lester Young yet retains its own individual sound and swing. After some of Hawkins's eccentric trumpet, Parrish's low-key piano and the ensemble end this piece with a very satisfyingly easy-rocking close.

Two other outstanding sides from the same July 18 session are "Weddin' Blues," by William Johnson, and an uncredited arrangement of Don Redman's "Cherry." After a piano introduction, the saxes open and close the Johnson piece with some lovely sectional work, which recalls the classical sonata's A-B-A form. In the "B" section, the listener is treated to Bascomb's muted wa-wa trumpet that offers a true blues feeling, as does Dash's brief tenor break. Bascomb returns for an open solo before the saxes, led by Henry's baritone, end the performance with a quiet closure that may suggest that someone either regrets the marriage (a rival for the bride or groom) or that one of the two repeating the vows is somewhat apprehensive. Whatever the case, the piece achieves a delicious sense of the bittersweetness of such an event. Something of the same sad pleasure is communicated by the eighteen-year-old vocalist, Ida James, who recorded "What Do You Know about Love?" with the Hawkins orchestra on October 20, 1938. James's sensuous, girlish sound on this tune proves the most fetching of her three performances from 1938 and 1939. The other vocalist for Hawkins was his drummer, James Morrison, who sings the lyrics on the recording of Redman's "Cherry." Aside from the vocal rendition, which is only generally well done, this is an impressive performance, with Johnson's silken alto setting the mood effectively and later leading the sax section in an affective workout, followed by Bascomb's growling trumpet break and then the ensemble accompanying Hawkins's stirring high-note outchorus.

Of the three primary arrangers it was Sammy Lowe who most consis-

tently turned in swinging, engaging charts. Even Lowe's version of an op-
eretta tune, "Let the Punishment Fit the Crime," from the session of
October 20, 1938, manages to swing the rather boring melody from Gilbert
and Sullivan's *Mikado*, aided by Henry's fine baritone, Bascomb's talking
mute-work, and Dash's capable running of the changes. Hawkins plays a
series of modulations at the end, and this in itself is an unusual feature,
something rare in a Sullivan score. It seems curious that Johnson would
have arranged such an unlikely piece as this Sullivan tune, but at about this
time more and more big bands began to "swing the classics." Perhaps more
typical of Lowe is his original composition, "No Soap (A Jitterbug Jamboree)," recorded on May 14, 1939, although this is essentially a solo
feature for Julian Dash's tenor. After another rather formal introduction,
the piece takes off with a few bars of Haywood Henry's rousing baritone,
which often sets the pace for the orchestra's recordings. Also heard at the
beginning is some of Hawkins's blazing, up-tempo trumpet, as well as a
rare bit of Leemie Stanfield's string bass. But it is Dash to whom most of
the side is given over, and he takes full advantage of the opportunity. At
first he smoothly runs the changes, but then gets after it with some swirling
figures reminiscent of Chu Berry, some alternate fingering that recalls Lester
Young's occasional use of this technique, a striking shake, and, after the
orchestra rallentandoes, a type of sweeping cadenza, at the end of which
he holds a low honk to close the side. One other Lowe arrangement, of
"You Can't Escape from Me," recorded on October 2, 1939, also features
some excellent Dash and a very nice open solo by Bascomb. The rhythm
section on this number really drives, and this may be the result of the
appearance by Clifton "Skeeter" Best, who replaced William McLemore
on guitar.

Both Albert McCarthy and Gunther Schuller have identified Lowe as an
admirer of Sy Oliver, the main arranger for the Lunceford band.[284] An
earlier side like "Rockin' Rollers Jubilee," from September 12, 1938, exhibits the Oliver influence, with the opening trombone figure seemingly
lifted right out of Lunceford's 1937 "Annie Laurie," as arranged by Oliver.
Also, the sax section trills sound very close to those frequently employed
by the Lunceford reeds. Likewise, the muted trumpets after Hawkins's dramatic introduction in Avery Parrish's "Swing Out," from April 8, 1939,
also seem an obvious borrowing from Lunceford, as do certain sax figures
that recall the Oliver arrangement of "Four or Five Times" from 1935.
Like the Lunceford orchestra, the Hawkins, as Schuller says, was clearly
"well rehearsed and played with considerable discipline in respect to intonation and orchestral balance."[285] But one important difference between
these two orchestras was the level of solo work, for the Hawkins sidemen
tended to be more imaginative and daring in their choruses, which were
for the most part longer than those taken by the Lunceford soloists.

Other, earlier recordings by the Hawkins orchestra that recall the Lunceford manner include the first side cut by the group, "It Was a Sad Night in Harlem," from July 20, 1936. This mood piece also owes something to Ellington, as the title would suggest. More fully influenced by Lunceford is "It Will Have to Do until the Real Thing Comes Along," also from July 20, with the sax section reminiscent of Jimmie's reeds. Also in the Lunceford vein is "Swinging in Harlem," from September 8, 1936, although this piece also recalls Ellington when the trombonist clearly imitates Tricky Sam Nanton's style and sound. Curiously, it was the Hawkins orchestra that first applied a two-beat approach to "Coquette," a tune best known from the later Lunceford version of January 26, 1937. The Hawkins "Coquette," from September 8, 1936, contains strong trumpet work by the leader and some fine baritone from Henry. In the case of " 'Way Down upon the Swanee River," from April 19, 1937, this Hawkins version comes almost two years after the Lunceford recording of the same tune and is nothing special. More impressive are two sides that compete on the same level with performances by the Ellington orchestra, that is, "Dear Old Southland" and "Uproar Shout." The Ellington orchestra recorded the former on December 4, 1933, and the Hawkins group cut its version at the April 19 session. Hawkins's open trumpet is controlled but also exhibits some fancy "finger" work and some great shakes, Dud Bascomb's talking muted trumpet is excellent, and brother Paul Bascomb's tenor is very fine. Although William Johnson's "Uproar Shout" was not recorded by Ellington, the swing generated on the Hawkins recording from April 19 is comparable to the best swing numbers cut by the Duke and his men. Henry's baritone playing, though different from the style of Harry Carney, is equally wonderful in its exuberance and inventiveness, and is supported by excellent background figures. (On "Swing Out," Henry shows in his baritone break considerably more imagination than Lunceford's Jock Carruthers usually managed, although it must be said that the latter was offered few opportunities to solo.) The saxes on "Uproar Shout" are answered by Hawkins in a marvelous swing exchange. All in all, this piece seems worthy of greater praise than some of the sides singled out by Schuller and McCarthy as particularly outstanding. Finally, "If You Leave Me," another Johnson original recorded at the April 19 session, recalls Sy Oliver's "Dream of You," as recorded by Lunceford in October 1934. Both tunes are poignant, although the Oliver melody is definitely the more affective.

To return to "Rockin' Rollers Jubilee," from September 12, 1938, this side has been cited by Albert McCarthy as exhibiting good breaks by trumpeter Bascomb and tenorist Dash, and Dash's is especially fine, whereas Hawkins's own solo toward the end is characterized by the English critic as marked by "convoluted high note wanderings."[286] Hawkins may have been guilty, as Schuller says, of "bombastic high-note grandstanding," but his solo on this same tune certainly infuses some vigor into the performance, which is frequently the case with his showy but driving trumpet.[287]

When Hawkins restrains himself, as he does on "I Found a New Baby," from August 12, 1937, he adds to the overall quality of the performance. Here Hawkins and his men produce a fine swing version of this Dixie or hot jazz standard, with Paul Bascomb and Haywood Henry both playing with verve and the ensemble digging in with some solid drive. On occasion, however, the leader as a soloist becomes overbearing and spoils what would otherwise be some very strong recordings, as on "Carry Me Back to Old Virginny," "Who's Sorry Now?," and "Lost in the Shuffle," all from February 25, 1938, and even "Miss Hallelujah Brown" from September 12, 1938, which Schuller finds, along with "Hot Platter" from July 18, 1939, to be in the Hawkins's band's own style that "combines music ideal for swing-style dancing with eminently *listenable* scores."[288]

Unlike the "angelic" leader, Julian Dash consistently contributes satisfying moments to the orchestra's sides, especially on such a recording as "Gin Mill Special," also from the July 18 session. But on the recording of "Sweet Georgia Brown," from June 10, 1940, Paul Bascomb would be the featured tenorist, and he dominates from the opening bars and throughout the rest of this swinging side. Bascomb, who had been with the Hawkins band before 1938 and returned in 1940 with what Schuller calls "a much more virile, aggressive approach," does not quite belong in any particular category of swing tenorists, the closest to his style perhaps being Chu Berry, although Schuller suggests that he was influenced by Ben Webster on Ellington's "Cotton Tail," of May 4, 1940, and that Bascomb's "hot, thrusting style also reminds one of the later [Paul] Gonsalves with Ellington."[289] Something of Bascomb's same assertiveness had already been evident on an unlikely tune titled "I Can't Escape from You," recorded at the Collegians' first session of July 20, 1936. It is revealing of Bascomb's early leanings toward a more aggressive approach to compare this 1936 recording and what Schuller would call its confusion of styles—including a "hotel band" sound, a crooning vocal, and "sweet" cup-mute fills—with the unit's solidly swinging version of a similarly titled tune, "You Can't Escape from Me," recorded on October 2, 1939.[290] On the former Bascomb departs from the "commercial" style with some daring, "thrusting" tenor, whereas on the latter, which has nothing of the "hotel band" tendency about it, both Hawkins and Dash turn in splendid solos, as the orchestra, backed by the rhythm section, riffs with a drive as rousing as that of a Basie entourage. Along with Bascomb's extended tenor solo on "Sweet Georgia Brown," Schuller also praises his outing on "Hey Doc!" from August 8, 1941.[291] Bascomb's solo work on "Hey Doc!" certainly stands comparison with Chu Berry's break on the same piece as recorded by the Cab Calloway Orchestra on July 24, 1941. Both tenorists come across as relaxed, with the Calloway version at an even slower tempo and Berry more mellow than Bascomb. Although the Hawkins side emphasizes a more rocking feel, the main difference between the two tenorists in this instance is that Bascomb presses his improvisation into more exploratory notes, phrases, and scales, his attack and tone purposely gruffer than Berry's, and his overall sound and drive more intense.[292]

Guitarist William McLemore does not solo on the recording by the Hawkins orchestra of Benny Goodman's "Soft Winds," from November 6, 1940, but his few tasteful fills would seem to indicate that he had heard Charlie Christian on the Goodman Sextet side from November 22, 1939. This piece as rendered by the Hawkins orchestra is certainly not a "soft" version of Goodman's 1939 sextet number, for screaming trumpets and a wailing clarinet make this a hard-driving side. In a more relaxed vein are two pieces featuring pianist Avery Parrish—on his own tunes "After Hours" and "Blackout," from June 10, 1940, and May 15, 1941, respectively. "After Hours" was a huge hit, but today seems a very lightweight effort, especially compared with sides featuring Dud Bascomb, Paul Bascomb, and Julian Dash. Sammy Lowe's "Easy Rider," from October 20, 1938, also is a relaxed number, but Hawkins's penetrating trumpet is in contrast to the "easy" swing of the orchestra and Dash's smoothly driving tenor, whereas Bascomb's muted trumpet talks softly yet, as it were, "carries a big stick." Just as the Hawkins "Soft Winds" holds up well alongside the Goodman original, some of the earlier sides by the Collegians stand comparison with the work of other name bands, in particular "Big John's Special," a Horace Henderson chart first recorded by the Fletcher Henderson Orchestra on September 11, 1934. The Hawkins version, from September 8, 1936, features a fine muted solo by Dud Bascomb and some Walleresque piano by Parrish. Both Dud Bascomb and Haywood Henry are especially good on "A Swingy Little Rhythm" (credited to Bascomb-Johnson-Hawkins), from the same September 8 session, with Henry's extended baritone solo very "swingy" and the entire performance marked by excellent section work based on fine writing and playing, reminiscent again of the Henderson units.

Other sides singled out as exceptional by McCarthy and Schuller include "Nona," from November 11, 1940 (although McCarthy prefers a 1950 version of this tune with Julian Dash on tenor rather than Paul Bascomb from the 1940 side), and "Shipyard Ramble," from May 15, 1941.[293] Schuller's view that Bascomb combines something of the 1940 Webster and the later Gonsalves is supported fully by the tenorist's solo on "Nona." The influence of Basie on the Hawkins band can be heard in the piano fills on "I Know a Secret," and the impact of Lunceford is apparent especially in the sax figures on "S'posin' " and "Tonight You Belong to Me," all three from the session of November 20, 1940, which also produced a typical swing-era instrumental entitled "Riff Time." These last four sides, despite their indebtedness to Basie and Lunceford, are all impressive in their own right and offer some fine touches that are peculiar to the Hawkins band. "Keep Cool, Fool," from the session of January 22, 1941, shows that the trombone soloist had been listening closely to Lunceford's Trummy Young. The Hawkins band was now up to three trombones for the first time, with Richard Harris added to Edward Sims and Robert Range. The trombone break on "No Use Squawkin,' " from the same date, is the most adventuresome and aggressive for any Hawkins trombonist to this point and includes some allusive phrases that forecast the bebop penchant for witty asides. "Uncle Bud," from the session of May 15, 1941, finds Dud Bascomb's bluesy, muted trumpet in fine form, with Julian Dash contributing a tasteful tenor break, and the trombone soloist in a nicely contrastive style that once more is quite forward looking. The entire ensemble swings solidly on the out passage. Equally effective is "Blue Sea," from the same date, with its easy but driving swing, which features half-a-dozen soloists, in addition to the sax section. Again, the outpassage is marked by a solid ensemble swing.

"Shipyard Ramble," as McCarthy suggests, is outstanding, with Haywood Henry on baritone as the featured soloist from the opening of the tune through the first minute and a half of this three-and-half minute side. It must be said, however, that the guitar solo toward the end does not hold up the earlier drive of this piece and the outpassage cannot compare with the closures of "Uncle Bud" and "Blue Sea." One of the more satisfying features for Hawkins's trumpet comes from the session of May 27, 1941, with "So Long, Shorty," where the leader is more restrained and thus more affective in his playing. Paul Bascomb contributes on the same date another fine solo on "I'm in a Low-Down Groove," although not on the same level of interest as his outings on "Nona" and "Hey Doc!" The final side cut in 1941 came with the session of December 22, with vocalist Ida James singing in the popular romantic style of the day on Sammy Lowe's arrangement of "I Don't Want to Walk without You," which offers an effective blend of ballad melody, orchestrated ensemble, and brief solo breaks by Dud Bascomb and Haywood Henry. What must have been a winning combination at the time can still appeal as a sentimental yet strongly realized piece of music that conveys the ballad's emotional meaning through instrumental virtuosity and conviction.

Almost no jazz critics other than Albert McCarthy and, following the English critic's lead, Gunther Schuller have discussed the recordings of the Hawkins orchestra, which seems rather strange. For, as Schuller points out, the Hawkins style, established largely by arrangers Parrish and Lowe, was "sonorically/harmonically rich" and "audiences could easily relate to and dance to" its "slow and medium tempos." Also, as Schuller observes, and this is fully supported by the recorded evidence, Hawkins and his orchestra achieved and maintained a "balance between creative integrity and popular appeal. . . . Very rarely did they falter in their mission to provide both a solidly functional dance music (Harlem style) and a relatively distinctive musical conception."[294] Hawkins continued to lead various groups through the 1940s and into the 1950s, and like so many of the successful black bands that made a substantial contribution to the Swing Era, Hawkins's sidemen stuck with him, in particular two of his principal soloists, tenorist Julian Dash and baritone saxophonist/clarinetist Haywood Henry, who were with the leader when the unit broke up in 1953.[295] Although the Hawkins orchestra did not make the kind of deeply significant impact of an Ellington or Basie band nor establish as unique a style as that of Lunceford, the "Twentieth Century Gabriel" certainly earned a place in the second tier of swing-era bands, by virtue not only of his group's original version of "Tuxedo Junction" but also through the impressive solo work of his sidemen, the solid section work of his ensembles, and the inspiring arrangements and/or originals of his arrangers, Avery Parrish, William Johnson, and Sammy Lowe. More so than a number of the lesser bands that have been remembered on big-band anthologies, the Hawkins orchestra deserves greater recognition for its creation of real jazz in a popular swing-era setting.

BOOTS DOUGLAS

Another territory band noticed by Albert McCarthy and Gunther Schuller is that of Clifford "Boots" Douglas, who was born in Temple, Texas, on September 7, 1908. A drummer from the age of fifteen, Douglas played his first job in 1926 at Turner's Park in San Antonio and organized his own band in that city in 1932. Unlike Erskine Hawkins and the 'Bama State Collegians, Douglas's band, called Boots and His Buddies, did not leave its home state of Texas but remained a territory band during the entire period of its existence. Schuller has characterized Douglas as "at his best—a kind of western Chick Webb" and originally considered his band, as recorded from 1935 to 1937, "one of the most exciting and spirited of the mid-1930s."[296] The first commentator to discuss the Douglas band was the seminal critic of jazz in the Southwest, Franklin Driggs, who found it "frequently out of tune," which Albert McCarthy allows to be true, saying that "the ensemble playing gives the listener some anxious moments," yet the English critic goes on to note that "there is an engaging quality about [the band's output] that results from the extrovert swing of the group and the presence of a number of good soloists."[297] After hearing more of the Douglas band as recorded in 1937 and 1938, which were the band's final appearances at recording sessions in San Antonio, Schuller "realized that the band made many absolutely atrocious sides and that it had begun to deteriorate badly by 1937." Nevertheless, Schuller also asserts that despite the fact that Boots and His Buddies never found their "own style . . . at its best the Boots band could be a very exciting group, resplendent with a number of outstanding soloists and espousing a relatively sophisticated modern style (as good as that, say, of Andy Kirk or Claude Hopkins)."[298]

Jazz critic Ross Russell has pointed out that the Douglas band "lacked the cohesion and originality that marks the work of the later Bennie Moten orchestras and Count Basie," but at least in its earliest recordings, there is a sense of cohesion and a certain originality of conception.[299] Although the debt owed to the Moten band is immediately evident from the first three sides recorded by Boots and His Buddies on August 14, 1935, there is still a tremendous drive that is peculiar to the Douglas band. "Rose Room," arranged by Eddie Heywood Jr., exhibits what Schuller calls "a certain earthy southwestern roughness," and this clearly goes back to the 1932 recordings by Moten.[300] However, the energy generated by Boots and His Buddies differs from that of the Moten recordings, for the Douglas drive derives largely from the drummer's very active role in the proceedings, the dynamic ensemble's "shouted" background figures and foreground passages (which are certainly reminiscent of those of the Moten sides but are even more spirited), and from the hard-charging tenorist, Baker Millian, who has been compared with Basie's Herschel Evans, originally from Texas and an early member of another of San Antonio's several territory bands, that of Troy Floyd.[301] This performance is truly as energized as any of the Moten recordings from 1932, and Millian is as impressive in his delivery as any of the soloists on those classic sides. Millian's ideas are developed beautifully even as he surges with a rhythmic drive and a technical control that would seem difficult to maintain while still working out a musical line of thought that is so clear and inventive. A.J. Johnson's piano also adds to what is a many-layered performance that swings powerfully throughout. The lyrics on "How Long?—Part 1" are sung by Celeste Allen, who is obviously beholden to Jimmy Rushing, even though the latter's own version of this Leroy Carr tune was not recorded until June 24, 1939.[302] Although the Douglas recording of "How Long?" does not contain a masterful chorus by Buck Clayton on trumpet or a wonderful trombone obbligato by Dickie Wells, it does offer a fine muted obbligato by one of the four trumpets (probably Charles Anderson) and a very compelling open-horn solo by the same or another trumpeter.[303] Johnson's opening on piano, his accompanying figures, and a brief solo following Allen's vocal are also an effective part of the overall performance. "Riffs," the third side recorded at the band's first session, is, like "Rose Room," a vibrant number in the same 1932 Moten vein. Douglas is again active on his drum set and two fine breaks by Anderson soar and drive, as do the trumpet section's "shouted" figures. The reed section also can "shout" to good effect. On the basis of these three sides, Schuller was certainly right to judge the Douglas band as one of the most exciting of the mid-1930s.

Unfortunately, Boots and His Buddies were not consistently inspired nor technically precise, and, as a result, one must pick and choose among their performances to find them "at their best." Fortunately, a terrible piece like the overly sweet "Wild Cherry" is countered somewhat by the rollicking

"I Love You Truly," both from the recording session of August 14, 1935. But more satisfying is a tune like "Georgia" from the session of February 25, 1936. Here again A.J. Johnson's piano sets the furious pace from the opening and a muted Anderson stokes the fire, while the sax section keeps the piece on track, followed by Millian on tenor, more of Johnson's stride-like piano, and the ensemble's driving outchorus, kicked along by the fine drumming of the leader. "The Swing," from February 25, also moves with infectious drive, and even among the weaker pieces, which are overly influenced by the white bands, there is an especially impressive moment now and then, as on "Coquette," when to end the side Anderson on trumpet plays a series of high notes with superb articulation. "Sweet Girl," also from this date, although a bit syrupy, features Johnson's rippling piano runs, some affective changes played by string bassist Walter McHenry, and a rather touching phrase by altoist Alva Brooks to close off the side. A year later, on February 27, 1937, the band recorded "Jealous," with the sax section showing its unity and drive and Millian and Douglas both contributing to the forward swing of this up-tempo performance. Although ultimately not much comes of this last piece, as McCarthy says, the group's "honest, straightforward approach provides good entertainment."[304] This is especially true of "Rhythmic Rhapsody" from the same February 27 session, on which Brooks delivers an excellent and impressive chorus, as does Charles Anderson, whom Schuller compares with Roy Eldridge and Dizzy Gillespie "of those years."[305] Brooks also is in fine form on "San Antonio Tamales," which Schuller identifies as the George Brunies tune "Angry" from the early 1920s. Once again, Anderson is strong, although Millian regretfully turns in a less than remarkable break.[306]

Baker Millian's best solo efforts are found on sides recorded at the session of September 17, 1937. Here, too, Alva Brooks on alto and Charles Anderson on trumpet contribute some especially fine solos. In general, Albert McCarthy sees the band "at its best on blues material such as 'How Long' and 'Blues of Avalon,' " and this is in line with what LeRoi Jones claims about black bands as compared with white bands: "Swing music, which was the result of arranged big-band jazz, as it developed to a music that had almost nothing to do with blues, had very little to do with black America, though that is certainly where it had come from." Jones even goes so far as to assert that "[s]wing simply does not exist in the history of the development of Negro music," meaning, it would seem, to associate the development of swing with white big bands and thereby to suggest that it was not integral to black music.[307] The Douglas band's "Blues of Avalon," a slow blues that shows the influence of Ellington, opens with Millian on tenor in one of his most adventuresome and relaxed solos, with an occasional telling blue note. He is followed by Anderson on trumpet and then Alva Brooks on alto, who recalls to some extent the alto work of Johnny Hodges. Brooks certainly reveals his blues roots in his unsentimental, probing chorus. Douglas closes this very satisfying performance with a clopping rhythm on Chinese wood blocks that lends a final touch from an earlier period, which perhaps fits well with Jones's view that true jazz originated prior to the Swing Era. If, as Jones alleges, swing is not an essential part of black music, "The Goo" by Boots and His Buddies demonstrates nonetheless how superior black swing could be. Here Brooks opens with some of his Hodges-inspired alto, and, after Celeste Allen and the chorus do a bit of their "swingaroo," Charles Anderson digs in with his very finest effort, which justifiably has been notated by Gunther Schuller as one example of the trumpeter's "remarkably advanced solos."[308] Millian takes eight bars before Anderson returns for another break, after which the ensemble really swings it out, with Boots Douglas kicking the band along. Another eight bars by Millian abruptly concludes this swinging piece. A more erratic solo by Anderson is found in "The Weep," along with solos by two different tenors, it would seem, as well as another trumpet. Unfortunately, this side grows far too dependent on repeated riffs that go nowhere.

Trumpeter L.D. Harris is featured on the ballad entitled "The Sad," also from September 17, 1937, where his solo displays an impressive range that yet remains restrained in its showmanship. This is true as well of Baker Millian's tenor solo, which again concludes this piece yet not so suddenly but rather with a rallentandoed cadenza. Schuller also notates Harris's solo, revealing his use of sixteenth notes, "not as ornaments or passing tones on the underlying slow-ballad quarter-note beats, but as 'eighth notes' in an implied, fast doubled-up tempo, in other words two rhythmic levels up from the base tempo."[309] (Harris, who is pictured on the CD insert booklet to *Boots and His Buddies 1937–1938*, is shown fitted with a prosthetic right hand, making his playing all the more impressive and admirable.) Although Harris, Anderson, Brooks, and Millian may not represent major stylists or soloists "of the first quality," they do stand as solid performers in at times a superb band far removed from the jazz centers.[310] Of course, through radio, recordings, and touring groups, such a band was in touch with developments elsewhere in the country. Nonetheless, it is still remarkable that this band and its sidemen managed to achieve such a high level of sophistication, technical skill, and on occasion even a quality of performance and invention that could equal those of the name bands. On Fats Waller's "Ain't Misbehavin'," again from September 17, the four principal soloists once more turn in splendid performances. In addition to the instrumental soloists, Cora Woods renders Andy Razaf's lyrics with finesse and exuberance. This relaxed version of Waller's classic tune swings wonderfully, with the two trumpet soloists providing contrasting styles in their very driving, imaginative solos and Millian showing his fine sense of time and his ability to toss off some unusual phrases that are not imitative of any of the major tenor stars. Alva Brooks's very tasteful, beautifully controlled alto break is certainly on a high, if not the highest, level of performance on his instrument.[311] As Schuller suggests, the Douglas band could indeed compete with bands such as those of Andy Kirk and Claude Hopkins, and in some ways its four soloists represent a more varied, more imaginative array of styles than offered for example by Kirk's Clouds of Joy.

"The Somebody," from the same session of September 17, 1937, also finds the band and its soloists in fine mettle, with an excellent opening trumpet chorus by Anderson. After Celeste Allen sings the lyrics of "Somebody Loves Me," the sax section shows its stuff, followed by the brasses, with the two sections joining forces for a driving ensemble passage. A short break by Millian is the only solo other than the opening one by Anderson. Still from the same session, "The Happy" (another title shortened from the original tune—this time "Sometimes I'm Happy") is not so successful, partly because the trombone soloist is less skilled. Even so, Anderson's trumpet break is notable, as is the ensemble's work, another short break by Millian, and the supportive drum work of Douglas. "The Raggle Taggle," the last side from this September 17 session, has been criticized by Schuller, among other sides, for Douglas's "rhythmically listless work" when he seems to be *following* the band rather than *leading* it."[312] Even so, this piece has its appeal, and Douglas's very active drumming is definitely part of the driving swing generated by the group, with intense tenor and trumpet breaks that fuel the high-energy performance. "A Salute to Harlem," from the session of April 6, 1938, is notable for Cora Woods's vocal that is sung in unison with the instruments playing the theme. Again, this piece swings nicely, and the trumpet solo adds to the rocking rhythm. A brief appearance by Millian on tenor is on a level with his better efforts, as are his short breaks on "Gone," where unfortunately the trumpet solo is quite weak and so, too, is the vocal by Henderson Glass. By this date Charles Anderson is no longer with the band, and perhaps as a result intonation problems now afflict the performance of "A Salute to Harlem" (especially in the trumpet section). But it must be said that this piece (by an unknown arranger) is rather ambitious in its harmonic demands, as well as its unusually jagged melody line. Gunther Schuller notes that the band was not given any alternate takes on its recording sessions, and this could account in part for the poor intonation and the raggedness of some of the playing.[313] Cora Woods's vocal on "Do-Re-Mi" has some of the spirit and quality of the work of Ellington's Ivie Anderson, and on this same tune, Baker Millian again takes another commendable break. But overall, the level of performance and musical interest has fallen off dramatically and would only rarely recover during the final recording session of October 28, 1938. The intonation problems became even more serious on pieces such as "Lonely Moments," from the April 6 session, although again this is principally in the trumpet section, for the saxes manage to execute their passages well enough and Millian solos admirably, whereas the trumpeter, apparently "Chubby" Jones, is rather pathetic. The latter is featured on "Chubby," a piece obviously named for him and one of what Schuller refers to as the band's "shockingly bad" sides.[314] George Corley's trombone is almost as weak as Jones's trumpet. Why L.D. Harris no longer solos is unclear.

It is quite unfortunate that Douglas was not able to retain Charles Anderson, for whatever reason, or to find a worthy replacement, because the band was still mostly composed of its original members, including Alva Brooks, Baker Millian, A.J. Johnson, and Walter McHenry. "True Blue Lou," the last side recorded at the session of April 6, 1938, does offer some worthy moments, despite the rather erratic nature of the performance. For one thing, it contains a curious solo by Brooks on alto, full of unexpected twists and turns, and Corley on trombone does a much better job with his solo opportunity. Corley's solo even recalls the brass figures in Duke Ellington's "Showboat Shuffle." Although the Boots version of "Blue Lou" may not be of a quality equal to the renditions by Chick Webb or Fletcher Henderson, it is in some respects not so far behind those superior performances.

By the time of the final Douglas session on October 28, 1938, Brooks was gone, and the soul of the group seems to have departed with him. The vocal by Henderson Glass on "I Don't Stand a Ghost of a Chance with You" is simply dreadful. "Boots Stomp" is a better effort, with Corley on trombone at his best and the trumpet (either Lonnie Moore or Percy Bush) creditable; also, here at least the ensemble playing is improved so far as intonation is concerned. "Careless Love" uses a rhumba rhythm and features the old-fashioned clarinet of Clifton Chatman, and Millian offers one of his lesser efforts and the trumpet is nothing special. The last side recorded by the group was "Remember," on which the sax section shows that it could manage to play as a unit and swing effectively and Millian maintains his fairly consistent high standard, whereas George Corley and a trumpeter are merely acceptable.

Gunther Schuller has expressed the great disappointment one feels in hearing a band such as Boots and His Buddies on its final recording sessions, a group that began with such a "high potential."[315] The explanation for what Schuller calls an apparent "complete demoralization of the entire band" may rest with the departure of Charles Anderson, who played such a vital role in providing solid solo work and in leading the trumpet section. Although Anderson was not the type of ascendant star around whom many of the name bands built their organizations, he obviously was a crucial figure. Alva Brooks, as well, must have contributed to the band more than just through his solo work. Baker Millian served as a dependable soloist on the level at times of a Dick Wilson and approaching even on occasion a Chu Berry. Certainly the Douglas band lacked an outstanding composer-arranger who could create for the unit a more individual style, and in no way did the band influence other bands around the country. Yet the group did make its mark as a unit capable at its best of matching the drive and invention of such bands as those of Moten and Kirk. The gradual wasting away of the band's energy, imagination, and execution points up the difficulties in maintaining a high level of performance over a long period of time. Few of the outstanding swing bands actually managed to do so, and often the problem was one of retaining key figures. This was frequently the case when a band featured a soloist who achieved such acclaim that he was encouraged to front his own band. As we shall see, this was especially true of members of the Goodman organization. But it was equally true of a black soloist such as Oran "Hot Lips" Page and a black soloist/composer-arranger such as Benny Carter. With regard to Boots and His Buddies, listeners are fortunate at least to have recordings of this group's efforts from 1935 to 1937 when it produced a number of quite impressive performances. One other observation is worth making: by remaining in Texas, Douglas and his sidemen enabled regional audiences to experience a quality local band, to hire local talent, and to inspire, if only indirectly, regional artists such as Texas reedman Leo Wright, whose father Mel played with Boots and His Buddies before the leader disbanded in the early 1940s.

ORAN "HOT LIPS" PAGE

With the success of Benny Goodman in 1935, many outstanding sidemen who succumbed to the lure of leadership ultimately proved themselves incapable of meeting the demands of such a difficult position. This was particularly true of many of the white leaders of big bands during the latter part of the decade. Soon after Goodman almost single-handedly created a nationwide craze that translated into a burgeoning market for big bands, and especially those led by musicians who first made their names with the Goodman organization, managing agents such as Joe Glaser, who had promoted and guided the career of Louis Armstrong, were on the lookout for luminaries of the same or a similar order. In Oran "Hot Lips" Page, the featured trumpet of first Bennie Moten and later Count Basie (but before the latter had landed a recording contract), Glaser found a promising star to front a big band as both its soloist and vocalist. Unlike the talented musicians in the big band of Boots Douglas, Lips Page had left his native Texas almost from the beginning of his career (which reportedly began at age thirteen in 1921), and had toured with Ma Rainey, the "Mother of the Blues," in the early to mid 1920s.[316] First recorded in 1929 with the Oklahoma Blue Devils, Page took probably his greatest solos on the seminal 1932 recordings with the Moten band, and had he remained with Basie's outfit he might have developed into an even greater soloist. But the attraction of stardom was apparently too much to resist, and Page opened with his own big band in August 1937 at Smalls' Paradise in Harlem. Page's short-lived career as a big-band leader—his group not even surviving to the middle of 1938—illustrates perhaps more than anything else the exigencies of the job and the type of temperament required for such a role.

In contrast to a number of the successful name-bandleaders such as Ellington, Goodman, Lunceford, and Basie, Lips Page lacked the qualities that resulted in the longevity of the bands led by those major figures. Although the sidemen with Ellington tended to remain with him throughout the 1920s and 1930s and the same goes for the Lunceford and Basie bands of the 1930s, the musicians with Goodman fairly quickly began to feel the itch to lead their own outfits. The exodus from Goodman's organization may have been due in large part to his rather tyrannical approach to leadership. Known as a taskmaster who would not settle for less than perfection—demanded of himself as a performer and of those he led—Goodman was a disciplined leader whose band has been called "at its peak . . . a near-perfect musical unit."[317] But Goodman also enjoyed the support and recommendations of John Hammond, who encouraged and even cajoled Goodman into hiring a number of key members of the organization, including Gene Krupa and Charlie Christian. Even though Lunceford tended to treat his men rather shabbily in terms of their pay, his leadership was so remarkable that most of his sidemen endured the substandard salaries in order to play under his almost magical baton. Like Goodman, Lunceford was a disciplinarian, and the band's usual precise execution was one of the outstanding features of its recorded performances. Certainly Lunceford benefited from the sectional leadership of Willie Smith, his alto saxophonist. Ellington, of course, had the advantage of being a great composer who knew how to utilize so effectively the various timbres and personalities of his instrumentalists. Over many years Ellington maintained a close-knit unit and could in this way develop a distinctive sound and a level of performance excellence rarely matched by any other big band. As for Basie, his seemingly easygoing style obviously went hand-in-hand with an assured notion of the type of relaxed swing he wished to achieve. Although his many soloists offered very individual and often contrasting approaches to the music, Basie was able to meld them into a unified force that still gives the impression of a natural, spontaneous outpouring, even as the group depends so fully on riff material that when played by most big bands grew monotonous and downright boring. All these name-bandleaders managed to bring together and for the most part keep together topflight musicians who responded to their directing styles with performances that still engage the listener, both on individual and group levels, as examples of the most satisfying forms of swing.

Although Lips Page has been considered one of the fine trumpet soloists of the 1930s and one of the few genuine players and singers of the blues, as the leader of his own big band he left much to be desired. Soon after

Page formed his twelve-piece band, he must have discovered that it was up to him to serve as the principal attraction, or perhaps he felt that this was his proper role rather than merely fitting into a group and contributing as just one of a number of soloists, which he had done while with Moten. As a soloist, Lips may have been an attractive showman, but his style was perhaps too close to that of Armstrong to set him apart in his own right. This is evident on a piece such as "The Pied Piper," recorded by Page and his band on June 24, 1938, on which the leader is essentially the only soloist. In addition to his vocal, Page's trumpet sound, his notes falling off or shaken, and his upward rips, all immediately recall Armstrong. Yet this was not really Page's style when he recorded with Moten, for during that earlier period the trumpeter shaped his solos more as musical ideas rather than as imitations of Armstrong's dramatic technique and his high-note exhibitions. Arthur Jackson has tried to make the case that Page's "clean-cut trumpet style, the no-vibrato tone and straight-ahead melodic phrasing may have stemmed from Louis in the first place but Lips' fiery attack and rhythmic flair . . . were his own. And vocally there is more of the great blues shouters than of Armstrong."[318] The fieriness is certainly heard on occasion in the big-band sides, but the bluesiness is almost entirely absent. Little of Page's penetrating blues approach survived once he took over as a leader.

Even the vocal material sung by Page was largely in the novelty vein. For example, "The Pied Piper" was rendered by Page in a manner somewhat reminiscent of Fats Waller, but without the latter's infectious humor. Compared with the Bunny Berigan version of the same song, recorded with his own big band on June 8, 1938, Page's "The Pied Piper" does not offer the listener of the period the necessary ingredients for popularity. Berigan's vocalist, Ruth Gaylor, must have appealed not only through her sweet, swinging style but also by the appropriate way in which her lines are responded to by Berigan's trumpet. Page echoes the words of the same verses by doing a type of scat singing to suggest a trumpet break, which does not offer the same variety as Berigan's actual trumpet interpolations, which are more convincingly illustrative of the lyrics. Also, Berigan's trumpet solo after the vocal—although a bit flawed in execution—derives more suitably from the song itself and the swing generated by the band, which plays a much greater and more vital part in the performance. Page's band is almost nonexistent, with none of the sidemen taking a real solo (only a clarinet providing some unswinging fills), whereas Georgie Auld on the Berigan side contributes a pulsing tenor break and the three trombones add an excellent piece of sectional work. This one recording by Page and his band suggests a number of the basic reasons for his failure as a leader.

The exceptions to Page's failed leadership—or the instances in which he and his band recorded even mildly satisfying sides—are limited to less than a handful of performances. Most notable is "Jumpin'," the first side recorded on April 27, 1938, which swings from start to finish. Solos by a tenor, clarinet, and Lips himself are all strong outings, and the absence of any vocal makes this one of the rare examples of a purely instrumental side by the Page unit—another being "Skull Duggery," as arranged by Harry White. "Feelin' High and Happy" also includes an effective tenor solo and Lips's Armstrong-influenced trumpet is more identifiably his own in its light but powerful drive. Even though the tenor soloist is effective, it is clear that without Lips there would not be anything particularly outstanding about this or the other sides recorded by the band. Although Lips is at first overly close to Armstrong on "At Your Beck and Call," the leader's trumpet really sparkles on this piece, which nevertheless has nothing to distinguish it from other recordings of the period, no real style to set it apart as exceptional. Page's vocal on this number is quite charming as delivered in his best relaxed manner, yet even so, this would not have been enough to make the performance stand out from so many similar recordings of the period. When the band attempts to "cover" a classic by Ellington—his "I Let a Song Go Out of My Heart"—the results can in no way compare with the original. Although the altoist on the Page performance is acceptable, he does not achieve the lilting, affective approach of a Johnny Hodges, and even Lips's open and then wa-wa offerings are not really in his style. More appealing is "If I Were You," from June 24, 1938, on which Delores Payne does a commendable job with the vocal and Lips tries something different with his own trumpet work, producing a more jumping swing than elsewhere on his big-band sides. The alto and tenor solos also add to the overall performance, but once again this is an exception among mostly unremarkable numbers.

The duration of Page's time as a leader of a big band was not only short-lived but the number of successful recordings by his outfit was severely circumscribed. Sides such as "(A Sky of Blue, with You) And So Forth" and "Will You Remember Tonight Tomorrow?," from the same session of June 24, 1938, represent the band at its worst, with the former not even featuring Lips in any solo capacity that might have salvaged a few bars from the realm of otherwise fully deserved oblivion. "And So Forth," a typical sentimental ballad with a trombone theme statement imitative of white leaders such as Tommy Dorsey and Glenn Miller, is made doubly dreadful by a sappy and poorly played clarinet trio behind Delores Payne's very weak vocal. Ben Bowers sings the vocal on "Will You Remember Tonight Tomorrow?," from the same date, and this again is a side best forgotten.

In general, Hot Lips Page's career as a big-band leader points up the fact that even when such a figure was blessed with instrumental and/or vocal talents, this did not guarantee success in fronting a full-sized swing-era organization. Although Page's sidemen may have been capable of better work, had they been offered more opportunities to solo and superior material on which to base their improvisations, the evidence of most of their appearances argues against their achieving any distinguishable place in the roll call of outstanding sidemen. The other fact revealed by Page's experience as a big-band leader is that not every talented musician was meant to serve in this very challenging capacity. Indeed, Page turned in his best performances as a sideman rather than as a leader, or at least not as a leader of a large unit. Prior to forming his twelve-piece band, Page had recorded, on March 10, 1938, with a sextet, and the results are far more engaging. Two of the pieces are blues ("Down on the Levee" and "Old Man Ben") and a third ("He's Pulling His Whiskers") finds Page in his very excellent trumpet solo employing blue notes to marvelous effect. Curiously, the combination of clarinet, tenor, and trumpet on "Down on the Levee" produces a fuller, more appealing sound than anything on the recordings by the twelve-piece band. On all four sides issued from the March 1938 session, Page is clearly in his element, whereas in the role of big-band leader he was simply out of place.

As we shall see in Chapter 6 on The Small Swing Groups, Page would serve in 1940 as the leader on a number of fine octet sides. He also would star in 1941 with the Artie Shaw orchestra, as both soloist and vocalist. In the same year, Page participated in some of the incipient bebop dates captured on wire recorder at various Harlem nightspots where he would make a name for himself as a champion of the jam session. But as the leader of a big band, Page obviously was not cut out for the job, which demonstrates the difficulty of competing with so many driven leaders such as Goodman, Miller, Lunceford, Shaw, and Ellington who demanded or expected perfection of their sidemen and who each dedicated himself to the creation of a unique style that would keep the dancers on the floor, the fans rocking in the aisles and balconies, and the devoted listeners glued to their radios or shelling out for the latest 78 release. Lips Page's brief career as a leader makes it clear that directing a big band was no simple feat and that to make it to the top with a big band or even to survive for a number of years required more than talent and a desire for acclaim and monetary gain.

Page was not alone in failing to find his niche as a big bandleader—even a major figure such as Coleman Hawkins was, as a bandleader, "always up in the clouds," according to the account of his pianist Gene Rodgers, who served as Bean's straw boss.[319] Various reasons have been given why "Hawkins's career as a bandleader didn't flourish," and one of these is that the tenorist did not offer a balanced fare for his general listeners, either too much riff jazz, not enough instrumental ballads, or too few vocal features.[320] So many considerations went into the making of a successful big band that, once again, sheer musical talent did not determine who would manage to succeed in a field that by 1941 was beginning to be—or already was—replete with scrambling bands. And Page and Hawkins were not the only prominent figures who were affected by the vagaries of the big-band enterprise. As John Chilton reveals, a highly regarded pianist-arranger such as Teddy Wilson never quite recovered from having to disband his unit from "failure to win over the public," and both Bunny Berigan and Jack Teagarden "bankrupted themselves trying to launch their own big bands."[321] In some ways, Page, Hawkins, and Teagarden, at least, may have been better off departing as they did from the big-band scene, which was fast approaching the end of its predominance. These three improvisers would instead find a place for themselves in smaller groups—Page in the jam sessions and in combinations that called for his more personal expression instrumentally and vocally, Hawkins paired with many of the horn-playing giants of his own and every succeeding generation, and Teagarden with the Armstrong All-Stars and other stellar groups. In joining with combos or units of fewer members, these jazzmen were given freer rein for their imaginative flights, and at greater lengths, which provided them it would seem with more challenging settings and outlets for their formidable artistic talents.

BENNY CARTER

More than Hot Lips Page, multi-instrumentalist, composer-arranger, and sometimes singer Benny Carter best exemplifies the elusive nature of success for a talented musician who took it upon himself to organize and direct a swing-era big band. The personal attributes that seemed to afflict a Fletcher Henderson in his handling of a jazz orchestra—which have been characterized as resulting in an almost tragic story of the fall of this big-band king from a position of respect and achievement, or in his never fully achieving the recognition he deserved—are in some ways repeated in the career of Benny Carter. However, the "tragic flaw," if this is not carrying the metaphor too far, was, unlike Henderson's apparent indifference and even bad luck, more a matter of pride in Carter's case. One secret of the success of such men as Ellington, Lunceford, and Basie would appear to have been their willingness to play a supporting role—big as they were—and to guide their sidemen into performances that proved, by and large, superior to those they gave under the direction of any other leaders. With Carter, either he felt the need to be a type of one-man band, despite his role as the leader of various ensembles, which included at times quite capable sidemen, or he was encouraged by his agents or the venues where he performed to place himself in the starring role at every opportunity. In contrast to what tended to be a fiasco in terms of Carter's career as a bandleader, his contributions as sideman and/or composer-arranger to big bands such as those led by Henderson and Benny Goodman and his participation in small group sessions where he was but one of many outstanding soloists are marked by exceptional performances, both by Carter as a soloist and of his compositions, which, as played by his own bands, never quite offer the same level of quality or stimulation.

Born in New York City on August 8, 1908, Carter was largely self-taught, which in itself is remarkable in that he mastered so many instruments. Long considered one of the premier alto saxophonists of the 1930s, Carter also was adept as a trumpeter and clarinetist. His work as a big-band arranger and composer often places him among the originators of the big-band style, which include Don Redman and Horace and Fletcher Henderson. Having served as a sideman with many of the leading big bands of the late 1920s and early 1930s, such as Duke Ellington, Fletcher Henderson, Chick Webb, and McKinney's Cotton Pickers, Carter first recorded with his own unit in 1932. "Tell All Your Day Dreams to Me," from circa June 23, did not bode well for his success as a leader, for this piece has little to recommend it, despite the presence among his personnel of such fine musicians as Dicky Wells, Chu Berry, Teddy Wilson, and Sid Catlett. This is pretty awful stuff; even Carter's playing, although his alto tone is exceptional, remains in a rickety style that is barely jazz, if even that, rather than in the smooth swing we would expect by 1932. The vocal by an "unknown girl" is truly wretched, and the entire piece is clearly influenced by Paul Whiteman's concert sound. In contrast to Carter's work in 1929 and '30 with small groups billed as the Chocolate Dandies, this is definitely a very weak showing.

With an almost entirely different personnel (with the exception of Sid Catlett still on drums and Chu Berry on tenor), Carter's next orchestral session, held on March 14, 1933, proved quite an improvement. Indeed, the first of four sides, "Swing It," does just that, and although Carter's vocal lines—"Swing it morning, noon, and night. . . . If you don't swing it it don't mean a thing"—had already been definitively enunciated by Ellington on February 2, 1932, this version of thirties swing is certainly the real thing. "Synthetic Love" is a nice enough ballad in its way, especially in the form of the dreamy opening theme statement by the trumpet. The trombone solo, by George Washington or Wilbur de Paris, is solid, and Carter's clarinet break is okay, while his vocal is rather "inauthentic" as if in keeping with the title of the tune. Chu Berry's distinctive sound on tenor closes out the soloing. The third side, "Six Bells Stampede," certainly offers good swing, with Berry digging in with a very driving break, yet the sax writing is perhaps something of a throwback to a twenties kind of jerkiness and the concert-type ending is rather corny. Even so, Albert McCarthy considers this the best of the four sides from this session.[322] Although this 1933 band may exhibit "all the basic gestures that Carter had helped to establish," such as "homophonic section scoring (especially four-part saxophone writing), antiphonal exchanges between sections, riff patterns, and balanced formal schemes," it is difficult to believe that the "commercial failure" of the Carter band was due to the "flexible manner" in which these "gestures" were used, as a trio of Carter critics has suggested.[323] A certain lack of polish in some of the performances, perhaps even at times dated ensemble writing, poor choices of material, and tasteless vocals—these, too, must have contributed to the band's nonsuccess. The fourth and last side from the March 14 session was a Carter original, entitled "Love You're Not the One for Me," and this, too, may indicate another reason for the band's inability to catch on with the listening public: the piece is typical of the very unappealing, unmemorable titles often given to Carter's own frequently very fetching compositions. Also, although the leader's alto solo is quite affective, his vocal is simply terrible. Finally, the Whiteman ending, complete with vibraphone shimmer, is flatly a disappointment from a musician who must have known better—to be explained only by the fact that at this time Carter's band was playing opposite Paul Whiteman's at the Empire Hall in New York City.[324]

One month later, Carter arranged for a series of recording sessions with his band under the leadership of the young Irish composer Spike Hughes. This was a curious development in jazz history and in many ways a unique occasion that resulted in fourteen fascinating sides. Held on April 18 and May 18 and 19, 1933, these sessions are marked by some excellent playing by Coleman Hawkins, Chu Berry, Dicky Wells, and Henry Allen. Hughes had been the composer of "Six Bells Stampede" from the March 14 session and would account for five original tunes for the April-May session. The first side, Hughes's "Nocturne," reveals the Irishman's indebtedness to Ellington and Gershwin, who were certainly models worthy of his emulation. But Hughes's use of some advanced chords lends this work a distinctive sound of its own, and the solo by Hawkins fits beautifully into the rhapsodic texture of the piece. "Someone Stole Gabriel's Horn" displays some of Sid Catlett's fine drumming, a typically high-quality outing by Hawkins, and a Carter vocal that is better than usual and a brief alto break that is really quite good. Carter is especially fine on Hughes's "Pastorale," as is Dicky Wells with his wonderful talking trombone. On what John Chilton calls "the lively, unhackneyed version of 'Bugle Call Rag,' " Carter produces in his alto solo "a model of graceful playing."[325] Wells again is sui generis with his emotive sliding trombone phrases, and Catlett's drums add to this spirited side, which in its closing bars shows once more Hughes's indebtedness to Ellington's superb style of ensemble swing. "Arabesque," another Hughes's composition, once again features Wells's conversational horn, which Chilton correctly says "sounds startlingly daring and totally original," and as usual Hawkins rhapsodizes handsomely. "Fanfare" exhibits Wells in a shaking blues mode, while Chu Berry and Hawkins turn in complementary tenor breaks, with Chilton hearing in Chu's "altered substitute chords . . . a musical ploy that later came to fruition in the bebop era."[326] Henry "Red" Allen adds his glowing trumpet both to "Fanfare" and "Sweet Sorrow Blues," whereas Hawkins is at his most impressive on "Sweet Sue," where he really lets loose with some of his most unbuttoned blowing. On "Music at Midnight," where the ensemble writing is again heavily influenced by Ellington, the Hawk really rocks and soars. Wayman Carver's flute, Wells's swirling trombone, and Carter's alto are all outstanding on "Sweet Sue," although Benny's solo is not entirely coherent, which was often the case with his improvisations.

For the May 19 session with Hughes as director, the Carter band recorded the last of the Irish composer's originals: "Donegal Cradle Song" and "Firebird." Along with these two originals, Hughes also contributed an arrangement of "Music at Sunrise," and the band also recorded "Air in D Flat" and "How Come You Do Me Like You Do?" "Air in D Flat" features more of Dicky Wells's tremendous trombone on this relaxed swinger. The ensemble background writing and playing is excellent in this piece and shows once more how closely Hughes had studied the Duke's scores. "Donegal Cradle Song" is a bit of Irish nostalgia for a jazz band, with a clarinet trio and some muted brass supported by bowed bass that add to the elegiac effect, which feeds wonderfully into what Chilton calls "one of the high points" in Hawkins's career—an emotive solo with the tenorist's patented rapturous tone.[327] "Firebird," an intriguing piece, with Carter on soprano sax, truly swings in a most unusual way, including saxophone trills that may suggest the bird of the tune's title (reminiscent of Stravinsky's ballet, of course). Wells's trombone style fits in beautifully and recalls something of Lawrence Brown of the Ellington organization, and the swing of this piece once again owes much to the influence of that master's orchestral touch. "Music at Sunrise" features some tricky figures for the reeds, and is highlighted by a brief break by Hawkins. The mark of Gershwin is on the closing section of this Hughes's arrangement, revealing once more the arranger's good taste in choosing his American mentors. The final side from this delightful session is "How Come You Do Me Like You Do?," which includes a catchy, partly scatted vocal by Henry Allen. But the main attractions of this performance are the magisterial solo by Wells, who, as Chilton accurately observes, "rarely play[ed] better," and Hawkins's smoothly swinging, sailing break. Chu Berry and Wayman Carver also add effectively to the overall success of this marvelous side. Had the Carter band been able to maintain such a high level of work, perhaps he would have achieved the popularity his peers felt that he should have attained. But it seems clear that it was Spike Hughes who was the real inspiration here, and not Carter, who probably belonged all along in a supportive role rather than one of leadership. The impact of Hughes is best indicated by Dicky Wells's comments, as quoted by Chilton: "No one in the outfit had the idea that [Hughes] had so much hell in that valise until we started rehearsing. It still shakes me to think of such swinging notes coming from England back in those days."[328] Hughes himself credited Carter with understanding his music better than other "American Negro bands," but it still seems evident that it was Hughes who understood what he wanted and that it was he who was able to utilize Carter's fine sidemen in order to realize his own musical vision.[329]

In October 1933 a new version of the Carter orchestra recorded on the 16th, with a totally different sax section, except for Wayman Carver on alto and flute, who is featured on Carter's "Devil's Holiday." The second of three Carter compositions, "Lonesome Nights" offers reed work that is not so appealing or engaging as that of the Lunceford orchestra, which this piece recalls. Ironically there is little of true jazz in this work as compared with the Hughes-directed sides. Albert McCarthy praises the performance as excellent and the reed scoring as "beautifully rich," but the Carter section (here and on "Devil's Holiday") is showy without being musical in the way that the Lunceford saxes were.[330] "Symphony in Riffs," also considered excellent by McCarthy, owing especially to the "brilliance of the saxophone passages," does not quite cohere nor does it flow smoothly or effectively.[331] The piece tends to stop and go without hanging together for any particular effect. J.C. Higginbotham's solos, although good in themselves, are rather out of place in this attempt at a more sophisticated type of jazz, as suggested by the piece's title. As for "Blue Lou," this is a sort of lazy treatment of the Edgar Sampson classic and does not muster as much punch as compared with the versions by Chick Webb and Benny Goodman. The brass punctuations are rather overly loud and somewhat ragged. Even Teddy Wilson's piano is too syncopated and jerky. This group did not include players of the caliber of Hawkins or Wells, and even those such as Higginbotham and Wilson, who could in another context produce highly satisfying work, do not perform effectively under Carter's guidance—Wilson even uncharacteristically misses notes.

Carter's inability to take advantage of the talents of sidemen who not only played individually on a high level but worked so well as a unit under the direction of other leaders is illustrated by the recording session of December 13, 1934. Much of Fletcher Henderson's band made up the Carter orchestra for this date, which opened with "Shoot the Works." This Carter original does offer some nice sax work by the reed section that included Ben Webster and Russell Procope; it also swings to a certain extent, though in a kind of popular rather than jazz mode. Teddy Wilson is in a Hines groove but still has his problems with missed notes. "Dream Lullaby," a Carter original like the previous side, is saved from the maudlin by a felt and technically daring solo from Webster, and Wilson's rippling arpeggios are more under control. Still, this piece is a weak offering and cannot compare with the leader's later "Melancholy Lullaby." As Albert McCarthy correctly assesses this session, "Everybody Shuffle" is the best of the four sides recorded, with a fine outing by Webster, and yet this piece is something of a throwback to the twenties. "Synthetic Love," which is another version of the George Washington and Carter tune recorded on March 13,

1933, is not improved by having Charles Holland substitute for Carter as the vocalist. Benny Morton's trombone solo is solid, and shows what Henderson's men could do, even with a rather paltry piece like this. The December 13 session marked the last by Carter before he left for Europe, where he was to remain until 1939.

Carter's years in Europe do not strictly concern us here; suffice it to say that there was little if anything during that period that could equal the sides recorded by the Carter band under the direction of Spike Hughes. Certainly Carter exhibited his multi-instrumental talents, recording extensively on trumpet and alto (and occasionally on clarinet) with the backing of groups in France, England, the Netherlands, Denmark, and Sweden. Although Carter was welcomed with all the honors he deserved and obviously had a stimulating effect on the European jazz community (hear, for instance, his sax section on "Skip It" recorded August 17, 1937, in The Hague), his own development of jazz as an art form did not necessarily benefit from his stay abroad. To compare a tune such as "Swingin' the Blues" (a Carter original and not the Basie-Durham tune recorded in 1932 with the Moten orchestra) is to hear how far Carter's work in Europe was from the mainstream development of jazz in the United States. His trumpet work is dated and is marred by fluffs, which is at times the case with a number of his solos on this instrument. Frequently, as on "When Day Is Done," from a late April 1936 date in London, Carter merely recalls Louis Armstrong, and Gunther Schuller has pointed out that it was "uncanny how perfectly Carter could imitate Armstrong's famous upward glissandoes."[332] Schuller considers two examples of Carter's best early work on trumpet to be the recording of his original tune "Once upon a Time," from October 10, 1933, with the Chocolate Dandies, and his version of "Stardust," with the Willie Lewis Orchestra in Paris on January 17, 1936. But this critic finds that although Carter's trumpet playing could be lyrically elegant and clean technically, ultimately it was "not *true* trumpet playing, in the sense that Roy Eldridge's or Buck Clayton's or Harry James's is."[333] The rhythm sections on Carter's European recordings were generally feeble, especially on the English sides, as Gunther Schuller has noted.[334] This is the case on "Swingin' the Blues," and even more so on "Swingin' at the Maida Vale," another Carter original recorded in London on April 15, 1936. There could be some very decent performances by certain British soloists, as on such Carter originals as "Gin and Jive" and "I'm in the Mood for Swing" from January 1937, but as would be expected, it is Carter's solos that are the most outstanding, as with his alto break on "Nagasaki" from the same session, where Al Craig on drums is not so plodding and monotonous as other British percussionists and the trombonist does a good imitation of Jack Teagarden. Carter's vocals on "Nagasaki" and "There's a Small Hotel" are an improvement over his earlier singing in the

United States. The rhythm section on a group of sides cut in Laren, Holland, on March 24, 1937, is not bad, and Carter's alto solo on "New Street Swing" demonstrates his great fluidity on the instrument. Nevertheless, as Schuller remarks, Carter's "fifty-odd recordings made in Europe . . . did not add much substance to Carter's output."[335]

Carter's first recording session back in the United States came on June 29, 1939, and the difference between the three sides cut on this occasion and Carter's work in Europe is dramatic. This is evident from the first side from this date, a tune titled "Plymouth Rock," which is more modern sounding than anything Carter recorded in Europe. The ensemble writing is in line with advanced developments being made by Jimmy Dorsey and Artie Shaw's arrangers and perhaps looks forward somewhat to Stan Kenton, even as the piece combines in spots the modern with a boogie style and rhythm, which was coming into vogue at the time. Despite the progressive features of the arrangement, Carter's alto solo is not really contemporary sounding; although it is technically competent, there are no ideas worth bragging about. This is in contrast to the fine solos on the second side recorded on this date, Carter's "Savoy Stampede," which has a very up-to-date tenor solo by Ernie Powell; a trumpet solo by Joe Thomas that shows how outmoded Carter's playing both on alto and trumpet had been during his years in Europe and continued to be on this June 1939 session; and a well-constructed vibraphone solo by Tyree Glenn, which also contrasts with the often erratic, unfocused solos by Carter.

Prior to cutting the sides with his new orchestra, Carter had performed at the Savoy Ballroom on May 20, and an air check from the broadcast includes Carter's theme song, "Melancholy Lullaby," which "supplied the necessary feature of a popular big band" and has been called "surely one of the best themes of that entire era."[336] Carter and his orchestra recorded the theme on June 29, and the leader plays his alto theme statement just as he had on the radio broadcast from the Savoy. It is a lovely, romantic sound Carter creates on his ballad, but his solo work in general tends to be overly showy, with little or no substance to it. This is true as well of his version of "I'm Coming Virginia" from a recording made in Paris, on March 7, 1938, with Djano Reinhardt and other European musicians. Carter's solo on "I'm Coming Virginia" has no unity to its structure, is again too showy, and does not compare favorably even with Frankie Trumbauer's rather peculiar piece of work on the 1927 recording with Bix Beiderbecke. This is true as well of Carter's alto solo on "Scandal in A Flat," made at the same June 29 session. Here the playing is all show, with no guts to the solo. In fact, an earlier version of this Carter original was recorded in mid-June 1936 with an English orchestra (including Ted Heath on trombone), and Carter's Hawkins-inspired solo on tenor is better conceived and more engaging than his 1939 improvisation on alto. By and large, Carter's alto work is rather frivolous, and it is telling in this regard that Gunther Schuller does not devote a section of *The Swing Era* to Carter as one of "The Great Soloists."

Carter's orchestra of 1939 does show that it could offer selections very much in the swing idiom made popular by Henderson, Goodman, and the other name bands. The more imaginative and sweet sides of Carter's alto playing are exhibited on "When Lights Are Low" and "The Favor of a Fool," respectively, from the August 31 session, both of which are Carter originals. In much of his alto playing, however, Carter tends to represent the case of a black musician who seems to be imitating the white jazzmen or those who transformed jazz into pop music. On the other hand, Joe Thomas's trumpet is outstanding on the August 31 session, and Henry Morrison's percussion work, especially on Carter's "Riff Romp," demonstrates the vast difference between most European drummers and those of the United States. In general, though, so many of the Carter offerings of this period sound like a pastiche of big-band phrases and clichés—there is nothing distinctive about the Carter approach. Gunther Schuller points to one tune, "More Than You Know," from the session of November 1, 1939, as representing one of Carter's "finest hours on the trumpet."[337] But even his playing here is not really jazz in the way that Joe Thomas's improvisations are; rather, Carter's solo is an exhibition of his technical skills and his ability to turn a ballad into a typical trumpet showpiece.

During 1940, the Carter orchestra remained fairly stable as far as its personnel was concerned. Coleman Hawkins did join for a session on January 30, replacing Ernie Powell, but pianist Eddie Heywood stayed on with Carter, as did Joe Thomas, trombonists Vic Dickenson and Jimmy Archey, as well as Hayes Alvis on bass, James Powell and Carl Frye on alto, and Ulysses Livingston on guitar. "Sleep" and "Among My Souvenirs" find Thomas on trumpet still the most attractive of the soloists, along with a brief Hawkins on the latter side. Hawkins is given more space on Carter's "Fish Fry," and the Hawk is his dependable self, turning in another imaginative break. Something of a rip-off of "Tuxedo Junction," Buck Ram's "Slow Freight" is by comparison with the Erskine Hawkins piece rather dull and pointless. On May 20, the Carter orchestra cut four more sides, all of them Carter originals, and for this date trumpeters Bill Coleman and Shad Collins replaced Joe Thomas and Lincoln Mills, with Russell Smith the only remaining trumpet from the January session. Collins is featured on "Pom Pom," as is Sammy Davis on tenor, who replaced Hawkins, and the replacements do well enough but do not have the same sharp edge to their playing. Carter on clarinet is again too close to the popular white leaders such as Goodman and Shaw. "O.K. for Baby" swings well and trumpet soloist Bill Coleman is effective, although there is no comparison here with his sparkling efforts elsewhere, as when he recorded with Fats Waller & His Rhythm. Previously Coleman had recorded with Carter in the Willie Lewis Orchestra in Paris. On October 15, Coleman formed part of Carter's eight-piece All-Star Orchestra, but neither are his solos here representative of his finest efforts. "Serenade to a Sarong" is a rather lame ballad, something of a half-hearted attempt at a progressive orchestration, with Sandy Williams on trombone not up to his best work and Carter's alto solo merely technically expert. Certainly Carter's orchestra was not a real class act, and it perhaps symbolizes the tired repertoire of so much swing music at the time, with only Basie and Ellington still offering top-notch work in this now largely enervating jazz mode.

One indication that Carter's leadership was not up to that of an Ellington or Basie is that the personnel changed drastically between May and the orchestra's recording session of October 23. Only Russell Smith, trombonist Milton Robinson, tenor saxophonist George James, pianist Sonny White, Hayes Alvis, and drummer William "Keg" Purnell remained from that earlier date, and none of these was a topflight soloist. Added to the group is The Mills Brothers, who sing on "By the Watermelon Vine" and "Lindy Lou," along with vocalist Roy Felton, for a treatment of pop material that only a Lunceford would have been able to convert into swinging jazz. Jonah Jones, who had joined on trumpet, saves this piece from being a total waste, as does tenorist Stafford Simon, another new member of the group. Another possible indication that Carter was merely coasting is that more of the material is made up of second-rate pop tunes rather than his own writing. On "Boogie Woogie Sugar Blues," Jones's trumpet and Sonny White's piano are obvious attempts to cash in on the boogie revival, with Simon's tenor solo a worthy contribution. Three of the four sides recorded on October 23 feature Roy Felton with unexceptional vocals so popular at the time. Little in the way of true jazz comes through on this or the November 19 session. Carter simply seems to be going through the motions instead of putting his heart and soul into the sides recorded at the end of 1940. A trombone theme statement on "All of Me" is purely imitative of Dorsey, the sax scoring is clearly influenced by Miller, and Carter's clarinet is almost embarrassingly a copy-cat version of Shaw. Chauncey Haughton, who seems to be the altoist on "Cocktails for Two," does a splendid job of stating the theme and embellishing it, which makes so many of Carter's own outings pale by comparison. The Classics CD that contains this side does not list Carter as playing alto on this session, but Morroe Berger writes that this is "a wonderful example of [Carter's] ability to never lose sight of the original melody even though his variation becomes increasingly ornate."[338] Albert McCarthy also credits Carter with this solo, writing that "Carter takes a quite stunning melodic alto solo with some fine melodic variations."[339] If this is indeed Carter, it is one of his finest solos from this or any other period of his career, far beyond anything he recorded in Europe, more substantial, more structured, and directed in its overall shape and execution.

The first side recorded in 1941 was Carter's "Cuddle Up, Huddle Up," and this session of January 21st is marked immediately by the superb drumming of J.C. Heard, who obviously stimulated the band to a burst of energy. "Babalu" also exhibits Heard's fine drumming, as well as an energized solo by trumpeter Sidney de Paris and a decent tenor solo, and to top it off a boogie piano break by Sonny White. But as Gunther Schuller observes, "the band's playing was now uneven at best, deteriorating at worst. . . . Carter and the band became increasingly ensnared in the prevailing swing formulas."[340] The group's April 1 session includes quality vocals by Maxine Sullivan and a swinging Carter original titled "My Favorite Blues," on which the leader takes a quite imaginative muted trumpet solo, Benny Morton adds a break that recalls his fine work with Fletcher Henderson, and Ernie Powell had returned to provide the band with a really rocking tenorist. Clearly the leader still had the ingredients for a successful band, he could write with the best of the swing composers, his solo talents remained intact and even seemed to be improving, and his sidemen were making solid contributions. Carter may have become more aware of the importance of having a variety of solos from his sidemen rather than focusing so much of the solo space on his own improvisations. But then a piece like his "Lullaby to a Dream" again spotlights him almost exclusively in a basically nonjazz trumpet feature.

The band's final recording session for 1941, on October 16, opens with a lively version of "Sunday," on which Carter delivers a more driving and daring alto solo than usual. The sax section writing is also more inventive than had been the case. "Ill Wind" finds Carter once again playing his alto in a ballad style influenced by the white bands, as are the figures for the reed section. Carter's "Back Bay Boogie" is of little interest as a tune, and even though Albert McCarthy praises the leader's alto break for its surprising drive and Gunther Schuller refers to Carter as charging into the solo "like a colt dashing out of a stall," it is only mildly interesting and is probably upstaged by William Lewis's electric guitar appearance that shows the swinging impact of Charlie Christian.[341] As Schuller implies, Carter's "Tree of Hope," which was rejected by Bluebird records, was ironically the end of the line for Carter's band.

Although the autumn of 1941 spelled the close of Carter's career as a bandleader, the multi-instrumentalist continued to make his talents available to other groups, doing arrangements for the Count Basie band and recording with the major players of his own and the next generation, such as Ben Webster, Budd Johnson, and Dizzy Gillespie. Referred to at times as a "Jazz Giant" and "The King," Carter may have been a claimant to such titles, but it was not as a bandleader nor perhaps as a soloist on any one instrument that he would have earned these epithets. Only as a composite musician who could play a number of different horns at a very high level of proficiency, a dependable contributing sideman, and a prolific composer-arranger can Carter be considered a major figure in jazz. None of his bands recorded a single side that could compete with the best or most popular productions of his peers in the 1930s. And although Carter has been regarded as one of the finest stylists among jazz alto saxophonists, he did not ascend to the heights achieved by Johnny Hodges of his own generation. By 1940, even Carter's virtuosity on the instrument had already been fully supplanted by the first recordings made with Charlie "Yardbird" Parker as a sideman. Parker not only surpassed every other altoist in jazz but equaled and some believe outstripped every soloist in the music's history. Above all, Parker brought to his instrument and jazz a vibrant swing and a musical imagination that contrasted completely with what critics such as Albert McCarthy and Gunther Schuller hear in Benny Carter's playing and compositions as "invariably somewhat detached and concerned more with producing shapely, poised solos than expressing emotion" and as maintaining a "disconcerting remoteness," as having about them "something mildly antiseptic."[342] Parker not only allows the listener into his thrilling solos but also draws him in both with a virtuosic handling of the alto and with deeply felt connections with the songs on which he based his ingenious improvisations.

JAY McSHANN

The last of the great Kansas City bandleaders, Jay McShann only arrived on the jazz scene at the tail end of the swing era's glory years, yet he and his band proved the very epitome of swing, summing up the best of the period's music and forecasting in many ways what was to come with the advent of bebop. McShann and his sidemen represented both a renewal of the Kansas City and Southwestern blues tradition and an expansion of the possibilities for improvisation through innovative interpretations of standard pop tunes that had become more and more the expected material of the successful swing units. Not only did the McShann orchestra transform the pop song into driving, inventive jazz but it also did so without gimmicks or enlarged forces (such as an added string section); instead, the McShann orchestra was rooted in the ability of a Kansas City big band such as Count Basie's to sound, as Buddy Tate put it, "like five pieces."[343] In a sense, the McShann orchestra recovered the true spirit of big-band jazz, even as it pointed the way for the bebop revolution, which also in a sense represented a return to the small-group, hot tradition of the music's formative 1920s decade.

Born in Muskogee, Oklahoma, on January 12, 1909, Jay McShann first developed as a boogie and blues pianist, and the repertoire of his big band, which he led beginning around 1937, always offered a diet heavy on that traditional southwestern fare. Touring the South and Midwest in the late 1930s, with a group made up primarily of Kansas City and Texas musicians, McShann and his band were recorded in Wichita, Kansas, on November 30, 1940, at a local radio station, KFBI. The fortunate preservation of the music of such an important band was made possible through the enthusiasm of Bud Gould, a staff musician at KFBI, who convinced the management to record McShann and his men in the station's studios. The results were historic for many reasons, but above all because the recording session caught Charlie Parker at the beginning of his formidable career.

In addition to Parker, the Wichita transcriptions captured the powerhouse playing of trumpeters Buddy Anderson and Orville Minor, the Herschel Evans–influenced tenorist Bob Mabane, and the solid rhythm section of McShann on piano, Gene Ramey on bass, and Gus Johnson on drums. From the very first tune, "I Found a New Baby," it is clear primarily that here is a totally new conception of the alto saxophone, even though, as Dan Morgenstern suggests, elements of Parker's "sound and phrasing definitely stem" from having listened to and worked with Buster "Prof" Smith, the clarinetist, alto saxophonist, and arranger who had been an important member of the Oklahoma Blue Devils and the Moten and early Basie bands. The first band in which Parker had played was in fact that of Buster Smith. Morgenstern also notes that Parker's solos on "Honeysuckle Rose" and "Oh! Lady Be Good" reveal the influence of Lester Young's "melodic and rhythmic freedom" and Coleman Hawkins's "drive and harmonic strength."[344] The speed and fluidity of Parker's playing still sound phenomenal after sixty years. Even on the slow "Body and Soul," Parker's magnificent ballad style is already evident, even though in this genre he will achieve a much higher level of artistry later in the decade. On "Coquette," Parker sings as Carter never could and works the chord changes on "Moten Swing" for all they're worth, developing musical phrases and ideas that had not been heard before. The other soloists on the session also create a series of highly imaginative, expressive solos that puts much of the work of Carter's sidemen in the shade, and certainly is superior to most of the solo work of the better-known white bands. Had the McShann orchestra recorded no more than the seven tunes from the Wichita transcriptions, these would have earned him and his men a place in the history of swing and of embryonic bebop.

The McShann orchestra also recorded on April 30, 1941, in Dallas, Texas. Only three sides of a Decca album—"Swingmatism," "Hootie Blues," and "Dexter Blues"—were devoted to the big band, with the other three sides given over to the rhythm section as a trio. Of the three big-band pieces, only two feature solos by Parker, and neither of the solos can compare with his work on the Wichita transcriptions. There is neither Parker's spirited drive nor his flowing musical ideas that characterize the 1940 session. On the other hand, the 1941 band as a whole exhibits a control that is not so present on the earlier transcriptions. It may be that Parker's performances were less inspired partly because he was not basing his impro-visations on pop tunes with more varied chord changes. The popular songs that predominated in the repertoire for the Wichita transcriptions gave way on the Dallas recording to an almost exclusively blues-based material. In the case of "Swingmatism," this rather more progressive piece of big-band arranging would appear to have been well suited to Parker's advanced con-ception, but in fact, as Gunther Schuller points out, the altoist "seems a little uncertain of his ideas, especially at the end of his solo . . . where he is stymied by the somewhat ambiguous and admittedly ill-advised dimin-ished chord."[345] Nonetheless, there are signs of the Parker to come in what Loren Schoenberg indicates is an effortless "striding across the bar lines with a degree of finesse previously heard only in the work of such masters as Benny Carter, Louis Armstrong, Earl Hines, Art Tatum, and Lester Young."[346]

McShann's piano is more prominent on the Dallas sides, beginning with his Basie-Hines-inspired opening to "Swingmatism." His playing is in many ways the principal focus of this recording session, which in hindsight is regrettable. As for the sidemen who solo, other than Parker, these tend not to generate the same intensity as they did in the Wichita studios. Only John Jackson, who takes the alto solo on "Dexter Blues," produces a notable improvisation, yet one wishes nonetheless that the break had been given to Parker. Orville Minor on trumpet offers some effective growl work, but it seems a bit out of place in the company of Parker, whose very open, direct approach—almost crystalline in its pure and penetrating sound—has intro-duced a modernity that dispenses to a large degree with earlier effects aimed at through artificially altering an instrument's tone and imitating human emotions on a more primitive level. Parker has moved away from swing's gimmickry and is attempting to communicate musical ideas of a sophisti-cated order. As a result of his emphasis on a greater seriousness in the production of sound and in the structuring of intellectually and aestheti-cally conscious solos, jazz would soon change forever. Although Armstrong had been the first jazz instrumentalist to construct solos that combined both solid swing and profound artistry in terms of note choice and placement and expressive phrasing, Parker carried these beyond anything heard be-fore, to a greater outflowing of musical ideas, to a seemingly inexhaustible rhythmic drive matched by a level of imagination that had perhaps been unthought of as possible in the field of jazz.

NOTES

1. Collier, *The Making of Jazz*, p. 158.
2. Dan Morgenstern, insert notes to *Louis Armstrong: The Complete RCA Victor Recordings* (RCA Victor 09026–6868–2, 1997), p. 16. Morgenstern espe-cially takes exception to Collier's charges of racism on the part of his manager Joe Glaser. Responding to Collier's view that the three-day RCA Victor recording ses-

sion in January 1933 was "evidence that [Armstrong] was being treated contemptuously by 'the white men who were overseeing his career,' " Morgenstern counters by saying that "in any case, racism had nothing to do with it," because "long recording sessions were nothing out of the ordinary. Touring was an essential element in the life of any working band, and thus the most was made of available time in cities with good studio facilities" (p. 22). Morgenstern adds that a Benny Goodman one-day session in 1935 produced fifty-one tunes "for which the sidemen were paid the kingly sum of one dollar per song." Morgenstern made the same point in his review of Collier's biography, *Louis Armstrong: An American Genius* (New York: Oxford University Press, 1983); the review is reprinted in *Reading Jazz: A Gathering of Autobiography, Reportage, and Criticism from 1919 to Now*, and the relevant passage appears on p. 1036.

   3. Schuller, *The Swing Era*, p. 170. This side is included on *Louis Armstrong: Mahogany Hall Stomp* (Living Era AJA 5049, 1987).

   4. "You're Lucky to Me" is included on *Louis Armstrong: Mahogany Hall Stomp* and "Chinatown, My Chinatown" is on *Louis Armstrong: Stardust*.

   5. Schuller, *The Swing Era*, p. 177.

   6. "Between the Devil and the Deep Blue Sea" and "Home" are both on *Louis Armstrong: Stardust*.

   7. According to Dan Morgenstern, the straight was the only type of mute that Armstrong utilized because this variety "least colors the open tone" (notes to *Louis Armstrong: The Complete RCA Victor Recordings*, p. 20).

   8. Schuller, *The Swing Era*, p. 186.

   9. Ibid.

   10. "Swing That Music" is included on a number of CDs, among them *Louis Armstrong and His Orchestra 1936–1937* (Classics 512, 1990) and *Louis Armstrong & His Orchestra: Heart Full of Rhythm, Vol. 2* (Decca, GRD-620, 1993).

   11. These sides are included on the CDs cited in footnote 10 above.

   12. "Mexican Swing" is included on *Louis Armstrong & His Orchestra, Vol. III: Pocketful of Dreams* (Decca GRD-649, 1995).

   13. Collier, *The Making of Jazz*, p. 156. "Hobo" is included on *Louis Armstrong: The Complete RCA Victor Recordings*.

   14. Morgenstern, *The Complete RCA Victor Recordings*, p. 20.

   15. Hart Crane, *The Complete Poems of Hart Crane* (New York: Doubleday, 1958), p. 17.

   16. Morgenstern, *The Complete RCA Victor Recordings*, p. 15.

   17. Ibid., p. 20. The four tunes recorded with the Webb orchestra are all on *The Complete RCA Victor Recordings*. The alternate take of "Hobo" finds Charlie Green's trombone just as hot, and his solo on the alternate take of "You'll Wish You'd Never Been Born" is also excellent.

   18. Quoted by Dan Morgenstern from a 1959 *Down Beat* interview, on p. 21 of *The Complete RCA Victor Recordings*.

   19. Avakian is quoted by George T. Simon in his liner notes to *A Rare Batch of Satch: The Authentic Sound of Louis Armstrong in the '30s* (RCA Victor Records, LPM-2322, 1961); Dan Morgenstern, "Louis Armstrong: An American Genius," in *Reading Jazz*, p. 1037.

   20. The sides discussed in this paragraph are included on *The Complete RCA Victor Recordings*.

21. This side is included on *Louis Armstrong & His Orchestra, Vol. III: Pocketful of Dreams*.

22. Both takes are available on *Pocketful of Dreams*.

23. Schuller, *The Swing Era*, p. 185.

24. These sides are included on *Louis Armstrong and His Orchestra 1936–1937*.

25. George Avakian, "Louis Armstrong," in *The Jazz Makers*, p. 50.

26. Schuller, *The Swing Era*, p. 189.

27. These and the other sides with the Dorsey orchestra are included on *Louis Armstrong and His Orchestra 1936–1937*.

28. "Hell's Bells" is on *Jimmie Lunceford: Jimmie's Legacy 1934–1937* (MCAC-1320, 1980); "Hi Spook" is on *Jimmie Lunceford: The Classic Tracks* (KAZ CD 317, 1996).

29. Schuller, *The Swing Era*, pp. 191–192.

30. Ibid., p. 192.

31. This side is included on *Louis Armstrong and His Orchestra 1936–1937*.

32. These recordings are included on *Louis Armstrong and His Orchestra 1936–1937*.

33. These sides are all included on *Louis Armstrong and His Orchestra 1936–1937*.

34. Schuller, *The Swing Era*, p. 193.

35. Ibid., pp. 192–193; Collier, *The Making of Jazz*, pp. 156–157. Both these tunes are included on *Louis Armstrong & His Orchestra: Heart Full of Rhythm, Vol. 2*.

36. Schuller, *The Swing Era*, p. 193; Richard Sudhalter, insert notes to *Heart Full of Rhythm*.

37. Schuller, *The Swing Era*, p. 193.

38. The 1927 version is included on *Louis Armstrong: The Greatest Hot Fives & Hot Sevens* (Living Era, AJA 5171, 1995).

39. Ibid., insert notes by Ray Crick.

40. Collier, *The Making of Jazz*, p. 157.

41. Harrison, *The Essential Jazz Records*, p. 341; Schuller, *The Swing Era*, p. 181.

42. Harrison, *The Essential Jazz Records*, p. 341.

43. Both the 1941 "It's Sleepy Time Down South" and the 1940 "Cain and Abel" are included on *Louis Armstrong and His Orchestra 1940–1942* (Classics 685, 1993).

44. Ibid.

45. Ibid.

46. Schuller, *The Swing Era*, p. 187.

47. McCarthy, *Big Band Jazz*, p. 84.

48. Ibid., p. 82; Schuller, *The Swing Era*, p. 187. This side is included on *Luis Russell and His Orchestra 1930–1934* (Classics, 606, 1991).

49. McCarthy, *Big Band Jazz*, p. 83. These two sides are included on *Luis Russell and His Orchestra 1930–1934* and on *The Luis Russell Collection, 1926–1934* (Collector's Classics, COCD-7, 1992).

50. Schuller, *The Swing Era*, p. 619.

51. McCarthy, *Big Band Jazz*, p. 82.

52. Hodeir, *Jazz: Its Evolution and Essence*, p. 75.

53. McCarthy, *Big Band Jazz*, p. 83. All four sides are included on *Luis Russell and His Orchestra 1930–1934* and on *The Luis Russell Collection, 1926–1934*.

54. Schuller, *The Swing Era*, p. 187.

55. Ibid.

56. Albert McCarthy has asserted that "Saratoga Shout" "must rate as one of the Russell band's greatest achievements" (*Big Band Jazz*, p. 82); James Lincoln Collier declares that the Russell Orchestra "can be heard at its best on 'Saratoga Shout,' based on the familiar chords of 'When the Saints Go Marching In,' and especially 'Panama,' a romping flag-waver with typically fine solos, particularly by Higginbotham and the little-known tenor saxophonist Greeley Walton" (*The Making of Jazz*, p. 187). Nonetheless, "Saratoga Shout" and "Panama" hark back more to the 1920s rather than looking forward to the mid and later '30s. The frantic nature of "Panama" is almost freakish. Another side that represents the later developments of the decade is "Muggin' Lightly," also from September 5, 1930. Here the sax section is given quite a workout, being featured throughout and demonstrating the great strides achieved by Russell's unit in terms of what would become a dominant role for the swing-era reeds. This side is available on *Luis Russell and His Orchestra 1930–1934*.

57. These sides are included on *Luis Russell and His Orchestra 1930–1934* and on *The Luis Russell Collection, 1926–1934*.

58. Schuller, *The Swing Era*, p. 188.

59. "You Rascal, You" is included on *Luis Russell and His Orchestra 1930–1934* and on *The Luis Russell Collection 1926–1934*.

60. Chilton, *The Song of the Hawk*, p. 74. The first take is available on *Fletcher Henderson: Tidal Wave* and takes two and three are on *Fletcher Henderson: The Crown King of Swing*.

61. Schuller, *The Swing Era*, pp. 187, 624. I would note that on "Saratoga Drag" Allen has already begun to harness his energy and to direct it more in the shaping of his solos.

62. McCarthy, *Big Band Jazz*, p. 84.

63. Ibid.

64. Schuller, *The Swing Era*, p. 188. These sides are included on *Luis Russell and His Orchestra 1930–1934* and on *The Luis Russell Collection 1926–1934*.

65. Ibid.

66. Ibid.

67. Loren Schoenberg, insert notes to *Spinnin' the Webb*.

68. Burt Korall, *Drummin' Men: The Heartbeat of Jazz* (New York: Schirmer Books, 1990), p. 2.

69. Ibid., p. 34; McCarthy, *Big Band Jazz*, p. 268.

70. Ibid., p. 24.

71. Ibid., p. 12.

72. Schuller, *The Swing Era*, p. 294.

73. "Heebie Jeebies" and "Darktown Strutters' Ball" are included on *Chick Webb and His Orchestra 1929–1934* (Classics 502, 1992), and "Heebie Jeebies" is also included on *Chick Webb: Spinnin' the Webb*.

74. McCarthy, *Big Band Jazz*, pp. 265–266. All these 1931 and 1933 recordings are included on Classics 502.

75. McCarthy, *Big Band Jazz*, p. 267.

76. Schuller, *The Swing Era*, p. 296. The sides mentioned in this paragraph are all on Classics 502.

77. McCarthy, *Big Band Jazz*, p. 228.

78. Schuller, *The Swing Era*, p. 296.

79. These sides are on Classics 502, and the September "Blue Minor" remake, "Lona," and "Blue Lou" are on *Spinnin' the Webb*. The Decca reproduction is superior to the Classics.

80. Andy Kirk, quoted in Korall, *Drummin' Men*, p. 19.

81. Eric Thacker, in *The Essential Jazz Records*, p. 306.

82. Korall, *Drummin' Men*, p. 32.

83. Schuller, *The Swing Era*. p. 297. The sides mentioned in this paragraph are included on *Spinnin' the Webb*.

84. "Love and Kisses" is not included on the Classics series of Webb recordings, which purportedly reproduce all of his sides from 1929 to 1938. Nor is it included on *Ella Fitzgerald with Chick Webb* (Swingsation GRD-9921, 1998).

85. Bill Grauer and Orrin Keepnews, notes to the Benny Goodman recording of "Sing Me a Swing Song" on *The RCA Victor Encyclopedia of Recorded Jazz*, Album 5.

86. "Sing Me a Swing Song" and "Vote for Mr. Rhythm" are on *Ella Fitzgerald with Chick Webb*, as are all the sides discussed here with Fitzgerald and Webb.

87. See especially Helen Oakley Dance in Korall, *Drummin' Men*, p. 23.

88. This illustration appears in Korall, *Drummin' Men*, p. 7.

89. Ibid., p. 23.

90. See Korall, *Drummin' Men*, pp. 31–32, for comments by drummer Alvin Stoller and trumpeter Joe Newman.

91. McCarthy, *Big Band Jazz*, p. 268.

92. Schuller, *The Swing Era*, p. 300.

93. Beverly Peer and Artie Shaw, quoted in Korall, *Drummin' Men*, pp. 30 and 18. These three sides are all included on *Spinnin' the Webb*.

94. Quoted in Stanley Dance, *The World of Earl Hines* (New York: Scribner, 1977; rpt. Da Capo, 1983), p. 184.

95. Collier, *The Making of Jazz*, p. 212.

96. John S. Wilson, "Earl Hines," in *The Jazz Makers*, p. 80.

97. Norman Field, insert notes to *Hot Jazz: New York and Chicago, 1928–1930* (Nimbus Records, HRM 6004, 1987).

98. McCarthy, *Big Band Jazz*, p. 238; Stanley Dance, liner notes to *Earl Hines: The Grand Terrace Band* (RCA Victor, LPV-512, 1965). *Sweet Ella May* is available on *Hot Jazz: New York and Chicago, 1928–1930*.

99. Schuller, *The Swing Era*, pp. 273–274.

100. McCarthy, *Big Band Jazz*, p. 238.

101. Quoted on liner notes to *Earl Hines: The Grand Terrace Band*.

102. The Hines sides between 1932 and 1937 are included on *Earl Hines and His Orchestra 1932–1934* (Classics 514, 1990) or *Earl Hines and His Orchestra 1934–1937* (Classics 528, 1990).

103. Schuller, *The Swing Era*, p. 275.

104. Ibid.

105. Ibid., p. 274.

106. Williams, liner notes to *Count Basie in Kansas City: Bennie Moten's Great Band of 1930–1932*.

107. McCarthy, *Big Band Jazz*, p. 238. It seems fairly certain that McCarthy confused the 1933 with the 1934 recording, because the latter does have an Armstrong-influenced vocal by Walter Fuller. However, on the 1933 version, Simeon does, as McCarthy indicates, solo on both baritone and alto—opening the piece with the theme statement on baritone. Gunther Schuller reports that there were four takes of "Rosetta" recorded by Columbia, with Darnell Howard on alto taking "a full chorus . . . abounding with elegant turns and lithe, florid lines" (*The Swing Era*, p. 276), which sounds like the Simeon alto solo identified by McCarthy as recorded by Brunswick in 1933. McCarthy identifies Howard as soloing on clarinet rather than on alto. It would appear that what Schuller heard is not the same as the Classics reissue sides of the Brunswick date, which McCarthy obviously had in mind.

108. Schuller, *The Swing Era*, p. 276.

109. Stanley Dance, liner notes to *Hines Rhythm* (Epic Records, 22021).

110. Wilson, "Earl Hines," *The Jazz Makers*, p. 81.

111. Dance, *The World of Earl Hines*, p. 72.

112. Ibid.

113. Schuller, *The Swing Era*, p. 279.

114. Dance, liner notes to *Hines Rhythm*.

115. Schuller, *The Swing Era*, pp. 279–280.

116. Ibid., p. 276.

117. Ibid., p. 280.

118. "Julia" and "Darkness" are on Classics 514 and "Stratosphere" is on *Jimmie's Legacy 1934–1937*.

119. Schuller, *The Swing Era*, p. 238n.

120. Ibid., p. 277.

121. Dance, *The World of Earl Hines*, pp. 189–190.

122. McCarthy, *Big Band Jazz*, p. 238.

123. Schuller, *The Swing Era*, p. 280.

124. Ibid.

125. Ray Spencer, liner notes to *Earl Hines and His Orchestra: Bubbling Over* (Official 3044, 1989).

126. The Classics CD lists only three saxes, but the sound is too full for that, and the Official album's listing of Jimmy Mundy on tenor as the fourth voice makes more sense.

127. Quoted in Schuller, *The Swing Era*, p. 284.

128. McCarthy, *Big Band Jazz*, p. 238.

129. Ibid., p. 239.

130. Schuller, *The Swing Era*, p. 285.

131. Ibid.

132. Dance, liner notes to *Hines Rhythm*.

133. Schuller, *The Swing Era*, p. 285.

134. McCarthy, *Big Band Jazz*, p. 239.

135. These two 1938 sides are on *Hines Rhythm*.

136. Dance, liner notes to *The Grand Terrace Band: Earl Hines*.

137. Stanley Dance, insert notes to *Earl Hines—Piano Man: Earl Hines, His*

Piano and His Orchestra (RCA Victor Bluebird 6750–2-RB, 1989). "'Gator Swing" is included on *The Grand Terrace Band: Earl Hines.*

138. "XYZ" is included on *The Grand Terrace Band: Earl Hines*; the other 1939 cuts are on *Earl Hines—Piano Man.*

139. Dance, liner notes to *The Grand Terrace Band: Earl Hines.*

140. Schuller, *The Swing Era*, p. 289.

141. McCarthy, *Big Band Jazz*, p. 211; Charles Edward Smith, liner notes to *Cab Calloway* (Epic LN 3265, n.d.).

142. Schuller, *The Swing Era,* p. 330.

143. Ibid., p. 332.

144. McCarthy, *Big Band Jazz*, p. 210.

145. Schuller, *The Swing Era*, p. 329.

146. Frank Driggs, liner notes to *The Most Important Recordings of Cab Calloway* (Official 3041–2, 1989).

147. McCarthy, *Big Band Jazz*, p. 211; Frank Driggs, liner notes to *The Most Important Recordings of Cab Calloway.* The recordings from 1930–1932 are included on *Cab Calloway and His Orchestra 1930–1931* (Classics, 516, 1990) and *Cab Calloway and His Orchestra 1931–1932* (Classics, 526, 1990).

148. McCarthy, *Big Band Jazz*, p. 211.

149. Ibid.; Schuller, *The Swing Era*, pp. 332, 334, and 336.

150. Ibid., p. 333n.

151. Ibid.

152. Ibid., p. 332.

153. Ibid., p. 331.

154. Ibid., p. 335.

155. McCarthy, *Big Band Jazz*, p. 211; Schuller *The Swing Era*, p. 331.

156. Schuller, *The Swing Era*, p. 337.

157. Ibid., pp. 339 and 331.

158. Ibid., p. 622.

159. Anatol Schenker, insert notes to *Cab Calloway and His Orchestra 1932* (Classics, 537, 1990).

160. Schuller, *The Swing Era*, p. 337.

161. Ibid., p. 331; McCarthy, *Big Band Jazz*, p. 211.

162. Schuller, *The Swing Era*, p. 332.

163. The recordings discussed here from 1932–1934 are included on *Cab Calloway and His Orchestra 1932–1934* (Classics 544, 1990).

164. Schuller, *The Swing Era*, p. 639.

165. Ibid., p. 340.

166. Ibid., pp. 333 and 331.

167. McCarthy, *Big Band Jazz*, p. 211.

168. Schuller, *The Swing Era*, pp. 342–343.

169. McCarthy, *Big Band Jazz*, p. 211.

170. Schuller, *The Swing Era*, p. 344.

171. Stowe, *Swing Changes*, p. 33.

172. Schuller, *The Swing Era*, p. 337.

173. "Weakness" and the tunes discussed here from 1935–1937 are on *Cab Calloway and His Orchestra 1934–1937* (Classics, 554, 1990).

174. Schuller, *The Swing Era*, p. 334.

175. Driggs, liner notes to *The Most Important Recordings of Cab Calloway*.

176. McCarthy, *Big Band Jazz*, p. 212.

177. Schuller, *The Swing Era*, p. 580.

178. Peter McSloy (pseudonym of Pete Townsend), *For Jazz: 21 Sonnets* (Lafayette, CA: hit & run press, 1995), p. 15.

179. McCarthy, *Big Band Jazz*, p. 212.

180. Beginning with "Swing, Swing, Swing" of March 3, 1937, and ending with "Azure" from March 23, 1938, the sides discussed for this period are on *Cab Calloway and His Orchestra 1937–1938* (Classics, 568, 1991).

181. The discography for Classics 568 lists Webster as the tenor for the sessions of December 10, 1937, and the January 26 and March 23, 1938, which is clearly in error, because both Brian Rust and Albert McCarthy identify Chu Berry as the tenor for these three dates and Calloway himself, on "I Like Music (With a Swing Like That)," can be heard to call upon Berry by name to solo.

182. Sudhalter, insert notes to *Heart Full of Rhythm*, p. 10.

183. McCarthy, *Big Band Jazz*, p. 212.

184. Leonard Feather, *The New Edition of The Encyclopedia of Jazz* (New York: Bonanza Books, 1960), pp. 135 and 457.

185. Schuller, *The Swing Era*, p. 348.

186. Ibid.

187. Ibid.

188. McCarthy, *Big Band Jazz*, p. 212.

189. See Williams, liner notes to *King Oliver in New York*.

190. McCarthy, *Big Band Jazz*, p. 213.

191. Ibid.

192. Schuller, *The Swing Era*, p. 344. On *The Most Important Recordings of Cab Calloway*, "Ratamacue" of February 20, 1939, is listed as being on this album, but the corresponding band (number 1, side 4) has "A Smooth One" from March 11, 1941, which is not one of the titles printed on either the liner or the disc itself. "Ratamacue" is included on Classics 576.

193. Korall, *Drummin' Men*, p. 316; Schuller, *The Swing Era*, p. 344.

194. Schuller, *The Swing Era*, p. 345.

195. "Cupid's Nightmare," in an expanded rendition, is included on *Cruisin' with Cab* (Alamac QSR 2407, n.d.), which derives from a radio transcription of a broadcast from the "Meadowbrook" in Cedar Grove, New Jersey. The shorter version is from August 28, 1940, and is on Classics 614.

196. McCarthy, *Big Band Jazz*, p. 214.

197. Schuller, *The Swing Era*, p. 346.

198. "Limehouse Blues" and "King Porter Stomp" are included on *Cruisin' with Cab*.

199. Schuller, *The Swing Era*, p. 349.

200. "Boog It," as included on Classics 614, is not the same performance as the one on *Cruisin' with Cab*, for only the latter has Chu Berry playing a "honk" in his solo.

201. For more on George Morrison, see Schuller, *Early Jazz*, Appendix, pp. 359–372.

202. Andy Kirk, as told to Amy Lee, *Twenty Years on Wheels* (Ann Arbor: University of Michigan Press, 1989), p. 25.

203. Ibid., pp. 24–25, 50.

204. Anatol Schenker, insert notes to *Andy Kirk and His Twelve Clouds of Joy 1929–1931* (Classics, 655, 1992).

205. Kirk, *Twenty Years on Wheels*, pp. 55 and 57.

206. Ibid., pp. 46–47.

207. Ibid., pp. 61–62.

208. Charles Fox, liner notes to *Andy Kirk & His 12 Clouds of Joy: March 1936* (Mainstream Records MRL 399, n.d.).

209. Kirk, *Twenty Years on Wheels*, p. 71.

210. McCarthy, *Big Band Jazz*, p. 243.

211. Ibid., p. 242.

212. Ibid., p. 243.

213. Ibid.

214. Kirk, *Twenty Years on Wheels*, p. 71.

215. Ibid., p. 66.

216. Schenker, insert notes to *Andy Kirk and His Twelve Clouds of Joy 1936–1937* (Classics, 573, 1991).

217. McCarthy, *Big Band Jazz*, p. 244.

218. Schuller, *The Swing Era*, p. 353.

219. Fox, liner notes to *Andy Kirk & His 12 Clouds of Joy: March 1936*.

220. Schuller, *The Swing Era*, p. 354.

221. Ibid.

222. Ibid.

223. McCarthy, *Big Band Jazz*, p. 245.

224. Schuller, *The Swing Era*, p. 354. Schuller writes that "it is not unreasonable to imagine [Wilson] having a significant impact on the next generation of saxophonists had he, like Prez, lived longer and been presented in as favorable a setting as the Basie band."

225. Ibid., p. 359.

226. Ibid., p. 354.

227. Fox, *The Essential Jazz Records*, p. 295.

228. Anatole Schenker, insert notes to *Andy Kirk and His Twelve Clouds of Joy: 1938* (Classics, 598, 1991).

229. McCarthy, *Big Band Jazz*, p. 245.

230. Anatole Schenker, insert notes to *Andy Kirk and His Twelve Clouds of Joy 1937–1938* (Classics, 581, 1991).

231. Schuller, *The Swing Era*, p. 360.

232. McCarthy, *Big Band Jazz*, p. 246.

233. Mary Lou Williams, autobiographical account, in *Reading Jazz*, p. 108.

234. Ibid., p. 115.

235. Orrin Keepnews, "A Bad Idea, Poorly Executed," in *Reading Jazz*, p. 1053.

236. Stanley Crouch, "Jazz Criticism and Its Effect on the Art Form," in *New Perspectives on Jazz*, ed. David N. Baker (Washington, D.C.: Smithsonian Institution Press, 1990), p. 81.

237. McCarthy, *Big Band Jazz*, p. 245.

238. Anatol Schenker, insert notes to *Andy Kirk and His Twelve Clouds of Joy 1939–1940* (Classics, 640, 1992).

239. Schuller, *The Swing Era*, p. 356; Fox, *The Essential Jazz Records*, p. 294.

240. Fox, *The Essential Jazz Records*, p. 169.

241. Ibid., p. 295.

242. Schuller, *The Swing Era*, p. 651.

243. Ibid., p. 358.

244. Ibid., p. 354.

245. The Calloway version of "Fifteen Minute Intermission" is included on Classics 614.

246. McCarthy, *Big Band Jazz*, p. 246.

247. Dance, liner notes to *The Ellington Era 1927–1940*.

248. Rex Harris, liner notes to *Andy Kirk: Twelve Clouds of Joy* (Ace of Hearts, AH 160, 1967).

249. For more on this side, see my *Texan Jazz*, pp. 33–34.

250. Schuller, *The Swing Era*, p. 360.

251. Ibid. and footnote 27.

252. Harris, liner notes to *Andy Kirk: Twelve Clouds of Joy*.

253. Fox, *The Essential Jazz Records*, p. 295; McCarthy, *Big Band Jazz*, p. 246.

254. McCarthy, *Big Band Jazz*, p. 172.

255. Schuller, *The Swing Era*, pp. 397, 396, and 394.

256. Ibid., p. 395.

257. Ibid., pp. 394 and 397.

258. Ibid., p. 394.

259. Ibid., p. 396. All sides from 1937 and 1938 mentioned here are included on *The Complete Lionel Hampton Vol. 1/2 (1937–1938)* (RCA 66500–2 B, Jazz Tribune No. 61, 1993).

260. Schuller, *The Swing Era*, p. 396.

261. Chilton, *The Song of the Hawk*, p. 159.

262. Morroe Berger, Edward Berger, and James Patrick, *Benny Carter: A Life in American Music* (Metuchen, N.J.: Scarecrow Press and the Institute of Jazz Studies, Rutgers University, 1982), p. 97.

263. Chilton, *The Song of the Hawk*, p. 159.

264. Ibid., p. 160.

265. Schuller, *The Swing Era*, p. 394.

266. Chilton, *The Song of the Hawk*, p. 160.

267. Ibid.

268. The 1939 sides discussed thus far are all included on *Lionel Hampton: Hot Mallets, Vol. 1* (RCA Victor Bluebird 6458-2-RB. 1987). Like Chilton in *The Song of the Hawk*, Leonard Feather in his insert notes to this CD identifies Ben Webster as the tenor soloist on "Early Session Hop."

269. Schuller, *The Swing Era*, pp. 394 and 395.

270. Neil Tesser, insert notes to *Lionel Hampton: Tempo and Swing, The All-Star Groups. Volume 3 (1939–40)* (RCA Victor Bluebird 66039-2, 1992).

271. Chilton, *The Song of the Hawk*, p. 167.

272. Schuller, *The Swing Era*, p. 394.

273. Ibid., p. 510.

274. Ibid., p. 395. The tracks from December 19 and 20, as well as the other Hampton sides discussed here, are included on *Lionel Hampton and His Orchestra 1940–1941* (Classics, 624, 1992).

275. Schuller, *The Swing Era*, p. 399.

276. McCarthy, *Big Band Jazz*, p. 233.

277. Schuller, *The Swing Era*, p. 405.

278. McCarthy, *Big Band Jazz*, p. 234.

279. Anatol Schenker, insert notes to *Erskine Hawkins and His Orchestra 1938–1939* (Classics, 667, 1992).

280. Clora Bryant, a trumpet player born in Denison, Texas, in 1927, reports that when she went to college at Prairie View A & M near Houston that she created her own solos "except on some songs they expected to hear the same solo that was on the record, the solo on Erskine Hawkins's 'Tuxedo Junction.' " See *Central Avenue Sounds: Jazz in Los Angeles* (Berkeley, California: University of California Press, 1998), p. 345.

281. McCarthy, *Big Band Jazz*, p. 233; Schuller, *The Swing Era*, pp. 407–408.

282. Schuller, *The Swing Era*, p. 408 n10.

283. McCarthy, *Big Band Jazz*, p. 234.

284. Ibid.; Schuller, *The Swing Era*, p. 407.

285. Schuller, *The Swing Era*, p. 408.

286. McCarthy, *Big Band Jazz*, p. 234.

287. Schuller, *The Swing Era*, p. 407.

288. Ibid., p. 408.

289. Ibid., p. 409.

290. Ibid., p. 407.

291. Ibid.

292. *Erskine Hawkins and His Orchestra 1940–1941* (Classics, 701, 1993).

293. Schuller, *The Swing Era*, pp. 407–409; McCarthy, *Big Band Jazz*, p. 235.

294. Schuller, *The Swing Era*, pp. 405 and 407.

295. Ibid., p. 408 n.10; McCarthy, *Big Band Jazz*, p. 235.

296. Schuller, *The Swing Era*, p. 799 and 799 n25.

297. Driggs, "Kansas City and the Southwest," in *Jazz: New Perspectives on the History of Jazz by Twelve of the World's Foremost Jazz Critics and Scholars*, p. 216; McCarthy, *Big Band Jazz*, p. 109.

298. Schuller, *The Swing Era*, pp. 799–800. In *Jazz Style in Kansas City and the Southwest* (Berkeley, Calif.: University of California Press, 1973), Ross Russell judges the soloists in the Douglas band as "not of the first quality" (p. 58), but both McCarthy and Schuller credit two of the soloists (tenorist Baker Millian and trumpeter Charles Anderson) with making contributions of "a high order" (McCarthy, *Big Band Jazz*, p. 109) and with being "remarkably advanced" (Schuller, p. 801).

299. Russell, *Jazz Style in Kansas City and the Southwest*, p. 58.

300. Schuller, *The Swing Era*, p. 799.

301. Arnold Schenker, insert notes to *Boots and His Buddies 1935–1937* (Classics, 723, 1993).

302. Rushing's performance of "How Long Blues" is on *The Essential Count Basie, Volume 1* (Coumbia CJ40608, 1987).

303. The personnel of the Douglas band as given by Albert McCarthy in his *Big Band Jazz* and on an album entitled *San Antonio Jazz* (International Association of Jazz Record Collectors, LP No. 3, n.d.) includes Charles Anderson on trumpet beginning with the first Douglas recording session of August 15, 1935. The Classics CD number 723 lists the trumpet section as including L.D. Harris instead of Charles

Anderson, whereas the IAJRC album lists L.D. Harris as only appearing on the session of September 17, 1937, which is when the Classics CD has Anderson joining the Douglas band. Gunther Schuller in *The Swing Era* follows McCarthy and the IAJRC in crediting to Anderson most of the trumpet solos beginning in 1935.

The eight recordings made in 1936 by another San Antonio band, that of Don Albert, are included on the same IAJRC album along with eight tunes by the Douglas band. McCarthy indicates that Albert's band was "the first to use the word 'swing' in its title," billing itself as "Don Albert and His Music, America's Greatest Swing Band" (McCarthy, *Big Band Jazz*, p. 107).

304. McCarthy, *Big Band Jazz*, p. 109.

305. Schuller, *The Swing Era*, p. 801.

306. Ibid., p. 800.

307. Jones, *Blues People*, pp. 164–165 and 221.

308. Schuller, *The Swing Era*, p. 801.

309. Ibid.

310. Russell, *Jazz Style in Kansas City and the Southwest*, p. 58.

311. There appear to be two versions of the Waller tune recorded by the Boots band, one of which is included on *San Antonio Jazz* and the other on *Boots and His Buddies 1935–1937* (Classics, 723, 1993). Brooks's solo on the Classics recording of "Ain't Misbehavin' " differs from and is superior to the one on *San Antonio Jazz*.

312. Schuller, *The Swing Era*, p. 799.

313. Ibid., p. 800 n26. As noted above, it does appear that there are two existing versions of "Ain't Misbehavin'," which would suggest that alternate takes were recorded.

314. Ibid., p. 799.

315. Ibid., p. 800.

316. Arthur Jackson, insert notes to *Hot Lips Page 1938–1940* (Official 83 047, 1989).

317. Nat Shapiro, "Benny Goodman," in *The Jazz Makers*, p. 183.

318. Jackson, insert notes to *Hot Lips Page 1938–1940*.

319. Chilton, *The Song of the Hawk*, p. 179.

320. Ibid., p. 181.

321. Ibid., p. 184.

322. McCarthy, *Big Band Jazz*, p. 215.

323. Berger, *Benny Carter: A Life in American Music*, pp. 109–110.

324. Ibid., p. 113.

325. Chilton, *The Song of the Hawk*, p. 80.

326. Ibid., p. 82.

327. Ibid.

328. Ibid., p. 83.

329. Berger, *Benny Carter: A Life in American Music*, p. 116.

330. McCarthy, *Big Band Jazz*, p. 215.

331. Ibid.

332. Schuller, *The Swing Era*, p. 379.

333. Ibid., p. 380.

334. Ibid., p. 378.

335. Ibid.

336. Berger, *Benny Carter: A Life in American Music*, p. 189. The air checks are available on *Benny Carter and His Orchestra: Live Broadcasts 1939 / 1948* (Jazz Hour JH-1005, 1990).

337. Schuller, *The Swing Era*, p. 379.

338. Berger, *Benny Carter: A Life in American Music*, p. 97.

339. McCarthy, *Big Band Jazz*, p. 216.

340. Schuller, *The Swing Era*, p. 383.

341. McCarthy, *Big Band Jazz*, p. 216; Schuller, *The Swing Era*, p. 383.

342. McCarthy, *Big Band Jazz*, p. 216; Schuller, *The Swing Era*, p. 381.

343. Quoted in John Chilton, *The Song of the Hawk*, p. 171.

344. Dan Morgenstern, insert notes to *Early Bird: Charlie Parker with Jay McShann and His Orchestra* (Stash Records, ST-CD-542, 1991).

345. Schuller, *The Swing Era*, p. 795.

346. Loren Schoenberg, insert notes to *Blues From Kansas City: Jay McShann Orchestra Featuring Charlie Parker & Walter Brown* (Decca, GRD-614, 1992).

Duke Ellington (Library of Congess).

Benny Goodman and Gene Krupa in 1938 (Library of Congress).

Glenn Miller (Library of Congress).

Louis Armstong, 1937 (Library of Congress).

Glenn Miller (Library of Congress).

Louis Armstong, 1937 (Library of Congress).

Cab Calloway, 1933 (Library of Congress).

Benny Carter (The Benny Carter Colletion).

Gene Krupa (Library of Congress).

Coleman Hawkins performs with the Coleman Hawkins Quartet, 1965 (Library of Congress).

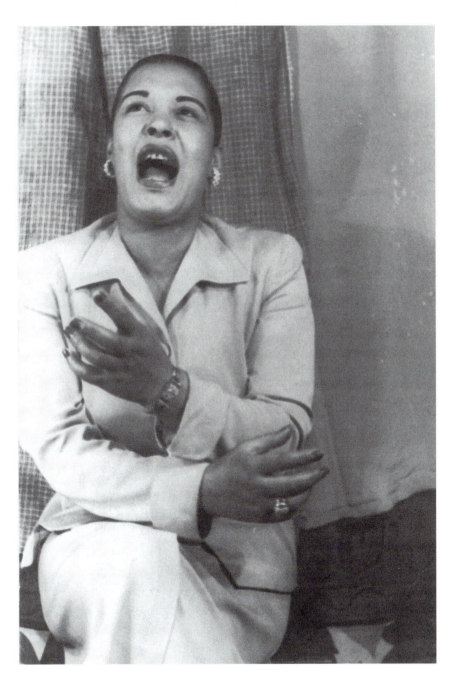

Billie Holiday, 1949 (Library of Congress).

Lester Young, 1956 (Library of Congress).

Fats Waller, 1938 (Library of Congress).

Chapter 5

Other White Bands

As noted at the beginning of Chapter 3, the Paul Whiteman Orchestra and the Casa Loma Orchestra were two of the early successful white big bands that led the way for the white name bands of the 1930s. It also was pointed out that many of the white musicians who achieved fame and relative fortune had their starts with the Whiteman organization. Not only this, but both the Whiteman and Casa Loma orchestras influenced in some ways the name black bands, even though this may be considered to some extent regrettable. Despite the segregation enforced on musicians, there was nothing that kept them from listening to and often admiring and learning from one another. Indeed, in terms of repertoire, it seems clear that the early white bands introduced a number of tunes that eventually became jazz classics as played both by the black and the white name bands, and in this regard the white bands' influence was important in suggesting the possibilities for innovative swing arrangements and in some ways for the advancement of the art of improvisation. Although the early white bands did not contribute so significantly in the area of improvisation as did the black bands, there were exceptions, beginning, as we have seen, with Bix Beiderbecke, and, as we shall see, continuing with such figures as Bunny Berigan and Jack Teagarden, who would themselves become leaders of two of the second tier of white bands just below those of Goodman, the Dorsey brothers, Shaw, and Miller. Often, when white sidemen were able to record in smaller groups, and their improvisational skills were allowed greater latitude, they proved fully capable of achieving high levels of technical virtuosity and artistic expression. As we have seen in the case of arranger Bill Challis of the Jean Goldkette organization, white arrangers also impressed their black counterparts and influenced their choice and handling of music materials. Although the white bands may not have had so profound an effect on swing jazz as the black bands, the former certainly had an impact on the directions the music took and its development as a genre, as well as its widespread acceptance by dancers and listeners of the swing age.

PAUL WHITEMAN

The first fact to be recalled about Paul Whiteman is that, as noted in Chapter 4, the future bandleader was the son of Wilberforce Whiteman, a music teacher in Denver, Colorado, where Paul was born on March 28, 1890. Wilberforce Whiteman not only taught his son, but also, as Paul reports in his 1926 autobiography, *Jazz*, his father also was the teacher of a number of musicians who would belong to the son's famous "Concert Orchestra."[1] In addition, as also noted in Chapter 4, Whiteman Senior taught two important black band leaders, Jimmie Lunceford and Andy Kirk. Although neither Whiteman father nor son was a jazz musician himself, the impact of each on the history of jazz is undeniable, and especially in the case of the latter, even though in a sense, as Albert McCarthy asserts, "it would be true to say that [Paul] Whiteman never made a real jazz record in the whole length of his band-leading career...."[2] If Paul Whiteman was not himself a jazz musician, he nonetheless was the first major white figure to consider jazz a fledgling art form. Through his popular concert orchestra, Whiteman attempted to interest prominent classical composers and musicians in jazz as an American music that he considered to be as serious as classical music and equal if not superior in its technical demands. In this regard Whiteman succeeded in enlisting in his and jazz's cause the likes of Leopold Stokowski, Fritz Kreisler, and, perhaps indirectly if not directly, Darius Milhaud and Igor Stravinsky. Whiteman himself claimed that only after his orchestra had performed George Gershwin's "Rhapsody in Blue" in 1925 did music critics begin to take seriously this jazz-inspired composer. Although Whiteman has been lambasted rather mercilessly for the photograph in his autobiography that shows him being crowned "The King of Jazz" and for his feature role in the 1930 film of the same title, his book remains a delightfully readable account of his first years as a bandleader and touches on many of the basic issues relating to jazz, including its origins, its development, and its impact on listeners worldwide. As Albert McCarthy also observes, Paul Whiteman's orchestra, although not of significance as a jazz unit in itself, influenced some of the most "irreproachable jazz groups" in the music's history, including those of Fletcher Henderson and Earl Hines, a fact that "most jazz followers are not anxious to admit."[3]

The problem with Whiteman's version of jazz is that it he based it primarily on his view that the music required composers and arrangers who could give it symphonic form. Writing in the mid-1920s, Whiteman felt that only through the efforts of composers and arrangers had the music been able to advance "from the day of discordant early jazz to the melodious form of the present."[4] Whiteman in no way claimed that he had invented jazz but only that he had orchestrated it, and by doing so had "put jazz on a real musical footing."[5] Although in one section in his book Whiteman credits jazz with having originated in New Orleans "along the water front among natural Negro musicians," he also contrasts those be-ginnings with "the soft jazz rhythms" created by his orchestra, which, he says, represent "great progress from the crudities of ten years ago."[6] De-spite this misconception, Whiteman did seem to recognize that the creation of jazz is not merely a matter of orchestration or of being written out for well-trained musicians. For he does speak of "the indefinable thing . . . that spontaneous jazzing . . . that will make the music talk jazz as a native tongue."[7] Unfortunately, Whiteman was not actually fluent in the jazz lan-guage and probably for this reason did not emphasize in his form of concert music the improvisational or spontaneous aspect of jazz. As a result, his performances tend to amount to no more than pastiche, a smattering of popular, classical, and novelty strains with an incidental bow now and then to jazz by way of a hot chorus from a jazzman of the caliber of Bix Bei-derbecke or Jack Teagarden.

In describing how one orchestration was developed, a piece titled "Oh, Katharina," scored for the Whiteman orchestra by Frank Barry, the leader points out that the composition is marked by a "German atmosphere," because it combines "In Tiefen Keller" (a German drinking song), "Sol-dier's Farewell" (a German folk song), "Oh Tannenbaum," and "Ach Du Lieber Augustine," with—before and after—"some counterpoint with a German tune," "a half chorus in jazz," and "a half chorus of hot jazz."[8] More often—and this is true from the first recordings by Whiteman in 1920—there is not even a four-bar burst of spontaneous jazz in White-man's offerings. An example would be the very popular "The Japanese Sandman" from August 19, 1920, which the leader returned to in 1932 when he included it in one of his typical medley performances.[9] Neither recording contains a jazz feeling or an ad lib solo but simply plays the theme with a rhythmic pulse that was patterned after that of the Original Dixieland Jazz Band. Nor is there any real difference between the 1920 and 1932 versions, except that the latter is at times more staccato and at other times—in keeping with the new swing trend—smoother.

The popularity of the Whiteman formula for "jazz," along with the fact that he had proven that jazz was marketable on an economic level unheard of before, made him the envy of many an orchestra leader. Not only this, but as Richard Sudhalter has pointed out, Whiteman attracted even a gen-uine jazz musician like Bix Beiderbecke, and this was owing largely to the classical, more complex aspects of some of the Whiteman scores. Sudhalter suggests that as Beiderbecke was developing in his solos a "deepening of thought and content . . . the Whiteman Orchestra, even in its overcooked 'symphonic jazz' efforts, somehow seems the most fertile environment [Bei-derbecke] could have asked for in his quest to explore these depths."[10] One wonders what Whiteman would have made of Beiderbecke and his role in the leader's scheme of things had Whiteman written his autobiography after the cornetist's death or during the time that he was an active member of the Whiteman organization. As it is, of course, Beiderbecke, having joined Whiteman after 1926, is not mentioned in *Jazz*, but then neither is any other jazz or even quasi-jazz soloist. What Whiteman does discuss on many occasions is his conception of the relationship between jazz and classical music, and in doing so he indicates not only his own leanings as a band leader but also accounts perhaps for his influence on another white leader such as Tommy Dorsey and even a black leader like Jimmie Lunceford.

Significantly, Whiteman believed that jazz could be based on any type of music, which would seem to anticipate the wide-ranging repertoire of the swing-era bands. In seeking to make the point that jazz could legitimately draw on the classical tradition to "improve" itself as an art form, Whiteman reveals that beneath a number of popular songs lies the "pilfered music" of the classical masters.[11] The leader advocates the use of classical music as a source for "jazzing," just as classical music had early on depended on folk music for its own artistic development. But a single example of Whiteman "pilfering" the classics is his version of "Song of India," recorded on April 25, 1929, and subsequently recorded by Tommy Dorsey and his orchestra on January 29, 1937.[12] A melody from the Russian composer Rimsky-Korsakov, "Song of India" was arranged for Whiteman by Ferde Grofé, composer of the often performed *Grand Canyon Suite* and orchestrator of George Gershwin's "Rhapsody in Blue." The Whiteman version of "Song of India" has no real connection with jazz or big-band music as such but opens rather with a symphonic sound; however, this is quickly modified by the tuba playing on the down beat and the banjo on the up beat, lending something of a rocking rhythm to the woodwinds' theme statement, which is either punctuated by the brass or sweetened by the strings. Again, there is no jazz connection to speak of, because the side contains no improvised solo nor any attempt at a call-and-response pattern between brass and reed sections. The Dorsey rendition of the same melody, arranged by Carmen Mastren and Red Bone, with suggestions from Bud Freeman and under the direction of the leader, differs very little from the Whiteman version in the sense that it opens with a treatment uncharacteristic of jazz but one more in the semiclassical vein, although the drummer sets something of a swing rhythm for the soft woodwinds that enter and are then "answered" by a typical big-band burst from the brasses. Once Dorsey on muted trombone states the theme—backed by a "riff" that is basically the same as that used for "Who?" which was recorded by Dorsey on October 14, 1937, where the leader also plays the theme on his muted trombone—the sound and feeling of this version of "Song of India" is very close to that of Whiteman: an essentially straight statement of the melody, simply reproducing Rimsky-Korsakov's classical theme. The one major difference is found in the break played by Bunny Berigan. As Gunther Schuller has noted, were it not for Berigan's improvised solo, the Dorsey version of "Song of India" would not lie "well within the jazz arena" but would be merely a "more or less successful well-performed commercial recording" along the lines of the Whiteman.[13]

Tommy Dorsey had worked for Whiteman during the 1920s, appearing, for example, ten years earlier on the Whiteman recording of "Whiteman Stomp," from August 11, 1927, a Fats Waller tune arranged on commission from Whiteman by none other than Don Redman.[14] This particular piece illustrates much about the impact of Whiteman, both on white and black jazz musicians of the 1920s and '30s. The classical leanings of Whiteman are evident in Redman's arrangement, which was actually recorded earlier by the Fletcher Henderson orchestra, on May 11, 1927, with both versions—the Whiteman and Henderson—being basically identical. Both recordings feature an excerpt from Gershwin's "Rhapsody in Blue" (as does Whiteman's ur-swing version of "The Birth of the Blues" from August 12, 1926) and what Gunther Schuller calls Redman's "ingenious way with a variety of 3/8 and 3/4 figures (all in the 4/4 jazz meter, of course)."[15] What is notable about the Whiteman performance of an arrangement that Schuller considers "brashly intricate" is that the white musicians manage to make the piece cohere better than the Henderson band, and the breaks on trombone (perhaps by Tommy Dorsey) and alto sax (surely by brother Jimmy) are as effective in the context of the Whiteman rendition as are the breaks by Jimmy Harrison on trombone and Coleman Hawkins on tenor sax in the Henderson version.[16] Even though both Harrison and Coleman are more robust and assertive in an elemental jazz manner, there is nothing shy nor anemic about the Dorsey brothers' very impressive breaks. But aside from presenting evidence that the white musicians could perform effectively as a unit and could, when called upon, handle the jazz idiom quite impressively, "Whiteman Stomp" mostly indicates that the tune's namesake was primarily interested in arrangements that emphasized complex writing and contained allusions to or were based on classical works. And it was such arranging tendencies that would become most widespread among white bands of the late 1930s, when the arranger became more and more the determining factor in big-band productions.[17] Tommy Dorsey's work with Whiteman affected, one would think, his own inclination toward the use of a classical repertoire on occasion, combining the true jazz solos of Bunny Berigan with more commercially viable arrangements such as that of "Song of India," just as in 1928 Whiteman had utilized Bix Beiderbecke in the midst of a symphonic-like arrangement of "Sweet Sue."

As we saw in Chapter 1, the Whiteman orchestra was capable of recording a more purely jazz performance, such as "Happy Feet," from February 10, 1930, which features a jazz solo by violinist Joe Venuti, as well as a respectable break by Frankie Trumbauer and a fine Bixish cornet solo by Andy Secrest. Often Whiteman led the way in featuring a pop tune such as "Happy Feet," which later was recorded by Horace Henderson and His Orchestra on October 3, 1933, with outstanding solos by Dickie Wells and

Coleman Hawkins. If Whiteman did not offer the truest or purest form of jazz, he did anticipate certain tendencies in jazz and in that sense pointed the way for later, more authentic jazz performances. That is, Whiteman's eclectic range of materials contributed to the openness of jazz and its incorporation of all types of music as a basis for arrangement and, more importantly, for purposes of improvisation.

One area in which Whiteman was something of an advanced guard is exemplified by his version of Gershwin's "Somebody Loves Me," from July 11, 1924.[18] Even this early performance contains a number of decent jazz breaks, probably by Frank Siegrist on trumpet, Ross Gorman on alto, and Wilbur Hall with a doo-wacka-doo trombone solo. (Hall may actually be the trombone soloist on "Whiteman Stomp.") Just as Whiteman's influence on jazz in the thirties derives from his classical bent and from his allowing for such hot soloists as Beiderbecke, Venuti, and Secrest, Whiteman also affected the development of jazz by his early introduction of Broadway musical numbers into the jazz repertoire. This is especially true in the case of "Body and Soul," which was composed by John W. Green for a 1930 revue and was recorded by Whiteman's orchestra on September 10 of the same year.[19] "Body and Soul" would become a touchstone for all tenor saxophonists following Coleman Hawkins's recording in 1939, but even before this date, a number of recordings of this song would seem to follow Whiteman's lead. For example, Louis Armstrong made a version of "Body and Soul" on October 9, 1930, one month after Whiteman's. Certainly the Whiteman version, with its heavy use of violins and its sappy vocal by Jack Fulton, does not represent genuine jazz at the level of an Armstrong performance, and yet it does include two legitimate improvised solos, probably by Andy Secrest (another Beiderbecke imitation) and Frank Siegrist. Even though Armstrong manages to suggest the possibilities for improvisation on "Body and Soul," the saccharine orchestra backing the trumpeter does tend to hinder the master's rendition of this pop tune. In general, Gunther Schuller credits Armstrong with an "uncanny ability to ferret out the best material" and "even more . . . to enhance . . . songs with his own creativity, often improvising fantastic new melodies on top of the original."[20] Although the soloists on the Whiteman side cannot quite compare with Armstrong, they nonetheless do a creditable job, and in this sense Whiteman, too, may be accounted "uncanny" in recognizing both the commercial and artistic potential for such a pop song as "Body and Soul."

Another song that Whiteman introduced was "All of Me," which he recorded on December 1, 1931, with Mildred Bailey as the vocalist.[21] Not only would Bailey become "the world's first resident female vocalist" in a big band (Frank Tirro declaring that "her success was partly responsible for the subsequent fact that nearly every swing band from the '30s through the '50s had to have a woman vocalist"), but also her performance predates by almost two months Louis Armstrong's first recording of "All of Me" on January 27, 1932.[22] Andy Secrest's open trumpet break is once again in a very convincing Beiderbecke vein, and the ensemble writing and playing that follow the vocal are rather remarkable. As for Bailey's vocal, it exhibits some of the affective falls at the ends of notes later heard in the singing of Billie Holiday, as well as some of the same innocent sexuality that would be evoked by Holiday's singing. Like so many of Whiteman's recordings, "All of Me" was a number one hit, remaining so for three weeks. An even longer-running number-one Whiteman hit was his recording of Jerome Kern's "Smoke Gets in Your Eyes," from the musical stage play *Roberta*, which opened on November 18, 1933, fifteen days *after* the Whiteman recording.[23] Whiteman's version of the Kern song is in a classic Broadway musical style, with Bob Lawrence's vocal sounding like so many Broadway crooners of succeeding years. Whiteman already had recorded other Kern hits, such as his "Ol' Man River," which, on January 11, 1928, had featured a Bing Crosby vocal, as well as a nifty C-melody solo by Frankie Trumbauer.[24] Yet another Whiteman recording of Kern's "Ol' Man River" was made on March 1, 1928, with bass Paul Robeson and tenor Lambert Murphy.[25] This latter recording also includes more of Whiteman's penchant for alluding to semiclassical and classical works, in this case (once again) to Gershwin's "Rhapsody in Blue" but also Dvorak's *New World Symphony*.

None of the songs recorded by Whiteman exhibits much in the way of a jazz interpretation, except for those sung by Mildred Bailey, who represented the truest jazz voice in the Whiteman organization. This is evident from her October 4, 1931, recording of "When It's Sleepy Time Down South," which perhaps owes something to Armstrong's shaking, falling-off notes on his version of the same tune (first recorded by Louis on April 20, 1931), as well as a hint of Holiday's bittersweetness to come.[26] Although on the Whiteman recording of "When It's Sleepy Time Down South" Bailey may emphasize, as Richard Sudhalter observes, "the song's inherent sentimentality," the vocalist had earlier recorded the same tune with the Casa Loma Orchestra (on September 15, 1931) and took "a tougher-minded view, enhanced by a faster tempo and a more rhythmic approach by the band."[27] Nonetheless, Bailey's work with the Whiteman orchestra remains both appealing and satisfying. As for the leader, his early recordings of so many enduring pop songs, delivered by a wide variety of vocalists, show him to have been indeed "an innovator, a promoter of talent, a genial wizard, a magnetic, charismatic personality who drew the finest musicians to his ranks and earned their affection because he treated them with respect."[28]

As for Whiteman's support of many songwriters of the 1920s, this may have helped attract the public to their work, and in the 1930s may have drawn the attention of big-band leaders such as Jimmie Lunceford, among others, to the particular songs recorded by Whiteman. Two songs waxed by Whiteman, Vincent Rose's "Linger Awhile," from November 23, 1923, and Walter Donaldson's "My Blue Heaven," from July 6, 1927, were subsequently recorded by Jimmie Lunceford, in 1935 and 1937, respectively, and it seems clear that it was Whiteman's early versions that must have caught Lunceford's ear.[29] Certainly Lunceford would have been interested in the Whiteman recordings, both from having, as noted earlier, studied with Paul's father Wilberforce, and from sharing with Paul, as he did, the role of an orchestra conductor rather than a featured jazz soloist. Lunceford, like so many other black band leaders, must have admired the precision playing of Whiteman's musicians and the varied repertoire offered by Whiteman on his numerous recordings.[30] With respect to the specific Lunceford performances of "Linger Awhile" and "My Blue Heaven," they have little in common with the Whiteman versions, because, especially in the case of "Linger Awhile," the Lunceford generates a driving swing through crisply played sectional work, something the early Whiteman recordings rarely achieved. Whiteman's version of "Linger Awhile" is dated by the use of a banjo and perhaps would also have turned off the swing-era audience with its slide-whistle theme statement, although earlier the baritone saxophonist plays the theme with an admirable robustness. As for "My Blue Heaven," the Whiteman rendition does at times manage a smooth, lively swing, in between some of the leader's "symphonic jazz." No improvised solos are offered in either Whiteman recording, whereas several of Lunceford's sidemen take breaks on "My Blue Heaven" (Joe Thomas on tenor, Jock Carruthers on baritone sax, and Russell Bowles on trombone). On the other hand, the semiclassical opening of Lunceford's recording of "My Blue Heaven" (which seems to contain an echo of Gershwin's "Rhapsody in Blue") may indicate in this regard a possible direct Whiteman influence. Lunceford's affinity for vocal groups also may be traced back to Whiteman, whose "My Blue Heaven" was sung by a quintet, including Bing Crosby. Despite these rather incidental parallels, the differences are dramatic between Whiteman's essentially pseudojazz and Lunceford's very substantial swing that involves sectional exchanges, solo breaks, ensemble drive, and a rhythm section free of oompahing tuba, tinny banjo, and saccharine strings (although on Lunceford's "My Blue Heaven" regular guitarist Al Norris does ad lib on violin behind the vocal trio).

Following the death of Beiderbecke and the departure of the Dorsey brothers, two of the talented sidemen attracted to Whiteman's profitable system were trumpeter Bunny Berigan and trombonist Jack Teagarden. Berigan is present on the 1933 Whiteman recording of "Smoke Gets in Your Eyes," where he takes a muted solo prior to Bob Lawrence's vocal. This is not an outstanding break by Berigan, although quite effective in the context of the Broadway setting; in fact, little that Bunny recorded with Whiteman can compare with his solos on recordings by Benny Goodman and Tommy Dorsey or with Berigan's own units. Even a small-group recording made with some of Whiteman's sidemen, serving as accompanists to Mildred Bailey's singing of Hoagy Carmichael's "Rockin' Chair," does not show Berigan at his best, although this particular recording of August 18, 1932, as Richard Sudhalter has written, "establishes Mildred Bailey beyond dispute as one of the strongest vocal presences in the early '30s."[31] Despite the fact that Jack Teagarden and Louis Armstrong are more popularly associated with "Rockin' Chair," it is Bailey's rendition of the Carmichael piece that is far more satisfying and artful than either the 1931 version by Teagarden's orchestra (with Eddie Gale doing the vocal) or the duet version by Armstrong and Teagarden from 1947.[32] Teagarden's voice on the 1947 "Rockin' Chair" is definitely appealing, but the hoakum of that recording ruins the overall effect, whereas Bailey's performance is thoroughly earnest and affective. As for Teagarden's time with Whiteman, this was, like Berigan's, not at all representative of his finest work. In many ways, as Gunther Schuller has suggested, it was Jack's brother Charlie who contributed the most consistently inventive solos during the five years the two men were with "the King."[33]

Jack Teagarden joined the Whiteman organization at the end of 1933, and a recording of Johnny Mercer's "Fare Thee Well to Harlem" was made with Jack and his brother Charlie on February 16, 1934.[34] Jack sings Mercer's lyrics effectively, despite the rather corny asides by the songwriter. The trombonist's instrumental break is nothing much, and this was too often the case with Jack's horn solos while with Whiteman. On August 18, 1934, Jack and Charlie participated in the recording of a piece written by Frankie Trumbauer, titled "Itchola." Here the trombonist takes two rather aggressive breaks, although in complete control of his instrument. Technically Jack's playing is impressive on this as on so many occasions, but it his brother Charlie who turns in the more appealing solo, at least in terms of its continuity and its overall contours and sound. Likewise, on the Whiteman version of the New Orleans Rhythm Kings' classic "Farewell Blues," recorded on September 7, 1935, Charlie takes a fine muted solo with his clean, penetrating drive. Brother Jack does not solo here but is part of the superb ensemble work that makes this side the equal of most any recording produced by a name swing-era band. Certainly nothing can compare with the wonderful sound of Paul Mares's muted trumpet or Leon Roppolo's weaving clarinet, but it is notable that whereas the original NORK recording of August 1922 is dominated in many ways by Lou Black's banjo, Whiteman has dispensed with this instrument, and his star banjoist, Mike Pingitore, has now taken up the rhythm guitar; Art Miller has replaced Whiteman's sometime string bassist Steve Brown, who was on the original NORK recording of "Farewell Blues"; and Larry Gomar has occupied the drum stool in the place of Herb Quigley. The rhythm section of Whiteman's 1935 orchestra swings as never before, and the reed section performs some intricate passages with the greatest precision and drive. In addition to Charlie Teagarden's outstanding muted trumpet solo, this performance also includes a delightful, rugged break by (it would seem) Charles Strickfaden on tenor. This one side, despite something of a concert opening and a clarinet trio at one point in the arrangement, belies any total characterization of the Whiteman orchestra as incapable of swinging with real intensity, of being simply a watered-down version of jazz. "Farewell Blues" may not be a purely jazz recording, but it certainly at times manages to exhibit the best elements of that music: solid swing, creditable improvisation, and superb sectional execution.

The Whiteman version of "Farewell Blues" also may be seen as in advance of the tendency of a number of swing-era groups to revive the Dixieland genre. As we shall see, the Bob Crosby orchestra created its own special niche by reverting to earlier jazz styles such as Dixieland, boogie woogie, and the blues. Although the Crosby orchestra did not record NORK's "Farewell Blues," it did cut a version of "Tin Roof Blues," which NORK had recorded in 1923.[35] As noted in Chapter 3, both Benny Goodman and Glenn Miller's orchestras cut versions of "Farewell Blues," in 1938 and 1939, respectively. These versions by two of the name white bands are exceptionally good recordings, with fine solos by Harry James on the Goodman and Tex Beneke, Clyde Hurley, and Glenn himself on the Miller. Not that any of these orchestras necessarily was influenced by Whiteman in this regard, but even so, Whiteman did precede these more fully swing groups in performing as part of his repertoire a work that represented something of a back to the jazz basics. In this and other respects, Whiteman was often ahead of the pack, which suggests that from the first and continuing into the thirties, the leader was "uncanny" in his ability to anticipate many of the directions that jazz, and especially swing, would take. It should be noted that at the same time the Casa Loma Orchestra likewise was recording a number of Dixieland tunes, such as "Clarinet Marmalade" (1931), "Milenberg Joys" (1934), and "Royal Garden Blues" (1936).[36]

Unfortunately, the 1935 Whiteman unit as represented by "Farewell Blues," and to a lesser extent by a version of "The Darktown Strutters' Ball," from July 10, 1935, is the exception among so many of the orchestra's performances of the mid to late 1930s. Even if Whiteman pointed the way, he did not follow through. And although a true jazz soloist such as Jack Teagarden was amply featured during these years, both as a rather soothing vocalist and an essentially hot trombonist, as on "The Darktown Strutters' Ball," more often than not Jack's instrumental work with Whiteman consisted mainly of ready-made licks that he played regardless of the song. This is made evident by more than a dozen radio recordings dating from 1936 and 1938. On "The Music Goes 'Round and 'Round," from January 12, 1936, the trombonist sounds like something of a self-parody of himself, whereas brother Charlie, who opens the piece with a brief solo, steals the show with his direct, unadorned swing. "Announcer's Blues," from January 19, is more notable, owing primarily to the drummer's supercharged stick work. On "Got a Bran' New Suit," from the same date, Jack's vocal is quite appealing and his trombone solo is undeniably impressive. The Whiteman version of "St. Louis Blues," from February 16, 1936, again features some fine stick work by the drummer, a mixed bag of sax and clarinet passages, and so-so contributions by the Teagardens. Whiteman also features on these radio broadcasts "The Three Ts," a reference to the Teagarden brothers along with Frankie Trumbauer. Although Trumbauer's break on "I Hope That Gabriel Likes My Music," from March 22, 1936, is a curiosity of sorts and the brothers perform dependably, this and so much of the Whiteman music is in the novelty vein and rarely gets down to the true business of jazz.

There are definitely exceptions to the novelty format, as with Charlie Teagarden's hot break on the Whiteman rendition of "Alexander's Ragtime Band," from May 24, 1936. On the other hand, brother Jack's virtuosic display on "I'm Coming, Virginia," from June 24, 1938, offers little in the way of a meaningful jazz feeling or interpretation. Despite the fact that Whiteman is performing classic jazz numbers, the pieces do not satisfy on the level of high-quality jazz. Many of the radio recordings are marred by slight flaws in Jack's playing, as in his cadenza on the performance of "Small Fry," from September 28, 1938. King Oliver's "Aunt Hagar's Blues," another early classic like "Farewell Blues" and "I'm Coming, Virginia," was performed by the Whiteman orchestra on September 21, 1938 (almost exactly ten years after the original recording of September 12, 1928), and again this is mostly a novelty number, even though Jack's vocal is delivered sincerely in between the almost offensive singing of a vocal quartet. As for the trombonist's high notes in his break on the Oliver tune, these are beautifully executed, as are those on an overorchestrated, pastiche version of "St. Louis Blues" from October 19, 1938. "Jeepers Creepers," from December 7, 1938, has a very likable vocal by Jack and a short but solid break by the trombonist. "Christmas Night in Harlem," from December 21, contains some excellent ensemble work, although it is fairly generic by this date. "John Peel," from the 28th, is in no way jazz, except for a four-bar break by Jack. So many of these radio recordings are Whiteman at his commercial worst, and even a classic jazz repertoire and the presence of capable jazzmen such as the Teagarden brothers could not salvage the performances from a popular mode that ultimately is fatal in terms of true jazz.

Although a performance by the Whiteman orchestra from 1942 is slightly beyond the range of years of this volume, it is appropriate to close the present commentary on Paul Whiteman and His Concert Orchestra with his recording of "Trav'lin' Light," from June 12, with Billie Holiday as the vocalist. In many ways this side brings the Whiteman recordings from 1930 to 1941 somewhat full circle in that they almost began (in 1931) with Mildred Bailey and nearly ended (in mid 1942) with Billie Holiday. "Trav'lin' Light" opens with a muted trombone theme statement, which obviously owes much to Whiteman's former sideman Tommy Dorsey and shows the reciprocal effect of one band leader on another. When Holiday enters, she is backed by what was almost from the first a Whiteman combination of strings, muted brass, and reeds, and although this is a commercial setting, the vocalist creates an immediate sense of authenticity of feeling through timing, note placement, and expressive emphasis. Although Whiteman never actually integrated his orchestra on a regular basis, he did record with such black singers as Paul Robeson and Billie Holiday, as well as with the part Native American Mildred Bailey. Whiteman's sidemen and singers hailed from all over, including, as we have seen, the leader's native Colorado and Jack and Charlie Teagarden's Texas, where Whiteman was invited to open Fort Worth's Casa Mañana in 1936 and where he showed how at home he was in the West, as indicated by a publicity photo in *Jazz* picturing him in sheepskin chaps, a cowboy hat in his hand, and a six-shooter on his hip.[37] The eclecticism of Whiteman's music is evident throughout his career, and his openness to every style, period of musical history, type of musician, and race says much in favor of this man who, as a friend phrased it, has been "demonized" for corrupting great jazzmen such as Beiderbecke and Teagarden, for not creating pure jazz, and for crowning himself the monarch of a musical form for which he had no understanding or true appreciation. None of this seems completely accurate, but even if it were, the undeniable fact remains that Paul Whiteman was a force in the creation and promulgation of jazz, that he preceded and predicted many of its developments in the 1930s, and that he promoted the careers of innumerable musicians who went on to become leaders, in their own right, of some of the era's most prominent big bands.

CASA LOMA ORCHESTRA

Formed originally in 1929 as one of the Jean Goldkette orchestras and denominated the Orange Blossoms, the Casa Loma Orchestra in the same year renamed itself after a Toronto nightclub and reorganized as the first jazz corporation, with stock owned by its members, who elected saxophonist Glen Gray as their president and leader. Commentators Bill Grauer and Orrin Keepnews have considered the Casa Loma Orchestra to be "best described as a highly jazz-conscious offshoot of the dance band style of the 1920s." These critics go on to say that the Casa Loma "helped pave the way for Goodman and others who came after."[38] According to Richard Sudhalter, another important contribution of the Casa Loma Orchestra was that it "helped free dance bands, black and white, from their traditional secondary role as traveling vaudeville units. . . . For the first time, the music—and an inherent elegance of presentation—seemed to be enough."[39] Both Sudhalter and Gunther Schuller suggest that the Casa Loma Orchestra influenced the Bennie Moten band, with both critics referring in this regard to "Toby" and "Lafayette" as recorded by Moten in 1932.[40] Schuller points out, for instance, that the Casa Loma recording of "Maniac's Ball," from December 18, 1931, was recorded a year before the Moten sides and established arranger Gene Gifford's highly influential approach of writing for listening more than dancing.[41] On the other hand, Rob Bamberger suggests that although "Casa Loma retained an enviable degree of popularity and musicianship into the later '30s and '40s, it was eclipsed by Benny Goodman and other leaders who refined the musical vocabulary of swing into distinct musical identities of their own, interpolating more Fletcher Henderson, perhaps, than Gene Gifford."[42] One side that Moten and the Casa Lomans have in common is their respective versions of Hoagy Carmichael's "New Orleans," recorded by Moten on December 13, 1932, and by Casa Loma on December 27, 1932.[43] There are crucial differences between these two recordings that reveal that the Casa Loma Orchestra was "a highly jazz-conscious offshoot of the dance band style of the 1920s," whereas the Moten band was a true jazz organization with soloists of the first rank who played with deep feeling and with note choices that are more musically expressive than almost anything played by the Casa Lomans.

As suggested in Chapter 1, Hoagy Carmichael's classic songs, such as "Stardust," "Rockin' Chair," and "Georgia on My Mind," have figured significantly in the history of jazz. Others of his tunes, such as "Lazy River" and "Lazy Bones," the latter recorded by the Casa Loma Orchestra on June 5, 1933, also exerted an impact on the development of jazz, especially as noted earlier in the case of "Lazy Bones," which in many ways forecast the coming of the Goodman and other big bands of the mid to late thirties. But "New Orleans" as recorded by Moten and the Casa Lomans shows that such black and white groups were miles apart in their treatment of such a Carmichael tune as this one. The fact that Moten recorded it first also suggests that there could not have been much, if any, influence, at least in this instance, coming from the Casa Lomans. The Grauer-Keepnews characterization of the Casa Loman style as deriving from the 1920s is illustrated by their rendition of "New Orleans," where the prominent use of violin and xylophone or celeste recalls the Whiteman approach, as does the sort of concert-style opening. Although the Moten version of "New Orleans" also employs at times a few xylophone-sounding notes, these are quite incidental and not at all sweet as they are on the Casa Loman side. The vocals, as sung by (probably) Pee Wee Hunt for the Casa Lomans and (definitely) Jimmy Rushing for Moten, are both quite effective in their differing styles, although the Moten is rather unusual in having the altoist (probably Eddie Barefield) accompany Rushing by playing essentially the same notes along with or slightly behind the singer. The muted trumpet

theme statement on the Casa Loman version is nicely done and even somewhat close in spirit to the open-horn trumpet statement on the Moten,
although the Casa Loma trumpeter is backed by a sweet ensemble sound
and the Moten is more in the hot vein.

The principal differences between the Moten and Casa Loma recordings
of "New Orleans" lie in the latter's concert-style ensemble, its rather dated
rhythm section, its saccharine violin that ends the side, and the fact that
on the Casa Loma version there are no real solos, other than a brief, very
straight passage by clarinetist Clarence Hutchenrider, versus the very intense, full-bodied, highly imaginative, and technically innovative solos and
the wonderfully relaxed but driving ensemble on the Moten side. Both Ben
Webster on tenor and Hot Lips Page on trumpet deliver solos on the Moten
that are cutting-edge jazz, with Page incorporating into his solo blue notes
that are tremendously telling in their artfully aesthetic and soulful selection.
Webster in 1932 is beyond anything any of the reed players in the Casa
Loma Orchestra ever achieved or even attempted, and he is original even
in comparison with other black tenorists. As Martin Williams observed,
Webster's "eruptive moment on the verse of the piece . . . sounds a lot less
like Coleman Hawkins here than he is supposed to have sounded at this
early point in his career," by which Williams would seem to suggest that
this solo already shows Webster to have a distinctive tenor sound of his
own, and if so, that is precisely the case with Ben's profoundly emotive
performance.[44] Finally, the overall Moten rendition of "New Orleans" is
purely jazz, not a commercial effort as the Casa Loman recording was
clearly intended to be.

Even though the "New Orleans" example may not be fair to the Casa
Lomans, it does help answer the troubling question raised by Gunther
Schuller as to why the white group, if it was such an important early influence, did not have the staying power of the Moten band, or at least of
those members who would form the Count Basie Orchestra and affect the
development of jazz for generations to come.[45] Despite the obvious "jazz-
conscious" emphasis of the Casa Lomans, there were other problems with
the orchestra's offerings. Although an early swing-era anthem such as
composer-arranger Gene Gifford's "Casa Loma Stomp," from December
6, 1930, became "the full-blown progenitor of hundreds of swing-style
offspring," the first two solos by the trombone and tenor are so dated that
it is hard to listen to such stiff playing after fluent musicians such as Jack
Teagarden and Coleman Hawkins had already shown the way to a
smoother, more affective line.[46] The muted trumpet and the clarinet are
definitely an improvement over the first pair of soloists, but after this, the
ensemble's call-and-response patterns grow repetitious and circus bandlike,
until the piece ends with a kind of concert conclusion that makes all the
earlier drive rather pointless. Although this number is taken at a fairly
moderate tempo, it still comes off as a bit frantic and directionless, which

is never true of a Moten or Basie side, even when they take a piece at breakneck speed. A little over two years later, on February 17, 1933, the Casa Lomans rerecorded their "Stomp" and, as Schuller indicates, such remakes become "increasingly mechanical and rigid," even though the trumpet solo, probably by Sonny Dunham, and the clarinet break by Hutchenrider are quite fluid at this point, and drummer Tony Briglia is relying more on a type of ride-cymbal that lends the performance a smoother flow.[47] Another Gifford tune, "White Jazz," was recorded on March 24, 1931, some four months after "Casa Loma Stomp," and already there is better solo production from the two trombones, Pee Wee Hunt and Bill Rauch, and Briglia's drumming helps stimulate the group to greater intensity without so much of a frantic feel, even though this latter tendency continued to plague the orchestra's performances.[48]

An exception to the all-out, mad-dash numbers that predominated among the Casa Lomans' recordings is Gifford's arrangement of "Smoke Rings," from March 18, 1932.[49] Here especially is a fluent solo by Clarence Hutchenrider that predates so many similar romantic excursions by clarinetists of the later swing era. Also, there apparently is one of Pat Davis's finest efforts on tenor in a subdued vein rather than what Gunther Schuller calls his "inconsistent, eccentric, and at times downright corny" manner.[50] Nonetheless, Davis's solo here is not really an example of what Schuller praises as his "combined technical command and range," and it does not contradict Albert McCarthy's claim that for the most part Davis "was a rather mediocre soloist" whose "jerky method of phrasing was inimical to genuine swing" and whose "illusion of excitement" substituted "for real ideas."[51] A more representative side by the Casa Loma Orchestra is "Limehouse Blues," from February 24, 1934, for here the group is in its rather typically frantic mode, which, as McCarthy suggests, takes the place of "real ideas."[52] Certainly this is an effective treatment of the tune, and the muted trombone at the beginning, and later in conjunction with some intriguing clarinet-led reed figures, is quite well done; also, Hutchenrider's two breaks on alto saxophone are rather impressive from a technical point of view. Davis's tenor break supports Schuller's estimation that the sideman could be energetic in an "odd-ball way," and the concluding ensemble section does generate considerable drive, even if the piece ends without the sense of a satisfying closure.[53] Although the Casa Loma version has its moments, compared with renditions of "Limehouse Blues" by Duke Ellington and Fletcher Henderson, the Casa Loma performance is definitely on a lower level of artistry and musical meaning.

Whereas the Casa Loma's "Limehouse Blues" opens with something of an American Indian motif, the Ellington version, from around three years earlier (June 16, 1931), is treated at the beginning, as Stanley Dance has observed, to some Chinese-style decor at a very much slower tempo, and the piece closes with this same treatment, complete with a gonglike cymbal to round off the composition.[54] Although the latter may be a rather elementary device for shaping the Ellington performance, it yet lends the recording a sense of logical completion. More significant are the solos on the Ellington, which include a highly affective break from Tricky Sam Nanton on his muted trombone that truly "speaks," superb alto work by Johnny Hodges, which at the time was beyond that of any other soloist on the instrument, a wailing Barney Bigard on clarinet, and an inimitable Harry Carney on baritone. As for the Henderson version of September 11, 1934 (arranged by Benny Carter), this is closer to the Casa Loma recording in terms of tempo, yet the effect is not of a frenetic attempt to create a "killer-diller"; rather, the Henderson side manages to maintain a momentum that builds to the very last bars and the trumpet's high-note ending. Along the way on the Henderson side, there are soaring breaks by Henry "Red" Allen on trumpet, Buster Bailey on clarinet, Keg Johnson on trombone, and Ben Webster on tenor, with the last of these really pouring it on. As Schuller has judged the situation, the Casa Loma soloists simply "were no match for those in Henderson's great band or Ellington's," and comparison of the three versions of "Limehouse Blues" fully supports the critic's judgment.[55]

The Casa Lomans, to their credit, surely appreciated the superior talents of an Ellington, as indicated by the homage they paid to the master in recording a version of his "Sophisticated Lady." Cut on June 5, 1933, less than three weeks after the Ellington original of May 16, the Casa Loman reading of "Sophisticated Lady" is in many ways an admirable tribute to Ellington and his composition.[56] The original opens with a sedate concert-type introduction, and Ellington's magisterial piano solo late in the recording also gives the piece a very serious, semiclassical feeling. So that it is perhaps not inappropriate that the Casa Loma version places the theme in the hands of violinist Mel Jenssen, even though this tends to make the piece somewhat cloying rather than rendering it as sophisticated sentiment. Nonetheless, the Casa Loman reading is quite serious and beautifully performed—from the reeds, with their advanced, highly unified sectional sound, to pianist Howard Hall, who does an excellent job of suggesting the Ellington touch, even if the Casa Loman in no way approaches Duke's technical and affective heights. But what most fully sets off the Ellington from the Casa Loma imitation are the soloists, which in the latter's case are limited to the violin theme statement and a brief appearance on clarinet by Clarence Hutchenrider, who shows his technical ability but little in the way of meaningful expression. Nothing in the Casa Loma version can compare with the emotive sound of Lawrence Brown's trombone, Barney Bigard's warm lilting clarinet, or Otto Hardwick's magnificent alto sax flutterings that bring the side to a wonderful yearning close. Whereas the Ellington achieves a deeply romantic effect, the Casa Loman stands as essentially a quite proficient, sensitive response to one of the composer's most enduring works, even though the Casa Loman version ultimately lacks the artistry and profound feeling manifest in the original recording.

Another instance of the Casa Lomans paying tribute to great jazz can be heard in the fine swing generated on "That's How Rhythm Was Born," from August 7, 1933.[57] (Unfortunately, the lyrics rather condescendingly account for the origin of black rhythm by referring to "darkies" washing their sins in the river where "cold water made them all shiver.") Although conceived in a Dixieland style, the piece yet has an easy rhythmic drive, and the two soloists on alto and tenor are more in the flowing swing vein than the earlier hot type of articulation. Most impressive are the two alto breaks by Clarence Hutchenrider, who originally had wanted to play this instrument but was pressured by relatives and a local bandmaster into taking up the clarinet instead.[58] In some ways this seems regrettable, in light of what seems a rather unusually substantial outing by Hutchenrider on alto. Even more impressive in terms of substance are the sideman's breaks on baritone, to be sampled, for instance, on the Casa Loma version of "I Got Rhythm" from December 30, 1933, where Hutchenrider "takes two supple (and clarinet-like) . . . choruses."[59] His baritone solo truly coheres and makes musical sense from beginning to end, at the same time that it is not marred by the shrill sound production heard later when Hutchenrider switches to clarinet. Too often on clarinet Hutchenrider was squeally, his note choices never having quite the penetrating effect of a Goodman's, the Casa Loman's playing always a bit too frantic, never really achieving a relaxed swing. An exception can be heard on the recording of "Avalon," from August 16, 1934, where the clarinetist stays at first in the lower register and creates a warmer, more intimate sound until he eventually works his way into the upper reaches of the instrument where he then grows rather strident.[60] On this same side, which exhibits some exceptionally smooth swing from soloists and ensemble alike, the opening break, probably by Sonny Dunham, is particularly striking, and Pat Davis on tenor turns in a wonderfully driving effort. A late recording by the Casa Lomans, of Dunham's composition titled "Come and Get It," from September 28, 1939, does not feature a solo by the composer but does offer an example of the orchestra's aggressive swing, along with fluid but hot breaks by Hutchenrider (who has obviously listened closely to Goodman) and a few bars of Davis's booting tenor.[61] The sax and brass sections really dig in on this number and show that the orchestra could keep up with the competition so far as execution and enthusiasm were concerned. However, the piano is an anachronism here and is accompanied by some dated drumming by Briglia. For the most part, this is the same group that began recording in the early thirties, except for an additional trombone, another alto, and replacements for Gene Gifford and trumpeter Bobby Jones.

One of the sidemen who remained with the original group from at least

1932 was trumpeter Grady Watts, whose solo on "I Got Rhythm" is outstanding and suggests that when given the opportunity most of the Casa Lomans were capable of turning in a fine accounting of themselves. Pee Wee Hunt and Billy Rauch were consistently dependable performers, if not in the same class with the Ellington and Henderson trombonists. Throughout the decade, the Casa Lomans were up to playing most every type of chart with finesse and spirit. Known for being well rehearsed, the orchestra maintained its high degree of professionalism throughout the period and supplied its listeners with delightful music, spiced with moments of second-level jazz. Probably the ultimate cause for the Casa Loma Orchestra not to achieve lasting prominence lay not so much with its personnel but rather in the area of composition. Apart from a few originals by Gene Gifford, such as "Casa Loma Stomp" and "White Jazz," there was not much that was distinctive about the Casa Loma book, and neither of these tunes really endured as a jazz standard. "White Jazz," recorded March 24, 1931, is mainly another frantic flag waver that did not represent the principal direction the swing movement would take, even though by the end of the decade "killer-dillers" were briefly all the rage.[62] Certainly, as Gunther Schuller has indicated, the Casa Lomans "brought jazz as an orchestral instrumental music (not mere *dance* music) out of its previous exclusively black domain over to white audiences," but as the critic also suggests, the group did not quite develop the "elusive rhythmic element" in swing but only managed something of a "driven, mechanical rigidity, muscle-bound in its all-too-obvious exertion."[63] This is clearly the case with "White Jazz," which in many ways sums up the main difference between white and black swing.

BUNNY BERIGAN

To succeed in the Swing Era, a band needed a hit number that would provide name recognition, a number that would gain a recording contract, make the juke boxes, and bring invitations from hotels, theaters, ballrooms, and nightclubs in cities across the nation. Once a band had secured a series of one-nighters at the various music venues or a residency at a prominent hotel or club, a hit number helped maintain a band's popularity. Radio was vital to keeping a band's music before the public from coast to coast, and in this regard as well, a hit number was essential as a theme song for purposes of identification. As Thomas Hennessey points out,

Radio was one of the few segments of the economy to escape severe damage from the depression. National networks began in the late 1920s, and their new sponsored programs . . . created profits and national impact. Both networks and local stations had plenty of open time, much of it filled by late night and late afternoon sustaining (non-sponsored) broadcasts from hotels, nightclubs, and ballrooms.

Hennessey goes on to quote a *Chicago Defender* article that reported how such radio broadcasts " 'so popularized good music that the smaller towns want and are willing to pay to hear good bands in person.' "[64] The other important ingredient for success, it would seem, was a name musician leading the band, and in some ways it may be that the Casa Loma Orchestra suffered from not having in its elected leader, Glen Gray, a star attraction. Of course, Whiteman was not a prominent soloist and neither was Lunceford, but most of the white bands were led by headliners whose names and reputations proceeded them. This was clearly the case with Bunny Berigan, the Wisconsin-born trumpeter who gained widespread popularity through his hit number, "I Can't Get Started," first recorded in 1936 by Berigan and a sextet and then with his own orchestra in 1937. Before this, Berigan had made a name for himself while with Whiteman in 1932–1933 and Benny Goodman in 1935, through the *CBS Saturday Night Swing Club* broadcasts in 1936, and during two months with Tommy Dorsey at the beginning of 1937.

Berigan's appeal to listeners is illustrated by an interview conducted by Richard Sudhalter with trumpeter Jim Maxwell: " 'I used to hear him on the radio. . . . I was still in high school, and I'd sometimes stay home from school to hear him. I'd never heard anybody play so lyrically: a good deal like Louis, I felt, but looser. . . . He had the most gorgeous sound, big and beautiful from top to bottom, and the most beautiful, liquid vibrato.' "[65] Sudhalter indicates the appeal of Berigan's hit number when he reports that "so total was the association of man and song in the public mind that fans request it often as 'Bunny Berigan's I Can't Get Started,' " even though the tune was written by Vernon Duke and the timeless lyrics by Ira Gershwin.[66] It also seems clear that Berigan's recordings helped make Duke's song a jazz classic, which includes in its line of interpretations at least two other masterpieces, one by Billie Holiday with the Count Basie orchestra from November 3, 1947, and one by Dizzy Gillespie with his all-stars from January 1945. Berigan's first recording of "I Can't Get Started" under his own name was on April 13, 1936, with Bunny singing the lyrics with a dreamy, very personal delivery that must have been part of the allure of this classic performance.[67] Yet it is clearly Berigan's amazing trumpet solo, with its contrast between his stirring upper-register sound and his emotive low notes, that made this first recording an ear-catching experience, to which listeners would have immediately and permanently attached the musician's name. The second recording came some four months after his first studio session with his own orchestra, on April 1, 1937.[68] On August 7, Berigan opened the more widely known version of what has been called his "anthem" with a virtuosic cadenza that sets up his lovely but not at all saccharine statement of the theme. After the saxes repeat the theme with a rather overly sweet lushness, Berigan sings the lyrics with a quite affected emphasis compared with the simplicity of the first recording. If Berigan's singing is not so satisfying here, his trumpet work is certainly more impressive than on the 1936 side, especially in the lower register, where he draws out the bittersweet flavor of the theme for all it's worth. The ending is less impressive because it leans in the direction of grandstanding, and is even marked by a few missed or imperfectly played notes. Nonetheless, this performance set the pattern for numerous trumpet showcases in the Swing Era, followed in particular by the spectacular exhibitions of Harry James. In addition, Berigan's solo ensured a place for his orchestra in the now highly competitive big-band market.

The problem, of course, was that one tune could not support a band forever, and unless the group as a whole could produce a continuous string of attractive recordings, its future was not secure. Prior to the establishment of his own orchestra, Berigan recorded a number of pieces under his own name with a pick-up group.[69] One side cut on February 17, 1937, of Cole Porter's classic "Let's Do It," offers an easy swing that is definitely infectious, and Berigan's solo is a wonderfully jaunty, obviously happy piece of playing on the leader's part. The ensemble execution is strikingly together, and the dynamic contrasts are delightful. The other soloists (Ford Leary on trombone and Matty Matlock on clarinet) are quite adequate and even pleasing, if not so thrilling as the leader is. Once Berigan had organized his own orchestra, he and his men cut two sides on June 25, 1937, and these continue the solid swing heard from the February 17 pick-up group. "Frankie and Johnnie" finds both the trumpeter and the band's other principal soloists, tenorist Georgie Auld (only eighteen years old at the time) and clarinetist Joe Dixon, blowing with gusto, while drummer George Wettling adds greatly to the performance's exuberant drive. Auld quotes Lester Young in the longer of his two breaks and shows that he knew the work of the most important new tenor voice in jazz. Certainly Auld was not himself among the elite on his instrument, but he could at times turn in something of a rousing break, as he does here. And although Joe Dixon was not blessed with an individual voice on his instrument, he, too, could contribute workmanlike solos on occasion. This particular side boded well for Berigan's orchestra, but in some ways it was not characteristic of its recordings during the next year and a half. Neither was the other side recorded on June 25, "Mahogany Hall Stomp," a tune made famous in jazz annals by Louis Armstrong, who first recorded it on March 5, 1929, and subsequently on January 28, 1933, and May 18, 1936.[70] As Gunther Schuller avers of Armstrong's pure and rich tone, "no jazz player has ever matched him in this domain (even Bunny Berigan)."[71] On Berigan's version of "Mahogany Hall Stomp," he plays the theme with a mute, which does not show off his special tone quality, but once he removes the mute for a break, he does not attempt to emphasize his glowing open sound as he does on "I Can't Get Started." In fact, few of his recorded solos reveal the loveliness of his tone so well as his "anthem." Mostly, the orchestra's recordings of the traditional "Frankie and Johnnie" and "Armstrong's" "Mahogany Hall Stomp" differ significantly from so much of Berigan's repertoire that would be drawn from the weakest pop songs of the day, with the result that too often the group's numbers were in the lightweight, novelty or plain saccharine vein. So many of the sides recorded by Berigan and the band offer little in the way of engaging or original arrangements; most sound generic and uninspired and certainly do not hold up well in comparison with the work of the name bands of the period.

Two exceptions to the orchestra's poor repertoire were "The Prisoner's Song," on the flip side of "I Can't Get Started" from August 7, 1937, and Irving Berlin's "Russian Lullaby" from a recording session on December 23.[72] Here Berigan and his soloists take extended breaks that amount to more than they ordinarily did in the coming months when they were hampered by rather dismal pop tunes and were restricted to very brief solo appearances. "The Prisoner's Song" opens with Berigan's muted trumpet imitating an Ellington mood, before the orchestra shifts into a typical swing piece closer to the Goodman style. The trumpeter's solo playing is essentially flashy, with little substance to it, which was too often the case during this period. On the other hand, Richard Sudhalter hears in Berigan's second chorus "an eight-bar phrase that presages the complexities of bebop," which may be true enough.[73] Auld is much better than usual; this was due, it would seem, to his having a chance to stretch out. Dixon also develops his ideas further than he was normally allowed. The trombone solo by Sonny Lee is better as well, although his break does not come to much, especially compared with the work of so many other trombonists of the era. On Berlin's "Russian Lullaby," Berigan really cuts loose, and although the breaks by Auld and Dixon are briefer, both blow more substantial solos than they did when they were so often limited to eight bars or less. The trumpeter soars at times and works well in conjunction with the orchestra, which again is rather the exception among the group's recordings. The entire performance holds together better than usual, and again points up the irony that despite Berlin's holding swing in low esteem it appears likely that this tune would not have survived except through the Berigan orchestra's recording. This is probably the case as well with Berlin's "He Ain't Got Rhythm," as recorded by Jimmie Lunceford.

Two other sides, from the session of December 23, 1937, are "Trees" and "Can't Help Lovin' That Man."[74] The first piece is almost purely a dance number with a sweet sound and a very imitative type of big-band swing. Berigan does solo well, and the band performs the arrangement with precision. Richard Sudhalter considers the leader's solo to be "less an improvisation than a poetic commentary on both the text [by Joyce Kilmer] and Oscar Rosbach's lovely, brooding melody." Sudhalter also points out that the solo covers three octaves, "including a low concert Eb that's not even on his horn," which Gunther Schuller had indicated was true of the trumpeter's solo on "Blues" from a jam session held on March 31, 1937.[75] "Can't Help Lovin' That Man" mostly contains clichés in the solos by Berigan and Auld, whereas Dixon actually comes across as more appealing than the leader. Berigan is, as so often, technically impressive, but there is little substance to his solos. This is certainly the case on the many novelty tunes recorded in 1938, beginning with the January 26 "Piano Tuner Man," where during some corny banter with vocalist Gail Reese, Berigan even tells her, "I've had about enough."

Another novelty tune from January 26 is "Heigh-Ho (The Dwarfs' March Song)," which, as "Whistle While You Work," was used in the famous Disney movie of *Snow White and the Seven Dwarfs*. Here Berigan seems unable to make anything out of the material, and although Auld is somewhat better, his break is so brief that nothing much comes of it. Sentimental songs such as "A Serenade to the Stars" and "Outside of Paradise" from the same date seem to limit Berigan's improvisational abilities, whereas Armstrong was clearly capable of mining even such minor works for more than they were worth. Gail Reese's vocals are extremely unappealing, and Dixon's clarinet breaks cannot compare with those of Goodman or Shaw, much less Barney Bigard or even Buster Bailey. On "Down Stream," from March 15, 1938, Berigan's low register is just not meaningful on such a weak tune, and on a Parish-Hudson piece such as "Sophisticated Swing" from the same date, again not much comes of even this better effort.[76] Reese sings the tricky melody well enough, but her vocal has no real emotive force, in contrast to anything sung by Holiday. (Berigan's accompaniment of Holiday certainly demonstrates the beneficial effect on his own playing of such a true jazz vocalist.) Auld tends to imitate the black tenors, and Berigan is merely showy with no real point to his improvisation. On the session of May 26, 1938, the band recorded "The Wearin' of the Green," which Sudhalter calls a "well-crafted arrangement" and Schuller praises for Berigan's solo with its "almost eerie sense of drama and daring, floating in out of nowhere on high notes."[77] But somehow this is largely another novelty piece that seems rather silly, with the clarinets arranged after the Irish manner and Auld's tenor break lifted almost verbatim from an earlier solo by Lunceford's Joe Thomas.

A piece such as "Rinka Tinka Man," from March 16, 1938, immediately gives away its lightweight character. Not even Dave Tough on drums can save this terrible novelty number, which perhaps only Whiteman could have turned into something more mildly interesting than Berigan managed. The leader tries, but it is no go, and Auld gets nowhere with his imitation shaking tenor. "An Old Straw Hat" from the same session does find the group generating more swing, more interaction between the sections than was usual on most of its recordings. Here Berigan's solo jumps, although he seems to become lost at one point, and even Reese's vocal swings better. "I Dance Alone," also from March 16, seems satisfied with a meager effort, no more than was expected of another dance number, with Berigan offering only what was sufficient for a commercial appeal.[78] On April 21, 1938, the orchestra recorded "Never Felt Better, Never Had Less," and one wonders how well this title applied to the band, when in fact there is nothing memorable about this side, nothing challenging intellectually, even though vocalist Ruth Gaylor is an improvement over Reese and the band seems more supportive in its playing behind the new singer. Here at least Auld is deeply into his solo, whereas Berigan just seems to be going through the motions. On "I've Got a Guy," from the same date, Berigan plays a nice open solo (his second, the first being muted), but in many ways he is repeating himself and is certainly not so "explorative" here as he had been while with Goodman and Dorsey, or as one would expect of "unquestionably one of the trumpet giants of the thirties."[79] A May 26 session produced "Wacky Dust," another novelty number, which, aside from Ella Fitzgerald's version, could only have been brought off successfully by a Lunceford. "Somewhere with Somebody Else," also from this date, opens with an unusual mood set by the arrangement (probably by trombonist Ray Conniff), but it quickly turns into a typical commercial dance band vocal. Berigan achieves a fine high-note ending, but this does not seem like real jazz, just as on "It's the Little Things That Count," also from May 26. Berigan swings well enough at the beginning, but the piece is fundamentally commercial music. The trumpeter's solo simply features half-valve work and upward rips, nothing very consequential, and even includes several muffed notes. As Gunther Schuller points out, most of Berigan's fluffs come in very conservative solos, not those in which he was more adventuresome.[80] Both as leader and featured soloist of his own band, Berigan ultimately was not that effective. The consensus seems to be that because Berigan was not a disciplinarian, his orchestra suffered from attention to detail as well as "a stultifying lack of variety in regard to style and format," and his own playing remained at a lower level of intensity and imagination largely because he "was to the fore in balling it up" and because of his growing alcoholism.[81]

The question arises as to why a fine sideman like Berigan wanted to lead a big band. Gunther Schuller has offered one response when he writes of Berigan that, "like Armstrong, he was merely interested in fronting a band, using it as a vehicle and a backdrop for his solo work."[82] Richard Sudhalter quotes one of Berigan's drummers, Johnny Blower, who considered Bunny "a marvelous sideman. In fact, he was always a sideman, never a leader in the strict sense of the word. He wanted to play, drink, enjoy life."[83] Sudhalter also quotes clarinetist Joe Dixon to the same effect: "Emotionally I don't think he ever thought of himself as a leader. It made him uncomfortable, isolated him from the men."[84] The sad thing is that Berigan never really developed his potential as a soloist once he became a nominal leader. Nor did he promote his sidemen the way other leaders normally did. Although some sidemen of the period could make do with only a few bars, for the most part Berigan's soloists were stifled by the limited space they were allotted for improvisation and, as noted before, by the poor selection of repertoire. But it is not clear if they necessarily would have produced more meaningful music had they been given longer breaks or been able to base their improvisations on more inspiring material. Even when the Berigan orchestra did explore more classic jazz works such as Ellington's "Azure," Jelly Roll Morton's "Jelly Roll Blues," Bix Beiderbecke's "Davenport Blues," and Juan Tizol's "Night Song," or even a promising pop song such as "I Cried for You," the results were mixed.

The Berigan orchestra's recording of Ellington's "Azure," from April 21, 1938, points up dramatically the difference between the two leaders' handling of an artful piece of music.[85] Ellington's composition was originally recorded by his orchestra on May 14, 1937, and the work is in the tradition of his earlier "Mood Indigo," with clarinet combined with muted trumpet and trombone to create a subtle blue atmosphere. Harry Carney on baritone sax plays but a few notes, and yet they say so much in the context of this haunting piece. On the other hand, the Berigan version is strictly commercialized and in no way attempts to re-create the blue mood of the original. Berigan's flashy break seems completely out of keeping, and the arrangement moves from one style to another, with nothing really fitting together to evoke the feeling of Ellington's composition. The ending, which is so effective and emotive in the Ellington version, is simply dumb in the Berigan. Auld plays nothing of interest, and Dixon, like Berigan, is in a showy mode far-removed from Ellington's artful work. The Berigan recording of "Jelly Roll Blues," from November 22, 1938, is for the most part a corny, parodic arrangement, although the section following the leader's solo is an improvement and the abrupt ending is a nicely appropriate touch.[86] Berigan does tend to pay tribute to Morton in his solo, which is more serious than much of the arrangement. Richard Sudhalter, for his part, praises Berigan for finding through his solo "emotional depths in the piece that even Morton himself probably never knew existed."[87] On November 30 a small group from the band recorded Beiderbecke's "Davenport Blues," and in this case the return to an earlier jazz classic proved an ameliorative choice.[88] Berigan's solo is outstanding, as are the solos of the other sidemen, although Ray Conniff's trombone break is merely adequate and Berigan does muff a few of the key notes in Bix's tune. Later, almost a year to the day, on November 28, 1939, Berigan and his men recorded Juan Tizol's "Night Song," and they do render this serious jazz composition quite effectively. Berigan's muted solo is more subdued and introspective than usual, not just a flashy bit of technique, even though it does include some quite impressive high notes. Al Jennings on trombone turns in a fine solo as well. There is more substantive music here than on most of the 1938 sides. However, "I Cried for You," from November 22, 1938, did elicit from Berigan a solo more in the mode of his 1937 version of "I Can't Get Started," and Auld on tenor proved a worthy soloist on this occasion.[89] But by 1939, Berigan's alcoholism began to take its toll, and in December he was hospitalized. In early 1940 he disbanded and declared bankruptcy.

Although Berigan organized another band in September 1940, it was not distinctive, and his own playing was deteriorating rapidly. By this time, even when audiences requested his hit number, "I Can't Get Started," he would have to beg off, explaining that he could no longer reproduce his original solo.[90] Gunther Schuller has suggested that Berigan's was a "star-crossed art," and sadly this seems to have been the case most often during his years of fronting his own band.[91] Albert McCarthy does allow that Berigan's contributions while leading his band should make a listener "grateful that his band entered the studios with such frequency from 1937 to 1939," but it seems that had the trumpeter remained a sideman with a Goodman or a Dorsey, under their disciplined approaches he might have lived longer and produced more significant jazz than he did as a leader.[92] The lure of leadership or the distaste for playing under someone else's direction may have been detrimental to Berigan's health and his artistic achievement. Yet as Richard Sudhalter has pointed out, perhaps too much emphasis has been placed on Berigan's production during his leadership period and that his overall career should be considered in evaluating his place in the pantheon of creative jazz musicians. Sudhalter concludes that "no one, listening to the dozens of solos recorded by Berigan between 1931 and 1936, can fail to perceive the eloquence and consistent beauty, allied to great strength and technical command."[93] And, of course, there were the exceptional solos on sides such as "Frankie and Johnnie," "I Can't Get Started," and "Russian Lullaby" from 1937, "Jelly Roll Blues" from 1938, and "Night Song" from 1939 that remain evidence of Berigan's status as a giant among trumpeters in the 1930s and in the history of jazz. And as we shall see in the chapter on The Small Swing Groups, Berigan, like many other jazz musicians, did some of his finest work in the more congenial combo setting.

THE BOB CROSBY ORCHESTRA

The importance of name recognition to any musical organization is perhaps best represented by the case of Bob Crosby and the orchestra for which his name served as the identifying moniker. Although Crosby was known in the midthirties through his vocals with the Dorsey Brothers Orchestra, he was a commodity as a bandleader mostly by virtue of his kinship to his more famous brother Bing, the early star crooner with Paul Whiteman. Although Bob was possessed of a fine baritone voice, which Gunther Schuller considers "similar to brother Bing's but enhanced by an intriguing, attractive, slight quaver," the younger man apparently was more valuable to the orchestra for being a Crosby than for his singing or for his "leading" of the group, because, at least in the latter regard, he had no real talent for fronting an instrumental ensemble, no conception of "even how to start off a number."[94] Basically Bob Crosby served as an indifferent or prudent headliner who left his musicians to their own devices; in the words of critic and promoter John Hammond, Bob had "a healthy respect for the musical whims of his band" and allowed "the boys to blow as loud or as soft" as they liked.[95]

The personnel of the Bob Crosby Orchestra consisted of disaffected side-men from Ben Pollack's band, from which they resigned in 1934, intending beforehand to remain together as a team. For their business manager, they chose Gil Rodin, who had handled the Pollack band, and with talented arrangers such as Deane Kincaide, Matty Matlock, and Bob Haggart—all former members of Pollack's unit—the Crosby Orchestra developed into what Schuller considers to have been "the first 'jazz repertory orchestra,' " playing a combination "of the new big band sound of swing with the free-dom and loose-textured spontaneity of small-group Dixieland."[96] The suc-cess of this revival of a 1920s, New Orleans–inspired repertoire in a big-band setting was remarkable, in light, according to some critics, of its retrograde nature and its appearance in the very midst of a swing move-ment that emphasized sectional writing rather than a contrapuntal type of group improvisation. In many ways, the Crosby Orchestra forecast the bit-ter feud in the forties between the "moldy figs" who advocated "pure" jazz of the 1920s or earlier and the new beboppers who sought to escape from the limitations of swing and any conservative effort (particularly among white jazzmen) to return to an outmoded format.

In October and November 1955, Billy May, an arranger for the Charlie Barnet Orchestra of the late 1930s, recorded an album titled *Sorta-Dixie*. Two of the soloists on this album, clarinetist Matty Matlock and tenorist Eddie Miller, had originally performed many of the tunes on this recording as members of the Bob Crosby Orchestra. But more to the point, the title phrase of this 1955 recording aptly describes the hybrid music of the Crosby Orchestra, even though, as Gunther Schuller observes, the vast ma-jority of its sides (some 280 out of over 300) were devoted to "pop tunes, sentimental vocals, and a dozen or so swing instrumentals."[97] Nonetheless, it is the Crosby Orchestra's "genuine Dixieland jazz" that has endured and is now the entire feature of the group's music on available compact discs of recordings reissued in recent years.[98] How close to the early Dixieland material the Crosby Orchestra actually hewed is indicated by Deane Kin-caide's arrangement of the 1927 Bix Beiderbecke version of "Royal Garden Blues" by Spencer and Clarence Williams.[99] Richard Sudhalter reports that Bob Haggart commented to him that the Kincaide arrangement re-created the lead line played by Bix because often the band members did not know the original melodies. "We only knew the tunes from what we'd heard on the old records. I did it too, in orchestrating things that had been played by Louis' Hot Five. We pretty well figured that if Bix or Louis had played it that way, that was how the tune ought to be played."[100] In fact, the Dixieland arrangements by the Crosby Orchestra are only "sorta-dixie," as illustrated by their version of "Royal Garden Blues," from August 19, 1936. On this recording the sound is fuller; the "contrapuntal" lines merely hinted at (with the clarinet filling in here and there as the larger ensemble states the theme); swing-era chords or modulations alter the original harmony; the solos by Matlock, trombonist Warren Smith, trumpeter Yank Lawson, and tenorist Eddie Miller are in the Dixieland style but modernized; and the outpassage has a full big-band sound and swing that departs noticeably from the small-group feel of Bix's 1927 recording. As Schuller says, this represents a "compromise," both an authentic revisiting of jazz's New Orleans roots and a "new big band sound," although there is nothing "forward-looking" about the orchestra's "musical policy" that was "safe and conservative."[101] Clearly, this compromise was the key to the orchestra's success, and with its very capable and dedicated sidemen such as Lawson (whose trumpet break is not merely imitative but is a deeply felt and personal expression in the earlier style), the group's formula updated jazz's "venerable history" and its "accumulated artistic tradition" for a swing-era audience.[102]

One of the first rave reviews received by the Crosby Orchestra came from George Simon, who in 1936 wrote in *Metronome* magazine that the group was "one of the swing greats of the country today." Years later, Simon would admit that his view was "one with which not all readers agreed. To some, two-beat jazz was and always would be old-fashioned and corny."[103] Although the Crosby Orchestra is remembered mostly for its Dixieland sides, the group's theme song was George Gershwin's "Summertime," in Simon's view "a seemingly incongruous selection for a group that swung as much as this one did." Yet as he goes on to say, "it made an ideal theme, not only because it signified good music but also because its long, mournful melodic lines offered such an exciting contrast with the rousing numbers that invariably opened and closed each Crosby band broadcast."[104] Eddie Miller's tenor solo on "Summertime" represents one of the fullest examples of what Gunther Schuller calls Miller's "lithe tone" that can "remind one of Lester Young," although the critic allows that Miller was "not as spontaneously creative and rhythmically loose as Young." Aside from the tenor's limited embellishment of the theme statement, the orchestra's version of "Summertime," from October 21, 1938, is, according to Schuller, "a wooden hotel-band type of arrangement" that marks the first low point in the band's "jazz quotient," when "pop ballads and novelty tunes threatened to take over."[105] One example of an inane adaptation of Dixie to a big-band setting is Bob Haggart's "March of the Bob Cats," from March 10, 1938, on which Miller offers little more than meaningless doodles, while the orchestration, as Schuller remarks, is "filled with swing and pseudo-jazz clichés."[106] But to the credit of the group, and supportive of Simon's rave review, the Crosby unit offered works that sampled the various prejazz or early jazz genres, such as gospel, blues, military march, boogie woogie, stride, and stomp. Not all of the orchestra's attempts to recapture these black musical styles are successful, but several do manage to achieve a genuine appreciation and a re-creation of such vital expressions of black music.

One of the most moving pieces by the Crosby Orchestra is Haggart's instrumental arrangement of "I'm Prayin' Humble," which was inspired when the arranger heard the Southern vocal group, Mitchell's Christian Singers, perform this gospel song.[107] George Simon reports that Haggart remembered how he was "knocked out the way they did it and the way they swung even without any accompaniment. So I decided to write it for the band."[108] The plunger cornet part, although conceived as a feature for Yank Lawson, was played at the recording session of October 19, 1938, by Sterling Bose, who also had been a member of the Ben Pollack band and was available when Lawson left to join the Tommy Dorsey Orchestra. Bose evokes the true feeling of the gospel or spiritual-like quality of the song and thus pays an authentic tribute to the work of Mitchell's Christian Singers and to a profound black musical tradition. The arrangement also exhibits Haggart's sensitive response to the deep emotional expression of the Singers' performance. Richard Sudhalter quotes Haggart as having noted that even though the Singers "knew nothing about [formal] music . . . all their performances had this kind of wonderful dissonant sound," which Sudhalter attributes to "simple devices . . . open fourths and fifths . . . evocative of a southern gospel 'shout.' "[109] The one distraction on this otherwise very laudable performance is Ray Bauduc's dull drumming, which even Haggart regretted by noting, "We were trying to get a kind of rolling gospel feel, but Ray got on his tomtoms and stuck to that beat all the way through, with the result that it never quite got off the ground the way I'd hoped."[110] Bauduc's drumming often is quite stimulating for the orchestra, but on this occasion and at other times he can be hyperactively overbearing.

Another somewhat moving side is the Crosby Orchestra's recording of Haggart's original tune, "Dogtown Blues," from November 16, 1937. This too is an authentic attempt at replicating an early or prejazz musical genre, both in its expressive feeling for the blues form and in its imitation of the original New Orleans style of jazz. Yank Lawson plays the trumpet part, which opens the piece and later includes a stop-time chorus, the latter a typical feature in New Orleans–based performances by such trumpet stars as King Oliver and Louis Armstrong. (On its early recording session of April 13, 1936, the Crosby Orchestra had reproduced "Riverside Blues," the Oliver-Armstrong classic from 1923, in an arrangement by Haggart titled "Dixieland Shuffle.") Lawson is effective in reproducing the patterns established by earlier black jazzmen, especially in his brilliant sound, but there is little if anything in his ideas or mode of expression that can approach the emotive force of his forebears. A better job of digging into the blues feeling is turned in by Eddie Miller on clarinet. As for Haggart's orchestration in "Dogtown Blues," this proves at times rather boring and even a bit corny, so overly bent does he seem on updating the form for a big-band effect. One other version of this same early jazz form is the Crosby Orchestra's rendition of a Jelly Roll Morton classic, "Wolverine Blues," first recorded in 1923 by the New Orleans Rhythm Kings. On February 18, 1938, not long before the composer himself would resurface to make in June 1938 his late Library of Congress recordings with Alan Lomax, the Crosby Orchestra cut their version of Morton's "Wolverine Blues," which unfortunately does not, in Matty Matlock's orchestration, pay proper tribute to the composer's masterpiece. The Crosby take tends to trivialize the original work, with Miller on clarinet sounding rather flippant, Ray Bauduc's drumming merely showy, and the clarinet trio sounding simply trite.[111] Of course, for listeners who did not know the NORK side from 1923 or Morton's 1925 duet recording with Volly De Faut on clarinet, they would not have known the difference, or if they had heard such recordings they surely would have been more taken with the Crosby Orchestra's "updating" of Morton's "outmoded" sort of music.

Two other sides produced at the session of November 16, 1937, "South Rampart Street Parade" and "Panama," are tunes subsequently recorded in 1955 by Billy May.[112] Clearly the Crosby Orchestra's versions of these pieces were the inspiration for May's later arrangements, for the first of these classic Dixieland numbers opens on the Crosby, as does the May, with the striking up of the marching band, an early source of New Orleans jazz. With the 1937 version, Crescent City native Eddie Miller revisits the clarinet tradition of his hometown to re-create its combination of rousing street parade style and classical symphony technique, which characterized the work of so many New Orleans players who employed the Albert clarinet system.[113] In this piece, Gunther Schuller especially singles out trumpeter Lawson's leading of "his troops to triumphant joyous victory," which the critic considers an instance of "the incomparable joy and excitement of collective music-making in the hands of a group of highly compatible musicians, led with irresistible fervor by a musician of Lawson's calibre and integrity."[114] The other classic Dixie piece, "Panama," also finds the orchestra "in full cry," or as Richard Sudhalter describes it: "here is the ability of the larger group to swing . . . with the same looseness and freedom that typified performances by the Crosby band-within-a-band, the Bobcats."[115] (Sudhalter is referring to the orchestra's small group consisting of a frontline of trumpet, clarinet, trombone, and tenor saxophone, accompanied by piano, bass, guitar, and drums.) On this occasion Eddie Miller returns to his tenor to take quite an exuberant break, as does Warren Smith on trombone. These are both excellent examples of the Crosby Orchestra's big-band form of Dixieland swing, which Albert McCarthy was probably the first to describe as "a surprisingly successful blend of big band sound with the freedom of a Dixieland small group."[116]

In 1938 and 1939, the Crosby Orchestra recorded a number of boogie-woogie pieces, after which this revived form became de rigueur for swing bands in the last years of the decade. Among many other boogie woogie arrangements for big band, there were Woody Herman's "Indian Boogie Woogie" and "Chips' Boogie Woogie" from December 1938 and September 1940.[117] Of course, Mary Lou Williams had written "Roll 'Em" for the Benny Goodman Orchestra, which recorded it on July 7, 1937, but as Gunther Schuller says, no other band was so dedicated as Crosby's to re-discovering the earlier music of New Orleans and Chicago (the latter being the principal center for boogie woogie from the mid to late '20s), and as a result it was probably the Crosby Orchestra's sides that led most to the boogie revival.[118] Schuller finds the Crosby Orchestra's "Boogie Woogie Maxixe," of August 29, 1939, with Joe Sullivan on piano, a "pleasant Latin-flavored" piece; two other boogie numbers are based on specific classic boogie woogie recordings.[119] "Yancey Special," of March 10, 1938, derives from the boogie style of Chicagoan Jimmy Yancey, who in October 1929 recorded, for example, his "Slow and Easy Blues" with boogie's characteristic repeated left-hand bass. The Crosby Orchestra's "Yancey Special" features pianist Bob Zurke, who sets the *ostinato* bass line, over which he plays the melody, after which the orchestra continues with a clarinet-trio repetition of the melody while the trombones take over the repeated bass line. Zurke returns and then the orchestra does its variations on the theme, with Ray Bauduc contributing some subtle punctuations on what is probably a perforated cymbal with metal cylinders to lend it a lush ring. The other classic boogie piece, "Honky Tonk Train Blues," is based on Meade Lux Lewis's composition, which he recorded on November 21, 1935, under the influence of Jimmy Yancey and other boogie-blues piano men of the '20s.[120] Zurke definitely captures the spirit of the original, even though he takes the piece at a much faster clip than Lewis. On the other hand, the orchestra fills tend to belittle the number, and Zurke's ending, although it follows the original Lewis recording in slowing down like a train, is a bit sentimental after all the headlong drive of the rest of the recording. Generally speaking, the Crosby version loses some of the earthiness of the original, owing to the almost parodic orchestral sections and the rather frivolous last measures that depart from the bittersweet bluesy ending by Lewis. The greatest difference between the Crosby versions and the originals is that the former are basically flashy pieces whereas the latter are more a combination of the joyous and sad that makes such boogie numbers inherently emotive rather than merely showy.

Pianist Joe Sullivan contributed to the Crosby book a tune titled "Little Rock Getaway," which was recorded by the orchestra on November 5, 1937. However, the piano part was performed by Bob Zurke, who had replaced Sullivan when he developed tuberculosis. Zurke opens this piece in something of a stride style reminiscent of James P. Johnson and Fats Waller, but also at times close to the shouting piano of Earl Hines. Later Zurke displays what Gunther Schuller calls the "astonishing independence of his two hands and ten fingers" which could lead "him into the most complicated contrapuntal mazes . . . from which he would always extricate himself just in time." Schuller also contrasts Zurke's "vertical, stomping, hell-bent playing, with wrong notes that somehow didn't sound wrong," with the "controlled, precise, linear playing" of tenorist Eddie Miller.[121] An example of the latter also is present on "Little Rock Getaway" when Miller delivers a solo of which George Simon writes that he has "seldom heard a more swinging or more beautifully-constructed tenor sax chorus than the one Eddie Miller plays here."[122] The rhythm section is appropriately subdued on this side, giving the pianist and tenorist a chance to shine without being overwhelmed, especially by Bauduc's often domineering drums. Zurke's overly busy piano-playing and Bauduc's excessive drumming ruin in many ways the two-part version of "Diga Diga Doo," from November 19, 1938, on which Eddie Miller contributes some very solid swing and Haggart shows that "even riff writing can be intelligent and absorbing."[123] Although "Little Rock Getaway" is a neatly played piece—the two soloists performing their parts admirably and without a hitch—the side comes off ultimately as derivative, as somewhat unimaginative in the sense that it is all prepackaged. Little that the Crosby Orchestra recorded gives the listener a sense that original musical thinking is taking place, that the musicians are doing any more than repeating certain patterns that already existed and had been played with a greater depth of feeling and a more engaging creativity. Of course, a jazz figure such as Fats Waller certainly employed set patterns or those that he tended to use from one recording to the next, which derives in part from the ragtime tradition of repeated strains on which stride was basically patterned, along with the added expressiveness of the blues. However, even though Zurke and Miller gave such patterns their own personal touch, the results remain largely secondhand, lacking in the innovative qualities of the first exponents of the style.

Two sides based on the early stomp style—"Stomp Off and Let's Go" and "Air Mail Stomp"—were both recorded in 1939.[124] By this time, according to Gunther Schuller, the orchestra "seemed to have lost its inspiration" and was consolidating its "fusion of Dixieland and swing" for purposes of pleasing "a wider audience spectrum." But Schuller does allow that the "stunning" performance of "Air Mail Stomp" represented "a momentary high point," whereas "Stomp Off and Let's Go" was an example of the orchestra's "simplistic Dixieland nonsense."[125] Clarinetist Irving Fazola, another New Orleans native, demonstrates his smooth technique and a certain melodic inventiveness on "Air Mail Stomp," whereas Eddie Miller on tenor tends toward the frantic and his break perhaps overemphasizes speed in place of statement. Meanwhile, trumpeter Shorty Sherock reveals how influenced he was by Roy Eldridge in offering a more modern style of intensely driving lines. The most meaningful solo on the side is probably taken by bassist Bob Haggart, who varies his approach, contrasting faster and slower phrases to good effect and choosing more telling notes than his fellow sidemen. Ray Bauduc, who opens the piece on his tom tom (as he did on "Big Noise from Winnetka" of October 14, 1938), takes a drum break that is certainly stimulating, and his rapid-fire percussive work seems to excite the ensemble into one of its most killer-diller conclusions.[126] (Haggart and Bauduc's popular duo recording of "Big Noise from Winnetka" was, as Sudhalter puts it, "a gimmick" rather than an inventive work of jazz improvisation.[127]) "Stomp Off and Let's Go," which was composed by Elmer Schoebel, pianist with the New Orleans Rhythm Kings of the early '20s, features a solo by Eddie Miller on tenor that perhaps saves this side from being an otherwise rather dated affair. Although Ray Bauduc's drum-rim routine behind Miller may have energized the tenorist, it does tend to lend an old-timey touch to the solo, as does elsewhere Bauduc's use of the cowbell (for instance on "Swingin' at the Sugar Bowl," from October 19, 1938, which also is saved by Miller's break on tenor).[128] A side such as "Stomp Off and Let's Go" at once set the Crosby Orchestra apart from all the white groups that were, in Haggart's words, "trying to sound like Ellington and Basie and Lunceford"; yet it also suggests that even by 1939, as Gil Rodin would only decide in 1942, "the Crosby dixieland style had worn out its welcome."[129] The happy, swinging mode of the Crosby Orchestra was obviously attractive to listeners of the late depression and during a period when war in Europe was threatening to engulf the rest of the world, including the then isolationist United States. But the Crosby group also could produce more introspective sides, which reflected the public's growing sentimental mood as the likelihood of war increased and took the edge off the lightheartedness brought on by the improving economic conditions.

With Bob Zurke replaced by Jess Stacy on piano, the Crosby Orchestra recorded, on November 6, 1939, a piece by Stacy entitled "Complainin'," orchestrated by Bob Haggart. More contemplative than Zurke or Sullivan before him, Stacy perhaps represents something of a shift to a less Dixie-dominated style. Stacy's very relaxed Earl Hines–and Teddy Wilson–influenced piano is certainly far removed from Zurke's "rhythmically compelling" approach.[130] For Richard Sudhalter the move away from the Dixieland emphasis was largely unfortunate, and he approves the Crosby Orchestra's return in early 1942 to its more successful Dixie repertoire, writing that "the band was happy and comfortable reclaiming this musical ground."[131] But even before Stacy's arrival, the orchestra had recorded other sides that differ rather dramatically from its Dixie predilection, including Haggart's "What's New?" (originally entitled "I'm Free"), from October 19, 1938, written especially for trumpeter Billy Butterfield, and "My Inspiration," a feature for Irving Fazola, recorded on the following day, October 20.[132] Just as "I Can't Get Started" made Bunny Berigan a household name, "What's New?" did the same for Butterfield among big-band listeners, so much so that, as Albert McCarthy reports, the inevitable requests for the trumpeter to play "What's New?" caused him to "become heartily sick of the number."[133] Butterfield's pure, penetrating sound is pleasant to hear, but it is perhaps lacking in the "brooding style" of Berigan that is so much more than simply well-played notes or a lyrical flow. "Brooding style," a phrase of George Frazier's, aptly captures the special undercurrent of melancholy in Berigan's playing; Frazier also described Bunny's style as "fire rather than merely warmth," which contrasts well with Butterfield's warmth rather than fire.[134] Nonetheless, "What's New?" did provide Butterfield with a meditative framework in which to showcase his singing lines, which, again, differ notably from the Dixie style of most of the Crosby Orchestra's hit recordings. Here Haggart's orchestration is richly modern, with what would seem to be his bowed bass adding a darker, deeper, full-bodied undertone. Haggart's melody is in itself bitter-sweet, and against the rather somber ensemble, the trumpet's theme statement, with its broad vibrato, creates a ballad that is probably the closest the Crosby Orchestra and its mostly Dixie-inclined soloists ever came to a "brooding style."

In a similar introspective mode is the opening of Haggart's "My Inspiration," featuring Irving Fazola's warm, technically pristine sound on clarinet. In the New Orleans tradition of clarinetists such as Jimmy Noone, Barney Bigard, Omer Simeon, and Leon Roppolo, Fazola reflects the tonal control and flawless execution of that Crescent City school. "Even at faster tempos," as Richard Sudhalter observes, Fazola tends "to speak in a tranquil voice," which is the case following the slow, musing first part of "My Inspiration" when the piece speeds up and the clarinetist goes into some exercise-like figures that yet swing intensely and exhibit, in Haggart's words, Fazola's "pure and unadorned, tonally rich" approach.[135] Against Haggart's equally rich ensemble background, Fazola first weaves his relaxed and lovely lines, and then, with the tempo doubled, he wails with the ensemble in something of a Dixie-like concerto jam. Fazola's mellifluous purity also can be heard on Haggart's adaptation of Waldteufel's "The Skater's Waltz," subtitled "In Swingtime" and recorded on January 23, 1939.[136] As Albert McCarthy remarks, at this time the Crosby Orchestra had three fine clarinetists in Fazola, Matty Matlock, and Eddie Miller, although on "The Skater's Waltz," as on most other sides, Miller takes a tenor solo, making for a fine contrast between his own slightly rough, more decorative, happy-go-lucky style and sound and the smooth, open-throated, singing tone of Fazola. Although the Crosby Orchestra did not enjoy the services of truly brilliant jazz soloists, all were quite capable performers who seemed to fit beautifully into whatever format the arrangers created, from Dixieland and the various early jazz forms to lyric pieces such as "What's New?" a solid swing number such as "Air Mail Stomp," the adaptation of a semiclassical work such as "The Skater's Waltz," and the instrumental version of a pop song such as "Between the Devil and the Deep Blue Sea," from February 8, 1937, which features notable solos by Miller, Yank Lawson, and Matlock.[137]

The Bob Crosby Orchestra was certainly a distinctive ensemble whose soloists did have identifiable voices. Although the group's music was derivative of earlier styles, it re-created those styles with infectious enthusiasm and, for the most part, impressive authenticity. And even though the orchestra did not contribute to the development of jazz in terms of innovation, it did pay dignified and well-deserved homage to the rich heritage of this American music. In many ways the Crosby Orchestra was important in making listeners aware of jazz's legacy. I personally recall that my introduction to the classic tunes of Jelly Roll Morton was through two 45-inch records in an album of the music of that New Orleans master as performed in the 1950s by the band of Yank Lawson and Bob Haggart. From that album I discovered Morton's magnificent music, only later coming across the original sides on which the Lawson-Haggart band had based their own recordings. Although I found the originals much more engaging, I could still appreciate how well those members of the late 1930s Bob Crosby Orchestra had captured the fun and joy of Morton's earlier music. I continued to thank Lawson and Haggart for having made me familiar with that composer's name and with the memorable tunes and unforgettable titles of Jelly Roll's marvelous jazz. Lawson and Haggart's devotion to the work of Morton, King Oliver, Louis Armstrong, Bix Beiderbecke, and other early giants is admirable in itself, but their ability to re-create its spirit through their own considerable musical talents—and those of their fellow sidemen such as Eddie Miller, Matty Matlock, Bob Zurke, and Irving Fazola—was and remains a remarkable achievement that leaves all listeners to the music of the Swing Era enriched by and indebted to the "repertory" concept behind the Bob Crosby Orchestra.

CHARLIE BARNET

If the Bob Crosby Orchestra set out to distinguish itself from most other swing orchestras that were attempting to sound like Ellington, Basie, and Lunceford, Charlie Barnet, with his orchestra of the late 1930s, intentionally based his conception of a big band on the recordings of his black mentors. Born in New York City on October 26, 1913, Barnet was active in music professionally by age sixteen when he performed as a saxophonist at various spots around his native city. In 1930, it was curiously Barnet who, according to Albert McCarthy, inexplicably played the chimes on the famous Duke Ellington recording of "Ring 'Dem Bells."[138] It is clear from this early contact with Ellington that Barnet was drawn from the first to Duke's music, which explains why in the late '30s and early '40s Barnet not only recorded such Ellington-inspired pieces as "The Duke's Idea" and "Wings over Manhattan" but also such Ellington originals as "The Gal from Joe's," "Echoes of Harlem," "Merry-Go-Round," "Rockin' in Rhythm," "Harlem Speaks," and "Things Ain't What They Used to Be." Through Barnet's allegiance to the Ellington orchestra and other name black bands, the leader and his orchestra "gained a reputation as the blackest-sounding of the white bands."[139] Although Gunther Schuller opines that Barnet's versions of black jazz were as stylized as the music of Glenn Miller, but not "self-created" as Miller's was, Albert McCarthy finds that Barnet's black-influenced pieces, in particular those inspired by Ellington, "demonstrate how to retain the spirit of the originals without indulging in imitation," that Barnet's recordings are "valid performances in their own right."[140]

Charlie Barnet's first big band, formed in 1933, was a society orchestra that played mostly "dance and Dixieland numbers at top New York hotels and high-society venues."[141] During this year the leader's group also substituted for his friend Benny Carter's band at the Apollo Theatre, reportedly being the first white band to appear at that Harlem site.[142] In 1934, Barnet recorded with Red Norvo's Swing Septet, a mixed group that included Artie Shaw on clarinet and Teddy Wilson on piano. From a side titled "Tomboy," recorded on October 4, Barnet can be heard sounding on tenor like Coleman Hawkins, although in the late '30s Barnet's approach would move away from the rather florid, full-bodied sound of Hawkins to what Albert McCarthy describes as "a slightly drier tone and a staccato phrasing that imparts to his solos the agitated quality of the jump style."[143] In 1935, Barnet dissolved his big band and tried his hand at acting in Hollywood movies, but by 1936 he had formed another group, recording in that and the following year for RCA Victor and Variety. In 1938, Barnet secured a new contract with Victor, under which his band held its first recording session on January 20, 1939. But it was not until July 17, when the group recorded "Cherokee," a Ray Noble tune arranged by Billy May, that Barnet and his band vaulted into the national spotlight with the biggest hit of the leader's career.[144] Ironically, the producer for the session was unimpressed with the performance of "Cherokee," but extensive radio and jukebox exposure of the tune brought Barnet and his men almost instant fame. Opening in something of a subdued Glenn Miller mode, with wa-wa-ing plunger-muted trumpets, "Cherokee" moves to Barnet's tenor theme statement that immediately reveals his deep jazz affinities, as he swings solidly but with fine restraint. May's arranging already is marked by his signature phrasing, with the muted trumpets playing a type of chromatic pickup. Trombones repeat the theme while the muted trumpets play something of a countermelody and then the saxes also state the theme with trumpets punctuating brightly. Barnet returns for another tenor break, in which he employs his "jump style" and quotes a bugle call phrase. At times Barnet's allusions are a bit corny, but on the whole his solos are quite satisfying and seem always to suit the tune being played, whether he solos on tenor, alto, soprano sax, or clarinet.

The success of "Cherokee" was primarily due, it would seem, to the radio, a cause-effect relationship that Barnet obviously could appreciate even before the fact. For on the same session of July 17, 1939, the band cut another side entitled "The All-Night Record Man," a piece dedicated to radio personality, "stay-up all-night" Stan Shaw. As Stanley Dance observes, Barnet "was one of the first musicians to recognize the value of disc jockeys," and this is evident from the lyrics of this tune, sung by vocalist Judy Ellington.[145] The verses of the song refer to night owl fans out in the hinterlands who listen to the radio to catch their favorite bands, with not even the disc jockey knowing how far or to where the music reaches. Barnet's fluid alto solo, with its very unusual contours, may have caught Charlie Parker's ear—certainly we know that the future bop star listened closely to "Cherokee," on which Parker first discovered how to employ the chords of a song in order to create his own melodic lines. Barnet's own influences on his various instruments in the reed family clearly included, at first, Coleman Hawkins on tenor, later Ellington's featured altoist, Johnny Hodges, very likely Basie's star tenorist, Lester Young, perhaps Sidney Bechet on soprano sax, and apparently Jimmie Lunceford's tenor soloist, Joe Thomas. Not only can the influence of Hodges and probably Young be heard on "The Duke's Idea" and "The Count's Idea," two recordings made by Barnet and his band on September 10, 1939, but these two sides also "represent the two primary Barnet influences" in terms of his big-band conception: Ellington and Basie.[146]

Gunther Schuller suggests that it is easier to imitate Count Basie's simpler riff style than Duke Ellington's subtle, wide-ranging sonorities, which in the critic's view helps explain why Barnet was more capable of "emulating" Basie in "The Count's Idea" than he was Ellington in "The Duke's Idea."[147] On the other hand, Albert McCarthy finds that it is "The Duke's Idea" rather than "The Count's Idea" that "evokes more successfully the spirit of the musician honoured."[148] In any case, both recordings are highly effective in conveying the styles of Barnet's mentors, and even though it is true that, as Schuller observes, the soloists on the Basie take do not approach so closely the "subtleties" of their models, they do manage to recreate something of their idols' characteristic modes.[149] On "The Duke's

Idea," Barnet plays a Hodges-like solo that pays ample homage to that artist, while the reed section captures a bit of Ellington's low, mellow tonal richness, even, it would seem, without the aid of a baritone sax. Trumpeter Bobby Burnet essentially quotes phrases often played by Cootie Williams and reproduces a simulacrum of the latter's growl technique. Ultimately, however, the Barnet performance is not a simple imitation but more of a tribute, one that is appropriately serious but yet not subservient. Likewise, "The Count's Idea" opens with a Basie-like piano by Bill Miller that precedes the riff theme, which, following Burnet's muted break that alludes to Buck Clayton's manner, is then reiterated. Here Barnet's jump tenor does not really approximate Lester Young's legato style, but he does employ alternate fingerings for the same note as Pres would on occasion. Barnet also resorts to this same lesser Pres technique on "The Right Idea," another Basie sound-alike recorded on October 9, 1939, as well as on the Basie classic, "Clap Hands, Here Comes Charlie!" recorded by the Barnet unit on December 11, 1939, and "taken at a punishing up-tempo."[150] For the most part, Barnet's break on "The Right Idea" is in his own style, not beholden to any other tenorist of the period. Trombonist Spud Murphy's solo makes a half bow to Dickie Wells, whereas Burnet's open trumpet solo salutes to a certain extent Buck Clayton, although there also is in Burnet's approach something of the exuberant, extrovert style of trumpeter-leader Erskine Hawkins. Meanwhile, the Barnet rhythm section cooks after the all-American fashion of Basie's Jo Jones, Walter Page, and Freddie Green.

Also on the October 9 session that produced "The Right Idea," the Barnet band recorded "Cuban Boogie Woogie," which shows once more the popularity of this earlier jazz form. However, little more than the title, and a reference in the lyrics (sung by Judy Ellington) to a Cuban band that had come to town playing boogie woogie, suggests this style, for the piece mostly tries to get "the rhumba rhythm right," as the verses have it. In some ways this number looks forward to the incorporation by Dizzy Gillespie in the mid to late 1940s of Cuban elements in his big-band bebop style. The only solo is by Barnet, briefly on tenor, to no particular effect, yet the sectional work is quite fine, as it consistently was with Barnet's band of this period. Another Barnet recording that incorporates boogie more directly is "Scrub Me, Mama, with a Boogie Beat," from December 3, 1940, but as Stanley Dance notes, the band does not "take it seriously."[151] Only the pianist really plays in a boogie style, although once again the emphasis is more on a rhumba beat. Trumpeter Ford Leary, serving as vocalist, sings a phrase that refers to musicians who "knock each other out" with their playing, although on this occasion there is nothing especially noteworthy about the performance. Another side in a similar vein is "Redskin Rhumba," recorded on October 14, 1940. Here the influence of Lunceford is heard in Barnet's tenor solo that recalls the style of Joe Thomas, although wa-wa patterns in the trumpets and trombones and Billy

May's growl trumpet show the influence of Ellington. For the most part, this piece conveys neither "redskin" nor a "rhumba feeling." More aptly entitled and in general more impressively performed are "Comanche War Dance" and "Southland Shuffle," from January 3, 1940, and "Leapin' at the Lincoln," from March 21, 1940.[152] On all three of these cuts, drummer Cliff Leeman drives the band with great verve and steadiness, and with quite a modern conception, as he adds to the forward momentum of the music without ever becoming overbearing or simply showy.

Leeman opens "Comanche War Dance" with Native American–style drum patterns, which establish the atmosphere before the band enters with a type of Indian riff. Leeman helps build up the ensemble's intense drive until Barnet enters on tenor, slows things down, and rather takes the air out of the whole proceedings. Afterward the side ends suddenly and disappointingly. On "Southland Shuffle," jaunty trombones open this jump piece, with the saxes continuing the jauntiness before they are joined by Barnet, whose brief tenor break alludes to the popular Popeye hornpipe motif. The feeling of peppiness (somewhat reminiscent of the Lunceford two-beat manner) is carried throughout this side, right up to Barnet's semi-cadenza that neatly ends the number. In between, Bobby Burnet solos exuberantly, again in something of the Erskine Hawkins style, and Barnet takes another of his delightful jump-style breaks, including a surprising upward rip. The relaxed swing of "Leapin' at the Lincoln" also recalls Lunceford, and Burnet's opening trumpet solo is close once again to Erskine Hawkins's extrovert manner, although there also are touches of Rex Stewart's half-valve technique. Burnet also sounds like both Hawkins and Stewart on "Charleston Alley," a Horace Henderson arrangement recorded on January 7, 1941; Burnet ends this side unexpectedly but pleasingly with a half-valve phrase.[153] For Barnet's part, he again employs the alternate fingering technique, but mostly his two separate solos are given over to the jump style with its joyous "leaping" around the horn. Not here but on at least two other sides, " 'Deed I Do," from March 21, 1940, and "Peaceful Valley," from June 19, 1940, Barnet seems to exhibit once again the influence of Lunceford's Joe Thomas, especially on the latter side, although Barnet's ballad style is broader and perhaps more romantic than Thomas's. On "Southern Fried," from September 17, 1940, Burnet again sounds very close to Erskine Hawkins.[154] Despite certain similarities between Barnet and Thomas and Burnet and Hawkins, both the white players are not merely imitative but infuse their solos with recognizable personalities of their own.

The Barnet Orchestra's recording session of January 7, 1941, marked the debut of torch singer Lena Horne. Although Horne only stayed with the band for four months, she would acknowledge that it was during her time with Barnet that she "began to develop her distinctive style."[155] On "Good-for-Nothin' Joe," she exhibits her tight vibrato, her falling off from notes somewhat after the emotive Billie Holiday manner, and her low and high notes that are so full bodied, with the words enunciated so clearly and feelingly. Even more evocative is Horne's rendition of "You're My Thrill," from the same date.[156] Here she not only falls off her notes to lend them a sensual sound, but she hums at times, creating a truly thrilling effect. Although Horne's style is more pop than jazz, it is undeniably appealing, and quite convincingly expressive in its rendering of a song's lyrics. In addition, Barnet's soprano sax theme statement beautifully complements Horne's singing by paralleling the vocalist's expressive style with what Stanley Dance terms the leader's "sultry" solo.[157] Unfortunately, Barnet's vocalists were not always so impressive as Horne or even Judy Ellington. Bob Carroll's version of "I Hear a Rhapsody," from October 14, 1940, is simply dreadful.[158] Only electric guitarist Bus Etri's brief jazz break saves this side from being a total waste, which is regrettable, as the tune is quite lovely and can be heard to fine effect on an album by the Ray Conniff orchestra and singers recorded in the 1950s.[159] Singer Mary Ann McCall also could have her less than inspiring moments, as on the side titled "Wanderin' Blues," from March 21, 1940.[160] Here a boogie-type piano opens the piece, with a bass continuing the rhythm while the reed section creates a rich harmonic passage that maintains nicely the blues feeling, as does Bus Etri's electric guitar. But in contrast, McCall's vocal comes across as a bit affected rather than sincere, although she sings her notes quite competently. Burnet's growly, muted trumpet alludes to Cootie Williams's talking style and concludes the side well enough within the blues mode, but even this attempt at capturing the spirit of the original form is not entirely satisfying. In general, the more successful jazz-oriented efforts of the Barnet band came with its purely instrumental sides, even those that remained heavily influenced by Barnet's black mentors.

An example of a Barnet recording that both pays tribute to one of his principal influences and to an important degree updates the original is his version of Ellington's "Rockin' in Rhythm," from June 19, 1940. Although Gunther Schuller faults the Barnet side with not quite being able to "duplicate the joyous relaxed rhythm and articulation that the Ellington band could give this piece," the Barnet version has its own valid qualities that are different from those of the original.[161] Arranged by Andy Gibson, the Barnet rendition does not so much attempt to reproduce the "rockin' " rhythm as it strives to create a hard-swinging drive that builds up to the orchestra's tremendous vocal shout. Likewise, Barnet's tenor solo that follows—as well as his earlier break—is in an entirely different spirit, one more characteristic of the ecstatic last years of the decade rather than the relaxed style of Ellington's 1930 original. The Barnet version certainly does justice to Ellington's wonderfully rocking themes, playing them with accuracy and with respect for their inherent worth. But the Gibson arrangement in some ways "modernizes" the Ellington piece by making it more contrapuntal, that is, by having different members of the orchestra play simultaneously in a style that is not at all Dixieland but rather is complex in its involvement of quite distinct motifs that yet combine for a fully unified effect. A less successful effort along these lines is "Pompton Turnpike," a Billy May arrangement recorded on July 19, 1940, inspired by a period when the band played an engagement at the Meadowbrook in New Jersey.[162] Stanley Dance calls the exchange between Barnet on soprano sax and May on muted trumpet an "animated dialogue," but this is largely an Ellington pastiche and comes off as far too clever and not really respectful of its source.[163] More conscientious in evoking the Ellington aural image is "Wings over Manhattan," recorded on September 17, 1940.[164] Originally intended for a joint appearance by the Barnet and Ellington orchestras, which did not materialize, "Wings over Manhattan" is a type of Ellingtonian suite or extended composition in several short movements. The opening section has a type of concert buildup to the Ellington-like sound of the saxes, after which the second blueslike section is related to a number of Ellington's mood pieces, with Barnet's tenor and Burnet's muted trumpet both re-creating something of the master's style. In the third section, Bus Etri's electric guitar leads to Barnet's clearly Hodges-inspired soprano solo. The fourth section begins with a marchlike introduction that quickly moves into a rather Broadway musical type of everything goes, with whinnying trumpet and trilling clarinet, before the piece concludes with again a type of concert sound. This is neither an entirely successful nor satisfying piece, but the Ellington-influenced sections are evocative and suitably ceremonious.

During 1941, Barnet recorded a number of arrangements by black arrangers, in particular Horace Henderson, whose "Charleston Alley" has already been mentioned. On April 29, the Barnet band cut Henderson's arrangement of "Ponce de Leon," which in theme sounds somewhat like "Flat Foot Floogie." Cliff Leeman's drumming is effective in giving the band a lift to a higher level of intense drive. Growling trumpets are one feature of the piece, along with a fine trombone break on a par with the work of Fletcher Henderson's sidemen. However, Barnet's tenor solo is not one of his better efforts and, in fact, his playing after this point does not seem to have developed beyond the high points reached in pieces such as "Leapin' at the Lincoln" and "Rockin' in Rhythm" of early to mid 1940. Barnet's own tune, "Wild Mab of the Fish Pond," from September 17, 1940, finds him—against a background of pedal trombones—mostly using gimmicks such as shaking, alternate fingerings, and a type of squawk, rather than shaping a meaningful solo.[165] On August 14, 1941, the band recorded "Swingin' on Nothin'," which apparently is a Sy Oliver composition arranged by Billy Moore.[166] Certainly the Lunceford influence seems present in the use of a vocal trio, in its rather relaxed swing, and in some of the sax figures, but this piece does not generate the kind of punch that even a lesser effort by the Lunceford orchestra could achieve. Barnet's alto solo employs more of his shaking, but other than a few stirring high notes, he creates little of interest, and the side ends abruptly with a few bars by Bus Etri on electric guitar. The title of this work seems to indicate aptly that the group was by this time not swinging in any way to compare with its work in 1939 and 1940, even if black arrangers were being depended on for much of the band's book. Although new blood would arrive during the late '40s, the Barnet band had by and large produced its most remarkable recordings by the end of 1940, even though the leader's own "Skyliner" (arranged by Billy Moore) would in 1944 give him another enduring hit to match the earlier "Cherokee," the classic that first secured his name as a top swing-era competitor.

GENE KRUPA

Like several of Benny Goodman's sidemen, Gene Krupa left to form his own big band, partly on the basis of his vast popularity as a showman drummer but perhaps mostly as a result of the friction that developed between leader and sideman. For many fans of the big-band craze, Krupa, whose career had begun in the mid '20s, was the epitome of the Swing Era, which is indicated by the enthusiastic reception he received on first appearing with his own outfit.[167] According to Albert McCarthy, soon after Krupa left Goodman in March 1938, his own band opened on April 16 at the Steel Pier in Atlantic City to a crowd of some four thousand. Even so, McCarthy asserts that Krupa's group from 1938 to 1940 "was not an outstanding unit," his best bands being those of 1941–1942 and 1944–1945.[168] Although Gunther Schuller claims that the Krupa band "never let jazz out of sight for very long," so many of its recordings are pure schmaltz, especially when vocalist Howard Dulany sang popular songs of the day.[169] In 1941, Krupa secured the services of a fine vocalist in Anita O'Day and of trumpet star Roy Eldridge, and their presence on a number of the band's recordings supports Schuller's view that indeed Krupa was committed to jazz, even though far too many of his sides fail to give much evidence that in terms of a "true commitment to jazz" the leader's orchestra rates "second only to Barnet's" among the white big bands.[170]

As a drummer, Krupa himself is rarely heard from, his showmanship hardly evident on his band's recordings, his drive as a member of the Goodman unit replaced by a surprising reserve. Even on the few pieces where Krupa features himself as a drummer, his playing does not come across as jazz and does not show off any very impressive drumming skills. The leader seems content to restrain himself and inspire the band as merely part of the rhythm section. Paired with Roy Eldridge on several sides from 1941, Krupa does support Schuller's view that the leader "was even more of a jazz fan than his thousands of admirers" and "thrived on that rhythmic feeling that separates jazz, in his case in the form of swing music, from most other forms of music."[171]

Although Krupa utilized the work of a number of black arrangers, his orchestra's performances never rise above a generic big-band sound and his soloists, aside from Roy Eldridge, are not exceptional. Albert McCarthy says of vocalist Irene Daye that she was a "reasonably proficient popular singer," which is apparent on such sides as "The Lady's in Love with You" and "Some Like It Hot," recorded on February 26, 1939, and "My Hands Are Tied," from March 10, 1939. Yet sometimes the vocal material is so bad that Daye can do nothing with it, which is true of "Sweetheart, Honey, Darlin' Dear," from July 24, 1939. As for the ensemble playing, this can vary from mildly stimulating—which applies to "Dracula," from March 10, and amazingly so to "Sweetheart, Honey, Darlin' Dear," despite the dripping saccharinity of its title and lyrics—to a performance that sounds tired and totally uninspired, which is the case with "Swanee River" as arranged by Jimmy Mundy, and even to a performance that is flat boring, which is true of "Hodge Podge," a tune by Johnny Hodges arranged by Duke Ellington. In no way can the Krupa version of "Swanee River," from March 10, compare with the Lunceford rendition of the same Stephen Foster tune from September 1935. "Hodge Podge," from April 16, 1939, contains a decent trumpet break, and tenorist Sam Donahue solos adequately, sounding a bit beholden to Lunceford's Joe Thomas. One of Donahue's best showings comes on "The Madam Swings It," from February 26, where he turns in a splendid, quite exciting effort. Another Stephen Foster song, "Old Black Joe," from July 24, 1939, also arranged by Jimmy Mundy, swings better than usual, but still it offers nothing out of the ordinary. In general, the Krupa orchestra's sides lack drama, contrast, or surprise of any kind. Even a piece such as "Jungle Madness," from April 17, 1939, an original by another black arranger, Chappie Willett, is a pseudoprimitive number with some faux tribal drumming by Krupa, which recalls his tom-tomming on "Sing, Sing, Sing," and with Sam Musiker's clarinet breaks that consist of out-of-place Middle Eastern melodic lines. The whole affair reeks of fakery, the concoction not even halfway as authentic as Ellington's so-called jungle music. Tunes arranged by tenorist Sam Donahue prove more appealing than those arranged by Mundy, Willett, or Ellington, and yet even Donahue's "Quiet and Roll 'Em" and "Challenger Chop," from February 26 and March 10, 1939, respectively, are standard big-band fare, and other bands such as those of Basie, Lunceford, and Erskine Hawkins easily could have played these pieces with more energy and drive.[172]

On occasion, Krupa's band could certainly swing, as it does on "There'll Be Some Changes Made," from January 17, 1941, with the vocal delivered spiritedly by Irene Daye. But contrary to the title of this tune, Krupa's band made no significant changes; essentially it followed the tried and true formula of sectional exchange, with, for example, brass answered by reeds on "Fool Am I," from March 12, 1941, and with Anita O'Day doing the vocal effectively enough, even though the lyrics are quite corny. By this date, the whole big-band formula has simply been run into the ground. Krupa's recordings contain few solos, or if, as on "Fool Am I," the sidemen do take breaks (here clarinet and tenor solo), their offerings more often than not amount to very little. Even when a sideman such as Shorty Sherock, who had been, as we have seen, with the Bob Crosby Orchestra, takes a virtuoso-type break on "Siren Serenade," also from the March 12 session, it lacks any real musical ideas, any development of a structured, meaningful solo. This is true as well of the breaks by the sidemen on trombone, clarinet, and tenor. This particular piece opens with Krupa on drums, after which a trumpet imitates a siren; it ends (following the unengaging series of solos that is at least greater in number than on most of the band's other sides) with the same trumpet's siren imitation, a neat package but ultimately rather pointless. So much of the material of the Krupa band is comprised of sentimental pop songs, such as "Little Man with a Candy Cigar," from March 19, 1941, or "Don't Cry, Cherie," from April 11, 1941. Both these songs are sung by Howard Dulany, whose vocals have nothing to do with jazz. The most that can be said about the latter of these two recordings is that historically it indicates, through the opening strain from the "Marseillaise" and its allusive lyrics, that France had fallen to Nazi Germany. High notes in the trumpets are meaningless, although one would gain the impression that they must have been appealing to audiences because at the time they had become so fashionable with most every big-band arranger. In general, there is little creativity involved in the Krupa band's music making. Even a peppy tune such as "I Take to You," from the April 11 session, offers such a tired formulaic pattern that Anita O'Day cannot overcome its predictability, and even a perhaps interpolated analogy between the love situation in the lyrics and the band leader—"like the Krupa takes to drumming I take to you"—does not save this piece from sounding as though the group is just going through the motions.[173]

Although Gunther Schuller suggests that Krupa "maintained a fine roster of jazz soloists, foremost among them tenor saxophonist Sam Donahue, clarinetist Sam Musiker, [and] trumpeters Corky Cornelius and Dave Schultz," they must have been for the most part bored out of their gourds by the material they had to play.[174] A piece such as "Let's Get Away from It All," from March 19, 1941, is simply dull stuff and defeats even a fine singer like Anita O'Day because the lyrics are so dreadful. When O'Day was given something worth her effort, such as Hoagy Carmichael's "Georgia on My Mind," she, probably Sam Musiker on tenor, and a muted Shorty Sherock, all turn in engaging performances.[175] To some extent, O'Day's vocal style is reminiscent of Billie Holiday's, although in the case of this particular tune, O'Day actually recorded her version of the Carmichael classic nine days before Holiday cut her own rendition on March 21, with a group that included Lester Young on tenor, Shad Collins on trumpet, and Eddie Heywood on piano. Only Heywood solos on the Holiday side, for the focus is on the vocalist's warm, affective singing, which features her very emotive delivery that lends each note and word a special sound and sense. The Krupa version swings nicely, partly because it is taken at a faster tempo than on the Holiday side and with a brighter feeling created by the clarinet-led reeds and muted trumpets. As for O'Day's singing, it has its own special appeal, which differs from Holiday's in that Anita consciously swings her vocal lines in a more lighthearted style, with her voice embellishing or rephrasing the melody in catchy ways. As Schuller points out, O'Day's vocal style "derived from jazz as an *instrumentalist's* art, rather than the vocalist's art of communicating words and stories." Schuller goes on to contrast Holiday and O'Day in terms of the depth of feeling they convey and finds that Billie is more expressive than Anita, that the "quasi-instrumental creative expression" of the latter's singing has to it "a certain abstractness, an emotional aloofness . . . that at once saves it from ever becoming sentimental but also prevents it from probing very deeply."[176]

"Alreet," another side recorded with Anita O'Day at the March 12 session, also demonstrates the vocalist's instrumental-like style, with its emphasis on the notes more than the lyrics' meaning, which basically disappears because a listener is engaged more in the way the singer handles the notes than in what she is saying. Again, the Krupa band swings nicely, with the leader's role restricted to one of driving his group with solid rather than showy drum work, with the exception of a very brief break. On "Slow Down," from March 19, the lyrics play a more important part in O'Day's vocal, for here she illustrates (along with the band) the contrast that she is recommending: "Say brother, you've been travelin' too fast. . . . You better slow down / before there's a showdown, / or else our love is going to break down." Krupa and the band effectively reinforce the vocalist's words with corresponding rhythmic responses. The tenor's solo, with Krupa backing him up, is more meaningful in the context of the song than is usual with the group's solo breaks. Although "Slow Down" presents contrasting fast and slow sections, most of the Krupa recordings do not offer much in the way of variety within specific sides. Overall, however, the band's offerings are fairly varied with regard to the types of material offered, from boogie woogie, novelty, and pop ballad to Latin-flavored pieces such as "María Elena," "A Rendezvous in Rio," and "Green Eyes." Like "Don't Cry, Cherie," the band's rendition of "Boogie Woogie Bugle Boy," from January 17, 1941, alludes in its lyrics sung by Irene Daye to World War II through references to "gone with the draft" and Company B, as well as the opening bugle call played by the orchestra and swung by a trumpeter at the end of the song. The eight-to-the-bar piano is, of course, characteristic of the boogie fashion, whereas the open trumpet break (probably by Shorty Sherock) shows the growing influence of Roy Eldridge, who would himself soon join the Krupa band as trumpeter and vocalist. Another boogie piece from the same date is "Drum Boogie," which, as Albert McCarthy indicates, is "less of a drum showcase than the title implies."[177] Here there are stirring solos by tenor and trumpet, with Krupa kicking the band along with sticks on his snare drum before he takes two short breaks with rolls and other drum patterns, the second break leading to the band's climactic chord. Although there is nothing new or outstanding about these boogie sides, they are performed with discipline and a certain driving verve.[178]

Rather than introduce anything novel, the Krupa band tended to "cover" tunes or styles already recorded or established by other white big bands. An early example of this is the orchestra's version of "Moonlight Serenade," from July 24, 1939, with the lyrics sung by Irene Daye, who delivers this kind of sentimental piece convincingly. But the Krupa version lacks the sophistication and the wonderful reed sound of the Miller orchestra, which had recorded the number over three months earlier, on April 4, 1939.[179] There are no soloists on the Krupa side, and once again the performance lacks drama and contrast, which the Miller offers in abundance. Opening with a trombone imitation of Tommy Dorsey is a piece of romantic schlock titled "Where You Are," from April 11, 1941, whereas "María Elena" and "Green Eyes," from April 11 and May 8, 1941, respectively, cover Jimmy Dorsey hits that had featured Bob Eberly and Helen O'Connell.[180] "María Elena," as recorded by Dorsey on March 19, 1941, and sung by Bob Eberly, is in no way an example of jazz, not even when Dorsey takes a clarinet break. But the Dorsey version of "Green Eyes," from the same date, approaches jazz in the alto solo of the leader, and Helen O'Connell's vocal at least swings a bit. The Krupa version of "María Elena" is about as low on Latin flavor as the Dorsey, but the Krupa does put more punch into the performance. Howard Dulany also tries to swing the vocal more than Bob Eberly and actually does a fairly decent job of it, especially for him. As for the Krupa version of "Green Eyes," it is a true jazz rendition, at least once Roy Eldridge has entered the picture; before the trumpeter's appearance, however, this is merely a society orchestra recording. Armstrong's influence can be heard in Eldridge's solo, yet there are original touches that identify the younger man as an innovative figure. Also, Eldridge seems to energize the band with his entry, to lift it to a higher level of intensity. Although Dulany opens "Green Eyes" with a quite unstimulating vocal, O'Day closes it with some of her infectious phraseology that carries through from Eldridge's driving trumpet chorus. Eldridge and O'Day also teamed up on the May 8 recording of "Let Me Off Uptown," mostly for some vocal banter. Anita's singing is delightful, but it is the trumpeter's solo that makes this side worth hearing.[181] The band itself sounds like so many other units at the end of the thirties and the beginning of the forties, but Eldridge's opening blast, which is echoed wonderfully by Krupa's drums, is a fresh salvo, and the trumpeter finishes off with a solid high note that punctuates his solo statement not so much with an exclamation point as with a declaration, as if to say that he has had his technical say in no uncertain terms.

On July 2, 1941, Eldridge was the featured soloist in a type of concerto with the Krupa band, playing Hoagy Carmichael's "Rockin' Chair," as arranged by Benny Carter. Gunther Schuller rightly asserts that this "is actually a strong and at times tremendously moving performance, spoiled only by the opening and closing cadenzas, the latter unforgivably aping the corniest of operatic cadenza traditions." Schuller especially praises the trumpeter's use of

a raspy, buzzy tone, which enormously heightens his playing's intensity, emotionally and dynamically. . . . Hear the almost uncontainable ardor of both first notes in the bridge and the last "eight" respectively (Roy's first chorus). It was also meant to hurt a little, to be disturbing, to express unfathomable stress.[182]

Although this was one side of the Krupa band's repertoire, more frequently the group's recordings were dominated by performances of pieces such as "Flamingo," with Howard Dulany singing the vocal. Obviously, despite Krupa's "commitment to jazz," the leader felt it imperative to keep Dulany for the sappy ballads that must have been expected by the band's audiences. Once again, there is no connection with jazz in the Krupa band's rendition of "Flamingo," from May 8, 1941, which in this case, especially, is quite disappointing, because one cannot help but compare this recording with such a masterpiece of modern jazz as Charles Mingus's version of "Flamingo" from 1957.[183] Of course, this is not only unfair, because the two works belong to two distinct periods, but admittedly the intent of the Krupa recording was to appeal to a totally different audience than was the Mingus. Such a comparison would hold the Krupa band accountable for commitment to a different type of jazz and would ignore the fact that during the Swing Era jazz largely existed in the interstices of a popular music which aimed at maintaining a large band full time rather than developing experimental works within a small-group workshop setting. Given the demand at this period by a mostly white audience for popular music with its mix of schmaltz and jump swing, it must be acknowledged that the Krupa band succeeded within this context and thus satisfied the needs of its listeners. Also, by providing a wide range of material, some of which, at least in the case of sides with Eldridge and O'Day, survives as representative of the leader's genuine love for the music, Krupa and his sidemen not only earned a living but managed in the process to entertain a nation still enamored of swing.

HARRY JAMES

With Gene Krupa's departure from the Benny Goodman Orchestra in March 1938, Harry James remained as the featured sideman, the star performer of the most popular big band of the day. But by the end of 1938, James, too, had left to form his own unit, one which, according to the new leader, would "swing, but also . . . be easy to dance to."[184] As a matter of fact, the formula of the James Orchestra proved to be a musical dichotomy, as the unit produced a limited number of swinging, jazz-inclined sides, and on the other hand, a rash of sentimental, even saccharine, recordings that had essentially nothing to do with jazz. Although some of the group's recordings of pop songs, even those on which four violins are added, may swing after a fashion, the effect is merely of a quasi-jazz dance rhythm, with little or no emphasis on improvisation or of inventive sectional interplay. Increasingly the focus of the James Orchestra, from its first recording sessions in 1939 to its last at the end of 1941, was on gaining popularity, by whatever means possible, and more and more this meant with less and less of an affinity with jazz. The higher the orchestra ascended in the popularity ratings the lower the percentage of jazz-related music it produced. In many ways this was the pattern for most of the white big bands, and the James Orchestra represents as dramatically as any white organization the decline of jazz-infused big-band music by the end of the period covered by the present volume.

Like other big-band leaders, James's response to criticism of his abandonment of a purer jazz was that the jazz purists "weren't in charge of the payroll."[185] But for listeners who know James's earlier jazz leanings, his astounding trumpet wizardry that can still thrill when he takes a solo and when he leads a trumpet section with power and precision, the trade-off seems especially regrettable. But then, James's tenure as a trumpet luminary and big-band leader did not conclude with 1941, for he would go on to record once again in a truer jazz vein in the late 1940s. And certainly in 1939, he and his band showed themselves to be "an exciting, driving swing band," even if by 1941, they may have preferred their position as "one of the country's most popular and commercially successful orchestras."[186]

The first recording session of the Harry James Orchestra came on February 20, 1939, and even here the Janus-faced nature of its music is indicated by such pieces as "Sweet Georgia Brown" and "Ciribiribin." On Hoagy Carmichael's classic, the group is put through its paces as perhaps never again. One has the impression that James had been held back by Goodman and was raring to go, even though this was probably not the case. But leading his own orchestra must have lit an even greater fire in the trumpeter, for he sets the performance of "Sweet Georgia Brown" at a daunting tempo and yet handles it with his usual aplomb and panache. This side also shows off James's leadership of the trumpet section, which had been an important aspect of his work with Goodman. As the orchestral arranger of Carmichael's song, James makes clear that he was under the influence of Basie, even though the band sounds thin compared with the Count's unit, owing largely to an emphasis on the horns and little support from the rhythm section. Pianist Jack Gardner is in something of a Fatha Hines groove, whereas altoist Dave Mathews's break comes together better than most of his efforts and certainly generates a good deal of energy. Claude Lakey on tenor is not particularly distinctive, but he has some of the same emotive moves associated with Basie's Herschel Evans. Certainly the intense swing of this piece is beyond anything Krupa recorded as a band leader.

As for "Ciribiribin," despite its "impurity," this side—with its Italian folk melody in waltz time that suddenly breaks into 4/4 swing—undeniably placed James above all other trumpeters of the Swing Era for sheer virtuosity on his instrument, much the same way that Louis Armstrong's "West End Blues" established him as far and away the most dynamic, technically secure trumpeter of the 1920s. Of course, such a comparison is only valid in terms of mere technique, because Armstrong's cadenza on "West End Blues" involves expressive qualities of a jazz-oriented order not present in James's basically semiclassic routine. James was more in the jazz tradition on a piece such as "Two O'Clock Jump," from March 6, 1939, which is a version of Count Basie's "One O'Clock Jump." Here James's opening solo is solid jazz improvisation, and the band swings the Smith-Page-Durham theme with conviction and drive, including again a strong showing from the trumpet section. On "Indiana," from April 6, 1939, James once more turns in a fine opening jazz break, followed by a full chorus by Lakey on tenor, which is more developed than any solo offered by Krupa's tenors. James returns for a fabulously virtuosic finale that combines his technical prowess with real swing trumpet.

On June 7, 1939, the orchestra cut their swinging version of "Avalon," which is indebted in part to Eddie Durham's arrangement recorded by the Lunceford unit. Claude Lakey contributes a fine tenor break and James pitches in with a thoughtful muted solo. Another example of James's jazz-inclined playing is heard on "Feet Draggin' Blues," from August 31, 1939, which demonstrates the leader's genuine feeling for the blues, even if he cannot quite bring it off on the same level of such classic blues trumpeters as Bubber Miley and Hot Lips Page. James's own tune, "Flash," from November 8, 1939, exhibits a fine instance of full-bodied big-band swing, with Gardner's opening piano solo paving the way. Claude Lakey's tenor break fuels the swing wonderfully, in contrast to Sam Donahue's tendency to take the drive out of a Krupa performance. Here, too, the James rhythm section, with Red Kent chording nicely on guitar, really cooks, lending the side a more Basie-like foundation. Kent also chords effectively on "Cross Country

Jump," also from November 8, with a muted James accompanied at first only by the rhythm section and showing that in such a small-group setting he could really dig in rather than simply rely on his technique. Moaning saxes and shouting trombones build up an intense drive that rivals even that of Basie's great band. Finally, a muted and later open James also proves that he could improvise to a true boogie beat on "Back Beat Boogie," from November 30, 1939, which again generates an intense drive. All these sides in the traditions of blues, boogie, and riff-based swing make it evident that James and his band were quite capable of producing legitimately jazz-based recordings.[187]

But after 1939, and even during this same year, the James Orchestra cut many sides that represent the worst kind of sentimental slop. "Orchids for Remembrance," of July 18, 1940, is but one of many examples, and even another classic composition by Hoagy Carmichael, his lovely "The Nearness of You," is rendered as a saccharine side by vocalist Dick Haymes, by James's trumpet, and by the syrupy orchestration. Haymes's pronunciation of words such as "you," "conversation," and "sensation" is affected and obviously intended to convey deep feeling but only suggests the falsity of the delivery and interpretation.[188] By contrast, the vocals of Frank Sinatra, who was discovered by James, indicate that from the first this singer's distinctive style was already set. "All or Nothing at All," recorded on August 31, 1939, has been considered "Sinatra's best recording with James," and although it "sold only 16,000 copies when it came out in 1940," it would sell "close to one million" after Sinatra had gained "top billing" while singing three years later with the Tommy Dorsey Orchestra.[189] Even on a piece like "To You," taped off a radio broadcast from the Panther Room of the Sherman Hotel in Chicago during October-November 1939, Sinatra is able to make musical sense of corny, clichéd lyrics.[190] On June 17, 1939, Sinatra recorded with the James Orchestra a song entitled "It's Funny to Everyone but Me," which opens with James's highly romantic muted trumpet.[191] By contrast, Sinatra's entrance is startlingly simple, and even though the lyrics and the singer's sensitive utterance indicate that this is a sentimental ballad, his singing has nothing of the saccharine about it. Sinatra's control and careful placement of his notes, in combination with a very natural phrasing, immediately reveals a new approach to balladry, which, if not exactly jazz, emphasizes a blend of musicality and meaningful interpretation of the lyrics that is fresh and appealing. Claude Lakey's tenor break continues the same feeling of the vocalist's delivery and suggests Lakey's awareness of such leading tenorists as Hawkins, Berry, and Webster. Unfortunately, after Sinatra left, James seemed to lose his way, as revealed by a piece like "Maybe," from July 18, 1940, whose title is even indicative of the leader's uncertainty.[192] His own playing seems to have lost its strength, and his choice of material departs dramatically from any jazz orientation. In addition, Claude Lakey was moved to alto to make way for tenor star Vido Musso, who in no way offered the same level of imaginative, tasteful solos as had Lakey.

So many of the sides from 1940 find the band fallen into a sentimental bog, suffocating from so much romantic mush. Even when the band plays more standard jazz-related tunes such as "Four or Five Times," "Super Chief," "Swanee River," or "Exactly Like You," the results are only mixed.[193] "Four or Five Times," from May 4, can certainly not compare with the Lunceford version; although on the James side the saxes and brasses play well enough, there is no zip to the performance. The vocal interlude by the band members fails to evoke the type of fun trios of Lunceford's men, and the lack of instrumental solos makes the whole production merely a big-band ensemble exercise. Ironically, a pop-tune side from August 12, "I Wouldn't Take a Million," which was rejected by the Varsity label that James had changed to after leaving Brunswick, contains a rather swinging, more natural vocal by Haymes, a fine break by one of the three trombonists, and a fetching solo by James.[194] "Super Chief," from May 9, opens with Vido Musso bursting at the seams, but in general his solos tend to sound like a lot is going on but ultimately they offer little in the way of ideas or surprising phraseology—they turn out to be rather pat arpeggios. James's trumpet breaks are mostly for show, with again little of significance or of a freshness of phrasing. The James version of "Super Chief" predates that of Count Basie from May 31, but it pales when compared with the latter's energetic ensemble work. Musso's solo cannot hold a candle to Buddy Tate's well-conceived break, nor for meaningfulness can James's solo match the one by trumpeter Harry Edison.[195] "Swanee River," from August 12, certainly beats the Krupa version, and although the James arrangement is basically lifted from the Lunceford rendition of 1935, the James version is quite decent. Here Musso's tenor breaks are even quite good, for him. A muted trombone solo remains rather too close to the melody to mean much, but drummer Mickey Scrima kicks the ensemble along very nicely, as he does on "Exactly Like You," from the same date.[196] Both Musso (if he in fact takes the tenor break) and James (in something of a Bixish mode) contribute solid solos on this piece that is played with, for this band, an unusually relaxed swing.

By January 8, 1941, the James Orchestra sounds tired and uninspired. On "I Never Purposely Hurt You," the piece seems to drag, although this could be a wrong impression created by the sentimental nature of the song, with its sappy vocal by Haymes. By this date, one notable addition to the band is Chuck Gentry on baritone, whose horn can be heard anchoring the reeds and giving the section a full, robust sound in the ensemble sections, especially on the tune's final chord. At the same session, the orchestra recorded "Montevideo," another rather lame Latin-flavored piece that seemed so in vogue at this time among the big bands. Nothing about the side makes it a jazz production, which is true as well of "La Paloma" from January 22. Also on the January 8 session, the orchestra recorded "Music Makers," a James original arranged by Margie Gibson, who somewhat emulates Glenn Miller in the sense of being attracted to a kind of fade away before the orchestra ends with a loud finale. This is a mildly catchy tune, but as arranged it seems too cutesy and the various sections of the arrangement do not really cohere. Gibson again employs the fade away on "Answer Man," recorded on January 22. Here the arrangement recalls Lunceford and, indeed, after another type of fade away, the orchestra quotes Lunceford at the end. On "Answer Man," James is more into his jazz manner, as he is on "Ol' Man River," also from January 22.[197] For the Kern classic, James is muted and supported by the rhythm section, and here again, this small-group type of setting seemed to challenge the trumpeter to think more musically than when he was backed by the large ensemble. Indeed, James's work with a contingent from the Basie band, recorded on December 1, 1937, and January 5, 1938, produced some of the trumpeter's best jazz of the period.[198] He also was effective in a Teddy Wilson–led small group on October 31 and November 9, 1938, backing up vocals by Billie Holiday.[199]

On March 26, 1941, the James Orchestra recorded a piece by Dave Mathews titled "Duke's Mixture," a tribute to Ellington, Mathews's avowed idol. The boogie beat in the piano is the only touch that seems out of character for an Ellington homage; otherwise, James imitates Cootie Williams, the saxes evoke the Ellington reed sound, trombonist Dalton Rizzotto reproduces Nanton's plunger tricks, Vido Musso bows in the direction of Ben Webster, and just at the end Mathews on alto tips his hat to Johnny Hodges. The band really takes to this piece and gives it a rousing performance from start to finish. Another Matthews chart, "Jeffries' Blues," from April 28, 1941, shows that he, like Margie Gibson, knew his Lunceford, lifting from the latter a sax riff played behind the first appearance of James's open trumpet. Musso is given an extended solo but does little with it, except for his second series that ends with a stirring high note. Musso does little better on "Sharp as a Tack" from the same date, while James really opens up on this piece and blows an imaginative first break, only to come back toward the end of the number for another of his flashy displays. On "Aurora," from May 20, 1941, a Latin-flavored number with Brazilian allusions, James swings with authority. Nonetheless, in the context of his own band, James is never quite up to his work with Goodman. More often than not, James only offers pop tunes that spotlight his ballad style, as on "You Made Me Love You," from the same May 20 session. Of course, this piece of balladry made him more famous than any of his jazz solos, and the arrangement, including four strings, was a huge hit. Nonetheless, tunes such as "Yes Indeed," from July 2, 1941, and "Nobody Knows the Trouble I've Seen," from October 6, 1941, could return James to the roots of jazz, and in the process his playing improved in its swing and musical sense. "Yes Indeed," by Lunceford's Sy Oliver, as arranged here by Leroy Holmes, is a type of spiritual shout, with the lyrics declaring "when the spirit moves you you'll shout hallelujah. . . . When that jazz starts jumping let me in there." Even Dick Haymes does a decent job of delivering his lines, and James's closing cadenza is quite convincing. But his performance on "Nobody Knows the Trouble I've Seen" offers even more of a genuine jazz feeling, along with some of his spectacular tone quality. The orchestration does, unfortunately, deteriorate near the end, but overall this is an indication of James's understanding of and appreciation of the jazz tradition.[200]

On the other hand, any number of schmaltzy tunes such as "Minka," "Misirlou," and "Nothin' "—all dating from September 8, 1941—come to very little, as the last title would suggest. But again, it was via such romantic numbers that the James Orchestra made its biggest splash, especially through a piece such as Gershwin's "But Not for Me" as sung by vocalist Helen Forrest on December 30, 1941. Forrest had joined James in October 1941, after leaving Goodman, and on October 25 she recorded "The Man I Love" with the James Orchestra. According to Peter K. Johnston, "Record collectors and music fans in general have come to regard [Forrest] as the greatest vocalist of the 'Big Band Era.' "[201] On November 16, 1941, Forrest sang Ellington's "I Got It Bad," accompanied by strings, and although this side is good, it does not come up to the performance by Ivie Anderson as recorded with the Ellington Orchestra on January 26 of the same year. The Gershwin tune seems more suited to Forrest's sensual sound, and the strings are perhaps more appropriate on this particular selection. By contrast, the strings on "The Mole," by Leroy Holmes, recorded on December 30, 1941, make this number pure Hollywood mood music, even including young seventeen-year-old Corky Corcoran's tenor break. Before this, on December 11, 1941, the first James session after Pearl Harbor, the band recorded Holmes's "B-19," which finds the trumpet leader in superb form.[202] But this is such macaronic music—such a mishmash of saccharine strings, big-band swing, and a kind of Arabic-like theme—that it is difficult for a listener fully to enjoy James's playing in the middle of so much nonjazz arranging. If the title refers to the bomber that would figure so prominently in the war effort, the music in no way suggests this connection. The whole performance is finally rather ludicrous, which is the feeling one is left with here at the end of the 1930–1941 period.

Looking back over the James Orchestra's recording career up to this point, and peering ahead to the effects of the reaction to big bands that was beginning to set in, it is instructive to return to a side recorded by the James unit on May 20, 1940, of that classic song by Hoagy Carmichael, "The Nearness of You." As noted earlier, Dick Haymes sings the lyrics in an affectedly romantic manner, and James accompanies with a mushy muted trumpet. All this is dramatically far from the origins of jazz, and yet Carmichael's song could and did serve for quite stimulating, swinging improvisation fifteen years later when the same piece was recorded by Gerry Mulligan and his pianoless quartet, featuring trumpeter Chet Baker.[203] But obviously by 1955 much had changed on the jazz scene, and even though Harry James continued to lead a big band at that time and until his death in 1983, the emphasis in jazz had shifted almost entirely to the small group, to bop-derived performances, and to a greater degree of interchange between musicians such as Mulligan and Baker in terms of a return to the polyphonic lines of 1920s jazz, although admittedly with a boppish difference. That James was capable of performing effectively in the context of small-group jazz is clear not only from his participation in recording sessions with members of the Count Basie band but also from passages on his own big-band sides where he and his rhythm section alone would create more intimate, more engaging music. Indeed, James was never limited to any one approach in his creation of swing-era jazz. His orchestra could at times swing on a level near that of the name bands, and he himself could, as Gunther Schuller has indicated, deliver an "exuberant swing," "blistering drive," the "hat trick" of a virtuoso piece such as "Flight of the Bumblebee" or "Carnival of Venice," as well as romantic ballads with "a bit of class."[204] All this made the trumpet-leader both one of the most popular figures of the Swing Era and, by the end of his career, one of the musicians longest active in the history of jazz.

NOTES

1. Paul Whiteman and Mary Margaret McBride, *Jazz* (New York: J.H. Sears & Company, 1926), p. 25.
2. McCarthy, *Big Band Jazz*, p. 187.
3. Ibid., p. 189.
4. Whiteman and McBride, *Jazz*, p. 94.
5. Ibid., p. 26.
6. Ibid., pp. 267, 278.
7. Ibid., p. 120.
8. Ibid., pp. 218–219.
9. "The Japanese Sandman" of 1920 is included on *Say It with Music: Paul Whiteman and His Orchestra* (Living Era, DC AJA 5291, 2000); the medley version is included on *Paul Whiteman "The King of Jazz": His Greatest Recordings 1920–1936.*
10. Sudhalter, *Lost Chords*, p. 427.
11. Whiteman and McBride, *Jazz*, p. 180.
12. Whiteman's "Song of India" is included on *Paul Whiteman "The King of Jazz."*
13. Schuller, *The Swing Era*, p. 470.
14. "Whiteman Stomp" is included on *Paul Whiteman & His Orchestra 1920/*

1935 (Jazz Archives No. 37, AD 052, 1991). Richard M. Sudhalter reports that Redman received two thousand dollars from Whiteman for twenty arrangements, including "Whiteman Stomp" and "Sensation Stomp," the latter also recorded by Whiteman on August 8, 1927. See *Lost Chords*, p. 800 n.20.

15. Schuller, *Early Jazz*, p. 266. "The Birth of the Blues" is included on *Say It with Music: Paul Whiteman and His Orchestra*.

16. Ibid.

17. Ted Gioia, in his *The History of Jazz*, compares Redman's "Whiteman Stomp" to Heisenberg's quantum physics of the period, asserting that the composition espouses "a jagged, pointillistic style in which all continuities are called into question. This piece . . . cannot be called a success. But it is a masterful failure, sounding like the jazz of some alternative universe" (p. 113).

18. "Somebody Loves Me" is included on *Say It with Music: Paul Whiteman and His Orchestra*.

19. "Body and Soul" is included on *Say It with Music*.

20. Schuller, *The Swing Era*, p. 167.

21. "All of Me" is included on *Say It with Music*.

22. Peter Dempsey, insert notes to *Paul Whiteman and His Orchestra: Say It with Music*; Tirro, *Jazz: A History*, p. 321. Richard Sudhalter reports that Bailey became "the first woman to sing regularly with a band," making "her official debut on the Old Gold network radio show of Tuesday, August 6, 1929, singing 'Moanin' Low' in an arrangement written for her by Roy Bargy and featuring solos by Bix and Frank Trumbauer" (*Lost Chords*, p. 660).

23. "Smoke Gets in Your Eyes" is included on *Say It with Music*.

24. "Ol' Man River" is included on *Say It with Music*.

25. This later version of "Ol' Man River" is included on *Paul Whiteman "The King of Jazz."*

26. "When It's Sleepy Time Down South" is included on *Paul Whiteman "The King of Jazz."*

27. Sudhalter, *Lost Chords*, p. 663.

28. Dempsey, insert notes to *Paul Whiteman "The King of Jazz."*

29. These two sides are included on *Say It with Music*.

30. "Muddy Waters," another tune recorded by Whiteman, was also done later by Lunceford, on October 14, 1936, almost ten years after the Whiteman side made on March 7, 1927.

31. Sudhalter, *Lost Chords*, p. 663. This recording is included on *Paul Whiteman & His Orchestra 1920/1935*.

32. Teagarden's 1931 recording of "Rockin' Chair" is included on *Jack Teagarden and His Orchestra 1930–1934* (Classics, 698, 1993).

33. Schuller, *The Swing Era*, p. 605 n10.

34. "Fare Thee Well to Harlem" is included on *Jack Teagarden: I Gotta Right to Sing the Blues* (Living Era, CD AJA 5059, 1989).

35. Sudhalter, *Lost Chords*, p. 390.

36. These three sides are included on *Casa Loma Orchestra: Maniac's Ball* (HEP, CD 1051, 1996).

37. Whiteman and McBride, *Jazz*, photo facing p. 38.

38. Bill Grauer Jr. and Orrin Keepnews, *The RCA Victor Encyclopedia of Recorded Jazz*, Album 5.

39. Sudhalter, *Lost Chords*, p. 347. This pretty much echoes what Gunther Schuller had said in *The Swing Era* about Gene Gifford's "Casa Loma Stomp" doing "more than any other piece in the early thirties to advance the idea of jazz instrumentals, at least in the guise of frenetic 'killer-dillers,' meant to be listened to *as* music, rather than as background for dancing" (p. 634).

40. Sudhalter, *Lost Chords*, p. 347; Schuller, *The Swing Era*, p. 642. Again, Schuller had made this observation prior to Sudhalter. Indeed, most of Sudhalter's major points in his book are simply restatements of what Schuller had earlier said, and this applies as well to most everything I myself have to say in the present volume. Alastair Robertson's notes for a CD entitled *Casa Loma Orchestra: Stompin' Around* (HEP, CD 1062, 1999) are essentially based on Schuller, although the critic is in no way credited.

41. "Maniac's Ball" is included on *Casa Loma Orchestra: Maniac's Ball*.

42. Rob Bamberger, insert notes to *Casa Loma Orchestra: Maniac's Ball*.

43. The Casa Loma version of "New Orleans" is included on *Maniac's Ball*.

44. Williams, liner notes to *Count Basie in Kansas City: Bennie Moten's Great Band of 1930–1932*.

45. Schuller, *The Swing Era*, p. 632. Schuller wonders how the Casa Loma Orchestra's impact could be "at once enormous and yet negligible (or at least short-lived)."

46. Ibid., p. 633. Schuller points out that in the case of Fletcher Henderson's inept version of "Casa Loma Stomp," from March 11, 1932, Coleman Hawkins "cannot even produce a solo equal to the one by Pat Davis, the Casa Lomans' tenor soloist" (p. 324). The first version of "Casa Loma Stomp," from 1930, is included on *Casa Loma Orchestra: Casa Loma Stomp* (HEP, CD1010, 1997).

47. Ibid., p. 643. The later version of "Casa Loma Stomp," from February 17, 1933, is included on *Stompin' Around*.

48. "White Jazz" is included on *Maniac's Ball*.

49. "Smoke Rings" is included on *Stompin' Around*.

50. Schuller, *The Swing Era*, p. 643.

51. Ibid., p. 644; McCarthy, *Big Band Jazz*, p. 193.

52. "Limehouse Blues" is included on *Stompin' Around*.

53. Schuller, *The Swing Era*, p. 644.

54. Stanley Dance, liner notes to *Duke Ellington: Daybreak Express* (RCA Victor LPV-506, 1964).

55. Schuller, *The Swing Era*, pp. 637–638.

56. This version of "Sophisticated Lady" is included on *Stompin' Around*.

57. "That's How Rhythm Was Born" is included on *Stompin' Around*.

58. Sudhalter, *Lost Chords*, p. 348.

59. Ibid., p. 349. Once again Gunther Schuller had already noted Hutchenrider's baritone solo on "I Got Rhythm" and rates it as "one of his best improvisations" and indicates that it is "a full two choruses . . . absolutely unheard of" at the time. Schuller considers Hutchenrider's clarinet work as "capable but somewhat uneven" and even "somewhat erratic technically" (*The Swing Era*, pp. 643–644). "I Got Rhythm" is included on *Stompin' Around*.

60. "Avalon" is included on *Stompin' Around*.

61. "Come and Get It" is included on *Stompin' Around*.

62. "White Jazz" is included on *Maniac's Ball*.

63. Schuller, *The Swing Era*, pp. 634–635 and 638.

64. Thomas J. Hennessey, *From Jazz to Swing: African-American Jazz Musicians and Their Music, 1890–1935* (Detroit: Wayne State University Press, 1994), p. 131.

65. Sudhalter, *Lost Chords*, p. 497.

66. Sudhalter, insert notes to *Bunny Berigan: The Pied Piper 1934–40*.

67. In *The Swing Era*, Gunther Schuller points out that "I Can't Get Started" was recorded ten days earlier than the date of April 13, 1936, but under Red McKenzie's name and with Berigan only playing a straight melodic statement (p. 471 n.27).

68. Berigan's versions of April 13, 1936, and August 7, 1937, are both included on *Bunny Berigan: His Best Recordings 1935–1939* (Best of Jazz, 4021, 1995).

69. Three of these sides discussed here, "Let's Do It," "Frankie and Johnnie," and "Mahogany Hall Stomp," are all included on *Bunny Berigan: His Best Recordings 1935–1939*.

70. Sudhalter, in *Lost Chords* (p. 508), refers to "Frankie and Johnnie" as having been recorded at the first studio session of April 1, but the discography for *Bunny Berigan: His Best Recordings 1935–1939* lists the date as June 25, 1937. Albert McCarthy in *Big Band Jazz* also dates this side from June 1937 (p. 209).

71. Schuller, *The Swing Era*, p. 182.

72. "The Prisoner's Song" and "Russian Lullaby" are included on *Bunny Berigan: The Pied Piper 1934–1940*.

73. Sudhalter, insert notes to *Bunny Berigan: The Pied Piper 1934–40*.

74. These two sides are included on *Bunny Berigan and His Orchestra 1937–1938*.

75. Sudhalter, insert notes to *Bunny Berigan: The Pied Piper 1934–40*; Schuller, *The Swing Era*, pp. 470–471. This version of "Blues" is included on *Bunny Berigan: His Best Recordings 1935–1939*. Another "Blues," from December 13, 1935, is included on *Bunny Berigan and His Boys 1935–1936* (Classics, 734, 1993).

76. The four sides from January 26 and March 15 are included on *Bunny Berigan and His Orchestra 1937–1938*.

77. Sudhalter, insert notes to *Bunny Berigan: The Pied Piper 1934–40*; Schuller, *The Swing Era*, p. 475.

78. These three sides are included on *Bunny Berigan and His Orchestra 1937–1938*.

79. Schuller, *The Swing Era*, pp. 465 and 463. Earlier, Albert McCarthy had already considered Berigan "undoubtedly one of the greatest trumpeters of the swing era, and, along with Bix Beiderbecke, one of the outstanding white trumpeters in jazz's history," as well as concluding that "Berigan, with his adventurousness as a soloist, remarkable instrumental command, and brilliance of tone and execution, was a giant of his era" (*Big Band Jazz*, pp. 207 and 210). The two sides from April 21 are included on *Bunny Berigan and His Orchestra 1937–1938*.

80. Schuller, *The Swing Era*, p. 464. The three sides from May 26 are included on *Bunny Berigan and His Orchestra 1937–1938*.

81. Schuller, *The Swing Era*, p. 474; McCarthy, *Big Band Jazz*, p. 209.

82. Schuller, *The Swing Era*, p. 474.

83. Sudhalter, insert notes to *Bunny Berigan: The Pied Piper 1934–40*.

84. Sudhalter, *Lost Chords*, p. 507.

85. "Azure" is included on *Bunny Berigan and His Orchestra 1937–1938*.

86. "Jelly Roll Blues" is included on *Bunny Berigan: The Pied Piper 1934–40*.

87. Sudhalter, *Lost Chords*, p. 510.

88. Berigan and the orchestra also recorded four of Beiderbecke's piano pieces, but the results are not exactly jazz. "Candlelights," from November 30, 1938, is representative, although, as Albert McCarthy observes, "the wistfulness of Berigan's playing during *Candlelights* . . . is not recreated on any other of his recordings" (*Big Band Jazz*, p. 209). Gunther Schuller argues that the four Joe Lippmann arrangements of Bix's piano pieces stand for "a concept of jazz-as-composition and jazz-as-repertory that was far ahead of its time and antithetical to most jazz musicians' views then and, alas, even now" (*The Swing Era*, p. 475). "Davenport Blues" is included on *Bunny Berigan: His Best Recordings 1935–1939*, and "Candlelights" is included on *Bunny Berigan: The Pied Piper 1934–40*.

89. "Night Song" and "I Cried for You" are included on *Bunny Berigan: His Best Recordings 1935–1939*.

90. McCarthy, *Big Band Jazz*, p. 210.

91. Schuller, *The Swing Era*, p. 473.

92. McCarthy, *Big Band Jazz*, p. 210.

93. Sudhalter, *Lost Chords*, p. 516.

94. Schuller, *The Swing Era*, p. 652; Sudhalter, *Lost Chords*, p. 386.

95. John Hammond, "Pollack Veterans with Crosby's New Band," in *Down Beat* (August 1935), quoted in Sudhalter, *Lost Chords*, p. 387.

96. Schuller, *The Swing Era*, pp. 652–653.

97. Ibid., p. 653 n19.

98. Ibid.

99. "Royal Garden Blues" is included on *Bob Crosby and His Orchestra: South Rampart Street Parade* (Decca, GRD-615, 1992).

100. Sudhalter, insert notes to *Bob Crosby and His Orchestra: South Rampart Street Parade*.

101. Schuller, *The Swing Era*, p. 653.

102. Ibid., p. 652.

103. George T. Simon, *The Big Bands*, 4th ed. (Garden City, N.Y.: Doubleday, 1981); quoted in Sudhalter, *Lost Chords*, p. 388.

104. George T. Simon, liner notes to *The Best of Bob Crosby* (MCA Records, MCA2-4083, 1975). It is a striking instance of how little Bob Crosby figures in the music of "his" orchestra, as reissued some forty years later, that this album contains not a single example of his vocal work.

105. Schuller, *The Swing Era*, pp. 656 and 658. Both "Summertime" and "March of the Bobcats" are included on *The Best of Bob Crosby*.

106. Ibid., p. 658.

107. "I'm Prayin' Humble" is included on *Bob Crosby and His Orchestra*.

108. Simon, liner notes to *The Best of Bob Crosby*.

109. Sudhalter, *Lost Chords*, p. 396.

110. Sudhalter, insert notes to *Bob Crosby and His Orchestra*.

111. "Dogtown Blues," "Dixieland Shuffle," and "Wolverine Blues" are included on *Bob Crosby and His Orchestra*.

112. Both pieces are included on *Bob Crosby and His Orchestra*.

113. Michael Ullman, "The Clarinet in Jazz," in *The Oxford Companion to*

Jazz, ed. Bill Kirchner (New York: Oxford University Press, 2000), p. 586. Ullman notes that the Albert system was preferred by New Orleans clarinetists over the Boehm, but that the "rough-and-ready clarinet style often heard in the twenties gave way to the elegance of Goodman and Shaw" who would have utilized the Boehm system because it "has more keys and allows more fluency."

114. Schuller, *The Swing Era*, p. 656.

115. Ibid.; Sudhalter, insert notes to *Bob Crosby and His Orchestra*.

116. McCarthy, *Big Band Jazz*, p. 217.

117. Both these Herman sides are included on *Boogie Woogie Stomps* (Living Era, AJA 5101, 1993).

118. Schuller, *The Swing Era*, p. 652.

119. Ibid., p. 658.

120. "Yancey Special" is included on *Boogie Woogie Stomp* and "Honky Tonk Train Blues" is included on *The Best of Bob Crosby*.

121. Schuller, *The Swing Era*, pp. 656–657.

122. Simon, liner notes to *The Best of Bob Crosby*.

123. Sudhalter, *Lost Chords*, p. 399.

124. "Stomp Off and Let's Go" is included on *The Best of Bob Crosby* and "Air Mail Stomp" is on *Bob Crosby and His Orchestra*.

125. Schuller, *The Swing Era*, p. 658.

126. "Big Noise from Winnetka" is included on *Bob Crosby and His Orchestra*.

127. Sudhalter, liner notes to *Bob Crosby and His Orchestra*.

128. "Swingin' at the Sugar Bowl" is included on *Bob Crosby and His Orchestra*.

129. Sudhalter, insert notes to *Bob Crosby and His Orchestra*; *Lost Chords*, p. 404.

130. Schuller, *The Swing Era*, p. 657.

131. Sudhalter, *Lost Chords*, p. 406. Some of the 1942 sides that reclaimed the terrain of early jazz forms include "Jimtown Blues," "Milenberg Joys," and "Chain Gang," the last of these a highly effective type of concert-movie music version of a black form of folk song. The other two sides are among the most swinging performances the band ever produced.

132. "Complainin'," "I'm Free," and "My Inspiration" are included on *Bob Crosby and His Orchestra*.

133. McCarthy, *Big Band Jazz*, p. 218.

134. George Frazier, "Homage to Bunny," in *Reading Jazz*, pp. 477 and 476.

135. Sudhalter, *Lost Chords*, p. 400; Haggart quoted by Sudhalter in the insert notes to *Bob Crosby and His Orchestra*.

136. "The Skaters' Waltz" is included on *Bob Crosby and His Orchestra*.

137. "Between the Devil and the Deep Blue Sea" is included on *Bob Crosby and His Orchestra*.

138. McCarthy, *Big Band Jazz*, p. 198.

139. Stanley Dance, insert notes to *Big Bands: Charlie Barnet* (Time-Life Music 4TBB-07, 1983).

140. Schuller, *The Swing Era*, p. 716; McCarthy, *Big Band Jazz*, p. 198.

141. Peter Dempsey, insert notes to *Charlie Barnet & His Orchestra: Cherokee* (Living Era CD AJA 5288, 1999).

142. Ibid.; McCarthy, *Big Band Jazz*, p. 198.

143. McCarthy, *Big Band Jazz*, p. 198. "Tomboy" is included on *Knockin' on Wood: Red Norvo* (Living Era CD AJA 5341, 1999).

144. "Cherokee" is included on *Charlie Barnet & His Orchestra: Cherokee* (Living Era, AJA 5288, 1999).

145. Dance, insert notes to *Big Bands: Charlie Barnet*. This cassette includes "The All-Night Record Man."

146. Ibid. Both tunes are included on *Charlie Barnet & His Orchestra: Cherokee*.

147. Schuller, *The Swing Era*, p. 717.

148. McCarthy, *Big Band Jazz*, p. 200.

149. Schuller, *The Swing Era*, p. 717.

150. Dance, insert notes to *Big Bands: Charlie Barnet*. Both these tunes are included on *Charlie Barnet & His Orchestra: Cherokee*.

151. Ibid. Both tunes are included on *Big Bands: Charlie Barnet*.

152. These three sides plus "Redskin Rhumba" are all on *Charlie Barnet & His Orchestra: Cherokee*.

153. "Charleston Alley" is included on *Charlie Barnet & His Orchestra: Cherokee*.

154. " 'Deed I Do," "Peaceful Valley," and "Southern Fried" are included on *Big Bands: Charlie Barnet*.

155. Dance, insert notes to *Big Bands: Charlie Barnet*.

156. "Good-for-Nothin' Joe" is included on *Big Bands: Charlie Barnet* and "You're My Thrill" is on *Charlie Barnet & His Orchestra: Cherokee*.

157. Dance, insert notes to *Big Bands: Charlie Barnet*.

158. "I Hear a Rhapsody" is included on *Charlie Barnet & His Orchestra: Cherokee*.

159. Ray Conniff, *'S Marvelous* (Columbia CL 1074, n.d.).

160. "Wanderin' Blues" is included on *Charlie Barnet & His Orchestra: Cherokee*.

161. Schuller, *The Swing Era*, p. 717.

162. "Rockin' in Rhythm" and "Pompton Turnpike" are included on *Charlie Barnet & His Orchestra: Cherokee*.

163. Dance, insert notes to *Big Bands: Charlie Barnet*.

164. "Wings over Manhattan" is included on *Big Bands: Charlie Barnet*.

165. "Ponce de Leon" and "Wild Mab of the Fish Pond" are included on *Big Bands: Charlie Barnet*.

166. "Swingin' on Nothin' " is included on *Charlie Barnet & His Orchestra: Cherokee*.

167. McCarthy, *Big Band Jazz*, p. 247.

168. Ibid., pp. 247–248.

169. Schuller, *The Swing Era*, p. 725.

170. Ibid., p. 724.

171. Ibid.

172. The sides discussed in this paragraph are included on *Gene Krupa and His Orchestra 1939* (Classics, 799, 1994).

173. The sides discussed in this paragraph are included on *Gene Krupa and His Orchestra 1941* (Classics, 960, 1997).

174. Schuller, *The Swing Era*, p. 724.

175. These two sides are included on *Gene Krupa and His Orchestra 1941*.

176. Ibid., p. 725.

177. McCarthy, *Big Band Jazz*, p. 247.

178. The sides discussed in this paragraph are included on *Gene Krupa and His Orchestra 1941*.

179. "Moonlight Serenade" is included on *Gene Krupa and His Orchestra 1939*.

180. These sides are included on *Gene Krupa and His Orchestra 1941*.

181. "Let Me Off Uptown" is included on *Gene Krupa and His Orchestra 1941* and on *Roy Eldridge: His Best Recordings 1935–1946* (Best of Jazz, 4051, 1997).

182. Schuller, *The Swing Era*, p. 461. "Rockin' Chair" is included on *Roy Eldridge: His Best Recordings 1935–1946*.

183. Krupa's "Flamingo" is included on *Gene Krupa and His Orchestra 1941*; the Mingus version is on *Charlie Mingus: Tijuana Moods* (RCA Victor, LPM-2533, 1957).

184. Quoted by Ian Crosbie, insert notes to *Harry James: Record Session '39–'42* (HEP CD 1068, 1999).

185. Ibid.

186. Peter K. Johnston, liner notes to *The Young Harry James* (Jazz Archives, Ja-31, 1976).

187. "Ciribiribin" is included on *Big Bands: Harry James* (Time Life Music, 4TBB-04, 1983); the other sides discussed in this paragraph are on *Harry James: Record Session '39–42*.

188. "Orchids for Remembrance" and "The Nearness of You" are included on *Harry James and His Orchestra 1940–1941* (Classics, 1014, 1998).

189. Len Lyons, insert notes to *Big Bands: Harry James*. "All or Nothing at All" is included on *Harry James and His Orchestra 1939* (Classics, 936, 1997).

190. "To You" is included on *The Young Harry James*.

191. This side is included on *The Essence of Harry James* (Columbia/Legacy, CK 57151, 1994).

192. This side is included on *Harry James and His Orchestra 1940–1941*.

193. These sides are included on *Harry James and His Orchestra 1940–1941*.

194. This side is included on *Harry James and His Orchestra 1940–1941*.

195. Jimmy Dorsey performed "Super Chief" on several occasions in 1946 (January 12 and 23 and April 13), and one of these performances is reproduced but not identified by date on a German CD, titled simply *Jimmy Dorsey* (TKO Records, UAE 30382, 1996). See the 1946 Dorsey listings in Tom Lord's *The Jazz Discography*, p. D468. The arrangement of January 12, 1946, is credited to Sonny Burke, but on the Jazz Roots Count Basie CD, *Jumpin' at the Woodside, 1937–1943*, "Super Chief" is credited to Carter, Dorsey, and Ellis. Whoever did the arrangement on the *Jimmy Dorsey* CD, whether Benny Carter or Sonny Burke, the Dorsey Orchestra's performance of this version of "Super Chief" is exceptional: Dorsey's hot clarinet break is impressive; an electric guitarist sounds like Charlie Christian; the maneuvers of the reed section are marvelous; and the brass punctuations are scintillating.

196. "Swanee River" and "Exactly Like You" are included on *Harry James and His Orchestra 1940–1941*.

197. The sides discussed in this paragraph are included on *Harry James and His Orchestra 1940–1941*.

198. See *Count Basie-Harry James: Basie Rhythm* (HEP Records, CD 1032, 1991).

199. See *The Quintessential Billie Holiday Volume 6 (1938)* (Columbia, C 45449, 1990).

200. The sides discussed in this paragraph are included on *Harry James and His Orchestra 1941 Vol. 2* (Classics, 1092, 1999).

201. Johnston, liner notes to *The Young Harry James*.

202. The sides discussed in this paragraph are included on *Harry James and His Orchestra 1941 Vol. 2*.

203. The Mulligan-Baker version of "The Nearness of You" is included on *Gerry Mulligan Quartet* (Pacific Jazz, PJ-1207, 1955).

204. Schuller, *The Swing Era*, pp. 750, 746. "Flight of the Bumblebee" is included on *Harry James and His Orchestra 1941 Vol. 2* and "Carnival of Venice" on *Harry James and His Orchestra 1939–1940* (Classics, 970, 1997).

Chapter 6

The Small Swing Groups

At the same time that big bands were dominating the music scene in the 1930s, small groups were "quietly" creating some of the most innovative jazz of the decade. Unlike the swing bands that slowly became larger, played louder, reached for higher notes (especially the trumpet sections but also some of the saxophonists), and featured vocalists more and more prominently, the small groups tended toward subdued performances, concentrated on individual and often more extended improvisation, and, if they included a vocalist such as Mildred Bailey or Billie Holiday or even Fats Waller, emphasized jazz singing rather than pop crooning. Even though the small-group sides were not million-selling hits or anything near, a number of them represented highly influential recordings that would profoundly affect the future of jazz.

Some of the musicians who made such important small-group recordings were also well known for their work with the big bands, but it was often only through sessions with groups smaller than ten members that such figures as Coleman Hawkins, Benny Carter, Lester Young, Lionel Hampton, Benny Goodman, Artie Shaw, Bud Freeman, Jack Teagarden, Bunny Berigan, Harry James, Charlie Christian, Roy Eldridge, Teddy Wilson, and many others were able to reveal and develop their talents free of the limitations of a big-band format. In the mid to late '20s, Louis Armstrong had established his reputation through his small-group recordings, but during the '30s he mainly presented himself in the context of larger ensembles. However, other important soloists, especially those developing the vital role of the saxophone in jazz, carried on Armstrong's small-group initiative and contributed significantly to the ongoing creation of the music's artistry. As the big bands slowly drifted toward enervation, the small groups often grew more innovative with regard to their importance as training grounds for the next generation of jazzmen who would extend swing into bebop and beyond.

One extremely significant aspect of the small-group session was that it allowed for a mixing of the races. Because black musicians were not allowed to appear in public in mixed groups, the big bands did not begin to integrate until late in the decade, and only then on a very limited scale, usually with a single star like Roy Eldridge. But within purely studio recordings, it was possible to break down the color line, which had in fact been broken as early as 1923 when Jelly Roll Morton recorded in Gennett's Indiana studio with the New Orleans Rhythm Kings. By the '30s, this practice became more widespread, and the results were quite notable in a number of cases. In fact, on certain occasions when Coleman Hawkins or Billie Holiday joined forces with a white group, the black instrumentalist and vocalist both seemed especially inspired by the setting and the white musicians likewise responded with some of their finest efforts. Jazz critics have lamented that more of these integrated sessions were not recorded, but at least the growing number of mixed studio recordings signaled the beginning of a major movement toward greater integration in the arts. Certainly it is clear that in many ways it was jazz in the Swing Era that was most responsible for breaching the racial barriers. Although the real challenge to segregation came when the white big bands dared to integrate, the small groups were crucial in indicating how beneficial to the musicians and the music was a mixing of the races. In a very real sense, hearing how musicians, regardless of skin color, could interrelate, inspire one another, and work together literally in harmony argued for a change in attitude that began in the '30s to sway the views of a new generation of Americans. Not only did small-group sessions contribute substantially to the development of jazz as an art form but also they served as a powerful force for social evolution.

COLEMAN HAWKINS

Undoubtedly the first major saxophonist in jazz was Coleman Hawkins, whose 1929 recordings with the Mound City Blue Blowers indicated a new direction for this member of the reed family, in particular the tenor saxophone. Although other important saxophonists were active in the 1920s, including Duke Ellington's premier altoist, Johnny Hodges, and the white C-melody saxophonist Frankie Trumbauer, it was Hawkins who single-handedly began to establish the tenor saxophone as a solo instrument on a par with the trumpet, trombone, and clarinet, especially as represented by the work in the later '20s of such soloists as Louis Armstrong and Bix Beiderbecke, Jimmy Harrison and Jack Teagarden, and Barnie Bigard and Benny Goodman. Continuing from his path-breaking session with the Mound City Blue Blowers of November 14, 1929, Hawkins recorded again on June 30, 1931, with the same white group, or at least under the same name and the same leader, Red McKenzie, but with different sidemen other than Eddie Condon on banjo and Jack Bland on guitar. But prior to Hawkins's session with McKenzie's group, the tenorist had recorded with a mixed group led by trumpeter Jack Purvis, which cut three sides on April 4, 1930.

The Purvis combo included trombonist J.C. Higginbotham, bass-saxophonist Adrian Rollini, Frank Froeba on piano, Will Johnson on guitar, and Charles Kegley on drums. Despite the presence of Higginbotham and Hawkins, this session has more of a commercial feel to it, especially the guitar chording of Will Johnson. Here Froeba's piano playing is markedly dated, is in fact not really jazz, and both Purvis and Higginbotham are quite behind the times in their improvisations. Purvis is overly indebted to Armstrong, is often rather erratic, and not at all into the smoother swing mode. Only Hawkins provides an advanced sound and conception, yet even he is not so inspired by this group as he obviously was by the Mound City Blue Blowers. None of the soloists on the Purvis date can compare with those on the November 1929 session, except on "Down Georgia Way," where, as Richard Sudhalter observes, Purvis does achieve a certain "sense of drama," yet on this number Johnson's guitar interferes with Hawkins' solo.[1] As is evident from this particular session, mixed groups did not necessarily produce outstanding recordings.

On the session of June 30, 1931, with the Mound City Blue Blowers, Hawkins was clearly more comfortable with and stimulated by the company he was keeping. On this occasion, however, Red McKenzie tends to sing mostly without his comb, which is not nearly so effective. Nonetheless, and more importantly, Al Morgan, a New Orleans string bass player, bows supportively behind Hawkins' "huge-toned, majestic solo" on "Georgia on My Mind," and Jimmy Dorsey contributes a romantic clarinet solo that hints at the emerging swing style.[2] Dorsey also plays with fine fluidity and with an impressive technical control on "The Darktown Strutters' Ball." Even though Dorsey can tend to lose his way a bit, he must have been inspired by Hawkins to try something a little more daring. On "I Can't Believe That You're in Love with Me," Hawkins plays with tremendous passion, at the same time that he ventures around his horn with amazing intrepidity, reaching for harmonies beyond the ordinary patterns. On "The Dark Town Strutters' Ball," Hawkins is working out a very forward-looking conception, described by John Chilton as "a complex legato phrase that combines passion with ingenuity." Chilton also asserts that this is "one of the most impressive fast solos of [Hawkins'] career."[3] "You Rascal, You," which Hawkins recorded more than once with the Fletcher Henderson Orchestra during the same summer of 1931, does not come up to the swing of the Henderson recordings. Partly this is because Hawkins is not given much space to work out his ideas; even so, he still manages to swing more than the rest of the group. Dorsey sounds rather influenced by Benny Goodman at this point, whereas Jack Russin on piano is not much better than Frank Froeba on the Purvis date. However, overall this is a more revealing session for the development of what Chilton calls Hawkins's "formidable strength," presenting the tenorist more fully in this regard than his big-band recordings with Henderson.[4]

On September 29, 1933, Hawkins recorded for the first time with a small group of his own, which included once again J.C. Higginbotham. Here the trombonist displays a more contemporary approach, joining Hilton Jefferson on clarinet and alto for some smoothly flowing breaks that are more compatible with Hawkins at his rhapsodic best. With "The Day You Came Along," the tenorist embellishes the theme with rapid, highly inventive phrases, then ends the piece with a type of cadenza backed by the rhythm section. John Chilton compares the way Hawkins "soars up to a G sharp" to "a great opera singer," and the critic adds that the tenorist "manages to impart a feeling of sweet adieu to his final two notes."[5] On "Jamaica Shout," a Horace Henderson original, Hawkins demonstrates his immaculate technique and swing, and once again Higginbotham unreels a smoothly complementary break. Especially impressive are the fine contrasts that Hawkins creates in his solo, both in style and dynamics. On his own original, "Heartbreak Blues," the tenorist is simply in a class all by himself, exhibiting a control and meaningfulness in his playing that was untouched by any other reedman of the day. Hawkins's note choices are so telling— romantically inclined yet in no way saccharine. With wonderful pacing, he pours out his blues while remaining in complete control of his instrument. Speaking of Hawkins's development during this period, Chilton comments that the tenorist shows "that he had perfected the ingenious style of rhapsodizing," and that although "many of those who followed in his footsteps dispensed with the ornateness of the original . . . they retained his method."[6]

Shortly before Hawkins departed for England, where he would remain for the next five years, the tenorist recorded three sides accompanied only by Buck Washington on piano. Dating from March 8, 1934, these unusual recordings document Hawkins's growing adventurousness, his desire to test the technical resources of his instrument and to plumb the depths of his own imagination. This would not have been possible within the confines of a big-band setting, and perhaps not even within the format of one of the small ensembles with which he previously recorded. Although the simple backing of a piano leaves the tenorist somewhat undersupported, somewhat overexposed, so that the least flaw is made vividly apparent, this is offset by the boldly exploratory nature of his playing. On Hawkins's own original, "It Sends Me," the tenorist only slowly feels his way into what John Chilton calls "an indifferent composition," but as the critic observes, after stating the theme "eloquently" although "uneventfully," Hawkins's imagination "immediately after the piano solo . . . suddenly catches fire. He plays a dazzling reentry phrase and moves on impressively to create a descending figure that blends ingenuity with excitement. He maintains this level of inspiration right through to the last notes, signing off with a break that was to be used later by countless saxophonists."[7] The other two sides, "I Ain't Got Nobody" and "On the Sunny Side of the Street," also contain evidence of Hawkins's daring, searching mind, as he takes chances and extends the range of his instrumental technique even as he advances the frontiers of emotive expression. It is evident from these recordings why Hawkins's dissatisfaction with his limited role in the Henderson orchestra prompted him to try his luck abroad, in order to test further the reaches of his technical and imaginative prowess.

In July 1939, Hawkins returned from his sojourn in Europe and in September recorded on a Lionel Hampton session discussed in Chapter 4. In October, Hawkins had formed his own eight-piece unit, and on the 11th he and his group recorded four sides, including his monumental touchstone version of "Body and Soul."[8] John Chilton finds that unfortunately the Hawkins orchestra was "a nine-piece band trying too hard to sound like a sixteen-piece unit" and that the two rifflike compositions by the leader, "Meet Doctor Foo" and "Fine Dinner," were "untuneful and therefore unmemorable."[9] Part of the problem on "Meet Doctor Foo" is that Hawkins takes four short breaks and none really amounts to much, perhaps because he seems unfocused and as a leader is concerned to furnish his sidemen with solo space. On "He's Funny That Way," with nineteen year-old Thelma Carpenter handling the vocal like a seasoned veteran, Hawkins is described by Chilton as becoming "bogged down by repetitive patterns and the last part of his chorus is little more than a high-class example of a great musician simply marking time."[10] On the other hand, Dan Morgenstern characterizes Hawkins's contribution on this piece as a "majestic full chorus and closing embellishments."[11] But certainly Chilton is closer to the mark when one compares Hawkins on this piece with his magisterial performance on "Body and Soul."[12] On the latter there are no superfluous phrases to be heard, and the show is entirely the tenorist's, except for a marvelous piano introduction by Gene Rodgers that sets the mood beautifully. (Both Chilton and Morgenstern praise Rodgers as a much underrated pianist.) As for the rhythm section, it remains unobtrusive, while the band supports Hawkins merely by playing a background of whole notes, allowing the soloist to work his magic.

By this point in Hawkins's career, the delicacy of his tenor playing seems to have taken a page from Lester Young's book of relaxed drive, but still there is nothing quite like the Hawk's impassioned sound toward the end of "Body and Soul." For the young generation of tenor players, what came through most radiantly was the fact that, as George Hoefer indicates, Hawkins "improvises two choruses with such originality that he is actually writing a new tune."[13] For Chilton, Hawkins "achieved the apotheosis of his entire career, creating a solo that remains the most perfectly conceived and executed example of jazz tenor-sax playing ever recorded."[14] What also is striking about this historic recording is that it was totally unplanned—the request of an employee for RCA Victor—and that Rodgers's piano introduction was a completely spur-of-the-moment response. Perhaps this accounts for the effect of spontaneity, of deep, unpremeditated feeling. As Rodgers recalled, "There was no shackles of an arrangement; he just played with no interruption, flat-footed, and he probably didn't even hear the accompaniment. His eyes were closed and he just played as if he was in heaven."[15] The impact on listeners was not limited merely to jazzmen, for Hawkins's recording was "adored" as well "by the general public."[16] As Gunther Schuller points out, Hawkins's recording "was the first true jazz performance to become a big seller . . . every note is virtually inevitable and inexorable. There is hardly anything like it in the annals of recorded jazz."[17]

Hawkins's last recording session of 1939 came on December 21, when once again he joined with a mixed group, this time including Benny Carter on trumpet, Edmond Hall on clarinet, Joe Sullivan on piano, Freddie Green on guitar, Art Bernstein on bass, Zutty Singleton on drums, and on vibes Lionel Hampton, who had organized the date. Here Hawkins plays another version of the Beiderbecke-Trumbauer classic, "Singin' the Blues," and this time the Hawk's "near-tender solo," as John Chilton describes it, "is couched in a breathy subtone that many young tenorists began to copy."[18] But the most outstanding side from this session was "Dinah," which opens with an exceptionally fine chorus by Carter. Hawkins follows with what is a vintage tenor solo, exhibiting the Hawk's proclivity for repeated phrases that build climactically and generate such a robust swing. Chilton rates this chorus as "among Hawkins's greatest achievements."[19] After Lionel Hampton hammers away on his vibes, the side closes with the vibist-leader playing with Hawkins's "same remarkable level of rhythmic intensity . . . over the front line's incisive riff."[20] Chilton observes that this final session of 1939 was "a momentous one, symbolizing [Hawkins's] continuous progress." The critic explains that, despite the tenorist's absence from "the fountains of jazz" in the United States, he had been listening avidly to classical music and discovering that "the harmonic riches in that music had hardly been tapped by any jazz saxophonist and becoming increasingly determined to rectify that situation."[21]

In 1940, Hawkins would record with another mixed group that included clarinetist Danny Polo, who himself had spent some ten years in Europe, following his early work with the Jean Goldkette Orchestra in the '20s, and who had, like the Hawk, just returned in 1939. This session of January 3 well illustrates Chilton's point about Hawkins' "continuous progress," for here on "The Sheik of Araby" the tenorist takes his break at an uptempo that, as George Hoefer indicates, makes it clear that "he is trying to get away from his former rhapsodic style. The pattern of his attack is changing and a new Hawkins phase is in the making."[22] This is demonstrated as well by the first tune recorded, "When Day Is Done," which Dan Morgenstern points out was a fitting choice, as "the tune is of European origin, discovered and imported by Paul Whiteman during a 1926 tour."[23] Even on this rather sentimental tune, Hawkins's style is now less florid, less embellished, less impassioned, leaner and more direct. It's as if with "Body and Soul," Hawkins knew that he had recorded his definitive statement on the rhapsodic, ornate style of tenor playing and was moving on. Danny Polo also reflects a more direct style of clarinet playing, rather far removed from either the curlicued Dixieland manner or the soaring approach of so many of the swing clarinetists. Although "My Blue Heaven" ends with something of a Dixieland tag, the solos on this piece also tend to be direct and unornamented. On the one original tune, "Bouncin' with Bean," which Morgenstern says "is a themeless jam on 'I've Found a New Baby,' " each of the frontline players, as well as a sprightly Gene Rodgers on piano, ably takes his turn, with Hawkins, the "Bean, bringing up the rear but showing that he had left the best for last."[24] This is a new kind of impassioned tenor playing, driving, decisive, and intensely "in your face."

As ever, Hawkins challenged all comers, putting them on notice that there was more to come from "The World's Greatest Saxophonist," as he was advertised by Joe Glaser, his and Louis Armstrong's agent, who had secured New York's Arcadia Ballroom for the Hawkins orchestra in late 1939. For many, Coleman Hawkins still retains the title by which Glaser billed him, not only for his recording of "Body and Soul" but also for the "continuous progress" he made throughout a career that stretched from 1922 to 1969 and was perhaps marked by more pace-setting changes than that of any other musician in jazz history.

JACK TEAGARDEN

The first full-blown modern trombonist was surely Jack Teagarden, even though some listeners have made claims for Jimmy Harrison as either preceding Teagarden in this respect or as his equal. But the evidence seems clearly to indicate that it was Teagarden who revolutionized trombone playing and introduced even in the 1920s a smooth swing style comparable on the unwieldy trombone to that of Louis Armstrong on the trumpet. Unfortunately, Teagarden never achieved the kind of star status enjoyed by other figures in the Swing Era, even those with less ability on their respective instruments. Tommy Dorsey not only gained fame and fortune as a bandleader, but he also established a romantic trombone sound that appealed more widely than Teagarden's distinctive jazz accent. As a bandleader, Teagarden was essentially a failure, his orchestra neither creating its own identifiable style nor serving as an effective showcase for the trombonist's considerable talents. On the other hand, as a vocalist, Teagarden was almost always successful in lending whatever lyrics he sang a mellow, welcome sound. As Vic Bellerby notes, "Teagarden's charm as a vocalist became known to millions who had no interest in, or knowledge of, his instrumental genius."[25] Teagarden's best work as a trombonist was done in smaller mixed groups rather than with his own big band or that of Paul Whiteman. Indeed, Teagarden was among the earliest white jazzmen to record with a mixed group, doing so in 1929 with a small group led by Louis Armstrong, and on such occasions the trombonist seemed to rise above his normal, relaxed output. Although Teagarden was never quite an ensemble player who contributed to the larger effort of group improvisation, he did respond well to other small-group players, both inspiring and being inspired by them. When Teagarden was on, he could elevate a performance, both his own and that of his fellow musicians. Whether in mixed or purely white small groups, Teagarden was a key member of the unit, and most listeners awaited eagerly his solo with its always dramatic entrance.

Just as Coleman Hawkins, in recording "The Sheik of Araby" in 1940, revealed a new direction in his playing, so Jack Teagarden recorded the same tune on June 3, 1930, and showed at that time that there was both an updated way to play the trombone and to sing.[26] Teagarden cut this side with a "small" unit led by Red Nichols and billed as usual as His Five Pennies, even though the group numbered a dozen in all. In truth, most of the groups that Teagarden recorded with throughout his career were larger than the small units in which so much innovative jazz was developed in the '30s. But even though an ensemble such as Nichols' Five Pennies could number as many as a dozen members, it never represented a big-band approach, for there were no sax sections answered by brass sections but rather a series of solos with only limited backing from rhythm section and a few horns, or, in the case of "The Sheik of Araby," a lone trombone, played by Glenn Miller, laying down the melody against which Teagarden improvises so brilliantly.

Teagarden apparently was quite a gregarious type, and rarely did he allow himself to record where he was the only soloist and could stretch out. Perhaps for this reason he did not really develop his artistry much beyond what it was in the 1920s. But on a piece such as "The Sheik of Araby," he did feature himself in a muted solo that demonstrates the ease with which he could handle his demanding instrument. The piece opens with Teagarden interrupting a sappy vocal by banjoist Treg Brown to say "Wait, wait, wait, man. What in the world are you singing about? Don't you know that's all out of date?" Big T then proceeds to sing in a more natural voice about "better ways to catch a queen" and follows that up with his trombone embellishments of the theme, including difficult figures on the instrument tossed off casually. Although many of Teagarden's vocals were of the novelty variety, he seemed quite serious about his trombone breaks, never stooping to the kind of corny tactics adopted by many other trombonists. But unfortunately one has to wait through dreadful vocals such as the one sung by Eddie Gale on the October 1, 1930, rendition of "You're Simply Delish," with Teagarden's ten-piece orchestra, before the trombonist takes a virtuoso break that demonstrates his technically masterful execution and his unique form of easy swing.[27]

When Teagarden joined forces with pianist Fats Waller, novelty vocals always tended to preponderate on the sides, and in the case of "You Rascal, You," from October 14, 1931, it is Jack's brother Charlie who somewhat steals the show with his fine trumpet solo. The trombonist opens this tune—which, as we have seen, Coleman Hawkins also recorded—with something of a brief cadenza before Charlie drives the ensemble and Jack actually contributes to the group improvisation. The repartee between Big T and Waller is pure vaudeville, with Jack taking the part of the straight man to Fats's humorous lines. This is true as well of their exchanges on "That's What I Like about You," from the same date.[28] Here again Charlie Teagarden delivers a fine solo (interrupted by a Pee Wee Russell break before the trumpeter continues), while Jack and Fats offer examples of their respective trombone and piano styles that were both basically a happy form of swing.

Another smaller group session was held on October 22, 1931, led by Eddie Lang and Joe Venuti. On this occasion, the eight-piece unit, comprised of brother Charlie, Benny Goodman, Frank Signorelli on piano, Harry Goodman on bass, and Ray Bauduc on drums, along with the two leaders on guitar and violin, respectively, recorded four sides that all feature Jack Teagarden as vocalist and/or trombonist. The first number, "Someday Sweetheart," opens with a Venuti and Lang duo, followed by two short breaks by Teagarden, muted but assertive. Brother Charlie delivers the fullest solo, which is quite fine. Jack hardly takes part in the concluding jam, which is rather typical of his non-Dixie approach. His vocal on "Beale Street Blues" is one of his most famous, with its lyrics that refer to being born in Texas and raised in Tennessee. In general, however, a piece such as this does not allow Teagarden to show off his trombone artistry, and in fact he does not solo on this side. Even "After You've Gone," on which he opens with a muted solo and later sings an excellent vocal, does not provide a setting that inspires his instrumental virtuosity. "Farewell Blues" finds Teagarden doing a limited bit of ensemble work, as he did at the very close of "After You've Gone." His solo on the former is far and away the most interesting of the session but frustratingly brief.[29]

More engaging than anything to be heard on the Venuti-Lang date is Teagarden's participation in the first recording sessions for Billie Holiday, held on November 27 and December 18, 1933. Along with Holiday, these sessions included a mixed group of musicians—with trumpeter Shirley Clay present among what was billed as Benny Goodman and His Orchestra, a nine-piece unit backing up the eighteen-year-old singer. Although again all too brief, Teagarden's breaks on "Your Mother's Son-in-Law" and "Riffin' the Scotch" are, apart from Holiday's vocals, the highlights of these sides.[30] The trombonist's driving, no frills solos are models of their kind in maintaining throughout both swing and meaningful invention. The second piece also includes a type of very brief cadenza by Teagarden, something of a signature statement that closes the side as if to say this is what jazz trombone is all about. Of course, Dickie Wells also had something to say about the way the instrument was to be played, but it was Teagarden who first established the easy swing that all trombonists would emulate.

Just prior to the Holiday sessions and before Teagarden joined the Paul Whiteman Orchestra in mid 1934, he recorded with another group led by Benny Goodman. On October 18 and 27, 1933, the nine-piece unit, which included Jack's brother Charlie and Manny Klein on trumpets, Goodman on clarinet, Art Karle on tenor, Joe Sullivan on piano, Dick McDonough on guitar, Artie Bernstein on bass, and Gene Krupa on drums, cut four sides that feature the trombonist as both vocalist and instrumental soloist.[31] The first tune, "Texas Tea Party," is an original blues by Teagarden and Goodman, with a play on the popular name for marijuana. Big T's vocal is warm and bluesy in his inimitable drawl, and his trombone break is also sui generis—full of expert turns that sound so natural and effortless. His vocal on "Ain't Cha Glad" is equally warm, but here he takes no trombone solo other than once again his signature coda; brother Charlie is the star soloist on this side. "Dr. Jeckle and Mr. Jibe" finds Big T's smooth swing much in evidence, both with his open horn and later for a muted ride that is immediately identifiable as his alone. Finally, his vocal on "I Gotta Right to Sing the Blues" is but one of many versions he sang throughout his career, which resulted in the tune becoming more fully associated with Teagarden than with any other singer. For many listeners, Teagarden was the greatest of all white bluesmen. On his trombone break, T's big, full sound is perhaps bigger and fuller than ever, and toward the end he is more forceful than was normally the case, his approach usually being extremely relaxed, rarely so assertive as here. Working with Goodman on these sessions of late 1933 seemed to bring out the best in Teagarden and reveal the many sides to his vocal and instrumental personality.

Of the few freelance sessions in which Teagarden participated while he was under contract to Whiteman, one of these was held on October 23, 1934, with a group led by Adrian Rollini. On this occasion Teagarden joined Bunny Berigan on trumpet, Benny Goodman on clarinet, and brothers Arthur and Adrian Rollini on tenor and bass sax, respectively, along with five other sidemen. Two tunes made famous by Bix Beiderbecke, "Davenport Blues" and "Riverboat Shuffle," are given treatments that differ essentially from the Dixieland style, especially when it comes to the trombone part, which with Teagarden is never of the tailgate variety.[32] In fact, this is clearly an arranged version far from the group improvisation of Dixieland, beginning with a subdued break by Teagarden that introduces the piece's very laid-back interpretation. Teagarden also closes the side with a characteristically mellow solo accompanied only by Stan King on drums. Arthur Rollini's tenor solo is quite un-Dixie as well, and indeed very much in the swing mode. For "Riverboat Shuffle," the pace picks up slightly to a jaunty bounce, and here Teagarden contributes another of his so-called "lazy" solos that mixes the smoothest swing with a technical facility that seems to belie the fact that the instrument being played is a trombone. Teagarden is the main soloist on this side, with only brief appearances by Adrian Rollini, Goodman, Berigan, and pianist Fulton McGrath. Again, Teagarden's relationship to the other members of the group does not actually involve anything much in the way of interchange. He essentially was a soloist, but his best work was done in conjunction with groups like this where he was merely a sideman rather than a leader. Such smaller groups definitely brought out the fullest artistry of this trombonist who obviously felt more at ease in his role as sideman and could therefore play with greater freedom and imagination.

From 1934 to 1938, Teagarden was with Paul Whiteman, after which he formed his own big band and first recorded in February 1939. In the beginning, Teagarden had with him a number of outstanding musicians, including reedman Ernie Caceres and trumpeter Charlie Spivak, but his was never a progressive jazz orchestra, and by 1940 Caceres and Spivak were both gone. During 1940 and 1941, the orchestra was mostly filled with inexperienced sidemen. As Anatol Schenker reveals, the orchestra's records "sold poorly since they had little to commend them, despite Teagarden's usually inspired solos."[33] As a matter of fact, Teagarden for the most part did not solo enough, leaving the spotlight to such singers as Kitty Kallen or Marianne Dunne, and when he did solo, it was hardly up to the work he had done with smaller, more jazz-oriented groups.

At the end of 1940, Teagarden recorded with what was labeled his Big Eight, a pick-up unit consisting of three members of the then Duke Ellington Orchestra: Rex Stewart on cornet, Barney Bigard on clarinet, and Ben Webster on tenor. On piano was Billy Kyle, who at the time formed part of the John Kirby sextet; the rhythm section was composed of Brick Fleagle on guitar (possibly the organizer of the session), Billy Taylor on string bass, and Dave Tough on drums. Although this eight-piece ensemble did not make path-breaking jazz, it certainly allowed Teagarden to open up and even prompted him to participate at times in a Dixie-type jam that for the trombonist was largely out of the ordinary. If the Ellington men do not quite equal the level of work they produced under the Duke's direction, they by no means embarrass themselves, and it would seem that they inspire Teagarden to extend himself beyond the rather generic big-band performances he had been giving with his own orchestra.

"St. James Infirmary," the first of four sides recorded on December 15, 1940, opens with Rex Stewart's cornet in a fittingly haunting mood, and then Webster shows why he was then one of the most respected tenors next to Hawkins, as Ben creates wonderful contrasts in phrasing and feeling.[34] Teagarden's vocal is convincingly expressive of the lyrics' melancholy content, and his trombone break is truly exquisite. Kyle's piano leads to a jam, after which Teagarden closes with one of his signature cadenzalike codas. The group's rendition of "The World Is Waiting for the Sunrise" is probably the most impressive of the entire session. It opens with Teagarden's smoothly swinging theme statement, followed by Bigard, who carries on admirably, even though he uncharacteristically misses a note, as he does on "The Big Eight Blues." Ben Webster then digs in and turns in one of his most exuberant breaks. Stewart's mute work is representative of his fine pixieish playing and works as well here as it did with Ellington. Kyle definitely puts his best foot forward on this number, swinging all the way. Teagarden returns, and he is really his old amazing self, combining great, flowing swing with his technical prowess, as he tosses off phrases that were the envy of every trombonist, and still are. Then the group rides out in a jam that features in the middle a driving eight by Webster and some notably urgent contributions by Teagarden. "The Big Eight Blues" is more relaxed and finds Webster in the bittersweet groove that gained for him his greatest fame. Bigard is good but not up to his best. Big T then delivers a masterful blues that he of all white players was most capable of bringing off. Stewart closes the side, as he had opened it, with his wah-wahs and growls to fine effect. The other outstanding side of the session is "Shine," the tune made famous by Armstrong. Here all eight of the musicians give a fine accounting of themselves, beginning with one of Teagarden's immediately identifiable declaratory openings. Webster is once more bursting at the seams, Kyle follows with a fine piano solo, and then an open Stewart does some of his joyous half-valve tricks. Bigard is at his best on this number, both in his jumping break and in doing his Dixie bit in the jam that follows his solo. Again Teagarden takes part in the jam before he offers another expansive break, after which the group rides out in a final enthusiastic group improvisation.

It is regrettable that Jack Teagarden was not heard more often in this kind of small-group setting. It clearly highlighted his remarkable talents in a way that his appearances fronting his own big band almost never did. Also, it would appear that in playing with such a mixed group that Teagarden was challenged to give of himself more fully. The basically "Big Eight" Dixie and blues sides present the trombonist as indisputably one of the major voices in jazz history, even if as a bandleader during the '30s he did not make his mark as a significant figure. Fortunately, he did leave proof of his mastery of his instrument and his understanding of the jazz idiom through a number of smaller group recordings, such as the memorable Benny Goodman–led sessions of the early '30s and the 1940 gathering with three of Ellington's most vital sidemen. In later years, Teagarden would join the original Louis Armstrong All-Stars and still later would lead successful world tours with another version of his own band. But in the period between 1930 and 1941, it was with pick-up groups in recording studios that Teagarden created many of his most important contributions to jazz and the era of swing.

BENNY GOODMAN

As we have seen, Benny Goodman was quite active with small studio groups during the early 1930s. But it was through the formation in 1935 of his Trio with Teddy Wilson on piano and Gene Krupa on drums, in 1936 of his Quartet with the addition of Lionel Hampton on vibraphone, in 1939 of his Sextet with Charlie Christian on electric guitar, and in 1940 of his Septet with Cootie Williams on trumpet that Goodman made his greatest impact as a small-group leader. From a chance meeting with Wilson at a party at the home of Mildred Bailey, Goodman enlisted the pianist as the first black jazz musician to work regularly in a mixed group. The Trio's initial recordings were made on July 13, 1935, and these affected the history of jazz in a number of ways. For one thing, Goodman has been credited deservedly with breaking down the racial barrier in jazz, which would result in whites in other fields following his example. In addition, his Trio changed jazz by making it more classically oriented, that is, revealing that the music could be played with restraint, refinement, and virtuosic precision, and yet still swing. His Quartet and Sextet introduced two major soloists in Hampton and Christian, who would each play a significant role in the history of jazz. Just as Goodman's big band expanded the audience for jazz, so, too, did his small groups. In addition, Goodman's smaller ensembles paved the way for a number of units that also came to emphasize a quieter, cooler approach to the music. Finally, Goodman also offered an alternative to the big bands and in that sense looked forward to what would become a growing tendency toward jazz created by smaller units that gave way eventually to the bebop revolution.

Although the Goodman Trio was itself somewhat revolutionary in reducing the size of a regularly working unit to three members in the midst of the big-band movement, its music was not especially pioneering, except from the viewpoint of its focusing on precision playing along the lines of a classical chamber ensemble. In this latter regard, the group immediately proved to be highly compatible, particularly Goodman and Wilson. The pianist's light, striding style complements perfectly Goodman's fluid, flawless clarinet. Krupa's frequent use of brushes keeps his playing inobtrusive even as it adds greatly to the group's overall swing. On "My Melancholy Baby," from the Trio's first recording session, Wilson's masterful left hand serves as the group's bass, feeding and driving both Goodman and Krupa on their solo breaks. At the same time, Wilson's left hand on his own solos is wonderfully active, at times creating countermelodies with their own inherent interest. "After You've Gone," another of the four sides recorded on July 13, was a tune made for the Trio, with its light, rhythmically jaunty theme such a perfect fit for Goodman's lightly swinging style, which at times mixes in some gruffness to lend it more of a jazz flavor. Wilson's responses to the clarinetist are utterly natural, so much so that it is almost as if Goodman has switched to piano. Likewise, as a rhythm section, Wilson and Krupa exhibit a rapport that translates into a special ease in the midst of simultaneous execution. Another side from this first date is "Body and Soul," the tune that Coleman Hawkins would make his own in 1939. Here in 1935 there is nothing especially advanced about the interpretation, although perhaps surprisingly this take is more impressive than the Trio's version recorded at the famous Carnegie Hall concert of January 16, 1938.[35] In 1935, Wilson was still indebted to Earl Hines, which accounts perhaps for his solo's greater jazz swing rather than his more filigreed treatment of 1938. Otherwise, not much changed in the Trio's approach over the two-and-a-half year period. Although Goodman was "dirtier" in 1935, even then his playing for the most part was essentially a tame version of jazz. In some ways both he and Wilson had made their music appealing almost on the level of a cocktail lounge refinement.

The group recorded next on April 24, 1936, and once again Wilson's pristine piano style serves as a wonderful complement to Goodman's clean-lined clarinet. On "More Than You Know," another tune perfectly suited to the clarinetist's style of embellishing swing, Goodman begins in the low, Chalumeau range of his instrument and then leaps or rips to the higher register, yet all the while maintaining the mellow quality of the song. From the same date, Wilson's phenomenal technique is displayed on "China Boy," where his rapid but impeccable runs and his amazing left hand leave the listener breathless. Also, his playing is quite witty in a very urbane way. Meanwhile, Goodman can match the pianist with his own flawless runs and impresses as well with his high notes that are always right on the money. Nonetheless, there is little from these sessions that advances the state of jazz. Compared with a recording date in November 1936 by a Basie small group, featuring Lester Young, the Goodman sides remain rather old-fashioned. Although a piece like "Oh, Lady Be Good!" recorded by the Trio on April 27, 1936, shares something of the low-keyed form of jazz that is heard on the Lester Young version of the same tune, from November 9, 1936, Goodman's Trio lacks the intense swing and the imaginative reach of the tenorist and his group. Goodman is more in his element on a tune such as "Sweet Sue, Just You," recorded on November 18, 1936, which exhibits the relaxed swing of the Quartet, with Lionel Hampton soloing effectively and adding to the overall drive of the unit. But there is little in the way of a climax on the Goodman sides, with their endings often so pat that they reduce the performances to a predictable formula. Also, on a side like the December 2 Quartet version of "Stompin' at the Savoy," the group plays this standard number in a rather quiet, refined manner that, although it can swing a bit, mostly tends to belabor the point by running on to twice the length of any normal recording of the period. For almost six minutes, the group indulges in the excesses that would later mar so many long-play recordings, especially those of the Jazz at the Philharmonic series. Even more meaningless is the version of "Stompin' at the Savoy" recorded at the 1938 Carnegie Hall concert, which reveals that the Quartet did not develop significantly as a group nor with regard to the quality or significance of its improvisations.

Earlier, in 1937, the Quartet also had been recorded live, and at that time the team work between Wilson and Goodman was truly quite impressive, especially in their playing of the theme of "Runnin' Wild" from February 3.[36] However, by this time Krupa was beginning to overdo his drum part, encouraged and stimulated by the audience. Here the tendency is more toward the ecstatic than the thoughtful, although on "My Gal Sal," from a live performance in November 1937, Hampton's break is at least more meaningful and Krupa is more restrained. On "Vibraphone Blues," which may be from August 26, 1936, rather than November 1937, Goodman and Wilson both do a decent job, but this form is not really their forte.[37] The November 1937 Trio version of "Nice Work If You Can Get It" again shows the group working well together, and in fact the mind-reading, synchronized interplay between Goodman and Wilson is perhaps unlike anything else in jazz, or is something of a swing-era equivalent of the mid-'20s Oliver-Armstrong duo. Here, too, Wilson is more under the beneficial influence of Hines, and Krupa is effectively supportive. From the same live performance, a Quartet rendition of "Killer Diller" is just that, with Krupa far too overbearing. On "Benny Sent Me," Hampton stirs up the crowd with his billy goat–like noises, but such antics serve no real musical purpose. On "I'm a Ding Dong Daddy from Dumas," the group mostly reveals its high level of skill, but the content of its playing is limited to virtuosity rather than offering any memorable music making. Perhaps the most satisfying performance from the November live recording comes on the Trio version of "Have You Met Miss Jones." Here Goodman produces some of his trademark relaxing swing, while Wilson offers up his clean, rapid keyboard runs. Again, the two men play almost as one, showing how compatible their approaches were and how well black and white musicians could work together.

By the time of the Carnegie Hall concert of January 16, 1938, the Trio and Quartet had already had their say. The performance of "I Got Rhythm" has been praised by Irving Kolodin for being "a special instance of the rhythmic tag the ensemble played with its listeners," but the group's stopping and then starting again when the audience thinks the men have finished the piece has little value other than as a crowd-pleasing tactic.[38] Nothing new in the way of jazz is really taking place, and most of the effort is put into frantic showmanship rather than meaningful music. With the departure of Gene Krupa in the spring of 1938, the Trio and Quartet no longer recorded, but by the fall of 1939, Goodman had formed his Sextet that would feature Charlie Christian's trailblazing electric guitar. On October 2, the Sextet, which consisted then of Goodman, Christian, Hampton, Fletcher Henderson on piano, Artie Bernstein on bass, and Nick Fatool on drums, cut four sides: "Flying Home," "Stardust," "Rose Room," and "Memories of You."[39] Goodman had first heard Christian's guitar playing at the instigation of John Hammond, but only after the leader had rejected the idea of auditioning Charlie and only through the good services of his own sidemen, who smuggled the guitarist onto the bandstand and jammed with him on "Rose Room" for forty-eight minutes.[40] Prior to his first recording session with Goodman, the guitarist took part in a session with a Hampton small group on September 11, discussed in Chapter 4. Although the Hampton date has been singled out by André Hodeir for producing a masterpiece in "When Lights Are Low," "the apex of the ascending curve that symbolizes the evolution of swing," Christian does not solo here but only contributes to the "incomparable homogeneity of the accompaniment."[41] On "Rose Room," recorded with the Goodman Sextet on October 2, Christian takes a full chorus that is described by Gunther Schuller as "a finely formed, logical composition" with a "splendid triplet eighth-note run." In considering the guitarist's contributions on all four tunes from this date, the critic concludes that they contain "all the essential elements of Christian's style: the clean uncluttered lines, often in arching shapes—his favorite phrase contour; his flawless time; his consistently blues-inflected melodic/harmonic language; the structural logic with which he invested form, whether in shorter segments (8-bar structures) or full choruses."[42]

Aside from Christian's presence on these Sextet performances, there is little new in Goodman's group, other than the quite different, less florid piano style of Fletcher Henderson. The tunes are all standards, except for "Flying Home," which in some corners has been credited to Christian but would become identified most fully with Hampton and his big bands. Although Christian makes an immediate impact through his innovative, very bluesy style, in the setting of these first somewhat antiseptic Sextet sides, the guitarist does not turn in his most impressive work. Even "Flying Home," which seems to inspire Christian's most swinging effort, cannot compare with some of his later performances. Here the guitarist does comp with urgency behind Hampton's vibraphone, but it does not seem to energize the group. Goodman's clarinet is good but has been heard hundreds of times before. Gunther Schuller finds that "Stardust," where the guitarist interpolates a bit of "Pretty Baby," "shows off Christian's full firm expressive tone at its expressive best," as well as his "extraordinary creativity" in superimposing on "Stardust" minor triads "set in a special blues-ish relaxed swing."[43] More swinging is the group performance of "Seven Come Eleven," a tune also credited to Christian. Recorded on November 22, 1939, this driving riff piece brings out Christian's ability to create longer-lined improvisations, and it even seems to lift Goodman to another level of performance, although once again the ending is rather too pat. Yet another tune credited to Christian is "Gone with 'What' Wind," recorded by the Sextet on February 7, 1940, but despite the presence of Count Basie on piano, this is not one of the guitarist's better outings. The two breaks played by Christian do provide evidence of his awareness of the work of Eddie Durham, his predecessor on the amplified guitar. Christian basically borrows a passage that Durham played on a Jimmie Lunceford recording of "Avalon," from September 30, 1935.[44]

The next month Christian would record with a group that included Goodman's then big-band tenorist, Jerry Jerome, along with Frankie Hines on piano and an unknown bass and drums. This session was caught in Minneapolis, Minnesota, and it finds Christian duplicating on "I Got Rhythm" some of what he had played on "Seven Come Eleven" with Goodman, and on "Stardust" his same interpolation of "Pretty Baby." But it also presents the guitarist in a more spirited setting, which not only offered him more space to stretch out but also more opportunities for his hard-driving comping in support of the piano and tenor. The obvious difference between Christian's playing in more of a jam atmosphere, with musicians who were looser in their approach, and the rather restrictive, polite context of the Goodman Sextet, is apparent here in the guitarist's more energetic and imaginative performances. On "Stardust," Christian especially ranges further from the tune's theme, revealing himself to be in the role of a precursor to the bop movement. Not only does he quote from "Pretty Baby" but also from Ellington's "I Let a Song Go Out of My Heart," thus exhibiting a penchant for quotation, one of the beboppers' favorite inclinations. On "Tea for Two," Christian comps wonderfully behind a honking, Young-inspired Jerome before Charlie takes off on his own highly venturesome solo.

One of the more effective Goodman Sextet offerings is "Boy Meets Goy," from April 16, 1940. Here Hampton delivers a fine vibraphone solo, and Johnny Guarnieri, who replaced Fletcher Henderson on piano, works into a boogie-woogie routine that seems to stir up Goodman's blood, as the leader really lets go. From a June 20 session, Christian plays a more down-home type of solo on "Six Appeal," whereas Hampton and Goodman offer very legitimate breaks but nothing spectacular. On November 7, 1940, Christian formed part of the Goodman Septet for a version of "Wholly Cats," with Cootie Williams on trumpet and Georgie Auld on tenor, along with Count Basie on piano. Here Christian again comps nicely, this time behind Auld and Basie, and then the guitarist gets into a groove before Goodman takes over, after which Cootie growls out with his muted trumpet over the riffing ensemble. With the same group, except for Ken Kersey sitting in on piano, Christian recorded "Breakfast Feud" on December 19, 1940, and here he digs in in a way that definitely sets him apart from the rest of the Septet members. Even though Cootie Williams is always impressive on the group's sides, and even Georgie Auld plays quite well, it is Christian who represents a jazz musician who is trying to create intensely each time he performs rather than just repeating himself as the other men tend to do—Cootie basically sounding as he did when he was with Ellington. Goodman does extend himself a bit on "Gilly," from the same date, but again it is Christian who sounds like he is from another jazz world. Cootie is perhaps best in his open-horn solo on "On the Alamo" from January 15, 1941. But both the trumpeter and Christian are most themselves on two impromptu sessions that just happened to be recorded by the Columbia studio engineers while the group was awaiting the arrival of Goodman. Titled "Blues in B" and "Waitin' for Benny" and captured on March 13, 1941, these two sides reveal the guitarist in a more natural setting, casually jamming and swinging beautifully on the first (in a difficult key) and on the second inspiring Cootie Williams to join in and really cut loose. As Al Avakian and Bob Prince have pointed out, Christian "rhythmically feeds Cootie Williams chords à la Basie, then riffs behind the trumpet, and Cootie proceeds with the only free, jamming swing-era trumpet he has ever recorded."[45]

The really telling fact about "Waitin' for Benny" is that its riff is based on Goodman's tune, "A Smooth One," which the group was waiting to record. The difference between the free swinging, imaginative jam carried on before Goodman's arrival at the studio and the Septet's recording of "A Smooth One" is dramatic and reveals how spirited the first is and how tame the second. In many ways the title of Goodman's piece also indicates how the small-group jazz he produced had become so smooth that it took the excitement out of the music. As Gunther Schuller has noted, the Goodman recording sessions had settled into "a certain mechanical routine quality," and as a result, the music had lost the stimulating, spontaneous-sounding, even surprising ingredients of true jazz.[46] Although the Goodman sides by his Trio, Quartet, Sextet, and Septet are full of proficiently swinging and technically superb performances, they tend to take the thrill out of jazz, to reduce the music to a predictable recipe. Nonetheless, it must not be forgotten that these sides represent historic occasions when the color line in jazz was crossed, bringing together such white musicians as Goodman, Krupa, Auld, and Guarnieri with black musicians such as Teddy Wilson, Lionel Hampton, Charlie Christian, Count Basie, and Cootie Williams. If the recordings of these groups do not offer so high a level of achievement in jazz as the recordings made by these same black musicians in conjunction with all-black groups, the Goodman sides stand as examples of more than competent jazz and signify a vital link in the process of integrating the arts and ultimately the nation.

BILLIE HOLIDAY

After Billie Holiday's first recording session in 1933, at which, as we have seen, Benny Goodman served as the leader of the ensemble backing up the vocalist, Teddy Wilson became the musician whose name would be linked inextricably with some of the finest recording dates of this greatest of all jazz singers. As the leader on many of Holiday's recording sessions during the Swing Era, Wilson was responsible for establishing a rapport with the vocalist that was unmatched, thereby assisting her to create some of the most unforgettable moments in her entire career. Glenn Coulter, a prominent Holiday critic, has written that

there never was such jazz as this for lyrical ardor and informal elegance, natural as breathing and yet as perfectly balanced as the most sophisticated art. Billie's choruses are utterly different in method and intention from their instrumental setting, a perfect counter-balance to the work of Teddy Wilson, for example, whose beautiful transformations of melodies force the listener into a seemingly permanent attitude of wonder and delight.[47]

Small groups other than those led by Wilson also backed up the singer, but on every occasion there were outstanding sidemen involved who turned in some of their finest improvisations in such "informal" settings. And once again, these small-group sessions frequently allowed for the simultaneous participation of both black and white musicians.

Among Holiday's most critically acclaimed recordings, two were made on July 2, 1935, under the direction of Teddy Wilson. "What a Little Moonlight Can Do" and "Miss Brown to You" have been singled out by Gunther Schuller as examples of, respectively, Holiday's "gritty and tart" voice and her ability to "highlight words or certain pitches," as when she lilts and rolls the "el" in such words as "little" and "lovable." Schuller goes on to say that Holiday's use of consonants, "apart from their uniqueness of enunciation, served to flavor and heighten the expression of certain syllables or words almost at will, all part of her instinctive improvisatory approach. Such consonantal emphases also were used as tiny subtle 'percussive' nuances, often adding enormously to her rhythmic swing."[48] Meanwhile, the instrumentalists on this date add immeasurably to the spirited performances. On both tunes, Benny Goodman opens on clarinet, and on "What a Little Moonlight Can Do," he especially turns in a finer piece of improvisation than on most any of the small-group sessions he himself led. On this same side, Wilson, Ben Webster on tenor, and Roy Eldridge on trumpet are simply marvelous, swinging as hard as anyone could, aided wonderfully by a solid rhythm section of Cozy Cole on drums, John Kirby on bass, and John Truehart on guitar. Eldridge and Goodman engage in some terrific Dixie-like jamming at the end of "Miss Brown to You" and on "What a Little Moonlight Can Do." Wilson is wonderfully active behind Billie's vocal, contributing tremendously to the swing with which the singer infuses her lyrics. Webster digs in and builds a terrific chorus, and then Wilson returns for a finely swinging break of his own. Unlike the endings of so many Goodman small-group sides, "What a Little Moonlight Can Do" concludes with much greater punch, with a powerful climactic finish. Also on this session, Holiday sings "I Wished on the Moon" with a voice tinged at times with her highly emotive gruffness. Once again Eldridge and Goodman, as well as Webster, engage in some lively group improvisation that ends this piece perfectly.[49]

Later in 1935, Holiday recorded two other numbers with a Wilson-led group, "If You Were Mine," a Johnny Mercer–Matty Malneck tune, on October 25, and "You Let Me Down," on December 3.[50] Surely Holiday's rendition must have been exactly what Mercer and Malneck would have wished for their song. The vocalist's romantically expressive, gruff delivery is so appealing without in the least lapsing into sappy sentimentalism. Behind her are Chu Berry on tenor, Wilson on piano, and then Benny Morton on trombone, each lending meaningful support to the singer's lines, especially Morton, who accompanies her in something of a duet. Morton also opens the piece and helps set the romantic mood, followed by Wilson, who does the same and in the process plays one of his loveliest solos. Not only must the composers of this tune have been taken with the vocalist's singing but equally with the Wilson-led group as a whole. Roy Eldridge's singing horn closes the side and completes the picture with a fully satisfying finishing touch. Among the instrumentalists on "You Let Me Down," Johnny Hodges is featured in a fine alto solo, and Dave Barbour on guitar takes a dandy break. Tom Mace on clarinet adds to what is a very unusual ensemble sound following Holiday's vocal. On this occasion the singer achieves a quite different tone to her delivery, both upbeat but also bittersweet, with at times a style reminiscent of Cab Calloway. Dick Clark on trumpet does not solo but plays an effective muted obbligato behind the vocalist.

Johnny Hodges, as well as his colleague Harry Carney from the Ellington orchestra, joined another Wilson group that recorded with Holiday on June 30, 1936. On this occasion the session produced a touching rendition of the standard, "These Foolish Things." Wilson opens with another of his appropriately romantic introductions, followed by Harry Carney, who blows one of his inimitable baritone solos, full of passion but with an easy swing. Hodges's fluttering obbligato alto adds greatly to the evocative nature of Holiday's delivery, with her special way of falling off emotively at the ends of certain word-notes. Jonah Jones on trumpet closes the piece nicely, even if a bit predictably. The next month, Holiday was accompanied by another small group, which consisted entirely of white sidemen with the exception of drummer Cozy Cole. On trumpet was Bunny Berigan and on clarinet Artie Shaw, both of whom turn in splendid solos that have nothing showy about them but are relaxed and thoughtful, indeed quite exceptionally so. The two sides cut on July 10, "Did I Remember?" and "No Regrets," seem tailor-made for Holiday's fresh, youthful voice, her combination of lilting swing and emotive enunciation.[51] In his accompaniment and solo breaks, Berigan is at his best as a bona fide jazz trumpeter. He opens "Did I Remember?" with his identifiably pure and ringing sound and on his break demonstrates the amazing range of his playing, from below the staff to above, with such a natural, flowing, singing quality. Joe Bushkin on piano also contributes a nice break, while Shaw's is simple but quite memorable. On "No Regrets," the two horn players engage in an extremely complementary piece of dual improvisation. On September 29, 1936, Berigan again recorded with Holiday, this time with Irving Fazola on clarinet and Clyde Hart on piano. However, the side cut on this date, a version of Jerome Kern's "A Fine Romance," does not find the group performing with quite the same infectious quality, even though Holiday's own vocal interpretation of the tune is thoroughly convincing, with her special way of imbuing her notes with a "gritty" jazz quality.

Teddy Wilson would return to the studios with Holiday in October and November 1936, along with much the same group that had backed up the vocalist in July 1935. In the place of Roy Eldridge, Irving Randolph or Jonah Jones was on trumpet, Vido Musso was on clarinet for one of the October sessions but Goodman was present on the others as well as on the November dates, and Allen Reuss replaced John Truehart on guitar. Of five sides cut during these two months, the first, "Easy to Love," from October 28, fully exemplifies Holiday's use of a slight vibrato, both on held notes and on those from which she falls off in a type of emotive quaver.[52] This technique also is found on "The Way You Look Tonight" from the same date, but here it includes as well a touch of the gruffness that adds to the emotive force of Holiday's delivery. As always, her enunciation is perfectly clear, even as she invests her lines with her own special rhythmic feel. On this number, Jonah Jones bends his notes beautifully, whereas Goodman, who opens the piece, produces more of his wonderfully rich sound and his easy, natural swing. On "Pennies from Heaven," recorded on November 19, Wilson displays his spectacular technique, but only at the service of the music. Ben Webster's tenor break is a beautiful piece of work full of fine contrasts. As for Holiday, she shows here that there has simply been no vocalist quite like her for control, for expressive power, and for a swinging rhythmic pulse. On "That's Life I Guess," also from November 19, Holiday is backed subtly by Webster and then by Goodman, while Wilson solos well with the support of Kirby's driving bass. Finally, on "I Can't Give You Anything but Love," from the same date, Holiday is once again superb, even though Jonah Jones is a bit off on this number, straining to reach his notes. Webster solos effectively, but it is the vocalist's delivery of the lyrics that is the outstanding feature of this side. Her version of this song that Fats Waller also sang so wonderfully is equally as good as his but in her own buoyant style.

In 1937, Wilson and Holiday were joined by Lester Young, who created some of his most appealing solos while in the company of both the pianist and the vocalist. The rest of the group for the two sides cut on January 25 consisted of Benny Goodman on clarinet, Buck Clayton on trumpet, and the Count Basie rhythm section of Freddie Green on guitar, Walter Page on bass, and Jo Jones on drums. On "This Year's Kisses," Young opens the piece with a masterfully constructed and flawlessly executed solo. Goodman plays obbligato behind the singer, who again exhibits her affective falling-away vibrato. Wilson and Buck Clayton on trumpet both take meaningfully breaks, and on "Why Was I Born?" it is Clayton who opens with a solo that is in its way as fine as Lester's on "This Year's Kisses," although the trumpeter sticks closer to the theme and his work is in that sense less original as a piece of improvisation. On June 1, both Clayton and Young returned to the studio to record with Holiday and Wilson, along with Buster Bailey on clarinet and the same Basie rhythm section. This date produced in "Easy Living" what Glenn Coulter rightly considers, in the "directness and intimacy" of Holiday's delivery, a rare instance of "true simplicity." Coulter also asserts that Wilson's solo work and his accompaniment of the other musicians "are enough by themselves to put this on any ten-best list, and Billie never surpassed this vocal with its repose and warmth."[53] Bailey opens effectively on clarinet, but it is Lester Young's tenor break that is especially poignant, while Clayton's obbligato trumpet responds beautifully to Holiday's vocal lines. Likewise, on "I'll Never Be the Same," from the same date, Lester's obbligato parallels and responds to Holiday with heartfelt expressivity. Wilson's filigreed but relaxed solo is accompanied wonderfully by the Basie rhythm section, as Teddy swings jauntily under the influence of Hines's "trumpet-style" piano.

Holiday worked with essentially the same small unit later in June and September 1937, but with Wilson replaced by James Sherman and Bailey by Edmond Hall on one session and Claude Thornhill on piano on another. Martin Williams considers two of the sides cut on June 15—"Me, Myself and I" and "A Sailboat in the Moonlight"—to be "among the great and revealing pleasures of the recorded jazz of the 'thirties" for "the simultaneous improvising of Holiday and Young."[54] The tenorist opens the first of these two cuts, and then Clayton's muted trumpet accompanies the vocalist. Hall's clarinet solo precedes an open-horned Clayton and a brief break by Wilson, before Holiday returns and she and Young engage in the "simultaneous improvising" referred to by Williams. On "A Sailboat in the

Moonlight," the piece begins with vocalist and tenorist together, and there certainly seems to be nothing else quite like these vocal-tenor improvisations. Both Clayton and Young also take fine solo breaks on this same side. Martin Williams singles out as well "Trav'lin' Alone," from September 13, as an instance of "perhaps the greatest paradoxical summary of this period . . . in which medium tempo and perfect swing are in suspenseful tension with the bitterness of [Holiday's] emotion."[55] Solos by Young and Clayton before the vocal establish the "medium tempo and perfect swing" and then Holiday maintains it but, as Williams says, hints at the bitterness through her tight, slightly falling vibrato and a certain high huskiness in her voice. It is indeed a touching example of what Williams calls a "suspenseful tension" that only Holiday's singing has ever achieved.

In January 1938, Wilson was back with essentially the same unit, changed only in that Benny Morton on trombone took over for Buster Bailey. It seems that Wilson's presence definitely made a difference, not only in terms of his own piano work but also in bringing out the best in the rest of the group. Lester Young, on "When You're Smiling" from January 5, is at the top of his game. On "If Dreams Come True," from January 6, the tenorist plays a delightful duet with Wilson, and Clayton accompanies Holiday's vocal with his lively muted trumpet. But Benny Morton takes the major solo on this side, a warm, imaginative chorus, followed by a fine open-horn break by Clayton. On January 12, the group recorded three additional sides, and these all offer more evidence of Wilson's crucial role as the session leader, inspiring the group members to a high level of artistic expression. On "Back in Your Own Backyard," Holiday and the rhythm section particularly swing this number, while Clayton accompanies with an agile obbligato. Following the first chorus, Young blows one of his coolly driving solos, encouraged by Jo Jones's punctuating drums. Wilson then backs up the vocalist marvelously as she returns for the closing chorus. A special treat is in store for listeners when the rarely featured, normally only rhythm guitarist Freddie Green opens "On the Sentimental Side" and then continues to be spotlighted until Morton takes a muted break, with Wilson's rippling runs in response. Green's ringing acoustic guitar passages are some of the richest in recorded jazz. The final song is "When a Woman Loves a Man," which opens with Young's cool, expressive tenor. Morton's muted trombone and Wilson's piano are heard behind Holiday, who offers more of her wonderfully clear, affective enunciation and her touching, rhythmic pulse. Without a doubt, these and other sides directed by Wilson are among the finest small-group recordings produced during the Swing Era. In addition to supporting Holiday, Wilson also recorded with vocalist Helen Ward, accompanied by a fine unit that included Harry James and Johnny Hodges, who both show themselves to be highly effective in such a supporting role.[56] It seems that no matter who played under Wilson's direction, the results were always superior for all concerned.

On January 30, 1939, Holiday sang a heartrending version of "What Shall I Say?" with the seven-piece orchestra once again led by Wilson.[57] Roy Eldridge on trumpet sets the stage with a lovely muted theme statement, and Ernie Powell on tenor adds quite an emotive solo. The slight huskiness in Holiday's vocal once again adds so emotively to her delivery, particularly of this song's sadly romantic lyrics. Wilson seems always to maintain perfectly the singer's mood, even as his rippling piano strains contrast beautifully with Holiday's basically unadorned style. On June 7, 1940, the pianist directed a nine-piece unit in support of the vocalist, and on this occasion Lester Young especially contributes some superb moments. By this time, Holiday's recordings are becoming more somber, which some listeners tend to prefer. The tempi of "I'm Pulling Through" and "Tell Me More" both rather drag in keeping with her renditions of a state of dejection. Young solos on the former and Wilson on the latter, but for the most part these sides do not feature the sidemen so fully, with Roy Eldridge only heard briefly, usually muted behind the vocalist. However, on the appropriately upbeat "Laughing at Life," Wilson takes a rocking solo, Young contributes nicely as usual, and Eldridge also solos briefly. "Time on My Hands" is back to a more morbid atmosphere and a slower-paced tempo. Both Holiday in singing and Wilson in his piano solo are more melancholy here, as are Young and Eldridge in their obbligatos behind the vocalist. This same type of mood characterizes Holiday's recordings in 1941.

On May 9, 1941, the singer produced one of her most famous, haunting recordings in "God Bless the Child," with the lyrics written by the vocalist herself. The pianist on this session was Eddie Heywood, and the only solo is a brief one by Roy Eldridge. On August 7, Teddy Wilson led the group that recorded three other sides, "I Cover the Waterfront," "Love Me or Leave Me," and "Gloomy Sunday."[58] Again, the tendency here is toward a rather melancholy mood, although on the second piece Holiday proves to be quite lively despite the dejected nature of the lyrics, or perhaps because of the words that assert that the singer "intends to be independently blue." On this side Jimmy Hamilton on tenor is the only soloist, and although quite good, he is not up to Young's high standard. As for "Gloomy Sunday," this represents perhaps one of the most depressive performances of Holiday's recording career from 1935 to 1941. There is essentially no participation by the ensemble other than to play a background role. Again, for some listeners this more melancholy side of the singer's career is the most appealing, whereas for others her greatest recordings date from the other end and middle of this period. Certainly the quality and degree of participation by the sidemen in the Holiday small-group performances declined after early 1939, even if the singer continued to deliver the lyrics of her songs with an expressiveness that is both remarkable and moving, maintaining, as Martin Williams aptly observed, the paradoxical, "suspenseful tension" of sadness and swing.

LESTER YOUNG

Along with Coleman Hawkins, tenorist Lester Young was the most in-fluential instrumentalist of the Swing Era. His cooler, more relaxed ap-proach to the saxophone, his ability to "tell a story" through his solos—these qualities deeply affected his own generation of jazz musicians as well as the next. Young, familiarly known as the President or Pres or Prez, acknowledged the impact on his playing of the C-melody saxophone style of Frankie Trumbauer, and most commentators believe that Bix Beider-becke, whose work Young would have heard in conjunction with Trum-bauer's, also must have influenced the tenorist's highly melodic, storytelling lines. As we have seen, Young was a prominent soloist with the Count Basie orchestra and participated significantly in the Billie Holiday recording sessions. But in some ways Young's most important recordings were the first he made, in November 1936, with a small group composed of mem-bers of the Basie band, nominally led by drummer Jo Jones and trumpeter Carl "Tatti" Smith. It was Young's performances on this seminal session with Jones-Smith, Inc. that clearly made the greatest impression on the next great jazz saxophonist, Charlie Parker, who reportedly learned Young's solos from this 1936 date note for note when the altoist was beginning to master his own instrument and discovering his own unique approach to jazz improvisation. In 1938, Young also took part in several small-group sessions headed up by another Basie sideman, trombonist-guitarist-composer-arranger Eddie Durham. Taken together, these small-group re-cordings document most fully Young's development of his innovative style, in the company of musicians sympathetic to and supportive of the tenorist's pioneering conception.

According to Chris Sheridan, compiler of the Count Basie biodiscogra-phy, the 1936 session that produced the four sides by Jones-Smith, Inc. "was perhaps the finest small band session of the 1930s," because from this date come "signposts to the way jazz would be played 10, even 20 years hence."[59] Included on this date was Basie blues singer Jimmy Rushing, who is featured on "Evenin'," which includes only a brief solo appearance by Young, yet one that shows the tenorist capable of more technique than he usually displayed, because normally he tended to hold back more than to let loose as he does here prior to Rushing's vocal. Basie opens this piece, and his unfrantic piano introduction is typical of his style and obviously responsible in large measure for the easy swing of this entire session. Carl Smith's muted riff behind Rushing is basic to the blues mode out of which this group's Kansas City tradition had evolved. "Boogie Woogie" repre-sents a genre that Sheridan notes "would become a staple of the Basie repertoire, but no version was fresher than this one."[60] Young's solo is just one example of his exuberant but relaxed style that so many other jazz musicians emulated and attempted to imitate. Carl Smith's muted break is wholly compatible with Young's approach—driving yet unhurried, a thoughtfully constructed "story" that keeps the listener's interest with every note. As for Basie, Sheridan credits the Count with being the genius behind the scene. The critic asserts that "one of the timeless lessons" of the group's rendition of "Shoe Shine Boy" is that it reveals Basie's understanding of the fact that "melody could become subservient to rhythm and therefore the notion of swing." Sheridan goes on to say that Basie "could deploy his instrument and that of Lester Young (and others) to make the results of that rhythmic drive singable."[61]

Gunther Schuller, for his part, has pointed to the "clarity of functions in the rhythm section" on "Shoe Shine Boy," calling such clarity "startling for its time." This critic emphasizes the "ideals pursued" by the group, which are "economy, 'less is more.' " He goes on to observe that,

at the same time, within these concepts the ensembles are flexible and diverse. Joe Jones "modulates" deftly from a variety of snare drum effects to all sorts of patterns and sounds on the hi-hat cymbal, always discreetly accompanying the soloist and blending with his rhythm partners. His playing on these four sides alone places him among the very best drummers of the period, for they reveal a degree of taste and sensitivity which few drummers have equalled.[62]

Schuller also finds that Basie, who opens "Shoe Shine Boy," toys "with a variety of pianistic approaches," including "sequences of full-blown two-handed stride piano."[63] Not only can one at times hear the influence of his old stride teacher Fats Waller but also in some of the Count's runs a speeded-up version of the later work of Thelonious Monk. In addition to his comments on Jo Jones and Basie, Schuller was one of the first to recognize the significant role played by Carl Smith, citing in particular the trumpeter's "exciting entrance on 'Shoe Shine Boy.' " The critic praises Smith's solo work as being "fluent, clear in thought and form, at times inspired . . . interesting in [its] note choices, fluent and well shaped in over-all form."[64] All these qualities are characteristic as well of the solos taken by Lester Young. On "Shoe Shine Boy," the tenorist manages to mix in almost every imaginable type of saxophone technique of the period: upward rips, drivingly repeated notes and phrases, bent notes within swinging arpeggios, something of a honk (supported by Jones's drums), and smoothly executed lines in which each note carries a level of swing hardly ever matched by any other saxophonist until Charlie Parker. Following the extended solos by Young and Smith, the two engage in a trading off of lively two-bar breaks, again complementing each other in the styles of their statements. Jo Jones takes a tasteful drum break, backed by Basie, that fits perfectly with the horn players' exchange. Then the group jams in a notably unified improvisation that yet allows for each voice to maintain its singular sound. After Young is left to have a final limited say, Jones to do just a bit on his drums, and Walter Page to work in a few solo notes, Smith then leads the group to a completely satisfying closure.[65]

Of all the four sides recorded on this date, the group's version of Gershwin's "Oh! Lady Be Good" is by consensus the highlight of the session. Gunther Schuller has fully analyzed Young's solo, transcribing it in order to reveal how it represents "a new artistic plateau in that the notes and general shaping of lines was now much more freed from the underlying harmonies. Again, horizontal and vertical had come together in a more symbiotic way, in which both aspects modified and complemented each other."[66] Chris Sheridan emphasizes the idea that Young's solo is a masterpiece in part because of the tenorist's "manner of harmonic anticipation."[67] Martin Williams demurs somewhat when he suggests that "one might say that [Young's] originality was not harmonic, but a-harmonic. He announced it on his very first recording date in the dense and ultimately self-justifying dissonances of 'Shoe Shine Boy,' rather different from the simple harmonic ignorance of some of his predecessors." As for "Oh! Lady Be Good," Williams stresses Young's "motific logic that is announced by his opening phrase."[68] More recently, critic Gary Giddins has written in an updated diction that the tenorist's two solos on these two sides represent "the most dynamic debuts in the history of records. . . . [Young's] wind-blown inventions combine vigorous riffs and piquant melodies, surfing the registers of the tenor, honking and crooning lean probing tales as narratively precise as a Hemingway story."[69]

Setting the stage for Young's masterpiece of lightly swinging yet intense improvisation, Basie typically sketches the theme of "Oh! Lady Be Good" with a minimum number of notes; also, he and Walter Page establish a wonderfully rocking rhythm. Throughout the tenorist's solo, Jo Jones lends support with a mixture of stick punctuations, rim shots, brief rolls on the snare head, and a steady but tightly controlled use of his cymbals. Likewise, Young's wide range of saxophone techniques is like a textbook of jazz tenor playing. His short opening phrase, followed by a pause, is dramatic but reservedly so, and when he takes up where he left off the entire phrase makes a thoroughly meaningful statement. In a way Young imitates Basie's opening of the piece, for the pianist starts by playing just a single note, and then goes on to finish the Gershwin melody, thus illustrating the claim that Basie could swing one note, for in this case he certainly seems to do so.[70] In the beginning Young is restrained but always swinging, then slowly builds until, through shakes, accented notes, upward rips, and drivingly repeated motifs with slightly altered pitches, his swing reaches an intensity that was matched by hardly any other soloist up to that point and by very few afterward. He ends his solo by returning to the less intense drive of his opening, coming full circle for an ending that feels totally fitting. Always there is a sense that everything Young plays is part of a larger design, even as each segment is captivating in its own right. There seems not to be a single wasted or superfluous note.

Gunther Schuller believes that Young's riffing behind Smith's solo is not very inspiring and in a way may have "straitjacketed" the trumpeter.[71] Even so, Smith maintains the same type of drive as the tenorist, as well as a similar level of invention. His muted sound is bright but also warm, both penetrating and consistently driving ahead. His note choices within the context of his motivic development, including a blues tinge here and there, are excellent, as Schuller observes, at the same time that he parallels the tenorist in never playing anything that does not add greatly to his own rhythmic conception and to the "storyline." The brief jamming of Young and Smith concludes the piece with absolute perfection.

During September 1938, Lester Young joined forces with five of his fellow Basieites to record four tunes arranged by Eddie Durham, who played electric guitar on this session. Known as the Kansas City Six, this group created a sound quite different from the one heard on the sides by Jones-Smith, Inc. Here Durham's arrangements make for a more relaxed setting, within which Young not only solos on tenor but also on clarinet, shaping on the latter a chorus that critic Nat Hentoff asserted he would trade for the collected works of, "yes, even Benny Goodman."[72] Hentoff considered the entire session of the Kansas City Six "among those half dozen collections I'd grab for if the building started to burn. I've been listening to the 78's off and on since they were first released and they are among those exceedingly rare works of man that do not become stale."[73] According to Leonard Feather, Young had recorded revolutionary solos with the Basie band that "were only the tip of a cool iceberg, one that came fully into view when the historic Kansas City combo dates were cut, starting in 1938."[74] On September 27, the Six opened their "revolutionary" session with a seemingly unlikely Dixieland number, "Way Down Yonder in New Orleans." Young's clarinet appropriately forms part of the theme statement, but there is nothing Dixieish about the cool, laid-back sound he produces on the instrument, quite different from the usual high-pitched, busy approach of most New Orleans–style clarinetists. The entire theme statement is in fact quite a departure from the customary "hot" Dixie manner, for Durham's arrangement emphasizes instead a cool ensemble treatment. Along with Buck Clayton's muted trumpet and Freddie Green's softly chording acoustic guitar, the group creates a wholly mellow instrumental blend. Clayton's very un-Dixieland muted solo, accompanied by Durham's low-toned electric guitar, is followed by Young on tenor with one of his most gently swinging choruses, completely removed from the Dixie style. Durham's solo is the first jazz on electric guitar to look forward to the smoother, longer lines that Charlie Christian would later exploit to such remarkable ends. As we shall see, Bob Dunn, another electric guitarist, with

Milton Brown and the Musical Brownies, already had recorded on the instrument as early as January 1935, but the results were Western Swing rather than the mainstream yet advanced jazz of this 1938 side.

If "Way Down Yonder in New Orleans" necessarily has about it the air of a Dixieland association, the next tune recorded by the Six, "Countless Blues," is a classic example of the Kansas City tradition of blues riffs, even without the presence of Count Basie on piano. This is especially true of Clayton's muted trumpet solo that begins by quoting the blues number made famous by Basie and Jimmy Rushing, "Sent for You Yesterday and Here You Come Today." Also in the Basie–Kansas City tradition is, following Clayton's very fine improvisation, the ensemble's quotation of the Basie theme song, "Jumpin' at the Woodside." "Countless Blues" opens with Durham's electric guitar setting a blues feel, and then the group riffing in a mellow groove, after which Durham plays a number of licks that may suggest that he had in fact been listening to Dunn, with the difference that at times Durham creates longer, smoother, more intricate melodic lines. Young on clarinet is fully, beautifully in the blues mode, except for what seems to be a quote from "Hold Tight," a pop tune made memorable by Fats Waller. Walter Page and Jo Jones are so subdued on this recording date that it is almost not until the group's recording of "Pagin' the Devil" that the listener is aware of the bassist's presence at the session. This last-mentioned side opens with Page's bass featured in a slow, deliberate pulse, aided by Jones's subtle cymbal. The whole piece, except for Young's solo on clarinet and Clayton's open horn, is played at the lowest level of perhaps any recording made in the entire Swing Era, which is such a dramatic contrast with the big-band tendency to go all out. The side closes as softly and quietly as it possibly could. Similarly, "I Want a Little Girl" is performed at a measured, leisurely pace, with Young's clarinet solo pitched at a much lower level than most solos of the day. Clayton's muted theme statement and subsequent solo, accompanied by warm chords from Green and very modern harmonies from Durham, are models of restraint and poignancy. Young's solo is somewhat less subdued but equally expressive, and so melodic as only he could be. Clayton's open horn closes the side with a contrastingly louder dynamic but still controlled in intensity, with only the final high note reaching a climactic point at which the piece effectively concludes.

On February 2, 1939, Lester Young would record one tune, "You Can Depend on Me," with another Basie group and including a vocal by Jimmy Rushing. For this date the trumpeter was Shad Collins, but the rhythm section again consisted of the "All-American" unit of Freddie Green, Walter Page, and Jo Jones. "You Can Depend on Me" opens with Basie's stride piano, with his own pointillistic, hard-driving version of this style established by James P. Johnson and Fats Waller.[75] Rushing's delightful shouted vocal is followed by a tenor chorus by Young that exhibits all his characteristic rhythmic and melodic qualities in their most identifiable form. Again he opens with a couple of attention-getting notes and then pauses before "leaping" fully into his driving solo. Here he is far more assertive and outgoing than on the sides recorded by the Kansas City Six. In some ways this is the Pres that so many other tenorists tried to imitate—the cool yet aggressive saxophonist who could create a narrative line that included a number of digressions that yet all contributed to the solo's overall design and effect. His sound is reminiscent of the one he attained on the clarinet, a higher-pitched, thinner tone than that of a Coleman Hawkins. Some commentators have even asserted that Young played the tenor like an alto. Certainly his sound was revolutionary in terms of the tenor, but also simply on the basis of his more linear, flowing style. Shad Collins's muted trumpet does not offer the same high level of performance of either a Carl Smith or a Buck Clayton, but his jamming with Young at the end is nonetheless similar in conception to that of his predecessors. This side is somewhat unusual in featuring a brief exchange among Basie's piano, the tenorist, and the trumpeter, who trade four-bar breaks which are very much in the Kansas City tradition of a spirited give and take.

Three other sides were cut on February 13, 1939, by an eight-piece group billed as Basie's Bad Boys, which included both Clayton and Collins on trumpet, the same "All-American" rhythm section, Basie on piano and also organ, and Dan Minor on trombone, along with vocalist Jimmy Rushing.[76] Basie opens "Goin' to Chicago Blues" on organ with an almost spooky sound, while the beat is kept by Page's pumping, near-muffled bass. Rushing's vocal is backed by obbligato passages from Young on clarinet, Minor on trombone (sounding close to Dickie Wells), and a muted Clayton. Riffing a type of jam, the group closes the side with a soft and easy swing. "Live and Love Tonight" again opens with Basie on organ, along with a muted Clayton. Basie then solos in a modified stride style, close to Fats Waller's organ sound except less ornamented with runs. Young on tenor, in combination with Basie's organ, achieves a mellow sound unlike anything heard before or perhaps since. As usual, the tenorist manages to swing hard with very few notes. Basie's close of the piece is almost churchy. For "Love Me or Leave Me," Basie switches to piano and, along with Page's bass, establishes a terrific swing at a medium-fast tempo. Clayton's open horn theme statement is bright and agile, whereas Young, as on the previous side, swings hard with few notes, as well as with some whooping upward rips. Collins takes a muted break, followed by brief passages from Young and Basie, and then an open Clayton closes the side. These are not among Young's most impressive recordings, but as small-group performances they all show that, as Stanley Dance has observed, "Young himself always remained essentially—as he affirmed years later—a *swing* musician."[77]

One of the most famous and well-considered sides recorded by Young,

"Lester Leaps In," was made on September 5, 1939, with a septet also drawn from the Basie big band. Two sides were cut by this group, with the only differences in the personnel from the February 13 date consisting of the replacement of Minor by Dickie Wells and the absence of Shad Collins. Wells's presence at the session is referred to in the title of the first tune, "Dickie's Dream," credited to Basie and Young. This number, with Green's comping guitar, is a classic riff of the kind that can be repeated almost endlessly without tiring the listener's ear. Clayton's fine muted break is followed by one of Young's most mellow offerings, limited to the middle range of his instrument yet swinging fiercely through his altering of his phrases, rhythms, and accents. He concludes by paraphrasing the riff, which is simultaneously picked up by Wells as he comes on like a runner grabbing the baton and holding on before he continues alone in a type of swing relay. This unique moment is the high point of the side, although Wells's entire solo is memorable, too, even if it lacks the trombonist's wildly dramatic contrasts, as André Hodeir indicates.[78] Basie's piano maintains the performance's interest before he plays another of his single "swinging" notes that signals the ensemble close. "Lester Leaps In," a tune credited to Young, is another riff that features the tenorist almost from first to last, including some rather showy stop-time passages. Gunther Schuller is correct in declaring that even though Young's work on this piece "has been hailed as a 'classic' for years by critics and musicians" that it is "marred by serious flaws."[79] For one thing, Young uncharacteristically plays a wrong note, perhaps caused by what Schuller suggests was an unintended intrusion by Basie. Nonetheless, Schuller concludes that even when all is said and done, Young's playing represents "a persistent quest for the new," which marked him as the most advanced jazz musician of the era.[80]

In late 1940, Young also recorded with a small group formed by Benny Goodman. On this occasion, on October 28, Charlie Christian joined Young for an exchange between two of the most revolutionary jazz artists of the day. Christian is most impressive in his brief solo on "Lester's Dream," on which Young is, as Schuller says, "a paragon of easy, relaxed, mellifluous swing."[81] Schuller also praises the tenorist's "laid-back breaks" on "Ad Lib Blues," but neither Christian nor Young seems especially inspired on this piece, perhaps because they felt inhibited by the overly arranged setting of a Goodman-led session.[82] Lester Young left Basie at the end of 1940 and for a short time played in a combo with his brother Lee, recording in 1941 at Kelly's Stable in New York City, as a backup for vocalist Una Mae Carlisle. Loren Schoenberg calls Young's obbligato and solo work with Carlisle "exquisite."[83] The tenorist also recorded with Sammy Price and His Texas Blusicians, on April 3, 1941, when he played not a great solo on "Just Jivin' Around" but, according to Schuller, a chorus that exhibits his "creamy smooth, gliding in on soft-tongued uncomplicated tonic repeated notes."[84] Young would go on to record many albums with his own small groups in the late 1940s and in the 1950s, continuing to influence a new generation of jazz musicians. But it was Young's small-group work in the late 1930s that remains his most vital contribution to swing, as well as to all the jazz movements that followed in the tenorist's pace-setting wake.

FATS WALLER

As one of the founders of the stride school of jazz piano and organ, Fats Waller was an important influence, as we have seen, on Count Basie. Also, Waller's vocal style—his singing both of songs he himself composed, such as "Ain't Misbehavin' " and "The Joint Is Jumpin' " (each with words by Waller's frequent lyricist, Andy Razaf), and of pop tunes of others to which he added his comedic asides, such as "I Can't Give You Anything But Love" and "Hold Tight"—was imitated by other vocalists with large and small ensembles alike. Although Waller appeared with various groups, such as the one led by Jack Teagarden in 1931, the pianist is best known for his own six-piece unit, billed as Fats Waller and His Rhythm, which first recorded in 1934. The sides made by Waller with His Rhythm range widely from the most banal pop tunes, such as "Hold Tight (Want Some Sea Food Mama)," to his own "The Joint Is Jumpin'," which re-creates the kind of rent party atmosphere at which stride piano was right at home, and included sentimental songs such as "Dream Man (Make Me Dream Some More)" and the seemingly unlikely "Porter's Love Song to a Chambermaid," with Razaf's witty verses. Not only do these sides reveal Waller's ability to turn what at times is pyrite into pure gold, but also they represent a style of swing that is at once smooth as silk and as infectious as any jazz ever produced.

Waller had first been under contract to the Victor company in 1929 when he recorded, with a mixed group that included Eddie Condon on banjo, one of the pianist-singer's approximately 360 original songs, "The Minor Drag." But then from 1931 to 1933, Waller recorded very little. In 1932 he first traveled to Europe, where he considered the "high point of that trip" to have been his playing of "the organ at Notre Dame in Paris, a privilege arranged by the cathedral's organist, Marcel Dupré."[85] Returning to New York almost before his continental tour had really begun, Waller started working soon after with a small group. On May 16, 1934, Waller and His Rhythm—comprised of Herman Autry on trumpet, Ben Whittet on clarinet and alto, Al Casey on guitar, Billy Taylor on bass, and Harry Dial on drums—recorded "Porter's Love Song to a Chambermaid," a delightful tune by Jimmy Johnson, with Razaf's lyrics developing an extended analogy between house cleaning and love: "Think of all the Mondays that we can rub-a-dub." Waller toys with the playful lyrics by changing his voice for various effects, as when he delivers as a knowing aside the line "thinking of you baby while I'm massaging those floors." In the beginning of Waller's vocal, Autry responds to the verses with his muted trumpet commentary, and later Whittet accompanies the singer on clarinet by doubling the melody line. Turning the order around, Autry's solo is a relaxed embellishing of the theme, and Waller accompanies the trumpeter with wonderfully precise piano interpolations and encourages his soloist by shouting "swing it" and "oh toot that thing." Like Holiday, Waller always enunciates the verses clearly, despite his comic inflections. After Autry and Whittet join in a leisurely jam, Waller ends the piece, as so often, with a phrase expressive of his satisfaction, in this case with his inimitable "yes yes yes."[86] This same phrase is used to urge on Autry in the group's recording of "Then I'll Be Tired of You," from August 17, 1934.[87] On this side the clarinetist-tenorist is Gene Sedric, who, along with Autry, would become a mainstay in Waller's Rhythm. The vocalist sings this sentimental ditty with a feeling that it is at once full of fun and genuine romance, and Waller's piano solo is almost classical in its delicate, seemingly effortless, flawless runs that yet swing so irresistibly. The muted solo by Autry exhibits his special drive, his use of shakes in the upper register that add so effectively to the group's intense but easy swing. Sedric's tenor break is more in the romantic vein, and represents the Rhythm's winning blend of sentiment and lighthearted drive.

The Rhythm was composed of a mixed group on September 28, 1934, when clarinetist Mezz Mezzrow and trombonist Floyd O'Brien replaced Gene Sedric for a recording of "How Can You Face Me." This side brings to the fore the lovely acoustic guitar of Al Casey, who accompanies Waller's vocal from the first, along with a muted Autry. Later Mezzrow also plays obbligato behind Waller, after which the singer swings out on piano in one of his great keyboard displays, including his trademark rippling runs, his ringing theme statement in the upper register, and his sudden left hand reaches into the bass. A muted statement of the melody by Floyd O'Brien is one of the most beautiful on records, with Waller playing the comedian who responds to the trombonist's "straight" lines by commenting "You dirty dog, get out get out. How can you face me now?" Waller continues his jibes as Mezzrow takes a short but touching break. Again, the mixture of sentiment, comedy, and subtle but solidly driving swing makes Waller's Rhythm at once movingly romantic and joyously uplifting.

The Waller combination of romance and uplifting joy is nowhere more fully realized than on "Dream Man," recorded with yet another change of personnel on November 7, 1934.[88] In place of Herman Autry, trumpeter Bill Coleman joined Waller and is the featured soloist on this unforgettable performance. Al Casey once more adds immeasurably to the group's relaxed but overwhelming drive. But it is Waller's vocal and Coleman's trumpet that have the most memorable effect. As usual, the singer is mischievous in delivering the song's sentimental lines and his own asides about a poor roomer dreaming of his beloved even as the landlady is knocking at his door for the rent. Waller's rippling runs and a subdued clarinet by Sedric open and set the romantic mood, which is then broken by Fats's jolly stride piano. Casey and Sedric accompany the vocalist, and then as if from the skies Coleman descends with a sound that is high pitched, thin, but ever so emotionally piercing. Like the O'Brien solo, there is nothing else quite like this solo by Coleman in all of recorded jazz. The inventiveness of the trumpeter seems endless, as each phrase of his solo is full of an unmatched freshness and vitality. He seems capable of going on and on without repeating himself, always ringing out the most natural and affective lines. After Waller returns to continue with his vocal, he and Coleman, who plays more of his same light but penetrating lines as an obbligato, create a type of counterpoint. As the trumpeter darts above, Waller shouts below: "Oh landlady, let me dream some more." Although Waller has been criticized for lowering himself as a comedian, for not taking his art more seriously, it is difficult to hear a piece such as "Dream Man" and not think that this kind of jazz is the height of sophistication, despite its humorous treatment of a pop tune. For this small-group side contains all the most engaging elements of swing: inventiveness, drive, and a clean, refreshing sound.

The introduction to "Sweet and Slow," recorded on May 8, 1935, is Waller at his most virtuosic, providing a cross-section of his varied styles of jazz piano.[89] Just as the title indicates, this piece is sweet and slow, with the pianist milking every note, every perfectly executed embellishment, chord, and trill for all the meaning and emotive quality his light, swinging touch can impart to the composition. His singing also exhibits an impressive range of inflections, from sincere to tongue-in-cheek and everything in between. "Us on a Bus," from April 8, 1936, is sheer unadulterated fun, as well as an example of Waller's ability to jazz a pop tune both as a vocalist and a pianist.[90] The first four notes of the theme, one for each of the title's four one-syllable words, reproduce the traditional sound of a vehicle horn, and the rest of the melody forms an ingenious up and down line ending with the same title words but in a different note arrangement. Accompanied by Autry's trumpet imitating a bus's humming exhaust, Waller sings the lyrics in a way that lends the words a rhythm and emphasis all his own, especially when he returns to sing the theme again following his sidemen's solos, concluding with obviously his own added phrase: "All out, Swing City." The happiness of his piano break is in everything he plays, from alterations of rhythms and sudden runs, to a kind of swaying and prancing that makes the listener feel that he really is on a bus, leaning with the curves and gently springing on the cushioned seat with the bumps and dips. With Waller it is always a joyride—not that he is reckless, quite the contrary when it comes to his steering at the keyboard, but he certainly is willing to take chances with the material, to surprise with humor and sudden shifts into low or high gear. Above all, Waller is the master of drive, making every bar swing from beginning to end. This is particularly true of his version of "Christopher Columbus," from the same session of April 8. Here Andy Razaf's lyrics, as with his "Porter's Love Song to a Chambermaid," are once again full of sexual innuendo, which Waller intimates with sly humor. His piano intro begins the swing and Casey's guitar feeds it, with Sedric's tenor solo building up to Waller's own piano break, which increases the intensity until he is joined by the entire jamming group that in its pandemonium mimics the ship's crew "making merry. Mary got up and went home." As Mike Lipskin has written, Waller and His Rhythm could generate an "infectious swinging quality which was found in few other hot combos of the time" and the pianist was capable of "the most powerful . . . choruses in any jazz recording."[91]

Again, some critics have lamented that Waller acted the clown, but he wore many masks, hiding perhaps the real man beneath his comedy, as Eudora Welty has suggested so brilliantly in her short story, "Powerhouse." Many of the songs Waller was either given to sing or chose himself would seem to reflect the jazzman's awareness of a double life, one of humor and one of deep feeling, and the relationship between the two. Irving Berlin's "You're Laughing at Me," from February 22, 1937, may be a prime example.[92] Using a celeste, as he did on occasion, Waller accompanies Sedric's romantic clarinet and helps set the stage for his own vocal, which after the opening is the focus of this side. Without seeing the lyrics, one never knows (to filch a Waller phrase) whether the singer is adding impromptu lines or if they are part of the song yet delivered by him as a wry commentary on the saccharine verses. It would certainly appear that Waller's asides in the Berlin song are his own, as when he tells the lady, "Baby, you know humor is death to romance." Perhaps such a blend is what bothers some critics, but it is Waller's unique capacity for evoking in the same song both romantic and sardonic responses to love that makes his singing so unsentimental and yet so genuinely moving. Berlin may be responsible to a large degree, because his lyrics do concern an attempt to be sentimental in the face of humor, but it is Waller's delivery that achieves for Berlin's song this seemingly incompatible combination that probably no other singer has ever quite managed or ever will. Once again, this mixture produced in part the special form of Waller's swing that has accounted for the longevity of a Berlin song that might otherwise have never endured.

More typical of Waller's joyous music is his own tune, "The Joint Is Jumpin'," from October 7, 1937. Here again he and His Rhythm re-create a scene of pandemonium, one in which the place "is in full swing" when police raid the party—one of those Harlem affairs where people gathered to help raise money to pay the rent. "The roof is rocking, the neighbors knocking" when a whistle and a siren are heard on the recording, a door slams, and dancers apparently scramble, as Waller wittily warns, "Don't give your right name, no no no." But again, Waller could present a contrastive style just as well, as on a Frank Loesser-Hoagy Carmichael song, "Two Sleepy People," recorded by the Rhythm on October 13, 1938.[93] Sentimental in the extreme, this is yet a touching picture of courtship that Waller can render with appropriate tenderness and simultaneous tongue in cheek, when necessary, as when the lyrics reveal that the couple had to marry in order to "get a bit of rest"—after so many nights "holding hands and yawning . . too much in love to break away." Waller's opening chords and his ringing piano figures against Autry's straight muted theme statement are once more both sentimental and playful, and it is this combination that makes such songs in Waller's hands and in his knowing tone of voice so completely winning.

Yet another side to the jazzman's personality is represented by recordings made during his trip to London in 1938. In August of that year, Waller performed on organ a number of Negro spirituals, including "All God's Chillun Got Wings" and "Swing Low, Sweet Chariot," as well as "Deep River" and "The Lonesome Road."[94] But undoubtedly, Waller is best known for such tunes as "Hold Tight (Want Some Sea Food Mama)" and "Your Feet's Too Big," both recorded in 1939.[95] The comic lyrics in both songs were made for Waller, but it is his own vocal shakes, falsetto tone, and mocking rhythms that all turn the January 19 performance of "Hold Tight" into a jazz interpretation. The same holds true to some extent of Waller's version of "Your Feet's Too Big," from November 3. Here the singer mostly "squawks," walks, and shouts, along with offering such asides as "I hate you because your feet's too big," "those things are gunboats," and, of course, "your pedal extremities really are obnoxious. One never knows, do one?" His piano introduction, after its mysterious first few bars suggesting that someone is tiptoeing around, is classic Waller, full of prancing rhythms and ringing chords. No other jazz "entertainer" could so successfully blend high jinx with virtuosity.

Waller may have been strapped with too many mediocre pop tunes, and he may not have recorded enough of his own compositions, but his repertoire was certainly varied. On July 16, 1940, he and His Rhythm, composed of a group that with the exception of Gene Sedric differs completely from his early units, cut "Original E-Flat Blues," one of the pianist's few recorded ventures into this genre.[96] Even here Waller does not seem able to take the lyrics seriously, singing them in his usual irreverent tone. Guitarist John Smith remains more faithful to the traditional sorrowfulness of the blues idiom, as do a muted John Hamilton on trumpet and Sedric on clarinet. The blues form itself does contain an inherent sense that, although the singer is suffering, love must be endured and not avoided, and in this respect is not tragic. Waller certainly seemed to express such a view in his singing of pop songs, even if here with the blues a listener may feel that the vocalist is being rather snide instead of sympathetic. But the blues do not appear to have been Waller's natural metier, for they do not so fully allow for the playfulness, the ironic asides (which he nonetheless does include in this performance), and the jauntiness that make up his most appealing "entertainments." In 1941, the pianist recorded a number of solo sides, showing again his keyboard virtuosity, but in some ways his solo work never satisfies or delights nearly so well as his piano displays in the midst of his combo recordings, where he drives his Rhythm on with witty remarks, rips off thrilling keyboard passages that fuel the overall performance, and swings with a gusto and elan that almost no other leader and his small group have equaled, then or now, or perhaps ever will.

MILTON BROWN

The influence of Fats Waller may have traveled as far as Texas during the same year that the pianist and His Rhythm first began to record. Although Cary Ginell claims that the "closest comparison" between vocalist Milton Brown and "a singer from that era would be big band vocalist/ entertainer Cab Calloway," there is an infectious quality to the Texan's singing, and to the Western Swing of his Musical Brownies, that suggests an awareness by the Texas combo of Waller and His Rhythm.[97] Ginell does note that Brown's hollering in his songs serves "as jazz exclamation marks (similar to those used by Fats Waller)."[98] However, Brown actually recorded with his group earlier than Waller did with his, if only by about six weeks. In any event, the two groups share certain similarities in the vocal styles of their leaders and in the easy swing and enthusiastic drive of their sidemen. Although Brown and the Brownies are closer in some respects to a Dixieland tradition, they, like Waller and his men, depended on Tin Pan Alley songs for much of their repertoire. Also, just as a sense of fun and good humor permeate the recordings of Waller and His Rhythm, so, too, do those same qualities pervade the sides cut by Brown and his aggregation. Beyond these possible connections, Brown and his six-piece western band purveyed an entirely different type of jazz, one which had received little attention in histories of the music before Jean A. Boyd made a case in 1998 for Western Swing as "The Jazz of the Southwest."[99] Previously, Gunther Schuller had briefly discussed Western Swing guitarists Leon McAuliffe, Muryel "Zeke" Campbell, and Bob Dunn as predecessors of Charlie Christian, but Brown and the Musical Brownies (apart from Dunn) receive only passing mention in a footnote in Schuller's *The Swing Era*.[100] Yet it does seem undeniable that Brown, with his sextet of string players and piano, did create a kind of improvised swing as inventive and captivating in its way as that of Waller and his unit, and of any number of other long-recognized small jazz ensembles.

Milton Brown, born near Stephenville, Texas, in 1903, was first recorded in 1932 by the Victor Company as part of the Fort Worth Doughboys, which included Bob Wills, the more famous exponent of Western Swing, on fiddle and harmony vocals. After playing over Fort Worth radio stations WBAP and KFJZ between 1930 and 1932, Brown and Wills split up when the sponsor of their radio show, W. Lee O'Daniel, refused to hire Brown's brother Derwood as a guitarist. In 1932, Milton Brown formed his own group, as Wills did in 1933, and the two musicians developed Western Swing in their separate ways. But prior to the separation, their first sides in 1932 represented a transition from the "dry, dusty sound of cowboy vocalists" to "a sophisticated, smoother sound, more associated with the big city," and Brown's vocals resembled "jazz/pop singers" rather than cowboy crooners.[101] At this point there were no real improvisations included on the recordings, but these would come when Brown established his Musical Brownies. Indeed, there is a dramatic difference between "Sunbonnet Sue" and "Nancy Jane," the two sides recorded by the Doughboys in 1932, and "Brownie's Stomp," the first side cut by the Musical Brownies on April 4, 1934.[102] Not only do the titles indicate a difference between country songs and a jazz-influenced style, but Cecil Brower on fiddle shows immediately that not only can he swing in a jazz mode but also that as a classically trained violinist he can handle his instrument as a pro not just an amateur picker. Also, Cary Ginell observes that Brower's "closing melody" is "a variation on 'Milenburg Joys,' " which indicates the soloist's awareness of jazz tradition.[103] Ocie Stockard on banjo really tears it up, and Fred "Papa" Calhoun on piano, although not in the same class with jazz pianists, can swing and does improvise. This piece starts with a tremendous burst of energy that lasts throughout the side. The next number, another purely instrumental piece, titled "Joe Turner Blues," demonstrates that from the first Brown and his Brownies would play the blues and do so with real conviction, with Brower's weepy fiddle and Calhoun's downhearted piano truly capturing the blues feeling. Stockard's banjo powers the opening of "Oh! You Pretty Woman," where Wanna Coffman on string bass backs up Brower's theme statement, while Calhoun's piano stomps and ripples behind Brown's lively vocal. Brower's improvised break is full of swinging trills and rips, and Brown sings with humor and fine rhythmic drive. A sentimental waltz such as "My Precious Sonny Boy" must have been popular with the depression crowd, especially with Brown's western delivery, which includes a straight talking section that yet conveys a rhythmic feel. With the leader's charming vocals and his Brownies' energetic swing, this was from the beginning a highly appealing unit that was rarely equaled by any other Western Swing ensemble.

At the annual meeting of the International Association of Jazz Record Collectors, held in San Antonio, Texas, in August 2000, Ron Sweetman of Canada presented a talk on the city's "Jazz and Blues Recording Sessions 1928–1938," in which he included the Brownies' "Garbage Man Blues." This side, recorded in San Antonio at the same session of April 4, 1934, also starts (after a comedy exchange) with a bang, and Brown's vocal is an example of powerhouse blues—that is, blues that is not slow and lowdown but fast and furious, full of booming and boisterous drive. Brown shouts and almost growls out the repeated line, "Get out your can, here come the garbage man," and as Ginell has suggested, even imitates something of Cab Calloway's tone of voice. Another piece that finds Brown in the Calloway vein is "Four, Five or Six Times," in which the vocalist scats the lyrics in the same style as Cab, echoed at times by the Brownies. The whole group furnishes an easy swing behind the singer, and Stockard takes a fine tenor guitar break. Perhaps more typical of the western style of the band is "Where You Been So Long, Corrine?" recorded on the session of August 8, 1934. Here Calhoun's piano obbligato is the jazziest part of this essentially country side. For the most part the ten sides recorded at this session are more in the country mode, but one piece, "Just Sitting on Top of the World," is blues tinged, and "Take It Slow and Easy" has to it something of a Dixie feel. On the latter, the breaks by Brower on fiddle and Calhoun on piano, especially their stop-time moments, are very much in the Dixieland style. "Get Along, Cindy" and "This Morning, This Evening, So Soon" both swing but with a country-western fiddling sound, except for Calhoun and Brower's breaks on the second side. "Trinity Waltz," "Loveland and You," and "Girl of My Dreams" are country-western waltzes, with the string harmonies quite rich on the first. "Loveless Love" contains two of Brower's best solo outings from this recording date.

As of the session of January 27, 1935, which took place in Chicago for the Decca label, the Brownies included for the first time amplified steel guitarist Bob Dunn, originally a trombonist who was a great admirer of Jack Teagarden. Dunn takes his first solo on "Put on Your Old Grey Bonnet," and although this is a very brief appearance, it is marked by the guitarist's honking, nasal tone quality that indeed suggests a trombone influence. On this session the Brownies cut a couple of Mexican standards, "In El Rancho Grande" and "Baile en Mi Rancho," revealing something of the wide range of material offered by the group. In his vocal on "Down by the O-Hi-O," Brown again recalls Calloway, whereas on "I Love You," Brower offers one of his more impressive fiddle solos—somewhat under the influence of jazz violinist Joe Venuti. Dunn takes a full chorus on "Sweet Jennie Lee," and although this is a curiosity not quite in the jazz mainstream, it is the earliest example of extended improvisation on the amplified guitar and is in its way quite fascinating. As sung by Brown, "St. Louis Blues" is not the W.C. Handy song, but it is in the blues mode, with Dunn soloing again not in the jazz tradition but with his own unique sound and style, including some sudden pinging leaps into the upper register, as also on "The Object of My Affection." Brown's vocal on this last piece is quite charming. Although brother Derwood croons in a western style on "Love in Bloom," he at times hints in his tone at a certain Waller affinity. Cary Ginell indicates, in fact, that Derwood Brown "was a big Fats Waller fan," which is revealed most fully on Derwood's recording of "Cross Patch" from February 19, 1937.[104] One of the swingingest sides from the session of January 27, 1935, is "Chinatown, My Chinatown," with Milton Brown singing well, Calhoun pounding it out on the piano, Dunn doing his thing nicely, and Brower turning in another of his splendid fiddle displays. The Brownies' version of "Copenhagen" contains in Brower's "take-off" (the Western Swing phrase for an improvised break) what Ginell says had become "a staple of Texas string bands": a " 'weeping fiddle' and the ubiquitous 'rockin' bow.' "[105] "Brownie Special" is a fun tour of towns on the Texas railroad line, complete with train whistle imitation and Brower's fiddle stoking the fire. "Some of These Days" is not in a class with the 1930 version by Calloway's orchestra, but it swings with an easy rock and Dunn contributes one of his erratic breaks full of unexpected dartings here and there. "Wabash Blues" also swings with a leisurely pulse, with Brower providing obbligato support to Brown's vocal and Dunn utilizing a touch of what Gunther Schuller refers to as the guitarist's "slidy Hawaiian effects, very popular on recordings going back to the late twenties."[106]

On January 28, 1935, the Brownies recorded twenty-two additional sides. From this session comes a number titled "Taking Off," which features Cecil Brower and Bob Dunn. Jean Boyd writes that "Brower's solo chorus . . . is the product of a jazz musician" and his "solo line, though idiomatic for the violin, is phrased like a horn solo."[107] This is not, however, one of Brower's better efforts, and in fact it is Dunn who is more adventuresome, including a few of his Hawaiian licks along with his usual nasal honk. Another jazz fiddler, J.R. Chatwell, produced on "Hot as I Am," recorded June 23, 1937, what is "still regarded as one of the definitive swing solos" on fiddle, and Chatwell's solo does indeed swing more intensely and inventively than any other such "take-off."[108] A number of the other sides from the Brownies' January 28 session feature tunes that are more traditionally associated with jazz performance, such as "I'll Be Glad When You're Dead You Rascal You," "Sweet Georgia Brown," "Darktown Strutter's Ball," and "Black and White Rag." Brower's take-off break on "I'll Be Glad" is in quite a different style from the many jazz versions of this number, and Brown's phrase, "you dirty dog you," although it recalls Waller's aside, does not carry the same humorous force despite its being a bit of clowning commentary during Dunn's break. On "Sweet Georgia Brown," Brower combines traditional breakdown fiddling with a Joe Venuti type of jazz violin swing. Cary Ginell has noted that "the Brownies' repertoire deemphasized traditional country music in accordance with [their] jazz-oriented interplay between the musicians and the vocals; and with their focus on current popular numbers, classic city blues, and sophisticated jazz instrumentals, the band totally transformed hillbilly music in Texas."[109] But insofar as being up to date in their "jazz-oriented interplay," the Brownies were not really, for a piece such as "Darktown

Strutter's Ball" has more of a Dixieland sound, especially with Stockard's banjo taking a prominent part. Also, Dunn's guitar lines are extremely stiff, his lines not really so smooth or flowing as those of Eddie Durham and especially not those of Charlie Christian. Of course, Dunn was ahead of the two jazz guitarists chronologically, although Durham would record on an amplified guitar later in 1935. Brower is the most fluid of the Brownies, but even he is into the syncopated style of the twenties more than the smoother swing of the thirties. Mainly it is the rhythm section, which is still rooted in a two-beat pattern, that is quite heavy compared with the four-beat swing of the jazz groups of this time period. The Brownies' version of "Black and White Rag" also is a rather backward-looking form of jazz by this date. And certainly the Brownies remained tied to a country idiom in such pieces as "Little Betty Brown," which is in the hoedown category, and "Going Up Brushy Creek," where Brower does another fiddle breakdown.

During its next three sessions recorded in New Orleans on March 3, 4, and 5, 1936—the final dates with Milton Brown as leader—the Brownies cut a tune identified with Jack Teagarden, "The Sheik of Araby." Brown's vocal does not offer so distinctive a rendition as Teagarden's, and here as elsewhere Calhoun's piano seems overly rudimentary. Brower still swings more smoothly than any other sideman in the group. For these New Orleans dates the Brownies added a second fiddle in Cliff Bruner, who at times could be rather fluent but in a more western style. Cary Ginell considers Brown's singing on "Beale Street Mama" to be "arguably" his "finest hot vocal performance," but by now Brown seems to have lost some of the special gusto he had exhibited on the 1934 sides.[110] In general, the group has not developed much beyond its first session, although at times Bob Dunn has definitely contributed some unusual breaks, as on the March 3 recording of "Somebody's Been Using That Thing." The difference between Brower and Bruner's fiddle styles is made most evident on the March 4 side titled "When I'm Gone, Don't You Grieve," which Ginell says has "possible origins as a traditional play-party song."[111] Here Bruner retains more of a western fiddle sound and technique, whereas Brower clearly belongs to the Joe Venuti school of jazz violin. One thing that can be said for Milton Brown and his jazz-oriented group is that the leader does include many tunes from the jazz-blues repertoire, such as "Beale Street Mama" (sung by Bessie Smith as "Beale Street Papa"), "Cow-Cow" Davenport's "Mama Don't Allow It," Big Bill Broonzy and the Hokum Boys' "Easy Ridin' Papa" and "Am I Blue?" (sung by Ethel Waters and Billie Holiday, respectively), "Memphis Blues" by W.C. Handy, "Somebody Stole My Gal," "Avalon," and "Sadie Green (The Vamp of New Orleans)." Brown's vocal on "Avalon" is not really jazz singing, but his rendition of "Sadie Green" is. One of his best blues vocals is on "Tired of the Same Thing All the Time," on which Brower also does a fine job with the blues and the group turns in a nice jam at the end. Unfortunately, the title of this tune can be applied to Bob Dunn's guitar take-off, which is very repetitious of the phrases he tended to play over and over. As for Calhoun, his piano break on "Am I Blue?" is certainly one of his strongest efforts. Brower shows his versatility on "I'll String Along with You" when he effectively plays the melody with a mute and tremolo. He also plays the theme on "Goofus" with a fine jazz rhythm, whereas Bruner is rather stiff and countrified.

Milton Brown's last side was "The Old Grey Mare," on which he and his brother Derwood sing a fine bit of harmony. After Milton's death from an auto accident, on April 13, 1936, Derwood kept part of the band together and replaced those who decided to join up with other outfits. Lefty Perkins took over for Dunn, continuing with the same honking, nasal sound on the amplified steel guitar and many of the same licks played by Dunn, although Perkins manages a smoother flow to his lines. "Buck" Buchanan on fiddle replaced Brower and, according to Cary Ginell, "helped usher in a new, more stylish era for western swing."[112] Calhoun and Stockard are their old reliable selves, and Johnny Borowski plays both fiddle and ocarini, the latter to great effect on "Cross Patch," recorded at the new Musical Brownies' only session, on February 19, 1937. Derwood Brown sounds fine on "Bring It on Down" and, as mentioned earlier, does a Fats Waller bit on "Cross Patch," ending the side with a "yeah" reminiscent of Fats. On "Louise Louise Blues," Derwood does a decent job and carries on his brother's tradition of including the blues, but this and a number of the other sides (such as the slow blues titled "I Just Want Your Stingaree") tend to drag and lack the spirit of the Milton Brown recordings. Some of the sides have lost a truer jazz quality, the two-fiddle sound is more syrupy and whiney, and Calhoun does not drive with the same urgency. Jimmie Davis's vocals on "High-Geared Daddy" and "Honky Tonk Blues" identify these tunes even more with the country mode, although Calhoun's piano take-offs are not bad, just not as inspired as before. Buchanan's take-off on "Honky Tonk Blues" is rather spiritless and countrified, although at one point in this piece the group does jam nicely. The only purely instrumental piece recorded by Derwood and the Brownies was "Rose Room," but this version has nothing special to recommend it and perhaps belongs more properly in the country category. Although Calhoun and Buchanan do contribute improvisations, they sound more like honky-tonk music that just happens to be jazz inflected. Ultimately, Western Swing may never be accepted in the jazz camp because it does retain so much of a country sound. Nonetheless, when Milton Brown led his group, especially in 1934, there was an excitement and energy to his music that at times places it squarely in the jazz tradition.

Jean Boyd has claimed that Joaquin Murphy of the Spade Cooley and later the Tex Williams band was in the same class of jazz improvisers with

Charlie Christian and Charlie Parker.[113] Murphy's work in the late 1940s is beyond the timeline for consideration here, but it is to be doubted that any Western Swing player will ever be considered a mainstream or major jazz soloist, for any number of reasons. Perhaps the context may always seem wrong, with a string sound that derives so greatly from the country tradition. Even so, it is possible that with time listeners with jazz-inclined ears will hear individual Western Swing soloists more sympathetically. It is true that in the case of a Texas jazzman such as Ornette Coleman that some of his work is country based, and jazz aficionados have not rejected his music on the basis of such an affiliation. Certainly jazz and Western Swing both originated primarily as a dance music that eventually incorporated improvisation to the delight of dancers and listeners alike. The level of invention and expressiveness may determine in the end whether Western Swing improvisers join the ranks of the jazz soloists so admired and emulated by the former. It may also depend on the type of band context in which the soloists performed their take-offs. In this regard, it seems apparent that a small group such as Milton Brown and His Musical Brownies, with its more fully committed policy of performing blues, stomp, rag, Dixieland, and swing, best represents the necessary justification for being included in this or any other history of jazz.

SUMMA CUM LAUDE, ET AL.

Despite the name for Bud Freeman's seven-piece group, neither his nor most of the other small ensembles to be considered in this section qualifies as having performed "with highest distinction" compared with the small units previously discussed. Certainly Freeman and His Summa Cum Laude Orchestra was not an avant-garde group in the way that Jones-Smith, Inc. and the various Goodman units were. In fact, for the most part, Freeman's orchestra remained rooted in the dixieland tradition of the 1920s, recording in 1940, for example, a version of "Sensation Rag," the tune reportedly played by Buddy Bolden's band before 1906, copyrighted in 1908 by Joseph F. Lamb, and recorded by the Original Dixieland Jazz Band during its London tour of 1919–1920.[114] Freeman's allegiance to a preswing conception is also clear from his own rather stiff, even corny tenor style, as evidenced as late as 1938 when he recorded with Eddie Condon & His Windy City Seven on "Love Is Just Around the Corner," a side that includes the original New Orleans Rhythm King's trombonist George Brunies. Freeman's various small-group recordings between 1933 and 1940 do reveal that he was struggling to discover his own voice and that during this period he did master his horn technically. Although Freeman's tenor solos with big bands such as those of Goodman and Tommy Dorsey represent superior swing performances, some of his small-group recordings demonstrate that his was a fairly unique approach to jazz in the 1930s and that he essentially stood apart from the styles represented by the swing leaders on his instrument, Coleman Hawkins and Lester Young.

To listen to Bud Freeman's very vertical tenor playing on a recording from December 8, 1927, of "China Boy," made by McKenzie & Condon's Chicagoans, is to realize how far he would come during the subsequent years. By the time of his appearance as part of Joe Venuti & His Blue Six on "Sweet Lorraine," from October 2, 1933, Freeman has developed into a much more swinging tenorist, even if his style is still and would continue to be a bit erect rather than smoothly horizontal as Benny Goodman's was on this same date.[115] The tenorist is even better on "Madame Dynamite," recorded on October 21, 1933, with Eddie Condon & His Orchestra, which also includes nice swing solos by Pee Wee Russell on clarinet, Floyd O'Brien on muted trombone, and Max Kaminsky on cornet. Most notable is the tenorist's sound on "Home Cooking," also from October 21. Here he is breathy rather than harsh, lighter than Hawkins, and in this sense forecasts Lester Young, even though it was not particularly a sound that Freeman continued to produce. By December 4, 1935, when Freeman recorded "The Buzzard" with his own Windy City Five, he is a bit stiff and awkward, and again even corny. His technique has improved, but he honks around and spoils the sense of a technical advance. It is apparent that he is struggling to find the sound that is right for him, for on "Tillie's Downtown Now," from the same date, he presents yet another sound, light and yet fuller, even though it is still somewhat stiff. On both of these sides, Freeman opens on clarinet, and definitely does not sound like Goodman or his imitators, and in fact Freeman's sound is more pleasant than the one he tended to produce on the tenor. His clarinet tone on the second side even looks forward to a certain extent to Jimmy Giuffre in the 1950s. One important aspect of these two recordings with Freeman's Windy City Five is that the drummer is Cozy Cole, who swings the group nicely and unobtrusively. By contrast, Freeman's choice of George Wettling as the percussion man for his later Trio sessions was quite unfortunate.

In 1938, Freeman cut three sides with Jess Stacy on piano and George Wettling on drums. On "I Got Rhythm," from January 17, Stacy is simply not very interesting and Wettling is positively oppressive. The drummer drowns out Freeman, whose tenor solo is once again stiff, even though technically he has improved, even to the point of overdoing it and becoming too showy. With "At Sundown," from April 13, Wettling again is overbearing, this time with his stick work that dates from the twenties. Freeman is basically corny and by this time sounds far behind the times considering that Young had been recording now for two years some of the most advanced solos of his formidable career. The best of the Trio sides is "Exactly Like You," also from April 13. Here Wettling finally relents to some extent, although Freeman is still rather corny, his form of swing in some ways stiffer than it was in 1933 and perhaps even in 1927! On the same day that Freeman first recorded with his Trio, January 17, he also joined Eddie Condon & His Windy City Seven for a recording session. On "Ja-Da," the tenorist is much more mellow, and his playing does suggest that in fact he had been listening to Young. Bobby Hackett on cornet is still under the Beiderbecke influence, although it is a rather forced, sweeter version. Hackett does better on "Love Is Just Around the Corner," while Pee Wee Russell is out of control, shrill, even weird, and yet he does manage to swing. Freeman is again stiff, playing in a basically Dixieland manner, but not even a particularly good one. As these various sides reveal, the tenorist was a very inconsistent player, seeming never to settle on a style that suited him or one that really fit into the Swing Era, at least not on a number of his small-group recordings.

Freeman's sides with his Summa Cum Laude Orchestra, from 1939 and 1940, show that he had definitely developed technically. On the first tune, "I've Found a New Baby," recorded on July 19, 1939, the tenorist displays his considerable technique, but there is little substance to his solo. He exhibits a greater degree of swing on "Easy to Get," from the same date, but his tone here is rather unpleasant and he offers the same little figures that sound somewhat artificial. His most famous and celebrated small-group side is "The Eel," from the same July 19 session. There is no denying that, technically speaking, this is a virtuoso performance, yet the exerciselike figures come to very little. Freeman was rarely a player with the expressive qualities of either a Hawkins or a Young, whose technique was always at the service of making meaningful music. Also, this side does not really swing, and Dave Bowman's piano is right out of the twenties. On these three 1939 numbers, it is Brad Gowans on valve trombone who swings more naturally than any of the other sidemen or even the leader. "Sensation Rag," from April 4, 1940, also finds Gowan contributing a fine muted chorus, whereas Freeman seems content to return to the Dixieland genre for more of his rather by now outmoded vertical tenor. He drives with verve but it just seems behind the times.

Richard Sudhalter has offered a very laudatory account of Freeman's career, and his estimate may bear more of the truth than the present overview. Sudhalter does admit that "not everyone was captivated. No other saxophone soloist of the '30s, in fact, seemed as able to polarize opinion as did Freeman: the very mention of his name in the trade magazines could bring on paroxysms of intemperate letter-writing." But the critic holds admirably to his own position, opining that on "Sensation Rag," Freeman "comes dancing out of the ensemble . . . equal parts wit and earnestness, swinging hard. No posturing: this is a chorus to define his 'third stream' of hot tenor, owing nothing to either Hawkins or Young."[116] Because we shall hear more from Freeman on other small-group sessions led by Bunny Berigan and Tommy Dorsey, it is only fair to leave the jury out on this eccentric swing-age personality.

Born in 1908 in Beardstown, Illinois, Red Norvo was the first musician to employ the xylophone in jazz, recording his initial solos in 1933 with a quartet that included Jimmy Dorsey on clarinet. Before this, Norvo had worked with Paul Whiteman and had met and married Mildred Bailey, who at the time was singing with the Whiteman orchestra. Norvo's early recordings suggest that he shared with Whiteman an interest in blending jazz with something of a classical tradition. The emphasis in several of Norvo's sides from 1933 is on a much smoother, cooler sound than perhaps any other jazz group had ever cultivated. So unjazz sounding were some of Norvo's 1933 sides that after their release, when Dave Kapp, the Brunswick manager, discovered that Norvo had made them at midnight after Kapp had left the studio, he was "furious."[117] Norvo would continue in this vein with larger groups later in the decade, but his 1933 recordings indicate the direction his work would take and represent probably the earliest examples of a chamber group–like mixture of jazz and classical music that in the 1950s would be termed "Third Stream."

Like so many of the white jazz musicians of the period who recorded with small groups, Norvo worked successfully with black musicians, such as Teddy Wilson and Chu Berry, as well as with many of the white swing-era stars, including Benny Goodman, Artie Shaw, and Harry James. Norvo's xylophone work has been compared favorably with the vibraphone playing of Lionel Hampton, and both were important leaders in the late Swing Era of small-group recording sessions along with those of their larger units.[118]

The first session headed up by Norvo came on April 8, 1933, when he recorded "Knockin' on Wood" with clarinet, piano, guitar, and string bass. Jimmy Dorsey's clarinet is smooth and cool, in keeping with the overall sound and style of the group. The chamber tendency of the combo is only broken at times by Fulton McGrath's boogie-woogie piano, as well as by Dorsey's hot lick at the very end of the side. Even more classically inclined are the two sides recorded on November 21, 1933, after Kapp had left the Brunswick offices. "In a Mist" is a marvelous quartet version of this Bix Beiderbecke piano piece, which in itself is close to Debussy and the classical impressionists. There is no improvisation, for this is simply a transcription for Norvo on marimba, Dick McDonough on guitar, Artie Bernstein on string bass, and Benny Goodman on bass clarinet. The last of these instruments adds to the "misty" effect of the transcription and of course to Beiderbecke's impressionist, basically nonjazz work. On "Dance of the Octopus," Goodman's bass clarinet again adds an impressionist touch, suggesting a kind of deep-sea setting. The two sides were obviously paired together consciously, with some of the same harmonies overlapping from the first to the second. Again, "Dance of the Octopus" is not jazz in the accustomed sense of the word, but rather more of a classical mood piece. It does exhibit a gentle swing, but that could be thought of as merely part of a gently rocking, wave effect. Bernstein's bowed bass also adds to a more chamber-oriented feeling, a low-toned, underwater sonority.

On October 4, 1934, Norvo recorded "Tomboy" with his Swing Septet, consisting of Teddy Wilson on piano, Charlie Barnet on tenor, and Jack Jenney on trombone, along with a rhythm section of guitar, bass, and drums. Even though Wilson is the only black sideman included, it is evident that Barnet is heavily influenced by Coleman Hawkins. It is also clear that Wilson swings better than any other member of the group. The same holds true of Norvo's Swing Octet recordings from January 25, 1935, which feature Wilson and Chu Berry as part of a mixed group that also included Bunny Berigan on trumpet, Jenney on trombone, and Johnny Mince on clarinet. The only white player who impresses on these sides is guitarist George Van Eps. On Waller's "Honeysuckle Rose," Wilson swings well and Berry makes a powerful tenor statement. Mince produces a generic clarinet sound that could easily be that of a Shaw or Goodman. Gene Krupa backs up Berry well, and Jenney is okay but not up to Teagarden's swing. On "Bughouse," Berigan is too hurried, too erratic, not smooth, and Norvo's outing is lightweight, with no real substance to his solo, as it relies too heavily on tremolos. Again, Eps is quite good, certainly better than Norvo. On Norvo's "Blues in E Flat," Berry and Wilson are really into this number, with Wilson's piano sound quite different from his usual approach, less florid and technical, but still impressive. Berigan has plenty of technique, but as with Norvo there is not much in the way of substance. The xylophonist is more attractive on "I Got Rhythm," from March 16, 1936, when he recorded with his Swing Sextette. It is clear that tenorist Herbie Haymer is under the influence of any number of black reedmen. As for trumpeter Stew Pletcher, he plays a few clams in his solo. This piece exhibits a smooth swing, but other than that there is not much to recommend the side, which simply offers little in the way of musical thinking.

Norvo is much more thoughtful on "Just a Mood," recorded again with a mixed group that included Wilson on piano, Harry James on trumpet, and John Simmons on bass. Cut on September 5, 1937, this Wilson original gave all the soloists a chance to stretch out, which was one of the advantages of such small-group sessions. Although James can be a bit too showy, at times overusing his vibrato and technique in his extended solo, he does manage in certain moments to develop the tune's blues feeling through some fine note choices and phrases. Wilson takes what may be his longest chorus during the thirties, and as he develops his ideas the solo becomes more and more intriguing. Norvo follows suit and turns in one of his best efforts on this side that runs to six minutes and fifty seconds. The xylophonist, who later in his career would switch to the vibraphone, continued to record with small groups into the forties and fifties, including sessions with Charlie Parker and Charles Mingus. Known for his "impeccable musical taste," Norvo certainly showed this when he chose to work with some of the most outstanding swing stars of the decade, and his own playing could at times demonstrate that he was an early exponent of a quieter approach to jazz that influenced many of the small groups of the thirties and beyond.[119]

Bunny Berigan and His Boys was a small group the trumpeter led prior to his forming a big band, and the sides produced by this six-or seven-piece unit present Berigan more impressively perhaps than at any other time of his career. Six sides Berigan made with Frank Froeba and His Swing Band, a mixed septet that included some of the same sidemen on the recordings issued by Berigan and His Boys, feature two fascinating vocalists, Tempo King and Midge Williams, but mostly these sides reveal the trumpeter's mature development as a soloist and ensemble leader.[120] A number of the most striking sessions with Berigan's own group included Cozy Cole on drums, and on the first recording session with His Boys the trumpeter teamed up effectively with altoist Edgar Sampson. These mixed groups accounted for several quite outstanding sides, especially those on which Cole served as the drummer. On one of the sides with Cole, Berigan recorded his first version of his most famous number, "I Can't Get Started."

On December 13, 1935, Berigan and His Boys cut four sides, including a version of the Beiderbecke-Trumbauer classic, "I'm Coming Virginia." But as noted earlier, here Berigan does not make any reference to the celebrated solo by Beiderbecke. Nor does this particular side show the trumpeter structuring a well-conceived solo of his own. Berigan does play the opening theme statement on "I'm Coming Virginia" with good drive, which his solo also exhibits even if it does not quite cut it. Although Eddie Miller's clarinet solo is rather nice, it is somewhat ruined by Ray Bauduc's overbearing drums. Berigan's opening muted theme statement on "You Took Advantage of Me" is also quite nicely done. For the most part, Berigan exhibits a good deal of technical proficiency on these sides but little imagination or real expressiveness. Edgar Sampson on alto and clarinet is effective enough, especially on "Blues," where he works more feeling into his solo. Eddie Miller takes fine breaks on tenor and clarinet, but in almost every case, Bauduc feels it necessary to back him up with some corny, obtrusive stick work. Berigan's solo on "Chicken Waffles" is a lively piece of playing, but it just doesn't come to much. Cliff Jackson on piano sounds like he has been listening to Fats Waller. At least on "Blues," Bauduc refrains from interfering with Miller's tenor solo, and Berigan's chorus on this last piece hints at some of his spectacular high-note work on "I Can't Get Started."

By the session of February 24, 1936, Berigan is truly developing into a powerful ensemble leader and is beginning to swing more than ever. However, it is perhaps ironic that the title of one piece, "I'd Rather Lead a Band," shows the leader faltering a bit, and up to this time the trumpeter has not quite achieved the same high level of some of his work recorded earlier in 1935 as a sideman with Goodman. Bud Freeman joined Berigan's Boys on "I'd Rather Lead a Band" and ends the piece with another of his rather eccentric breaks. Again ironically, the tenorist is more reservedly swinging on "Let Yourself Go." But it is Forrest Crawford who takes the most advanced solo on tenor, driving on "Swing, Mister Charlie" with a smoother but more gripping, at times ripping, swing. Berigan's most impressive lead role comes on this same side, where he effectively drives the group, with the aid of Dave Tough on drums and Mort Stuhlmaker on string bass. Here, too, Joe Bushkin contributes a fine piano chorus, with Tough banging away behind him but in a more tasteful manner than had Bauduc behind Miller.

With the session of April 13, 1936, Berigan is starting to show off some of the beautifully soaring tone quality and dazzling phraseology that made him such a favored trumpeter of the Swing Era. This is evident from the very first side, "A Melody from the Sky," which Richard Sudhalter rightly admires for Berigan's "full-blooded break and solo."[121] Cozy Cole's subdued drumming and steady beat make for a smoother swing, especially on "A Little Bit Later" and "Rhythm Saved the World." On the former, Paul Ricci takes a fine clarinet solo, and on the latter Forrest Crawford contributes two excellent tenor breaks. Berigan on "A Little Bit Later" sounds close to his inspired performance on "No Regrets" with Billie Holiday, which would be recorded the following July 10. Of course, "I Can't Get Started" is the side from this session that has garnered the most attention and commentary. Gunther Schuller observes that this "earlier sextet version has a pristine freshness and charm all its own" and that it exhibits "a masterful and instinctive use of dynamics, of musical characterization, or harmonic progression—in short of drama, of musical storytelling. It probably couldn't have happened without Armstrong's 'West End Blues' cadenza, but it was a noble first extension of it."[122] Likewise, Sudhalter would later declare that "there's no minimizing the importance of this three-minute tour de force. It's the apotheosis of Bunny Berigan's art as a soloist in the grand tradition established by Armstrong."[123] For Schuller, Berigan's vocal on this number is "relaxed and rhythmically free—like his middle register ballad trumpet-playing—and totally unpretentious," whereas for Sudhalter, Berigan's chorus is sung "in his high, light voice, his fast vibrato lending a sense of vulnerability."[124]

More personally satisfying to me is the vocal work of Tempo King on two sides cut four days later by Frank Froeba and His Swing Band. On April 17, Berigan joined Froeba, King, Joe Marsala on clarinet, Herbie Haymer on tenor, and a rhythm section to record "Just to Be in Caroline" and " 'Tain't Nobody's Biz'ness What I Do." On both these sides, all the participants perform well, with Berigan playing on the first tune a won-derfully structured solo. King's vocals are fine examples of jazz singing, with a happy, rhythmic quality to his treatments. On June 9, 1936, Berigan was back in the studio with His Boys, recording four more sides whose swing owes much once more to Cozy Cole's drumming. Berigan is espe-cially fine on "But Definitely," along with Jack Lacey on trombone (who exhibits a Teagarden influence) and Slats Long on clarinet. Berigan's lead on "If I Had My Way" is superb, described by Richard Sudhalter as "charging" and "abandoned."[125] Rejoining Frank Froeba for four addi-tional sides on August 27, 1936, Berigan is again in the steady, unobtrusive timekeeping company of Cozy Cole. In the place of Tempo King is vocalist Midge Williams, who does an equally enchanting job with the lyrics, be-ginning with "Whatcha Gonna Do When There Ain't No Swing?" The easy swing of the opening ensemble is quite notable, with Berigan leading the group vigorously into Williams's lilting vocal. The trumpeter plays a touch of obbligato behind the singer, and then Froeba contributes a nicely swing-ing piano chorus, full of florid runs that at times recall the Ellington style. Joe Marsala follows with a mellow clarinet solo, and then Berigan again strongly leads the ensemble until Cole inserts a brief drum break and Wil-liams finishes off with a little scat singing. One noteworthy feature of Beri-gan's closing ensemble passage is that before Cole comes in on drums the trumpeter plays something of a stop-time phrase that is the same one with which in 1927 Bix Beiderbecke had ended "I'm Coming Virginia."

The Froeba session continued with a stirring rendition of "Organ Grinder's Swing," which opens with the pianist doing once again a type of Ellington bit. Art Drelinger on tenor is as good as Forrest Crawford but even more driving and intense, while Midge Williams sings and scats in a style that looks forward to Ella Fitzgerald. Berigan apparently starts to come in ahead of time in the middle of the vocalist's chorus, perhaps be-cause he is simply supercharged, for when he does enter he cuts loose with one of his most spirited choruses. Williams returns for more singing and scatting, with Drelinger adding some fine obbligato work behind her. Froeba adds a piano chorus and then Berigan leads the ensemble into a rousing drum break by Cole that obviously stimulates Berigan, for after-ward he seems to jump for joy with his jamming horn. The group fades out on what is one of the finest mixed small-group recordings of the decade. But then "Rhythm Lullaby," too, is another splendid side, in a more re-laxed swing, with Cole adding wonderfully to the group's easy drive. Here Williams sings with a mellower voice that is quite striking and captivating. Berigan's lead is lovely, and Drelinger's few notes make one wish for more from this fine tenorist. Fortunately, Drelinger obliges—or Froeba allowed him to—on the final side, "It All Begins and Ends with You." Williams again sings with her enchanting voice and swinging rhythmic sense. Berigan reminds me here and elsewhere on this session of the excitement generated by Bill Coleman's work with Fats Waller. Drelinger on tenor, Artie Shapiro on bass, and Cole on drums add wondrously to the spirit of this side and to the overall performances of the session. For some reason, neither Gunther Schuller nor Richard Sudhalter mentions these four sides, and Schuller does not cite Drelinger at all in his *The Swing Era*, whereas Sudhalter in *Lost Chords* only refers to the tenorist as having worked with Berigan at the Famous Door on 52nd Street in NYC.[126] These sides only further confirm Berigan's already considerable stature and also serve to illustrate the high artistic achievement possible among racially mixed groups.

Yet another performance by a mixed group took place on March 31, 1937, when Berigan joined Fats Waller and Tommy Dorsey for what has been labeled "A Jam Session at Victor."[127] In doing Waller's classic, "Honeysuckle Rose," along with a tune titled "Blues," the group was essentially in a Dixieland groove of the type preferred by Dorsey's small group, The Clambake Seven. Dick McDonough contributes a fine guitar chorus, and George Wettling is on his best behavior. Of course, Waller steals the show with his stride piano, but Berigan follows with a solid solo and a fine ensemble lead. Dorsey is the weak link here, his trombone not quite in the spirit, either on the Waller tune or on "Blues." Berigan overdoes it a bit on the latter, and Wettling interferes with Waller's moving piano solo. In general this session can in no way compare with that of Frank Froeba and His Swing Band from August 27, 1936. One note about the ending of "Blues"—it, too, comes in the form of Beiderbecke's concluding phrase on "I'm Coming Virginia." It is clear that Bix's shadow was long, and although Berigan represents something of an extension of the Beiderbecke tradition, perhaps nothing he ever played—not even his solos on "I Can't Get Started"—has left the same kind of indelible mark as his forebear's unforgettable sound and phrasing. Nonetheless, Bunny Berigan remains one of the legendary figures of the Swing Era, and much of his finest work came with small units, in particular with small racially mixed groups that included an outstanding musician such as Cozy Cole and unheralded tenors such as Forrest Crawford and Art Drelinger. Despite the greater renown of the big bands, some of the more important jazz of the thirties is still to be heard on the period's little-known small-group recordings led, as in Frank Froeba's case, by almost totally unfamiliar names.

In addition to leading a big band, Tommy Dorsey also headed up a small group that he called his Clambake Seven. Formed in 1935, the group consisted in 1936 of Max Kaminsky on trumpet, Joe Dixon on clarinet, Bud Freeman on tenor, Dick Jones on piano, William Schaffer on guitar, Gene Traxler on string bass, and Dave Tough on drums. In addition, Edythe Wright served as the group's vocalist. In 1937, Pee Wee Erwin replaced Kaminsky, Carmen Mastren replaced Schaffer, and Johnny Mintz took Dixon's seat; in 1938, Maurice Purtill took over on drums for Dave Tough. Based largely on the Dixieland format, the group yet sounds and the soloists mostly swing in a very contemporary manner. Even so, the musical offerings of the Dorsey unit are often a mishmash, with the same piece containing Dixie jamming and abruptly the mood shifting to that of a romantic pop song. Part of the problem lies with the singer, who does not always fit into the unit's attempt at a principally Dixieland style; frequently Wright conflicts with this style when she fails to inject any kind of jazz feeling into her vocals. The sides recorded between 1936 and 1938 to be discussed here alternate between smooth swing and corny Dixieland, between the leader's sentimental bent and the group's hot breaks and jams, between Tin Pan Alley tunes and the latest dance rage. This provides for an eclectic assortment of styles but also at times a sense that nothing quite coheres, a feeling that the group mainly created a hodgepodge.

The first side on which Bud Freeman participated came on April 15, 1936, when the Clambake Seven recorded "At the Codfish Ball." The tenorist is introduced by Wright as the newest addition to the group, and he opens the side immediately, swinging nicely, not in an erratic but a smooth and inventive manner. Precisely one year from the same date, on April 15, 1937, Wright and the group recorded "At the Milkman's Matinee," and there is little in the singer's style that will appeal to a latter-day listener. Freeman, meanwhile, is very mellow and relaxed, quite a contrast to much of his work. Joe Dixon is a fine, if somewhat generic, swing-era clarinetist, and Pee Wee Erwin is overly brash on this particular side, which is a facet of his playing that too often takes over when he solos. From the same session, the group cut an arrangement by Dean Kincaide of "Twilight in Turkey," which is a piece of exotica that finds Tough doing a rather fake Middle Eastern rhythm behind Freeman's solo. Erwin again is overly brazen and even corny, and Dorsey's chorus alludes to "Mammy's Little Baby Loves Shortenin' Bread," which is not only "corny" but wholly out of place in even a faux Middle Eastern setting. Freeman is certainly the most attractive soloist on "He's a Gypsy from Poughkeepsie," also from April 15, but the tenor still tends to introduce unorthodox licks that do not quite belong in his overall chorus. One of Wright's better efforts comes on "Alibi Baby," from the same date. Likewise, Erwin's solo here is an improvement, more restrained and thoughtful. Freeman is a bit stiff in places, but basically his solo makes it. Clarinetist Dixon swings with a relaxed drive—he is far and away the most consistently satisfying soloist.

With the session of June 12, 1937, the group cut two sides that open in the Dixie style and a third that presents the popular dance form called "posin'." Erwin effectively leads the Dixie ensemble opening on "Is This Gonna Be My Lucky Summer," and Dorsey does a nice job on this number, while Freeman is his typically eccentric self. The ending is a classic Dixie tag. "Who'll Be the One This Summer," which pairs up well with the previous selection, also is given a Dixie treatment, except that the sound is definitely more Swing Era rather than from the twenties, smoother and with lusher harmonies. But suddenly Wright alters the whole feeling of the piece with her romantic mood. Dorsey's muted trombone chorus is again rather corny, and Tough's drumming seems to date from the previous decade. The band's rendition of "Posin' " predates the version by Jimmie Lunceford's orchestra by almost a month, but the Dorsey take totally lacks coherence. Wright addresses the various members of the group and asks them to supply something appropriate or that fits with a rhyme. She asks Dixon for "some corny playing and singing," and he supplies the same. This pretty well sums up this number. On July 20, 1937, Dorsey and His Seven recorded "All You Want To Do Is Dance," and here Dixon does what he does most consistently—swings well with a pleasant sound. Freeman once again is rather stiff. The side ends with some good traditional Dixieland jamming. The same session accounted for three other sides, and one of these, "Having a Wonderful Time," is very much a mixed bag. Dorsey's easygoing chorus opens the number very impressively, but then Wright's vocal is entirely wrong, contrasting too drastically with what the trombonist had just played. Freeman is all over his horn but it doesn't work, it's too erratic. Dixon is swinging nicely, and then Erwin is simply unpleasant. "After You" is a slow drag, semiboogie piece, with Wright once again totally wrong. This time Dorsey's muted solo doesn't fit either. Freeman makes the most of this tune, but in his own eccentric or perhaps witty way. The ending is again a nice enough Dixie jam. Finally, Wright is fairly dreadful on "Stardust on the Moon," whereas Erwin does better than usual, shaping his solo rather than coming on like gangbusters as he does so often.

Five more sides from August and September mix pop songs, a fine Tin Pan Alley tune, and the only purely instrumental number, all for another grab bag assortment. Wright's singing of "The Big Apple" is full of trite banter between her and the band's chorus, but this piece does serve the purpose of surveying many of the most popular dances of the period. After singing how everyone needs to learn the dance style known as the Big Apple, in order not to be taken for a "social dud," Wright employs such phrases and names for other dances as "truck around," "posin'," "lindy hop," and "peck alot," while the chorus responds with a Fats Waller phrase, "yes yes my my." Carmen Mastren's comping behind the singer is notable, and Dorsey's solo is decent. Wright is good—and almost who couldn't be—on the Rodgers and Hart classic, "The Lady Is a Tramp," and yet not even here is the singer a jazz vocalist. Dorsey's "sentimental gentleman" muted trombone is heard on "Tears in My Heart" and "Josephine," neither of which is jazz in any meaningful sense of the word. The level of interest has gone down, partly perhaps because not even the eccentric Freeman has been heard from for the last four numbers. He returns on the purely instrumental "If the Man in the Moon," but here his chorus is once again too stiff and forced, too much a matter of showing off with rather pat exercise figures. Even Dixon is too flashy on this side. Another fine Tin Pan Alley selection, from October 14, 1937, is Gershwin's "Nice Work If You Can Get It," yet Dorsey's theme statement makes it sound rather ricky-ticky, and Tough is up to his old-fashioned drumming again. Wright tends to cheapen the piece with her vocal and even Dixon doesn't do it justice. Only Freeman almost saves the day, but his appearance is too brief to do so. There is more of the "sentimental gentleman" on "You're a Sweetheart."

Two sides from 1938 close out this overview of the Clambake Seven, both of which are songs by Irving Berlin. "When the Midnight Choo-Choo Leaves for Alabam" is probably a forgotten tune, except perhaps for this recording, on which Wright swings pretty well. But Dorsey's chorus is rather blatant and cornball, whereas Dixon in the Chalumeau range of his clarinet works out a very nicely constructed solo. Freeman follows with another of his eccentric choruses. Likewise, on "Everybody's Doing It," Dorsey tends to make the whole thing rather trite, even overblowing, which he normally never did. Wright asks Dixon, "Isn't that music touching your heart?" and one will surely reply, not at all. Freeman repeats some of his favorite licks, typically erratic and eccentric. It should be clear that these sides are not the most highly recommended of the many produced by small groups in the 1930s. As for Bud Freeman, some of his performances here are quite fine, whereas others seem stiff or unpredictable or incoherent. Based on the lot of them taken together, it seems impossible to come to a decision as to Freeman's stature as a soloist—it's a hung jury.

Artie Shaw, like Tommy Dorsey with his Clambake Seven (as well as Bob Crosby with His Bobcats), subscribed to the idea of a "band-within-a-band," which in his case he formed from his big band and labeled his Gramercy Five. Having come to feel in 1940 that, because of the size of his latest version of a large orchestra (twenty-two pieces plus a nine-piece string section) and "the complexity of several of the arrangements, his jazz soloists were being somewhat stilted," Shaw selected four members of his unit to perform "head arrangements of both original and standard material. Nothing was committed to paper, which partly accounts for the loose feel" of the group, as well as the fact that "apart from the skillfully executed ensemble passages, everything played by these musicians was improvised."[128] Always one to come up with novel instrumental combinations, in 1936 Shaw had performed at the New York City Imperial Theater with an octet that included a string quartet. The leader decided for his Gramercy Five to have his regular pianist, Johnny Guarnieri, play a harpsichord, an instrument that had hardly been heard from before Wanda Landowska reintroduced it earlier in the century in her performances of works by Bach and other baroque classical composers. In addition to Shaw on clarinet, the other members of the Gramercy Five consisted of trumpeter Billy Butterfield, Al Hendrickson on guitar, Jud DeNaut on bass, and Nick Fatool on drums. Only eight sides were recorded by the original unit before Shaw disbanded his orchestra in March 1941, and it would be four years until a second version of the group recorded again in 1945. But the distinctive sound of the original combo would no longer be the same, because Dodo Marmarosa, who replaced Guarnieri, would play only piano instead of harpsichord.

The first side recorded at the initial session of September 3, 1940, was "Special Delivery Stomp," a head arrangement credited to Shaw. It opens with the almost startling sound of Guarnieri's "souped-up" harpsichord. Here the instrument is in no way timid, and later when the sideman solos, this keyboard is in his hands not at all tinkly, as one might expect. Shaw swings as he does throughout the session, while Al Hendrickson reveals his awareness of the work of Charlie Christian. (It should be noted that of course Benny Goodman also led small groups whose members were associated with his larger units, but strictly speaking, Teddy Wilson, Lionel Hampton, Charlie Christian, and Cootie Williams were not regular sidemen in Goodman's orchestra, so that to call his trio, quartet, sextet, or septet a "band-within-a-band" is not quite accurate. In any case, the influence of Goodman's small groups on Shaw's Gramercy Five is evident both through Christian and the overall sound of Goodman's various units.) The second side recorded by the Shaw unit was "Summit Ridge Drive," which begins with more of a chamber sound but then shifts as jazz rhythms set in. Primarily a riff tune, this piece can at times become a bit too shrill. More appealing is the very different sound the group attains on "Keepin' Myself for You," where Guarnieri's harpsichord is really quite lovely. Butterfield contributes a sweet muted solo and Hendrickson also a mellow, sweet sound on his guitar. Shaw's clarinet is lilting, and at the end of his solo, it melts into the sound of the harpsichord. The interrelationship among the members of the group is most impressive. Butterfield returns for a more improvised solo, and Guarnieri concludes the side with something of a classical flourish. "Cross Your Heart" is very much in the swing-era tradition of an easy-driving version of a highly romantic tune. What is most appealing about this performance is the interplay in the opening between Guarnieri and drummer Nick Fatool and later the improvised duet of Butterfield and Hendrickson. Fatool's use of cymbals is quite tasteful in conjunction with the harpsichord, as is his use of brushes throughout. Butterfield is muted, and Hendrickson sticks to the lower range of his guitar, producing a quite unusual sound. Guarnieri accompanies the improvised duet but very much in the background, adding subtly to the overall effect. Afterward, harpsichordist and bassist go into a boogielike routine, which does not jar at all but seems a natural extension of the previous section. This contrasts sharply with the Clambake Seven's melange of material that never quite comes together. Shaw as usual contributes some great swinging clarinet.

In contrast to the Dorsey group's version of "Twilight in Turkey," the

Gramercy Five's head arrangement of "Dr. Livingstone, I Presume?" recorded at the session of December 5, 1940, is a piece of exotica that does work. The unit cohesion is remarkable, as the group's various tonal colors complement one another in creating a uniquely unified sound. Here Hendrickson is very much into a Christian mode, while Guarnieri's solo style is reminiscent of Basie in its use of a limited number of notes yet making each a meaningful part of the whole. (In some ways Hendrickson's clearly Christian-influenced, down-home sound and style are not entirely right in the context of this mostly sophisticated chamber jazz.) The harpsichordist never shows off on his keyboard, never plays rapid runs or florid embellishments. The only slightly out-of-place passage on this side is Shaw's interpolation of a type of Jewish, Middle Eastern melody. "When the Quail Come Back to San Quentin," like its title, contains some rather overly cutesy bits, especially the main riff and the rather flippant ending. The most interesting section of this side is when Butterfield and Shaw play off against each other and then come together in a sort of resolution of their tonal differences. "My Blue Heaven" finds Shaw swinging wonderfully with the support of the rhythm section. Here again Guarnieri seems clearly influenced by Basie and Hendrickson by Christian, and the closing ensemble evokes the sound of Goodman's sextet. Shaw is himself quite close to Goodman in his clarinet style, as heard in Shaw's smooth execution of his final break on this particular number, as well as elsewhere on the Gramercy Five sessions. The group's rendition of Jerome Kern's "Smoke Gets in Your Eyes" elicits from the clarinetist his most beautiful tone. Guarnieri's touch is again forthright and charming on his first solo, whereas his second appearance evinces once more his indebtedness to Basie. Hendrickson plays a very mellow, relaxed solo, and Butterfield's muted trumpet is backed up solidly by the rhythm section.

Although the Gramercy Five produced a good deal of improvised jazz, which at times is quite inventive, it is the group's overall sound that is most attractive. No other small unit, with the exception perhaps of John Kirby and His Orchestra, managed to combine so well a classical chamber music approach with swinging jazz rhythms and tone colors.[129] Goodman's groups opened the way in this direction, but Shaw's choice of instrumentation gave his combo a special quality of finesse and inventiveness, of varied coloration and interplay between and among the instruments. The use of the harpsichord—and Guarnieri's subtle but swinging approach—made the group extraordinary, and it remains so to this day, because almost no other jazz unit—perhaps an Australian unit as I vaguely recall—has ever employed this precursor to the piano, certainly not with the same level of success. Although Shaw's group did not particularly affect the future of jazz, it did make a mark for itself as one of the most singular units in the Swing Era and even in the entire history of the music.

DUKE ELLINGTON

From the beginning of his career, Duke Ellington led small groups, which slowly evolved into his famous orchestra. But the leader was often attracted to the use of small units within his larger orchestra for purposes of experimenting with various tonal combinations. Only in 1936, however, did Ellington "adopt a recording policy which featured his major soloists in little units under their own names."[130] Ellington's small groups differed from those of the white bands in that Duke's did not perform in public but only in recording studios. The sides recorded by Ellington's men, whose groups sported their own peculiar names, make it possible to hear more of some of his star soloists than was permitted in the context of the larger orchestra. As one tune's title has it, these small-group recordings are "Jazz à la Carte," that is, each individual voice is separate from the main order of the usual Ellington big-band fare. At times there is not much difference between the large and small units, in that Ellington's presence ensures that the pieces "have shape, finish and continuity, and only rarely are the rough edges of the 'workshop' experiment audible."[131] On many occasions the sidemen do little more than embellish a theme, but on others the listener is able to hear a favorite figure in an extended solo, and even at times an infrequently recorded sideman such as Juan Tizol or Otto Hardwick in a role other than that of section player. Above all, some of the Ellington small-group sides afford an opportunity to experience more of Ellington as a pianist, and especially of the great string-bass revolutionary, Jimmy Blanton, in a setting that allows for hearing him more fully than when he served as a timekeeper and only sporadically as a soloist with the Ellington orchestra.

On March 8, 1937, one of the Ellington men's small-group sessions was billed as Cootie Williams and His Rug Cutters, and the first number recorded by the unit was "I Can't Believe That You're in Love With Me."[132] Here there is little improvisation involved. Harry Carney opens with an embellished theme statement, and Williams continues it, while Ellington himself does improvise on piano more than was usual with the leader when he performed with his orchestra, functioning there essentially as an ensemble player. Both "Tricky" Sam Nanton on trombone and Johnny Hodges on soprano sax basically state the theme as well. On "Downtown Uproar," Hodges improvises more fully, as does Nanton, while Ellington plays mostly an arranged part. On "Digga Digga Doo," Williams cuts loose more in the vein of his improvised work with Charlie Christian on the recording of "Waitin' for Benny" from 1941. "Blue Reverie" finds Ellington developing a moving blues improvisation and Carney extemporizing in his unique baritone voice. Here Williams sticks close to the theme, which is true as well for Hodges, who only slightly embellishes the melody. "Tiger

Rag," the final side from this session, is not much different from the El-lington orchestral version of January 1929. Most of the small-group sides do not present anything much in the way of a soloist's advanced ideas or even skills, because all these sidemen had established their individual voices and dexterity long before. What is most attractive about some of the sides is simply that a listener is able to hear more of a soloist such as Carney whose improvisation is never quite so repetitious as say that of Nanton, or Williams with his predictable growls. Hodges's florid soprano or alto re-mains fresh regardless of how many times one has heard it.

On April 29, 1937, Barney Bigard and His Jazzopaters recorded four sides, beginning with "Solace (Lament for a Lost Love)." As with most of these selections, which are credited to Ellington and one or more of his men, this one is by Bigard and Ellington. Carney on baritone and Rex Stewart on cornet take their turns playing the theme in a lovely, relaxed manner. Bigard also solos, but most of the side involves the group playing probably Ellington's arrangement of Bigard's melody. More of a free-for-all is entitled "Four and One-Half Street," a piece credited to Stewart and Ellington on which everyone improvises effectively. Sonny Greer on drums is heard from more prominently on this and the next number, "Demi-Tasse (Each Day)," where is he especially fine. The latter piece, by Carney and Ellington, finds Bigard's solo backed by a riffing ensemble. Stewart also solos, as he does on the final side, "Jazz à la Carte," credited to Ellington, Bigard, and Stewart. Here the cornetist plays with a mute in a twenties style, as does Bigard, while Ellington comes on with some stride piano. Whether Duke is playing ragtime, blues, or stride, his piano is always iden-tifiably his own. Likewise, Harry Carney is immediately recognizable for his burry-throated, full-throttle swing, and one of the greatest pleasures of all these Ellingtonian small-group sides is to hear the baritonist embellish, improvise, or simply sing a melody as only he could.

One session that definitely has a sound and feel to it different from the Ellington orchestra was held on July 7, 1937. Over a shuffle rhythm set down by Hayes Alvis on bass and Jack Maisel on drums, "The Back Room Romp (A Contrapuntal Stomp)," performed by Rex Stewart and His Fifty-Second Street Stompers (with the piece itself by Stewart and Ellington), has to it a much looser, more relaxed swing.[133] A muted Freddy Jenkins on trumpet backs up Carney and makes for an unusual combination, probably because Jenkins is playing in the lower register of his horn, blending with the baritone and sounding like a trombone but not quite. Toward the end the group jams in something of a Dixie style, but again, not quite. "Swing, Baby, Swing (Love in My Heart)," credited to Alvis and Ellington, is more of a mainstream swing number rather than an impressionistic work of the sort either Ellington so often composed or arranged or a sideman such as Juan Tizol would contribute to the orchestra (such as "Caravan"). This is definitely a small-group sound, not the full orchestra's expansiveness. Stewart leads the ensemble with a lively swing that is especially impressive. "Sugar Hill Shim-Sham," also by Stewart and Ellington, features another fine solo by Carney, whereas the group's rendition of "Tea and Trumpets," again by Stewart and Ellington, showcases, as might be expected from the clever title, the witty Stewart (on cornet rather than trumpet). On this occasion Stewart has a chance to demonstrate how well he could develop a germinal idea into an extended piece of driving, varied improvisation. Carney also solos nicely, with Alvis and Maisel urging the group on with a smooth, inspiring swing.

More of Cootie Williams and His Rug Cutters was made available by a session from October 26, 1937. The surprise here is that on "Jubilesta," Juan Tizol plays a longer solo than was normal for him in the orchestral setting. Although his is mainly a theme statement (of his own making it seems from the credits), it is marvelous to hear at length his fluid valve trombone. He again is featured on "Pigeons and Peppers," a piece purely by Ellington. Once more Tizol shows off his fine melodic flow, while Carney embellishes the theme with gusto. This piece is one more example of the wittiness of so many of the small-group titles, which taken together reveal a certain literary bent on the part of Ellington and his talented sidemen. In contrast, the final side of this session is a standard pop tune, "I Can't Give You Anything but Love," which features Cootie Williams in a muted theme statement. This is a classic piece of work by Williams; if not quite in the same category as his orchestral performance of "Concerto for Cootie," the trumpeter's playing here is certainly exceptional, full of feeling achieved by his marvelous timing and phrasing. Carney embellishes the theme more than Williams does, but both present the melody in a new light. Also adding his alto voice to the interpretation is Otto Hardwick, whose lovely tone is usually only heard as part of the Ellington reed section. Here it is clear that Hardwick had one of the most distinctive alto sounds of the Swing Era. It is owing to such small-group sessions that a listener is made more fully aware of the rich individual voices in the elegant Ellingtonian choir.

The other, more famous altoist was of course Johnny Hodges, who led a small group on September 1, 1939. Billed as Hodges and His Orchestra, this seven-piece unit alternated Ellington and Billy Strayhorn on piano and featured Cootie Williams, Lawrence Brown, and Harry Carney as the other horn players, along with Billy Taylor on bass and Sonny Greer on drums. The first side recorded bears the title "The Rabbit's Jump," a Hodges tune that refers to the altoist's nickname.[134] It is a typical Ellington-sounding number, largely because of Hodges's presence. Williams's muted growls, Carney's baritone, and Brown's melodious trombone also identify this as an Ellington unit, even though the pianist here is Billy Strayhorn. "Moon Romance," also credited to Hodges (as are all the selections), sounds like a number of Ellington works, and in fact the titles often changed, so that this may in fact be known by another name among the Ellington orchestral oeuvre. The altoist solos with his inimitable timbre and lifting phraseology. On "Truly Wonderful," Brown, Carney, and Williams take their turns before Hodges finishes up the soloing, all done over a riffing ensemble and a bit of Strayhorn piano. The final side is entitled "Dream Blues" and once again is typical Ellingtonia, with the maestro chording behind Hodges's theme statement. This is a prime example of why, before the coming of Charlie Parker, the Ellington altoist had something of a hold on the conception of the way the instrument should be played. Although Hodges could be florid, here on this blues number he is quite direct and unadorned, his tone singing but with no vibrato to speak of. Although Parker could be even more penetrating with his almost metallic tone, Hodges is clearly a forebear of the great bop progenitor.

On October 14, 1939, Hodges led the same group in another studio session, but this time with Jimmy Blanton replacing Billy Taylor on bass. This marked the initial recording association for Blanton with the Ellington organization. The first side is entitled "Skunk Hollow Blues," another original by Hodges. Williams's extended, muted blues chorus is authoritative, as is Hodges's that follows. Meanwhile, Blanton's bass can be heard feeding notes that are clearly new to the Ellington ensembles, and he concludes the piece with his amazingly identifiable tone. Blanton also contributes to the swing of the next side, "I Know What You Do," yet another Hodges original. Greer's drums and Blanton's bass power this performance as they would the Ellington big band. Other than Hodges's frequent but brief appearances, mostly this is a group effort that looks forward to several of the most famous sides of the Blanton era, such as "Jack the Bear," "Ko-Ko," and "Conga Brava." Ellington's own "Your Love Has Faded" features both Hodges and Brown in a very romantic mode. The final side, "Tired Socks," another Hodges number, showcases the leader on soprano, with the Williams-led ensemble punctuating on the beat. Although Blanton does not solo on any of these sides, he would when he recorded with only Ellington at the piano for a pioneering session during the next year. But already it is evident that the bassist's presence was beginning to change the sound of an Ellington unit, just as he would revolutionize the role of the bass in the subsequent history of jazz.

In Chicago on October 1, 1940, Blanton and Ellington recorded four sides as a duo—unusual even in this regard, but what is most remarkable is the work of the bassist, who demonstrates the virtuosic potential of his instrument, which heretofore had been limited almost entirely to a time-keeping role. Ellington opens the first number, his "Pitter Panther Patter," with one of his flowery runs, to which Blanton responds with some of his fast finger work on the strings. The pace is a medium fast tempo, but the bassist shows no difficulty in keeping up and at the same time even turning in some double-time passages. Later, Ellington goes into a bit of stride piano, to which Blanton again responds but with more swing this time and longer lines. Blanton can obviously handle anything the pianist dishes out; he even throws in what sound like allusive phrases. On "Body and Soul," Blanton seems to bow his strings in something of a response to Coleman Hawkins's pacesetting salvo sent out to the jazz world on October 11, 1939. After demonstrating the full range of his bowing capabilities, both technically and improvisationally, Blanton switches to a plucked piece of invention that displays how well the bassist's tone carries and how flawlessly he could execute the most intricate passages. Blanton's bowing is even more virtuosic on Ellington's "Sophisticated Lady." Here he trills, dips suddenly into the lowest range of his instrument, and phrases the theme with meaningful feeling and technical facility. Afterward he once again returns, as on "Body and Soul," to a plucking section that concludes the piece with greater swing and long, darting lines. The final selection is "Mr. J.B. Blues," which shows off the bassist's understanding of this genre and how well he could communicate its "message" on the bass. This time Blanton begins by plucking and then shifts to his bow, leaving no doubt that with either method he was a master. Here on piano Ellington sounds at times quite pointillistic, and in this regard the Duke looks forward to Thelonious Monk in the late forties. Meanwhile, Blanton becomes quite witty in his bowed improvisation, ending the side with what seems like the same phrase with which, the previous March, he had concluded his solo on the orchestral version of "Jack the Bear."[135]

Blanton would again participate in small-group sessions with the Ellington men later in 1940 and in the middle of 1941. Unfortunately, he never solos, but he can be heard prominently on two sides, "Squaty Roo," by Johnny Hodges and Orchestra, and "Subtle Slough," by Rex Stewart and Orchestra, both parenthetically "An Ellington Unit." On "Squaty Roo," a Hodges's composition from his session of November 2, 1940, Blanton's bass, to paraphrase Stanley Dance, imparts tremendous drive to this straight-ahead, swinging performance, whereas on Ellington's "Subtle Slough," the bassist states the theme on his instrument and then drives the group with his big tone and fine note choices.[136] Blanton also can be heard to some extent on "Poor Bubber," from the Stewart session of July 3, 1941, as well as backing up Ellington's solo on "Going Out the Back Way," from the Hodges session of November 2, and doing the same for Ben Webster on "Linger Awhile," from July 3. Blanton's bass is up high and all around on "Things Ain't What They Used to Be," from the Hodges session, and on "Passion Flower," he adds his full but not booming sound to Hodges's lyrically tender performance of Billy Strayhorn's mood piece. Throughout these sessions, Blanton's presence is felt if not clearly heard, as he maintains a subtle but solid beat. However, many of these sides tend to sound very much alike, and some, such as "Poor Bubber" and "My Sunday Gal" (from July 3), both by the Rex Stewart group, almost drag along in a rather spiritless "slough." (Stanley Dance explains that Ellington's use of the word "slough" in his title, "Subtle Slough," means "to shed," and does not refer to the "muddy hollow" in my previous sentence.)

In general, Ellington's men did not perform so well without his compositions to provide their solos with a more meaningful context. Even so, the leader was quite generous in his efforts to showcase the talents of his sidemen in small-group settings, and the results could be on occasion of a high quality. But overall, it must be admitted that the Ellington small-group sides do not hold up nearly so well as the leader's orchestral recordings. This may be due in part to the fact that within each number there is not enough contrast in the ways in which the soloists exploit the material. At times, as in the case of Rex Stewart's very lovely theme, "Some Saturday," recorded on July 3, the melody is so captivating that the soloists merely restate it one after another. It is certainly a contrast just to hear Stewart on cornet, Harry Carney on baritone, Lawrence Brown on trombone, and Ben Webster on tenor, each repeating the theme in his own unique voice, but even this can become somewhat redundant. At the end of "Some Saturday," Stewart does improvise in a type of call-and-response exchange with the ensemble that provides a bit of welcome variety. For listeners accustomed at the time to hearing so many of the killer-dillers of the big-band era, certainly the low-keyed, muted, softly swinging numbers by the two Ellington units (especially Stewart's fine "Linger Awhile") must have been in itself a dramatic change, but even so, after a while one now wishes for a little more excitement. Two slow, mood pieces featuring Hodges's alto, "Passion Flower" and "Day Dream," are undeniably beautiful but perhaps one of the two would have been enough. Also, after repeated use, Stewart's half-valve effects, especially on "Menelik (The Lion of Judah)," do not wear so well. Stewart is much better on a standard like "Without a Song," where he plays open with only a minimum of such tonal tricks. The contrast within this piece is provided by Carney's voice, which lamentably on this session is only lifted on rare occasions. Lawrence Brown is effective on "Good Queen Bess" (a somewhat copycat version of "Christopher Columbus") and "Junior Hop," both recorded by the Hodges group. The trombonist is particularly outstanding on "Linger Awhile." In the end, however, these are certainly less innovative sessions than the one with Ellington and Blanton, and do not quite compare with the small-group sides cut in 1937 and 1939. The time was obviously ripe for a change, which would soon come in the form of bebop.

ROY ELDRIDGE AND BUSTER SMITH

To find predecessors to Dizzy Gillespie and Charlie Parker in the Swing Era is a bit like looking for a needle in a haystack, especially in the case of Parker, whose alto playing seemed to burst on the jazz scene full blown and unprecedented. To find a trumpet and alto team comparable to Diz and Bird is perhaps even more difficult. Roy Eldridge and Buster Smith, who have been mentioned as precursors in one or other sense to the bebop giants, never recorded together, but they did cut a number of sides with figures who tenuously predict Gillespie and Parker. Little Jazz, as Eldridge was called, joined with altoist Scoops Carey in a 1937 studio session, and the Professor, as altoist Buster Smith was called, had recorded with Hot Lips Page since 1929 and would take part with the trumpeter in two important sessions in 1939 and 1940. In addition to these four swing-age trumpeters and alto saxophonists, there were various other swing musicians to whom it is possible to trace certain precedents for Gillespie and Parker's bebop, among them Coleman Hawkins, Lester Young, and Charlie Christian, but these men were not trumpet or alto players. Although Charlie Shavers and Russell Procope performed together on trumpet and alto, respectively, within the context of the John Kirby Sextet, there is little to connect them with bebop, even though, as Gunther Schuller observes, Gillespie learned Eldridge's solos from Shaver, whose "relation to bop lies more in its speed and rhythmic fluency, the technical razzle-dazzle of bop, than in its essence as a melodically/harmonically/rhythmically reconstituted . . . language of jazz."[137] Procope certainly does not suggest either Parker's sound or his melodic/harmonic/rhythmic conception. Perhaps the closest, then, that two sets of trumpet and alto players came to the team of Dizzy and Bird were the Eldridge-Carey and Page-Smith combinations. As we shall see, these pairs of late swing-era horn men at least hint at what was to come and represent in some ways the most advanced developments in jazz toward the end of the thirties and during the first year of the forties.

In 1940, Charlie Parker, as we have seen, recorded with the Jay McShann Orchestra a version of Gershwin's "Oh! Lady Be Good" that looks back to Lester Young's path-breaking recording of the same tune in 1936. In 1945, Parker would make jazz history when he recorded with Dizzy Gillespie a side titled "Koko," based on Ray Noble's "Cherokee," which Charlie Barnet had made famous in 1939 and which the Count Basie Orchestra recorded on February 3, 1939, five months before Barnet.[138] On the Basie version, Lester Young is the featured soloist, but although the tenorist's chorus is quite good, it does not forecast either the sound or phenomenal technique of Parker. Young's solo is, in fact, quite tame compared with his earlier, highly adventurous work in 1936. Reportedly, Parker himself liked to listen to altoist Rudy Williams play "Cherokee," but whether Williams was ever recorded playing this piece is unclear. As Charles Fox tells it, Parker "presumably recognized in [Williams] a fellow explorer of what were then, by jazz standards, unfamiliar extensions of the chords. But Williams lacked Parker's rhythmic and imaginative audacity, so he remains a transitional figure—fascinating and exciting to listen to, but only venturing so far."[139] Fox also mentions altoist Tab Smith in somewhat the same light.[140]

To hear a tone on the alto close to Parker's, and even something of his rhythmic "audacity," one can listen to a recording session with Roy Eldridge and His Orchestra from January 23, 1937. On "Wabash Stomp," not only can one begin to hear Eldridge "breaking through the previous boundaries of jazz trumpet," and in this regard standing as an influence on Gillespie, but also Scoops Carey on alto sounds like a harbinger of the Bird.[141] Although Carey's solo is brief, it yet presages Parker's crystalline tone, as well as something of the Bird's twists and turns. Eldridge's brother Joe takes the first alto solo on the side, and although his tone is rather hard-edged like Parker's, it does not suggest the Bird so much as does the second break by Carey, who especially at the end of his solo blows a phrase that almost flies after the manner of the Bird. But both Eldridge and Carey provide an even clearer picture of something new in the air on "Heckler's Hop." Carey really takes off in his two solos, doing flips and other acrobatics that would become the hallmark of Parker. Meanwhile, Eldridge, although still very much in the swing mode, suddenly leaps into the top range of his instrument as Gillespie would. The feeling of Little Jazz's whole performance has something of the hi-jinx character of Dizzy's trumpet antics, with even the title of the Eldridge-Edgar Battle tune suggesting such.

"That Thing," an Eldridge original recorded five days later, on January 28, 1937, is said to include two alto solos by Carey "representing a slightly more daring use of harmony, comparable to what Rudy Williams then was doing with the Savoy Sultans," but this may be Eldridge's brother Joe rather than Carey. Certainly the solos on "That Thing" by either Joe Eldridge or Scoops Carey do not suggest Parker in the same way as does the second alto break on "Wabash Stomp" and as the two breaks do on "Heckler's Hop."[142]

Sounding more like the soloist on "That Thing," Carey also can be heard with the Earl Hines big band, on December 2, 1940, taking a solo on "Jelly, Jelly."[143] Here again the altoist shows his ability to move around his horn more acrobatically, and his tone seems closer to that of Parker. Of course, by this date Parker had already outdistanced Carey or any other altoist of the Swing Era. Carey, by his own account, was responsible for inducing Hines to hire Parker in 1943, which Fatha did, although only a tenor seat was available. Gillespie also was in the Hines band at the same time. John Steiner reports that "Carey's high development of melodic eccentricity and harmonic discoveries ultimately brought him close to Charlie Parker," but that "despite resemblances," Carey himself told Steiner that "he and Parker were mature before meeting and that they probably were mutually compatible rather than influential for each other."[144]

A similar sound and technique to those in what seem to be 1937 solos by Scoops Carey are to be heard as well on sides recorded in 1939 and 1940 with Hot Lips Page on trumpet and Buster Smith on alto. The fact that in 1937 Smith and Parker sat next to one another in Smith's band, the first organized group in which the Bird was to play, would tend to support Buster's claim that Parker learned from him to "double up," or what Smith called that "double time stuff. . . . Only we called it double tongue sometimes in those days. I used to do a lot of that on clarinet."[145] Aside from this "hearsay" evidence, the most convincing corroboration of Smith's assertion is to be heard in the few recordings Buster made beginning in 1939. Performing with Hot Lips Page as part of Pete Johnson & His Boogie Woogie Boys, Smith recorded with this group two sides, "Cherry Red" and "Baby, Look at You," both cut on June 30, 1939.[146] After Joe Turner sings the lyrics on "Cherry Red," Buster Smith solos very briefly but definitely exhibits a smoothness and a soft metallic tone that are suggestive of Parker's. On "Baby, Look at You," Smith takes a longer solo after Turner's vocal, and here all the signs of the altoist's style point toward Parker as his pupil. Beginning with a swirl of notes and continuing with what Gunther Schuller calls "sleek downward runs," Smith develops a "beautiful and prophetic" solo, in which "Charlie Parker is clearly discernible . . . not only in the warmth and depth of tone but in the choice of notes, clean fluent lines, and easy swing."[147] Hot Lips Page's muted solo may not remind one so much of Gillespie, but there is a touch of Dizzy's muted sound and of his rapid-fire note production. Also, Page and Smith playing together at the end of the side represents one of the few early examples of a trumpet-alto team working in the manner of the alliance later formed by Dizzy and Bird.

Further examples of the Page-Smith amalgamation are to be heard from a session recorded on January 23, 1940, with Hot Lips Page and His Band. Out of eight sides cut on this date, Smith solos on alto on only two tunes, "I Ain't Got Nobody" and "Walk It to Me," but from these, and especially the first, it is clear that, as Budd Johnson stated, "Bird really came from Buster Smith."[148] Smith's sound and conception are fully in evidence with his solo on "I Ain't Got Nobody," where his ideas come flowing out ceaselessly and unexpectedly as in a Bird solo—from an unusual, dramatic entrance to many inventive melodic twists and turns that undoubtedly taught Parker so much when he sat beside the Professor back in 1937. On "Walk It to Me," Smith reveals from his first notes a newer feeling, a more fluent style. On November 30, 1940, as we have seen, Parker soloed on several sides with the McShann Orchestra, one of which was a version of Eddie Durham's "Moten Swing." Almost three weeks earlier, on November 11, 1940, Smith already had recorded a solo on this same tune, with a group led by fellow Texan Eddie Durham. Critic Thomas Owens has observed that "sitting next to Smith night after night apparently had its effect on Parker, for his solo on 'Moten Swing' is remarkably similar in tone quality and some melodic details to Smith's solo."[149] Although Charles Fox cautions against allowing hindsight "to read more into short solos like [Smith's] than they may deserve," even as slight as the evidence is, it seems to demonstrate that of all the alto players of the swing era, Buster Smith was the closest to Parker both literally and conceptually.[150]

Of course, no one in the period from 1930 to 1941 ever approached the technical and imaginative range of Charlie Parker, not even Benny Carter or Johnny Hodges for all their impressive command of the alto saxophone. But there is no doubt that Parker built on the facility and harmonic inventiveness of his forebears in the Swing Era and that without them the next era of jazz would not have been possible. As this volume has attempted to demonstrate, the jazz continuum is just that, with each period in no way abandoning entirely what came before and in many cases, as with the Dixieland revival, embracing earlier styles wholeheartedly. Although the big bands may slowly have drifted into enervation, the small groups throughout the '30s and into 1940 and 1941 carried the flame in advancing the art on many fronts, from greater technical skill to increased freedom of expression. At the same time, the small groups played a seminal role in the breakdown of racial barriers, in the creation not only of an integrated music, which it always had been, but also of a more racially integrated form of entertainment in the studio and ultimately in public appearances on stage and screen and in the previously segregated hotels and dance halls. In the coming war period, jazz, as a form of music, received and promoted without regard to race, would serve democracy around the world, and this political role as well was in many ways a reflection of the developments within the small mixed groups of the '30s and early '40s. Making both an aesthetic and a social impact, jazz in the Swing Era continued its great American tradition that began in the twenties and would be extended throughout the war and into the postwar periods beyond.

NOTES

1. Sudhalter, *Lost Chords*, p. 476.
2. Chilton, *The Song of the Hawk*, p. 73.
3. Ibid.
4. Ibid.
5. Ibid., pp. 87–88.
6. Ibid., p. 89.
7. Ibid., pp. 93–94. The Hawkins sides discussed thus far are included on *Coleman Hawkins 1929–1934* (Classics 587, 1992).
8. These four sides are included on *Coleman Hawkins: Body and Soul* (Bluebird, 5658–1 RB, 1986).
9. Chilton, *The Song of the Hawk*, p. 161.
10. Ibid., pp. 161–162.

11. Dan Morgenstern, liner notes to *Coleman Hawkins: Body and Soul.*

12. The four sides from this session are included on *Coleman Hawkins: Body and Soul.*

13. George Hoefer, liner notes to *Body and Soul: A Jazz Autobiography—Coleman Hawkins.*

14. Chilton, *The Song of the Hawk*, p. 162.

15. "Mississippi Rag" (January 1983), quoted in ibid., p. 163.

16. Chilton, *The Song of the Hawk*, p. 162.

17. Schuller, *The Swing Era*, p. 445.

18. Chilton, *The Song of the Hawk*, p. 167.

19. Ibid. "Dinah" is included on *Body and Soul: A Jazz Autobiography—Coleman Hawkins.*

20. Ibid.

21. Ibid., pp. 167–168.

22. Hoefer, liner notes to *Body and Soul: A Jazz Autobiography—Coleman Hawkins.*

23. Morgenstern, liner notes to *Body and Soul: Coleman Hawkins.*

24. Chilton, *The Song of the Hawk*, pp. 168–169.

25. Vic Bellerby, insert notes to *Jack Teagarden: I Gotta Right to Sing the Blues* (Living Era, CD AJA 5059, 1989).

26. "The Sheik of Araby" is included on *Jack Teagarden Vol. 1* (Jazz Archives No. 51, 157022, 1992).

27. "You're Simply Delish" is included on *Jack Teagarden and His Orchestra 1930–1934* (Classics 698, 1993).

28. Both these sides are included on *Jack Teagarden and His Orchestra 1930–1934.*

29. These four sides are included on *The Golden Horn of Jack Teagarden* (Decca, DL4540, n.d.).

30. These two sides are included on *Billie Holiday: The Golden Years.*

31. These four sides are included on *Benny Goodman and The Giants of Swing* (Prestige, PR 7644, 1969).

32. Both these sides are included on *The Golden Horn of Jack Teagarden.*

33. Anatol Schenker, insert notes to *Jack Teagarden and His Orchestra 1940–1941* (Classics 839, 1995).

34. These four sides are included on *Jack Teagarden and His Orchestra 1940–1941.*

35. All the sides from 1935 and 1936 discussed here are included on *The Jazz Collector Edition: Benny Goodman* (Laserlight, 15726, 1990). "Body and Soul" and "Dinah" are incorrectly labeled as cuts 9 and 2 but are in fact reversed on the CD. The Carnegie Hall sides from January 16, 1938, are included on *Benny Goodman: Live at Carnegie Hall.*

36. The sides from 1937 and 1938, except for the Carnegie Hall performances, are included on *Benny Goodman Trio and Quartet Live 1937–38* (Columbia Special Products, Cassette BT 13289, n.d.).

37. Neither the Laserlight nor the Columbia Special Products compilation provides dates for the recordings, but Brian Rust's *Jazz Records 1897–1942*, 2 vols. (Chigwell, England: Storyville Publications, 1975), has supplied the dates given here. Rust does not furnish a specific date for the November 1937 recordings and

says in fact that this is merely a supposition. The two recordings of "Vibraphone Blues" on Laserlight and the Columbia Special Products cassette may be one and the same; that is, the recording included in the Laserlight 1935–1936 compilation may be the same as the one on the CBS cassette of 1937–1938 performances, especially as both are live tapings, as indicated by the audience applause.

38. Kolodin, liner notes to *Benny Goodman: Live at Carnegie Hall*.

39. "Flying Home" and "Stardust" are included on *The Benny Goodman Sextet, Featuring Charlie Christian (1939–1941)* (Columbia, CK 45144, 1989); "Rose Room" and "Memories of You" are on *Solo Flight: The Genius of Charlie Christian* (Columbia, CG 30779, 1972).

40. The account of this episode is found in a number of sources, including *The Jazz Makers*, p. 323.

41. Hodeir, *Jazz: Its Evolution and Essence*, pp. 217 and 215. "When Lights Are Low" is included on *Lionel Hampton: Hot Mallets, Vol. 1* (Bluebird, 6458-2-RB, 1987), along with the other three sides from the session of September 11, 1939: "One Sweet Letter from You," "Hot Mallets," and "Early Session Hop." Leonard Feather claims that this session "may well have [had] the most distinguished saxophone foursome in recorded annals"—Coleman Hawkins, Chu Berry, Benny Carter, and Ben Webster. This collection offers many fine small-group sides, but they are for the most part very similar to Hampton's big-band recordings discussed in Chapter 4, and in fact on a piece such as Benny Carter's "I'm in the Mood for Swing," from July 21, 1938, the nine-piece group sounds essentially like a small big band. A number of these sides involve racially mixed groups and some very outstanding performances by members of the Basie, Ellington, Goodman, and Hines orchestras. From July 21, 1938, Harry James delivers a fine solo on "Shoe Shiner's Drag," while on "Ring Dem Bells" and "Don't Be That Way," from January 18, 1938, Edgar Sampson on baritone is something of a pleasant surprise. Contrary to Feather's claim, it sounds to my ear like Herschel Evans takes the second tenor solo on "Shoe Shiner's Drag" and Babe Russin the first. Herschel is even better on "Muskrat Ramble," also from July 21. Alvin Burroughs's drumming on "Down Home Jump," from October 11, 1938, is superfine. Chu Berry is a delight on "Denison Swing" and "Ain'tcha Comin' Home," from April 5 and June 9, 1939, respectively, while Hampton's amateurish two-finger piano can grow at times a bit annoying on the first but his vibraphone solo on the latter is quite a treat. Many of these pieces such as "Down Home Jump" generate some really superb, driving swing.

42. Schuller, *The Swing Era*, p. 567.

43. Ibid., p. 568.

44. Claude Carrière, insert notes to *Charlie Christian, Volume 6, 1940–1941* (Média, MJCD 68, 1994).

45. Al Avakian and Bob Prince, liner notes to *Charlie Christian with the Benny Goodman Sextet and Orchestra* (Columbia, CL 652, n.d.); reprinted in *The Art of Jazz*, ed. Martin T. Williams (New York: Grove Press, 1960), p. 183.

46. Schuller, *The Swing Era*, p. 576.

47. Glenn Coulter, "Billie Holiday," in *The Art of Jazz*, p. 165.

48. Schuller, *The Swing Era*, pp. 537–538.

49. All three of these sides are included on *Teddy Wilson: His Piano and Orchestra with Billie Holiday* (Living Era, CD AJA 5053, 1994).

50. Ibid.

51. All four sides discussed in this paragraph are included on *Billie Holiday: The Golden Years*. After this volume was in production in October 2001, a 10-CD box set appeared from Sony/Legacy, *Lady Day: The Complete Billie Holiday on Columbia (1933–1944)*. The quality of sound on this set is outstanding, and the collection incorporates all the sides referred to here by Holiday on Columbia records.

52. All five sides discussed in this paragraph are included on *Billie Holiday: The Golden Years*.

53. Coulter, in *The Art of Jazz*, p. 165. "Easy Living" is included on *Teddy Wilson: His Piano and Orchestra with Billie Holiday*; the other sides discussed in this paragraph are on *Billie Holiday: The Golden Years*.

54. Williams, *The Jazz Tradition*, p. 89. These two sides are included on *The Quintessential Billie Holiday Volume 4 (1937)* (Columbia, CJ 44252, 1988).

55. Williams, *The Jazz Tradition*, p. 88. This side is included on *Billie Holiday: The Golden Years*.

56. All five Holiday sides discussed in this paragraph are included on *Billie Holiday: The Golden Years*; the Helen Ward recording of "How Am I to Know?" is on *Teddy Wilson: His Piano and Orchestra with Billie Holiday*.

57. "What Shall I Say?" is included on *Roy Eldridge: His Best Recordings 1935–1946* (Best of Jazz, 4051, 1997).

58. The sides mentioned in this paragraph, except for "What Shall I Say?" are included on *Billie Holiday: The Golden Years*.

59. Chris Sheridan, insert notes to *Count Basie-Harry James: Basie Rhythm*.

60. Ibid.

61. Ibid.

62. Schuller, *The Swing Era*, p. 229.

63. Ibid., pp. 229–230.

64. Ibid., p. 230.

65. In his more technical analysis of "Shoe Shine Boy," Lawrence Gushee brings out several points regarding what he calls "oral composition . . . the distinctly mixed oral-written tradition called jazz." Gushee notes that Lester Young "transcends the repetitive, hierarchical structure of the tune and its harmonization" and creates through a number of organizing schemata two solos of "extraordinary profundity" and "coherence." See Gushee's "Lester Young's 'Shoe Shine Boy,' " in *A Lester Young Reader*, pp. 252–253.

66. Schuller, *The Swing Era*, pp. 230–232.

67. Sheridan, insert notes to *Count Basie-Harry James: Basie Rhythm*.

68. Williams, *The Jazz Tradition*, pp. 131–132.

69. Giddins, *Visions of Jazz*, p. 175.

70. Ibid., p. 170.

71. Schuller, *The Swing Era*, p. 230.

72. Quoted by Milt Gabler, in insert notes to *Giants of the Tenor Sax: Lester "Prez" Young & Friends* (Commodore, CCD 7002, 1988). All four of the Kansas City Six sides discussed here are included on this compact disc.

73. Ibid.

74. Leonard Feather, insert notes to *Giants of the Tenor Sax*.

75. This side is included on *Count Basie-Harry James: Basie Rhythm*.

76. These three sides are included on *The Essential Count Basie, Volume 1* (Columbia, CJ 40608, 1987).

77. Ibid., liner notes.

78. Hodeir, *Jazz*, p. 72.

79. Schuller, *The Swing Era*, p. 249.

80. Ibid., p. 251.

81. Ibid., p. 553.

82. Ibid.

83. Loren Schoenberg, "East of the Sun: The Changes of Lester Young," in *The Lester Young Reader*, p. 205.

84. Ibid. "Just Jivin' Around" is included on *52nd Street Swing: New York in the '30s* (Decca, GRD 646, n.d.).

85. Liner notes to *Fats Waller in London* (Capitol, T10258, 1961).

86. Mildred Bailey's version of this same song, recorded with her husband Red Norvo's orchestra on August 26, 1936, is interesting but does not have the same energy or sense of fun as Waller's. See *Red Norvo: Knockin' on Wood*.

87. "Porter's Love Song to a Chambermaid" and "Then I'll Be Tired of You" are included on *One Never Knows, Do One?: Fats Waller and His Rhythm* (RCA Victor, LPM-1503, 1957). Note: Waller's complete RCA Victor recordings have been reissued in CD form.

88. "How Can You Face Me" and "Dream Man" are included on *Handful of Keys: Fats Waller and His Rhythm* (RCA Victor, LPM-1502, 1957).

89. Ibid.

90. "Us on a Bus" is included on *One Never Knows, Do One?*

91. Mike Lipskin, liner notes to *Fractious Fingering: Fats Waller* (RCA Victor, LPV-537, 1967).

92. "You're Laughing at Me" is included on *Handful of Keys*.

93. "The Joint Is Jumpin' " and "Two Sleepy People" are included on *Ain't Misbehavin': "Fats" Waller and His Rhythm* (RCA Victor, LPM-1246, 1956).

94. These sides are all included on *Fats Waller in London*.

95. Both sides are included on *Ain't Misbehavin'*.

96. This side is included on *Handful of Keys*.

97. Cary Ginell, insert notes to *The Complete Recordings of the Father of Western Swing: Milton Brown and the Musical Brownies, 1932–1937* (Texas Rose Records, TXRCD1–5, 1995). Ginell also writes in his book-length study (*Milton Brown and the Founding of Western Swing* [Urbana: University of Illinois Press, 1994]) that Brown's "energetic vocals, affecting recitations, and Roaring Twenties 'hotcha' style suggest Ted Lewis or Cab Calloway on jazz tunes and Fred Astaire on Tin Pan Alley songs" (p. xxi). One tune not recorded by the Brownies but which Brown's brother Roy Lee reported the leader "put extra words to" was "What's the Reason (I'm Not Pleasin' You)," which Waller recorded on March 6, 1935 (p. 131). Milton's brother Derwood did record "There'll Be Some Changes Made," which was cut by Waller on June 24, 1935. Derwood Brown and his version of the Musical Brownies recorded the same piece in 1937.

98. Ginell, *Milton Brown and the Founding of Western Swing*, p. xxvi.

99. Jean A. Boyd, *The Jazz of the Southwest: An Oral History of Western Swing* (Austin: University of Texas Press, 1998).

100. Schuller, *The Swing Era*, p. 564 n.33.

101. Ginell, *Milton Brown and the Founding of Western Swing*, pp. 63–64.

102. All sides by Milton Brown and the Musical Brownies are included on the five-CD set, *The Complete Recordings of the Father of Western Swing: Milton Brown and the Musical Brownies, 1932–1937*.

103. Ginell, *Milton Brown and the Founding of Western Swing*, p. 281.

104. Ibid., p. 309.

105. Ibid., p. 289.

106. Schuller, *The Swing Era*, p. 564 n33.

107. Boyd, *The Jazz of the Southwest*, p. 41.

108. John Morthland, insert notes to *Texas Music Vol. 2: Western Swing & Honky Tonk* (Rhino, R2 71782, 1994).

109. Ginell, *Milton Brown and the Founding of Western Swing*, p. xxii.

110. Ibid., p. 296.

111. Ibid., p. 301.

112. Ibid., p. 309.

113. Boyd, *The Jazz of the Southwest*, p. 127.

114. Tirro, *Jazz: A History*, pp. 72 and 104.

115. All the Freeman sides discussed here are included on *Bud Freeman: Swingin' with 'The Eel'* (Living Era, CD AJA 5280, 1998).

116. Sudhalter, *Lost Chords*, pp. 247 and 267.

117. Vic Bellerby, insert notes to *Red Norvo: Knockin' on Wood*.

118. Richard Sudhalter cites the Norvo orchestra's recording of "Remember," an Irving Berlin tune arranged by Eddie Sauter, as "one of the most memorable performances of its age" (*Lost Chords*, p. 697). This side, from March 22, 1937 (included on *Red Norvo: Knockin' on Wood*), finds Norvo soloing in a manner that distinguishes his approach to his instrument and the music as more of a decorative, meditative improvisation rather than a jazz style of irresistible drive and invention as represented by the later work of Milt Jackson.

119. Schuller, *The Swing Era*, p. 527.

120. All these sessions are included on *Bunny Berigan and His Boys 1935–1936*.

121. Ibid. Sudhalter refers to this tune as "Just a Melody from the Sky," which differs from the title given on the Classics CD.

122. Schuller, *The Swing Era*, pp. 471 and 473.

123. Sudhalter, *Lost Chords*, p. 502.

124. Schuller, *The Swing Era*, p. 471; Sudhalter, *Lost Chords*, p. 502.

125. Sudhalter, *Lost Chords*, p. 503.

126. Sudhalter, *Lost Chords*, p. 496. The critic quotes Drelinger as having said that when Berigan was not stoned "he was the greatest player I'd ever heard" (p. 511).

127. Two sides from this session are included on *Bunny Berigan: His Best Recordings 1935–1939*.

128. John P. Callanan, insert notes to *Artie Shaw: The Complete Gramercy Five Sessions* (Bluebird, 7637–2-RB, 1989).

129. Gunther Schuller discusses the Kirby group and concludes that with its "kind of polite, refined, classically biased chamber music" that was intended to "capture that audience which was put off by the unpredictable spontaneity and alleged 'roughness' of most jazz," it "was hardly jazz at all," with only trumpeter Charlie Shavers, a true jazz improviser, who exhibited "a strong influence of high

quality classical trumpet-playing, exemplified by a fine tone, smooth legato, clean tonguing, and an even control of range" (*The Swing Era*, pp. 812–813).

130. Stanley Dance, liner notes to *Things Ain't What They Used To Be: Johnny Hodges and Rex Stewart* (RCA Victor, LPV-533, 1966).

131. Ibid.

132. All the sides discussed here, from "I Can't Believe That You're in Love With Me" through "Jazz à la Carte," are included on *Duke Ellington and His Orchestra 1937* (Classics, 675, 1992).

133. All the sides discussed here from "The Back Room Romp" through "I Can't Give You Anything but Love" are included on *Duke Ellington and His Orchestra 1937 Vol. 2* (Classics, 687, 1993).

134. All the sides discussed here from "The Rabbit's Jump" through "Tired Socks" are included on *Duke Ellington and His Orchestra 1939 Vol. 2* (Classics, 780, 1994).

135. All four of these sides, plus alternate takes, are included on *The Indispensable Duke Ellington*.

136. Dance, liner notes to *Things Ain't What They Used To Be*, which includes all the sides discussed here.

137. Schuller, *The Swing Era*, p. 814.

138. Basie's two-part "Cherokee" is included on *Count Basie-Harry James: Basie Rhythm*.

139. Fox, *The Essential Jazz Records, Vol. 1*, p. 304. Fox is reviewing an album by Al Cooper's Savoy Sultans, covering recordings by the group between 1938 and 1941.

140. Ibid., p. 382.

141. John Chilton, insert notes to *Roy Eldridge—Little Jazz* (Columbia, CK 54275, 1989).

142. Fox, *The Essential Jazz Records, Vol. 1*, p. 548. I am basing my hearing of Carey as the altoist on these two occasions on Graham Colombé's identification of Carey as the second alto soloist on "Wabash Stomp" (see Colombé's insert notes to *Roy Eldridge: His Best Recordings 1935–1946* (Best of Jazz, 4051, 1997).

143. "Jelly, Jelly" is included on *Earl Hines—Piano Man: Earl Hines, His Piano and His Orchestra*.

144. John Steiner, "Chicago," in *Jazz: New Perspectives on the History of Jazz*, p. 159. Incidentally, there seems to be no agreement as to the correct spelling of Scoops Carey's last name, which is given either as Carey or Carry. I have gone with Steiner and Colombé's spelling.

145. Quoted in Don Gazzaway, "Buster and Bird: Conversations with Buster Smith," part 3, *Jazz Review* 3, no. 2 (February 1960): 14.

146. These two sides are included on *The Real Kansas City of the '20s, '30s & '40s*.

147. Schuller, *The Swing Era*, p. 797.

148. Quoted in Gitler, *Swing to Bop*, p. 60. All eight of the Page sides are included on *Hot Lips Page and His Band 1938–1940* (Classics, 561, 1991).

149. Thomas Owens, *Bebop: The Music and Its Players* (New York: Oxford University Press, 1995), p. 9. "Moten Swing" by Eddie Durham and His Band is included on *Kansas City Jazz* (Decca, 8044, n.d.).

150. Fox, *The Essential Jazz Records*, Vol. 1, p. 549.

♪

A to Z

Allen, Henry "Red" (1908–1967). A trumpeter whose career began with recordings in 1929 with his own band and in 1930 with King Oliver, Allen developed into one of the fieriest of the swing improvisers. His work with the Luis Russell and Fletcher Henderson Orchestras in the early '30s is often spectacular, as on the 1930 Russell recording of "Louisiana Swing" and on the 1933 Henderson recording of "Queer Notions." Between 1933 and 1939, Allen often worked with smaller groups, which included such sidemen as J.C. Higginbotham, Chu Berry, and Dickie Wells, who all formed part of the Fletcher Henderson Orchestra at one time or another.

Anderson, Ivie (1905–1949). A vocalist with the Duke Ellington Orchestra beginning in 1931, Anderson first recorded with the organization on the seminal 1932 Ellington song, "It Don't Mean a Thing If It Ain't Got That Swing." Her recording in 1937 of "All God's Children" exhibits her fine sense of swing. Her ability to handle ballad material with a blues feeling is demonstrated by her 1941 recording of Ellington's lovely "I Got It Bad and That Ain't Good."

Apollo Theatre. Both the Apollo Theatre and the Savoy Ballroom hosted black and white bands, with Charlie Barnet's Orchestra appearing at the Apollo in 1934 as the first white unit and, according to *Metronome* magazine, "shatter[ing] all precedent and opening day records" (cited in David W. Stowe, *Swing Changes*, p. 43), although Barnet denies that this was the case (see his *Those Swinging Years: The Autobiography of Charlie Barnet with Stanley Dance*, p. 61). The Apollo held a regular Amateur Night, at which in 1934 Ella Fitzgerald was discovered by drummer-band leader Chick Webb.

Armstrong, Louis "Satchmo" (1901–1971). As a seminal figure in jazz, Armstrong influenced all individual musicians and groups by his ability to swing with an incomparable ease and a natural rhythmic flow, both as a trumpet soloist and a vocalist. He extended the range of his instrument, but above all he brought to jazz and the Swing Era rhythmic and emotional dimensions that made possible the music's worldwide appeal. James Lincoln Collier considers Armstrong's 1932 recording of "Hobo, You Can't Ride This Train" one of his finest of the 1930s (*The Making of Jazz*, p. 156), and Gunther Schuller rates Armstrong's versions of "Stardust" and "Between the Devil and Deep Blue Seas" from 1931 and 1932, respectively, "beyond anything he had previously achieved" (*The Swing Era*, p. 177). Although Armstrong's most historic recordings date from the 1920s, his playing during the '30s developed a greater instrumental range and perhaps reached deeper emotional levels than in any other period of his long, productive career.

Auld, Georgie (1919–1990). A tenorist with the Artie Shaw Orchestra, Auld was still a teenager when he joined the unit in 1938. Before that he had recorded with the Bunny Berigan Orchestra, and during 1940–1941, he worked with the Benny Goodman Orchestra, recording with the leader's septet that included Cootie Williams and Charlie Christian. Somewhat influenced by Lester Young, Auld could turn in quite effective breaks, as on the 1939 Shaw recording of "One Foot in the Groove" and the 1941 Goodman septet recording of "Wholly Cats."

Autry, Herman (1904–1980). A trumpeter with Fats Waller and His Rhythm, Autry seemed perfectly suited to the pianist's combination of comedy and lively, driving swing. Autry's lighthearted playing can be sampled on the 1934 Waller recording of "Porter's Lovesong to a Chambermaid."

Bailey, Buster (1902–1967). A clarinetist with the Fletcher Henderson Orchestra in the early part of the decade and at its end with the John Kirby Sextet, Bailey was a dependable if not entirely impressive soloist. Some of his more effective contributions can be heard on the 1934 Henderson recording of "Shanghai Shuffle" and the 1936 Henderson version of "Christopher Columbus."

Bailey, Mildred (1907–1951). Originally with the Paul Whiteman Orchestra, Bailey was the first big-band vocalist and has been considered among the finest singers of the 1930s, although on a level below the inimitable Billie Holiday. Married to vibraphonist Red Norvo, Bailey was featured with her husband's band from 1936 to 1939. Some of her more impressive appearances were with the Jimmy Dorsey Orchestra in 1933 and with a quartet in 1935 that included Bunny Berigan, Johnny Hodges, and Teddy

Wilson. Gunther Schuller credits Bailey with being "the first important white singer" and the first "to break away significantly from the essentially all-blues tradition." Schuller considers her strongest work to have been in conjunction with "a strong and progressive" arranger such as Eddie Sauter (for example, the 1937 "Smoke Dreams"), although he singles out "Thanks for the Memory," with a 1938 combo that included Chu Berry and Teddy Wilson, as "one of Mildred Bailey's finest and most representative vocals" (*The Swing Era*, p. 519). Richard Sudhalter asserts that "Bailey probably never made a bad record" (*Lost Chords*, p. 697).

Barnet, Charlie (1913–1991). Tenorist and big-band leader, Barnet was unusual among his white colleagues for openly emulating his black mentors, Duke Ellington and Count Basie. Barnet's most famous side was his 1939 recording of Ray Noble's "Cherokee." A respectable soloist on tenor, Barnet can be heard characteristically on "Cherokee," as well as on "The Count's Idea" (also from 1939), the latter revealing something of the influence of Lester Young.

Bascomb, Dud (1916–1972). A trumpeter with the Erskine Hawkins Orchestra, Bascomb took the more thoughtful jazz solos, while the leader tended to showboat. Bascomb can be heard on the band's most famous side, "Tuxedo Junction," from 1939, and is especially impressive on "Miss Hallelujah Brown" from 1938.

Bascomb, Paul (1910–1986). A tenorist with the Erskine Hawkins Orchestra, Bascomb, like his younger brother Dud, was an important member of the Hawkins unit. Bascomb is well represented by his solo on "Sweet Georgia Brown" from 1940.

Basie, Count (1904–1984). As a pianist and band leader, Basie helped establish a relaxed yet powerfully driving style of blues, riff-based big-band and combo jazz, which originated in Kansas City and drew on the competitive Southwestern tradition of touring territory bands. Basie's "Swinging the Blues," by composer-arranger Eddie Durham, has been taken as a title that aptly encapsulates the Basie form of swing-era jazz, which influenced developments during the Bop era and continues as one of the fundamental styles in jazz history. Martin Williams in *The Jazz Tradition* declares Basie's solo on his big band's 1938 recording of "Doggin' Around" to be "a classic of linking and occasionally contrasting melodic ideas, and is probably his masterpiece" (p. 128). Pianist-composer John Lewis observed that his own jazz ideals stemmed from the Basie band's "integration of ensemble playing which projected—and sounded like—the spontaneous playing of ideas which were the personal expression of each member of the band rather than the arrangers and composers" (quoted by Ralph J. Gleason in his liner notes to the 1956 Atlantic album, *Fontessa/The Modern Jazz Quartet*).

Beiderbecke, Bix (1903–1931). Even though Beiderbecke made his last recordings at the beginning of the Swing Era, his solos from 1927 continued to influence such cornet and trumpet players as Bunny Berigan and Bobby Hackett and perhaps the work of Lester Young, who listened closely to Frankie Trumbauer's saxophone on the 1927 Beiderbecke recordings and could not have helped but pick up on Bix's storytelling style. A late side from 1930, "Barnacle Bill the Sailor," shows Beiderbecke's drive and imagination even at that date not to be matched by any other white player and by few black players of any period.

Beneke, Tex (1914–2000). A tenorist with the Glenn Miller Orchestra, Beneke was often featured both as an instrumental soloist and as a vocalist. If not one of the great jazz soloists, Beneke contributed to the Miller success story through his warm, soothing voice and his at times energetic breaks on tenor. His vocal on the 1941 "I Gotta Gal in Kalamazoo" was one of the many Miller hits to which Beneke made a major contribution. His more jazz-oriented work is represented by his tenor break on the 1939 "Glen Island Special."

Berigan, Bunny (1908–1942). A trumpeter with the original Benny Goodman Orchestra and later a leader of his own big band, Berigan was afflicted by alcoholism, which led to an early death. His recorded output, however, was considerable, including both his work with large groups and with smaller units. His most famous solos came on two versions of "I Can't Get Started" from 1936 and 1937. Berigan's warm, emotive tone and his considerable technical control and expressiveness marked him as one of the most identifiable soloists of the era. Small group sides from 1936 with Billie Holiday ("No Regrets" and "A Fine Romance") and with Frank Froeba ("Organ Grinder's Swing" and "Rhythm Lullaby") reveal Berigan's special gift for melodic improvisation and bittersweet soulfulness.

Berry, Chu (1910–1941). One of a number of outstanding tenor saxophonists of the Swing Era, Berry as a stylist fell somewhere between Coleman Hawkins's surging, robust sound and Lester Young's more lightly swinging approach. Berry was featured on a number of fine recordings by the Fletcher Henderson Orchestra in 1936 and 1937, such as "Christopher Columbus" (written by Berry), and with the Cab Calloway Orchestra from 1937 to 1941, including "Jive" and "Tappin' Off."

Bigard, Barney (1906–1980). A clarinetist with the Duke Ellington Orchestra, Bigard was a product of the New Orleans clarinet tradition but fit perfectly into the sophisticated Ellington organization by virtue of his splendid technique, his soaring sound, and his fluid, faultless lines. Bigard solos on and adds to the eerie effect of the classic "Mood Indigo" from 1930, wails on "Daybreak Express" from 1933, and is featured in the concerto-like "Clarinet Lament" of 1936.

Blanton, Jimmy (1921–1942). A bassist with the Duke Ellington Orchestra, Blanton is considered the first modern-style, virtuoso player on his instrument. He broke away from the role of timekeeper to explore the solo possibilities of the bass, extending its technical and expressive range. Featured on Ellington's 1940 "Jack the Bear" and adding immensely to the driving swing of other sides recorded with the orchestra during the few years before his untimely death, Blanton can be heard most fully on four sides also recorded in 1940 but with only Ellington at the piano.

Braud, Wellman (1891–1966). A bassist with the Duke Ellington Orchestra from 1926 until 1935, Braud provided a firm foundation for the group with his big, round tone and his rocking beat. Braud's sound was always well recorded and can be heard clearly on all the Ellington sides, such as the 1933 "Jive Stomp" (reportedly the first use of the term "jive" on a record) and on the 1933 "Harlem Speaks" where he slaps the bass in the New Orleans style and swings with tremendous power.

Brown, Lawrence (1907–1988). A trombonist with the Duke Ellington Orchestra, Brown was a versatile soloist, capable of warm, romantic breaks but also highly effective at up-tempo swing. These two sides of his musical personality are apparent on the 1938 "I Let a Song Go Out of My Heart," where Brown is at his sentimental best, and on the 1932 "Slippery Horn," whose title was suggested by the trombonist who had just joined the orchestra and who shows here his ability to play beautifully in any register of his instrument.

Byas, Don (1912–1972). A tenor saxophonist with a number of bands during the '30s, at the end of the decade with Andy Kirk, and in 1941 with Count Basie, Byas is perhaps best known for his work with Dizzy Gillespie in 1946 on the classic "Night in Tunisia"; the tenorist also was captured at Minton's in 1941 playing with Thelonious Monk. Scott Yanow cites Byas's solo on "Stardust" from the 1941 "Minton's at Midnight" session (recorded by Jerry Newman) as a "stunning ballad statement" (*Swing*, p. 178). Byas's solo to open Basie's 1941 "Harvard Blues" is, as Gunther Schuller observes, "simple and affecting, poignant and languorous" (*The Swing Era*, p. 255).

Calloway, Cab (1907–1994). Although a singer of largely novelty numbers, Calloway made his mark as one of the most versatile vocalists of the Swing Era and as a leader of a highly popular and at times innovative big band, which featured toward the end of the decade such important figures as Chu Berry, Ben Webster, Dizzy Gillespie, and Milt Hinton. Calloway's jive scatting, his "hi-de-ho" and "Chinese" lingo, can be heard on such sides as the 1933 "Kickin' the Gong Around" and the 1934 "Chinese Rhythm." The latter also shows off his orchestra to fine advantage, with solid solos on clarinet, alto, and trumpet, as well as Al Morgan's driving bass.

Carmichael, Hoagy (1899–1981). Pianist-composer Carmichael contributed many of the most popular tunes of the Swing Era, including "Georgia on My Mind," "Lazy Bones," "Lazy River," "Rockin' Chair," "Sing Me a Swing Song," "Stardust," and countless others. "Two Sleepy People," a little-known Carmichael tune, with lyrics by Frank Loesser, was rendered inimitably by Fats Waller and His Rhythm in 1938.

Carney, Harry (1910–1974). Anchoring the Duke Ellington Orchestra with his vigorous baritone, Carney was a mainstay of the Ellington unit, remaining with his leader through six decades. As a soloist Carney was, during the Swing Era, the greatest improviser on his instrument. A personal favorite among his innumerable solos is his spine-tingling break on the 1935 "Merry-Go-Round."

Carter, Benny (b. 1907). A multi-instrumentalist (alto saxophone and trumpet), arranger-composer, and bandleader, Carter was the principal arranger for the Fletcher Henderson Orchestra at the beginning of the 1930s and contributed important arrangements to the Chick Webb Orchestra in 1931 and to the Benny Goodman Orchestra in 1934. He has been considered the master of block-chord writing for saxophones, and although his own band was well respected, it did not achieve the level of popular appeal enjoyed by the name bands, even though Carter's theme song for his orchestra, "Melancholy Lullaby," has been called one of the best of the Swing Era. As an alto soloist, Carter was one of the first virtuosos on his instrument.

Casey, Al (b. 1915). A guitarist with Fats Waller and His Rhythm, Casey added greatly to the easy swing of the pianist's combo. His guitar work under Waller's vocals has been called "masterful" and can be heard, for example, on the 1936 "I'm Sorry I Made You Cry." His ability to play to Waller's comic treatment of popular songs is illustrated by the guitarist's "harmonic mocking of the chords" (Mike Lipskin, liner notes to *Fractious Fingering*).

Catlett, "Big" Sid (1910–1951). A drummer's drummer, Catlett played with many of the finest black orchestras, including those of Fletcher Henderson, Benny Carter, Don Redman, Louis Armstrong, and very briefly Benny Goodman. Catlett was the drummer on several classic Henderson sides, including "Christopher Columbus," "Blue Lou," and "Stealin' Apples," which feature important solos by Chu Berry and Roy Eldridge. Catlett can be heard especially on the last of these, punctuating behind the soloists and driving the band with a steady beat.

Christian, Charlie (1919–1942). The revolutionary electric guitarist who starred with Benny Goodman's small groups from 1939 to 1941, Christian participated in after-hours sessions at Minton's that heralded the coming of Bebop. His long, highly inventive, blues-inflected lines influenced every subsequent guitarist, as did his ability to improvise endlessly from the simplest riffs, a number of which he himself created, such as "Flying Home," "Gone with 'What' Wind," and "Seven Come Eleven." One of the most satisfying sessions Christian recorded was with tenorist Jerry Jerome in Minneapolis in 1940, as he takes on this date several brilliant solos on three standards, "I Got Rhythm," "Stardust," and "Tea for Two."

Clayton, Buck (1911–1991). The star trumpeter with the Count Basie Orchestra, Clayton contributed immensely to Basie's Kansas City style of a small-group, integrated sound for big-band swing. Either muted or open, Clayton's trumpet added to the blues-derived feeling of the Basie unit, at the same time that his driving improvisations fueled the performances as much as any of the band's many distinguished sidemen. On one of the band's biggest hits, the 1937 "One O'Clock Jump," Clayton plays a trademark open solo, complete with bent notes and his slight growl approach, and on the 1937 "Topsy," he opens this Eddie Durham piece with a muted theme statement, again with bent notes as well as his own agile embellishments.

Cole, Cozy (1906 or 1909–1981). A drummer with a number of swing-era bands before joining Cab Calloway in 1938, Cole helped the Calloway rhythm section to become one of the best in the business. He was featured by Cab on several sides, in particular "Ratamacue" of 1939 and "Paradiddle" of 1940.

Cole, Nat "King" (1917–1965). Known as the pianist-leader of a fine swing trio during the last years of the thirties and the first two years of the forties, even before he achieved international fame as a vocalist, Cole played in an advanced style for the time, utilizing harmonic substitutions that would only become standard bebop fare later in the 1940s. The trio's first minor hit was "Sweet Lorraine," in 1940, and exhibits Coles's and guitarist Oscar Moore's vanguard voicings.

Coleman, Bill (1904–1981). A trumpeter who spent much of his career in France, Coleman recorded a few especially memorable sides with Fats Waller and His Rhythm. His penetrating tone and flexible, seemingly illimitable lines are forever a joy to hear. Although a 1943 recording is slightly beyond the period of this volume, *Classic Tenors: Coleman Hawkins/Lester Young* (Doctor Jazz, FW38446) fully exhibits on "Linger Awhile" and "I Got Rhythm" what Nat Hentoff in his liner notes calls Coleman's "particular kind of lyricism—crisp with a soft center, and flowing, always flowing." Also on this album is Dickie Wells at his most acrobatic.

Cotton Club. This Harlem nightclub for whites only featured floor shows with black entertainers and all-black orchestras, most prominently that of Duke Ellington, whose "jungle" music was developed there beginning in 1927. During the '30s, the nightclub also showcased the orchestras of Cab Calloway and Jimmie Lunceford. Residency at and radio broadcasts from the Cotton Club generally gained for any band a national reputation, although the appearance there of Claude Hopkins seems to have been an exception to the rule.

Crawford, Jimmy (1910–1980). The drummer with the Jimmie Lunceford Orchestra from its inception, Crawford was fundamental to the group's success. Because the Lunceford approach called for a wide variety of styles and sounds, it was essential that the drummer be highly adaptable, and Crawford was entirely so. In addition, he was a great show drummer, which also made him a natural for the Lunceford conception. Arranger Sy Oliver observed that Crawford "was never intrusive" but "swung a band without making a noise. I mean, you *felt* him" (quoted by Burt Korall, *Drummin' Men*, p. 320).

Crosby, Bob (1913–1993). Singer-leader of the Bob Crosby Orchestra and the small group called the Bobcats, Crosby essentially was taken on by the unit for the sake of name recognition. Brother of the more famous Bing Crosby, Bob managed to serve the orchestra well and allowed the group to achieve considerable success under his leadership.

Dash, Julian (1916–1974). A tenorist with the Erskine Hawkins Orchestra, Dash replaced Paul Bascomb when the latter left the group in 1938, and then the two men shared tenor duties when Bascomb returned in 1940. Along with the leader and William Johnson, Dash is credited with the creation of the classic tune, "Tuxedo Junction." On tenor, Dash soloed often and well, being featured on "No Soap (A Jitterbug Jamboree)" from 1939.

Dorsey, Jimmy (1904–1957). A talented reedman who impressed the likes of Charlie Parker, Dorsey may never have realized his potential as a jazzman, partly because he did not work at or feature his own playing as he probably should have but depended rather on less capable sidemen in his band that was an on-again off-again popular swing-era outfit. Neither he nor his band ever quite found an enduring musical identity, never developed any one style or approach deeply enough to make it personal and meaningful. When Dorsey did solo, as on the 1940 "Dolemite," he offers proof that he could have been quite a formidable altoist and suggests why Parker and a later altoist such as Leo Wright found Dorsey a model on their instrument.

Dorsey, Tommy (1905–1956). Like his brother Jimmy, Tommy was a talented musician, but unlike his brother, Tommy developed a distinctly romantic style of trombone playing that made him and his band a perennial favorite among dancers and listeners of the Swing Era. Tommy's music was only in a limited sense jazz, for the simple reason that it gave greater emphasis to mood making and less to creative improvisation. Some of Tommy's best work as an improviser can be heard when he recorded with his Clambake Seven, as on "Having a Wonderful Time" from 1937. Probably Tommy's most famous appearance with his full orchestra came with his trombone theme statement on the 1935 "I'm Gettin' Sentimental over You."

Douglas, Clifford "Boots" (1908–). Drummer-leader of his own group, Boots and His Buddies, Douglas has been called the Chick Webb of the Southwest. Largely unknown outside his home base of San Antonio, Texas, Douglas led a unit that on its first recordings from 1935 followed impressively in the tradition of the 1932 Bennie Moten band, but as the decade wore on the group's recordings lost their early level of quality and interest. One of the most driving of the band's sides was "Rose Room," cut in 1935, although "Ain't Misbehavin'," from 1937, still offered a spirited, imaginative effort, with solos that compete with the best of the period.

Durham, Eddie (1906–1987). A guitarist-trombonist-arranger-composer for several of the leading big bands of the era, Durham contributed significantly to the Bennie Moten, Jimmie Lunceford, Count Basie, and Glenn Miller orchestras, among others. He was one of the first musicians to record with an amplified guitar and had a direct influence on the work of Charlie Christian. Durham's recording of "Hittin' the Bottle" in 1935 with the Lunceford Orchestra featured his amplified guitar as well as his arranging skills. He composed and/or arranged a number of classic Basie tunes, including "Topsy," "Out the Window," "Swinging the Blues," "Blue and Sentimental," "Sent for You Yesterday," and "John's Idea."

Edison, Harry "Sweets" (1915–1999). A trumpeter with the Count Basie Orchestra, Edison was a more aggressive player than his section mate Buck Clayton. "Sweets" solos wonderfully on "Every Tub," a classic side from 1938 that exhibits the trumpeter's tendency to repeat his notes, driving them with increasing intensity, which is especially appropriate on this all-out swinger.

Eldridge, Roy "Little Jazz" (1911–1989). A trumpeter who brought a new approach to his instrument, Eldridge made his first impact through his work with the Fletcher Henderson Orchestra in 1936. He became the model for such bebop trumpeters as Dizzy Gillespie and Fats Navarro, impressing them with his technical range and imaginative flights that differed dramatically from the style of Louis Armstrong. One of Eldridge's most striking sessions was held in 1937 with a group billed as Roy Eldridge and His Orchestra. "Heckler's Hop" from this date shows the trumpet-leader breaking the sound barrier and reeling off electrifying runs full of vibrant invention.

Ellington, Duke (1899–1974). Active in every decade of jazz until his death, Ellington was and is considered the leader of the finest big band of the Swing Era. As performed by his own orchestra, Ellington's original compositions—such as "Merry-Go-Round," "Do Nothing Till You Hear from Me," "Solitude," "In a Sentimental Mood," and "Harlem Air Shaft"—remain unique works of the highest order of big-band jazz. Through his sidemen, Ellington contributed to jazz some of its most inimitable instrumental voices. His 1932 song "It Don't Mean a Thing If It Ain't Got That Swing" was in many ways the defining manifesto of the entire era. Yet Ellington was a creator of sketches in sound that encompassed more than enticing rhythms—he depicted people (including his own sidemen), places (the jungle, Harlem, Birmingham, East St. Louis, New Orleans, Dallas, Oklahoma), and machines (trains, riverboats, carousels) through a sonic palette unequaled by any other composer in jazz history.

Elman, Ziggy (1914–1968). A trumpeter with the Benny Goodman Orchestra, Elman was something of an eccentric soloist, but his playing could be quite effective and appealing. He did not have quite the same dramatic flair of a Harry James, and this is evident when the two men played basically the same notes on a solo, as in the case of their breaks on "Jam Session," recorded with Elman in 1936 and caught on a radio broadcast with James in 1937. Elman's work with various smaller groups led by Lionel Hampton was often stimulating, as on "The Object of My Affection" and "I Just Couldn't Take It Baby," both from 1937.

Evans, Herschel (1909–1939). A tenorist with the Count Basie Orchestra, Evans offered a contrast in style with that of Lester Young, the other tenor and the most outstanding soloist with the Basie group, which included such talented figures as trombonist Dickie Wells, trumpeter Buck Clayton, and Basie himself on piano. Evans represented the Coleman Hawkins tradition of tenor saxophone playing, even though Herschel achieved a rather unique sound in his own right: dramatic, stirring in a highly emotive vein, and swinging without resorting to a flurry of notes. In fact, most of the Basie soloists tended to limit themselves to a few notes that counted for much in terms of a heightened expressiveness. Evans was featured on "Blue and Sentimental" from 1938, but also served as an effective foil to Young on other of the Basie classics, such as "One O'Clock Jump" from 1937.

Fitzgerald, Ella (1917–1996). Beginning her career at eighteen in 1935 with the Chick Webb Orchestra, Fitzgerald helped catapult the Webb unit to its greatest prominence among the big bands of the day. Her 1938 singing with the orchestra of a children's tune, "A-Tisket, A-Tasket," became a nationwide hit. Fitzgerald's music career was long and eclectic, including scat singing, duets with Louis Armstrong, and classic renditions of songs by Rodgers and Hart. Colin MacInnes aptly characterizes what was from the first "an inborn sense of rhythm, so strongly felt that she can vary the beat to a preposterous degree without ever for a second losing it. Clear, precise diction, and a sixth sense for pace. Easy, assured and infinitely flexible phrasing, graceful, undulating and vivacious" (in *Reading Jazz*, pp. 247–249).

Forrest, Helen (1918–1999). A vocalist with the Artie Shaw and Benny Goodman orchestras before she joined Harry James in 1941, Forrest has been considered one of the finest singers of the big-band era. Her rendition of "Deep Purple" with Shaw in 1939 is as sensual as anything sung by a female vocalist of the period. Her version of "But Not for Me" with James in 1941 is equally feminine in its loveliness but less sensuous, more dramatic in the delivery, with some of her falling notes suggesting the influence of Billie Holiday. But Forrest is a different kind of singer, somewhat affected in terms of sentiment, yet effective in her own rather earnest way.

Foster, Pops (1892–1969). A bassist with the Luis Russell Orchestra, Foster had been active in the '20s with the likes of King Oliver, but in 1929 joined Russell and anchored the rhythm section with his booming sound and pulsing drive. He can be heard slapping his bass to great effect on "Saratoga Drag" from 1930 and rocking and rolling on "Mahogany Hall Stomp" from 1936.

Freeman, Bud (1906–1991). A tenorist with a number of important big bands of the era, Freeman was something of an enigmatic figure, and this is reflected in the different styles he tended to cultivate. He could adhere to the Dixieland manner at times and at others would sound as modern as the leading tenorists of the day, including Lester Young. His work with the Benny Goodman Orchestra was often quite solid, and the same can be said of his solos with the Tommy Dorsey Orchestra. According to Loren Schoenberg the tenorist "could be the most logical melodic improviser at times, but integrated elements of incoherence and eccentricity into his solos for narrative leavening" (notes to *Benny Goodman: Wrappin' It Up, The Harry James Years Part 2*). This can be heard in his brief solo at the end of "Wrappin' It Up" from 1938, and equally so in his break at the close of Tommy Dorsey's 1937 recording of "Marie." His small-group work has been praised by many commentators, especially with his Summa Cum Laude Orchestra of 1939.

Gale, Moe (1898–1964). Owner of the Savoy Ballroom, Gale was known as "the Great White Father of Harlem." He promoted Chick Webb, Cab Calloway, and Ella Fitzgerald, as well as managing and booking such bandleaders as Benny Carter and Erskine Hawkins.

Gifford, Gene (1908–1970). A composer-arranger with the Casa Loma Orchestra, Gifford created big-band arrangements that were admired by many bands at the beginning of the '30s. His "Casa Loma Stomp" of 1933 epitomized the driving, tightly arranged compositions that made the orchestra led by Glen Gray the envy of both black and white musicians.

Gillespie, Dizzy (1917–1993). A trumpeter active at the end of the 1930s, Gillespie joined in 1939 the Cab Calloway Orchestra, not only contributing formative trumpet solos but also writing and arranging "Paradiddle" as a feature for drummer Cozy Cole. Gillespie was just beginning to find his own approach to jazz, but his solo on "Pluckin' the Bass" from 1939 signaled "an already distinct and original voice" and his composition "Paradiddle" exhibited in 1940 "bold bop-ish harmonies and voicings" (Gunther Schuller, *The Swing Era*, pp. 344–45). Another Gillespie composition, "Pickin' the Cabbage," also from 1940, is "prophetic" of the bop movement in that his long trumpet solo utilizes "whole-tone scales" and "revolutionary rhythmic ideas" (Ross Russell, in "Bebop," *The Art of Jazz*, ed. Martin Williams, p. 205).

Glaser, Joe (1896–1969). Manager for Louis Armstrong, Lionel Hampton, Andy Kirk, Hot Lips Page, and others, Glaser worked for the second-largest booking office, Rockwell-O'Keefe, which "was regarded as more sensitive to its clients' musical goals, and controlled Glenn Miller, Artie Shaw, Woody Herman, Jimmy Dorsey, and Casa Loma (in its postcooperative incarnation)" (David W. Stowe, *Swing Changes*, p. 105).

Goodman, Benny (1909–1986). Crowned by a mass audience as "The King of Swing," Goodman earned his right to such a title on the basis of his fluid, silken-toned clarinet and his well-rehearsed orchestra with its superstar line-up headed by Harry James and Gene Krupa. If ultimately Goodman's oeuvre does not measure up to the work of Ellington and Basie in terms of imaginative jazz, his recordings and live appearances were crucial in making jazz of this period the most widely popular of any music in American history.

Grand Terrace. This Chicago nightclub opened in December 1928 with the Earl Hines Orchestra, which worked there regularly for over ten years. Other bands, such as those of Erskine Tate, Fletcher Henderson, and Count Basie, also were featured at this important venue, whose radio broadcasts helped attract a larger audience for swing jazz and helped ensure the longevity of a struggling band like that of Henderson when he signed off using his "Christopher Columbus" as a theme song.

Gray, Glen (1906–1963). Leader of the Casa Loma Orchestra, Gray proved to be an effective manager after being elected president by the orchestra members who formed the first big-band corporation.

Green, Charlie "Big" (1900–1936). An important accompanist on Bessie Smith's first recordings in 1924 and 1925, Green may have played a rather old-fashioned blues-style trombone during his final recordings with the Chick Webb band when it backed up Louis Armstrong in 1932, but his swinging, shaking solos are deeply moving in their emotive force.

Green, Freddie (1911–1987). A rhythm guitarist with the Count Basie Orchestra, Green formed an essential part of the so-called All-American Rhythm Section whose other members were Basie on piano, drummer Jo Jones, and bassist Walter Page. This unit set the pattern for a driving yet relaxed swing that characterized the Basie well-oiled machine. Green was rarely heard as a soloist but his steady strumming added immeasurably to the orchestra's unique form of Kansas City swing.

Greer, Sonny (1895–1982). A drummer with the Duke Ellington Orchestra, Greer utilized a variety of percussion instruments to achieve the subtle, evocative tonal shades that contributed so significantly to the Ellington sound. Greer could swing with the best of the period's drummers but also could add coloration that was rarely called for in other orchestras whose leaders were less creative and less willing to allow for individual participation in the overall musical effect. Greer can be heard working his magic to a marvelous degree in the 1940 masterpieces, "Harlem Air Shaft" and

"Cotton Tail," while his tom-tomming set the mood for the 1936 recording of Juan Tizol's classic "Caravan."

Hackett, Bobby (1915–1976). A cornetist who played at the famed Carnegie Hall Concert of 1938, Hackett reproduced the Bix Beiderbecke solo from the famous 1927 recording of "I'm Coming Virginia." A famous solo of his own is Hackett's scalar ascent on the Glenn Miller recording of "A String of Pearls" from 1941. His work with smaller groups includes a 1938 session with an Eddie Condon septet, with the cornetist leading the ensemble on "Ja-Da" and "Love Is Just Around the Corner," taking on the former a forceful (if somewhat forced) melodic solo. His later career was characterized by lush solo versions of classic pop tunes accompanied by romantic strings.

Haggart, Bob (1914–1998). A bassist and arranger-composer with the Bob Crosby Orchestra, Haggart created the classic "What's New?" and made perhaps even a bigger name for himself by whistling and plucking his bass simultaneously on "Big Noise from Winnetka." He was largely responsible for the Dixieland mode for which the Crosby Orchestra was best known.

Hammond, John (b. 1910). Probably the most important but frequently controversial promoter of jazz, Hammond is credited with furthering the careers of Benny Goodman, Count Basie, Charlie Christian, and Billie Holiday, among many others. Writing for British publications, Hammond helped bring American jazz to the notice of a European audience and also prompted Americans to pay more attention to their own homegrown music. Hammond encouraged Goodman to hire Fletcher Henderson as an arranger, brought Goodman and Charlie Christian together, and served as master of ceremonies at the 1938 "Spirituals to Swing" concert at Carnegie Hall. His detractors included Otis Ferguson, critic for *The New Republic*, whose writings Hammond admired, and Duke Ellington, whom Hammond attacked for ignoring the social and economic needs of his people. Hammond's autobiography, *John Hammond on Record* (1977), traces his career as a musical and political activist.

Hampton, Lionel (b. 1913). A drummer and pianist, Hampton was primarily a vibraharpist who, along with Red Norvo, established this instrument as a legitimate and very expressive medium for jazz. He was a member of the prestigious Benny Goodman Quartet, led many small-group sessions under his own name, and formed his own highly successful big band in 1940. He will forever be identified with the tune "Flying Home," which he recorded in February 1940 with a group that included Ziggy Elman and Budd Johnson, but it was a later 1942 version, with a solo by tenorist Illinois Jacquet, that linked the piece inextricably to both Hampton and Jacquet.

Harrison, Jimmy (1900–1931). A major jazz trombonist who only lived into the second year of the swing era, Harrison was with the Fletcher Henderson and Chick Webb orchestras during 1930 and 1931, respectively. Harrison's advanced conception can be heard on "Soft and Sweet" from March 1931 with the Webb Orchestra.

Hawkins, Coleman (1904–1969). The first important tenor saxophonist in jazz, Hawkins came into his own during his eleven years with the Fletcher Henderson Orchestra, from 1923 to 1934, developing into one of the first reed players to achieve a technical fluency and imaginative range of ideas that helped make improvised jazz a true art form. Recordings made with smaller groups beginning in 1929 show Hawkins moving beyond his role as a sideman and becoming a major jazz soloist. With his return from Europe at the end of the 1930s, Hawkins would solidify his position as the most inventive rhapsodist in all of jazz. His 1939 recording of "Body and Soul" is a touchstone of saxophone improvisation.

Hawkins, Erskine (1914–1993). A trumpeter-leader who was billed as "The Twentieth-Century Gabriel," Hawkins coauthored in 1939 the famous "Tuxedo Junction," which Glenn Miller capitalized on more successfully with his own version recorded in 1940. As a trumpet player, Hawkins took rather showy solos, but he also featured his very fine sidemen whose work was more artistically satisfying. Compared with the Miller orchestra, Hawkins's unit created more authentic, swinging jazz, especially in terms of improvised solos.

Henderson, Fletcher "Smack" (1897–1952). Recognized generally as the "Father of the Big Band," Henderson led one of the most admired units of the Swing Era. Such Henderson sidemen as Coleman Hawkins and Benny Carter went on to establish themselves as major figures in their own right. Henderson not only promoted these men, but he also selflessly encouraged and supported many of his competitors in the field. Some of his original compositions and arrangements have been credited with making possible in 1935 the phenomenal success of the Benny Goodman Orchestra, which resulted in Swing becoming the most popular music of the day. Henderson's arrangement and 1932 recording of "New King Porter Stomp" marked in many ways the advent of Swing as espoused by most every big band that followed his lead.

Henderson, Horace (1904–1988). Pianist-composer-arranger and brother to Fletcher Henderson, Horace wrote a number of classic tunes that were recorded not only by the Henderson Orchestra but also were picked up or commissioned by many other groups of the Swing Era. "Hot and Anxious" from 1931 (which contains the motif made famous by Glenn Miller's "In the Mood"), "Big John's Special" and "Rug Cutter's Swing" from 1934, and the arrangement of Chu Berry's "Christopher Columbus" from 1936 are but four of some thirty works that Horace created for his brother's group. Horace led his own orchestra from 1937 to 1941.

Higginbotham, J.C. (1906–1973). A trombonist who combined technical prowess with imaginative solo construction, Higginbotham helped lift every group with which he recorded to a higher level of energetic drive. His work with the bands of Luis Russell and Fletcher Henderson, as well as with many lesser-known, pick-up or all-star groups, is always satisfying and exhibits his impressive range, his facility for shakes, lip-trills, and two-octave leaps, and his immediately recognizable gruff, brawny sound that is at once authoritative and personable. Higginbotham's solos on the 1930 "Saratoga Drag" with the Russell band and on the 1932 "New King Porter Stomp" with the Henderson band represent the trombonist at his best.

Hill, Teddy (1909–1978). A tenorist and band leader, Hill is perhaps best known as the manager of Minton's Playhouse, but his orchestra, formed in 1932 as the NBC Orchestra (which sounds somewhat like a society outfit), included many outstanding soloists, among them Dickie Wells (who can be heard on the 1935 "A Study in Brown") and Roy Eldridge (on the 1935 "Lookie, Lookie, Lookie Here Comes Cookie," a rather corny piece except for Eldridge, Wells, and Chu Berry's breaks). Bill Coleman and Dizzy Gillespie also were among Hill's sidemen. The Hill orchestra lasted until 1940 when he disbanded and assumed the managership of Minton's.

Hines, Earl "Fatha" (1903–1983). Originator of the so-called "trumpet style" of piano playing, which was influenced by Louis Armstrong and which in turn influenced most every major jazz pianist (especially Teddy Wilson and Oscar Peterson), Hines was a highly successful big-band leader of the Swing Era, performing regularly with his orchestra for more than ten years at the Grand Terrace in Chicago. Hines's performance on the 1939 "Piano Man" finds the "King of Pianology" strutting his stuff.

Hinton, Milt (b. 1910). A bassist with the Cab Calloway Orchestra beginning in 1936, Hinton was featured on "Pluckin' the Bass" in 1939 and on "Ebony Silhouette" in 1941. At the time he was considered one of the most advanced musicians on his instrument, both plucking and slapping as well as bowing his bass in the process of his improvisations.

Hodges, Johnny (1906–1970). One of the premier alto saxophonists of the Swing Era, Hodges was a vital voice in the Duke Ellington Orchestra's reed section and a soloist of extraordinary beauty and technical facility. Ellington featured Hodges prominently and the saxophonist's lilting, fluttering sound helped establish something of Ellington's distinctive sonic aura. Hodges's romantic side is represented by his opening theme statement on the 1938 "I Let a Song Go Out of My Heart" and his more agile playing can be heard on the 1937 "All God's Chillun Got Rhythm."

Holiday, Billie (1915–1959). One of the truest jazz singers of all times, Holiday created a vocal style that paralleled in many ways the type of cool yet highly emotive approach represented among instrumental musicians by the playing of tenorist Lester Young, with whom Holiday recorded some of her most unforgettable performances. Her sessions with pianist Teddy Wilson as leader of small groups that often included Lester Young are exceptionable in showcasing both the beauty of Holiday's voice and the expressive quality of her interpretations of pop tunes of the day. Two of these sides, "Miss Brown to You" and "What a Little Moonlight Can Do," both from 1935, are often singled out as high points in her amazing if star-crossed career.

Hopkins, Claude (1903–1984). A pianist-leader, Hopkins led a fine orchestra in the early 1930s that did not live up to its potential, even with the likes of trombonist Snub Mosley, altoist Hilton Jefferson, and trumpeter Ovie Alston among its talented sidemen. Nonetheless, Hopkins and his group did record a number of fine performances, including a swinging rendition of "King Porter Stomp" from 1934. Earlier recordings and radio transcriptions from 1932 to 1933 include an arrangement by Jimmy Mundy of "Mush Mouth" from 1932 and "California Here I Come" from 1933 (a feature for Hopkins' stride piano).

James, Harry (1916–1983). Aside from Louis Armstrong and Bunny Berigan, James was the most conspicuous trumpeter of the Swing Era. Starring with the Benny Goodman Orchestra from 1937 to 1939, James was featured as a soloist, led the trumpet section with precision and punch, and contributed two of the group's best arrangements, "Peckin' " and "Life Goes to a Party," both recorded in 1937. James solos on his two arrangements with the spirited, even swaggering style that he made so famous during his stay with Goodman. In 1939, James formed his own orchestra, which became one of the most popular of the following decade.

Jefferson, Hilton (1903–1968). An alto saxophonist who was with King Oliver in 1930, with Fletcher Henderson from 1932 to 1934, with Chick Webb in 1934, 1936, and 1938, and with Cab Calloway beginning in 1940, Jefferson was never a prominent figure, but his solo and sectional work were always outstanding. He was featured by Calloway on "Willow Weep for Me" in 1941, and this one side reveals Jefferson's solid technique and tasteful artistry.

Johnson, Budd (1910–1984). A versatile multi-reedman with a number of groups during the thirties, but most prominently with the Earl Hines Orchestra in the latter part of the decade, Johnson was a complete musician, contributing to the history of jazz as soloist, composer-arranger, and straw boss for the Hines organization, as well as appearing as a sideman with the Louis Armstrong Orchestra and at recording dates for Lionel Hampton's pick-up sessions. On tenor Johnson could sound at times like Lester Young, on alto he was something of a precursor of bebop in his adventuresome flights, and on clarinet he even looked forward to the stratospheric style of a John Carter in the 1980s. Johnson's alto solo on the 1939 "Father Steps In" with the Earl Hines Orchestra remains freshly modern.

Jones, Claude (1901–1962). A section mate with Benny Morton in the Fletcher Henderson Orchestra, with Sandy Williams in the Chick Webb Orchestra, and with Keg Johnson in the Cab Calloway Orchestra, Jones recorded many outstanding solos, among them a fine break on "Keep a Song in Your Soul" with Henderson in 1930 and a superb solo on "Nagasaki" with Calloway in 1935.

Jones, Jo (1911–1985). A drummer with the Count Basie Orchestra, Jones was a member of what was considered the All-American Rhythm Section, along with Basie on piano, Freddie Green on guitar, and Walter Page on bass. Jones relied on his hi-hat cymbal for timekeeping and thus achieved a lighter sound, which allowed for Green's guitar and Page's bass to carry through more clearly and to create a richly harmonic and movingly driving swing. Representative of Jones's percussion work is his subtle drum break on the 1938 "Swingin' the Blues," his hi-hat work behind Lester Young, Dickie Wells, Basie, and the ensemble on the 1939 "Taxi War Dance," and his awesome breaks, punctuations, and drive on the 1939 "Clap Hands, Here Comes Charlie."

Kirby, John (1908–1952). A bassist with the Fletcher Henderson Orchestra from 1930 to 1933 and with the Chick Webb Orchestra from 1933 to 1935 before returning to Henderson for 1935–1936, Kirby formed his own Sextet in 1938, which was billed as "The Biggest Little Band in the Land." But it was Kirby's work with the Henderson and Webb orchestras that gained him a reputation as one of the finest bassmen of the Swing Era. His fluid, foundational support is evident on such sides as Henderson's 1930 "Somebody Loves Me" and Webb's 1933 "Darktown Strutters' Ball."

Kirk, Andy (1898–1992). Active in music as early as the midtwenties, playing string bass and tenor, Kirk became an important big-band leader when he took the place of Terrence Holder in 1929 and built what became known as the Twelve Clouds of Joy into a group that was in great demand throughout the country, especially following its 1936 hit recording titled "Until the Real Thing Comes Along."

Klink, Al (1915–1991). A tenorist with the Glenn Miller Orchestra, Klink was considered by many a superior soloist to the more frequently featured Tex Beneke. Klink and Beneke both appear as soloists on Miller's 1939 "In the Mood." Klink also solos effectively on "Johnson Rag" from 1939 and "Boulder Buff" from 1941.

Krupa, Gene (1909–1973). A drummer featured with the Benny Goodman Trio, Quartet, and Orchestra and a bandleader in his own right beginning in 1938, Krupa was one of the most popular jazz figures of the period. He was featured at the 1938 Carnegie Hall Concert on "Sing, Sing, Sing," which was a favorite of audiences from coast to coast. Perhaps surprisingly, Krupa did not feature himself so prominently when he became a band-leader. To his credit, he did spotlight two of his finest band members, trumpeter Roy Eldridge and singer Anita Day. Although as a show drummer Krupa epitomized for many listeners the entire Swing Era, he was not one of the great big-band drummers in the same category with a Jo Jones, Chick Webb, or Sonny Greer.

Lawson, Yank (1911–1995). A trumpeter with the Bob Crosby Orchestra, Lawson first worked with the Ben Pollack Orchestra in the early '30s but became a star with the Crosby group from 1935 to 1938. He joined Tommy Dorsey's Orchestra in 1938 but returned to the Crosby unit in 1941. Lawson takes a traditional stop-time solo on "Dogtown Blues" from 1937 and leads the ensemble with power on the 1937 "South Rampart Street Parade."

Lunceford, Jimmie (1902–1947). As a leader who was unique in not being an outstanding instrumentalist or vocalist, Lunceford led one of the finest and most popular big bands of the Swing Era. Serving almost exclusively as the director of his group, Lunceford was a disciplinarian who achieved a distinctive style marked by precision but also a powerful drive. Without the aid of any major sidemen, but with the assistance of such arrangers and able section men as Sy Oliver and Willie Smith, Lunceford managed to create an immediately recognizable sound that remains his alone. Like Ellington with his declaration that "It Don't Mean a Thing If It Ain't Got That Swing," Lunceford also issued a major manifesto during the Swing Era with his tune titled "Rhythm Is Our Business."

McShann, Jay (b. 1916). Pianist-leader of the last great Kansas City orchestra, McShann was primarily a player of blues and boogie woogie, although his orchestra proved something of a breeding ground for bebop, with dynamic improvisations by his sidemen on such tunes as "Body and Soul," "Oh! Lady Be Good," "Moten Swing," and "Honeysuckle Rose." Known mostly for featuring the work of young Charlie Parker, McShann's orchestra also included a number of other solid sidemen, such as tenorist Bob Mabane, trumpeter Orville Minor, bassist Gene Ramey, and drummer Gus Johnson. The band's soloists are all featured on "Oh! Lady Be Good" from 1940, with Parker responding to Lester Young's revolutionary recording of the same tune in 1936 with the young alto saxophonist's own soon-to-be-recognized revolutionary sound and style.

Miller, Glenn (1904–1944). By the end of the 1930s, Miller's orchestra had emerged as the number one big band in popularity. His orchestra's smooth, rich sound and the all-American themes of his songs appealed widely during a period of great uncertainty in the land and throughout the world. Although Miller had been active in jazz circles from the 1920s, he eschewed for the most part the improvisatory dimension of jazz and focused more on arrangements that featured his reed section with a clarinet lead that created a seductively romantic sound. For many listeners the Miller recordings stand as the most representative of the Swing Era and the nostalgia it evokes for a time of togetherness during the dark days before another imminent world war.

Mills, Irving (1884–1985). As the manager for Duke Ellington, Mills is credited with steering the composer-bandleader in the right direction in terms of business transactions, national and international tours, public relations, and music publication. Beginning in 1937, Mills also managed Cab Calloway, as well as organizing the Mills Blue Rhythm Band to substitute at nightspots such as the Cotton Club for Ellington and Calloway. However, a figure like Benny Carter did not have the same beneficial relationship with Mills as did Ellington and Calloway. Mills's purchase of Carter's jazz standard, "Blues in My Heart," for $25, was unfortunately typical of the shabby treatment many black jazz musicians received at the hands of managers and record company executives.

Minton's Playhouse. This New York Harlem nightspot was the scene of many jam sessions that allowed jazz musicians to play in whatever style they wished. Here, at what was referred to by some as Minton's University of Bebop, experimentalists such as Thelonious Monk, Charlie Christian, and Dizzy Gillespie began to work out some of the directions of the new music. In general, the jazz at Minton's was in contrast to that performed by the big bands—the focus was on smaller groups and on more extended, complex improvisation.

Morton, Benny (1907–1985). A fine trombonist who worked with two of the top big bands (those of Fletcher Henderson and Count Basie), Morton always turned in solid solos with tremendous drive and inventiveness. He can be heard on the 1931 Henderson recording of Oliver's "Sugar Foot Stomp" and the 1938 Basie recording of "Swingin' the Blues."

Morton, Ferdinand "Jelly Roll" (1885?–1941). Even though the active career of this self-proclaimed inventor of Swing essentially ended in 1930 with his final recording session for RCA Victor, Morton played a vital role in the Swing Era through recordings by most every big band of his "King Porter Stomp," a composition dating possibly from as early as 1902.

Mundy, Jimmy (1907–1983). Known primarily as an arranger, although he played tenor saxophone and other instruments, Mundy worked for a number of big-band leaders, including Earl Hines, Benny Goodman, and Count Basie. Among his more notable arrangements are "Cavernism" for Hines, "Jam Session," "Solo Flight" (with Charlie Christian on electric guitar), "Air Mail Special" for Goodman, and "Super Chief" for Basie.

Nanton, "Tricky" Sam (1904–1946). A trombonist with the Duke Ellington Orchestra, Nanton provided the talking, plunger-mute growls so closely identified with the Ellington sound. Nanton solos on the 1932 seminal Ellington statement, "It Don't Mean a Thing (If It Ain't Got That Swing)"; appears twice on the 1933 "Harlem Speaks"; and is entrusted with an anguished wa-wa statement of the theme in the important 1940 "Ko-Ko."

Norvo, Red (1908–1999). Xylophonist with Paul Whiteman at the beginning of the '30s, Norvo made a name for himself with small-group recordings and later as the leader of a big band, with arrangements done by Eddie Sauter, who emphasized a softer sound, as exemplified by the 1937 "Remember." As a soloist, Norvo can be heard playing his characteristically smoothly flowing lines with his Swing Sextette on "I Got Rhythm" from 1936 and with his Orchestra on the 1937 "Jivin' the Jeep."

Oliver, Joseph "King" (1885–1938). The mentor of Louis Armstrong and the creator in the 1920s of such classics as "Dippermouth Blues" (also known as "Sugar Foot Strut" or "Stomp") and "Snag It," which were arranged and performed by almost every band of the Swing Era, Oliver remained a vital figure in the development of jazz during this period, even though his own active career had ended in 1930.

Oliver, Sy (1910–1988). A trumpeter, composer, arranger, and singer with the Jimmie Lunceford Orchestra, Oliver was responsible in large part for the Lunceford style and the unit's consequent popular success. Oliver's arrangement of the 1937 "For Dancers Only" is typical of the two-beat syncopation that stamped the Lunceford style and was ideal for dancing.

Another side to Oliver's work is represented by his 1934 "Dream of You," a haunting tune arranged with remarkable taste. Oliver left Lunceford for the Tommy Dorsey Orchestra in 1939, contributing to the creation of more jazz-oriented pieces than Dorsey had previously performed, such as the 1941 "Yes Indeed."

Onyx Club. Owned by Joe Helblock, the Onyx Club was "one of the most popular hot spots on New York's West 52nd Street" (Chris Albertson, insert notes to *Begin the Beguine: Artie Shaw and His Orchestra*). Helblock invited Artie Shaw to play briefly at a Swing Music Concert in 1936 at the New York Imperial Theatre, and Shaw's performance with a string quartet helped launch the clarinetist's career as a bandleader.

Page, Oran "Hot Lips" (1908–1954). A trumpeter-vocalist whose career in the 1930s began with the Bennie Moten Orchestra, Page was one of the most dynamic soloists on the historic 1932 recordings by the Moten Orchestra. Leaving the Count Basie Orchestra before it achieved prominence, Page was managed by Joe Glaser and groomed as another Louis Armstrong, but as a bandleader Page never achieved success. Many of his most impressive performances (both on trumpet and as a blues singer) came with smaller groups, including appearances at jam sessions at Minton's. In 1941, he began a brief association with the Artie Shaw Orchestra. Perhaps his greatest contributions remain his solos on such Moten sides as "Moten Swing" and "New Orleans."

Page, Walter (1900–1957). A bassist with the Count Basie Orchestra, Page was first with the Bennie Moten Orchestra, but his most important period was during the late thirties when he teamed with Basie on piano, Jo Jones on drums, and Freddie Green on guitar to form the so-called All-American Rhythm Section. The rich sound that Page created on his instrument was uniquely his own, and his steady, round-toned bass lines smoothly propelled the Basie band in conjunction with the other members of its inimitably driving rhythm section.

Palomar Ballroom. Located in Los Angeles, California, the Palomar was the site in August 1935 of Benny Goodman's overnight success as a bandleader. The crowd came more to listen to the jazz numbers that the Goodman Orchestra offered (many arranged by Fletcher Henderson) than to dance, and this marked the beginning of a greater interest by white audiences in the music for its own sake.

Parker, Charlie (1920–1955). In his recordings from 1940, Parker shows himself to have been at the time still in the swing tradition, even though his sound on alto saxophone was already sui generis. Parker's fluent command of his horn, his seemingly endless flow of fresh ideas, and his fluid swing all made him the unsurpassed technical and intellectual master of the period, even before he became the nonpareil bebop artist of the mid to late 1940s. Starting from Lester Young's 1936 revolutionary recording of "Oh! Lady Be Good," Parker indicated with his own 1940 version of the Gershwin song a further development of Young's relaxed swing, melodic invention, harmonic structure, and rhythmic complexity.

Redman, Don (1900–1964). Credited with the creation almost single-handedly of the orchestral format for the big band with its sectional responses to one another, Redman emphasized the mobility of the reeds in arrangements based on pop songs of the day. His work with the Fletcher Henderson Orchestra before 1927 and his years as director of McKinney's Cotton Pickers from 1927 to 1929 set the pattern for most big bands of the Swing Era. Recordings by the Cotton Pickers from 1930 onward are not so interesting as they were prior to the thirties.

Roseland Ballroom. This Manhattan venue for whites only was originally the home of the Fletcher Henderson Orchestra when it achieved its status as the top band in the East. Other groups would perform here as well, but it was primarily identified with the early success of the Henderson organization.

Rushing, Jimmy (1903–1972). A blues singer with the Count Basie Orchestra, Rushing was the most important big-band blues shouter of the period. In his rich, expressive voice, he would belt out the lyrics above the swinging Basie band with authority and passion. Among his more famous vocals is the 1938 "Sent for You Yesterday and Here You Come Today." His singing of the 1941 "Harvard Blues" is a blues in a class all its own.

Russell, Luis (1902–1963). A pianist-leader, Russell had one of the more swinging outfits during the early 1930s. But when Russell and his unit fell on hard times financially, they took on the role of back-up orchestra for star trumpeter-singer Louis Armstrong. The Russell Orchestra's early recordings from 1930 to 1934 are impressive as examples of the evolution of swing from a New Orleans combo style to that of a full-blown orchestra with dynamic soloists, such as trombonist Dickie Wells and cornetist Rex Stewart. Although serving in a secondary role behind Armstrong, the Russell group still managed to contribute outstanding solo and ensemble performances, as on the 1936 "I Come from a Musical Family," where Pops Foster's string bass and Paul Barbarin's drums are featured briefly, and on the 1938 "I Double Dare You," where trombonist J.C. Higginbotham takes one of his always intensely driving breaks.

Sampson, Edgar (1907–1973). Saxophonist and composer-arranger with the Fletcher Henderson and Chick Webb orchestras, Sampson contributed two of the Swing Era's best-known compositions, "Blue Lou" and "Don't Be That Way," the latter made most famous by Benny Goodman's performance of the piece at the 1938 Carnegie Hall Concert. As an altoist, Sampson could be quite an effective soloist, taking fine breaks in 1934 with the Webb Orchestra on another pair of his outstanding compositions, "When Dreams Come True" and "Let's Get Together."

Sauter, Eddie (1914–1981). As an arranger-composer for Red Norvo and Benny Goodman, Sauter introduced harmonically complex compositions, represented by his 1937 dissonant arrangement of "Smoke Dreams" for Norvo and his 1941 "Clarinet à la King," a concerto for Goodman with a blend of classical quotations and progressive chords and voicings.

Savoy Ballroom. Known as the "Home of Happy Feet," the Harlem Savoy was the scene of a number of highly publicized battles of bands, involving Chick Webb's resident orchestra. Each night there were two bands, one taking over from the other by playing the same song that the first had just finished performing. Some of the most popular black dance styles of the day, such as the Lindy Hop (named after Charles Lindbergh), were made famous at this integrated venue. Another ballroom of the same name was operated in Chicago but did not contribute to the Swing Era so significantly as did the New York version. After playing at the segregated Roseland, the Fletcher Henderson Orchestra would move over later in the evening to the Savoy, pleasing the dance-crazy crowd by opening up with King Oliver's "Sugar Foot Stomp."

Sedric, Gene "Honey Bear" (1907–1963). A clarinetist-tenorist with Fats Waller and His Rhythm, Sedric fit well into Waller's light-hearted style of small-group jazz. His fun tenor rocks on "Swingin' Them Jingle Bells" from 1936 and from the same year his clarinet mimics Waller's mocking of the lyrics to "Who's Afraid of Love?"

Shaw, Artie (b. 1910). Technically one of the most accomplished of the many clarinetists in jazz history, Shaw rarely used his facility on the instrument in the service of great jazz, and his orchestras generally lacked the depth of artistry that the black bands exhibited. Nonetheless, Shaw scored many successes as a soloist and bandleader, especially with his "Begin the Beguine." An experimentalist throughout his career, Shaw was an eclectic player who in many ways resisted being limited to the jazz field, and in many ways resented what he considered his doting public's ignorance of the music they loved to hear him play.

Sinatra, Frank (1915–1998). A vocalist with the Harry James and Tommy Dorsey orchestras, Sinatra achieved prominence as a singer through his rich, smooth voice and the naturalness of his delivery. Neither Sinatra nor Billie Holiday was an improvising (or at least scatting) singer, but both brought a special feeling to the lyrics and music of any song they sang. Sinatra began with James and gained valuable experience with a big band, and then under the tutelage of Tommy Dorsey, the singer, according to his own testimony, learned breath control from observing the trombonist performing on his horn the softest of passages. Sinatra's 1939 vocal on "It's Funny to Everyone but Me," with the James Orchestra, shows off well and early on the singer's very impressive talents that would endure for over fifty years.

Smith, Willie (1910–1967). An altoist with the Jimmie Lunceford Orchestra, Smith ably led and apparently disciplined the unit's reed section, soloed effectively, sang in the group's popular trio, and created some outstanding arrangements, among them his 1934 versions of "Rose Room" and of Ellington's "Mood Indigo" and "Sophisticated Lady."

Stacy, Jess (1904–1994). A pianist with the Benny Goodman Orchestra as early as 1935, Stacy was a big hit at the 1938 Carnegie Hall Concert when he soloed on "Sing, Sing, Sing." From 1939, Stacy was with the Bob Crosby Orchestra, which featured him on the 1939 "Complainin'."

Stark, Bobby (1906–1945). One of the many lesser known but highly impressive swing trumpeters, Stark was a vital member of the Fletcher Henderson Orchestra during the early 1930s. He can be heard on the important 1932 version of "New King Porter Stomp," but even earlier on the 1930 "Keep a Song in Your Soul," where the trumpeter sounds, according to Gunther Schuller, as Dizzy Gillespie would a full decade later (*Early Jazz*, p. 274). Stark's work with the Chick Webb Orchestra of the mid to late '30s includes outstanding breaks on "That Rhythm Man" from 1934 and "Spinnin' the Webb" and "Liza" from 1938.

Stewart, Rex (1907–1967). A cornetist with the Fletcher Henderson and Duke Ellington orchestras, Stewart created a readily identifiable style with his pixieish dartings and his half-valve effects. He can be heard on Henderson's 1931 recording of "Sugar Foot Stomp" and his important "New King Porter Stomp" of 1932. While with Ellington, Stewart soloed on the 1935 "Merry-Go-Round" and was featured on the 1938 "Boy Meets Horn," a concerto written by the Duke especially for the cornetist. Stewart also recorded on a number of small-group sessions with members of the Ellington unit. Just as Gunther Schuller found trumpeter Bobby Stark something of a predecessor of Dizzy Gillespie, so, too, the critic has suggested that "Dizzy's clownish trumpet humor may not have been entirely unaware of similar traits in Stewart" (*The Swing Era*, p. 103 n.33).

Strayhorn, Billy (1915–1967). A composer-arranger who, beginning in 1939, collaborated with Duke Ellington, Strayhorn was the composer of one of the Ellington Orchestra's greatest hits, the 1941 "Take the 'A' Train," which served as the group's theme song. He also composed the classic song, "Lush Life."

Tatum, Art (1910–1956). This premier pianist made his first solo recordings in 1932 and gained an international reputation by the mid thirties with his work at the Onyx Club on 52nd Street. A pianist's pianist and for many the greatest of all jazz pianists, Tatum was primarily a soloist whose improvisational genius was best expressed when he was free to "change tempo, key or rhythm without thought for any accompanist" (David Fleming, notes to *The Art of Tatum* [Living Era, AJA 5164, 1995], which includes twenty-five solo performances, twenty-four made between 1932 ["Tiger Rag"] and 1940 ["Humoresque" and ten other sides, among them another version of "Tiger Rag"]). Three examples of Tatum's shifting tempi are found on his 1934 recordings of his own composition, "The Shout," and of George Gershwin's "Liza," and his 1937 rendition of "Gone with the Wind." As David Fleming also points out, by way of a quote from Billy Taylor, Tatum was " 'a whole band complete in himself,' " which is true in particular of his version of "Liza." Because the pianist did not appear with the big bands (perhaps owing in part to the fact that he was 85 percent blind) and only rarely with small groups (until he formed a Trio in 1943), he is not discussed in the main body of this text. Gunther Schuller devotes over twenty-five pages to Tatum in his *The Swing Era*, while observing from the first that "in a large measure Tatum's art and his career developed parallel to but not really as a part of the jazz mainstream, whether in the thirties during the Swing Era or in later years when bop and modern jazz had evolved as the prevailing styles" (p. 477). Tatum's piano styles could range from a stride of the Fats Waller variety to a type of classics-jazz (as in his 1940 treatments of Massenet's *Elegie* and Dvorak's *Humoresque*), as well as to what Schuller considers, in the case of the soloist's 1933 version of Duke Ellington's "Sophisticated Lady," "extravagant chromaticisms and chord substitutions" that "overembroider Ellington's melody with so many high-register besequined runs and double-time intrusions that Ellington's suavely elegant lady becomes a garrulous overdressed flapper" (p. 483). Schuller's charge may be true as well of Tatum's 1934 version of Hoagy Carmichael's "Stardust," yet in both cases one remains astounded by the pianist's matchless technique and what is undeniably a special kind of musicality all his own that is both impressive technically and appealing on the level either of lively or touching swing.

Teagarden, Charlie (1913–1984). A trumpeter with the Paul Whiteman Orchestra, Charlie was overshadowed by his trombonist brother Jack, but the younger Teagarden was a fine soloist in his own right. He played in various aggregations headed up by his brother between 1931 and 1933, and can be heard soloing to good effect on "Farewell Blues" of 1931 (with the Eddie Lang–Joe Venuti All-Star Orchestra) and of 1935 (muted with the Paul Whiteman Orchestra).

Teagarden, Jack, (1905–1964). Probably the most famous trombonist in jazz, Teagarden was a force to be reckoned with in having revolutionized the playing of his horn in much the same way that Armstrong had changed the trumpet and subsequently all jazz instruments by placing the emphasis on solos rather than on ensembles. However, Teagarden was not primarily an ensemble musician, which makes one wonder all the more why he condemned himself to a five-year contract with the Paul Whiteman Orchestra beginning in 1934. As a bandleader, Teagarden was not particularly a success, and again this may have been because he was so solo-oriented. Some of his finest moments come with small groups, including the 1933 session with Billie Holiday, when Teagarden romps magnificently on "My Mother's Son-in-Law" and "Riffin' the Scotch." Teagarden also was effective as one of the finest white jazz singers of the Swing Era, especially on his 1931 recordings of "Basin Street Blues" and "Beale Street Blues" and his 1933 recording of "I Gotta Right to Sing the Blues."

Thomas, Joe (1909–1986). A tenorist with the Jimmie Lunceford Orchestra from 1933 to the death of the leader in 1947, Thomas seems to have been an influence on several other tenorists of the period. Although not particularly an inventive improviser, Thomas created original solos by virtue of his robust sound that he infused with a driving swing, even when he played a limited number of notes. Some of his representative outings can be heard on Lunceford recordings of "Stomp It Off," "Charmaine," "I'm Nuts about Screwy Music," "Annie Laurie," "Well All Right Then," and "Bugs Parade." Thomas also sang at times, as on the 1935 "He Ain't Got Rhythm," where he takes as well a fine tenor break.

Tizol, Juan (1900–1984). A valve trombonist with the Duke Ellington Orchestra, Tizol not only added a Latin tinge to the group's exotic palette but contributed a number of memorable compositions, including the timeless "Caravan" of 1937 and "Pyramid" of 1938 (his famous "Perdido" dating from 1942).

Trumbauer, Frankie (1900–1956). A C-melody saxophonist, Trumbauer made his permanent mark in jazz through his 1927 recordings of "I'm Comin' Virginia" and "Singin' the Blues" with cornetist Bix Beiderbecke. In the 1930s, Tram, as he was called, recorded extensively as a member of the Paul Whiteman Orchestra, including sides that featured the Three T's (Trumbauer and the two Teagarden brothers). Trumbauer's influence on Lester Young was acknowledged by the tenorist, who emulated the older man's ability to "tell a story" with his sax and to create a more naturally flowing line. Little that Trumbauer recorded during the thirties can in any way compare with his work from 1927.

Waller, Thomas "Fats" (1904–1943). A pianist, singer, composer, and combo leader, Waller was a masterful musician who seemed to toss off flawless runs effortlessly as he created in the stride manner a joyful, uplifting sound and rhythm. He was criticized after his death for having made his art subservient to his comedy, but as André Hodeir points out in *Jazz: Its Evolution and Essence*, Waller's jazz remains fresh when that of so many other musicians became afflicted with "sclerosis" (p. 175). Waller's recordings with His Rhythm offer an irrepressible sense of joie de vivre, even when the pianist-singer is obviously playing around with many of the pop song lyrics he parodies and mocks with his running vocal and pianistic commentary. His sidemen add immensely to the fun *and* musicality of a Waller performance, as is apparent on pieces such as the 1934 "Dream Man (Make Me Dream Some More)" and the 1936 "Christopher Columbus." "Honeysuckle Rose," one of over 300 songs composed by Waller (including "Ain't Misbehavin' "), was recorded by most every major figure from Fletcher Henderson (1932) and Count Basie (1937) to Charlie Parker (1940).

Webb, Chick (1907–1939). The complete drummer and a profound influence on all other jazz percussionists, Webb powered his band into a prominent position as the regular attraction at the Savoy Ballroom, where in 1937 he defeated the Goodman orchestra in one of the highly publicized battles of the Swing Era. With Ella Fitzgerald as his young vocalist, Webb reached new heights of popularity shortly before his early death of spinal tuberculosis.

Webster, Ben (1909–1973). The recording career of this major tenor star spanned most of the decade, beginning in 1932 with the classic sides cut by the Bennie Moten band and climaxing with Webster's solos on such tunes as "Cotton Tail" and "Just A-Settin' and A-Rockin' " with the Duke Ellington orchestra of 1940 and 1941. Related to the rhapsodic style of Coleman Hawkins, Webster's playing is distinguished from his colleague's by a warmer, more relaxed, lyrical approach that makes his sound and phrasing in some ways even more rhapsodic than the master's.

Wells, Dickie (1909–1985). One of the most distinctive trombonists of the Swing Era, Wells recorded with the Benny Carter, Horace Henderson, and Fletcher Henderson orchestras in 1933 and was with the Teddy Hill Orchestra from 1934 to 1937 before joining the Count Basie Orchestra in 1938, both as a strikingly original soloist and as an obbligatist to the vocals of Jimmy Rushing. André Hodeir has written the most enthusiastic treatment of Wells's artistry in *Jazz: Its Evolution and Essence*, calling his tone and style "majesty personified" (p. 67). "Dickie's Dream," recorded in 1939 by a Basie septet, contains a characteristic solo by Wells, as does the Basie big-band version of "Texas Shuffle" of 1938. His obbligato behind Rushing on the 1941 "Harvard Blues" is magisterial.

Whiteman, Paul (1890–1967). Although much of Whiteman's music has been relegated to the category of a businessman's bounce or considered an early instance of the Third Stream hybrid mixture of a symphonic style with jazz interpolations, the Whiteman formula was looked upon by many big bands of the Swing Era as a hopeful sign that jazz could achieve a broader appeal and greater financial rewards. Although such a hybrid formula was not adopted wholesale, there was a definite Whiteman influence to be heard in the work of Lunceford and even Ellington. Whiteman did employ such legitimate jazz masters as Bix Beiderbecke and Jack Teagarden and supported them out of a spirit of respect and generosity.

Williams, Cootie (1910–1985). Known primarily for his work with the Ellington Orchestra, Williams carried on the growl tradition established in the 1920s by Bubber Miley, putting his own stamp on this early technique. He is featured most famously on Ellington's 1940 "Concerto for Cootie," whose theme is better known as the Ellington tune titled "Do Nothing 'Till You Hear from Me." French critic André Hodeir has declared this work "a masterpiece" (*Jazz: Its Evolution and Essence*, p. 77). Williams also made significant sides with the Benny Goodman sextet, especially an impromptu jam with Charlie Christian on "Waitin' for Benny" from 1941.

Williams, Mary Lou (1910–1981). A pianist-composer-arranger with the Andy Kirk Orchestra, Williams was responsible to a large extent for the more jazz-inflected sides recorded by the Kirk organization. As a soloist, she was dependably solid and could swing after the stride manner of an Earl Hines and a Count Basie. Her style had its roots primarily in ragtime and boogie woogie but was an updated, swing-era version. One of her compositions in the boogie mode, "Roll 'Em," was written especially for the Benny Goodman Orchestra. Her late boogie-woogie work for the Kirk Orchestra can be heard in the 1941 recordings of "47th Street Jive" and "Big Time Crip." Gunther Schuller has characterized Williams as an "advanced conservative," and this was true both of her work during the 1930s and of her later career during the Bebop period (*The Swing Era*, p. 360).

Wilson, Dick (1911–1941). A tenorist with the Andy Kirk Orchestra, Wilson was certainly the star soloist of the unit, along with pianist-composer-arranger Mary Lou Williams. Wilson has been rated along with Chu Berry and Ben Webster as on the second tier among the finest tenorists of the Swing Era. His style has been considered something of a cross between the rhapsodic manner of Coleman Hawkins and the more sensuous lines of Lester Young. He was featured on Kirk's 1936 version of "Lotta Sax Appeal" and can be heard to fine effect on "Corky," also from 1936, "In the Groove" from 1937, and "Big Time Crip" from 1941.

Wilson, Teddy (1912–1986). One of the most distinctive piano stylists of the Swing Era, Wilson was prominent as a member of the Benny Goodman Trio and as the leader of small-group sessions with vocalist Billie Holiday. Classically trained, Wilson brought a new sophistication to jazz piano, at the same time that he maintained an easy swing with his technically polished embellishments. His piano work on the Holiday version of "What a Little Moonlight Can Do" from 1935 illustrates his flawless technique and his steady swing.

Young, Lester "Pres" (1909–1959). Along with Coleman Hawkins, Young was the most important tenor saxophonist of the Swing Era; however, his playing differed totally from the Hawk's. A self-confessed admirer of the vibrato-less, flowing, storytelling style of Frankie Trumbauer on his C-melody sax, Young adapted this approach to the tenor, adding to it a slightly behind-the-beat phrasing that gave his solos a paradoxically relaxed yet yearningly forward drive. Young's impact on the next generation of tenor players was greater than that of Hawkins. Just as Louis Armstrong had earlier influenced jazz musicians on every instrument, Young also had an effect on almost every player to follow him. His seminal recordings were made with small groups, but his fame came first from his solos with the Basie big band, especially on such tunes as the 1938 "Every Tub" and the 1939 "Clap Hands, Here Comes Charlie." Young's work with Billie Holiday also set him apart as the most sensitive accompanist since Armstrong had recorded with Bessie Smith in the 1920s.

Young, Trummy (1912–1984). A trombonist with the Jimmie Lunceford Orchestra, Young joined the group late in the decade but made an immediate impact with his high-note technique and his fetching vocal style with something of a comedic touch. Featured especially on the 1938 recording of "Margie," where Young reaches for a high F# at the end of his solo, the trombonist proved to be the orchestra's most virtuosic instrumentalist.

Zurke, Bob (1912–1944). A pianist with the Bob Crosby Orchestra, Zurke recorded in 1937 a hit side with the Crosby group when he replaced pianist Joe Sullivan (1906–1971) on the latter's composition, "Little Rock Getaway." Sullivan returned to the Crosby Orchestra in 1938, and thereafter Zurke led his own big band from 1939 to 1940. Although considered an artistic success, Zurke and His Delta Rhythm Band did not enjoy a popular following, and from then on Zurke worked as a solo act until his premature death at thirty-two.

♪

Selected Bibliography

Allen, Walter C. *Hendersonia: The Music of Fletcher Henderson and His Musicians: A Bio-Discography*. Highland Park, N.J.: n.p., 1973.

Armstrong, Louis. *Swing That Music*. London: Longmans, Green, 1936; rpt. Da Capo Press, 1993.

Baker, David N., ed. *New Perspectives on Jazz*. Washington, D.C.: Smithsonian Institution Press, 1990.

Baraka, Amiri (pseudonym of LeRoi Jones). *Blues People*. New York: William Morrow, 1963.

Barnet, Charlie. *Those Swinging Years: The Autobiography of Charlie Barnet with Stanley Dance*. Baton Rouge: Louisiana State University Press, ca. 1984.

Berger, Morroe, Edward Berger, and James Patrick. *Benny Carter: A Life in American Music*. Metuchen, N.J.: Scarecrow Press and the Institute of Jazz Studies, Rutgers University, 1982.

Boyd, Jean A. *The Jazz of the Southwest: An Oral History of Western Swing*. Austin: University of Texas Press, 1998.

Chilton, John. *The Song of the Hawk: The Life and Recordings of Coleman Hawkins*. Ann Arbor: University of Michigan Press, 1990.

Collier, James Lincoln. *Jazz*. New York: Oxford University Press, 1993.

———. *The Making of Jazz: A Comprehensive History*. New York: Houghton Mifflin, 1978; rpt. Delta, 1979.

Dance, Stanley. *The World of Earl Hines*. New York: Scribner, 1977; rpt. Da Capo, 1983.

Erenberg, Lewis A. *Swingin' the Dream: Big Band Jazz and the Rebirth of American Culture*. Chicago: University of Chicago Press, 1998.

Feather, Leonard. *The New Edition of the Encyclopedia of Jazz*. New York: Bonanza Books, 1960 and 1962.

Giddins, Gary. *Visions of Jazz: The First Century*. New York: Oxford University Press, 1998.

Ginell, Cary. *Milton Brown and the Founding of Western Swing*. Urbana: University of Illinois Press, 1994.

Gioia, Ted. *The History of Jazz*. New York: Oxford University Press, 1997.

Gitler, Ira. *Swing to Bop*. New York: Oxford University Press, 1995.

Gottlieb, Robert, ed. *Reading Jazz: A Gathering of Autobiography, Reportage, and Criticism from 1919 to Now*. New York: Pantheon Books, 1996.

Gridley, Mark C. *Jazz Styles: History and Analysis*. 2nd ed. Englewood Cliffs, N.J.: Prentice-Hall, Inc., 1985.

Harrison, Max, Charles Fox, and Eric Thacker. *The Essential Jazz Records, Vol. 1 Ragtime to Swing*. London: Mansell Publishing Ltd., 1984; rpt. Da Capo Press, 1988.

Hennessey, Thomas J. *From Jazz to Swing: African-American Jazz Musicians and Their Music, 1890–1935*. Detroit: Wayne State University Press, 1994.

Hentoff, Nat, and Albert J. McCarthy, eds. *Jazz: New Perspectives on the History of Jazz by Twelve of the World's Foremost Jazz Critics and Scholars*. New York: Holt, Rinehart & Winston, 1959; rpt. Da Capo Press, 1975.

Hodeir, André. *Jazz: Its Evolution and Essence*. Translated by David Noakes. New York: Grove Press, 1956.

Kirk, Andy, as told to Amy Lee. *Twenty Years on Wheels*. Ann Arbor: University of Michigan Press, 1989.

Korall, Burt. *Drummin' Men: The Heartbeat of Jazz*. New York: Schirmer Books, 1990.

Lord, Tom. *The Jazz Discography*. Vancouver, B.C., Canada: Tom Lord Reference Inc., 1992.

McCarthy, Albert J. *Big Band Jazz*. London: Barrie & Jenkins, 1974.

Mellers, Wilfrid. *Music in a New Found Land: Themes and Developments in the History of American Music*. New York: Alfred A. Knopf, 1965; rpt. Oxford University Press, 1987.

Meltzer, David, ed. *Reading Jazz*. San Francisco, Calif.: Mercury House, 1993.

Murray, Albert. *Stomping the Blues*. New York: Da Capo Press, 1987; rpt. of 1976 publication.

Oliphant, Dave. *Texan Jazz*. Austin: University of Texas Press, 1996.

Owens, Thomas. *Bebop: The Music and Its Players*. New York: Oxford University Press, 1995.

Porter, Lewis, ed. *A Lester Young Reader*. Washington: Smithsonian Institution Press, 1991.

Russell, Ross. *Jazz Style in Kansas City and the Southwest*. Berkeley: University of California Press, 1973.

Rust, Brian. *Jazz Records 1897–1942*. 2 Vols. Chigwell, England: Storyville Publications, 1975.

Schuller, Gunther. *Early Jazz: Its Roots and Musical Development*. New York: Oxford University Press, 1968.

———. *The Swing Era*. New York: Oxford University Press, 1986.

Simon, George T. *The Big Bands*. 4th ed. Garden City, N.Y.: Doubleday, 1981.

Stearns, Marshall W. *The Story of Jazz*. New York: Oxford University Press, 1970.

Stowe, David W. *Swing Changes: Big-Band Jazz in New Deal America*. Cambridge: Harvard University Press, 1994.

Sudhalter, Richard M. *Lost Chords: White Musicians and Their Contribution to Jazz, 1915–1945*. New York: Oxford University Press, 1999.

Tucker, Mark, ed. *The Duke Ellington Reader*. New York: Oxford University Press, 1993.

Williams, Martin. *The Jazz Tradition*. New York: Oxford University Press, 1983.

Williams, Martin T., ed. *The Art of Jazz*. New York: Grove Press, 1960.
Whiteman, Paul, and Mary Margaret McBride. *Jazz*. New York: J.H. Sears & Company, 1926.
Yanow, Scott. *Swing*. San Francisco: Miller Freeman Books, 2000.

Index

"Ach Du Lieber Augustine," 265
"Ad Lib Blues," 355
"After Hours," 224
"After You," 377
"After You've Gone," 211, 333, 338
"Ain't Cha Glad," 334
"Ain't Got a Gal in This Town," 182
"Ain't Misbehavin,'" 149, 229, 260n.311, 260n.313, 356, 405, 424
"Ain't She Sweet," 87
"Ain'tcha Comin' Home," 212
"Air in D Flat," 240
"Air Mail Special," 77, 417
"Air Mail Stomp," 293–94, 296
Alabamians, 177
Albert, Don, 39, 260n.303
Albertson, Chris, 418
"Alexander's Ragtime Band," 273
"Alibi Baby," 376
"Alice Blue Gown," 197
"All God's Chillun Got Rhythm," vii, 66–69, 71, 94n.95, 397, 413
"All God's Chillun Got Wings," 360
"The All-Night Record Man," 298
"All of Me, 118, 121, 150, 245, 268–69
"All or Nothing at All," 311
"All the Jive Is Gone," 199
"All Too Soon," 77–78
"All You Want To Do Is Dance," 377
Allen, Celeste, 227, 229–30

Allen, Charlie, 171
Allen, Henry "Red," 12, 43, 50–51, 91n.35, 156–59, 239–40, 278, 397
Allen, Moses, 80, 87
Allen, Walter, 19, 91n.29, 92n.61
"Alreet," 306
Alston, Ovie, 12, 413
"Altitude," 216
Alvis, Hayes, 74, 168, 215, 244–45, 382–83
"Am I Blue?," 365–66
"Amapola," 123
"Among My Souvenirs," 244
Anderson, Buddy, 248
Anderson, Charles, 227–31, 259n.298, 259–60n.303
Anderson, Ivie, xiii, 66, 68, 72–73, 94n.95, 120, 230, 314, 397
Andy Iona and His Islanders, 154
"Angeline," 183
"Angry," 173–74, 228
"Annie Laurie," 86–87, 221, 423
"Announcer's Blues," 273
"Answer Man," 313
"Any Old Time," 126
"Any Time at All," 211
Apollo Theatre, 40, 79, 297, 397
"Arabesque," 239
Archey, Jimmy, 150, 153, 159–60, 244
"Are You in Love with Me Again?," 187–89

Arlen, Harold, 122, 188
Armstrong, Louis, 2–3, 5–8, 12, 15–
    18, 21–22, 25, 40–41, 44–45, 47–
    48, 55, 60, 81, 106, 118–19, 124,
    129, 131, 134, 143n.71, 147–58,
    160, 162–63, 167, 174, 176, 183,
    186, 191, 209, 232, 234–35, 237,
    242, 249–50n.2, 268–69, 271, 282,
    284–85, 289–90, 296, 310, 325–27,
    331–32, 336–37, 339, 373, 397–98,
    403, 407–9, 412–14, 418–19, 423,
    426
Arodin, Sidney, 124
Ashby, Irving, 216
"A-Tisket, A-Tasket," 166, 407
"At Last," 135
"At Sundown," 127, 368
"At the Clambake Carnival," 192
"At the Codfish Ball," 376
"At the Darktown Strutters' Ball," 160
"At the Milkman's Matinee," 376
"At Your Beck and Call," 235
Auld, Georgie, 127–29, 234, 282–86,
    341–42, 398
"Aunt Hagar's Blues," 273
Austin High Gang, 14
Autry, Herman, 356–58, 360, 398
Avakian, Al, 342
Avakian, George, 76, 150, 152
"Avalon," 84, 186, 279, 310, 341,
    365
"Aw You Dawg," 182, 186
"Awful Sad," 69
"Azure," 192, 194, 286

"Babalu," 246
"Baby, Don't Tell on Me," 60
"Baby, Look at You," 389
"Baby Won't You Please Come
    Home," 87, 187–88, 211
Bach, J.S., 161, 378
"Back Bay Boogie," 246
"Back Bay Shuffle," 126
"Back Beat Boogie," 311
"Back in Your Own Backyard," 46,
    53, 347
"The Back Room Romp (A
    Contrapuntal Stomp)," 382

Bacon, Louis, 153, 162, 180
"Baile en Mi Rancho," 363
Bailey, Buster, 47–48, 51–53, 91n.29,
    210, 278, 284, 346–47, 398
Bailey, Mildred, 7, 13, 111, 268–69,
    271, 274, 316n.22, 325, 337, 370,
    398–99
Baker, Chet, 315
Baker, Harold, 206–8
Ballard, Red, 99
Ballew, Smith, 134
'Bama State Collegians, 217, 224, 226
Bamberger, Rob, 275
Barbarin, Paul, 27, 157–58, 419
Barbour, Dave, 344
Barefield, Eddie, 54–55, 182, 185–87,
    210–11, 275
Bargy, Roy, 9, 316n.22
Barker, Danny, 187, 212
"Barnacle Bill the Sailor," 5–8, 400
Barnet, Charlie, 40, 122, 288, 296–
    303, 371, 387, 397, 399
Barry, Frank, 265
Bascom, Wilbur "Dud," 218–22, 224–
    25, 399
Bascomb, Paul, 222–25, 399, 404
Basie, William "Count," x, 12, 21, 24,
    39–40, 52–66, 79–80, 86, 93n.80,
    100, 105–106, 108, 110, 115, 117,
    123, 126–28, 139, 142n.43, 147–48,
    157, 161–62, 165, 167, 170, 172,
    174, 176–77, 199, 202, 205–6, 208–
    11, 216, 220, 223–24, 226–27, 232–
    33, 237, 242, 245–48, 257n.224,
    276–77, 281, 294, 296, 298–99,
    304, 310–13, 315, 338, 341–42,
    346, 349–56, 380, 387, 399–401,
    403, 405–410, 414, 416–19, 424–26
Basie's Bad Boys, 354
"Basin Street Blues," 100, 134, 151,
    423
Battle, Edgar, 195, 388
"Battle of Swing," 74
Bauduc, Ray, 290–94, 333, 372–73
Bauza, Mario, 163–64
"Beale Street Blues," 333, 423
"Beale Street Mama," 365
"Beale Street Papa," 365

"Bearcat Shuffle," 199

Bechet, Sidney, 73, 155, 298

Beckett, Fred, 216–17

Beethoven, Ludwig van, 161

"Begin the Beguine," xi, 125–26, 128, 132, 420

Beiderbecke, Bix, 5–8, 15, 20–23, 25, 27, 34n.64, 44–45, 56–57, 90n.20, 97–98, 105, 112, 115, 129, 179, 198, 214, 243, 263, 265–70, 274, 286, 288, 296, 312, 316n.22, 318n.79, 319n.88, 330, 334, 349, 369–70, 372, 374–75, 400, 410, 424–25

"Belgium Stomp," 88

Bellerby, Vic, 332

Bellson, Louis, x

Beneke, Tex, 137–40, 272, 400, 415

"Benny Rides Again," 110

"Benny Sent Me," 339

Benson Orchestra, 9

Berger, Morroe, 245

Berigan, Bunny, 7, 13–14, 20–21, 50, 59–60, 65, 99–101, 104, 116–17, 124, 136, 154, 234, 237, 263, 266–67, 270–71, 280–87, 295, 318n.79, 319n.88, 325, 334–35, 345, 370–75, 398, 400, 413

Berlin, Irving, vii, xiiin.2, 29–30, 102, 107, 135, 283, 359, 378, 395n.118

Bernstein, Artie, 213–14, 330, 334, 340, 370–71

Berry, Chu, 49, 51–52, 66, 100, 189–92, 194–95, 198–200, 206, 212–13, 220–21, 223–24, 231, 238–40, 256n.181, 311, 344, 370–71, 397, 399–400, 402–3, 412, 426

Berry, Emmett, 52–53, 66

Berry, Leroy, 54, 56

"Bésame Mucho," 123

Best, Clifton "Skeeter," 221

Bestor, Don, 9

"Better Luck Next Time," 201

"Between the Devil and the Deep Blue Sea," 149, 182, 296, 398

"Bie Mir Bist Du Schon," 107

"The Big Apple," 377

"The Big Eight Blues," 336

"Big Jim Blues," 205

"Big John's Special," 106, 224, 411

"Big Noise from Winnetka," 294, 410

"Big Time Crip," 208, 426

Bigard, Barney, xii, 67, 69, 71, 190, 278, 284, 295, 326, 335–36, 382, 401

"Bird of Paradise," 81

"Birth of the Blues," 267

Bishop, Wallace, 169, 172–75

Black, Lou, 271

"Black and Tan Fantasy," xii, 81

Black and Tan Fantasy (film), 93n.95

"Black and White Rag," 364–65

Black Bottom Club, 162

"Black Bottom Stomp," 26

"Black, Brown, and Beige," 71

"Black Rhythm," 179, 181

"Blackout," 224

Blake, Jerry, 53, 66, 194

Bland, Jack, 326

Blanton, Jimmy, 69–71, 76–77, 103, 381, 384, 401

Blower, Johnny, 285

Blue, William Thornton, 187

"Blue," 172, 174

"Blue and Sentimental," 62, 405, 407

Blue Devils, 54, 56, 58, 61, 232, 248

"Blue Drag," 169–70

"Blue Illusion," 200

"Blue Lou," 26, 29, 51–52, 164, 231, 241, 403, 420

"Blue Minor," 164

"Blue Reverie," 106, 381

"Blue Room," 55, 107–8

"Blue Sea," 225

"Blue Skies," xiiin.2, 107

"Blues," 130, 284, 372, 375

"Blues in B," 342

"Blues in E Flat," 371

"Blues in My Heart," 162, 179–80, 416

"Blues of Avalon," 228

"B-19," 314

Bob Crosby Orchestra and His Bobcats, 115, 124, 287–96, 305, 378, 404, 410, 415, 421, 427

"Body and Soul," 46, 58, 107, 129, 248, 268, 329, 331, 338, 385, 415
"Bogo Jo," 216
"Bojangles," 71
Bolden, Buddy, 367
Bone, Red, 266
"Boog It," 195
"Boogie Woogie," x, 115, 349
"Boogie Woogie (I May Be Wrong)," 115
"Boogie Woogie Bugle Boy," 306
"Boogie Woogie Maxixe," 292
"Boogie Woogie on St. Louis Blues," 168
"Boogie Woogie Sugar Blues," 245
"The Booglie Wooglie Piggy," 140
Boone, Lester, 168
Boots and His Buddies, 226–27, 229, 231–32, 260n.311, 405
"Boots Stomp," 231
"Boo-Wah-Boo-Wah," 194
Bordewijk, Ferdinand, 82
Borowski, Johnny, 366
Bose, Sterling, 290
Boston Symphony, 196
"Boulder Buff," 139, 415
"Bouncin' with Bean," 331
"Bouncing at the Beacon," 216
Bowers, Ben, 235
Bowles, Russell, 81–82, 270
Bowman, Dave, 369
Bowman, Euday L., 34n.62
"Boy Meets Goy," 341
"Boy Meets Horn," 421
Boyd, Jean A., 361, 364, 366
"Braggin' in Brass," 75
Brahms, Johannes, 111
Braud, Wellman, 68, 70, 73, 172, 401
"Breakfast Feud," 342
"Breeze (Blow My Baby Back to Me)," 202
Bridge, The (poem), 151
Briglia, Tony, 25, 184, 277, 279
"Bring It on Down," 366
"Broadway Rhythm," 27
Brooks, Alva, 228–29, 231, 260n.311
Broonzy, Big Bill, 365
Brower, Cecil, 362–65

Brown, Andrew, 179, 195
Brown, Derwood, 17, 362–64, 366, 394n.97
Brown, Lawrence, 67–69, 71, 75, 77, 103, 207, 210, 212, 240, 278, 383–84, 386, 401
Brown, Les, 25, 51
Brown, Milton, 17, 179, 353, 361–67
Brown, Steve, 271
Brown, Treg, 332
Brown, Vernon, 106, 109
"Brownie Special," 364
"Brownie's Stomp," 362
Bruner, Cliff, 365
Brunies, George, 228, 367
Bryant, Clora, 259n.280
"Bubbling Over," 171, 174
Buchanan, Buck, 366
Buckner, Milt, 216–17
Buckner, Ted, 87–88
Bughouse "Bughouse," 371
"Bugle Blues," 191
"Bugle Call Rag," 101 181, 239
"Bugs Parade," 88–89, 423
Bullock, Chris, 157, 159, 183,
"Bumble Bee Stomp," 109
Bunn, Teddy, 215
Burke, Edward, 176
Burness, Les, 127
Burnet, Bobby, 299–301
Burroughs, Alvin, 175–77, 392n.41
Bush, Percy, 231
Bushell, Garvin, 187, 189–91
Bushkin, Joe, 345, 373
"But Definitely," 374
"But It Didn't Mean a Thing," 202, 204
"But Not for Me," 314, 407
Butterfield, Billy, 129, 131, 295, 378–80
Buzzard "The Buzzard," 368
"Buzzin' Around with the Bee," 210
"By the Watermelon Vine," 245
Byas, Don, 204–5, 401
"Bye Bye Blues," 192, 194–95
Byrne, Bobby, 119–21

Caceres, Ernie, 137, 335

Cahn, Sammy, 82, 200–201

"Cain and Abel," 155

Calhoun, Fred "Papa," 362–66

"California Here I Come," 413

"Call Me Happy," 176–77

"The Call of the Freaks," 158

"Calling All Bars," 194

Calloway, Blanche, 197–98

Calloway, Cab, 9, 39, 47–49, 78, 81, 147, 177–95, 206, 209, 212, 223, 256n.181, 344, 363, 400, 402–3, 408, 412, 414, 416

Camarata, Toots, 119–21

"Camp Meeting Blues," 50

Campbell, Muryel "Zeke," 361

"Candlelights," 319n.88

"Can't Help Lovin' That Man," 283–84

"Can't We Be Friends," 104

Cara, Mancy, 168

"Caravan," 67, 75, 382, 410, 423

"Careless Love," 231

Carey, Scoops, 387–89, 396n.142, 396n.144

"The Carioca," 128

Carlisle, Una Mae, 355

Carmichael, Hoagy, vii, 5–8, 24–25, 165, 188, 191, 271, 275, 305, 308–11, 314–15, 360, 402, 422

Carnegie Hall, 20, 40, 52, 105–8, 164, 338–39, 410, 415, 420–21

Carney, Harry, xi, 67–69, 72–73, 85, 102, 106, 168, 212, 222, 278, 286, 344, 381–84, 386, 402

"Carnival of Venice," 315

Carpenter, Thelma, 329

Carr, Leroy, 227

Carroll, Bob, 301

Carruthers, Earl "Jock," 83–86, 160, 222, 270

"Carry Me Back to Old Virginny," 223

Carter, Benny, 11, 15, 20, 28–29, 41–42, 65, 147, 162, 167, 177, 180, 183, 185, 194–95, 211–14, 232, 237–47, 249, 278, 297, 308, 325, 330, 390, 402–3, 408, 411, 416, 425

Carter, John, 177, 414

Carver, Wayman, 240–41

Casa Loma Orchestra, 7, 22–23, 81, 97, 124, 173, 184, 263, 269, 272, 274–81, 408

"Casa Loma Stomp," 23–26, 170, 173, 184, 276–77, 280, 317n.39, 317n. 46, 408

Casa Mañana, 274

Casey, Al, 213, 356–59, 402

"Casey Jones," 197

"Casey Jones Blues," 197

Catlett, "Big" Sid, 51, 53, 161, 238–39, 403

"Cavernism," 170–71, 174, 417

CBS Saturday Night Swing Club, 281

"Challenger Chop," 304

Challis, Bill, 9, 15, 20, 22, 130, 263

"Changes," 46, 90n.20, 104

"Chantez-les bas," 126

Chaplin, Saul, 200–201

Character (film), 82

"Charleston Alley," 122, 300, 302

"Charmaine," 84–85, 423

"Chasin' with Chase," 216

Chatman, Clifton, 231

"Chattanooga Choo-Choo," 138–40, 195

Chatwell, J.R., 364

Cheatham, Doc, 183–84, 186

"Cheatin' on Me," 87

Check and Double Check (film), 66, 70, 93n.95

"Cherokee," 297–98, 303, 387, 399

"Cherry," 220

"Cherry Red," 389

"Chickasaw Stomp," 78

"Chicken Waffles," 372

Chilton, John, 11, 42, 46, 90n.25, 213–14, 236, 239–40, 258n.268, 327–30

"China Boy," 108, 338, 368

"China Stomp," 210

"Chinatown, My Chinatown," 149, 364

"Chinese Rhythm," 186, 402

"Chips' Boogie Woogie," 292

"Chloe," 103

Chocolate Dandies, 238, 242

"Choo Choo," 67

"Chop, Chop Charlie Chan (From China)," 47–49

Christian, Charlie, 7, 28, 30, 58, 102, 110–11, 194, 212–13, 216, 224, 233, 246, 325, 337, 340–42, 352, 355, 361, 365, 367, 379–81, 387, 398, 403, 405, 410, 416–17, 425

"Christmas Time in Harlem," 273

"Christopher Columbus," 30n.1, 51–52, 99, 101, 171, 190, 199, 359, 386, 398, 400, 403, 409, 412, 424

"Ciribiribin," 309

Clambake Seven, 113, 115, 192, 375–79, 405

"Clap Hands, Here Comes Charlie," 64, 93n.91, 164–65, 299, 414, 426

"Clarinet à la King," 111, 420

"Clarinet Lament," 71, 401

"Clarinet Marmalade," 272

Clark, Dick, 344

Clark, Pete, 163, 165

Clarke, Herbert L., 160

Clarke, Kenny, 175

Clay, Shirley, 168, 333

Clay, Sonny, 196

Clayton, Buck, 57, 59–61, 63, 106, 227, 242, 299, 346–47, 352–55, 403, 406–7

Clinton, Larry, 51

"Close to Five," 204

"Cloudy," 200

Club Alabam, 40

"Cocktails for Two," 245

Coffman, Wanna, 362

Cole, Cozy, 193–95, 210, 212, 344–45, 368, 372–75, 403, 408

Cole, Nat "King," 84, 152, 215, 403–4

Coleman, Bill, 27, 90n.19, 244, 357–58, 375, 404, 412

Coleman, Oliver, 175

Coleman, Ornette, 367

Collier, James Lincoln, 15, 31n.3, 41, 43, 51, 53, 57, 63, 72, 77, 148–50, 154–55, 168, 249n.2, 252n.56, 398

Collins, Booker, 198, 208

Collins, Shad, 244, 306, 353–55

Coltrane, John, 22

"Comanche War Dance," 300

"Come and Get It," 279

"Come on with the 'Come On,'" 193

"Comin' On," 126

"Community Swing," 136

"Complainin'," 294, 421

"Concerto for Clarinet," 131

"Concerto for Cootie," 77–78, 383, 425

Condon, Eddie, 326, 356, 367–69, 410

"Conga Brava," 67, 384

"Congo," 189

Conniff, Ray, 129–30, 285–86, 301

"Contrasts," 118, 121–22

Cook, Will Marion, 5

Cooley, Spade, 366

"Copenhagen," 40, 173–74, 364

"Copper-Colored Gal," 188–89

Coquette "Coquette," 86, 222, 228, 248

Corcoran, Corky, 314

"Corky," 197, 199, 426

"Corky Stomp," 197

Corley, George, 231

Cornelius, Corky, 305

"Cornet Chop Suey," 150

Cotton Club, xi, 40, 66, 79, 178, 183, 404, 416

"Cotton Club Stomp," 85, 96n.164

"Cotton Tail," xii, 74, 77, 223, 410, 416

"Could You Pass in Love?," 21–22, 109

Coulter, Glen, 343, 346

"The Count," 207

"The Count's Idea," 298–99, 399

"Countless Blues," 353

Craig, Al, 242

Crane, Hart, 151

"Crawdad Blues," 91n.49

Crawford, Forrest, 373–75

Crawford, Jimmy, 79–80, 83, 85–88, 404

"The Creeper," 31n.12
Creole Jazz Band, 16–17, 54
"Creole Love Song," 179
"Creole Rhapsody," 71
"Crescendo in Drums," 193
Crosby, Bing, 148, 153, 269–70, 287, 404
Crosby, Israel, 52–53
"Cross Country Jump," 310–11
"Cross Patch," 364, 366
"Cross Your Heart," 379
Crouch, Stanley, 152, 203
Crowder, Robert, 176
Crumbley, Elmer, 84, 88
"Cuban Boogie Woogie," 207, 299
"Cuddle Up, Huddle Up," 246
"Cupid's Nightmare," 194–95, 256n.195

"Dallas Blues," 198
Dance, Stanley, 75, 80, 83, 88, 89n.14, 94n.95, 170–71, 175–76, 206–7, 277, 299, 301–2, 354, 385–86
"Dance of the Octopus," 82, 370–71
"Daniel's Blues," 35n.64
Daniels, Douglas, 215
"Danny Boy," 132, 135
"Darkness," 172
"The Darktown Strutter's Ball," 118, 120, 162, 272, 327, 364–65, 414
"Darling Nelly Gray," 154
Dash, Julian, 218–26, 404
Davenport, "Cow-Cow," 365
"Davenport Blues," 286, 334
Davis, Jimmie, 366
Davis, Leonard, 150
Davis, Miles, 130, 216
Davis, Pat, 24–25, 277, 279, 317n.46
Davis, Sammy, 244
Davis-Coots, 188, 190
"Day Dream," 386
"The Day You Came Along," 328
"Daybreak Express," xii, 71, 401
Daye, Irene, 304, 306–7
De Faut, Volly, 291
De Paris, Wilbur, 238, 246

"Dear Old Southland," 222
"'Deed I Do," 133, 300
"Deep Forest," 174
"Deep Purple," 130, 407
"Deep River," 360
Delacroix, Eugène, 161
"Demi-tasse (Each Day)," 382
DeNaut, Jud, 378
"Denison Swing," 212, 392n.41
Dent, Lafore, 83
"Devil's Holiday," 241
Dexter, Dave, 161, 163
"Dexter Blues," 248–49
Dial, Harry, 356
Dickenson, Vic, 27, 244
Dickerson, R.Q., 178
"Dickie's Dream," 59, 64, 355, 425
"Did I Remember?," 345
"Did You Mean It," 101
"Diga, Diga Doo," 127, 293, 381
"Dinah," 182, 330
"Dippermouth Blues," 2, 16–19, 134, 153, 417
"Disappointed in Love," 174
Dixie and/or Savannah Syncopators, 2
"Dixie Vagabond," 178
"Dixieland Shuffle," 291
Dixon, George, 172, 175–77
Dixon, Joe, 114, 282–86, 375–78
"Dizzy Spells," 108
"Do Nothin' Till You Hear From Me," 78, 406, 425
"Do-Re-Mi," 230
Dodds, Johnny, 18, 155, 178
"Doggin' Around," 63–64, 399
"Dogtown Blues," 290–91, 415
"Doin' the Rhumba," 179
"Doing the Reactionary," 191
"Dolemite," 118, 121–23, 405
"Dolly Mine," 158
"Dolores," 117
Dolphy, Eric, 185
Donahue, Sam, 304–5, 310
Donaldson, Walter, 270
"Donegal Cradle Song," 240
Donnelly, Ted, 199, 208
"Don't Be That Way," 26, 29, 105–6, 118, 120, 164, 211, 420

"Don't Cry, Cherie," 305–6
"Don't Get Around Much Anymore," 76
"Don't Know If I'm Comin' or Goin,'" 189
Dorsey, Jimmy, 6–7, 9, 17, 20, 39, 65, 112, 117–24, 127, 133, 143n.74, 153, 205, 243, 245, 263, 267, 307, 322n.195, 327, 370, 398, 405, 408
Dorsey, Tommy, ix, xi, xiiin.2, 6–7, 16, 22, 25, 39, 65, 73, 88, 102, 112–17, 119, 124, 127, 133, 166, 191–92, 235, 263, 266–67, 270, 274, 281, 285, 287, 290, 307, 311, 331, 367, 370, 375–79, 405, 408, 415, 418, 421
Dorsey Brothers Orchestra, 112, 287
"Dorsey Stomp," 120
"Double Check Stomp," 73
Douglas, Clifford "Boots," 39, 65, 226–32, 259n.303, 405
Dowell, Edgar, 162
"Down by the O-Hi-O," 363
"Down Georgia Way," 327
"Down Home Jump," 212, 392n.41
"Down in Honky Tonk Town," 156
"Down on the Levee," 236
"Down South Camp Meeting," 49–50, 103
"Down Stream," 284
"Downstream," 201
"Downtown Uproar," 381
"Dr. Jeckle and Mr. Jibe," 334
"Dr. Livingston, I Presume?," 380
"Dracula," 304
"Dream," x
"Dream Blues," 384
"Dream Lullaby," 241
"Dream Man (Make Me Dream Some More)," 356–58, 424
"Dream of You," 82, 222, 418
Drelinger, Art, 374–75
Driggs, Frank, 57, 178, 187, 190, 192, 226
"Drum Boogie," 307
"Drum Stomp," 210
Duke, Vernon, 59, 281

"The Duke's Idea," 297–99
"Duke's Mixture," 313
Dulany, Howard, 303, 305, 307–8
Dunham, Sonny, 276, 279
"Dunkin' a Doughnut," 203
Dunn, Bob, 352–53, 361, 363–66
Dunne, Marianne, 335
Dupré, Marcel, 356
Durham, Allen, 198
Durham, Eddie, 30, 54–55, 58, 61–64, 84–88, 117, 133, 138–39, 204–5, 242, 310, 341, 349, 352–53, 365, 389, 399, 403, 405
"Dusk," 70, 76
"Dusk in Upper Sandusky," 120
"Dusky Stevedore," 152
Dvorak, Antonin, 269, 422

"Eadie Was a Lady," 183
"Early Session Hop," 213, 258n.268,
"Ease on Down," 156–58
"Easy Living," 346
"Easy Rider," 224
"Easy Ridin' Papa," 365
"Easy to Get," 369
"Easy to Love," 345
Eberly, Bob, 123, 307
Eberly, Ray, 136
"Ebony Silhouette," 194, 412
"Echoes of Harlem," 71, 297
Eckstine, Billy, 177
Edison, Harry "Sweets," 62–63, 312, 406
"Edna," 2
Edwards, Eddie, 106
"The Eel," 369
El Torreon Ballroom, 197
Eldridge, Joe, 388
Eldridge, Roy, 6–7, 14, 51–52, 100, 228, 242, 294, 303–4, 307–8, 325–26, 343–45, 348, 386–88, 403, 406, 412, 415
Elegie, 422
"Elephant Wobble," 91n.49
Ellington, Duke, x-xii, 5–6, 21, 39–40, 48, 52, 54, 61, 65–81, 83, 85–87, 93n.95, 100, 103–6, 108, 117, 119–

21, 123, 129–30, 137, 148, 151,
160–62, 167–69, 172, 179–80, 182–
83, 188, 190, 192, 194–95, 205–
212, 218, 220, 222–23, 226, 228,
230–31, 233, 235–40, 245, 277–78,
280, 283, 286, 294, 296–302, 304,
313–14, 326, 335, 341–42, 344,
374, 381–86, 397, 399, 401–2, 404,
406, 408–10, 412, 414, 416–17,
421–25
Ellington, Judy, 298–99, 301
Elman, Ziggy, 101, 104, 107, 167,
210–15, 219, 406, 410
"Elmer's Tune," 136
Empire Hall, 239
Enoch, Tommy, 177
Erenberg, Lewis A., xiiin.9, 14–15, 22,
51, 98, 101, 107, 135
Erwin, Pee Wee, 116–17, 375–77
Escudero, Ralph, 5
Estes, Bud, 88
Estes, Buff, 215
Etri, Bus, 301–3
Evans, Gil, 76, 130
Evans, Herschel, 56–57, 59, 62–64,
128, 199, 211, 227, 248, 310, 406–
7
"Evenin,'" 184, 349
"Every Day's a Holiday," 190
"Every Tub," 62–63, 406, 426
"Everybody Loves My Baby," 211
"Everybody Shuffle," 241
"Everybody's Doing It," 378
"Everything I Love," 137
"Everything Is Jumpin,'" 127
"Ev'ntide," 152–53
Ewing, John, 176–77
"Exactly Like You," 312, 368
"Exposition Swing," 74

Famous Door, 375
"Fanfare," 239
"Fare Thee Well to Harlem," 271
"Farewell Blues," 9, 109, 133, 140,
179–80, 271–73, 333, 423
"Fat Babes," 173
"The Father Jumps," 177

"Father Steps In," 176, 414
Fatool, Nick, 340, 378–79
"The Favor of a Fool," 244
Fazola, Irving, 294–96, 345
Feather, Leonard, 134, 174, 192,
258n.268, 352, 392n.41
"Feelin' High and Happy," 235
"Feelin' No Pain," 33n.28
"Feet Draggin' Blues," 310
Felton, Roy, 245
Ferguson, Otis, 61, 410
"Fiddle Dee Dee," 216
"Fiddle Diddle," 212
Field, Norman, 168
"Fifteen Minutes Intermission," 206
Fillmore, Henry, 181
"Fine and Mellow," 205
"Fine Dinner," 329
"A Fine Romance," 345, 400
Finegan, Bill, 139–40
"Firebird," 240
"Fish Fry," 244
Fisk University, 78, 217
Fitzgerald, Ella, 102–3, 165–67, 397,
407–8, 424
"Flaming Reeds and Screaming Brass,"
78, 80
"Flamingo," 308
"Flany Doodle Swing," 174
"Flash," 310
"Flat Foot Floogie," 82, 302
Fleagle, Brick, 335
The Fleet's In (film), 123
Fleming, David, 422
"Flight of the Bumblebee," 315
Floyd, Troy, 227
"Floyd's Guitar Blues," 204
"Flying Home," xivn.17, 215, 217,
340, 403, 410
"Fool Am I," 305
"Foolin' with You," 192
"For Dancers Only," 86, 417
Forrest, Helen, 111, 130, 314, 407
Fort Worth Doughboys, 361
"47th Street Jive," 208, 426
Foster, Pops, 27, 150, 157, 182, 191,
407, 419
Foster, Stephen, 304

"Four and One-Half Street," 382
"Four, Five or Six Times," 363
"Four or Five Times," 84, 181, 214, 221, 312
Fox, Charles, 199, 201, 204–5, 208, 387–88, 390
Fox Folly, 217
Frank, Joe, 9
"Frankie and Johnnie," 282–83, 287, 318n.70
Franklin, William, 169
Frazier, Charlie, 119
Frazier, George, 295
"Freakish Blues," 158
"Freakish Light Blues," 158
Freedland, Michael, 29
Freeman, Bud, 6–8, 104, 107, 109–10, 114–17, 133, 266, 325, 367–70, 373, 375–78, 407–8
Freeman, Laurence, 198
"Frenesi," 128
"Frisco Flo," 188
Froeba, Frank, 327, 372–75, 400
"Froggy Bottom," 199, 203–4
Frye, Carl, 244
Fuller, Walter, 170, 172, 174, 176, 212, 254n.107
Fulton, Jack, 268

"G.T. Stomp," 175
Gaillard, Slim, 82
"The Gal from Joe's," 297
Gale, Eddie, 271, 333
"Garbage Man Blues," 362
Gardner, Ava, 125
Gardner, Fred, 34n.64
Gardner, Jack, 310
Garland, Joe, 138
Garland, Red, 216
Gately, Buddy, 112
"'Gator Swing," 176
Gaylor, Ruth, 234, 285
"Geechy Joe," 195
Gentry, Chuck, 312
George, Karl, 216
"Georgia," 7, 228
"Georgia on My Mind," 7–8, 275, 305, 327, 402

"Georgia Stomp," 2
"Georgia Swing," 1–2, 72
Gershwin, George, 27–29, 98, 107, 114, 128, 131, 167, 239–40, 264, 266–70, 289, 314, 351, 378, 387, 422
Gershwin, Ira, 60, 281
"Get Along Cindy," 363
"Get the Bucket," 30n.1
"A Ghost of a Chance," 193
"Ghost of the Freaks," 158, 160
Gibson, Andy, 195, 301
Gibson, Margie, 130, 313
Giddins, Gary, 85, 90n.23, 130, 351
Gifford, Gene, 22–25, 275–77, 279–80, 317n.39, 408
Gilbert and Sullivan, 221
Gillespie, Dizzy, ix, 28, 42, 49, 193–94, 207, 212–13, 228, 246, 281, 299, 386–89, 401–2, 406, 408, 412, 416, 421–22
"Gilly," 342
"Gin and Jive," 242
"Gin for Christmas," 214
"Gin Mill Special," 220, 223
Ginell, Cary, 361–66, 394n.97
Gioia, Ted, 9, 74–75, 98–99, 316n.17
"Girl of My Dreams," 363
"Git," 199
"Git Along," 183
Giuffre, Jimmy, 368
"Give Her a Pint (and She'll Take It All)," 200
"Give Me Some Skin," 216
Glaser, Joe, 148, 201, 232, 249n.2, 331, 408, 418
Glass, Henderson, 230–31
Gleason, Ralph, J., vii, 79–80, 85, 89, 400
Glen Island Casino, 40, 132, 136, 138
"Glen Island Special," 133, 139, 400
Glenn, Tyree, 194, 243
"Gloomy Sunday," 348
"Go Harlem," 164
"Go 'Long Mule," 40, 48
"Go South, Young Man," 190
"God Bless the Child," 348
Goddard, Paulette, 131

"Goin' to Chicago Blues," 354
"Goin' to Town," 157
"Going Out the Back Way," 385
"Going Up Brushy Creek," 365
Goldkette, Jean, 8–9, 15–16, 22, 27, 112, 263, 274, 330
Gomar, Larry, 271
"Gone," 230
"Gone With the Wind," 422
"Gone with 'What' Wind," 341, 403
Gonsalves, Paul, 223–24
"The Goo," 229
"Good-For-Nothin' Joe," 300
"Good Morning Blues," 61
"Good Queen Bess," 386
"Good Sauce from the Gravy Bowl," 187
"Goodbye," 99
Goodman, Benny, vii, viii, x, 6–7, 9, 12–16, 18, 20–28, 39–40, 42–43, 48, 50–53, 73, 97–112, 114, 116, 120, 123–25, 128, 133–36, 142n.43, 148, 161, 163–65, 168, 173, 175, 181, 189, 194, 209, 211, 215, 219, 223, 232, 236–37, 241, 244, 250n.2, 263, 270, 272, 274–75, 279, 281, 283–85, 287, 292, 303, 309–10, 313–14, 325–27, 329, 333–35, 337–46, 352, 355, 367–68, 370–71, 373, 379–80, 398, 400, 402–3, 406–11, 413, 415, 417–18, 420, 424–26
Goodman, Harry, 6, 23, 99, 333
"Goodnight My Love," 102
"Goodnight, Sweet Dreams, Goodnight," 175
"Goody Goody," 102
"Goofus," 366
Gordon, Dexter, 216
Gorman, Ross, 268
"Got a Bran' New Suit," 152, 273
"Gotta Go Places and Do Things," 184
Gould, Bud, 248
Gould, Morton, 140
Gowans, Brad, 369
Gramercy Five, 378–80
Grand Canyon Suite, 266

Grand Terrace, 39, 58, 167–68, 170–71, 409
"Grand Terrace Rhythm," 52
"Grand Terrace Shuffle," 176
Grappelli, Stéphane, 216
Grauer, Bill, 274–75
Gray, Glen, 134, 274, 281, 408–9
Gray, Jerry, 125, 130, 138, 140
Green, Charlie "Big," 47, 60, 151, 250n.17, 409
Green, Freddie, 59, 62, 108, 164, 214, 299, 330, 34647, 353, 355, 409, 414, 418
Green, John W., 268
"Green Eyes," 123, 306–7
Greer, Sonny, xi-xii, 67–68, 73, 75–76, 208, 211–12, 383–84, 409–10, 415
Gridler, Mark, 11
Grissom, Dan, 83, 85
Grofé, Ferde, 9, 115, 266
Guarnieri, Johnny, 341–42, 378–80
Gushee, Lawrence, 393n.65
Guy, Freddy, 172
"A Gypsy Without a Song," 67, 75

Hackett, Bobby, 20–21 106, 137, 369, 400, 410
Haggart, Bob, 288–91, 293–96, 410
Hall, Edmond, 12, 214, 330, 346
Hall, Howard, 278
Hall, Wilbur, 268
Hamilton, John, 360
Hammond, John, 14, 57, 98, 101, 105, 108, 233, 288, 340, 410
Hampton, Gladys, 215
Hampton, Lionel, 7, 20–21, 39, 65, 77, 102, 106, 108–10, 147, 209–17, 325, 329–30, 337–38, 340–42, 370, 406, 408, 410, 414
"Hampton Stomp," 210
Handy, W.C., 49, 126–27, 178, 363, 365
"The Happy," 230
"Happy Feet," 44–45, 179, 267
Harburg, Edgar Y., 188
Hardin, Lil, 155
Harding, Buster, 176–77, 195

Hardwick, Otto, 278, 381, 383
"Harlem Air Shaft," xii, 70–71, 406, 409
"Harlem Congo," 165
"Harlem Holiday," 183
"Harlem Lament," 171
Harlem Opera House, 217
"Harlem Shout," 85
"Harlem Speaks," 297, 401, 417
Harrington, John, 201, 208
Harris, Arville, 185–86
Harris, Joe, 100–101, 164
Harris, L.D., 229, 231, 259n.303
Harris, Leroy, 176
Harris, Richard, 225
Harrison, Jimmy, 10–12, 42, 162–63, 267, 326, 331, 411
Harrison, Max, 18, 15556
Hart, Clyde, 212–14, 345
"Harvard Blues," 61, 93n.77, 401, 419, 425
Haughton, Chauncey, 191–92, 245
"Have You Met Miss Jones," 339
"Having a Wonderful Time," 377, 405
"Hawaiian War Chant," x
Hawes, Pat, 115
Hawkins, Coleman, 4, 6, 9–12, 14, 18–19, 2, 25, 42–43, 45–46, 50–52, 56–58, 62, 82, 90n.23, 129, 133–34, 137, 159, 179–80, 189–90, 192, 198–99, 212–15, 236–37, 239–41, 243–44, 248, 267–68, 276, 298, 311, 317n.46, 325–33, 336, 338, 349, 354, 368–69, 371, 385, 387, 400, 407, 411, 424, 426
Hawkins, Erskine, 40, 121, 217–26, 244, 259n.280, 299–300, 304, 399, 404, 408, 411
Hayes, Thamon, 54
Haymer, Herbie, 371, 373
Haymes, Dick, 311–12, 314
Hayton, Lennie, 22, 129–31
"He Ain't Got Rhythm," 29, 102, 159, 283, 423
Heard, J.C., 245
"Heartbreak Blues," 328
Heath, Ted, 243
"Heckler's Hop," 388, 406

"Heebie Jeebies," 162
"Heigh-Ho (The Dwarfs' March Song)," 284
Helblock, Joe, 124, 418
"Hello, Lola," 47
"Hell's Bells," 153
Hemingway, Ernest, 351
Henderson, Fletcher, 2–4, 8–20, 22–24, 27, 29, 39–54, 57–58, 62–63, 65–68, 78–79, 82, 84–86, 98–102, 104, 106–110, 123, 125–26, 134, 138–39, 148, 151, 153, 157–59, 161, 171–72, 175, 179–80, 183, 187, 198–99, 211, 214, 219, 224, 231, 237–38, 241–42, 244, 246, 264, 267, 275, 277–78, 280, 297, 302, 317n.46, 327, 340–41, 397–98, 400, 402–3, 406, 409–14, 416, 418–21, 424–25
Henderson, Horace, 28, 41–46, 51, 98, 106, 108, 122, 139, 224, 238, 267, 300, 302, 328, 411–12, 425
Hendrickson, Al, 378–80
Hennessey, Thomas, 280
Henry, Haywood, 218–26
Hentoff, Nat, 103, 352, 404
Herfurts, Skeets, 119
Herlihy, Ed, ix
Herman, Woody, 292, 408
"He's a Gypsy from Poughkeepsie," 376
"He's a Son of the South," 151
"He's Funny That Way," 329
"He's Pulling His Whiskers," 236
"Hey Doc!," 223, 225
Heywood, Eddie, Jr., 227, 244, 306, 348
"The Hi-De-Ho Miracle Man," 188
"Hi Spook," 88, 153
Hickman, Art, 9
Higginbotham, J.C., 12, 14, 19, 27, 53, 156–58, 167, 241, 252n.56, 327–28, 397, 412, 419
"High-Geared Daddy," 366
"High Tension," 156, 158
Hill, Alex, 103
Hill, Alexander, 180
Hill, Teddy, 27, 412, 425

Hines, Earl "Fatha," 39, 65, 101, 103, 147–48, 155, 161, 167–77, 197, 208, 211, 241, 249, 264, 293–94, 310, 338, 346, 388, 409, 412–14, 417, 425

Hines, Frankie, 341

Hinton, Milt, 172, 187–89, 192–95, 212, 402, 412

Hite, Les, 25, 149, 209

"Hittin' the Bottle," 84, 86, 405

"Hobo, You Can't Ride This Train," 150, 398

"Hocus Pocus," 51, 159

Hodeir, André, 45, 63, 77, 79, 157, 213, 340, 355, 424–25

"Hodge Podge," 304

Hodges, Johnny, xii, 67–69, 72–77, 102, 106, 121, 157, 160, 163, 172, 207, 210–11, 228–29, 235, 246, 278, 298–99, 302, 304, 313, 326, 344, 347, 381–86, 390, 398, 412–13

Hoefer, George, 51, 213, 329–30

"Hokus Pokus," 158–60

"Hold Tight (Want Some Sea Food Mama)," 63, 353, 356, 360

Holder, Terrence, 196, 414

Holiday, Billie, 7, 30, 59–60, 98, 102, 117, 120–21, 126, 152, 181, 205, 215, 269, 273–74, 281, 284, 300, 305–6, 313, 325–26, 333–34, 343–49, 357, 365, 373, 398, 400, 407, 410, 413, 421, 423, 426

Holland, Charles, 242

Holmes, Charlie, 27, 412, 425

Holmes, Leroy, 314

"Home (When Shadows Fall)," 149

"Home Cooking," 368

Homer, 9, 161

"Honey, Do!," 151

"Honey, Just For You," 198

"Honeysuckle Rose," 11, 57, 106, 248, 371, 375, 415, 424

"Honky Tonk Blues," 366

"Honky Tonk Train Blues," 292

"Hootie Blues," 248

Hopkins, Claude, 9, 12–13, 65, 103, 109, 226, 230, 404, 413

Horne, Lena, 300–301

"Hot and Anxious," 41–42, 138, 411

"Hot as I Am," 364

Hot Club of Paris, 216

Hot Five and Hot Seven, 8, 24–25, 167–68, 289

"Hot Mallets," 213

"Hot Platter," 220, 223

"Hot Toddy," 183

"Hot Water," 184–85

"Hotcha-Razz-Ma-Tazz," 185–86

"Hotter Than 'Ell," 51

"House of David Blues," 42–43

"How Can We Be Wrong?," 202

"How Can You Face Me Now," 357

"How Come You Do Me Like You Do?," 240

"How High the Moon," 111

"How Long Blues," 60

"How Long—Part 1," 227

Howard, Darnell, 169–70, 172, 174–75, 254n.107

Howard, Paul, 209

Howell, Tom, 34n.64

Hudson, Will, 81, 85, 159, 183–85, 284

Hughes, Paul, x-xi

Hughes, Spike, 68, 239–42

"Humoresque," 422

Humoresque, 422

Hunt, Pee Wee, 24–25, 184, 275, 277, 280

Hurley, Clyde, 137–40, 145n.153, 272

Hutchenrider, Clarence, 25, 36n.81, 276–79, 317n.59

Hutton, Marion, 139

"I Ain't Got Nobody," 187–88, 329, 389

"I Cant' Believe That You're in Love with Me," 327, 381

"I Can't Dance (I Got Ants in My Pants)," 163

"I Can't Escape from You," 223

"I Can't Face the Music," 119–20

"I Can't Get Started," 59, 124, 213–14, 281–83, 287, 295, 318n.67, 372–73, 400

"I Can't Give You Anything But Love," 104, 346, 356, 383

"I Come From a Musical Family," 150, 419

"I Cover the Waterfront," 131, 348

"I Cried For You," 120, 286

"I Dance Alone," 284

"(I Don't Believe It but) Say It Again," 204

"I Don't Stand a Ghost of a Chance," 231

"I Don't Want to Walk without You," 225

"I Double Dare You," 155, 419

"I Dream I Dwelt in Harlem," 139

"I Found a New Baby," 223, 248

"I Got It Bad and That Ain't Good," 68, 314, 397

"I Got Rhythm," 27–29, 90n.19, 107, 118–19, 279–80, 317n.59, 339, 341, 368, 371, 403–4, 417

"I Gotta Gal in Kalamazoo," 400

"I Gotta Right to Sing the Blues," 151, 183, 334, 423

"(I Guess) I'll Never Learn," 204

"I Hear a Rhapsody," 301

"I Hope That Gabriel Likes My Music," 273

"I Just Couldn't Take It Baby," 406

"I Just Want Your Stingaree," 366

"I Know a Secret," 224

"I Know What You Do," 384

"I Let a Song Go Out of My Heart," 75–76, 235, 341, 401, 413

I Like Jazz, 68

"I Like Music (with a Swing Like That)," 191–92, 256n.181

"I Lost My Gal from Memphis," 197–98

"I Love to Sing," 187, 189

"I Love You," 363

"I Love You Because I Love You," 169

"I Love You Truly," 228

"I Never Knew," 64

"I Never Purposely Hurt You," 312

"I Surrender Dear," 126

"I Take to You," 305

"... I Wanna Count Sheep Till the Cows Come Home," 41

"I Wanna Go Where You Go—Do What You Do Then I'll Be Happy," 205

"I Wanna Hear Swing Songs," 88

"I Want a Little Girl," 353

"I Want a Lot of Love," 170–71

"I Want to Be Happy," 103, 166

"I Wished on the Moon," 344

"I Wonder Who," 152

"(I Would Do) Anything for You," 103

"I Wouldn't Take a Million," 312

"I'd Rather Lead a Band," 373

"If Dreams Come True," 347

"If I Had My Way," 374

"If I Were You," 235

"If It Ain't Love," 164

"If the Man in the Moon," 377

"If We Never Meet Again," 152–53

"If You Leave Me," 222

"If You Were Mine," 344

"I'll Always Be in Love With You," 110

"I'll Be Glad When You're Dead You Rascal You," 364

"I'll Never Be the Same," 346

"I'll Never Smile Again," x, 117

"I'll String Along With You," 366

"Ill Wind," 246

"I'm a Ding Dong Daddy from Dumas," 339

"Imagination," 163

"I'm Alone With You," 88

"I'm Always in the Mood for You," 190

"I'm an Old English Village," 191

"I'm Beginning to See the Light," 78

"I'm Coming Virginia," 5, 8, 20–21, 35n.70, 106, 243, 273, 372, 374–75, 410, 424

"I'm Crazy 'Bout My Baby," 42 179–80

"I'm Free," 295

"I'm Getting Sentimental over You," xi, 73, 112–13, 405

"I'm in a Low-Down Groove," 225

"I'm in an Awful Mood," 87–88
"I'm in the Mood for Swing," 242
"I'm Just a Jitterbug," 166
"I'm Nuts About Screwy Music," 84–85, 423
"I'm Prayin' Humble," 290
"I'm Pulling Through," 348
"I'm Shooting High," 113
"I'm Sorry I Made You Cry," 402
"In a Mellotone," 76
"In a Mist," 370
"In a Sentimental Mood," xii, 73, 117–19, 121, 406
"In El Rancho Grande," 363
"In My Wildest Dreams," 201
"In the Groove," 201, 426
"In the Groove at the Grove," 167
"In the Mood," ix, 42, 76, 133, 138, 411, 415
"In Tiefen Keller," 265
"Indián Boogie Woogie," 292
"Indiana," 310
Inge, William, 185
"Interlude in B-Flat," 124
"Intermission Riff," 89
International Association of Jazz Record Collectors, 362
"Invitation to the Dance," 100
Irwin, Cecil, 168, 174
"Is This Gonna Be My Lucky Summer," 376
"I'se a Muggin,'" 200
"It All Begins and Ends With You," 374
"It Don't Mean a Thing (If It Ain't Got That Swing)," 72, 87, 212, 397, 406, 415, 417
"It Had To Be You," 110
"It Sends Me," 328
"It Was a Sad Night in Harlem," 222
"It Will Have to Do until the Real Thing Comes Along," 222
"Itchola," 271
"It's Funny to Everyone but Me," 311, 421
"It's the Blues," 9
"It's the Little Things That Count," 285

"It's the Talk of the Town," 90n.23
"It's You I'm Talking About," 114
"I've Found a New Baby," 213, 331, 369
"I've Got a Guy," 285
"I've Got the World on a String," 183
"I've Got to Sing a Torch Song," 46, 90nn.23, 25

"Jack and Jill," 136
"Jack the Bear," 71, 76, 384–85, 401
Jackson, Arthur, 234
Jackson, Cliff, 372
Jackson, Franz, 177
Jackson, John, 249
Jackson, Marion, 197
Jackson, Pee Wee, 175, 177
Jacquet, Illinois, xii, xivn.17, 176, 215–16
"Ja-Da," 369, 410
"Jam Session," 101, 406, 417
"A Jam Session at Victor," 375
"Jamaica Shout," 328
James, Elmer, 28, 48
James, George, 245
James, Harry, x-xi, 16, 18–19, 21, 24–25, 39, 42, 50–51, 65, 91n.35, 101, 103–9, 117, 122, 128, 142n.39, 167, 189, 209, 211, 219, 242, 272, 282, 309–15, 325, 347, 370–71, 406–8, 413, 421
James, Ida, 220, 225
"Jangled Nerves," 52
"Japanese Sandman," 174, 264
"Jazz à la Carte," 381–82
"Jazznocracy," 82
"Jealous," 228
"Jeepers Creepers," 273
Jefferson, Hilton, 2, 28, 48, 50, 193, 328, 413
"Jeffries' Blues," 313
"Jelly, Jelly," 177, 388
"Jelly Roll Blues," 160, 286–87
Jenkins, Freddy, xii, 73, 382
Jenney, Jack, 129, 131, 371
Jennings, Al, 286
Jenssen, Mel, 278

Jerome, Jerry, 110, 213, 215, 341, 403
"Jersey Bounce," 89
"Jess's Natu'lly Lazy," 188
"Jingle Bells," 100, 136
"Jitter Bug," 185
"Jive (Page One of the Hepster's Dictionary)," 192–93, 400
"A Jive Spiritual," 116
"Jive Stomp," 73, 401
"Jivin' the Jeep," 417
"Jivin' the Vibes," 210
"Joe Turner Blues," 362
John Kirby and His Orchestra (Sextet), 380, 387, 395n.129, 398, 414
"John Peel," 273
"John Silver," 120
Johnakins, Leslie, 201
"John's Idea," 62, 64, 405
Johnson, A.J., 227–28, 231
Johnson, Budd, 57, 151, 174–77, 196, 211–12, 215, 246, 389, 410, 413–14
Johnson, Gene, 12
Johnson, Gus, 248, 416
Johnson, James P., 171, 293
Johnson, Jimmy, 356
Johnson, Keg, 28, 151–52, 187, 192, 195, 278, 414
Johnson, Walter, 11, 19, 28, 43, 45, 52–53
Johnson, William, 218–22, 226, 327, 404
"Johnson Rag," 140, 415
Johnston, Peter K., 314
"The Joint Is Jumpin'," 356, 359
Jolson, Al, 179
Jones, Bobby, 279
Jones, Claude, 18, 42, 82, 159, 180, 186–87, 414
Jones, "Chubby," 231
Jones, Dick, 375
Jones, Henry, 160
Jones, Isham, 9, 206
Jones, Jo, 60, 62–63, 161, 166, 299, 346–47, 349–50, 353, 409, 414–15, 418
Jones, Jonah, 194, 211, 245, 344–46

Jones, LeRoi (Amiri Baraka), vii, 228–29
Jones, Maggie, 49
Jones, Reunald, 163
Jones, Richard M., 4
Jones, Slick, 213
Jones-Smith, Inc., 349, 352, 367
Joplin, Scott, 173
Jordan, Paul, 129–30
Jordan, Taft, 162–63, 167
"Josephine," 377
"Jubilee," 154–55, 191
Jubilee(show), 125
"Jubilesta," 383
"Julia," 172, 174
"Julius Caesar," 202
"Jump Jack Jump," 202
"Jumpin'," 234
"Jumpin' at the Woodside," 62, 64, 110, 353
"The Jumpin' Jive," 195
"Jumpy Nerves," 138
"Jungle Madness," 304
"Junior Hop," 386
"Just a Mood," 371
"(Just an) Error in the News," 191
"Just A-Settin' and A-Rockin'," 78, 424
"Just Blues," 41, 43
"Just for You," 217
"Just Jivin' Around," 355
"Just Sitting on Top of the World," 363
"Just to Be in Caroline," 373

Kallen, Kitty, 335
Kaminsky, Max, 114, 368, 375
Kansas City Six, 352–54
Kapp, Dave, 370
Karle, Art, 334
"Keep a Song in Your Soul," 11, 41, 414, 421
"Keep Cool, Fool," 224
"Keep That Hi-De-Hi in Your Soul," 187
"Keepin' Myself for You," 379
Keepnews, Orin, 10, 203, 274–75
Kegley, Charles, 327

Kelly's Stable, 355
Kent, Red, 310
Kenton, Stan, 43, 89, 243
Kern, Jerome, 160, 269, 313, 345, 380
Kersey, Ken, 342
Keyes, Joe, 54
"Kickin' the Gong Around," 402
Kilmer, Joyce, 283
Kincaide, Deane, 115, 288, 376
King, Martin Luther, Jr., 166
King, Paul, 199, 201
King, Stan, 154, 335
King, Tempo, 372–74
King of Jazz (film), 44, 264
"King of Spades," 68
"King Porter Stomp," 2, 9–15, 26, 32n.28, 33nn.29, 48, 34n.54, 43, 50, 58, 63, 66, 99–100, 117–18, 133, 194, 218–20, 413, 417
Kirby, John, 3, 10–12, 19, 26, 28, 42–43, 51–52, 163–64, 211, 335, 344–45, 380, 387, 414
Kirk, Andy, 39, 195–98, 226, 230, 232, 264, 401, 408, 414, 425–26
Kirkpatrick, Don, 162, 164
"Kiss Me Again," 197
Klein, Manny, 334
Klink, Al, 137–40, 415
"Knockin' on Wood," 370
"Ko-Ko," 76, 384, 417
"Koko," 387
Kolodin, Irving, 21, 339
Korall, Burt, 165, 193, 404
Kreisler, Fritz, 264
Krise, Ray, 120
Krupa, Gene, 6–7, 65, 98, 101, 103–4, 106–8, 110, 161, 165–66, 209, 233, 303–10, 312, 334, 337–40, 342, 371, 408, 415
Kuhn, John, 9
Kunzel, Erich, x
Kyle, Billy, 335–36

"La Paloma," 313
La Rocca, Nick, 106
Lacey, Jack, 374
Ladnier, Tommy, 4
"The Lady Is a Tramp," 377

"The Lady Who Swings the Band," 200
"The Lady's in Love with You," 304
"Lafayette," 55, 275
Lakey, Claude, 310–12
Lamb, Joseph F., 367
Landowska, Wanda, 378
Lang, Eddie, 6–7, 333, 423
Langford, Frances, 153
Laughin "Laughin' Louie," 152
Lawn, Richard, 90n.25
Lawrence, Bob, 269–70
Lawson, Harry "Big Jim," 198–99, 205–6, 208
Lawson, Yank, 289–91, 296, 415
"Lazy Bones," 7, 24, 188, 275, 402
"Lazy River," 7, 275, 402
"Leapin' at the Lincoln," 300, 302
Leary, Ford, 282, 299
Lee, Peggy, 111
Lee, Sonny, 283
Leeman, Cliff, 300, 302
Leonard, Harlan, 56–57
Leonard, Jack, 114, 116–17
Leonardo da Vinci, 161
Leslie, Nat, 43
"Lester Leaps In," 59, 64, 355
"Lester's Dream," 355
"Let 'Er Go," 66
"Let Me Off Uptown," 307
"Let That Be a Lesson to You," 104
"Let the Punishment Fit the Crime," 221
"Let Yourself Go," 373
"Let's Dance," 100, 110–11
Let's Dance (radio show), x, 100
"Let's Do It," 282
"Let's Get Away from It All," 305
"Let's Get Together," 163, 420
Lewis, Ed, 56
Lewis, John, 399–400
Lewis, Meade Lux, 292
Lewis, Ted, 21, 106
Lewis, William, 246
Lewis, Willie, 242, 245
"Life Goes to a Party," 106, 128, 413
"Limehouse Blues," 194, 277–78

Lincoln Center Jazz Orchestra (LCJO), xi, 61
Lindsay, John, 3
"Lindy Lou," 245
"Linger Awhile," 90n.19, 270, 385–86, 404
Lippmann, Joe, 122, 319n.88
Lipskin, Mike, 359, 402
Lissner, John, 121
"Little Betty Brown," 365
"A Little Bit Later," 373
"Little Brown Jug," 132, 137
"Little Joe from Chicago," 202
"Little Man with a Candy Cigar," 305
"Little Miss," 206
"Little Posey," 71
"Little Rock Getaway," 293, 427
"Little White Lies," 117
"Live and Love Tonight," 354
"Livery Stable Blues," 5
Livingston, Ulysses, 244
"Liza," 28–29, 167, 421–22
"Loch Lomond," 107
Loesser, Frank, 360, 402
Lombardo, Carmen, 25
Lombardo, Guy, 23, 25
"Lona," 164
"The Lone Arranger," 195
"Lonely Moments," 230
"Lonesome Moments," 164
"Lonesome Nights," 193, 195, 241
"The Lonesome Road," 87, 360
Long, Slats, 374
"Long about Midnight," 185
"Lookie, Lookie Here Comes Cookie," 412
"Loose Ankles," 198
Lopez, Vincent, 134
"Lost in the Shuffle," 223
"Lotta Sax Appeal," 197, 199, 426
"Louise," 110
"Louise Louise Blues," 366
"Louisana Swing," 156–57, 397
"Love and Kisses," 165
"Love in Bloom," 363
"Love Is Just Around the Corner," 367, 369, 410
"Love Is the Reason," 188

"Love Is the Thing," 205
"Love Jumped In," 64
"Love Me or Leave Me," 348, 354
"Love, You Funny Thing," 25, 150
"Love You're Not the One for Me," 239
"Loveland and You," 363
"Loveless Love," 34n.64
"Lover, Come Back to Me," 128, 201
Lowe, Sammy, 219–21, 224–26
Lucie, Lawrence, 53
"Lullaby in Rhythm," 109
"Lullaby to a Dream," 246
Lunceford, Jimmie, ix, 22–24, 30, 39–40, 43, 61, 66 78–89, 100, 102, 109, 115–16, 122–23, 126–27, 137, 158–62, 168, 172–73, 175–76, 181–82, 186, 196, 199, 202–4, 208, 217–18, 221–22, 224–26, 233, 236–37, 241, 245, 264, 266, 269–70, 283–85, 294, 296, 299–300, 303–4, 310, 312–14, 316n.30, 341, 377, 404–5, 415, 417–18, 421, 423, 425–26
"Lush Life," 422
"Lyin' to Myself," 152–53

Mabane, Bob, 248, 416
Mace, Tom, 344
MacInnes, Colin, 407
"Madame Dynamite," 368
"The Madame Swings It," 304
"Madhouse," 172
Madison, Bingie, 30n.1, 150, 153
"Mahogany Hall Stomp," 150–52, 28283, 407
Maisel, Jack, 382–83
Malneck, Marty, 344
"Mama Don't Allow It," 365
"Mama, I Wanna Make Rhythm," 190
"Mammy's Little Baby Loves Shortenin' Bread," 376
"The Man From Harlem," 183
"The Man I Love," 107, 314
"Manhattan Jam," 190
"Maniac's Ball," 275
Manone, Wingy, 42, 138
"Maple Leaf Rag," 173
"March of the Bob Cats," 289

Mares, Paul, 110, 271

"Margie," 87, 109, 186, 427

"María Elena," 123, 306–7

"Marie," x, xiiin.2, 116, 408

Marmarosa, Dodo, 379

Marsala, Joe, 373–74

Marsalis, Wynton, xi–xii, 61

Marshall, Kaiser, 11, 215

Marx Brothers, 66, 94n.95

"Mary Had a Little Lamb," 52

"Mary's Idea," 198, 204

Massenet, Jules, 422

Massey, Billy, 198

Mastren, Carmen, 266, 375, 377

Mathews, Dave, 50, 109, 211, 310, 313

Matlock, Matty, 124, 282, 288–89, 291, 295–96

Maxey, Leroy, 182–84, 186, 189–90, 192–93

Maxwell, Jim, 281

May, Billy, 288, 291, 297–300, 302

"Maybe," 311

McAuliffe, Leon, 361

McCall, Mary Ann, 301

McCarthy, Albert J., 30n.1, 46, 53, 79–80, 90n.23, 156–59, 162–64, 169–70, 173–75, 178, 181, 183, 185, 187, 191, 193–94, 197, 199–200, 204, 206, 208, 218–19, 221–22, 224–26, 228, 238, 241, 245–47, 252n.56, 254n.107, 256n.181, 259n.298, 259n.303, 264, 277, 287, 292, 295, 297–98, 303–4, 307, 318n.79, 319n.88

McDonough, Dick, 334, 370, 375

McEachern, Murray, 101–2, 104–5

McGhee, Howard, 46

McGrath, Fulton, 335, 370

McGregor, Chummy, 140

McHenry, Walter, 228, 231

McKenzie, Red, 318n.67, 326–27, 368

McKinley, Ray, 18, 119–20, 122

McKinney's Cotton Pickers, 2, 46–47, 238, 419

McLemore, William, 221, 224

McMickle, Dale, 139

McNeil, Edward, 198

McPartland, Jimmy, 48, 133

McRae, Teddy, 165

McShann, Jay, 65, 247–49, 387, 389, 415–16

McSloy, Peter (pseud. of Pete Townsend), 34n.64, 189

McVea, Jack, 217

McWashington, Willie, 54–56

"Me, Myself, and I," 346

Meadowbrook (New Jersey), 302

"Meet Doctor Foo," 329

"Melancholy Lullaby," 241, 243, 402

Mellers, Wilfrid, 4

"A Mellow Bit of Rhythm," 201

"A Melody From the Sky," 124, 373

"Memories of You," 209, 340

"Memphis Blues," 49, 365

"Memphis Rag," 78

"Menelik (The Lion of Judah)," 386

Mercer, Johnny, 24, 100, 271, 344

"Merry-Go-Round," 68, 86, 297, 402, 406, 421

"The Merry-Go-Round Broke Down," 86

"Mess-a-Stomp," 197, 202–4

"Mexican Swing," 150

Mezzrow, Mezz, 151, 357

Michelangelo, 161

"Midnight Stroll," 206

"Mighty River," 152

Mikado, 221

"Milenberg Joys," 134, 272, 362

Miley, Bubber, 5–7, 67, 81, 106, 158, 310, 425

Milhaud, Darius, 264

Miller, Art, 271

Miller, Bill, 299

Miller, Charlie, 61

Miller, Eddie, 288–89, 291, 293–96, 372–73

Miller, Glenn, ix, 9, 15–16, 22, 25, 27, 39, 42, 48, 65, 76, 97–98, 132–40, 145n.139, 160, 195, 205, 218–19, 235–36, 245, 263, 272, 297, 307, 313, 332, 400, 405, 408, 410–11, 415–16

Millian, Baker, 227–31, 259n.298

Mills, Irving, 127, 163, 416

Mills, Lincoln, 244
Mills Blue Rhythm Band, 416
Mills Brothers, 138, 154, 245
Mince, Johnny, 371
Mingus, Charles, 308, 372
"Minka," 314
"Minnie the Moocher," 178–79, 184
"Minnie the Moocher's Wedding
    Day," 183
Minor, Dan, 54–55, 354–55
Minor, Orville, 248–49, 416
"A Minor Breakdown (Rustle of
    Swing)," 191–92
"The Minor Drag," 356
Minton's, 110, 401, 403, 412, 416,
    418
Mintz (Mince?), Johnny, 375
"Misirlou," 314
"Miss Brown to You," 343–44, 413
"Miss Hallelujah Brown," 223, 399
"Miss Otis Regrets," 81, 187
"Mississippi Basin," 152
Missourians, 177–78
"Misty Morning," 69
Mitchell, George, 168
Mitchell's Christian Singers, 290
"Moanin' Low," 316n.22
The Modernaires, 136, 138, 140
"The Mole," 314
Monaco, James V., 62
Mondello, Toots, 213, 215
Monk, Thelonious, 350, 385, 401, 416
"Montevideo," 312
"The Mooche," 35n.64
"Mood Indigo," 69–70, 76, 81, 117,
    179, 286, 401, 421
"The Mood That I'm In," 210
"Moon Glow," 185–86
"Moon Ray," 130
"Moon Romance," 383
"Moonlight Blues," 209
"Moonlight Cocktail," 139
"Moonlight Rhapsody," 185
"Moonlight Serenade," ix–x, 133–34,
    136, 139–40, 307
Moore, Billy, 88, 203, 302–3
Moore, Lonnie, 231
Moore, Oscar, 215, 404

"More Than You Know," 244, 338
Morgan, Al, 182–88, 185–86, 189,
    327, 402
Morgantini, Jacques, 46
Morgenstern, Dan, 143n.71, 148, 152,
    248, 249n.2, 329, 331
Morris, Marlowe, 215
Morrison, George, 196–97
Morrison, Henry, 244
Morrison, James, 220
Morrow, Buddy, xi-xi
Morton, Ferdinand "Jelly Roll," 1–3,
    5, 9–15, 24, 26–27, 30n.1, 31n.4,
    58, 65, 72, 79, 99, 117, 160, 168,
    171, 178, 194, 196, 218–19, 286,
    291, 296, 325, 417
Morton, Benny, 18–19, 59, 82, 242,
    246, 344, 347, 414, 416–17
Mosely, Snub, 150, 413
Moten, Bennie, 22, 53–58, 61, 63, 65,
    100, 128, 162, 170, 180, 183, 188,
    196, 199, 227, 232, 234, 242, 248,
    275–77, 405, 418, 424
"Moten Swing," 55, 117–18, 199,
    248, 389, 415, 418
Mound City Blue Blowers, 6, 46, 133,
    326–27
Mozart, Wolfgang Amadeus, 31n.4,
    161
"Mr. J.B. Blues," 385
"Muddy Waters," 316n.30
"Muggin' Lightly," 252n.56
"Muggles," 167
Mulligan, Gerry, 315
Mundy, Jimmy, 13, 62, 64, 101, 107,
    109–10, 147, 168, 170, 173–75,
    177, 304, 413, 417
Munson "The Munson Street
    Breakdown," 213–14
Murphy, Joaquin, 366–67
Murphy, Lambert, 269
Murphy, Spud, 100, 299
"Mush Mouth," 413
"Music at Midnight," 239
"Music at Sunrise," 240
"Music Goes 'Round and 'Round,"
    272
"Music Makers," 313

Musical Brownies, 17, 179, 353, 361–67

Musiker, Sam, 304–5

"Muskrat Ramble," 211

Musso, Vido, 101, 104, 312–13, 345

"My Blue Heaven," 79, 84, 127, 159–60, 270, 331, 380

"My Buddy," 214

"My Favorite Blues," 246

"My Gal Mezzanine," 188–89

"My Gal Sal," 339

"My Hands Are Tied," 304

"My Honey's Lovin' Arms," 179, 181

"My Inspiration," 295

"My Melancholy Baby," 337

"My Precious Sonny Boy," 362

"My Sunday Gal," 183–84, 385

"My Sweet Tooth Says I Wanna but My Wisdom Tooth Says No," 41, 89n.11

"My Wish," 217

Myers, Evelyn, 216

"Nagasaki," 187, 242, 414

Nance, Ray, 175

"Nancy Jane," 362

Nanton, "Tricky" Sam, 7, 67–68, 72–73, 76, 84, 106, 222, 278, 313, 381–82, 417

"Naughty Man," 40

Navarro, Fats, 406

"The Nearness of You," 311, 314

Nelson, Ozzie, 134

"Never Felt Better, Never Had Less," 285

"New King Porter Stomp," 11, 14–15, 43, 411–12, 421

"New Orleans," 275–76, 418

New Orleans Rhythm Kings (NORK), 5, 9, 109, 140, 271–72, 291, 294, 325, 367

"New Street Swing," 243

New World Symphony, 269

Newman, Jerry, 401

Newman, Joe, 216

"Nice Work If You Can Get It," 339, 378

Nicholas, Albert, 27

Nichols, Red, 21, 27, 98, 133, 332

"Night in Tunisia," 401

"Night Song," 286–87

"No Regrets," 60, 345, 373, 400

"No Soap (A Jitterbug Jamboree)," 221, 404

"No Trumps," 34n.64

"No Use Squawkin,'" 225

Noble, Ray, 134, 297, 387, 399

"Nobody Knows," 60

"Nobody Knows the Trouble I've Seen," 313–14

"Nobody's Sweetheart," 187

"Nocturne," 131, 239

"Nola," 217

"Nona," 224–25

Noone, Jimmy, 295

Norman, Fred, 12, 109, 130

Norris, Al, 270

Norvo, Red, 13, 82, 297, 370–72, 398, 410, 417, 420

"Nothin,'" 314

"Now I Lay Me Down to Sleep," 206

"Number 19," 176

"The Object of My Affection," 211, 363, 406

O'Brien, Floyd, 357–58, 368

O'Connell, Helen, 121–23, 307

O'Daniel, W. Lee, 362

O'Day, Anita, 303, 305–6, 308, 415

"Oh! Boy," 84

"Oh! Eddie," 54

"Oh, Katharina," 265

"Oh! Lady Be Good," 128, 248, 338, 351, 387, 415–16, 419

"Oh Tannenbaum," 265

"Oh Yes, Take Another Guess," 166

"Oh! You Pretty Woman," 362

"Oh! You Sweet Thing," 169

"O.K. for Baby," 244

"Ol' Man River," 160, 269, 313

"Old Black Joe," 304

"The Old Grey Mare," 366

"Old Man Ben," 236

"Old Man Blues," 73, 160

"An Old Straw Hat," 284

"Old Yazoo," 183

Oliver, Joe "King," 1–5, 10, 14–19, 30n.1, 50, 53–54, 65, 68, 79, 105, 158, 161, 167, 182, 186, 193, 198, 273, 290, 296, 339, 397, 407, 413, 417, 420
Oliver, Sy, ix, 29, 81–88, 115–17, 160, 181, 221–22, 302, 314, 404, 415, 417
"On the Alamo," 342
"On the Sentimental Side," 347
"On the Sunny Side of the Street," 162, 210, 329
"Once Upon a Time," 242
"One Big Union for Two," 191
"One Foot in the Groove," 127, 398
"One Hour," 46, 58, 90n.23, 133
"One More Time," 30n.1
"One O'Clock Jump," x, 59, 105–6, 117–18, 310, 403, 407
"One Sweet Letter from You," 213
Onyx Club, 124, 418, 422
"Oodles of Noodles," 121
"Open House," 216
"Opus No. 1," ix, 117
Orange Blossoms, 274
Orchestra Wives (film), 135
"Orchids for Remembrance," 311
"Organ Grinder's Swing," 85, 116, 374, 400
Original Dixieland Jazz Band (ODJB), 5, 21, 106, 265, 367
"Original E-Flat Blues," 360
Ory, Kid, 3
"Out the Window," 62–63, 405
"Outside of Paradise," 284
Owens, Thomas, 389

"Pagan Love Song," 140
Page, Oran "Hot Lips," 54–56, 58, 129–30, 147, 232–37, 276, 310, 387, 389, 408, 418
Page, Walter, 54–56, 58–59, 62, 108, 299, 346, 351, 353–54, 409, 414, 418
"Pagin' the Devil," 353
Paige, Patty, xi
Palmer Brothers, 174

Palomar Ballroom, viii, 13, 23, 43, 98–100, 130, 418
"Panama," 156, 158, 252n.56, 291
Panassié, Hugues, 4
"Papa's Gone," 35n.64
"Parade of the Milk Bottle Caps," 118
"Paradiddle," 193, 403, 408
Parish, Mitchell, 7, 82, 284
Parker, Charlie "Yardbird," ix, 25, 28, 56, 118, 121–22, 157, 247–49, 298, 349–50, 367, 372, 384, 386–90, 405, 415–16, 418–19, 424
Parrish, Avery, 219–21, 224–26
Pascal, Milton, 188
"Passion Flower," 385–86
"Pastel Blue," 126
Pastor, Tony, 125–26, 130
"Pavane," 140
Payne, Benny, 182, 184, 186–87, 192
Payne, Delores, 235
"Peaceful Valley," 300
"Peckin'," 104, 187, 189, 413
"Pennies From Heaven," 153, 345
"Pennsylvania 6–5000," 137
"Perdido," 67, 423
Peretti, Burton W., xiiin.10, 14
Perkins, Lefty, 366
Perry, Ray, 216
Peter Johnson & His Boogie Woogie Boys, 389
Peterson, Oscar, 412
Philburn, Al, 154
"Piano Man," 176, 412
"Piano Stomp," 210
"Piano Tuner Man," 284
"Pianology," 175
"Pickin' the Cabbage," 408
Picnic (film), 185
"The Pied Piper," 234
The Pied Pipers, 117
"Pigeon Walk," 62, 86–87
"Pigeons and Peppers," 383
Pingitore, Mike, 271
"Pitter Panther Patter," 384
Pla-Mor Ballroom, 197–98
"Plantation Joys," 158
"Please Believe Me," 113

"Please Don't Talk About Me When I'm Gone," 205
Pletcher, Stew, 371
"Pluckin' the Bass," 193–94, 408, 412
"Plymouth Rock," 243
Poe, Edgar Allan, 118
Pollack, Ben, 15, 23, 47–49, 97, 109, 112, 123–24, 133, 189, 288, 290, 415
Polo, Danny, 330–31
The Polynesians, 154
"Pom Pom," 244
"Pompton Turnpike," 302
"Ponce de Leon," 302
"Poor Bubber," 385
"Poor Butterfly," 202
"Pop-corn Man," 104
"Popeye the Sailor Man," 120, 300
Porgy and Bess, 131
Porter, Cole, 81, 125, 282
"Porter's Love Song to a Chambermaid," 356, 359, 394n.86, 398
"A Portrait of Bert Williams," 71
"A Portrait of Freddy Jenkins," 72
"Posin'," 66, 86, 377
"Potato Head Blues," 3
Powell, Ernie, 243, 246, 348
Powell, James, 244
"Powerhouse," 359
"Prelude to a Kiss," 78
"Pretty Baby," 340–41
Price, Sammy, 355
"Primitive," 157, 160
Prince, Bob, 342
Prince, Earres, 178
Prince, Wesley, 215
"Prince of Wales (or Wails)," 55, 183
"The Prisoner's Song," 283
Procope, Russell, 20, 28, 241, 387
"Puddin' Head Serenade," 200
Purnell, William "Keg," 245
Purtill, Maurice, 138, 140, 375
Purvis, Jack, 327
"Put on Your Old Grey Bonnet," 86–87, 363
"Pyramid," 67, 75, 423

"Queen Isabelle," 190
"Queer Notions," 43, 82, 397
"Quiet and Roll 'Em," 304
Quigley, Herb, 271

"The Rabbit's Jump," 383
"Radio Rhythm," 42–43, 183
"The Raggle Taggle," 230
Rainey, Ma, 49, 232
Ram, Buck, 244
Ramey, Gene, 248, 416
Ramey, Hurley, 177
Randall, William, 175
Randolph, Irving "Mouse," 48, 187, 189–92, 195, 212, 345
Randolph, Zilmer, 25
Range, Robert, 219, 225
"Ratamacue," 193, 403
Rath, Franz, 196
Rauch, Billy, 25, 277, 280
Razaf, Andy, 148, 186, 229, 356
Red Hot Peppers, 1–3, 24, 26, 168, 171
"Red Nose," 152–53
"Red Sails in the Sunset," 158
Redman, Don, 4, 16–17, 41, 43, 46–47, 49–50, 53, 84, 134, 138, 160, 168, 194–95, 220, 238, 267, 316n.14 and 17, 403, 419
"Redskin Rhumba," 299
"Reefer Man," 183
Reese, Gail, 284–85
Reeves, Reuben, 179
Reinhardt, Django, 216, 243
"Remember," 231, 395n.118, 417
"Reminiscing in Tempo," 71
"A Rendezvous in Rio," 306
Reuss, Alan, 103, 210–11, 345
"Rhapsody in Blue," 114, 264, 266–67, 269–70
"Rhapsody Jr.," 81
"Rhythm Is Our Business," 82, 415
"Rhythm Lullaby," 174, 374, 400
"Rhythm of the Tambourine," 53
"Rhythm, Rhythm," 210
"Rhythm Sundae," 175
"Rhythmic Rhapsody," 228
Rich, Buddy, 127–28, 161

Richards, Chuck, xiiin.4, 163
Richmond, June, 120, 204–8
"Ridin' a Riff," 175
"Riff Medley," 176
"Riff Romp," 244
"Riff Time," 224
"Riffin,'" 52
"Riffin' the Scotch," 334, 423
"Riffs," 227
"The Right Idea," 299
Rimsky-Korsakov, Nikolai, 115, 266
"Ring Dem Bells," 70–71, 100, 172, 207–8, 211, 297
"Rinka Tinka Man," 284
"Rite Tite," 56
"The River," 151
"Riverboat Shuffle," 334–35
"Riverside Blues," 290
Rizzotto, Dalton, 313
Roberta (stage play), 269
Roberts, Claude, 168, 177
Robeson, Paul, 269, 274
"Robins and Roses," 114
Robinson, Bill, 71
Robinson, Fred, 168, 206–7
Robinson, Milton, 245
Robinson, Ted, 204
"Rock-a-bye Basie," 64
"Rock and Rye," 173
"Rock Hill Special," 212
"Rockin' Chair," 6, 271, 275, 308, 402
"Rockin' in Rhythm," 72–73, 104, 297, 301–2
"Rockin' Rollers Jubilee," 221–22
Rodemich-Conley, 48
Rodgers, Gene, 236, 329–31
Rodgers and Hart, 377, 407
Rodin, Gil, 288, 294
Rogers, Shorty, 21
"Roll 'Em," 104, 115, 202, 292, 425
Rollini, Adrian, 99–100, 164, 210, 327, 334–35
Rollini, Arthur, 334–35
Roppolo, Leon, 271, 295
Rosbach, Oscar, 283
Rose, Vincent, 270

"Rose Room," 82, 120, 227, 340, 366, 405, 421
Roseland Ballroom, 8, 22, 27, 40, 57, 419
"Roseland Shuffle," 58
"Rosetta," 103, 170, 254n.107
Royal, Ernie, 216
Royal, Marshall, 216–17
"Royal Garden Blues," 115, 272, 288
"Rug Cutter's Swing," 51, 139, 411
Rugolo, Pete, 32n.28, 82
"Runnin' Wild," 339
"Running a Temperature," 85–86, 188
Rushing, Jimmy, 54, 60–61, 63, 102–3, 121, 180, 227, 275, 349, 353–54, 419, 425
Russell, Luis, 3, 27, 65, 150, 152–63, 191, 252n.56, 397, 407, 412, 419
Russell, Pee Wee, 7, 333, 368–69
Russell, Ross, 227, 259n.298, 408
"Russian Lullaby," 109, 283, 287
Russin, Babe, 106, 211–12
Russin, Jack, 327
Rust, Brian, 256n.181
Ryan, Jack, 122

"The Sad," 229
"Sadie Green (The Vamp of New Orleans)," 365
"A Sailboat in the Moonlight," 346
"A Salute to Harlem," 230
Sampson, Edgar, 13, 21, 25–26, 42, 51, 56, 89n.11, 105, 108, 117, 119, 147, 161–64, 211, 241, 372, 420
"San Antonio Tamales," 228
Sands, Bobby, 12
"Santa Claus Came in the Spring," 100
"Saratoga Drag," 156–58, 407, 412
"Saratoga Shout," 158, 252n.56
"Saratoga Swing," 72
"Satin Doll," 78
"Saturday," 198
Sauter, Eddie, 111, 399, 417, 420
"Savage Rhythm," 190
"Save It, Pretty Mama," 214
Savoy Ballroom, 25, 40, 79, 147, 161,

164, 172, 217–18, 243, 397, 408, 420, 424
"Savoy Stampede," 243
Savoy Sultans, 388
"Say the Word," 158
"Scandal in A Flat," 243
"The Scat Song," 180–82
Schaap, Phil, 9
Schaffer, William, 375
Schenker, Anatol, 335
Schertzer, Hymie, 210
Schoebel, Elmer, 9, 294
Schoenberg, Loren, 21–22, 56, 105, 110, 249, 355, 408
Schuller, Gunther, viii-ix, xi, 10–13, 15–16, 23, 25, 41–44, 50–51, 54–59, 63–64, 69–77, 79, 81–86, 88–89, 90n.23, 91n.29, 94n.95, 98–99, 104, 108, 110–13, 116–21, 123–26, 128–37, 140, 148–60, 162–65, 167, 169–73, 175, 178–79, 181–85, 187–88, 192–93, 199–202, 204–6, 208–13, 215–19, 221–31, 242–44, 246–47, 249, 254n.107, 257n.224, 259n.298, 260n.303, 266–68, 271, 275, 277, 282–85, 287–94, 297–98, 301, 305–6, 308, 315, 317nn.39, 40, 46, 59, 319n.88, 330, 342–43, 350–52, 355, 361, 364, 373, 375, 387, 389, 398–99, 401, 421–22, 426
Schultz, Dave, 305
Schutz, Buddy, 110, 122
Schwartz, Wilbur, 134
"Scratching the Gravel," 206
Scrima, Mickey, 312
"Scrub Me, Mama," 299
Sears, Jerry, 131
Second Chorus (film), 131
Secrest, Andy, 44, 267–69
Sedric, Gene, 357–60, 420
"Sensation Rag," 106, 367, 369
"Sensation Stomp," 316n.14
"Sensational Mood," 170
"Sent for You Yesterday and Here You Come Today," 62–63, 353, 405, 419
"Sepia Panorama," 71, 76

"Serenade to a Sarong," 245
"Serenade to a Savage," 128
"A Serenade to the Stars, 284
"Seven Come Eleven," 340, 403
Severinsen, Doc, x-xi
"Shades of Jack," 215
"Shake It and Break It," 193
Shakespeare, William, 9, 71, 86, 161
"Shanghai Shuffle," 47–49, 91n.29, 398
Shapiro, Artie, 375
"Sharp as a Tack," 313
Shavers, Charlie, 387, 395n.129
Shaw, Artie, xi, 14, 16, 22, 24–25, 39, 60, 65, 107, 110, 114, 120, 123–32, 135, 138, 167, 236, 243–45, 263, 284, 297, 325, 345, 370, 378–80, 398, 407–8, 418, 420
Shaw, Stan, 298
"She's Tall, She's Tan, She's Terrific," 190
"The Sheik of Araby," 98, 330, 332, 365
Sheridan, Chris, 349–51
Sherman, James, 346
Sherock, Shorty, 119, 294, 305, 307
"Shine," 336
"Shipyard Ramble," 224–25
"Shoe Shine Boy," 52, 350
"Shoe Shiner's Drag," 211
"Shoot the Likker to Me, John Boy," 125
"Shoot the Works," 241
"The Shout," 422
"Showboat Shuffle," 71, 231
"Shufflin' at Hollywood," 212
Siegrist, Frank, 268
Signorelli, Frank, 333
Simeon, Omer, 169–70, 172, 254n.107, 295
Simmons, John, 371
Simms, Edward, 176
Simon, George, 289
Simon, Stafford, 245
Sims, Edward, 225
Sims, J.B., 217
Sinatra, Frank, x, 111, 113–14, 117, 311, 421

"Sing Me a Swing Song (And Let Me Dance)," vii. 102, 165, 402
"Sing, Sing, Sing," 52, 104, 106, 304, 415, 421
"Sing You Sinners," 53
"Singapore Sorrows," 48
"Singin' the Blues," 5, 8, 20–21, 42, 57, 112, 129, 214, 242, 330, 424
Singleton, Zutty, 168, 330
"Siren Serenade," 305
"Sittin' Around and Dreamin'," 202
"Sittin' in the Dark," 151
"Six Appeal," 341
"Six Bells Stampede," 238–39
"Six or Seven Times," 179, 181
"The Skater's Waltz," 295–96
"Skeleton in the Closet," 153
"Skip It," 242
"Skull Duggery," 235
"Skunk Hollow Blues," 384
"(A Sky of Blue, with You) And So Forth," 235
"Skyliner," 303
Slack, Freddy, 120
"Sleep," 244
"Sleepy Time Gal," 83
"Slip Horn Jive," 133, 139
"Slippery Horn," 401
"Slow and Easy Blues," 292
"Slow Down," 306
"Slow Freight," 139, 244
"Small Fry," 273
Smalls' Paradise, 233
"Smart Aleck," 216
Smeck, Roy, 183
Smith, Bessie, 60, 98, 153, 365, 409, 426
Smith, Carl "Tatti," 349–52, 354
Smith, Charles Edward, xiiin.9
Smith, Floyd, 204, 206, 208
Smith, Henry "Buster," 23, 56–58, 248, 310, 386–87, 389–90
Smith, Howard, 115
Smith, Jimmy, 180, 182
Smith, Joe, 4, 60
Smith, John, 360
Smith, Pinetop, 115
Smith, Russell, 53, 244–45

Smith, Tab, 388
Smith, Warren, 289, 292
Smith, Willie, 79–83, 85–88, 122, 196, 233, 415, 421
"Smoke Dreams," 399, 420
"Smoke Gets in Your Eyes," 116, 269–70, 380
"Smoke House," 109
"Smoke Rings," 25, 277
"A Smooth One," 194, 342
"Snag It," 2–5, 31n.12, 198, 417
"Snake Rag," 31n.12
"So Little Time," 155
"So Long, Shorty," 225
"So Sweet," 178
"So You're the One," 136
"Soft and Sweet," 162, 411
"Soft Winds," 224
"Soldier's Farewell," 265
"Solid Mama," 175
"Solitude," xi, 81, 406
"Solo Flight," 110, 417
Solomson, Shorty, 122–23
"Some Like It Hot," 304
"Some of These Days," 178, 364
"Some Saturday," 386
"Some Sweet Day," 151
"The Somebody," 230
"Somebody Loves Me," 10, 230, 268, 414
"Somebody Stole My Gal," 170, 365
"Somebody's Been Using That Thing," 365
"Someday Sweetheart," 333
"Someone Stole Gabriel's Horn," 239
"Sometimes I'm Happy," 99–100, 104, 106
"Somewhere with Somebody Else," 285
"Song of India," x, 115–16, 266–67
"Song of the Volga Boatmen," 137
"Sophisticated Lady," xii, 71, 77, 81, 278, 385, 421–22
"Sophisticated Swing," 284
"Sophomore," 198
"South Rampart Street Parade," 291, 415
"Southern Echoes," 217

"Southern Fried," 300
"Southland Shuffle," 300
"Special Delivery," 195
"Special Delivery Stomp," 379
Spieldock, Al, 215
"Spinnin' the Webb," 167, 421
"Spirituals to Swing," 108, 410
Spivack, Charlie, 335
"S'posin,'" 224
"Squaty Roo," 385
St. Cyr, Johnny, 155
"St. James Infirmary," 179, 195, 336
"St. Louis Blues," 126–27, 134, 152, 178, 273, 363
"St. Louis Shuffle," 46
Stacy, Jess, 103–4, 108, 210–11, 294–95, 368, 421
Stafford, Jo, 116
"The Stampede," 4, 52–53
Stanfield, Leemie, 221
"Star Dust," 7, 9, 22, 25, 32n.21, 36n.75–77, 117, 128, 135–37, 149, 275, 340–41, 398, 401–3, 422
"Stardust on the Moon," 377
Stark, Bobby, 10–12, 14, 42, 45, 164, 167, 421
"Stealin' Apples," 52, 403
Stearne, Marshall, 4–5, 61, 65
Steiner, John, 388
"Steppin' into Swing Society," 75
"Steppin' Pretty," 199
Stevenson, Tommy, 82–83
Stewart, Dee, 54
Stewart, Rex, 4, 9, 18–20, 22, 42, 52, 67, 71, 159–60, 212, 300, 335–36, 382–83, 385–86, 419, 421–22
Still, William Grant, 128, 130
Stockard, Ocie, 362–63, 365–66
Stokowski, Leopold, 264
"Stomp It Off," 82, 423
"Stomp Off and Let's Go," 293–94
"Stompin' at the Savoy," 25–27, 29, 108, 117–19, 163, 339
"Stompology," 210
"Stop Crying," 30n.1
"Stormy Weather," 185
Stowe, David W., 6, 61, 86, 101, 166, 183, 397, 408

"Stratosphere," 43, 82, 172
Stravinsky, Igor, 240, 264
Strayhorn, Billy, 76, 78, 130, 137, 194, 383–85, 422
Strickfaden, Charles, 272
"Strictly Cullud Affair," 182
"Strictly Swing," 219
"A String of Pearls," 133, 137, 410
Strong, Jimmy, 168
"Struttin' with Some Barbecue," 154–55
"A Study in Blue," 219
"A Study in Brown," 412
Stuhlmaker, Mort, 373
"Subtle Lament," 76
"Subtle Slough," 385–86
Sudhalter, Richard, 9–10, 14–15, 20 23–24, 90n.20, 106, 109, 112, 114, 120, 124, 128–29, 131, 142n.54, 154, 191, 265, 269, 271, 274–75, 280–81, 283–88, 290–91, 294–95, 316nn.14, 22, 327, 369, 373–75, 395n.118, 399
"Sugar Foot Stomp" or "Strut," 16–20, 26, 42, 50, 66, 92n.61, 105, 417, 420–21
"Sugar Hill Shim-Sham," 383
Suggs, Peter, 53
"Suite No. 8," 129
Sullivan, Joe, 214, 292–93, 330, 334, 427
Sullivan, Maxine, 246
Summa Cum Laude Orchestra, 367, 369, 408
"Summertime," 289
"Summit Ridge Drive," 379
"Sumpin' 'bout Rhythm," 73
Sun Valley Serenade (film), 135
"The Sun Will Shine Tonight," 211
"Sunbonnet Sue," 362
"Sunday," 246
"Sunrise Serenade," 143–35
"Super Chief," 64, 312, 322n.195, 417
Super Sax, 83–84
"Swanee Lullaby," 183
"Swanee River," 84, 304, 312
Swayzee, Edwin, 185–86

"Sweet and Hot," 23

"Sweet and Slow," 358

"Sweet Chariot," 72

"Sweet Ella May," 168

"Sweet Georgia Brown," 223, 309, 364, 399

"Sweet Girl," 228

"Sweet Hearts on Parade," 25

"Sweet Jennie Lee," 179, 363

"Sweet Lorraine," 368, 404

"Sweet Mumtaz," 31n.12, 158

"Sweet Music," 41

"Sweet Sorrow Blues," 239

"Sweet Sue," 5, 46, 90n.20, 109, 114, 239–40, 267

"Sweet Sue, Just You," 338

"Sweetheart, Honey, Darlin' Dear," 304

Sweetman, Ron, 362

"The Swing," 228

"Swing Baby Swing (Love in My Heart)," 74, 382

"Swing It," 238

"Swing Low," 72

"Swing Low, Sweet Chariot," 360

"Swing, Mister Charlie," 373

"Swing Out," 221

"Swing, Swing, Swing," 190

"Swing That Music," 150, 152

Swing That Music, 118

"Swingin' at the Maida Vale," 242

"Swingin' at the Sugar Bowl," 294

"Swingin' Down," 172–73

"Swingin' on Lenox Avenue," 220

"Swingin' on Nothing," 302

"Swingin' the Blues," 62–63, 399, 405, 417

"Swingin' Them Jingle Bells," 420

"Swingin' Uptown," 82, 84

"Swinging at the Daisy Chain," 57

"Swinging in Harlem," 222

"Swingmatism," 248–49

"Swingtime in the Rockies," 107

"A Swingy Little Rhythm," 224

Symphony in Black (film), 94n.95

"Symphony in Riffs," 241

"Synthetic Love," 238, 241

"Tain't No Use," 101

"Tain't Nobody's Biz'ness What I Do," 373

"Tain't What You Do (It's the Way Hotcha Do It)," 87, 166

"Take It Easy," 171

"Take It Slow and Easy," 363

"Take the 'A' Train," x, 78, 137, 194, 422

"Take Those Blues Away," 205–6

"Taking Off," 364

"Tangerine," 121, 123

"Tantalizing a Cuban," 177

"Tappin' Off," 194, 400

"Tar Paper Stomp," 42, 138

Tate, Buddy, 64, 247, 312

Tate, Erskine, 409

Tatum, Art, 64, 167–68, 249, 422–23

"Taxi War Dance," 64, 414

Taylor, Billy, 67, 211–12, 335, 356, 383–84, 422

Taylor, J.R. 15, 52

Taylor, Paul, 138

Tchaikovsky, Peter Ilich, 137

"Tchaikovsky's Piano Concerto," 135

"Tea and Trumpets," 383

"Tea for Two," 58, 341, 403

Teagarden, Charlie, 98, 271–74, 333–34, 423–24

Teagarden, Jack, 5–7, 10–11, 23, 27, 65, 98, 100, 105, 111–12, 118, 120, 127, 140, 154–55, 183, 196, 237, 242, 263, 265, 270–74, 276, 325–26, 331–37, 356, 363, 365, 371, 374, 423–25

"Tears in My Heart," 377

"Tell All Your Dreams to Me," 238

"Tell Me More," 348

"Tempo and Swing," 215

"Temptation," 130

Terrell, Pha, 199–204, 206–7

"Terrific Stomp," 56

Texas Blusicians, 355

"Texas Shuffle," 63–64, 425

"Texas Tea Party," 334

"Thankful," 152–53

"Thanks for the Memory," 399

"That Man Is Here Again," 189

"That Naughty Waltz," 165
"That Rhythm Man," 164, 421
"That Thing," 388
"That's a Plenty," 173
"That's How Rhythm Was Born," 279
"That's Life I Guess," 345
"That's What I Like about You," 333
"Then I'll Be Tired of You," 357
"There Is No Greater Love," 206
"There'll Be Some Changes Made,"
    304
"There's a Small Hotel," 242
"There's Rhythm in Harlem," 138
"These Foolish Things," 102, 344
Thigpen, Ben, 198–99, 201, 204, 206,
    208
"Things Ain't What They Used to Be,"
    297, 385
"This Morning, This Evening, So
    Soon," 363
"This Year's Kisses," 346
Thomas, Joe (Lewis), 244
Thomas, Joe, 29, 82–83, 85, 87–88,
    137, 203, 243, 284, 298–300, 304,
    423
Thomas, Lorenzo, 44
Thomas, Walter, 179, 181, 195
Thompson, Butch, 30n.1
Thompson, Sir Charles, 216
Thornhill, Claude, 76, 346
"Three Swings and Out," 191–92
"The Three Ts," 273, 424
"Three-Quarter Boogie," 216
"Tickle Toe," 21, 36n.74
"Tiger Rag," 120, 381–82, 422
"Till Tom Special," 215
"Tillie's Downtown Now," 368
Tilton, Martha, 104, 107, 109
"Time Out," 62
"Time's A-Wastin'," 87
"Tin Roof Blues," 272
"Ti-Pi-Tin," 108
"Tired of the Same Thing All the
    Time," 365
"Tired Socks," 384
Tirro, Frank, 26, 268
Tizol, Juan, 67, 75, 286, 381–83, 410,
    423

"To a Broadway Rose," 129
"Toadie Toddle," 203–4
"Toby," 55, 128, 183, 275
"Tomboy," 297, 371
Tompkins, Eddie, 85
Tonight Show, xi
"Tonight You Belong to Me," 224
"Topsy," 62, 109, 403, 405
"Topsy Turvy (Hard Times)," 195
Tough, Dave, 108–10, 114–15, 284,
    335, 375–77
"Traffic Jam," 128
"Trav'lin' Alone," 347
"Trav'lin' Light," 273
Traxler, Gene, 375
Traylor, Rudy, 177
"Tree of Hope," 246
"Trees," 283
"Trinity Waltz," 363
"Troubled," 124
"Truckin'," 73–74
"True," 164
"True Blue Lou," 231
"True Confession," 155
Truehart, John, 52, 162–64, 344–45
"Truly Wonderful," 384
Trumbauer, Frankie, 8–9, 15, 20–21,
    44, 56–57, 97, 112, 118, 124, 129,
    198, 214, 243, 267, 269, 271, 273,
    316n.22. 326, 330, 349, 372, 400,
    424, 426
"Trumpet in Spades," 71
"Turn Left," 121–22
"Turn Right," 118, 121–23
Turner, Henry, 12
Turner, Joe, 389
Turner, Lana, 125
"Tuxedo Junction," 30n.1 132, 135,
    139, 218, 220, 226, 244, 259n.280,
    399, 404, 411
Twain, Mark, vii, 118, 143n.71
"Twelfth Street Rag," 34n.62, 93n.91,
    207, 212
Twelve Clouds of Joy, 39, 196–209,
    414, 425–26
"Twilight in Turkey," 376, 379
"Twinklin'," 202
"2:19 Blues," 156

"Two O'Clock Jump," 310
"Two Sleepy People," 360, 402

"Uncle Bud," 225
"Until the Real Thing Comes Along,"
    200–201, 414
"Up Jumped the Devil," 177
"Uproar Shout," 222
"Uptown Blues," 88
"Us on a Bus," 358

Van Eps, Bobby, 119
Van Eps, George, 102, 371
Vance, Dick, 49
Venuti, Joe, 6–7, 44, 112, 267–68,
    333, 363–65, 368, 423
"Vibraphone Blues," 339
"The Viper's Drag," 179–80
Virgil, 9
"Vote for Mr. Rhythm," 165–66

"Wabash Blues," 364
"Wabash Stomp," 388
"Wacky Dust," 166, 285
Wagner, Richard, 111
"Wah-Dee-Dah," 183
"Waitin' for Benny," 342, 381, 425
"Wake and Live, 190–91
Waldteufel, Emil, 295
"Walk It to Me," 389
"Walkin' and Swingin'," 198
"Wall Street Wail," 151
Waller, Fats, xiiin.2, 27, 42, 57, 62,
    87, 104, 106, 149, 164, 167–69,
    180–81, 183, 200, 202, 208, 224,
    229, 234, 244, 260n.311, 267, 293,
    325, 333, 346, 350, 353–54, 356–
    61, 366, 371, 375, 377, 394n.97,
    398, 402, 404, 420, 422, 424
Walters, Eddie, x–xi
Walton, Greely, 27, 150, 152, 156–59,
    252n.56
"Wanderin' Blues," 301
Ward, Helen, vii, 102, 165, 347
"Warm Valley," 71
Warner Brothers, 79
Warren, Earl, 63
Washington, Buck, 328

Washington, George, 238, 241
Washington, Jack, 54, 63–64
Washington, Leon, 175
Waters, Ethel, 365
Watson, Leo, 125
Watts, Grady, 280
"'Way Down upon the Swanee River,"
    222
"Way Down Yonder in New Orleans,"
    352–53
"The Way You Look Tonight," 345
"Weakness," 186
"Wearin' of the Green, The," 284
"Weary," 113
"Weather Bird," 3, 148, 167
Webb, Chick, 24, 26, 28–29, 39–40,
    52, 65, 105, 108, 119–20, 147, 150–
    51, 161–67, 170, 172, 179–80, 184,
    217–18, 226, 231, 238, 241, 397,
    402, 405, 407–9, 411, 413–15, 420–
    21, 424
Weber, Carl Maria von, 100
Webster, Ben, xii, 46, 49–51, 54–55,
    69, 73, 77–78, 103, 187–90, 192,
    208, 212–14, 223–24, 241, 246,
    256n.181, 258n.268, 276, 278, 311,
    313, 335–36, 343–46, 386, 424–26
Webster, Paul, 87–88
"Weddin' Blues," 220
"The Wedding of Mr. and Mrs.
    Swing," 188–89
"Wednesday Night Hop," 201
"Weely (A Portrait of Billy
    Strayhorn)," 71
"The Weep," 229
Weiss, Sam, 114
"Well All Right Then," 87–88, 116,
    423
Wells, Dickie or Dicky, 12, 43, 45, 60,
    63–64, 90n.19, 121, 131, 157–58,
    227, 238–41, 267, 299, 334, 354–
    55, 397, 404, 407, 412, 414, 419,
    425
Wells, Henry, 202, 207–8
Welty, Eudora, 359
"West End Blues," 129, 148, 167,
    310, 373

Weston, Paul, 115

Wettling, George, 282, 368, 375

"Wham (Re Bop Boom Bam)," 133, 139, 205

"What a Little Moonlight Can Do," 343–44, 413, 426

"What Do You Know about Love?," 220

"What Is This Thing Called Love?," 125

"What Shall I Say?," 348

"What Shuffle," 164

"What Would People Say," 202

"What's Mine Is Yours," 201

"What's New?," 295, 410

"What's the Reason (I'm Not Pleasin' You)," 394n.97

"What's Your Story, Morning Glory," 88, 203

"Whatcha Gonna Do When There Ain't No Swing?," vii, 35n.69, 374

Wheeler, De Priest, 178–80

"When," 22

"When a Woman Loves a Man," 347

"When Day Is Done," 242, 331

"When Dreams Come True," 163, 420

"When I'm Alone," 54

"When I'm Gone, Don't You Grieve," 365

"When It's Sleepy Time Down South," 104, 155, 269

"When Lights Are Low," 213, 244, 340

"When Ruben Swings the Cuban," 118

"When the Midnight Choo-Choo Leaves for Alabam," 378

"When the Quail Come Back to San Quentin," 380

"When the Saints Go Marching In," 252n.56

"When the Sun Comes Out," 122

"When You're Smiling," 189, 347

"Where You Are," 307

"Where You Been So Long, Corrine?," 363

"Wherever There's a Will, Baby," 46

Whetsol, Arthur, 71, 207

"While Love Lasts," 23, 78–81

"Whistle While You Work," 284

White, Harry, 182, 184, 186, 190, 192, 235

White, Morris, 180, 182–83, 185–86

White, Sonny, 245–46

"White Heat," 81–82, 173

"White Jazz," 25, 277, 280,

Whiteman, Paul, 5, 9, 15, 21–22, 42, 44–45, 97, 112–16, 121, 124, 157, 174, 179, 196, 219, 238–39, 263–75, 281, 284, 287, 316n.30, 331–32, 334–35, 370, 398, 417, 423–25

Whiteman, Wilberforce, J., 196, 264, 270

"Whiteman Stomp," 267–68, 315n.14, 316n.17

Whitman, Walt, 118

Whittet, Ben, 356–57

"Who?," 116, 266

"Who Ya Hunchin'?," 167

"Who'll Be the One This Summer," 376

"Wholly Cats," 341, 398

"Who's Afraid of Love?," 420

"Who's Sorry Now?," 223

"Why Should I Beg For Love," 163

"Why Was I Born?," 346

Wilborn, Dave, 168

Wilcox, Ed, 79–83, 85

"Wild Cherry," 227

"Wild Mab of the Fish Pond," 302

"Wild Party," 50

"Will You Remember Tonight Tomorrow?," 235

Willett, Chappie, 304

Williams, Clarence, 288

Williams, Claude, 198

Williams, Cootie, xi, 7, 67–68, 71, 76–77, 103–4, 106, 210–11, 299, 301, 337, 341–42, 379, 381, 398, 425

Williams, Elmer, 151, 162–63

Williams, John, 197

Williams, Martin, 55–56, 64, 74, 91n.35, 170, 276, 346–48, 351, 399

Williams, Mary Lou, 104, 115, 146, 197–98, 200–208, 211, 292, 425–26

Williams, Midge, xiiin.3, 372, 374

Williams, Roberto, 103
Williams, Rudy, 387–88
Williams, Sandy, 163–64, 166–67, 245, 414
Williams, Spencer, 288
Williams, Tex, 366
"Willow Weep for Me," 193, 195, 413
Wills, Bob, 170, 361–62
Wilson, Dick, 197–208, 231, 257n.224, 426
Wilson, Gerald, 88
Wilson, John S., 12, 17, 41, 168, 171
Wilson, Quinn, 169, 172–74, 176–77
Wilson, Shadow, 216
Wilson, Teddy, 7, 21, 60, 102–3, 107, 151, 167–68, 202, 209, 213, 215–16, 237–38, 241, 294, 297, 313, 325, 337–39, 342–48, 370–71, 379, 398–99, 412, 426
Windy City Five, 368
"Windy City Jive," 177
Windy City Seven, 367, 369
"Wings Over Manhattan," 297, 302
"With Love in My Heart," 201
"Without a Song," 386
"Without Rhythm," 180
Woods, Cora, 229–30
Woods, Sonny, 160
"The World Is Waiting for the Sunrise," 336
"Woverine Blues," 173–74, 291
"Wrappin' It Up," 49–50, 108–9, 408
Wright, Edythe, 113–14, 375–78
Wright, Lammar, 179, 182, 186, 195
Wright, Leo, 232, 405
Wright, Mel, 232
Wylie, Austin, 124

"Yaller," 179
Yancey, Jimmy, 292
"Yancey Special," 115, 292
"Yard Dog Mazurka," 89
"Yeah Man!," 46
"Yearning for Love," 71
Yellen-Ager, 45
"Yes Indeed," 115, 313, 418

"Yes! Yes! My! My!," 154
"You," 114
"You and Your Love," 110
"You Can Depend on Me," 49, 353
"You Can't Escape from Me," 221, 223
"You Can't Stop Me from Lovin' You," 181
"You Dog," 182, 186
"You Let Me Down," 344
"You Made Me Love You," xi, 313
"You Never Looked So Beautiful," 114
"You Rascal, You," 157, 159, 180, 198, 327, 333
"You Set Me on Fire," 204
"You Started Me Dreaming," 112
"You Took Advantage of Me," 372
"You'll Wish You'd Never Been Born," 151, 250n.17
"You're a Sweetheart," 378
"You're Laughing at Me," xiiin.2, 359
"You're Lucky to Me," 148
"You're My Thrill," 301
"You're Simply Delish," 333
"You're the Cure for What Ails Me," 187–88
Young, Lee, 216, 355
Young, Lester "Pres" or "Prez," 22, 56–60, 62–64, 90n.19, 93n.91, 106, 110, 116, 121, 126, 128, 174–76, 192, 199, 207, 214–15, 220–21, 248–49, 257n.224, 282, 289, 298–99, 306, 325, 329, 338, 341, 346–56, 368–69, 387, 398–400, 406, 408, 413–14, 416, 419, 424, 426
Young, Snooky, 88
Young, Trummy, 87–88, 122, 166, 168, 171, 174–76, 186, 225, 426–27
"Your Feet's Too Big," 360
"Your Love Has Faded," 384
"Your Mother's Son-in-Law," 334, 423

"Zaz Zuh Zaz," 184
Zurke, Bob, 292–94, 296, 427

About the Author

DAVE OLIPHANT is a lecturer at the University of Texas at Austin, where he teaches English and has edited a scholarly journal. He has written extensively on music, including his historical study *Texan Jazz* in 1996, and has published several volumes of his own poetry as well as translations of Latin American poetry.